AMERICAN LAW YEARBOOK 2010

A GUIDE TO THE YEAR'S MAJOR LEGAL CASES AND DEVELOPMENTS

ISSN 1521-0901

AMERICAN LAW YEARBOOK 2010

A GUIDE TO THE YEAR'S

MAJOR LEGAL CASES AND

DEVELOPMENTS

GALE
CENGAGE Learning

Detroit • New York • San Francisco • New Haven, Conn • Waterville, Maine • London

American Law Yearbook 2010

Project Editor: Jeffrey Wilson

Editorial: Kristin Key

Product Manager: Stephen Wasserstein

Editorial Support Services: Andrea Lopeman

Indexing Services: Janet Mazefsky

Rights Acquisition and Management:
Leitha Etheridge-Sims

Composition: Evi Abou-El-Seoud

Manufacturing: Rita Wimberley

Imaging: John Watkins

Product Design: Pam Galbreath

For product information and technology assistance, contact us at
Gale Customer Support, 1-800-877-4253.

For permission to use material from this text or product,
submit all requests online at **www.cengage.com/permissions.**
Further permissions questions can be emailed to
permissionrequest@cengage.com

While every effort has been made to ensure the reliability of the information presented in this publication, Gale, a part of Cengage Learning, does not guarantee the accuracy of the data contained herein. Gale accepts no payment for listing; and inclusion in the publication of any organization, agency, institution, publication, service, or individual does not imply endorsement of the editors or publisher. Errors brought to the attention of the publisher and verified to the satisfaction of the publisher will be corrected in future editions.

ISBN 978-1-4144-3881-8
ISBN 1-4144-3881-8
ISSN 1521-0901

Gale
27500 Drake Rd.
Farmington Hills, MI, 48331-3535

This title is also available as an e-book.
ISBN-13: 978-1-4144-6339-1   ISBN-10: 1-4144-6339-1
Contact your Gale, a part of Cengage Learning sales representative for ordering information.

Printed in the United States of America
1 2 3 4 5 6 7 12 11 10

CONTENTS

The need for a layperson's comprehensive, understandable guide to terms, concepts, and historical developments in U.S. law has been well met by *The Gale Encyclopedia of American Law* (*GEAL*). Published in a third edition in 2010 (in e-book format, and 2011 in print) by The Gale Group, *GEAL* has proved itself a valuable successor to West's 1983 publication, *The Guide to American Law: Everyone's Legal Encyclopedia.* and the 1997 and 2004 editions of *The West Encyclopedia of American Law.*

Since 1998, Gale, a part of Cengage Learning, a premier reference publisher, has extended the value of *GEAL* with the publication of *American Law Yearbook* (*ALY*). This companion volume series adds entries on emerging topics not covered in the main set. A legal reference must be current to be authoritative, so *ALY* is a vital companion to a key reference source. Uniform organization by *GEAL* term and cross-referencing make it easy to use the titles together, while inclusion of key definitions and summaries of earlier rulings in supplement entries whether new or continuations make it unnecessary to refer to the main set constantly.

UNDERSTANDING THE AMERICAN LEGAL SYSTEM

The U.S. legal system is admired around the world for the freedoms it allows the individual and the fairness with which it attempts to treat all persons. On the surface, it may seem simple, yet those who have delved into it know that this system of federal and state constitutions, statutes, regulations, and common-law decisions is elaborate and complex. It derives from the English common law, but includes principles older than England, along with some principles from other lands. The U.S. legal system, like many others, has a language all its own, but too often it is an unfamiliar language: many concepts are still phrased in Latin. *GEAL* explains legal terms and concepts in everyday language, however. It covers a wide variety of persons, entities, and events that have shaped the U.S. legal system and influenced public perceptions of it.

FEATURES OF THIS SUPPLEMENT

Entries

ALY 2010 contains 150 entries covering individuals, cases, laws, and concepts significant to U.S. law. Entries are arranged alphabetically and use the same entry title as in *GEAL* or *ALY* when introduced in an earlier *Yearbook* (e.g., September 11th Attacks). There may be several cases discussed under a given topic.

Profiles of individuals cover interesting and influential people from the world of law, government, and public life, both historic and contemporary. All have contributed to U.S. law as a whole. Each short biography includes a timeline highlighting important moments in the subject's life. Persons whose lives were detailed in *GEAL*, but who have died since publication of that work, receive obituary entries in *ALY*.

DEFINITIONS

Each entry on a legal term is preceded by a definition where applicable, which is easily distinguished by its sans serif typeface. The back of the book includes a Glossary of Legal Terms containing the definitions for a selection of the most important terms bolded in the text of the essays and biographies. Terms **bolded** but not included in the Glossary of Legal Terms in ALY can be found in the Dictionary volume of GEAL.

CROSS REFERENCES

To facilitate research, *ALY 2010* provides two types of cross-references: within and following entries. Within the entries, terms are set in small capital letters (e.g., First Amendment) to indicate that they have their own entry in *GEAL.* At the end of each entry, additional relevant topics in *ALY 2010* are listed alphabetically by title.

APPENDIX

This section follows the main body and includes a selection of primary documents related to cases discussed in ALY 2010, as well as a list of executive orders issued by President Obama so far in his administration.

TABLE OF CASES CITED AND INDEX BY NAME AND SUBJECT

These features make it quick and easy for users to locate references to cases, people, statutes, events, and other subjects. The Table of Cases Cited traces the influences of legal precedents by identifying cases mentioned throughout the text. In a departure from *GEAL,* references to individuals have been folded into the general index to simplify searches. Litigants, justices, historical and contemporary figures, as well as topical references are included in the Index by Name and Subject.

CITATIONS

Wherever possible, *ALY* includes citations to cases and statutes for readers wishing to do further research. They refer to one or more series, called "reporters," which publish court opinions and related information. Each citation includes a volume number, an abbreviation for the reporter, and the starting page reference. Underscores in a citation indicate that a court opinion has not been officially reported as of *ALY*'s publication. Two sample citations, with explanations, are presented below.

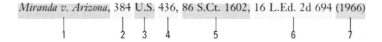

1. *Case title.* The title of the case is set in i and indicates the names of the parties. The suit in this sample citation was between Ernesto A. Miranda and the state of Arizona.

2. *Reporter volume number.* The number preceding the reporter abbreviation indicates the reporter volume containing the case. The volume number appears on the spine of the reporter, along with the reporter abbreviation.

3. *Reporter abbreviation.* The suit in the sample citation is from the reporter, or series of books, called *U.S. Reports,* which contains cases from the U.S. Supreme Court. Numerous reporters publish cases from the federal and state courts; consult the Abbreviations list at the back of this volume for full titles.

4. *Reporter page.* The number following the reporter abbreviation indicates the reporter page on which the case begins.

5. *Additional reporter citation.* Many cases may be found in more than one reporter. The suit in the sample citation also appears in volume 86 of the *Supreme Court Reporter,* beginning on page 1602.

6. *Additional reporter citation.* The suit in the sample citation is also reported in volume 16 of the *Lawyer's Edition,* second series, beginning on page 694.

7. *Year of decision.* The year the court issued its decision in the case appears in parentheses at the end of the cite.

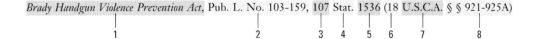

Brady Handgun Violence Prevention Act, Pub. L. No. 103-159, 107 Stat. 1536 (18 U.S.C.A. § § 921-925A)

1. *Statute title.*

2. *Public law number.* In the sample citation, the number 103 indicates this law was passed by the 103d Congress, and the number 159 indicates it was the 159th law passed by that Congress.

3. *Reporter volume number.* The number preceding the reporter abbreviation indicates the reporter volume containing the statute.

4. *Reporter abbreviation.* The name of the reporter is abbreviated. The statute in the sample citation is from *Statutes at Large.*

5. *Reporter page.* The number following the reporter abbreviation indicates the reporter page on which the statute begins.

6. *Title number.* Federal laws are divided into major sections with specific titles. The number preceding a reference to the U.S. Code stands for the section called Crimes and Criminal Procedure.

7. *Additional reporter.* The statute in the sample citation may also be found in the *U.S. Code Annotated.*

8. *Section numbers.* The section numbers following a reference to the *U.S. Code Annotated* indicate where the statute appears in that reporter.

COMMENTS WELCOME

Considerable efforts were expended at the time of publication to ensure the accuracy of the information presented in *American Law Yearbook 2010.* The editor welcomes your comments and suggestions for enhancing and improving future editions of this supplement to *The Gale*

Encyclopedia of American Law. Send comments and suggestions to:

American Law Yearbook

Gale

27500 Drake Rd.

Farmington Hills, MI 48331-3535

AFFIRMATIVE ACTION

Employment programs required by federal statutes and regulations designed to remedy discriminatory practices in hiring minority group members; i.e., positive steps designed to eliminate existing and continuing discrimination, to remedy lingering effects of past discrimination, and to create systems and procedures to prevent future discrimination; commonly based on population percentages of minority groups in a particular area. Factors considered are race, color, sex, creed, and age.

Ricci v. DeStefano

Affirmative action programs have been established by some employers to correct generations of racial DISCRIMINATION. However, there has been a constant tension between the means of achieving racial INTEGRATION through the use of examinations and the results that these exams produce. Employers may be presented with a legal dilemma: the threat of either a Title VII DISPARATE IMPACT lawsuit by non-white employees or a Title VII disparate treatment action by white employees. The SUPREME COURT addressed this situation in *Ricci v. DeStefano*, __U.S.__, 129 S. Ct. 2658, 174 L. Ed. 2d 490 (2009), ruling that the city of New Haven, Connecticut could not throw out the results of a firefighters promotion examination because the white and Hispanic candidates had outperformed the minority candidates.

New Haven used objective examinations to identify the best qualified firefighter candidates for promotion. In 2003, 118 New Haven firefighters took examinations to qualify for promotion to the rank of lieutenant or captain. Promotion examinations were infrequent, so candidates had additional pressures. The exam results would determine which firefighters would be considered for promotions during the next two years, and the order in which the candidates would be considered.

The examination results showed that white candidates had outperformed minority candidates. This led to a public debate as to what the city should do. Some minority firefighters argued the tests should be discarded because the results showed the tests to be discriminatory. They threatened a disparate impact discrimination lawsuit if the city made promotions based on the tests. White firefighters said the exams were neutral and fair. They threatened a disparate treatment discrimination lawsuit if the city, relying on the statistical racial disparity, ignored the test results and denied promotions to the candidates who had performed well. The city threw out the examination results, which led to a federal CIVIL RIGHTS lawsuit.

Some white and Hispanic firefighters who likely would have been promoted based on their test performance sued the city and some of its officials. They alleged that, by discarding the test results, the city and the named officials discriminated against the plaintiffs based on their race, in violation of both Title VII and the

Equal Protection Clause. The city and the officials defended their actions, claiming that if they had certified the results, they could have faced liability under Title VII for adopting a practice that had a disparate impact on the minority firefighters. The federal **district court** agreed with the city and dismissed the lawsuit. The Second **Circuit Court** of Appeals affirmed in a very brief opinion. The three-judge panel included Judge SONIA SOTOMAYOR, who was nominated to the Supreme Court shortly before the case was decided by the Court.

The Court, in a 5-4 decision, reversed the Second Circuit ruling. Justice ANTHONY KENNEDY, writing for the majority, noted the cursory appeals COURT OPINION. Therefore, he devoted a large part of his opinion to setting out the facts of the case. The promotion and hiring process was governed by the city charter, in addition to federal and state law. The charter established a **merit system** that required the city to fill vacancies in the classified civil-service ranks with the most qualified individuals, as determined by job-related examinations. After each examination, the New Haven Civil Service Board (CSB) certifies a ranked list of applicants who passed the test. Under the charter's "rule of three," the relevant hiring authority must fill each vacancy by choosing one candidate from the top three scorers on the list. Certified promotional lists remain valid for two years.

Under the union agreement with the firefighters, the city imposed other requirements. Applicants for lieutenant and captain positions were to be screened using written and oral examinations, with the written exam accounting for 60 percent and the oral exam 40 percent of an applicant's total score. To qualify for the examination candidates for lieutenant needed 30 months' experience in the department, a high-school diploma, and certain vocational training courses. Candidates for captain needed one year's service as a lieutenant in the department, a high-school diploma, and certain vocational training courses.

A private consulting firm prepared the examinations, which consisted of 100 objective questions. After consultant prepared the tests, the city authorized a 3-month study period. Candidates were provided a list that identified the source material for the questions, including the specific chapters from which the questions were taken. Oral examinations were also prepared, which were based on hypothetical situations to test incident-command skills, firefighting tactics, interpersonal skills, leadership, and management ability.

Seventy-seven candidates completed the lieutenant examination—43 whites, 19 blacks, and 15 Hispanics. Of those, 34 candidates passed—25 whites, 6 blacks, and 3 Hispanics. Eight lieutenant positions were vacant at the time of the examination. As the rule of three operated, this meant that the top 10 candidates were eligible for an immediate promotion to lieutenant. All 10 were white. Forty-one candidates completed the captain examination—25 whites, 8 blacks, and 8 Hispanics. Of those, 22 candidates passed—16 whites, 3 blacks, and 3 Hispanics. Seven captain positions were vacant at the time of the examination. Under the rule of three, 9 candidates were eligible for an immediate promotion to captain—7 whites and 2 Hispanics.

Justice Kennedy noted that the lawsuit involved "two provisions of Title VII to be interpreted and reconciled, with few, if any, precedents in the courts of appeals discussing the issue." The Court crafted its decision on the premise that the City of New Haven's "actions would violate the disparate-treatment prohibition of Title VII absent some valid defense. All the evidence demonstrates that the City chose not to certify the examination results because of the statistical disparity based on race—i.e., how minority candidates had performed when compared to white candidates." Without some other justification, the express, race-based decision-making violated Title VII's command that employers cannot take adverse employment actions because of an individual's race.

The Court concluded that the district court had mistakenly ignored this principle when it ruled that the city's "motivation to avoid making promotions based on a test with a racially disparate impact ... does not, as a MATTER OF LAW, constitute discriminatory intent." Justice Kennedy stated that the question is "not whether that conduct was discriminatory but whether the City had a lawful justification for its race-based action." He concluded that it should adopt the "strong basis in evidence" standard that it had used in EQUAL PROTECTION Clause cases. Under this standard, "certain government actions to remedy past racial discrimination—actions that are themselves based on race—are constitutional only where there is a 'strong basis in evidence' that the remedial actions were necessary." This standard constrains employers' discretion in making race-based decisions; it limits that discretion to cases in which there is a "strong basis in evidence of disparate-impact liability, but it is not so restrictive that it allows employers to act only when there is a provable, actual violation."

Applying this standard, the Court held the city lacked a strong basis in evidence. The city could not discard test results and thereby discriminate against qualified candidates on the basis of their race. There was no strong evidence that the tests were flawed because they were not job-related or because other, equally valid and less discriminatory tests were available to the city. Moreover, "Fear of LITIGATION alone cannot justify an employer's reliance on race to the detriment of individuals who passed the examinations and qualified for promotions."

ANTITRUST LAW

Legislation enacted by the federal and various state governments to regulate trade and commerce by preventing unlawful restraints, price-fixing, and monopolies, to promote competition, and to encourage the production of quality goods and services at the lowest prices, with the primary goal of safeguarding public welfare by ensuring that consumer demands will be met by the manufacture and sale of goods at reasonable prices.

American Needle, Inc. v. National Football League

The National Football League sought to be exempt from federal antitrust laws, just as Major League Baseball enjoys such an exemption. The league successfully made this argument before a federal **district court** in 2007 and again before the Seventh **Circuit Court** of Appeals in 2008. However, a unanimous SUPREME COURT disagreed with the league, concluding in a 2010 opinion that the NFL consists of 32 separate entities that competed with one another. Since the NFL was subject to antitrust laws, a lawsuit brought by the manufacturer of souvenir headwear will be allowed to proceed with its case against the league.

The NFL was founded as the American Professional Football Association in 1920. The league has had numerous teams during its 90-year history; as of 2010, the league consisted of 32 franchises. These franchises are separately owned and operated, and these teams compete in more than 250 games per season. The league's championship game, known as the Super Bowl, is one of the biggest single-day events in the world, garnering massive attention

An American Needle worker at the company office, June 2009.

AP IMAGES

not only from the press in the United States, but also from the press in dozens of other countries.

Given its enormous popularity that is still growing, the league's INTELLECTUAL PROPERTY is very valuable. During the 1960s, the teams in the league and the league itself sought to promote its brand collectively. To do so, the league formed NFL Properties in 1963 to spearhead its promotional efforts. NFL Properties is a corporate **entity** formed separately from the league, and the organization is charged with two principal obligations. First, NFL Properties develops, licenses, and markets the intellectual property the teams own, including the various logos, TRADEMARKS, and so forth. Second, the entity conducts and engages in advertising campaigns and promotional ventures on behalf of the league and its teams.

NFL Properties grants licenses to vendors so that these vendors can use the various teams' trademarks and insignia on merchandise, such as shirts and caps. For several years, NFL Properties granted licenses for several vendors to produce headwear. One of these vendors was American Needle, which had a license from NFL Properties for more than 20 years. However, NFL Properties in 2000 announced that it would grant an exclusive headwear license, and after a bidding war took place, NFL Properties granted an exclusive license to Reebok for 10 years. At that time, NFL Properties refused to renew American Needle's license.

American Needle responded by bringing a lawsuit against the NFL, NFL Properties, the different NFL teams, and Reebok. American Needle alleged that the NFL and the other defendants had violated the Sherman Antitrust Act, 15 U.S.C. § 1, which prohibits any "contract, combination … or CONSPIRACY, in restraint of trade." According to American Needle's argument, the NFL teams are separate, individual legal entities that collectively agreed to authorize NFL Properties to negotiate on the teams' behalf. According to American Needle, when NFL Properties decided on the teams' behalf to award an exclusive contract to Reebok, the defendants had conspired to restrain trade. Moreover, American Needle argued that by awarding an exclusive license, NFL Properties and the other defendants had created a **monopoly** for the sale of NFL merchandise and products in violation of § 2 of the Sherman Antitrust Act.

The NFL countered that the Sherman Antitrust Act did not apply to the league or the other defendants because all of these defendants were essentially part of one entity. The league based its argument on the Supreme Court's decision in *Copperweld Corp. v. Independence Tube Corp.*, 467 U.S. 752, 104 S. Ct. 2731, 81 L. Ed. 2d 628 (1984), in which the Court held that a parent corporation and a wholly owned subsidiary were a single entity for purposes of **antitrust law**. Since the concerns behind the Sherman Antitrust Act do not involve entities that are part of the parent-subsidiary relationship, the Court concluded that the act did not apply. Lower **federal courts** later extended this decision to apply to affiliated companies and individuals, even though the parties may not have had a parent-subsidiary relationship.

After a lengthy pretrial process, Judge James B. Moran of the U.S. District Court for the Northern District of Illinois agreed with the league regarding its single-entity argument. According to Moran, "[American Needle] is correct in asserting that a finding of 'single entity' does not in all circumstances doom a monopolization claim. But here the conduct of the 'single entity' relates to the licensing of intellectual property and the owner or controller of such property can license to one or many without running afoul of the antitrust laws. And the licensee can aggressively promote such an arrangement because it is only promoting what the licensor has a right to do." *American Needle, Inc. v. New Orleans La. Saints*, 533 F. Supp. 2d 7901 (N.D. Ill. 2007). Moran accordingly granted the NFL's motion for **summary judgment**.

American Needle renewed its arguments before a panel of the Seventh Circuit Court of Appeals. American Needle asserted that the Supreme Court's analysis in *Copperweld* should not apply to the NFL, because unlike a parent and subsidiary, the different NFL teams compete with one another. In an opinion written by Michael S. Kanne, however, the Seventh Circuit panel disagreed. According to the court, the NFL's activities can only be carried out jointly, and the league's joint efforts constitute one source of economic power. Kanne's opinion concluded, "Simply put, nothing in § 1 (of the Sherman Antitrust Act) prohibits the NFL teams from cooperating so the league can compete against other entertainment providers. Indeed, ANTITRUST LAW encourages cooperation inside a business organization-such as, in this case, a professional sports league-to foster competition between that organization and its competitors. Viewed in this light, the NFL teams are best described as a single source of economic power when promoting NFL football through licensing the teams' intellectual property, and we thus cannot say that the district court was wrong to so conclude."

Once again, American Needle appealed the decision, seeking a **writ** of **certiorari** from the U.S. Supreme Court. In a surprising move, the NFL agreed that the Court should review the case, with the league hoping that the Court would conclude that the Sherman Antitrust Act simply does not apply to leagues such as the NFL, National Basketball Association, and so forth. Instead, a unanimous Court reached the opposite conclusion. Justice Stevens, a former antitrust lawyer, wrote, "To a firm making hats, the Saints and the Colts are two potentially competing suppliers of valuable trademarks." Stevens rejected the NFL's single-entity argument, noting, "The teams compete with one another, not only on the playing field, but to attract fans, for gate receipts and for contracts with managerial and playing personnel."

Stevens reviewed the jurisprudence that had evolved in the Court to determine whether the NFL's argument about it being a single entity had merit. By concluding that the NFL teams each acted independently, the Court disagreed with the Seventh Circuit's assessment. Stevens noted that the decision did not effectively mean that the league was "trapped" by antitrust law. In some instances, the league's teams may need to make decisions collectively, and these collective decisions will not necessarily constitute violations of the Sherman Act. However, attempting to limit the sale of items through a single outlet was not a type of agreement that was exempt from the Sherman Act.

Commentators noted that American Needle's victory was the first by a PLAINTIFF in an antitrust case before the Supreme Court since 1992.

ARBITRATION

The submission of a dispute to an unbiased third person designated by the parties to the controversy, who agree in advance to comply with the award— a decision to be issued after a hearing at which both parties have an opportunity to be heard.

Jackson v. Rent-a-Center West

The U.S. SUPREME COURT ruled in June 2010 that the validity of an ARBITRATION agreement signed by an employer and an employee must be resolved by the arbitrator rather than a federal court under

the terms of the arbitration agreement itself. Commentators stressed that the decision could have significant implications on the law of dispute resolution, given that **federal courts** provide fair tribunals to review what could be unfair arbitration agreements. Under the Court's decision in *Rent-a-Center v. Jackson*, No. 09-497, 2010 WL 2471058 (June 21, 2010), a federal court can only review an arbitration agreement's provision about permitting an arbitrator to review a dispute.

Before beginning work at Rent-a-Center West in Nevada, Antonio Jackson signed an arbitration agreement. The agreement provided, "The arbitrator, and not any federal, state, or local court or agency, shall have exclusive authority to resolve any dispute relating to the interpretation, applicability, enforceability or formation of this Agreement including, but not limited to any claim that all or any part of this Agreement is void or voidable."

Jackson on February 1, 2007 filed a lawsuit in the U.S. **District Court** for the District of Nevada, claiming racial DISCRIMINATION and retaliation in violation of 42 U.S.C. § 1981. Based on the arbitration agreement, Rent-a-Center moved to dismiss the proceedings and compel arbitration. According to Rent-a-Center, an arbitrator should decide threshold question about whether the valid and enforceable rather than a federal district court. Jackson responded by arguing that the arbitration agreement was both procedurally and substantively **unconscionable** and thus unenforceable. Jackson further argued that the district court and not the arbitrator should rule on the unconscionability argument.

The dispute focused on the application of the Federal Arbitration Act (FAA), 9 U.S.C. §§ 1 **et seq.** Section 2 of this **statute** establishes that arbitration agreements "shall be valid, **irrevocable**, and enforceable, save upon such grounds as exist at law or in equity for the revocation of any contract." As a general matter, courts have held that arbitration agreements are subject to the same defenses to enforcement as other contracts. Thus, a party contesting an arbitration agreement can assert claims based on generally applicable contract defenses, such as unconscionability, **fraud**, or **duress**. The FAA further provides that a party may request that a federal court to stay an action on any issue that should be subject to arbitration. Moreover, the FAA allows a party to petition a federal court to order the parties to submit a dispute to arbitration.

The question in *Jackson* focused on the role the federal district court should play when an arbitration agreement provides that the arbitrator should decide the enforceability of the agreement. In a line of cases, the Supreme Court established that when a party challenges the validity of a contract as a whole rather than the specific arbitration provision, the arbitrator should make the decision rather than the court. Thus, for example, if a contract for professional services also contains an arbitration provision, and a party challenges the validity of the entire professional services contract, then an arbitrator should make this decision. Conversely, when a party challenges only the arbitration provision and not the contract as a whole, then a court should rule on the enforceability of the arbitration provision.

In 2007, Federal District Court Judge Larry R. Hicks ruled, "The Agreement to Arbitrate clearly and unmistakenly provides the arbitrator with the exclusive authority to decide whether the Agreement to Arbitrate is enforceable." Thus, "[t]he question of arbitrability is a question for the arbitrator. Accordingly, as it appears a valid arbitration agreement exists which would compel arbitration on the underlying issue disputed by the parties, the court orders all claims concerning the validity of the underlying arbitration clause be submitted to arbitration as agreed to by the parties." Hicks also ruled that even if the court could properly rule on the merits of Jackson's argument, the contract was not unenforceable based on unconscionability. *Jackson v. Rent-a-Center-Weste Inc.* No. 03:07-CV-0050-LRH, 2007 WL 7030394 (D. Nev. June 7, 2007).

A divided panel of the Ninth **Circuit Court** of Appeals reviewed the case. Judges Sidney R. Thomas, writing for the majority, analyzed several Supreme Court cases and concluded that the matter was relatively "straightforward" because the dispute focused entirely on the arbitration agreement and not on another larger agreement. Accordingly, the panel reversed the district court's decision and held that the district court should review Jackson's argument. Judge Cynthia Holcomb Hall dissented stressing that the decision would send run-of-the-mill arbitration cases to federal court for a mini-trial about whether the arbitration agreement is

valid. *Jackson v. Rent-a-Center West, Inc.*, 581 F.3d 912 (9th Cir. 2009).

The Supreme Court agreed to review the case. Writing for a 5-4 majority, Justice ANTONIN SCALIA reviewed the precedent cases regarding the differences between a party challenging an agreement to arbitrate and an agreement as a whole. Scalia stressed that Jackson had challenged the enforceability of the entire agreement and not only the section focused on the agreement to arbitrate. The fact that the entire agreement was an arbitration agreement made "no difference" according to Scalia; since Jackson did not specifically challenge the provision that delegated resolution of disputes to an arbitrator, the arbitrator had the power to resolve the question about whether the contract was UNCONSCIONABLE.

Justice JOHN PAUL STEVENS dissented and was joined by three other justices. Stevens disagreed with the majority's conclusion that it did not matter whether the entire contract was an arbitration agreement or something else. Stevens said the distinction should have made all the difference in the case's outcome.

Legal commentators, such as law professor Karen Halverson Cross of John Marshall Law School in Chicago, noted that the decision was a victory for business, because businesses are most typically the parties who prefer to include these agreement to arbitrate cases. Consumer protection advocates have stressed that the arbitration process can be unfair to both consumer and employees. After the Court's decision in *Jackson*, though, the arbitrator is the person to decide whether the arbitration agreement is fair. According to Cross, "If an agreement to arbitrate is unfair, the arbitrator shouldn't decide that question. There needs to be a basic level of court control of that process."

Stolt-Nielsen v. AnimalFeeds International

International maritime contracts, especially those involving cargo or parcel shipments, generally contain ARBITRATION clauses. However, many of those clauses are silent on whether or not class arbitration (i.e., consolidation of cases with similar issues and parties) can be imposed on all parties. In *Stolt-Nielsen v. AnimalFeeds International Corp.*, No. 08-1198, 559 U.S. ___ (2010), the U.S. SUPREME COURT held that imposing class arbitration on parties who have not agreed to authorize class arbitration is inconsistent with the

Federal Arbitration Act (FAA). Justice Alito delivered the 5-3 decision of the Court, with Justice Sotomayor taking no part in either deliberation or decision. In so holding, the Court reversed the decision of the Second **Circuit Court** of Appeals.

AnimalFeeds International Corporation, which supplied large quantities of raw ingredients such as fish oil to animal-feed producers around the world, regularly shipped its goods pursuant to a standard contract known in maritime trade as a charter party. Stolt-Nielsen was one of several shipping companies offering parcel tanker transportation services. In 2003, a U.S. DEPARTMENT OF JUSTICE criminal investigation concluded that Stolt-Nielsen and others were engaging in an illegal **price-fixing** CONSPIRACY. When Animal-Feeds learned of this, it filed suit in the U.S. **District Court** for the Eastern District of Pennsylvania against Stolt-Nielsen and several others, alleging multiple antitrust violations, particularly inflated prices, in furtherance of a "global conspiracy to restrain competition in the world market." Other charterers brought similar suits in different jurisdictions. Eventually, the Judicial Panel on MULTIDISTRICT LITIGATION ordered a consolidation of then-pending actions (including AnimalFeed's) in the U.S. District Court for the District of Connecticut.

All parties in the consolidated cases agreed that they must arbitrate their respective antitrust claims. However, AnimalFeeds served upon the defendants a demand for class arbitration seeking to represent the entire class of plaintiffs. Not all the charter parties had class arbitration clauses, i.e., they were silent on the issues of whether arbitration was permissible on behalf of a class. Therefore, the parties submitted that very question to arbitration.

The arbitration panel decided to allow class arbitration, after the parties agreed that the panel would apply rules of the American Arbitration Association. The district court vacated the class arbitration decision, ruling that such determination was in "manifest disregard" of the law. What the court was referring to was its conclusion that the arbitrators should have conducted a choice-of-law analysis, after which they would have applied the federal maritime law that required contracts to be interpreted in light of custom and usage.

The Second Circuit Court of Appeals reversed, holding that, since Stolt-Nielsen and others did not cite any authority that applied a maritime rule of custom and usage *against* class arbitration, the arbitrators' decision was not in "manifest disregard" of maritime law; nor had they disregarded New York law, which had not established a rule against class arbitration.

But the U.S. Supreme Court disagreed. In reversing the Second Circuit, the Court concluded that the arbitrators had exceeded their powers by imposing their own policy decision imposing arbitration on parties who had not agreed to authorize it. Justice Alito, writing for the majority, noted that while interpretation of arbitration agreements was generally a matter of state law, the Federal Arbitration Act (FAA), 9 U.S.C. §1 *et seq.* imposed certain rules, one of which declared that arbitration was a matter of consent, not coercion.

Said the Court,

> [A] party may not be compelled under the FAA to submit to class arbitration unless there is a contractual basis for concluding that the party *agreed* to do so.
> ... Here, where the parties stipulated that there was 'no agreement' on this question, it follows that the parties cannot be compelled to submit their dispute to class arbitration.

The Court then went on to note that an implicit agreement to authorize **class action** arbitration was not something an arbitrator could conclude solely from the fact that there was an agreement to arbitrate. To the contrary, the differences between a simple bilateral action versus a complex CLASS ACTION arbitration were too great for such a presumption.

The Court took time to explain the inapplicability of one of its previous cases, *Green Tree Financial Corporation v. Bazzle,* 539 U.S. 444, after which decision the American Arbitration Association developed its Class Rules. Class Rule 3, in accordance with the **plurality** opinion in that case, requires an arbitrator, as a threshold matter, to determine "whether the applicable arbitration clause permits the arbitration to proceed on behalf of or against a class." But the Court in the present case noted that no single rationale controlled a majority in *Bazzle,* and the plurality opinion in that case only decided whether the court or arbitrator should decide if contracts were "silent" on the class arbitration issue, concluding that it was the arbitrator rather than court. But that question had no bearing on the present case, in which the parties expressly assigned the issue to an arbitrator and none of the parties objected. In any event, the Court clarified that the *Bazzle* plurality did not establish the standard to be applied in deciding whether class arbitration was permitted, but rather left that question open.

Justice Ginsburg's DISSENT (joined by Justices Stevens and Breyer, opined that the Court prematurely took up the question, indulged in a *de novo* review, and "overturned the ruling of experienced arbitrators, substituting its own judgment for that of the decision-makers chosen by the parties."

ATTORNEY-CLIENT PRIVILEGE

In law of evidence, client's privilege to refuse to disclose and to prevent any other person from disclosing confidential communications between the client and his or her attorney. Such privilege protects communications between attorney and client made for the purpose of furnishing or obtaining professional legal advice or assistance. That privilege that permits an attorney to refuse to testify as to communications from the client though it belongs to the client, not the attorney, and hence the client may waive it. In federal courts, state law is applied with respect to such privilege.

Mohawk Industries, Inc. v. Carpenter

Federal and state **appellate** courts conduct their appeals using rules of procedure. These rules contain provisions that make clear to litigants that in most cases appeals courts will only review final decisions of trial courts. APPELLATE courts want to make sure that all matters have been resolved and a judgment entered before examining trial proceedings. Appellate rules generally prohibit parties from appealing trial court orders that deal with pre-trial matters such as discovery, for otherwise appellate courts would be swamped with appeals. Most matters can be resolved **without prejudice** by **appellate court** review of final decisions of the trial courts. The SUPREME COURT dealt with this issue in *Mohawk Industries, Inc. v. Carpenter*, __U.S.__, 130 S. Ct. 599, __L. Ed. 2d __ (2009). It ruled that a pre-trial order requiring the DEFENDANT to disclose attorney-client information was not immediately appealable under the "collateral order doctrine."

Norman Carpenter was a shift supervisor at a Mohawk manufacturing plant in Georgia. He claimed he was terminated after he told the human resources department that the company was employing undocumented immigrants. At the time he informed the company he was not aware of a pending class-action lawsuit against Mohawk for hiring undocumented workers. The company told Carpenter to meet with the lawyer it had retained for this case, who allegedly pressured Carpenter to recant his statements. Carpenter declined to do so, which he alleged led to Mohawk firing him under **false pretenses**. He filed a lawsuit in federal **district court** challenging his termination, which led the plaintiffs in the **class action** case to request an evidentiary hearing to explore Carpenter's allegations. Mohawk objected and presented its side of the story in its response. The company alleged Carpenter had been fire for attempting to hire an undocumented worker.

As the CLASS ACTION progressed, Carpenter's case entered the discovery phase. His lawyer filed a motion to compel the company to provide information about his meeting with the Mohawk lawyer and its termination decision. Mohawk objected, claiming the information was protected by **attorney-client privilege**. The district court ruled that the privilege applied to the information but granted the motion because Mohawk had implicitly waived the privilege when it discussed the matter in the class action lawsuit. Mohawk asked the court to certify its order so that it would be immediately appealable but the court refused. The company then filed both a notice of appeal and a petition for a **writ** of **mandamus** with the Eleventh **Circuit Court** of Appeals. The appeals court dismissed the appeal for lack of jurisdiction because the discovery order was not an immediately appealable **collateral** order. Under Supreme Court precedent, an order is appealable if, according to the appeals court, "(1) conclusively determines the disputed question; (2) resolves an important issue completely separate from the merits of the action; and (3) is effectively unreviewable on appeal from a final judgment." The order satisfied the first two conditions but not the third because "a discovery order that implicates the attorney-client privilege" can be adequately reviewed "on appeal from a final judgment." Because other circuit courts of appeal had ruled differently on this type of order, the Supreme Court accepted review.

The Court, in a unanimous decision, upheld the Eleventh Circuit ruling. Justice SONIA

SOTOMAYOR, writing for the Court, noted that the appeals courts "have jurisdiction of appeals from all final decisions of the district courts." Final decisions include not only judgments that end an action but also a small group of prejudgment orders that are "collateral to" an action's merits and "too important" to be denied immediate review. This group includes only decisions that are "effectively unreviewable on appeal from the final judgment in the underlying action." For a right to be effectively unreviewable, delaying review until a final judgment "would imperil a substantial public interest" or "some particular value of a high order."

Applying these principals, Justice Sotomayor agreed with the Eleventh Circuit that disclosure orders involving the ATTORNEY-CLIENT PRIVILEGE can be effectively reviewed by means other than the collateral order doctrine. The order could be included in a review of the trial court judgment and appellate courts could remedy an improper disclosure of privileged material by vacating the judgment and order a new trial with the protected material excluded from evidence. In addition, litigants could ask the trial court to certify an **interlocutory** appeal involving a "controlling question of law" the prompt resolution of which "may materially **advance** the ultimate termination of the litigation."

Justice Sotomayor also pointed out that Congress had enacted laws that designate rule-making as the preferred way for determining "whether and when prejudgment orders should be immediately appealable." The Court directed lawyers dissatisfied with the ruling to seek an amendment to the federal appellate rules of procedure.

ATTORNEY

A person admitted to practice law in at least one jurisdiction and authorized to perform criminal and civil legal functions on behalf of clients. These functions include providing legal counsel, drafting legal documents, and representing clients before courts, administrative agencies, and other tribunals.

Second Circuit Affirms Conviction of Civil Rights Attorney

In November 2009, the **Circuit Court** of Appeals for the Second Circuit upheld the 2005 conviction of CIVIL RIGHTS attorney Lynne Stewart for crimes associated with her LEGAL REPRESENTATION of, and association with,

convicted terrorist and radical cleric Sheikh Omar Abdel-Rahman. *United States v. Stewart*, 597 F.3d 514 (2d Cir. 2009). Most of the original charges centered on her violation of federal Bureau of Prisons regulations restricting her communication of any information learned during her visits with Abdel-Rahman in prison. She also was convicted of conspiring to provide, providing, and concealing material support to Islamic terrorists, PERJURY, and defrauding the federal government.

Practicing law (mostly as a PUBLIC DEFENDER) for more than 30 years on the New York legal scene, Stewart was a self-proclaimed "radical HUMAN RIGHTS lawyer" who publicly professed her support for armed revolutionary struggle. In the past, she had legally defended such controversial clients as the Black Panthers, various police killers, drug dealers, and accused terrorists. Notwithstanding, she maintained a respectable reputation for professional conduct over the years. Her troubles started with her legal representation of Abdel-Rahman in a 1995 trial that resulted in his conviction. He is serving a life sentence for his role in a thwarted 1993 plot to bomb the UNITED NATIONS, the FBI Building in Manhattan, the Lincoln and Holland Tunnels, and other New York landmarks. He also promoted the ASSASSINATION of Egypt's President Hosni Mubarak. Several of Abdel-Rahman's followers issued a series of threats against the United States demanding his release. Stewart and two other defendants, Ahmed Abdel Sattar and Mohammed Yousry, were accused of scheming to obtain his release.

Following Abdel-Rahman's conviction, he was placed in solitary confinement in a maximum security facility in Colorado. Additionally, he was subject to Special Administrative Measures (SAMs) which restricted his communications with individuals outside of prison, permitting communications only with his wife and his lawyers. As his lawyer, Stewart signed several documents pledging to obey the federal rules that barred her client from communicating with his followers and devotees.

Instead, she allegedly covered up secret conversations between Abdel-Rahman and his followers, actually SMUGGLING messages to and from him outside and into the prison during her visits with him. Government surveillance, both on audio recordings and video tape, confirmed Stewart's role in the message-relaying. At one

point, after conveying a message to him from some Islamic group members, she brought a responsive message back from him. She then contacted a media reporter and read him the statement, hoping to make a public announcement that Abdel-Rahman did not support the cease-fire between the Egyptian government and the Islamic group, a fundamentalist organization that carried out terrorist attacks on tourists and police officers.

Testifying on her own behalf, Stewart readily acknowledged violating government regulations, but argued that her conduct was within a lawyer's "bubble" to defend her client as she saw best. Therefore, she argued, her alleged misconduct amounted to no more than zealous representation of her client.

But at her trial, Stewart skirted questions regarding the violent anti-American preachings of her client. Prosecutors introduced more than 1,300 exhibits, including a videotape of Osama bin Laden vowing to "spill blood" if Stewart's client, Abdel-Rahman, was not released from prison. (Stewart's co-defendant Sattar later issued a fatwa urging followers to kill Jews everywhere.)

Ultimately, after 12 days of deliberation, the chosen jury (who served anonymously because of the terrorism-related charges at trial)

convicted Stewart on five counts of aiding TERRORISM. Tearful and pale at the reading of the verdict, she later vowed to fight her conviction, becoming indignant and unrepenting for her crimes. Federal prosecutors had asked for the maximum sentence of 30 years, but in 2006, Stewart was sentenced to just 28 months, based on her clean record of professional conduct up to this point. She remained free on bond pending her appeal.

Appellate counsel for Stewart included volunteer attorneys such as Duke Law School Professor Michael Tigar and New York attorney Joshua Dratel. They argued that the convictions and Stewart's 28-month prison sentence were politically motivated and influenced by the terror-related events of September 11, 2001.

But the Second Circuit disagreed. Not only did it affirm the convictions, it also ordered the **district court** to revoke Stewart's bail and ordered Stewart to surrender immediately. Said the Court,

> We conclude that the district court committed neither procedural error in calculating the applicable Guideline ranges, nor substantive error in varying from those ranges pursuant to its consideration of the factors set forth in 18 U.S.C. §3553(a) . . . [W]e direct the court to revoke Stewart's and Yousry's

bail pending appeal and to order them to surrender to the United States Marshal to begin serving their sentences **forthwith**.

Even more commanding in the APPELLATE court's 191-page opinion was its remand order. Finding that the district court failed to consider whether Stewart had committed perjury at trial, the court noted that her current 28-month sentence was "out of line with the extreme seriousness of her criminal conduct," and in a concurring opinion by Judge John Walker, suggested that Stewart serve 360 months.

Following her original sentencing in 2006, Stewart voluntarily resigned from practicing law in New York. However, in 2007, she was involuntarily disbarred, following rejection of her voluntary resignation.

ATTORNEY'S FEES

Astrue v. Ratliff

The Equal Access to Justice Act (EAJA), 28 U.S.C. §2412(d), provides, in relevant part, that "a court shall award to a prevailing party ... fees and other expenses ... in any civil action ... brought by or against the United States ... unless the court finds that the position of the United States was substantially justified." In *Astrue v. Ratliff*, No. 08-1322, 560 U.S. ___ (2010), the U.S. SUPREME COURT considered whether an award of "fees and other expenses" to a "prevailing party" under §2412(d) was payable to the litigant or to his attorney. The unanimous opinion of the Court held that the award was payable to the litigant and was therefore subject to a Government offset to satisfy a non-related debt owed by the litigant to the United States.

South Dakota attorney Catherine Ratliff represented litigant Ruby Willows Kills Ree in a successful claim for SOCIAL SECURITY benefits. The **district court** granted Ree's unopposed motion for a §2412(d) fees award totaling $2,112.60. However, prior to paying the fees award, the United States Government discovered that Rees had an outstanding debt owed to the U.S. Treasury. Under 31 U.S.C. §3716 (which subjects all funds payable by the United States to an individual to be offset by the amount of certain unpaid delinquent debts owed to the United States by that individual), it sought to have the fees award offset accordingly. But when the government notified Ree that it would apply the Treasury Department's Offset Program

(TOP) to the fees award, attorney Ratliff intervened. She challenged the offset on the grounds that §2412(d) fees belonged to the litigant's attorney, and therefore could not be used to satisfy the litigant's unrelated federal debts. Ratliff characterized the offset as an illegal seizure under the FOURTH AMENDMENT.

The district court held that because §2412 (d) fees were awarded to a "prevailing party," not the prevailing party's attorney, Ratliff lacked standing to challenge the offset. Ratliff appealed.

The Eighth **Circuit Court** of Appeals reversed. It held that under its precedent, EAJA attorneys' fees were awarded to prevailing parties' attorneys. The **appellate court** acknowledged that its decision was contrary to the holding of several other circuits. But, conceded Circuit Judge Michael Melloy, "Were we deciding this case in the **first instance**, we may well agree with our sister circuits and be persuaded by a literal interpretation of the EAJA, providing that 'a court may award reasonable fees and expenses of attorneys to the prevailing party.'" The U.S. Supreme Court granted **certiorari** to resolve the conflict among circuit courts.

Justice Thomas delivered the opinion of the Court. In holding that fees awarded under the EAJA's §2412(d) were payable to the litigant and not the litigant's attorney, the Court also found that such an award could be subjected to an offset to satisfy the litigant's pre-existing debt to the government. "Nothing in EAJA contradicts this Court's longstanding view that the term 'prevailing party' in attorney's fees statutes is a 'term of art' that refers to the prevailing litigant," wrote Justice Thomas. That the prevailing party's attorney may have a **beneficial interest** or a contractual right in the fees did not alter that conclusion.

The Court also rejected Ratliff's argument that the EAJA provisions, combined with the Social Security Act and the government's practice of paying some EAJA awards directly to attorneys in Social Security cases, rendered §2412(d) ambiguous as to the question presented in this case. The Court noted that subsection (d)(1)(B) as well as other provisions clearly distinguished attorneys and prevailing parties, treating attorneys in a category with other service providers in a manner that would foreclose a conclusion that they were singled out to receive direct payment of §2412(d)(1)(A) awards. With regard to Social Security fees awards payable directly to a prevailing party's attorney under 42 U.S.C. §406(b)(1)(A), the Court found this to actually undermine Ratliff's argument. Rather, said the Court, it showed that Congress knew how to create a direct fee requirement where it intended to do so. Finally, said the Court, its conclusion was supported by other cases interpreting 42 U.S.C. §1988, which contained language almost identical to that in §2412(d)(1)(A). (See, e.g., *Evans v. Jeff D.*, 475 U.S. 717 at 730-732.)

Justice Sotomayor wrote a separate concurring opinion, in which she was joined by Justices Stevens and Ginsburg. She agreed with the Court's opinion because the text of EAJA and the Court's precedents compelled such a conclusion. However, that conclusion, continued Justice Sotomayor, did not answer the question whether Congress intended the government to reduce awards from EAJA to offset a litigant's pre-existing and non-related debts. Justice Sotomayor noted that the TREASURY DEPARTMENT began to do this only as of 2005, pursuant to its authority under the Debt Collection Improvement Act of 1996, Pub. L. No. 104-134, 110 Stat. 1321. She opined that Congress likely did not consider that question at the time, and that, had it done so, it would not have wanted EAJA fee awards to be subject to offset. She further opined that such offsets undercut the effectiveness of the EAJA and hinted that perhaps Congress may address this in the future.

Perdue v. Kenny A.

Under the federal CIVIL RIGHTS law 42 U.S.C. §1988 a court may award "reasonable" attorney's fees for prevailing parties in a civil rights action. Since its enactment, the SUPREME COURT has had to determine when a party "prevails" and how the lower courts must calculate reasonable fees. By 2009 the Court had settled on what it called the "lodestar," which is the number of hours the lawyers and their employees worked multiplied by the hourly rates prevailing in the community. However, some courts have increased the lodestar for superior performance. When such enhancements are justified led to confusion. The Court attempted to resolve the confusion in *Perdue v. Kenny A.*, __U.S.__, 130 S. Ct. 1662, __L. Ed. 2d__ (2010). It held that courts may enhance lawyer fees for superior performance but only in extraordinary circumstances.

A civil rights lawsuit was filed on behalf of Kenny A. and 3,000 other children in the Georgia foster-care system. The **class action**, which named as defendants the governor and other state officials, claimed that the foster-care system in two counties near Atlanta were deficient and that these problems violated federal and state rights and laws. The federal **district court** ultimately referred the case to **mediation**, where the parties signed a CONSENT DECREE. The court approved the settlement, which resolved all issues other than the plaintiffs' attorneys fees that should be awarded under §1988. The lawyer submitted a request for $14 million in fees. Half of the amount based on the lodestar, which they justified on the prevailing market rates for legal services in Georgia. The other $7 million was based on the lawyers' claim that their fees be enhanced for superior work and results. They supported their request by claiming the lodestar amount "would be generally insufficient to induce lawyers of comparable skill, judgment, professional representation and experience" to litigate this case. The state objected to the overall fee request, arguing that the proposed hourly rates were too high, the hours claimed were excessive, and the enhancement included factors already reflected in the lodestar amount.

The district court awarded fees of approximately $10.5 million. The court concluded that the hourly rates were reasonable but some of the hours claimed could not be justified because of poor billing records and because of the hours claimed were excessive. The court cut non-travel hours by 15% and reduced the hourly rate for travel by half. The lodestar calculation resulted in fees of almost $6 million. However, the court enhanced this award by 75% because the lodestar calculation failed to take into account the $1.7 million of expenses the lawyers advanced over a three-year period and the fact their fees were contingent on them prevailing. The court lauded the lawyers' performance, calling it the best it had observed in 27 years on the bench. The enhancement added $4.5 million to the award. The Eleventh **Circuit Court** of Appeals upheld the award based on circuit precedent.

The Supreme Court, in a 5-4 decision, overturned the Eleventh Circuit decision. Justice SAMUEL ALITO, writing for the majority, restated the importance of following the lodestar calculation, as it was the most objective measurement for a reviewing court to use in assessing whether the fee award was correct. He noted that six rules guided its decision in the case. First, a "reasonable fee" was one "that is sufficient to induce a capable attorney to undertake the representation of a meritorious civil rights case." Second, there was a strong presumption that the lodestar calculation produced a sufficient fee. Third, the Court had never upheld an enhancement of a lodestar amount for performance. Fourth, the lodestar includes most, if not all, of the relevant factors constituting a reasonable fee amount. An enhancement may not be based on a factor subsumed in a lodestar calculation, such as a lawyer's performance. Fifth, the burden of proving the enhancement is borne by the lawyer seeking the award. Sixth, the lawyer seeking an enhancement must produce "specific evidence" supporting the award.

Applying these rules, Justice Alito concluded that while a fee determined by the lodestar calculation could be enhanced, it could only occur "in those rare circumstances in which the lodestar does not adequately account for a factor that may properly be considered in determining a reasonable fee." In this case the lawyers sought an enhancement for either the quality of their performance or the results they obtained. As to the latter, it was impossible to know if the result

was because of superior performance of the plaintiffs' lawyers or the inferior performances of the defense lawyers. Therefore, the key question was whether superior performance produced the outcome. Alito concluded that there were few circumstances in which superior lawyer performance was not already taken into account in the lodestar calculation, for a lawyer's hourly rate should reflect the person's stature and ability in the legal community.

The district court failed to provide proper justification for raising the lodestar by 75%. By doing so, the court increased the top rate for the lawyers to more than $866 per hour. However, the court did not provide evidence that showed this was the "appropriate figure for the relevant market." In addition, it did not calculate the amount of the enhancement based on the large advances of money that the lawyers made for three years. These and other deficiencies in the methodology used to calculate the fee award order prevented "meaningful **appellate** review." Though Alito did not question the sincerity of the district court's observations about the performance of the lawyers, he concluded that this "impressionistic" approach undermined the major purpose of the lodestar method: "providing an objective and reviewable basis for fees." The Court sent the case back to the lower courts for a new calculation of fees.

BANKRUPTCY

A federally authorized procedure by which a debtor—an individual, corporation, or municipality—is relieved of total liability for its debts by making court-approved arrangements for their partial repayment.

Hamilton v. Lanning

Debtors filing for protection under Chapter 13 of the BANKRUPTCY Code are "individual[s] with regular income" whose debts fall within **statutory** limits. 11 U.S.C. §§101(30) and 109(e). Unlike Chapter 7 debtors (who must **liquidate** their non-exempt assets to pay creditors), Chapter 13 debtors are allowed to keep their property, but must agree to a court-approved plan to pay creditors out of future income. A bankruptcy **trustee** is appointed to oversee the filing and execution of a Chapter 13 debtor's plan. If a proposed plan is objected to by either an unsecured creditor or bankruptcy trustee, the bankruptcy court may not approve the plan unless it specifies provisions for the full repayment of unsecured claims or, alternatively, "provides that all of the debtor's projected disposable income to be received" over the duration of the plan "will be applied to make payments in accordance with the terms of the plan." The Code did not define "projected disposable income" or mandate a method for determining it. That is precisely what the U.S. SUPREME COURT addressed in *Hamilton v. Lanning,* No. 08-998, 560 U.S. ___ (2010).

Stefanie Lanning's income in the six months immediately prior to her bankruptcy petition was significantly inflated because of a one-time buyout from her former employer. Her new job paid much less, and she now had a significantly reduced monthly income. Under the Code, "current monthly income" is calculated by averaging the debtor's monthly income during the six-month period preceding a bankruptcy filing.

Further, most bankruptcy courts calculated "projected disposable income" by using a mechanical approach: multiplying monthly income by the number of months in the plan, and determining the "disposable" portion of the result. In turn, "disposable" referred to the amount remaining after deduction of reasonable amounts necessary for the debtor's maintenance and support.

Lanning proposed a bankruptcy plan based on her actual current income with her new employer. Accordingly, she proposed payment to her creditors of $144 monthly for 36 months. The bankruptcy trustee objected, considering her income for the prior six months (the "mechanical approach") and arguing that the plan should be based on payments of $756 per month for 60 months. The bankruptcy court then modified Lanning's proposed plan, requiring payments of $144 per month for 60 months. Nonetheless, it held that the statute's requirement for the plan to be based on "projected" income meant that courts needed to consider the debtor's actual income at the time of the plan's approval. The bankruptcy court's decision was upheld by the Tenth Circuit Bankruptcy Appeals Panel. The Tenth **Circuit Court** of Appeals also affirmed, holding that, although a calculation of "projected disposable income" generally begins with a presumption that the prior-six-month historical figure is correct, that figure could be rebutted by evidence of a substantial change in the debtor's circumstances.

The U.S. Supreme Court also affirmed, ending a conflict among circuits. In an opinion by Justice Samuel Alito, the Court held that a bankruptcy court may properly account for changes in a debtor's income or expenses that are "known or virtually certain" at the time of confirmation. Such a forward-looking approach (rather than looking at the prior six months) was supported by the very meaning of the word "projected."

Even terms in §1325 clashed with a "mechanical approach," said the Court. This section expressly refers to projected disposable income "to be received in the applicable commitment period," which strongly favors a forward-looking approach. In the present case, Lanning would have far less than $756 per month in disposable income during the plan period, not accurately reflecting disposable income "to be received." Further, since §1325 requires projected disposable income to "be applied to make payments," such a directive clause would be rendered hollow if, as of the plan's effective date, the debtor lacked the income to pay creditors the calculated monthly amount. Other language in the **statute**, such as directing bankruptcy courts to determine disposable income "as of the effective date of the plan," i.e., the date the plan is confirmed (not the date of filing), further supported a more flexible approach.

Likewise, the Court found flaws in the trustee's other arguments supporting the mechanical approach (inflexible formula using the prior six months' income). The trustee had proposed that if using the mechanical approach proved too harsh on debtors, they could employ other strategies to reduce the effects of a higher income during the six-month period preceding the filing. For example, they could delay the filing of a bankruptcy petition so as to place any extraordinary income outside the six-month period, or, could seed leave of court to delay filing a schedule of current income, or, could

dismiss the petition and re-file during a more favorable period. Said the Court, "There is no reason to think that Congress meant for any of these strategies to operate as a safety valve for the mechanical approach."

In sum, the Court, in affirming, concluded,

> [W]e hold that when a bankruptcy court calculates a debtor's projected disposable income, the court may account for changes in the debtor's income or expenses that are known or virtually certain at the time of confirmation.

Justice Scalia was the lone dissenter. He found the Court's conclusion contrary to the Code's actual text, and opined that the Court should not carve out exceptional cases.

Milavetz, Gallop & Milavetz, P.A. v. U.S.

Individuals who are deeply in debt have been taken advantage of by agencies that deal with federal BANKRUPTCY filings. Congress sought to prevent unethical practices surrounding the filing of a bankruptcy petition, one of which was to advise the individual to take on more debt before filing the petition. The Bankruptcy Abuse Prevention and Consumer Protection Act of 2005 (BAPCPA), Pub. L. No. 109-8, 119 Stat. 23. amended the Bankruptcy Code to define a class of bankruptcy professionals as "debt relief agencies." 11 U.S.C. §101(12A). This class includes, with limited exceptions, any person who provides any bankruptcy assistance to an assisted person for payment, or who is a bankruptcy petition preparer. BAPCPA prohibits these professionals from advising an assisted person to incur more debt in contemplation of filing for bankruptcy. §526(a)(4). It also requires them to disclose in their advertisements that their services are with respect to or may involve bankruptcy relief, §§528(a)(3), (b)(2)(A), and to identify themselves as debt relief agencies, §§528(a)(4), (b)(2)(B). A law firm specializing in bankruptcy challenged these provisions of the BAPCPA as applied to lawyers. The SUPREME COURT, in Milavetz, Gallop & Milavetz, P.A. v. U.S., __U.S.__, 130 S. Ct. 3124, 176 L. Ed. 2d 79 (2010), ruled that lawyers were debt relief agencies if they practice bankruptcy law, and that the other provisions of the BAPCPA were similarly applicable to lawyers.

The law firm Milavetz, Gallop & Milavetz and several of its lawyers filed a federal lawsuit seeking a **declaratory judgment** that the

BAPCPA provisions did not apply to lawyers. They asked the court to hold that the firm was not bound by these provisions and therefore could freely advise clients to incur additional debt and need not identify itself as a debt relief agency in its advertisements. The **district court** agreed that lawyers were not debt relief agencies and that the other provisions dealing with identification and advertising of debt relief agencies were unconstitutional as applied to lawyers. The Eighth **Circuit Court** of Appeals reversed all but one part of the district court decision: it ruled unconstitutional the BAPCPA provision that "broadly prohibits a debt relief agency from advising an assisted person to incur *any* additional debt when the assisted person is contemplating bankruptcy," even when that advice constitutes prudent prebankruptcy planning not intended to abuse the bankruptcy laws." The Supreme Court agreed to accept review because other circuit courts of appeal had upheld the BAPCPA as applied to lawyers.

The Court, in a unanimous decision, reversed the Eighth Circuit on the incurring of additional debt issue and upheld the appeals court's other conclusions concerning the scope of BAPCPA. Justice SONIA SOTOMAYOR, writing for the Court, noted that the threshold question was whether lawyers could be considered debt relief agencies. The **statute** seemed clear on this point: "By definition, bankruptcy assistance' includes several services commonly performed by attorneys." In addition, when Congress listed specific exceptions to the definition of debt relief agencies, it did not demonstrate any intent to exclude lawyers. Milavetz had argued that the omission of lawyers from that section demonstrated the opposite conclusion. That omission stood in contract to the provision's explicit inclusion of "bankruptcy petition preparer[s]" a category of professionals that excludes attorneys and their staff. Sotomayor called this argument implausible, as it would exclude from the act all professionals except bankruptcy petition preparers.

Having established that lawyers can be debt relief agencies, the Court examined Milavetz's contention that the prohibition on advising a client to take on more debt before filing for bankruptcy was an unconstitutional content-based restriction on lawyer-client communications. Sotomayor rejected this analysis, siding with the government's more narrow reading of the provision. The restriction on advice to incur

more debt "in contemplation of" bankruptcy was most naturally read to forbid only advice to undertake actions to abuse the bankruptcy system. The phrase "in contemplation of" bankruptcy has long been associated with abusive conduct. The LEGISLATIVE HISTORY of BAPCPA included a finding that consumers were purchasing sizable quantities of goods and services on credit on the eve of bankruptcy in contemplation of obtaining a discharge in bankruptcy. The Court concluded that a debt relief agency violates BAPCPA "only when the impetus of the advice to incur more debt is the expectation of filing for bankruptcy and obtaining the attendant relief."

As to the BAPCPA disclosure requirements, the Court ruled that they did not violate the FIRST AMENDMENT rights of debt relief agencies. The law was directed at "misleading" commercial speech, which does not have the same constitutional protection of noncommercial speech. Congress had identified a "pattern of advertisements that hold out the promise of debt relief without alerting consumers to its potential cost." The likelihood of deception was not speculative and the purpose of the provision was reasonably related to the government's interest in preventing deception of consumers.

United Student Aid Funds, Inc. v. Espinosa

The U.S. BANKRUPTCY Code gives options to debtors as to how to restructure their finances. In many cases debtors will walk away from all that they owe, but Congress has placed restrictions on discharging student loans. It has put in place a procedure to allow debtors a chance to convince the bankruptcy court that continuing to pay on the loans would constitute an undue hardship. Sometimes debtors neglect to send the proper notice to the student loan creditors but the bankruptcy court mistakenly discharges all or part of the loan debt without finding undue hardship or conducting an adversary hearing. The federal circuit courts of appeal were divided on how to treat this oversight; some ruled that the order of discharge was void, while others concluded that creditors still had sufficient notice at the time to raise an objection and therefore the discharge was valid. The SUPREME COURT, in *United Student Aid Funds, Inc. v. Espinosa*, __U.S.__, 130 S. Ct. 1367, 176 L. Ed. 2d 158 (2009), held that in such cases the judgment of the bankruptcy court could not be voided.

Between 1988 and 1989, Francisco Espinosa obtained four federally guaranteed student loans for a total principal amount of $13,250. In 1992, he filed a bankruptcy petition under Chapter 13. Using Chapter 13 will result in a discharge of the debts listed in the plan if the debtor completes the payments the plan requires. Espinosa listed only the student loans in his plan and proposed to repay only the principal on that debt. The remainder of the debt—the accrued interest— would be discharged once he repaid the principal. The clerk of the bankruptcy court sent United Student Aid Funds a copy of Espinosa's filings along with a notice that informed the creditor of the deadline for filing objections to the plan. Under bankruptcy rules, Espinosa should have requested an adversarial proceeding to consider whether making him pay back the entire amount of the loans was an undue hardship. This would have required him to serve a copy of this request on United. Although he did not do so, United's only response was to file with the court a proof of claim for $17,832.15, an amount representing both the principal and the accrued interest on Espinosa's student loans. The company did not did not object to the plan's proposed discharge of Espinosa's student loan interest without a determination of undue hardship, nor did it object to Espinosa's failure to initiate an **adversary proceeding**. In 1993 the court confirmed Espinosa's plan without an adversarial hearing for finding undue hardship. After Espinosa paid off the principal amount in 1997, the court discharged the student loan interest.

Three years later the company sought to collect on the unpaid interest. In 2003, Espinosa filed motion asking the bankruptcy court to enforce its 1997 discharge order by directing United to cease all efforts to collect the unpaid interest on his student loan debt. United countered that the 1993 order should be set aside because of the failure of the court to conduct an undue hardship hearing. In addition, it claimed its due process rights had been violated by Espinosa's failure to serve a summons and complaint on the company for an adversarial proceeding. The court rejected both arguments. United then appealed to U.S. District Court for the District of Arizona, which sided with the company. The Ninth **Circuit Court** of Appeals reversed the **district court**, concluding that the bankruptcy court may have committed a legal error that United might have successfully appealed. However, any such legal error was not a basis for setting aside the confirmation order as void.

Because of the conflict over this issue in the circuits, the Supreme Court accepted review.

In a unanimous decision the Court upheld the Ninth Circuit ruling. Justice CLARENCE THOMAS, writing for the Court, stated that Federal Rule of **Civil Procedure** 60(b)(4), which permits the voiding of legal judgments could not be applied to cases such as Espinosa's. The bankruptcy court's 1993 order was a final judgment from which United did not appeal. The law respects the need for finality and will not undue final decisions absent compelling reasons. Under 60(b)(4), a judgment could only be voided if it is based "either on a certain type of jurisdictional error or on a violation of due process that deprives a party of notice or the opportunity to be heard." There was no jurisdictional error in this case—the bankruptcy court clearly had the authority to rule on the plan. As to the denial of due process, Justice Thomas agreed that United had been denied the required notice for a hearing on undue hardship but this did not reach the level of deprivation of due process. United had been provided with **actual notice** when the clerk sent the company the contents of Espinosa's plan. This "more than satisfied its due process rights."

The Court also held that the bankruptcy court did not lack authority to enter its 1993 order because it did not conduct a hearing on Espinosa's undue hardship plan. Although the court's failure to find undue hardship was a legal error, "the confirmation order is enforceable and binding on United because it had actual notice of the error and failed to object or timely appeal." Finally, Justice Thomas addressed United's claim that allowing such discharges would encourage debtors not to file for a hearing in hopes the court and creditors would overlook the proposal and not object. He stated that "such bad-faith efforts should be deterred by the specter of penalties" that debtors and lawyers face under various code provisions. If more deterrence was warranted, Congress could enact additional sanctions.

Schwab v. Reilly

The U.S. BANKRUPTCY Code provides that a business who files for Chapter 7 bankruptcy, which liquidates assets to pay creditors, may exempt certain assets. A dispute arose in the federal **circuit court** of appeals over whether a bankruptcy **trustee** must formally object to the proposed exempted assets within 30 days if the claimed amount was within the statute's dollar limit. With the court divided on this issue, the SUPREME COURT ruled in *Schwab v. Reilly*, __U.S.__, __ S. Ct. __, __L. Ed. 2d__, 2010 WL 2400094 (2010) that the trustee did not have to formally object. This allows trustees to auction off these exempted assets if they are valued higher than the debtor claimed, pay the debtor the claimed amount, and use the rest of the proceeds to pay creditors.

Nadejda Reilly filed for Chapter 7 bankruptcy when her catering business failed. Her filings included a Schedule C that listed property she claimed was exempt from creditors; she listed tools and equipment that she claimed were worth $10,718, which is below the maximum allowable amount of $10,225. On Schedule B she listed all of her assets, including the equipment. The bankruptcy trustee, William Schwab, had a duty to **liquidate** all the assets and pay the proceeds to the Reilly's creditors. Schwab did not object to the exempt property listed on Schedule C within the 30-day period required by the rules because the dollar value assigned to the equipment by Reilly was within the limits of the **statute**. However, Schwab had the equipment appraised and the value of the property was estimated to be as much as $17,500.

Schwab filed a motion with the bankruptcy court, asking for permission to auction the equipment so Reilly could receive the $10,718 she claimed as exempt, and the estate could distribute the equipment's remaining value (approximately $6,500) to her creditors. Reilly opposed the motion. She argued that by equating on Schedule C the total value of the exemptions she claimed in the equipment with the equipment's estimated **market value**, she had put Schwab and her creditors on notice that she intended to exempt the equipment's full value, even if that amount turned out to be more than the dollar amount she declared, and more than the Code allowed. Therefore, Schwab should have filed an objection if he disputed the amount claimed in question. The bankruptcy court sided with Reilly. Schwab filed an action in federal **district court** but again was denied permission to auction the equipment. The Third Circuit Court of Appeals upheld the ruling. The Supreme Court agreed to hear Schwab's appeal so as to resolve the split in the circuits on this issue.

The Court, in a 6-3 decision, reversed the Third Circuit. Justice CLARENCE THOMAS, writing for the majority, held that Schwab was not required to object to the exemptions in order to preserve the estate's right to retain any value in the equipment beyond the value of the exempt interest. Both sides had agreed that §522(l) of the Code governed the case. This section states that a Chapter 7 debtor must "file a list of property that the debtor claims as exempt under subsection (b) of this section," and that "[u]nless a party in interest objects, the property claimed as exempt on such list is exempt." Reilly contended that the "property claimed as exempt" referred to all of the information on Schedule C, including the estimated market value of each asset. Schwab countered that the Code defined such property as an interest, not to exceed a certain dollar amount, in a particular asset, not as the asset itself. Therefore, the value of the property claimed exempt should be judged on the dollar value the debtor assigned the interest, not on the value the debtor assigned the asset. Justice Thomas concluded that Schwab's reading of the law was correct. Schwab had no duty to object to the property Reilly claimed as exempt because its stated value was within the limits the Code allowed. The information contained in Schedule C was there to aid the trustee in administering the estate. It helped Schwab identify assets that might have value beyond the amount the debtor claimed as exempt, or whose full value might not be available for exemption.

Justice Thomas stated that to adopt Reilly's interpretation could "convert the Code's goal of giving debtors a fresh start into a free pass." By allowing a debtor to remove from the estate certain interests in property, up to certain values, Congress "balanced the difficult choices that exemption limits impose on debtors with the economic harm that exemptions visit on creditors." Therefore, the Court "should not alter that balance by requiring trustees to object to claimed exemptions based on form entries beyond those governing an exemption's validity under the Code." The decision in this case did not encourage trustees and creditors to "sleep on their rights." Instead, the ruling "encourages a debtor wishing to exempt an asset's full market value or the asset itself to declare the value of the claimed exemption in a way that makes its scope clear."

BANKS AND BANKING

Authorized financial institutions and the business in which they engage, which encompasses the receipt of money for deposit, to be payable according to the terms of the account; collection of checks presented for payment; issuance of loans to individuals who meet certain requirements; discount of commercial paper; and other money-related functions.

Cuomo, Attorney General of New York v. Clearing House Association LLC

Certain areas of the law produce legal frictions between state governments and the federal government. For example, Congress has given the federal government broad powers to deal with labor and bank regulation. This does not mean that states cannot address labor and banking issues, but they must be careful not to intrude on federal laws and regulations. The doctrine of federal **preemption** means that federal laws must take precedence over state laws. When a state enacts a law or takes regulatory action in an area where there is a clear statement of federal PREEMPTION, the stage is set for a lawsuit challenging the legality of the **state action**. Such was the case in *Cuomo, Attorney General of New York v. Clearing House Association LLC*, __U.S.__, 129 S. Ct. 2710, 174 L. Ed. 2d 464 (2009), where several national banks (chartered by the federal government) challenged requests "in lieu of a subpoena" issued by then New York attorney general Elliot Spitzer. (His successor, Andrew Cuomo, was later substituted as defendant.) Spitzer sought to determine whether these banks had violated state fair-lending laws. The SUPREME COURT rejected some of the preemption argument and concluded that while such requests were impermissible, the state was allowed to pursue an enforcement action in court.

The Clearing House Association, a banking trade group, and the federal Office of the **Comptroller** of the Currency (OCC), filed suit in New York federal **district court**, contending that the request was preempted by federal law and asking for an INJUNCTION prohibiting it. The OCC specifically pointed to an OCC regulation promulgated under the National Bank Act (NBA) that prohibits that form of state law enforcement against national banks. The district court agreed and entered an injunction prohibiting the attorney general from enforcing state fair-lending laws through demands for records or judicial proceedings. The Second **Circuit Court** of Appeals upheld the injunction.

The Supreme Court, in a 5-4 decision, upheld part of the injunction and overturned another part. Justice Anthony Scalia, writing for the majority, cited the pertinent section of the NBA, which deals with the "visitorial powers" that can be exercised over national banks. The provision states that: "No national bank shall be subject to any visitorial powers except as authorized by Federal law, vested in the courts of justice or such as shall be, or have been exercised or directed by Congress or by either House thereof or by any committee of Congress or of either House duly authorized." The OCC issued a regulation to implement the law which gives the OCC the sole power to exercise visitorial powers. State officials may not exercise these powers, which include conducting examinations, inspecting or requiring the production of books or records, or prosecuting enforcement actions, except in limited circumstances authorized by federal law.

Justice Scalia examined the history of the meaning of "visitorial powers," which originally dealt in England with the oversight of corporations by the sovereign. When the NBA was enacted in 1864, visitorial powers was understood as "[t]he act of examining into the affairs of a corporation" by "the government itself." Supreme Court **case law** has made a distinction between "visitation," which is the oversight of corporate affairs, and the power to enforce the law. The NBA only preempts states from exercising visitorial powers. The NBA itself allows some state substantive laws on banks to remain in effect yet the OCC rule states that a state may not enforce its "valid, non-preempted laws against national banks."

The Court made clear that when a state chooses to pursue enforcement of its laws in court, then it is not exercising its visitation powers and will be treated like a litigant. Recognition of this status does not deprive the federal government of its powers nor does it allow a state regulator to create unchecked mischief. Scalia pointed out that an attorney general acting as a civil litigant "must file a lawsuit, survive a motion to dismiss, endure the rules of procedure and discovery, and risk sanctions if his claim is frivolous or his discovery tactics abusive." In addition, judges have the power to prevent "fishing expeditions" by state officials. Therefore, the Court ruled that the OCC regulation did not comport with the NBA provision. Moreover, the OCC's interpretation of its own regulation did not comport with the text. The Comptroller sought to limit the broad sweep of the regulation by including in its statement of purpose language that Scalia found could not be reconciled with the regulation.

Applying these principles to the case, Justice Scalia upheld that part of the injunction barring the threatened issuance of an executive SUB-POENA. The Court vacated the other part of the injunction that barred the attorney general from bringing an enforcement action.

BLACKMAIL

The crime involving a threat for purposes of compelling a person to do an act against his or her will, or for purposes of taking the person's money or property.

David Letterman Part of an Extortion Plot

Late night talk show star David Letterman became the target in a $2 million EXTORTION plot conceived by a television producer who sought revenge for Letterman's affair with a female staffer. Letterman not only involved the authorities in the case, but he also confessed to the allegations of sexual conduct on his television show. The case led to a guilty plea by Robert "Joe" Halderman, who was sentenced to six months in prison.

Letterman has been a celebrity since first appearing on *Late Night with David Letterman* on NBC in 1983. His show followed the popular *Tonight Show* with Johnny Carson for a number of years before Letterman in 1993 moved to CBS to become the host of *The Late Show with David Letterman*. He is known for dry, sarcastic humor and self-deprecation, and he has won numerous awards for his performances. Letterman's first marriage ended in DIVORCE in 1977. He reportedly had a long-term relationship with one of the head writers and producers on the show before he began a relationship with Regina Lasko, a production manager, in 1986. Letterman and Lasko had a child together in 2003, and in 2009, the two finally married.

In 2005, Letterman was the target of another BLACKMAIL scheme when a painter who worked on Letterman's ranch in Montana concocted a scheme to extort $5 million from Letterman by KIDNAPPING Letterman's then 16-month-old

Robert J. Halderman, accused of blackmailing David Letterman, in court October 2009.
AP IMAGES

son, Harry. Agents with the FEDERAL BUREAU OF INVESTIGATION caught the man, Kelly A. Frank, before Frank could complete the kidnapping. Frank was caught when he pitched the idea to an acquaintance whom Frank was trying to bring in as a co-conspirator.

Halderman began his career as a producer on CBS and later became a foreign reporter. During the 2000s, he produced a number of television shows, including *48 Hours*. He won a total of seven Emmy Awards for his production work. His first marriage ended in divorce, and he was reportedly ordered to pay $6,800 to his former spouse in child and spousal support. He began a relationship with Stephanie Birkett, an assistant on Letterman's show who sometimes appeared in skits on the show's telecasts. Halderman and Birkett lived together for several years.

During the fall of 2009, Letterman noted on his show that he was being blackmailed. On October 1, he offered more specifics, noting that he had testified before a **grand jury** in New York. In the monologue, Letterman acknowledged that he had engaged in sexual relationships with female staff members in the past, though he offered no specifics. He apologized on air to both the women and to Lasko. All of Letterman's affairs reportedly occurred before Lasko and Letterman were married. Most commentators said that Letterman handled the on-air apologies well and that by admitting to the affairs on the air, Letterman probably saved himself from a public relations nightmare.

Stories about the extortion attempt became public shortly after Letterman's show. According to initial reports, Letterman received a package during September 2009. The package stated that the person who sent the package would reveal Letterman's indiscretions unless Letterman agreed to pay $2 million to the sender. On the air, Letterman told his audience that the letter he received said, "I know that you do some terrible terrible things and I can prove that you do these terrible things... and sure enough what was contained in the package was proof that I do terrible, terrible things." Letterman contacted his attorney and set up a meeting with the blackmailer. At a meeting, the blackmailer said that he had planned to write a book about Letterman's life, focusing on Letterman's sexual relationships. Letterman gave the blackmailer a fake $2 million check.

One day after Letterman's on-air admission, Manhattan District Attorney Robert Morgenthau identified Halderman as the person trying to blackmail Letterman. Morgenthau said that Letterman's attorney met with Halderman three times. At the press conference, the PROSECUTOR revealed that one of the staff members with whom Letterman was involved was Birkett, who had done production work with *48 Hours* before working on Letterman's show starting in 2003. Birkett began a relationship with Letterman shortly after arriving as a staff member, and this relationship continued even after Halderman and Birkett had moved in together. Halderman discovered the affair when he read Birkett's diaries.

According to prosecutors, Halderman had accumulated significant debts due in large part to his divorce, and these debts were part of Halderman's motivation for trying to blackmail Letterman. Halderman was also reportedly despondent over his ex-wife's decision to move to Colorado with their son, with whom Halderman had a close relationship. One of Halderman's friends noted that Halderman spent many hours teaching his son to play sports, and the friend expressed shock about the revelations that he was behind the plot. One source told the *New York Post* that Halderman's principal motivation for the plot was based on his anger towards Letterman. The source said, "This wasn't about money, not money alone. This was revenge. It was about making Letterman miserable."

In March 2010, Halderman pleaded guilty to a charge of second degree **grand larceny**. Although Halderman's lawyer maintained that Halderman had the right to sell the book idea regarding Letterman's affairs, Halderman apologized publicly to Letterman, Birkett, and others for the plot. Halderman faced up to 15 years in prison, but he received only a six-month sentence.

CABLE TELEVISION

D.C. Circuit Overturns FCC Cable Ownership Rule

The FEDERAL COMMUNICATIONS COMMISSION (FCC) is charged with regulating electronic media, including broadcast and CABLE TELEVISION. In 1993 the FCC issued a rule that barred cable companies from controlling more than 30 percent of the U.S. market. The FCC imposed the cap after Congress passed the Cable Television Consumer Protection and Competition Act of 1992, Pub. L. No. 102-385, 106 Stat. 1460, which said the agency must set "reasonable limits" on the number of customers a cable company can service. Since the law's enactment the number of cable networks has increased five-fold and satellite television companies, which were insignificant players then, now serve one-third of all subscribers. The FCC twice changed the formula it uses to determine the maximum number of subscribers a cable operator may serve, but the subscriber limit remained at 30 percent.

In 2001, the cable industry successfully challenged the formula the FCC used to calculate the 30 percent subscriber cap. On remand the FCC issued a new set of rules that the cable industry found constricting. It filed a new petition. In 2009 the **Circuit Court** of Appeals for the District of Columbia ruled in favor of the cable industry in *Comcast v. Federal Communications Commission*, 579 F.3d 1, (D.C.Cir.:2009). The appeals court labeled the rule "arbitrary and capricious" and faulted the FCC for not sufficiently considering the competition to cable companies from direct broadcast satellite providers DirecTV and Dish Network.

The dispute centered on how the FCC developed the formula that led to the 30 percent cap on any one company controlling the cable market. In 1993, the FCC used the "open field" approach that took into account three variables: (1) the "minimum viable scale"–the number of viewers a network must reach to be economically viable; (2) the relevant market–the total number of subscribers; and (3) the "penetration rate"–the percentage of viewers the average cable network reaches once a cable operator elects to carry it. The FCC sought to ensure a minimum open field of 40 percent and concluded that a 30 percent cap rather than a 60 percent cap was needed because the commission was concerned a cable network would not be viable if the two largest cable operators refused to carry it. In the 2001 decision by the D.C. Circuit, the court concluded that there was no evidence that cable operators were colluding to do deny access to cable programmers. In reversing the FCC rule, the court directed it to draft a new rule that took into account the massive growth of the DBA companies.

The FCC revisited the rule and again adopted a 30 percent subscriber limit. The new rule was premised on the commission's desire that no one single cable operator could cause a programming network to fail by refusing to carry it. In its recalculation of the minimum variable scale, the FCC relied on a study that used data from 1984 to 2001. The study concluded that a cable network needed 19 million subscribers to have a 70 percent chance of survival after five years. This was four million more than had been needed when designing the previous rule. The 19 million subscribers was based on a penetration rate that almost half the previous rate. Therefore, a cable programming network, to be viable, required an open field of 70 percent, which was up more than 40 percent of all subscribers from the previous rule calculation.

The appeals court noted that it could only set aside the new rule if it was arbitrary, capricious, an **abuse of discretion**, or not in accordance with law. If an **administrative agency** examines the relevant data and articulates a satisfactory explanation for its action, a court will not set it aside. However, in this case the court found that the FCC had not followed its previous mandate to take into account the growing rate of subscribers to DBS services. As of 2009, DBS companies served approximately 33 percent of all subscribers, yet the FCC analysis left out data on DBS penetration rate. The court agreed with Comcast that the FCC had offered no plausible reason for failing to take into account the competitive impact of DBS companies. Comcast produced evidence that the growing market share of DBS could be attributed in large part to exclusive arrangements with highly sought after programmers. Moreover, the number of cable programming networks had increased almost 500 per cent since 1992 and had grown faster since 2000.

The appeals court used these changing market conditions and the failure of FCC to deal with them to overturn the rule as arbitrary and capricious. The court, instead of again remanding the case to the FCC for a revision of the rule, vacated the rule. Such a step is unusual, but the court stated that the FCCs "dereliction in this case is particularly egregious." By ignoring the court's prior instructions, it was "apparent that the Commission either cannot or will not fully incorporate the competitive impact of DBS and fiber optic companies into its open field model." To allow the FCC another attempt would burden the FIRST AMENDMENT rights of cable programmers and operators. Sixteen years of a failed policy was enough. If,

for some reason, cable operators did corner the market, federal antitrust laws were sufficient to deal with such actions.

CAMPAIGN FINANCE

Citizens United v. Federal Election Commission

The Bipartisan Campaign Reform Act of 2002 (BCRA), 116 Stat. 81, which is usually known as the McCain-Feingold Law (Senator JOHN MCCAIN, R-Arizona and Senator Russell Feingold, D-Wisconsin were the SENATE sponsors), sought to remove "big money" from U.S. elections. The Court, in *McConnell v. Federal Election Commission*, 540 U.S. 93, 124 S.Ct. 619, 157 L.Ed.2d 491 (2003), upheld most of the law's provisions. However, in 2007 the Court struck down the law's ban on issue advertisements 30 days preceding a primary election or 60 days preceding a general election. In *Federal Election Commission v. Wisconsin Right to Life, Inc.*, 551 U.S. 449, 127 S. Ct. 2652, 168 L. Ed. 2d 329 (2007), the Court ruled that unless an ad could not reasonably be interpreted as anything other than an ad urging the support or defeat of a candidate, it could not be banned. In 2009 the Court heard arguments concerning the law's ban on corporate and union funding of broadcast, cable, or satellite communication that mentioned a candidate within 60 days of a general election or 30 days of a primary. However, it decided to rehear the case and questioned whether the provision on its face violated the FIRST AMENDMENT rights of corporations. In *Citizens United v. Federal Election Commission*, __U.S.__, 130 S. Ct. 876__L. Ed. 2d__ (2010), the Court ruled that the provision was unconstitutional. The decision dramatically changed the political playing field, as it set the stage for corporate-financed political campaigns.

Citizens United, a nonprofit corporation, accepts donations from individuals and corporations. In January 2008, Citizens United released a 90-minute film entitled *Hillary: The Movie*. It was a documentary about then-Senator HILLARY CLINTON, who was a candidate in the Democratic Party's 2008 presidential primary elections. The tone of the work was very critical of Clinton. The film was shown in theaters and released on DVD but Citizens United sought a wider distribution network. It sought to place it as a video-on-demand item on cable and satellite networks as a free movie yet it was concerned that by showing it within 30 days of any of the primary elections in early 2008, it would violate §441b of the McCain-Feingold law.

Section 441b prohibits corporations and unions from using general treasury funds to make direct contributions to candidates or independent expenditures that expressly advocate the election or defeat of a candidate, through any form of media, in connection with certain qualified federal elections. In addition, it bars any "electioneering communication" made within 30 days of a primary or 60 days of a general election. "Electioneering communications" is defined as "any broadcast, cable, or satellite communication" that "refers to a clearly identified candidate for Federal office."

To protect itself, Citizens United filed a federal lawsuit against the Federal Election Commission in December 2007, challenging the constitutionality of §441b as applied to *Hillary: The Movie*. The **district court** granted the FEC's motion to dismiss the lawsuit. The court reasoned that the provision was facially constitutional under *McConnell* and that §441b was constitutional as applied to the film. Citizens United then appealed to the SUPREME COURT.

The Court, in a 5-4 decision, overruled the district court and held that §441b violated the First Amendment rights of corporations. Justice ANTHONY KENNEDY, writing for the majority, focused on the Court's precedent in *Austin v. Michigan Chamber of Commerce*, 494 U.S. 652, 110 S. Ct. 1391, 108 L. Ed. 2d 652 (1990). In that case the Court ruled that corporations could be barred from using treasury money to support or oppose candidates in elections did not violate the First Amendment. Kennedy announced that the Court overruled *Austin*. The First Amendment prohibits Congress from fining or jailing citizens, or associations of citizens, for engaging in political speech, yet *Austin* would "permit the Government to ban political speech because the speaker is an association with a corporate form." Political speech was "indispensable to decisionmaking in a democracy, and this is no less true because the speech comes from a corporation." With this precedent now discarded, the Court held that there was no basis for allowing the government to limit corporate independent expenditures. Section 441b placed an "outright ban on speech, with criminal sanctions."

The Court also rejected the government's contention that corporate political speech can be banned to prevent corruption or its appearance. Justice Kennedy announced that the "Court now concludes that independent expenditures, including those made by corporations, do not give rise to corruption or the appearance of corruption. That speakers may have influence over or access to elected officials does not mean that those officials are corrupt. And the appearance of influence or access will not cause the electorate to lose faith in this democracy."

The Court did uphold McCain-Feingold's public disclaimer and disclosure requirements as applied to Citizens United's ads. The disclaimers, at minimum, "avoid confusion by making clear that the ads are not funded by a candidate or political party."

Justice JOHN PAUL STEVENS, in a lengthy dissenting opinion joined by Justices RUTH BADER GINSBURG, STEPHEN BREYER, and SONIA SOTOMAYOR, argued that the decision "threatens to undermine the integrity of elected institutions across the Nation. The path it has taken to reach its outcome will, I fear, do damage to this institution." As for the importance of corporate personhood, Stevens was dismissive: "The conceit that corporations must be treated identically to natural persons in the political sphere is not only inaccurate but also inadequate to justify the Court's **disposition** of this case." Corporations cannot vote or run for office and they can be run by nonresidents whose interests conflict with interests of eligible voters. Lawmakers had a "compelling constitutional basis, if not also a democratic duty, to take measures designed to guard against the potentially deleterious effects of corporate spending in local and national races." The majority's approach marked a "dramatic break" from the past.

CAPITAL PUNISHMENT

The lawful infliction of death as a punishment; the death penalty.

Smith v. Spisak

Though the SUPREME COURT recognizes the constitutionality of the death penalty, it has set conditions on how judges and juries consider a sentence of death. In a 1988 case the Court held that jury instructions and verdict forms violated the Constitution because they told the jury that it could not find a particular circumstance to be mitigating for the DEFENDANT unless all 12 jurors agreed that the mitigating circumstance had been proved to exist. This standard was applied was applied by a federal court of appeals to overturn the death sentence of an Ohio inmate but the Court, in *Smith v. Spisak*, __U.S. __, 130 S. Ct. 676, __L. Ed. 2d__ (2010), ruled that the state court had correctly upheld the validity of the jury instructions. Moreover, even if the **federal courts** could legitimately apply the 1988 precedent, the jury instructions and forms in question differed significantly from those in the earlier case.

In 1983, an Ohio state jury convicted Frank Spisak, Jr., of three murders and two attempted murders at Cleveland State University in 1982. The Ohio courts upheld the verdicts on both Spisak's direct appeal and state post-conviction appeal. He then sought a **writ** of **habeas corpus** in Ohio federal **district court**, contending that the sentencing part of his trial violated the U.S. Constitution in two ways. Spisak's first claims concerned the instructions and verdict forms that the jury received at the sentencing phase of his trial. He contended the instructions were unconstitutional because the forms required the jurors to unanimously agree to the presence of a mitigating factor. Such a practice had been ruled unconstitutional in *Mills v. Maryland*, 486 U.S. 367, 108 S. Ct. 1860, 100 L. Ed. 2d 384 (1988). Second, Spisak contended that his lawyer had provided ineffective counsel during the sentencing phase, in violation of the SIXTH AMENDMENT. The district court rejected Spisak's petition but in 2006 the Sixth **Circuit Court** of Appeals disagreed and ordered a conditional writ of HABEAS CORPUS forbidding his execution. The state then appealed to the Supreme Court.

The Court unanimously overturned the Sixth Circuit decision. Justice STEPHEN BREYER, writing for the Court, noted that for a federal court to overturn a state-court decision it must show that the state-court decision "was contrary to, or involved an unreasonable application of, clearly established Federal law, as determined by the Supreme Court of the United States." The Court concluded that Spisak's jury instruction claim did not satisfy this standard but assumed for the sake of argument that *Mills* was "clearly established Federal law." After examining the jury instructions and forms used in Spisak's case and comparing them to those used in *Mills*,

Breyer found that the Ohio documents differed significantly from those in *Mills*. The judge had told the Spisak sentencing jury that it could take into account the mitigating factors the judge had listed, including mental disease or defendant of Spisak, as well as "any other" mitigating factor that it found relevant to the issue of whether Spisak should be sentenced to death. In addition, he instructed the jury that the prosecution carried the burden of proving **beyond a reasonable doubt** that the aggravating circumstances outweighed the mitigating factors. The Court ruled that the judge's oral instructions and the printed materials "made clear that, to recommend a death sentence, the jury had to find, unanimously and BEYOND A REASONABLE DOUBT, that each of the aggravating factors outweighed any **mitigating circumstances**. But the instructions did not say that the jury must determine the existence of each individual mitigating factor unanimously. Neither the instructions nor the forms said anything about how—or even whether—the jury should make individual determinations that each particular mitigating circumstance existed. They focused only on the overall balancing question."

As for the ineffective counsel argument, Breyer stated that Spisak's lawyer at the sentencing phase was not so inadequate as to violate the Sixth Amendment. The lawyer's representation did not fall below an objective standard of reasonableness and that there was not the "reasonable probability that, but for counsel's unprofessional errors, the results of the proceeding would have been different." Spisak's lawyer had sought to ACQUIT his client on the basis of mental illness but failed. Spisak contended that during the lawyer's **closing argument** during the sentencing phase overly emphasized the gruesome nature of the killings and Spisak's threats to continue his crimes. Moreover, the lawyer understated the facts from experts concerning Spisak's mental illness, barely mentioned possible MITIGATING CIRCUMSTANCES, and made no explicit request to the jury not to sentence his client to death.

The Court assumed for argument that all of these claims were true but still found no "reasonable probability" that a "better CLOSING ARGUMENT without these defects would have made a significant difference." Any different, more adequate closing argument would have taken place in the context of Spisak's admission of three murders and two other shootings, a failed mental illness defense, and the calling of Spisak to the stand in hopes of demonstrating his mentally defective condition to the jury. The jury still held all of this gruesome and troubling information, including Spisak's "boastful and unrepentant confessions and his threats to commit further acts of violence. We therefore do not see how a less descriptive closing argument with fewer disparaging comments about Spisak could have made a significant difference."

CLASS ACTION

A lawsuit that allows a large number of people with a common interest in a matter to sue or be sued as a group.

Shady Grove Orthopedic Associates, P. A. v. Allstate Insurance Co.

For much of U.S. LEGAL HISTORY, the federal courts were able to impose a federal **common law** on litigants from two or more states when hearing state law claims. In 1938, the SUPREME COURT overturned this approach in *Erie R. Co v. Tompkins*, 304 U.S. 64, 58 S. Ct. 817, 82 L. Ed. 1188 (1938), ruling that **federal courts** must apply state law on substantive issues. Since that decision the Supreme Court has dealt with the scope and breadth of this ruling. In *Shady Grove Orthopedic Associates, P.A. v. Allstate Insurance Co.*, __U.S.__, 130 S. Ct. 1431, __L. Ed. 2d __ (2010), the Court had to determine whether a state law that barred class actions in certain circumstances prevented a federal **district court** from entertaining a **class action** under the Federal Rules of **Civil Procedure**. The Court concluded that the **statute** could not prevent the federal court from hearing the claim.

Shady Grove Orthopedic Associates provided medical care to a woman who suffered injuries in an automobile accident. As partial payment for this care, the woman assigned her rights to insurance benefits under a policy issued in New York by Allstate Insurance. Shady Grove submitted a claim to Allstate, which under New York law had 30 days to pay the claim or deny it. Allstate paid Shady Grove but not within the 30-day period. It refused to pay the **statutory** interest (two percent) that accrued on the overdue benefits. Shady Grove, which has locations in Maryland, filed a lawsuit in New York federal district court alleging that

Allstate routinely refused to pay interest on overdue benefits. Shady Grove sought to represent both itself and a class of all others to whom Allstate owed interest.

The district court dismissed the lawsuit for lack of jurisdiction, citing New York Civil Practice Law § 901(b), which prohibited class action lawsuits that sought to recover a "penalty." The district court concluded that under *Erie* it was compelled to follow the New York law, despite the fact that Rule 23 of the Federal Rules of CIVIL PROCEDURE governed class action lawsuits. It reasoned that statutory interest was a penalty under New York law. Without class-action status, Shady Grove conceded that the individual claims were worth no more than $500 and therefore could not meet the amount-in-controversy requirement for individual suits of $75,000. The Second **Circuit Court** of Appeals upheld the district court decision, finding that §901(b) was a **substantive law** within the meaning of *Erie*.

The Supreme Court, in a 5-4 decision, overturned the appeals court decision. Justice ANTONIN SCALIA announced the judgment of the Court but the five-member majority splintered on certain parts of the case. Justice Scalia noted that the Court must first decide whether Rule 23 answered the question in dispute. If so, the rule would govern despite the state law unless the rule "exceeds statutory authorization or Congress's rulemaking power." He cautioned that the Court does not "wade into *Erie's* waters unless the federal rule is inapplicable or invalid."

Justice Scalia stated that Rule 23 answered the question: Shady Grove could proceed as a class action. To maintain a class action, the rule requires that the lawsuit satisfy a series of criteria and must fit into one of three categories. If the PLAINTIFF can meet these two sets of requirements, federal courts must confer class-action status. This "one-size-fits-all formula" clearly gave Shady Grove class-action status unless Rule 23 exceeded the scope of federal law. Scalia disagreed with the Second Circuit's assertion that §901(b) and Rule 23 were not in conflict because they addressed different issues. The appeals court said that Rule 23 only dealt with whether a class should be certified; section 901(b) addressed a question that came before Rule 23 consideration: was the claim eligible for class treatment in the first place. Scalia rejected this argument, finding that the "line between eligibility and certifiability is entirely artificial. Both are preconditions for maintaining a class action." The courts do not have discretion under Rule 23 to make distinctions on this basis.

COMITY

Courtesy; respect; a disposition to perform some official act out of goodwill and tradition rather than obligation or law. The acceptance or adoption of decisions or laws by a court of another jurisdiction, either foreign or domestic, based on public policy rather than legal mandate.

Levin v. Commerce Energy

In *Levin v. Commerce Energy,* No. 09-223, 560 U.S. ___ (2010), Commerce Energy, a California-based retail natural gas supplier, joined others in filing a lawsuit accusing the State of Ohio of using a discriminatory tax system that unfairly offered tax exemptions to in-state tax suppliers. The plaintiffs argued that because four local natural gas distribution companies benefited from tax exemptions that did not benefit the plaintiffs, despite similar circumstances, the tax scheme was unconstitutional under the **Commerce Clause** and the **Equal Protection** Clause of the U.S. Constitution. The plaintiffs sought **declaratory judgment** and injunctive relief invalidating three tax exemptions that the state granted exclusively to local distribution companies (LDCs). Specifically, Commerce and other plaintiffs had to pay a commercial activities tax based on gross receipts, a separate gross receipts tax for gas sales from an LDC to a retail supplier, and other sales and use taxes. Under Ohio law, the LDCs were exempt from each of these taxes (although they paid a gross receipts **excise** tax and a "MCF tax" based on the amount of gas they sold and delivered). The plaintiffs argued that the Ohio tax exemptions violated the dormant COMMERCE CLAUSE by providing a discriminatory advantage to LDCs and also violated the EQUAL PROTECTION Clause by discriminating against similarly-situated businesses.

The case was filed in the U.S. **District Court** for the Southern District of Ohio. DEFENDANT Ohio Tax Commissioner Richard Levin sought to dismiss the suit, arguing that federal tax law prohibits state tax disputes from being heard in **federal courts**. Specifically, he argued that the Tax INJUNCTION Act (TIA), 28 U.S.C. §1341, prohibited lower federal courts from restraining "the assessment, levy, or collection of any tax under State law where a plain, speedy and efficient remedy may be had in the courts of such State ..." He also offered a similar argument, this one grounded in **comity**.

The district court found that plaintiffs' suit was not barred by the TIA. Notwithstanding, it also found that the doctrine of comity, which restrains federal courts from entertaining claims that risk disrupting state tax administration, prevented it from having jurisdiction over the case. It dismissed in favor of defendant Ohio Tax Commissioner Levin.

Now the case was before the Sixth **Circuit Court** of Appeals, which agreed with the district court's TIA holding, but disagreed on the comity ruling. It remanded the case for **adjudication** on the merits. In so ruling and remanding, the **appellate court** opined that it believed it was compelled to do so, based on a footnote in the U.S. SUPREME COURT case of *Hibbs v. Winn,* 542 U.S. 88, 124 S. Ct. 2276, 159 L. Ed. 2d 172 (2004). The footnote stated that the Court "has relied upon 'principles of comity' to preclude original federal-court jurisdiction only when plaintiffs have sought district-court aid in order to arrest or countermand state tax collection." Since plaintiffs in the present case were challenging only a few limited exemptions, their success on the merits would not significantly intrude upon Ohio's administration of its tax system.

The Supreme Court, in a unanimous opinion by Justice Ginsburg, reversed and remanded the case, noting that the comity doctrine was more expansive than the TIA in application. Justice Ginsburg characterized the question before the Court as "whether a federal district court may entertain a complaint of allegedly discriminatory state taxation, framed as a request to increase a commercial competitor's tax burden." The Court concluded, "Under the comity doctrine, a taxpayer's complaint of allegedly discriminatory state taxation, even when framed as a request to increase a competitor's tax burden, must proceed originally in state court."

The comity doctrine, said the Court, reflects

> "a proper respect for state functions, a recognition of the fact that the entire country is made up of a Union of separate state governments, and a continuance of the belief that the National Government will fare best if the States and their institutions are left free to perform their separate functions in separate ways." (Quoting *Younger v. Harris,*

401 U.S. 37, 91 S.Ct. 746, 27 L.Ed.2d 669, as reiterated in *Fair Assessment in Real Estate Assn., Inc. v. McNary.* 454 U.S. 100, 102 S. Ct. 177, 70 L. Ed. 2d 271)

As applied here, the Court stated that the *Hibbs* footnote relied on by the Sixth Circuit did not restrict the reach of the comity doctrine, but also stated that neither *Hibbs* nor any other decision of the Court considered the comity doctrine's application to the kind of case presented here. Nonetheless, said the Court, comity considerations warranted dismissal of plaintiffs' lawsuit. If Ohio's tax scheme was unconstitutional, the Ohio courts were better positioned to determine how to comply with the mandate of equal protection (at least, unless and until the Ohio legislature addressed the issue). Finally, noted the Court, "If the State voluntarily chooses to submit to a federal forum, principles of comity do not demand that the federal court force the case back into the State's own system." (Quoting from *Ohio Bureau of Employment Servs. v. Hodory,* 421 U.S. 471, 95 S.Ct. 1716, 44 L.Ed.2d 295 (1975))

Justice Kennedy wrote a separate concurring opinion, noting that he joined the majority with the understanding that it did not undermine the holding in *Hibbs,* to be left "for another day." Justice Thomas, joined by Justice Scalia, also wrote a separate opinion concurring in the judgment. He also expressed skepticism for *Hibbs,* but agreed "that it is not necessary for us to revisit that decision to hold that this case belongs in state court."

COMMERCIAL LAW

Congress Passes the Credit Card Accountability Responsibility and Disclosure Act of 2009

Congress in 2009 addressed concerns about the credit card industry by passing the Credit Card Accountability Responsibility and Disclosure Act of 2009, Pub. L. No. 111-24, 123 Stat. 1734. The **statute** imposes a number of requirements regarding the terms of credit card agreements. Although the legislation promises to save credit card holders billions of dollars per year in fees and interests, credit card companies quickly found new ways to make money that could be just as costly to customers in the long run.

For several years, consumer advocate groups have criticized various tactics used by credit

card companies regarding how these companies handle accounts. These companies were often unclear about the actual interest rates that consumers would be charged. Several credit card companies would only provide a range of possible rates rather than provide a clear statement of the actual rate. In some instances, the actual rate charged could be more than 20 percent. Another technique was the imposition of universal default provisions, under which a card company could increase a customer's fee to a default fee if the customer defaulted with a different lender, even though the customer had not defaulted with the company imposing the default rate.

Other concerns focused on billing practices used by credit card companies. Some companies allegedly mailed credit card statements right before the bill was due, and when the customer paid the bill late, the company would impose a fee. It was also difficult for credit card customers to determine how long it would take to pay off the amount owed in full. In many instances, a customer who only made minimum payments on a credit card might have to submit payments for several years due to interest rate charges and other fees.

Credit card companies also tended to target high-risk customers. One target of the customers were college students, even though these students had no income and no credit history. According to a survey conducted in 2008 by the U.S. PUBLIC INTEREST Research Group, 80 percent of college students polled said that they had received direct mail solicitations from credit card companies. Several companies offered students free T-shirts and other merchandise, and students often did not know that they were signing in up for a credit card. A number of reports show why the tactic is effective—many of the young students who received the credit cards started using them and eventually reached the maximum balance. Studies show that giving a college student a credit card builds brand loyalty, as these students often hold on to the same cards after they graduate. On the other hand, high credit card balances have led a few college students to commit SUICIDE.

On January 22, 2009, Rep. Carolyn B. Maloney (D.-N.Y.) introduced the Credit Card Accountability Responsibility and Disclosure Act of 2009 as H.R. 627. The House during the previous congressional session had approved an earlier version of the bill, and the House approved the bill by a overwhelming vote of 357-70 on April 30, 2009. The SENATE passed an amended version of the bill on May 19, and the House approved the Senate amendments the following day. President BARACK OBAMA signed the bill on May 22, 2009, with several of the bill's provisions becoming effective nine months after passage. At the time of signing, Obama said, "With this new law, consumers will have the strong and reliable protections they deserve. We will continue to press for reform that is built on transparency, accountability, and mutual responsibility—values fundamental to the new foundation we seek to build for our economy."

The statute addresses several of the concerns that have been raised in the past about practices of credit card companies. The legislation prohibits credit card issuers from increasing a credit card's interest rate during the first year after issuance unless: (1) the card has a variable interest rate; (2) the increase is due to the expiration of a time period during which a promotional rate applies; or (3) the card holder does not make the required minimum payment within 60 days after a due date. The bill also limits the ability of issuers to increase interest rates on existing balances, though the same basic exceptions that apply to the first year also apply to existing balances. The statute also places several limits on the fees and penalties that companies can charge. For instance, if an issuer increases a rate because a customer fails to make a minimum payment for 60 days after a due date, the issuer must restore the original rate if the customer makes minimum payments on time for six consecutive months afterward.

The new legislation places limitations on the credit card companies' practices of targeting young adults. Under the new law, a card company cannot issue a new card to someone under the age of 21 unless: (1) someone over the age of 21 cosigns for the card; or (2) the customer under the age of 21 provides information showing that he or she has independent means of paying for balance on a card. Moreover, the statute prohibits card issuers from sending prescreened card offers to those under 21 unless the person has opted to receive these offers. Moreover, card issuers are restricted from providing gifts to students who fill out a credit card application, and the statute requires colleges to publicly disclose marketing contracts between the colleges and card issuers.

Other provisions in the statute apply to notices that card issuers must give. Card issuers are required to disclose the time period required to pay off a balance and the total interest paid if a customer only makes minimum payments. The statute also requires issuers to give customers 45 days' notice before raising a card's ANNUAL PERCENTAGE RATE or changing terms in the credit card agreement. The legislation includes provisions applicable to gift cards. Under the new law, a gift card cannot expire less than five years after the card was purchased or after money was last added on the card, whichever is later.

The legislation is expected to cost the credit card industry up to $12 billion per year in lost revenue. Commentators expect card companies to try to recoup these lost revenues by imposing higher annual fees, higher balance-transfer charges, and increased charges for foreign transactions.

CONFLICT OF LAWS

Kawasaki Kisen Kaisha v. Regal-Beloit

In 2005, cargo being shipped from Shanghai and Hong Kong to the United States was allegedly damaged after a train carrying it derailed in Oklahoma. In *Kawasaki Kisen Kaisha v. Regal-Beloit,* No. 08-1553, 561 U.S. ___ (2010), the U.S. SUPREME COURT was asked to determine what laws apply when international shipments are damaged in transit within the United States. The Court, by a 6-3 margin, held that in this case, the parties' private contract, stipulating liability as well as designating a forum for adjudicating disputes, was controlling, and not the Carmack Amendment to the INTERSTATE COMMERCE ACT of 1887, 49 U.S.C. §11706 (rail **carriers**) and §14706 (motor carriers), as follows.

Regal-Beloit, a manufacturer of electric motors, and the owner of the cargo shipment in this case, contracted with Kawasaki Kisen Kaisha (K-Line) to ship its goods from China to inland United States destinations. K-Line issued to Regal-Beliot four "through bills of lading," i.e., bills of lading covering both the ocean and inland portions of transport all in a single document. The through bills issued to Regal-Beloit contained a standard "Himalaya Clause," which, among other things, contained clauses relevant here. Specifically, the Himalaya Clause permitted K-Line to subcontract out to complete the journey; it extended liability as well as available defenses to subcontractors; it provided that the entire journey (water and land) was governed by the Carriage of Goods by Sea Act (COGSA, which regulated bills of lading issued by ocean carriers engaged in foreign trade); and it stipulated a Tokyo court as the **venue** for any dispute.

K-Line, after issuing its through bills to Regal-Beloit, arranged for the entire journey. The cargo was to be shipped by K-Line vessels to California, at which point it would be loaded onto a Union Pacific train, subcontracted by K-line for rail shipment within the United States. (Regal-Beloit also sued Union Pacific in the present case. Union Pacific sued Regal-Beloit in a companion case, *Union Pacific Railroad Co. v. Regal-Beloit*, No. 08-1554, which the Supreme Court consolidated with this case.)

A train derailment occurred in Oklahoma, and Regal-Beloit sued both K-Line and Union Pacific, the case being removed to federal **district court** in California. Ultimately, the district court granted dismissal for the defendants, based on the parties' through bill contract, which stipulated Tokyo as the designated venue. Regal-Beloit, the PLAINTIFF, argued that the **bill of lading** clause should not apply because it was trumped by the Carmack Amendment.

On appeal, the question became whether the Carmack Amendment to the Interstate Commerce Act of 1887, which governs certain rail and motor transportation by common carriers within the United States, applied to the inland (domestic) rail portion of an intermodal shipment originating overseas, when the shipment was made pursuant to a "through bill" of lading, issued by an ocean carrier, that extended the Carriage of Goods by Sea Act, 46 U.S.C. §30701, to cover the entire journey.

The Ninth **Circuit Court** of Appeals reversed the district court, holding that carriers could not make private contracts that usurped or clashed with domestic law. Specifically, the **appellate court** ruled that the Carmack Amendment governed defendants' liability for the destruction of goods during the inland portion of the shipment. Further, the forum-selection found in the through bills of lading clause (designating Tokyo as the appropriate forum) was valid only if the parties expressly contracted out of the Carmack provisions under the authority of the Interstate Commerce Act, §10709 or §10502.

But a majority of the U.S. Supreme Court reversed. It held that the Carmack Amendment did not apply to shipments originating overseas under a single through BILL OF LADING. Therefore, the parties' contract to litigate their dispute(s) in Tokyo was binding.

By analysis and significance to the present case, the difference came down to this. K-Line and Union Pacific contended that the contractual through bills of ladings issued to Regal-Beloit expressly stated that the entire journey would be covered under COGSA (see above). COGSA requires carriers to issue bills to cargo owners that contain specified terms. Although COGSA generally covers only shipments from United States ports to foreign ports and vice versa, it permits parties to extend its terms "by contract" to cover the entire journey, including "period[s] of inland ... transport." Further. COGSA does not limit the parties' ability to contractually adopt a specified forum for disputes.

Conversely, Regal-Beloit urged that the Carmack Amendment applied to the inland portion of the transport (Oklahoma), where the alleged damage occurred. The purpose of the Carmack Amendment was to relieve cargo owners such as regal-Beloit from the burden of trying to identify and search out a particular negligent carrier from among the often numerous ones handling interstate shipment of goods. The Carmack Amendment expressly **assigns** liability for damage on the rail route to "receiving rail carrier[s]" and "delivering rail carrier[s]," regardless of which carrier caused the damage. Accordingly, the Carmack Amendment constrains carriers in their ability to limit liability by contract [§11706(c)] and limits the parties' choice of venue to federal and STATE COURTS [§11706(d)(1)].

But the Supreme Court agreed with K-Line (and Union Pacific). In reversing and remanding, Justice Kennedy, writing for the majority, held that the Carmack Amendment did not govern shipments originating overseas under a single through bill of lading. Therefore, the district court was correct in dismissing the case, and the parties would have to litigate in Tokyo. Of import, the Court noted that under the Carmack Amendment, a "receiving rail carrier" was the initial carrier. If it referred to any carrier receiving the property, each one would have to issue its own bill. This would be contrary to Carmack's purpose of making receiving and delivering carriers liable under a single, initial bill for damage caused by any carrier within a single course of shipment. Because the Ninth Circuit ignored Carmack's "receive[d] ... for transportation" limitation, it reached the wrong conclusion, said the Court.

Justice Kennedy was joined in the majority opinion by Chief Justice Roberts and Justices Scalia, Thomas, Breyer, and Alito. Justice Sotomayor filed a dissenting opinion, in which she was joined by Justices Stevens and Ginsburg. Justice Sotomayor opined that the Carmack Amendment applied to the inland leg of a multi-modal shipment. She would have remanded the case to see if the parties satisfied their obligations under the Interstate Commerce Act (see above) to contractually opt out of Carmack Amendment **purview**.

CONSTITUTIONAL LAW

The written text of the state and federal constitutions. The body of judicial precedent that has gradually developed through a process in which courts interpret, apply, and explain the meaning of particular constitutional provisions and principles during a legal proceeding. Executive, legislative, and judicial actions that conform with the norms prescribed by a constitutional provision.

Kiyemba v. Obama

The U.S. detainment facility at Guantanamo Bay in Cuba has caused a great deal of controversy throughout the 2000s and has led to a significant amount of litigation. Some of these cases have reached as high as the U.S. SUPREME COURT. In September 2009, the Court agreed to hear a case involving a group of Chinese Muslims whom the United States mistakenly believed were enemy combatants. The detainees were held at Guantanamo Bay since shortly after the September 11th attacks in 2001. In February 2009, the U.S. Court of Appeals for the District of Columbia ruled that only the executive or legislative branches could allow detainees to be released into the United States. However, before the Court heard oral arguments in the case, the Court dismissed the case because factual circumstances had changed since the time of the lower court's opinion.

At some point prior to the September 11th attacks in 2001, a group of 17 Chinese citizens left China and traveled to Afghanistan to join with other Chinese Muslims, known as Uighurs.

After the September 11th attacks, the United States bombed the camp where the Uighurs were staying. The Uighurs fled to Pakistan, but local villagers later turned over the Uighurs to U.S. military personnel. The United States determined that the Uighurs were enemy combatants and held the Uighurs at Guantanamo Bay beginning in June 2002. The Combatant Status Review Tribunals reviewed the cases of the Uighurs and determined that the the Uighurs had planned to fight against the Chinese government and had trained at the camp in Afghanistan for this reason. The hearings revealed that the camp was run by the Eastern Turkistan Islamic Movement, which the military believed was associated with either the al Qaida terrorist organization or with the Taliban. The United States later designated the Eastern Turkistan Islamic Movement as a terrorist organization, which allowed the United States to hold the Uighurs.

Guantanamo Bay detainees in general have had some success challenging their INCARCERATION in U.S. courts. One detainee who was part of the Uighars group challenged his incarceration. The D.C. **Circuit Court** of Appeals reviewed the case. The court found no evidence that the Eastern Turkistan Islamic Movement was associated with a terrorist organization and that there was no justification for holding the petitioner as an ENEMY COMBATANT. *Parhat v. Gates*, 532 F.3d 834 (D.C. Cir. 2008). U.S. authorities later determined that none of the other Uighur detainees could be held as enemy combatants.

The United States, however, had difficulty determining what to do with the detainees. One option was to return the detainees to China, but they would like face persecution, and the United States will not transfer individuals to nations were the individuals will be mistreated. The detainees initially failed to comply with U.S. IMMIGRATION laws, so they could not be released into the United States. By 2008, the United States had cleared each of the 17 detainees for release or transfer from the Guantanamo Bay facility, but the government was unable to find a third country to receive the detainees. Thus, the U.S. military continued to hold the Uighurs at the Guantanamo Bay base.

In July 2005, the detainees filed a petition for **habeas corpus** with the U.S. **District Court** for the District of Columbia. The cases were consolidated and heard before Judge Ricardo M. Urbina, who determined that the United States no longer had authority to hold the detainees. However, the court struggled with the appropriate relief. The authority for determining whether an alien should be admitted into the United States usually rests with the executive or legislative branches rather than with the courts. However, in some extraordinary instances, the courts are able to intervene. In the case of the Uighur detainees, the government's best efforts to resettle the detainees in another country had failed for more than four years. Moreover, the court did not believe that these efforts would succeed within the foreseeable future. Accordingly, Judge Urbina ruled that the detainees should be released into the United States. *In re Guantanamo Bay Detainee Litigation*, 581 F. Supp. 33 (D.D.C. 2008).

The government appealed the decision to the D.C. Court of Appeals, which heard oral arguments in November 2008. The **appellate court** opened its analysis by restating a principle established in the 19th century by the Supreme Court: the power of the government to exclude ALIENS is "inherent in sovereignty, necessary for maintaining normal international relations and defending the country against foreign encroachments and dangers—a power to be exercised exclusively by the political branches of government." *The Chinese Exclusion Case*, 130 U.S. 581, 9 S. Ct. 623, 32 L. Ed. 1068 (1889). Subsequent cases also reaffirmed the right of the executive and legislative branches to decide which aliens may or may not enter the United States. Two of three judges on the D.C. Circuit's panel agreed that the district court's decision was contrary to existing authority. In an opinion written by Judge A. Raymond Randolph, the court reversed the district court and remanded the case to the district court. *Kiyemba v. Obama*, 555 F.3d 1022 (D.C. Cir. 2009). A third judge, Judith W. Rogers, concurred in the judgment but disagreed that the decision was consistent with recent Supreme Court precedent related to detentions of enemy combatants.

The Uighur detainees sought a review of their case by the U.S. Supreme Court, and the Court granted the petition in September 2009. The case stood to be a major SEPARATION OF POWERS case, given that the heart of the case focused on the power of the judiciary compared with the power of the other branches of government. Some commentators suggested that Congress should have stepped in to allow the detainees to enter the United States, given the relatively large Uighur community already in the country. However, each of the detainees received an offer to resettle in a country other than the United States. Attorneys for the government argued that these offers changed the facts of the case significantly enough that the Court should dismiss the appeal. The Court agreed, and in a per curiam decision, the Court vacated the lower court's decision and remanded the case to the D.C. Circuit for further consideration. *Kiyemba v. Obama*, 130 S. Ct. 1235 (2010).

CONTEMPT

An act of deliberate disobedience or disregard for the laws, regulations, or decorum of a public authority, such as a court or legislative body.

Horne v. Flores

Federal courts have the power to order state and local governments to change how they operate. A familiar example is the use of an INJUNCTION to desegregate a school district. Since the 1970s federal courts have used their authority to oversee not only school districts but state prison systems, low-income housing programs, and the deinstitutionalize of mentally disabled persons. However, the SUPREME COURT has become increasingly skeptical about the scope and duration of federal court structural injunctions and since the 1990s has encouraged the lower federal courts to withdraw as soon as possible from state and local governance issues. This was again illustrated in *Horne v. Flores*, __U.S.__,129 S. Ct. 2579, 174 L. Ed. 2d 406 (2009), where the Court concluded that the lower courts had not properly examined whether the state of Arizona should be held in CONTEMPT for failing to fund English Language-Learner (ELL) programs are required by the federal **district court**. The Supreme Court made clear that the courts need to conduct a proper analysis as to whether the court order should be lifted.

In 1992 a group of ELL students in the Nogales Unified School District and their parents filed a class-action lawsuit in federal district court, alleging that the state was violating the Equal Educational Opportunities Act of 1974 (EEOA), which requires a state to "take appropriate action to overcome language barriers that impede equal participation by its students in its instructional programs." They sued on behalf of all minority "at risk" and limited English proficient children and asked for a **declaratory judgment** that the state was violating the EEOA by providing inadequate ELL instruction in Nogales. The case moved slowly for seven years, as the parties settled a number of issues. The case went to trial in 2000 on the remaining issues and the court sided with the plaintiffs. It entered a DECLARATORY JUDGMENT that the defendants were violating the EEOA because the amount of funding Arizona allocated for the special needs of ELL students was arbitrary and not related to the actual funding needed by the Nogales district for ELL instruction. The defendants did not appeal this order.

In 2001 the court extended the order to apply to all of Arizona and set a deadline of January 31, 2002 for the state to provide funding that "bear[s] a rational relationship to the actual funding needed." The state took no action and in January 2005 the court gave the state 90 days to fund the ELL programs as required by the previous court orders. After the state failed again to comply, the court held the state in contempt. It ordered the state legislature to comply within the first 15 days of its 2006 session, even though the legislature was not then a party to the lawsuit. If the legislature failed to act, the court threatened to impose an escalating schedule of fines that could lead to $2 million per day. The legislature did not act and by March 2006 the fines amounted to over $20 million. At that point a bill was passed and the governor allowed it to become law without her signature. However, court approval was needed for it to become effective.

The district court denied the state's motion to be purged of contempt or, alternatively, that under Federal Rule of **Civil Procedure** 60(b)(5) the underlying order should be changed due to changes in circumstances. The district denied both arguments and concluded the funding bill was defective in several ways. The Ninth **Circuit Court** of Appeals upheld the lower court rulings, concluding that while the Nogales district had made "significant strides" since 2000, the progress did not warrant the lifting of the injunction. Moreover, it rejected the state's claim that the enactment of the No Child Left Behind Act of 2001 (NCLB) constituted a changed legal circumstance that warranted Rule 60(b)(5) relief.

The Supreme Court, in a 5-4 decision, overturned the Ninth Circuit ruling. Justice SAMUEL ALITO, writing for the majority, held that the lower courts had not conducted a proper Rule 60(b)(5) analysis. The rule permits a party to seek relief from a judgment or order if "a significant change either in factual conditions or in law" renders continued enforcement "detrimental to the public interest." As with other cases involving structural, institutional reform, injunctions often remain in force for many years. During this time circumstances may change enough to require the court to reexamine its original judgment. In addition, the Arizona case displayed FEDERALISM concerns, as the federal court was dictating budget priorities to state legislators and the governor. Therefore, the court must take a "flexible approach" to Rule 60(b)(5) motions to insure that its turns back to the state the powers it held over areas properly within the governance of the state. The key question in this case was whether the EEOA violation had been remedied.

The Ninth Circuit had also failed to address this question properly. The appeals court imposed too strict a standard on what constitutes changed circumstances for Rule 60(b)(5) relief. The court "should have ascertained whether the 2000 order's ongoing enforcement was supported by an ongoing EEOA violation." Instead, it focused on a particular funding mechanism and improperly substituted its own policy judgments for those of the state and local officials entrusted with the decisions. Therefore, the case needed to be remanded to the district court for a "proper examination" of at least four factual or legal changes that might warrant relief. One major change was the enactment of NCLB, as it led Arizona to make significant structural and programming changes in its ELL programming and it "significantly increased federal funding for education in general and ELL programming in particular." In addition, it provided evidence of the progress and achievement of Nogales' ELL students through its assessment and reporting requirements. Finally, it marked a shift in federal education policy.

COPYRIGHT

An intangible right granted by statute to the author or originator of certain literary or artistic productions, whereby, for a limited period, the exclusive privilege is given to the person to make copies of the same for publication and sale.

Music Publishers' Association Files Copyright Infringement Suits Against Online Publishers of Song Lyrics

During the 2000s, much of the focus regarding COPYRIGHT INFRINGEMENT on the Internet involved services that allowed users to listen to protected songs or watch protected videos in violation of the copyright holder's rights. In 2009, the National Music Publishers' Association went after another target, bringing two suits against websites that post lyrics to several thousand songs. One of the cases was settled out of court, while the other appeared to be headed for trial as of April 2010.

Music publishers and organizations representing these publishers have had success in the courts protecting copyrights. In *MGM Studios, Inc. v. Grokster, Ltd.*, 545 U.S. 913, 125 S. Ct. 2764, 162 L. Ed. 2d 781 (2005), the U.S. SUPREME COURT ruled that two file-sharing companies could be sued for marketing software that allowed Internet users to trade music files with one another. The decision effectively shut the websites of those companies down. Music publishers continued to go after other entities and individuals in a continued effort to put an end to copyright infringement. For example, the Recording Industry Association of America (RIAA) has filed more than 20,000 lawsuits for copyright infringement. In June 2009, a jury ordered a single mother to pay $1.92 million for illegally sharing more than 1,000 music files. Due to the negative publicity surrounding the suit, the RIAA announced that it would no longer sue individuals who trade small quantities of songs and would instead seek to shut down the trading with the cooperation of Internet service providers (ISPs).

In addition to sites that provide access to audio and video files containing copyrighted works, dozens of websites also provide the text of the lyrics of songs. On many of these sites, users post the lyrics, and as a result these lyrics may be incomplete or inaccurate. Many of these websites earn revenue from the sites by placing advertisements on the pages next to the lyrics. One of the more popular advertising platforms is Google Adsense. When the owner of a website registers as an Adsense "partner," the owner is given a HTML code to place on the site.

Google's servers determine which advertisements would be most relevant to the site and places ads on the site that correspond with the site's subject matter. When an Internet user clicks on an ad, both Google and the website owner make money. This practice can be lucrative for owners of websites with song lyrics, given the popularity of Internet searches for the song lyrics.

In 2007, the National Music Publishers' Association (NMPA) expressed concern about lyric websites and complained to Google. The NMPA is the largest trade association representing U.S. music publishers and has more than 700 members. A spokesperson for NMPA said that the organization had sent copyright notices to commercially oriented sites but that this strategy was somewhat successful. Other strategies would focus on contacting ISPs to try to shut down the sites that contained copyrighted lyrics. A significant part of the NMPA's motivation for addressing the infringing lyric sites was the development of an online lyrics service that received rights from music publishers to republish the lyrics.

Between 2007 and 2010, the NMPA sent hundreds of cease and desist notices to sites that displayed protected lyrics. In several cases, the sites either discontinued their operations or received licenses to operate legally. However, a few sites ignored the notices and continued operating. The resistance of the owners of these sites to shut down their operations led the NMPA in August 2009 to file lawsuits in two different federal district courts. At the time these suits were filed, NMPA president and CEO David Israelite said, "Unlicensed web sites exploiting song lyrics for profit have become a significant problem. These sites are profiting on the backs of songwriters. It is unfortunate that copyright holders must so frequently divert energies to protect their rights to license and distribute their works. However, the demand for music prompts a seemingly endless stream of illegal business models."

One of the suits focused on a company named Motive Force, L.L.C. and its owner, Sean Colombo. Motive Force operated a website called "LyricWiki," which displayed lyrics to hundreds of thousands of songs, according to the NMPA. Lyrics to the songs were added by users, and the site allowed users to distribute lyrics to other websites and to download the lyrics to user computers. The suit against Motive Force and Colombo was filed in the U.S. **District Court** for the Western District of Pennsylvania. The parties settled the dispute in January 2010. Motive Force and Colombo agreed to pay a judgment of $150,000 and to cease infringing activity. As of April 2010, LyricWiki still existed, displaying lyrics that were licensed through a company named Gracenote.

The second lawsuit was filed in the U.S. District Court for the Central District of California against LiveUniverse and Brad Greenspan, the site's owner. Greenspan was one of the founders of MySpace and participated in running LiveUniverse, which allegedly runs several lyric websites that contain copyrighted lyrics. According to the suit, the site Lyricdownload.com is one of the largest music sites in the world, with more than 700,000 lyrics from more than 28,000 artists. Other sites owned by LiveUniverse likewise contain thousands of unlicensed lyrics. In addition to damages, the NMPA has also sought to enjoin these sites from displaying the lyrics.

According to Israelite, "Music fans are the biggest losers when licensed businesses, like LyricFind, Gracenote and TuneWiki can't survive and prosper because unlicensed, illegal businesses are allowed to thumb their noses at the law. We are confident the courts will conclude that, like Napster and Grokster before them, these sites are simply freeloading off artists and fans."

Reed Elsevier, Inc. v. Muchnick

The federal COPYRIGHT Act governs INTELLECTUAL PROPERTY rights in the U.S. By registering a work with the Copyright Office the copyright holder may file a copyright INFRINGEMENT suit in federal court. In the 1990s a class-action lawsuit was filed by authors against a group of publishers who took their works and converted them for use in electronic databases such as LexisNexis and Westlaw. The SUPREME COURT, in *N.Y. Times Co. v. Tasini*, 533 U.S. 483, 122 S. Ct. 2381, 150 L. Ed. 2d 500 (2001), ruled that these publishers had infringed on the authors' copyright work. Following the decision similar lawsuits were consolidated into one proceeding and the parties began settlement discussions. Though the federal **district court** approved the settlement, some authors disliked the terms and appealed the decision. The court of appeals, on its own initiative, concluded that the district

court lacked jurisdiction to hear the case and approve the settlement because some of the authors in the class had not registered their works as required by federal law. The Supreme Court, in *Reed Elsevier, Inc. v. Muchnick*, __U.S.__,130 S. Ct. 1237, 176 L. Ed. 2d 17 (2010), overruled the appeals court and held that the registration requirement was not jurisdictional.

Settlement negotiations with the authors and publishers led to an agreement in March 2005. The parties asked the New York federal district court to approve the agreement but ten freelance authors, including Irvin Muchnick, objected. The court overruled these objections and certified the settlement of $18 million. On appeal to the Second **Circuit Court** of Appeals, Muchnick and his fellow authors renewed their objections. All parties to the appeal asserted that the district court had subject-matter jurisdiction to approve the settlement, even though it included unregistered works. The Second Circuit, relying on its precedents ruled that the district court lacked jurisdiction because of the inclusion of the unregistered works. In a rare occurrence, both sides appealed this ruling to the Supreme Court. The Court granted review and appointed a lawyer to defend the Second Circuit decision.

The Court overturned the ruling in a unanimous decision. Justice CLARENCE THOMAS, writing for the Court, stated that the courts had become confused over whether a statute's requirements are "jurisdictional" or only "claim-processing rules." Jurisdiction refers to a court's "adjudicatory authority" and a **statutory** requirement is considered jurisdictional if Congress clearly states that it counts as jurisdictional. If Congress fails to assert this condition, then the condition ins nonjurisdictional and a court may hear the case. Thomas cited as an example the requirement in Title VII of the CIVIL RIGHTS Act of 1964 that an action could only be brought against employers with fifteen or more employers. The Court had ruled that the employee's lawsuit could be heard in federal court because the civil rights provision did not clearly state that the numerosity requirement was jurisdictional. Moreover, the requirement was not located in separate jurisdiction-granting section of Title VII.

Justice Thomas applied this same approach to the Copyright Act provision, §411(a). Like the Title VII requirement, §411(a) did not clearly state that is registration requirement was jurisdictional. Although it did use the word "jurisdiction" in its last sentence, that sentence spoke to a "court's adjudicatory authority to determine a copyright claim's registrability and says nothing about whether a federal court has subject-matter jurisdiction to adjudicate claims for infringement of unregistered works." In addition, §411(a)'s registration requirement was located in a provision separate from those granting **federal courts** subject-matter jurisdiction over different types of claims.

The lawyer representing the Second Circuit had contended that Court should uphold the decision even if it disagreed with the appeals court ruling because some of the parties had previously asserted that copyright registration was jurisdictional. Under the doctrine of judicial **estoppel** a court will rule against a party if it has "succeeded in persuading a court to accept that party's earlier position, so that judicial acceptance of an inconsistent position in a later proceeding would create the perception that either the first or the second court was misled." Justice Thomas declined to apply ESTOPPEL because the parties made their statements during the negotiations of the settlement agreement and this was a proper bargaining tool. Second, the parties had argued before the Second Circuit that the district court did have jurisdiction. Therefore, the Court held that the

district court did have the authority to hear the case and approve the settlement. Muchnick and his fellow plaintiffs could now appeal the merits of the settlement to the Second Circuit.

CORRUPTION

Conviction of Former Congressman William Jefferson

In August 2009, former Louisiana Congressman William J. Jefferson was convicted on 11 counts of corruption in U.S. **District Court**, Alexandria, Virginia, following a jury trial. In November 2009, he was sentenced to 13 years in prison (followed by three years of supervised release) and **forfeiture** of $470,000. Jefferson, 62, had served in Congress as Democratic representative for the New Orleans district for 18 years until being defeated in 2008. The charges and convictions centered on his misuse of power associated with his Congressional office for personal gain and enrichment. This manifested in a series of bribes and payoffs involving business ventures in Africa.

The federal jury deliberated five days before returning guilty verdicts for BRIBERY, CONSPIRACY to commit bribery, money **fraud**, RACKETEERING under the Racketeer Influenced

William Jefferson and his wife Andrea, leave court after his sentencing, November 2009.

AP IMAGES

Corrupt Organization Act (RICO), 18 U.S.C. § 1961–1968, and violations of the Foreign Corrupt Practices Act (FCPA), 15 U.S.C. §§ 78dd-1 et seq. (involving the bribery of foreign government officials). Jefferson was acquitted on three charges, including one for OBSTRUCTION OF JUSTICE.

Perhaps the most distinguishing and memorable fact associated with this case, going back to 2005, was the seizure by the FBI of $90,000 in cash, neatly wrapped in aluminum foil and stashed in Boca Burger and Pillsbury boxes, from Mr. Jefferson's refrigerator freezer at his residence. Another distinguishing fact was the FBI raid on his congressional office. The execution of a SEARCH WARRANT upon the office of a sitting Congressman was apparently the first in the 200-year history of the Constitution.

In July 2006, the U.S. District Court for the District of Columbia issued a 28-page opinion upholding the FBI raid. *In re: Search of the Rayburn House Office Building Room Number 2113 Washington, DC 20515,* No. 06-1231 M-01 (2006). The government's application for a search warrant was supported with an 83-page AFFIDAVIT outlining the evidence against Jefferson thus far obtained. The application also set forth "special search procedures" to minimize the chance that any politically-sensitive materials or documents that "may fall within the **purview** of the SPEECH OR DEBATE CLAUSE [Article I, §6 of the U.S. Constitution] . . . or any other pertinent privilege" would be compromised. Indeed, several House leaders from both parties objected that the raid also violated the SEPARATION OF POWERS between executive and legislative branches.

In considering the scope of legislative privilege, the U.S. **Circuit Court** of Appeals for the D.C. Circuit affirmed the district court's denial of Jefferson's motion for the return of all documents obtained in the search of his office. *United States v. Rayburn House Office Building,* 497 F.3d 654 (D.C. Cir. 2007). However, it ordered the return of all *privileged* documents, to be determined by the district court. This decision undermined the district court's original holding that the entire **search and seizure** did not violate the Speech or Debate Clause. The U.S. SUPREME COURT denied review (07-816, 2008).

Jefferson was the first African-American congressman to be elected in Louisiana since the RECONSTRUCTION following the Civil War. As former co-chairman of congressional caucuses on Nigerian and African trade, he led official delegations to Africa and corresponded with American and foreign officials to promote ventures in Nigeria, Ghana, and Equatorial Guinea in which he had a financial interest. These included TELECOMMUNICATIONS deals (Nigeria, Ghana), oil concessions (Equatorial Guinea), and satellite transmission contracts in Botswana, Equatorial Guinea, and the Republic of Congo.

The government's case against him relied partly on testimony from former Jefferson aides and business associates who had pleaded guilty and agreed to testify against him. Brett M. Pfeffer, a former congressional staff member for Jefferson, and Vernon L. Jackson, a Louisville, Kentucky businessman, both pleaded guilty to charges of conspiracy to commit bribery and the payment of bribes to a public official, and were sentenced to 96 months and 87 months in prison, respectively. Jackson, the CEO of a Kentucky telecommunications company, iGate Inc., told officials that he paid more than $400,000 to a company controlled by Jefferson's family. An iGate investor, who cooperated with the FBI and wore a surveillance wire device during meetings and telephone conversations with Jefferson, was videotaped handing Jefferson a briefcase containing $100,000. The money was reportedly to be used as a bribe for the VICE PRESIDENT of Nigeria. It was this money (all but $10,000 of it) that was later found in Jefferson's freezer.

Evidence at trial showed that Jefferson sought millions in bribes, by performing official acts (such as leading official business delegations to Africa and using congressional staff members to promote the business ventures), in return for things of value. The value received included payments from monthly fees or retainers, consulting fees, percentage shares of business revenues and profits, flat fees, and stock ownership in the companies seeking his assistance and promotion. (Although prosecutors believed he sought millions, they also believed that he actually received less than $400,000.)

In a November 2009 press release from the U.S. Attorney's Office following the sentencing, DEPARTMENT OF JUSTICE, Principal Deputy Assistant Attorney General Mythili Raman said, "In a stunning betrayal of the public's trust, former Congressman Jefferson repeatedly used his public office for private gain. The lengthy prison sentence imposed on Mr. Jefferson today is a stark reminder to all public officials that the consequences of accepting bribes can and will be severe."

Former New York Police Commissioner Sentenced to Prison

Bernard B. "Bernie" Kerik had been a popular New York City police commissioner who, along with former New York City mayor and Republican presidential candidate Rudolph "Rudy" Guiliani, became a national hero for leadership during the September 11, 2001 terrorist attacks in that city. In the political aftermath, fame quickly turned to scandal. Finally, in February 2010, Kerik was sentenced to four years in prison after PLEADING guilty to eight **felony** charges. The guilty pleas were entered on record in November 2009, just days before criminal trial was to commence. Between the November plea and the February sentencing, Kerik remained on strict HOUSE ARREST in his New Jersey residence. Kerik was the first New York City police commissioner in history to admit to felony crimes.

Of the 15 charges scheduled for trial, Kerik pleaded guilty to two counts of tax **fraud**, one count of making a false statement on a loan application, and five counts of making false statements to the federal government while being vetted for senior positions. In addition to the prison sentence, U.S. **District Court** Judge Stephen C. Robinson ordered Kerik to pay $187,931 **restitution** to the INTERNAL REVENUE SERVICE.

The guilty plea stemmed from a November 2007 federal INDICTMENT charging Kerik with 16 counts of corruption, **mail fraud**, tax FRAUD, OBSTRUCTION OF JUSTICE, and lying to the government. The 30-page criminal complaint charged, among other things, that within months of Kerik's appointment by Guiliani as New York City's prisons commissioner, he was already accepting payments from a New Jersey company (later identified as Interstate Materials)eager to earn lucrative contracts with the city. The company allegedly provided $250,000 in marble bathrooms, a whirlpool tub, and a grand marble rotunda in Kerik's Bronx apartment. In exchange, Kerik set up meetings with city officials to vouch for the company's reputation and help it get city contracts. The indictment further alleged that both Kerik and the company concealed their relationship. (At the same time, Interstate Materials was under

investigation for financial ties to ORGANIZED CRIME and the Gambino crime family. Ultimately, the company was barred from bidding on all city contracts.)

The indictment had further charged Kerik with "selling his office" for hundreds of thousands of dollars when he was prisons commissioner and police commissioner, then lying to cover up the schemes. Finally, the indictment had charged that over a six-year period, Kerik failed to report $500,000 in income to the Internal Revenue Service, and falsely claimed several thousands of dollars in tax deductions. He was also charged with coaxing witnesses to lie to investigators about payments he received and with providing false information to a state **grand jury** that was investigating similar charges.

In 2006, Kerik pleaded guilty to two state **misdemeanor** charges in the Bronx division of State SUPREME COURT; those charges tied to the renovation of his apartment. He paid $221,000 in fines and penalties but was not sentenced to jail.

Bernie Kerik had become a household name as a onetime close aide to Guiliani, under whom Kerik was serving as police commissioner. In 2003, Kerik was appointed by the Pentagon to serve as interim minister of the interior in Iraq, under the Coalition Provisional Authority set up by the U.S. DEPARTMENT OF DEFENSE to run Iraq after the fall of Saddam Hussein.

It was not until President GEORGE W. BUSH, impressed, nominated Kerik to succeed Tom Ridge as Secretary of Homeland Security, that Kerik's colorful past came to light. During the vetting process, Kerik insisted that while completing documents required for SENATE confirmation, he discovered that he had not paid required employer taxes for his nanny. Upon then discovering that the nanny, an illegal alien, was using a friend's SOCIAL SECURITY number, Kerik notified the White House that he needed to withdraw from consideration. Although President Bush announced his disappointment the following day, an avalanche of damaging tabloid and mainstream stories flooded the news media.

Kerik pleaded not guilty at his court ARRAIGNMENT and vowed to fight the charges, claiming that the media had distorted his past. Then in January 2008, the district court disqualified Kerik's longtime personal attorney, Kenneth Breen, citing CONFLICT OF INTEREST, in that Breen might be called as an adverse witness in the trial against Kerik.

In return for the federal plea, prosecutors agreed to drop the most serious charges against Kerik, mail and wire fraud. They also agreed to recommend 27 to 33 months for a prison term. However, at the February 2010 sentencing, U.S. District Court Judge Stephen C. Robinson departed from that recommendation and meted out a longer prison term, citing Kerik's betrayal of the public's trust. As reported by the *New York Times,* Judge Robinson noted that he admired much about Kerik, particularly his leadership in the aftermath of 9/11. But "the fact that Mr. Kerik would use that event for personal gain and aggrandizement is a dark place in the soul for me," said the judge.

CRIMINAL LAW

A body of rules and statutes that defines conduct prohibited by the government because it threatens and harms public safety and welfare and that establishes punishment to be imposed for the commission of such acts.

NBA Star Gilbert Arenas Pleads Guilty to Gun Charge

Professional basketball star Gilbert Arenas ran into problems off-the-court when he was charged with carrying a weapon without a license in violation of gun-control laws in the District of Columbia. The charges led the league to suspend Arenas for the remainder of the 2009-2010 season, and he was later forced to spend 30 days in a halfway house after PLEADING guilty to the charge.

Arenas was a star basketball player in both high school and college. He was originally drafted by the Golden State Warriors in 2001 and spent three seasons with the team. In 2003, he signed with the Washington Wizards, and he became an NBA all-star by 2005. Arenas suffered an injury late in the 2007 season that kept him out of action for most of the 2007-2008 and 2008-2009 seasons. He returned to play full-time at the beginning of the 2009-2010 season.

On December 24, 2009, Arenas and team-mate Javaris Crittenton became involved in a dispute over a gambling debt that Arenas allegedly owed to Crittenton. At some point, both men pulled guns on the other, and reports indicated that Arenas pulled his gun first. Later reports indicated that a total of five witnesses were in the locker room at the time of the incident. Two of the witnesses said that Crittenton had loaded his weapon and chambered a round, though he never pointed the gun at Arenas. The witnesses also said that Crittenton also began to taunt Arenas while Crittenton had the weapon in his hand.

The dispute took place on a practice day, so it was not clear immediately whether other players were around. One day after the incident occurred, a team spokesperson relayed a message indicating that Arenas had brought the guns to his locker around December 10, which was just after the birth of Arenas' daughter. Arenas reportedly commented, "I decided I didn't want the guns in my house and around the kids anymore, so I took them to my lockbox at Verizon Center. Then like a week later, I turned them over to team security and told them to hand them over to the police, because I don't want them anymore." As of December 25, the Washington police department refused to comment on the case.

News that the players had pulled guns on one another was reported as early January. The league at that time would only refer to authorities, and by then, the case had attracted the attention of federal agents as well as local police. According to Wizards' General Manager Ernie Grunfeld (a former player), "We're going to get to the bottom of this, if there is a bottom to this." Federal authorities were reportedly interested in the case due to the possible ties between the gun possession and the gambling. The NBA has been subject to scrutiny about illicit gambling since former referee Tim Donahgy admitted in 2007 to making bad calls that affected the point spreads of games he officiated.

ESPN noted that the NBA had taken a public-relations blow as a result of the Arenas incident. Though the league's **collective bargaining agreement** allows players to possess firearms legally, players cannot bring guns to facilities or while traveling on league-related business. In 1997, Washington team owner Abe Pollin changed the franchise name from the Bullets to the Wizards out of concern that the Bullets' name had a negative connotation.

At first, Arenas would not take the charges seriously. Shortly after the incident occurred, he remarked sarcastically to teammates, "You guys, I wanted to go rob banks, and I wanted to be a bank robber on the weekends." He later joked about the incident on his Twitter account. On January 5, a photographer caught Arenas pointing his index fingers towards teammates as if he had guns in his hands. Although reports described Arenas' behavior as "playful," NBA Commissioner David Stern did not find humor in Arenas' actions. On January 6, Stern suspended Arenas indefinitely without pay, and the suspension eventually covered the remainder of the entire season. The Wizards supported the move, with a statement issued by the team noting that Arenas' behavior had been unacceptable. Arenas issued a statement as well, saying that he had "put the NBA in a negative light" and had let his teammates down through his behavior.

On January 15, the U.S. Attorney for the District of Columbia charged Arenas with **felony** gun possession. Arenas avoided a trial and a lengthy process by pleading guilty to a felony of carrying an unlicensed pistol outside his home or business. He faced a sentence of up to five years, though most commentators expected a sentence of less than six months. Arenas had maintained that he and Crittenton were joking around when the incident occurred, but Crittenton had indicated to others that he had felt threatened and pulled his gun for his own protection. Nevertheless, Crittenton pleaded guilty to a **misdemeanor** gun possession charge, and when Stern suspended Arenas for the remainder of the season on January 27, he also suspended Crittenton for the same duration.

In February, Arenas wrote a piece that was published by the *Washington Post*. Arenas acknowledged his wrongdoing and said that he was learning to be a better role model. On March 26, a judge sentenced Arenas to two years PROBATION. Though Arenas avoided prison time, he had to spend 30 days in a halfway house in Maryland. He started his stay at the facility on April 9 and was released on May 7. With his suspension ending after the 2009-2010 season, Arenas will be able to continue his NBA career, and he will reportedly return to the Wizards.

CRIMINAL PROCEDURE

The framework of laws and rules that govern the administration of justice in cases involving an individual who has been accused of a crime, beginning with the initial investigation of the crime and concluding either with the unconditional release of the accused by virtue of acquittal

Gilbert Arenas entering court, January 15, 2010.
AP IMAGES

(a judgment of not guilty) or by the imposition of a term of punishment pursuant to a conviction for the crime.

Black v. United States

Mail fraud is the subject of criminal statutes codified at 18 U.S.C. §§ 1341 **et seq.** Four individuals who were convicted of mail **fraud** related their scheme to steal money from the corporation they ran challenged their conviction on grounds that the **district court** had erred in instructing the jury about the charges. The individuals appealed the case to both the Seventh **Circuit Court** of Appeals and to the U. S. SUPREME COURT. The Supreme Court on June 24, 2010 ruled in the defendants' favor, holding that the defendants had not forfeited their right to object based on their decision to request a **general verdict** rather than special verdicts related to the charges. *Black v. United States*, No. 08-876 (June 24, 2010).

The four defendants in the case were senior executives with Hollinger International, an American company that owned several newspapers. A Canadian company known as Ravelston controlled Hollinger; Ravelston in turn was controlled by Conrad M. Black, who was also the CEO of Hollinger. Other defendants also owned stock in Ravelston. Any money funneled from Hollinger to Ravelston thus served to benefit the defendants who owned stock in Ravelston. One of Hollinger's subsidiaries sold several newspapers until it had only one left, which was a tiny weekly paper focusing on Mammoth Lake, California. The defendants devised a scheme through which executives were paid $5.5 million not to compete with the tiny newspaper. Neither the audit committee at Hollinger nor Hollinger's board of directors approved the transaction. The defendants later said that Hollinger owed Ravelston the money for management fees and that the $5.5 million was really compensation for these fees. The defendants said they characterized the fees as compensation for the noncompetition agreement in the hopes that the Canadian government would not treat the money as **taxable income**.

Under 18 U.S.C. § 1341, "Whoever, having devised or intending to devise any scheme or artifice to DEFRAUD ... places in any post office or authorized depository for mail matter, any matter or thing whatever to be sent or delivered by the Postal Service ... shall be fined under this title or imprisoned not more than 20 years, or both." In 1988, Congress added 18 U.S.C. § 1346, which defines "scheme or artifice to defraud" to include "a scheme or artifice to deprive another of the intangible right of honest services."

Based on these statutes, prosecutors charged the executives with MAIL FRAUD. One theory that the prosecution advanced was that the Hollinger executives had committed mail FRAUD through theft of money or other property by way of misrepresentations and misleading omissions. Under a second theory, prosecutors argued that the defendants had violated the **statute** by deprived Hollinger and its shareholders of "their intangible right to the honest services of the corporate officers, directors or controlling shareholders of Hollinger." The U.S. District Court for the Northern District of Illinois instructed the jury on both of these theories. Regarding the second of these theories, the defendants objected the court's instruction that a person commits honest-services fraud by misusing "his position for private gain for himself and/or a co-schemer" and "knowingly and intentionally" breaching a duty of loyalty.

Prosecutors requested that the court use a special-verdict form, which would mean that the jury would specify which theory, if any, on which it based its theory. The defendants, however, urged the court to use a GENERAL VERDICT form, which means that the jury could convict the defendants based on either theory. After a four-month trial, the jury returned a guilty verdict on the mail-fraud charges.

The defendants appealed their conviction to the Seventh Circuit Court of Appeals. In support of their position, the defendants cited *Yates v. United States*, 354 U.S. 298, 77 S. Ct. 1064, 1 L. Ed. 2d 1356 (1957). In *Yates*, the Supreme Court held that a general verdict should be set aside when a jury's verdict is supportable on one ground by not a second ground, and it is impossible to determine the ground on which the jury made its decision. According to the defendants, the district court had erred in making its instruction regarding honest-services fraud. Since it was impossible to tell which theory the jury used to base its decision, the defendants argued that the general verdict should be set aside.

The Seventh Circuit noted that had the court used the special-verdict form instead of the general-verdict form, the issue of the jury instructions would have been moot because it would have been clear about the theory the jury used. The court stressed that the defendants and not prosecutors had objected to the use of the special-verdict form. According to the **appellate court**, this constituted a **forfeiture** of the defendants' right to object because the defendants bore responsibility for the court using the general-verdict form. Therefore, the Seventh Circuit affirmed the district court's decision. *United States v. Black*, 530 F.3d 596 (7th Cir. 2008).

The Supreme Court agreed to review the case along with the case of *Skilling v. United States*, No. 08-1394 (June 24, 2010), and the Court decided both cases on the same day. In *Skilling*, the Court ruled that 18 U.S.C. § 1346 only applies to schemes to defraud that involve bribes or kickbacks. In *Black*, the district court indeed erred in defining honest-services fraud. Justice RUTH BADER GINSBURG, who wrote the majority opinions in both *Skilling* and *Black*, turned to the question of whether the defendants in *Black* had forfeited their right to object based on their failure to acquiesce to the prosecution's request for special verdicts. Ginsburg reviewed applicable provisions in the Federal Rules of **Criminal Procedure** and found no support for the Seventh Circuit's FORFEITURE analysis. Ginsburg concluded that because the defendants had properly objected to the jury instruction at trial that they had secured the right to challenge the instructions on appeal. Accordingly, the Court vacated the Seventh Circuit's judgment.

The Court's decisions in both *Skilling* and *Black* called into question whether the convictions of the defendants would hold up in the lower courts. Defense lawyers and other commentators also said the decision would likely lead to appeals by many of those who have been convicted under the law. However, other commentators noted that because Black was convicted on other grounds as well, the Court's decision may provide a glimmer of hope that his sentence could be reduced. A spokesperson for the Justice Department noted that part of the law remained intact and that federal prosecutors would continue to pursue cases under the honest-services law.

DEATH AND DYING

Death *is the end of life.* Dying *is the process of approaching death, including the choices and actions involved in that process.*

Numerous Legal Issues Surround Michael Jackson's Death

After years of being at the center of many controversies, pop music star Michael Jackson planned for a triumphant return as he prepared during the summer of 2009 for a new concert series. On the morning of June 25, however, Jackson's doctor found Jackson in bed having difficulty breathing. Efforts to resuscitate Jackson failed, and Jackson died that afternoon. His untimely death caused a number of legal issues related to his estate, CUSTODY of his children, and the cause of his death. Some of these issues may not be resolved for years.

Jackson was born on August 29, 1958 in Gary, Indiana. He earned acclaim as a child as the lead singer of the Jackson 5, which also featured four of Jackson's older brothers. By the late 1970s, Jackson had emerged as a solo artist, leading to the 1982 release of the album *Thriller*, which became the best-selling album of all time. Over the course of his career, Jackson earned 15 Grammy Awards and 26 American Music Awards. He earned numerous lifetime achievement awards, and the *Guinness Book of World Records* states that Jackson is the most successful entertainer in history.

During the 1990s and 2000s, Jackson's life became the subject of tabloid headlines. In 1993, he was accused of molesting a boy who sometimes stayed at Jackson's home. Charges were never filed in that case, but Jackson faced similar charges in 2003. In 2005, a judge cleared Jackson of the charges, but Jackson's reputation had been tarnished. He had a total of three children, including two from his second wife, Debbie Rowe, and a third from a surrogate mother. Jackson reportedly made about $500 million earnings during the course of his career. Jackson held substantial interests in music catalogs, and these interests were worth hundreds of millions of dollars.

In June 2009, Jackson was preparing for a concert series entitled *This Is It*. Jackson had previously hired Conrad Murray as a personal physician at a rate of $150,000 per month. On the evening of June 25, he rehearsed at the Staples Center in Los Angeles before returning home after midnight. The next morning, Murray entered Jackson's room and discovered that the singer was not breathing. Murray said that Jackson still had a slight pulse and was still warm. Murray attempted to conduct CPR on Jackson, but nobody called 911 until about 30 minutes had elapsed from the time that Murray first found Jackson. Paramedics finally arrived at Jackson's house at 12:26 p.m. and tried to administer CPR before taking Jackson to the RONALD REAGAN UCLA Medical Center. Resuscitation efforts failed, and Jackson was pronounced dead at 2:26 p.m.

Michael Jackson's physician, Dr. Conrad Murray, appears in court on charges of involuntary manslaughter, April 2010.

AP IMAGES

Reports conflicted about Jackson's health at the time of his death. Some reports indicated that Jackson was frail and had many needle marks around his body. Several stories indicated that Jackson was taking a number of sleeping and anti-anxiety medications. However, Jackson's family denied the reports that he was in poor health. The Los Angeles Coroner's office conducted an AUTOPSY on June 26, and the Jackson family arranged for a second private autopsy. Although initial reports suggested that no foul play was involved, the CORONER later classified the death as a HOMICIDE.

Investigators, along with Jackson's family, focused their attention on Murray. The doctor told investigators that he had given Jackson a variety of medications, including the drug propofol, which is typically used by anesthesiologists during surgery. Murray said that he was trying to wean Jackson off the drug and had been giving Jackson doses of other sedatives. Two days before Jackson's death, Murray gave Jackson doses of the sedative and withheld the propofol. On the night of Jackson's death, Murray gave Jackson several drugs before finally administering propofol due to Jackson's insistence. Authorities were unable to find evidence that Murray had obtained propofol under his medical license. However, the authorities found a bottle of propofol in Murray's medical bag,

and they found a number of other drugs at Jackson's house. These drugs were prescribed by several doctors, including Murray.

In February 2010, prosecutors formally charged Murray with **involuntary manslaughter** for his role in Jackson's death. Judge Keith Schwartz set bail at $75,000, and though Murray was allowed to continue to practice medicine, he could not administer any anesthetic agents, including propofol. Jackson's family attended the hearing as well as another procedural hearing in April. Murray has an active practice that covers the states of California, Nevada, and Texas, but attorneys with the California Attorney General wanted to revoke his California license. If that happened, he would most likely also lose his license in Texas and Nevada as well.

For several months after Jackson's death, several reports focused on who would obtain custody of Jackson's three children. The two oldest—12-year-old Prince Michael I and 11-year-old Paris—were also the children of Rowe, who had given up parental rights. However, Rowe reportedly had resumed contact with the children, and some speculated that she could obtain custody. A third child, seven-year-old Prince Michael II, was conceived through a surrogate mother. Although Rowe's attorney initially indicated that she would seek custody, Rowe later agreed not to challenge a court's decision to grant custody to Jackson's mother, Katherine.

The subject of Jackson's estate has proven to be more complicated. On July 6, 2009, attorney John Branca filed Jackson's will at the Los Angeles County courthouse. Jackson's reported NET WORTH as of 2007 was $236.6 million, but he also had debts of $331 million. Settlement of these debts could take years, according to some reports. Jackson's share of the Sony/ATV MUSIC PUBLISHING company's catalog constitute a significant portion Jackson's assets. Some speculated that creditors could force a sale of Jackson's assets, including his interest in the catalog, which would reduce the value of his estate.

In late 2009, Columbia Pictures released a video entitled "This Is It," which ran in theaters in October and was later released on home video. Sony also announced that it would release several posthumous albums, with a significant percentage of the proceeds going to Jackson's estate.

DEBTOR AND CREDITOR

A debtor is one who owes a debt or the performance of an obligation to another, who is called the creditor; one who may be compelled to pay a claim or demand; anyone liable on a claim, whether due or to become due.

In bankruptcy law, a person who files a voluntary petition or person against whom an involuntary petition is filed. A person or munici- pality concerning which a bankruptcy case has been commenced.

Jerman v. Carlisle

Creditors are restricted in their methods and practices of debt-collecting pursuant to the Fair Debt Collection Practices Act (FDCPA), 15 U.S.C. §§1692, *et seq.* The Act imposes civil liability for violations. In *Jerman v. Carlisle,* No. 08-1200, 559 U.S. ___ (2010), the U.S. SUPREME COURT ruled against a debt collector who alleged his mistake fell under the "bona fide error" provision of the Act, when he informed a homeowner that a mortgage debt would be considered valid unless she disputed the claim in writing. Newly-appointed Justice SONIA SOTO- MAYOR wrote the opinion of the Court in a 7-2 decision finding that the debtor had violated the FDCPA. The case was an important and timely one as an increasing number of homeowners across the country faced **foreclosure** on their homes.

In April 2006, the law firm of Carlisle, McNellie, Rini, Kramer & Ulrich, L.P.A., and one of its attorneys, Adrienne Foster (hereinafter "Carlisle") filed a complaint in an Ohio state court on behalf of client Countrywide Home Loans, Inc. The lawsuit sought FORECLOSURE on a mortgage held by Countrywide in real property owned by Karen Jerman. Attached to the complaint was a "Notice," later served on Jerman, which advised her that unless she disputed the mortgage debt in writing, the debt would be assumed to be valid.

Jerman retained a lawyer, who sent a letter disputing the debt, after which Carlisle attempted to verify the debt from Countrywide. In fact, Countrywide acknowledged that Jerman had already paid the debt in full, and Carlisle withdrew the lawsuit.

Through counsel, Jerman then filed her own lawsuit, seeking class certification and damages under the FDCPA. Her complaint alleged that Carlisle, by sending notice requiring her to dispute the debt in writing, and by not maintaining procedures to avoid such errors, had violated the Act. While acknowledging Carlisle's error, the U.S. **District Court** for the Northern District of Ohio found that it fell under the "bona fide error" defense of the Act, §1692k. In relevant part, that provision excuses from liability any debt collector who can show, by a **preponderance of evidence**, that (1) the violation was not intentional, and (2) it was the result of a **bona fide** error notwithstanding the maintenance of procedures reasonably adapted to avoid such errors. The district court granted Carlisle **summary judgment**.

On appeal, the Sixth **Circuit Court** of Appeals affirmed the district court. Although it acknowledged a contrary majority position adopted by the 2nd, 8th and 9th Circuits, it sided with the 10th Circuit in holding that the availability of the "bona fide error" defense was applicable not only to clerical or procedural errors, but also to mistakes of law.

Not so, said Justice Sotomayor for the Supreme Court's majority opinion. In reversing the Sixth Circuit, the high court expressly held that "[t]he bona fide error defense in §1692k(c) does not apply to a violation resulting from a debt collector's mistaken interpretation of the legal requirements of the FDCPA." Ignorance of the law would not excuse any person, civilly or criminally, said the Court.

In analysis, the Court noted that a debt collector's misinterpretation of the legal requirements of the Act did not constitute "unintentional" error. The majority further noted that, by way of comparison, administrative penalty provisions of the FEDERAL TRADE COMMIS- SION Act (FTC), expressly incorporated into the FDCPA, applied only where a debt collector acted with "actual knowledge or knowledge fairly implied on the basis of objective circumstances" that the FDCPA prohibited such an action or practice. The absence of similar language in §1692k leads to a reasonable inference that Congress intended that injured consumers could recover damages for "intentional" conduct such as that deemed in the present case. Moreover, Congress did not confine the reaches of liability under the FDCPA to "willful" violations, a term understood in the civil context to exclude mistakes of law. In fact, the inclusion of language requiring a debt collector to show that it maintained "procedures reasonably adapted to avoid any such error" implies procedures that would avoid mistakes like clerical or factual errors. Indeed, said the Court, Congress had not expressly included mistakes of law in any parallel "bona fide error" defenses anywhere in the entire **U.S. Code**.

Justice Sotomayor was joined by Chief Justice Roberts and Justices Stevens, Thomas, Ginsburg, and Breyer (who filed a concurring opinion). In his concurrence, Justice Breyer noted that any fears that lawyers acting in the best interests of their clients might be liable for their interpretive mistakes were expressly alleviated by the fact that they could turn to the FTC for an **advisory opinion** at any time. Justice Scalia also wrote a separate opinion, both concurring and concurring in the judgment, but disagreeing with the Court's tracing of Congress's actions outside of the FDCPA to determine Congressional intent.

In his DISSENT, Justice Kennedy (joined by Justice Alito) opined that a more reasonable, "straightforward," and "quite reasonable" interpretation of the statute's plain terms would have excused good-faith mistakes, whether in law or in fact.

DEPORTATION

Banishment to a foreign country, attended with confiscation of property and deprivation of civil rights.

The transfer of an alien, by exclusion or expulsion, from the United States to a foreign country. The removal or sending back of an alien to the country from which he or she came because his or her presence is deemed inconsistent with the public welfare, and without any punishment being imposed or contemplated. The grounds for deportation are set forth at 8 U.S.C.A. § 1251 and the procedures are provided for in §§ 1252-1254.

Carachuri-Rosendo v. Holder

Under the IMMIGRATION and Nationality Act (INA), 8 U.S.C. §§1101, *et seq.*, a lawful permanent resident may apply for discretionary cancellation of removal proceedings if, among other things, he "has not been convicted of any aggravated felony." §1229b(a)(3). However, as between statutes of the United States, the definition of "aggravated felony" is complex.

Under §1101(a)(43)(B) of the INA, the term is defined to include, *inter alia*, "illicit trafficking in a controlled substance ... including a drug trafficking crime" as defined in 18 U.S.C. §924 (c), which, in turn, defines a "drug trafficking crime" as a "felony punishable under," *inter alia*, "the Controlled Substances Act (21 U.S.C. §§801 et seq.)."

Simple possession offenses are generally treated as misdemeanors with shorter sentences, but under §924(c), a conviction "after a prior conviction under this subchapter [or] the law of any State ... has become final," a "recidivist" simple possession offense can be "punishable" as a **felony** and subject to a two-year sentence. Importantly, to charge (i.e., elevate) a "recidivist" simple possession offense as an "aggravated felony" under §1101(a)(43), a PROSECU-TOR must charge (i.e., allege) the existence of the former (prior) conviction. This provides notice and an opportunity to challenge its validity, mandatory prerequisites to a successful prosecution seeking to "authorize" a felony punishment based on the fact of the prior conviction, for what would otherwise constitute a simple possession offense.

In *Carachuri-Rosendo v. Holder*, No. 09-60, 560 U.S. ___ (2010), Carachuri-Rosnedo, a lawful permanent resident of the United States since he was five years old, now faced DEPORTA-TION under federal law for two **misdemeanor** drug possession offenses in Texas. The first involved possession of less than two ounces of marijuana, for which he received 20 days in jail. The second offense was for possession of a single tablet of a common anti-anxiety medication (Xanax), without prescription, and he received 10 days in jail. After the second offense, the federal government initiated removal proceedings against him.

Carachuri-Rosendo acknowledged that he was removable, but claimed he was eligible for discretionary relief from removal under §1229b(a)(3), his eligibility for such relief premised upon not having been convicted of any "aggravated felony." The Immigration Judge denied his request, holding that his second conviction of simple possession was an aggravated felony. The Board of Immigration Appeals affirmed, as did the Fifth **Circuit Court** of Appeals. The **appellate court** cited *Lopez v. Gonzales*, 549 U.S. 47, 127 S. Ct. 625, 166 L. Ed. 2d 462 (2006), to support the premise that, to be an "aggravated felony" for immigration law purposes, a state drug conviction must be punishable as a felony under federal law. The **appellate** court then created a "hypothetical approach," reasoning that since Carachuri-Rosendo's conduct could have been prosecuted as a recidivist simple possession under state law, it qualified as a felony under federal law. In other words, since the second drug conviction could have been punished as a felony under the Controlled Substances Abuse Act (if prosecuted in federal court), the conviction qualified as an "aggravated felony" making him ineligible for cancellation of removal proceedings.

A unanimous SUPREME COURT reversed the judgment of the Fifth Circuit. Simply put, the Court held that if Texas did not specifically prosecute the second conviction based on the fact of a prior conviction, then that second conviction was not an "aggravated felony" under the Immigration and Nationality Act (INA), 8 U.S.C. §1101. Texas law, like federal law, did provide for sentence enhancement if the state proved that the DEFENDANT had been previously convicted of a similar offense. But in this case, Texas did not seek such an enhancement, and Carachuri-Rosendo was not tried as a recidivist nor was his offense characterized as a recidivist second offense. Attempting to characterize the prior conviction as such, at a later date, in a different forum, would not suffice to deny Carachuri-Rosendo's petition. To do so would ignore the INA's text, which limited cancellation powers of the Attorney General only when, *inter alia,* a non-citizen "has … been convicted of a[n] aggravated felony." Determination of what one has been convicted of does not contemplate what might have, or should have, been charged; neither does it allow for conviction by analogy. The immigration court could not, after the fact, enhance the state offense **of record** just because facts known to it would have authorized a greater penalty.

Writing for the Court, Justice Stevens noted that one did not usually think of a 10-day sentence for unauthorized possession of a single prescription pill as an "aggravated felony." He cautioned that the Court must be wary in this case, because the government sought a result that "the English language tells [the Court] not to expect." Besides, added the Court, any ambiguities in criminal statutes that are referenced in immigration laws should be construed in favor of the non-citizen.

Justices Scalia and Thomas wrote separate opinions concurring in the judgment. Justice Scalia came to the same conclusion as the Court, but with different reasoning. He concluded that a misdemeanor offense with a sentencing factor that could raise it to the felony level under the Controlled Substance was not the same as an offense that qualified for purposes of determining what elements an alien had been "convicted of." Here, Carachuri-Rosendo was only "convicted of" possession of a controlled substance without a valid prescription, a Class A misdemeanor under Texas law. Since the elements of that crime did not include "recidivism," the immigration court could not add that element to his conviction in order to enhance the offense to felony level under 21 U.S.C. §844(a). Justice Thomas concluded that a proper reading of the **statutory** text supported the result reached by the Court.

DISPARATE IMPACT

Lewis v. City of Chicago

Title VII of the CIVIL RIGHTS Act of 1964, 42 U.S.C. §§2000e *et seq.* prohibits employers not only from acts of intentional DISCRIMINATION, but also from using employment practices that cause a DISPARATE IMPACT on protected groups. In order to bring a federal lawsuit under the Act, plaintiffs must show that the first filed a timely charge of discrimination with the EQUAL EMPLOYMENT OPPORTUNITY COMMISSION (EEOC) within 300 days after their claims accrued. In *Lewis v. City of Chicago, Illinois,* No. 08-974, 560 U.S. ___ (2010), the U.S. SUPREME COURT considered whether a PLAINTIFF who does not file a timely charge challenging the *adoption* of an employment practice may nonetheless later assert a disparate impact claim in a timely EEOC charge challenging the employer's later-date *application* of that practice.

The case involved the City of Chicago's ("City") written examination (given in 1995) to applicants seeking firefighter positions. In 1996, the City announced that it would randomly draw candidates from the pool of applicants who had scored at least 89 of 100 points on the examination (they were designated by the City as "highly qualified"). Those who scored between 65 and 88 ("qualified") were advised that it was unlikely they would be called for further processing, but that the City would keep them on the eligibility list for as long as it was utilized. Those who scored below 65 on the examination were informed that they had failed and would not be considered further. Shortly thereafter, the City began hiring candidates from the top "highly qualified" group.

In 1997, several African-American applicants who scored in the middle group (65-88, "qualified") filed discrimination charges with the EEOC and received right-to-sue letters in 1998. They filed suit in federal **district court**, which certified them as a plaintiff class (ultimately the class consisted of more than 5,000 African-American applicants who scored between 65 and 88 on the examination).

The City sought **summary judgment**, arguing that plaintiffs had failed to file EEOC charges within the requisite 300-day period from the accrual of their claims. The district court denied the motion, holding that the City's continuing reliance on the 1995 test results constituted a "continuing violation" of Title VII. Following a **bench trial**, the court rejected the City's "business necessity" defense (after stipulating that the scoring process had a disparate impact on the plaintiff class) and ruled in favor of plaintiffs. It ordered the City to hire 132 randomly-selected applicants from the plaintiff class and awarded backpay to be divided among the remaining class members. The City appealed.

In 2008, the Seventh **Circuit Court** of Appeals reversed. It sided with the City, holding that the lawsuit was untimely because the EEOC charge was filed more than 300 days after the only discriminatory act: sorting the scores into three categories. According to the **appellate court**, the hiring of applicants from the top group was only a consequence of the test scores and did not constitute a new act of discrimination.

But a unanimous U.S. Supreme Court disagreed. In reversing the Seventh Circuit, Justice Scalia, writing for the Court, held that plaintiffs could assert a disparate impact claim in a timely charge that challenged the employer's later *application* of an earlier *adopted* practice not timely challenged, if plaintiffs could allege all elements of a disparate impact claim. But determining whether a charge is timely necessarily requires the identification of the specific unlawful employment practice complained of. Here, said the Court, all agreed that the challenged practice was the City's selection of firefighters on the basis of the 1996 sorting into three score groups.

With the exception of the first selection round, all subsequent hiring selections from the list occurred within 300 days of the first charge filed with the EEOC. Said the Court, "It may be true that the city's January 1996 decision to adopt the cutoff score (and to create a list of the applicants above it) gave rise to a freestanding disparate impact claim ... But it does not follow that no new violations occurred—and no new claims could arise—when the city implemented that decision down the road."

The real question before it, said the Court, was not the timeliness of the claim, but whether the challenged practice could be the basis for a disparate impact claim. Characterized as the exclusion of passing applicants whose scores fell below 89 when selecting potential candidates for hire, the employment practice qualified as one that could be challenged. Next, the Court reiterated that to establish a **prima facie** claim for disparate impact, a plaintiff must show that an employer "uses a particular employment practice that causes a disparate impact" on one of the prohibited bases. After agreeing that, in this case, the term "employment practice" clearly encompassed the conduct complained of, the Court found that plaintiffs stated a PRIMA FACIE violation. (Whether they proved a violation was not before the Court.)

After noting that this was not a claim of disparate treatment (which requires a showing of discriminatory intent), the Court left it to the Seventh Circuit, on remand, to determine whether the judgment of the district court needed to be modified, in that it had awarded relief based on the first round of hiring, which occurred outside of the EEOC charging period.

DIVERSITY JURISDICTION

Hertz Corp. v. Friend

Under the Constitution, the **federal courts** are open to disputes involving parties from different states. Diversity jurisdiction is important because out-of-state defendants believe that federal courts are friendlier places than STATE COURTS. Therefore, when an out-of-state DEFENDANT is sued in state court, the defendant will file a motion in that state's federal district courts to "remove" the case to federal court. When individual defendants are involved, the question of removal is usually straightforward. However, when a business with multiple locations in the United States is the defendant, things become much more complicated. Congress enacted an amendment to the federal diversity jurisdiction **statute**, 28 U.S.C. §1332(d)(2), which states that diversity will be based on a corporation's "principal place of business." However, this phrase did not improve diversity analysis by the courts. The SUPREME COURT stepped in and settled the matter in *Hertz Corp. v. Friend*, __U.S.__, 130 S. Ct. 1181, __L. Ed. 2d__ (2010). The Court held that in determining a corporation's principal place of business, the courts must use the "nerve center" approach. This would be the place where a corporation's officers direct, control, and coordinate the corporation's activities.

In 2007, Melinda Friend and John Nhieu, two California citizens, sued the Hertz Corporation in a California state court. They sought damages for what they claimed were violations of California's wage and hour laws. They also requested relief on behalf of a potential class composed of California citizens who had allegedly suffered similar injuries. Hertz filed a notice seeking removal to a federal court, arguing that the plaintiffs and the defendant were citizens of different states. Hertz submitted a declaration that sought to show that Hertz's "principal place of business" was in New Jersey, not in California. Hertz operated facilities in 44 States. The state of California—which had about 12% of the nation's population—accounted for 273 of Hertz's 1,606 car rental locations; about 2,300 of its 11,230 full-time employees; about $811 million of its $4.371 billion in annual revenue; and about 3.8 million of its approximately 21 million annual transactions. Hertz's corporate headquarters were located in Park Ridge, New Jersey but some executive and administrative functions were conducted in Oklahoma City, Oklahoma.

The federal **district court** agreed that the submitted facts were undisputed but denied removal to federal court because of the Ninth **Circuit Court** of Appeals' precedent that requires courts to identify a corporation's "principal place of business" by first determining the amount of a corporation's business activity state by state. If the amount of activity is "significantly larger" or "substantially predominates" in one state, then that state is the corporation's "principal place of business." If

there is no such state, then the "principal place of business" is the corporation's "nerve center." This is the place where "the majority" of its executive and administrative functions are performed. The district court applied the test and found that the "plurality of each of the relevant business activities" was in California, and that "the differential between the amount of those activities" in California and the amount in "the next closest state" was "significant." Therefore, the lawsuit must remain in California state court. The Ninth Circuit upheld the ruling and the Supreme Court accepted review to resolve a conflict in the circuit courts of appeal over the definition of "principal place of business."

In a unanimous decision, the Court rejected the Ninth Circuit approach and endorsed the use of the "nerve center" approach as the sole means of analyzing corporate diversity issues. Justice STEPHEN BREYER, writing for the Court, noted that Congress had inserted the phrase "principal place of business" to prevent corporations from manipulating federal-court jurisdiction as well as to reduce the number of diversity cases. Despite its best intentions, Congress did not improve the quality of legal analysis with this amendment. If a corporation's headquarters and executive offices were in the same state in which it did most of its business, the test seemed clear. The "principal place of business" was in that state. But if those corporate headquarters, including executive offices, were in one state, while the corporation's plants or other centers of business activity were located in other states, the answer was more difficult. A number of circuit courts embraced the "nerve center" approach but it was not helpful when a corporation's operations were not far-flung but rather limited to only a few states. The circuits developed their own tests, focusing more heavily on where a corporation's actual business activities are located. Over time these various tests became increasingly complex.

Justice Breyer announced that the Court had settled on using the nerve center approach. The nerve center would be where a corporation's officers "direct, control, and coordinate the corporation's activities. In practice it should normally be the place where the corporation maintains its headquarters." Although the approach was admittedly "imperfect," Breyer pointed to three sets of considerations in its favor: the diversity statute supported this approach, administratively simplicity, and it was less complex than the approach taken by the circuits, including the Ninth. However, the Court would not tolerate jurisdictional manipulation of the nerve center location. If the alleged "nerve center" was "nothing more than a mail drop box, a bare office with a computer, or the location of an annual executive retreat, the courts should instead take as the 'nerve center' the place of actual direction, control, and coordination, in the absence of such manipulation." Although the nerve center approach clearly showed Hertz was located in New Jersey, and thus qualified for diversity jurisdiction, the Court remanded the case to the lower courts for that determination.

DOUBLE JEOPARDY

Bobby v. Bies

The SUPREME COURT, in *Atkins v. Virginia*, 536 U.S. 304, 122 S. Ct. 2242, 153 L. Ed. 2d 335 (2002), ruled that the EIGHTH AMENDMENT ban on **cruel and unusual punishment** prohibits the execution of mentally retarded offenders. Prior to this decision, mental retardation could be considered as a mitigating factor against imposing the death penalty but there was no absolute bar on CAPITAL PUNISHMENT. In light of *Atkins*, some inmates already on death row have sought to claim mental retardation as a means of overturning their death sentences. The Supreme Court, in *Bobby v. Bies*, __U.S.__, 129 S. Ct. 2145, 173 L. Ed. 2d 1173 (2009), addressed whether the Fifth Amendment's **Double Jeopardy** Clause prevents a court from conducting a hearing on such an inmate's mental capacity to determine whether the death sentence should be set aside. The Court concluded that such a hearing was constitutional.

In 1992, Michael Bies was tried and convicted in Ohio of the aggravated MURDER, KID-NAPPING, and attempted RAPE of a ten-year-old boy. The jury was instructed at the sentencing stage to weigh **mitigating circumstances**, including evidence of Bies' mild to borderline mental retardation, against aggravating factors including the brutality of the crime. The jury recommended the death penalty and the trial court imposed it. The Ohio Supreme Court reviewed Bies' case and upheld the conviction and the sentence, concluding that his mild to borderline mental retardation merited consideration but was outweighed by the aggravating factors. Following the *Atkins* decision, the Ohio

trial court ordered a hearing on the question of Bies' mental capacity. The trial court was to follow an Ohio Supreme Court ruling that required Bies to prove "(1) significantly subaverage intellectual functioning, (2) significant limitations in two or more adaptive skills, such as communication, self-care, and self-direction, and (3) onset before the age of 18."

However, prior to the hearing, Bies filed a federal **habeas corpus** action in federal **district court**, seeking an immediate vacation of his death sentence. The court granted his petition and the state appealed to the Sixth **Circuit Court** of Appeals. The appeals court upheld the district court, finding that the Ohio Supreme Court's recognition of Bies' mental retardation gave Bies a "legal entitlement to a life sentence." Under the Double **Jeopardy** Clause of the U.S. Constitution, the state court was barred from making any renewed inquiry into the matter of Bies' mental state. The state then appealed to the U.S. Supreme Court.

The Supreme Court, in a unanimous decision, overturned the Sixth Circuit decision. Justice RUTH BADER GINSBURG, writing for the Court, stated that the lower **federal courts** had "fundamentally misperceived the application of the DOUBLE JEOPARDY Clause." In this case there were no serial prosecutions of Bies for the same crime but rather "serial efforts by the prisoner to vacate his capital sentence." Moreover, mental retardation for purposes of *Atkins* and mental retardation as "one mitigator to be weighed against aggravators," were discrete issues.

The Sixth Circuit had based its ruling on the doctrine of **issue preclusion**. ISSUE PRECLUSION bars successive LITIGATION of "an issue of fact or law" that "is actually litigated and determined by a valid and final judgment, and . . . is essential to the judgment." If a judgment does not depend on a given determination, relitigation of that determination is not precluded. Justice Ginsburg first noted that it was unclear that the Ohio courts had made a ruling on the issue of Bies' mental retardation at trial or on direct review. The courts had not found that Bies suffered "significant limitations in two or more adaptive skills." In addition, the state contested whether Bies could be classified as mentally retarded.

More importantly, the Court ruled that it was clear that the courts' statements regarding Bies' mental capacity were not necessary to the judgments affirming his death sentence. The

Sixth Circuit had concluded that the Ohio courts determined Bies' mental capacity pursuant to their "mandatory duty" to weigh the aggravating and MITIGATING CIRCUMSTANCES. Weighing these factors could not have happened, according to the Sixth Circuit, "unless the court first determined what to place on either side of the scale." Justice Ginsburg disagreed. The state courts' review of mental retardation was at best a "subsidiary finding that, standing alone, is not outcome determinative. Issue preclusion cannot transform Bies' loss at the sentencing phase into a partial victory."

Finally, the Court ruled that even if the requirements for issue preclusion had been met, an exception could have been applied. The *Atkins* decision altered the way prosecutors treated claims of mental retardation by defendants. When mental retardation was just a mitigating factor, prosecutors did not vigorously contest the evidence because the jury could view this as an aggravating factor of future dangerousness as well. Therefore, the change in law "substantially altered the State's incentive to contest Bies' mental capacity, applying preclusion would not **advance** the equitable administration of the law."

DRUGS AND NARCOTICS

Drugs *are articles intended for use in the diagnosis, cure, mitigation, treatment, or prevention of disease in humans or animals, and any articles other than food intended to affect the mental or body function of humans or animals.* Narcotics *are any drugs that dull the senses and commonly become addictive after prolonged use.*

California Supreme Court Strikes Down Legislative Amendment to Medical Marijuana Law

California and 14 other states have enacted medical marijuana laws. Under these statutes a person may legally be prescribed a certain amount of marijuana by a physician. Law enforcement officials have expressed concern that such laws could be used as a cover for illegal drug dealing. California enacted an amendment to the law that placed limits on the amount of marijuana a person could possess but the law was challenged as a violation of the initiative provision of the California Constitution. Under this provision, voters may directly enact laws.

Unlike other states with initiative clauses in their constitutions, California's places strict limits on what the legislature may do to modify the law. The California SUPREME COURT, in *State v. Kelly*, 222 P.3d 186 (2010), ruled that the amendment was invalid because it went beyond its lawful authority under the initiative provision.

In 1996, California voters passed an initiative measure, labeled Proposition 215, that placed into law the Compassionate Use Act (CUA). CUA provides that the **criminal law** provisions dealing with the possession and cultivation of marijuana do not apply to a patient or to a patient's primary caregiver who possesses or cultivates marijuana for the "personal medical purposes of the patient upon the written or oral recommendation or approval of a physician." Therefore, the CUA provides an **affirmative defense** to prosecution for the crimes of possession or cultivation. However, the CUA does not grant IMMUNITY from arrest for those crimes. CUA does not specific the amount of marijuana that a patient may possess or cultivate. The law merely states that the marijuana must be for the patient's "personal medical purposes." A 1997 California appeals court decision construed this to mean that the amount "should be reasonably related to the patient's current medical needs.

In 2003 the legislature received reports that the CUA's lack of specificity as to the amount of marijuana made drug laws difficult to enforce. In response, it enacted the Medical Marijuana Program (MMP) law. The law added 18 provisions that addressed the general subject matter covered by the CUA. One major provision created a voluntary identification card that provided protection against arrest for marijuana-related crimes. A person could obtain a card by registering and then renewing the card annually. However, the law also established quantity limitations for card-holders and non-card-holders. Under the law a patient could possess no more than eight ounces of dried marijuana and could only maintain no more than six mature or 12 immature marijuana plants. The law allowed for greater amounts in certain situations.

Patrick Kelly suffered from a number of debilitating ailments. For ten years he unsuccessfully treated himself for pain caused by his ailments, using injections, nerve stimulators, and various medications. In early 2005 he met with a doctor who recommended that he use marijuana for one year. The doctor did not recommend a dosage and Kelly did not register for an ID card. Kelly could not afford to purchase marijuana, so he cultivated plants at his home. He consumed one to two ounces per week and found that it lessened his nausea. In October 2005 an unidentified informant told a law enforcement officer that Kelly was growing marijuana. A law officer went to Kelly's home and observed marijuana plants growing in the backyard. He obtained a SEARCH WARRANT and returned to the home with seven to 9 other officers. Besides the plants, the officers found seven plastic bags of dried marijuana and a small amount of the drug in a plastic jar. They concluded Kelly had 12 usable ounces of marijuana. There was no evidence that Kelly was a dealer (scales, pagers, large amounts of cash, etc.). Kelly produced the doctor's written recommendation for medical use of marijuana but that did not prevent him with being charged with possessing marijuana for sale and for cultivating the plant.

Kelly was convicted of a lesser offense of possessing marijuana and of cultivating marijuana, and sentenced to three years' PROBATION. He appealed to the California Court of Appeals, which ruled the MMP provisions unconstitutional. The state then appealed to the California Supreme Court.

The Court upheld the court of appeals' decision. It based its ruling on the state constitution's initiative provision. The provision expressly stated that the legislature could not amend voter-approved laws; to do otherwise would allow the legislature to undo "what the people have done, without the electorate's consent." A long line of court cases had made clear that the legislature had very little opportunity to tinker with initiative laws. Turning to the 2003 law, the court noted that CUA ballot statements did not quantify the amount of marijuana a patient could possess. In contrast, the 2003 law did just that. The legislature recognized that it had gone too far with this change, when in 2004 it amended the law to remove the amount. However, Governor Arnold Schwarzenegger vetoed the law, believing the original quantity amounts were reasonable. By the time the case reached the supreme court, the state agreed that quantity standards unconstitutionally amended the law. A DEFENDANT who possessed more than the **statute** allowed could not use CUA as an AFFIRMATIVE DEFENSE.

The court reviewed the history of initiative statutes in California and pointed out that the state has from the beginning placed the greatest restrictions on the legislature's ability to amend initiative statutes. Of the 21 states that permit voter initiatives, 12 place no limitations upon the authority of the legislature to **repeal** or amend an initiative statute. Eight other states place some limitations on the authority of the legislature, but they are not as restrictive as California. Since initiative became part of the state constitution in 1911, a number of attempts have been made to amend the provision to allow some legislature action. These efforts have proved unsuccessful. The court concluded that under the constitution, the legislature could not amend CUA as to the specific amount of marijuana a patient could possess.

EDUCATION LAW

The body of state and federal constitutional provisions; local, state, and federal statutes; court opinions; and government regulations that provide the legal framework for educational institutions.

Forest Grove School District v. T.A.

In *Forest Grove School District v. T.A.*, __U.S.__, 129 S. Ct. 2484, 174 L. Ed. 2d 168 (2009), the SUPREME COURT ruled that the Individuals with Disabilities Education Amendments of 1997 (IDEA), Pub. L. No. 105-17, 111 Stat. 37. did not categorically prohibit reimbursement for private-education costs if a child has not "previously received special education and related services under the authority of a public agency." The decision could force public school systems to make high tuition payments for students whose parents believe that a private education would better meet their needs.

T.A. attended public schools in the Forest Grove School District, which is located in Oregon, from the time he was in kindergarten through the winter of his junior year of high school. From kindergarten through eighth grade his teachers observed that he had trouble paying attention in class and completing his assignments. When T.A. entered high school, his difficulties increased. During his freshman year his mother met with the school counselor to discuss her son's schoolwork. At the end of the school year, T.A. was evaluated by a school psychologist. After interviewing him, examining his school records, and administering cognitive ability tests, the psychologist concluded that he did not need further testing for any learning disabilities or other health impairments, including attention deficit hyperactivity disorder (ADHD). The psychologist and two other school officials discussed the evaluation results with his mother and all agreed that T.A. did not qualify for special-education services.

T.A. completed his sophomore year at Forest Grove High School, but his problems worsened during his junior year. His parents discussed with the school district the possibility of T.A. completing high school through a partnership program with the local community college. They also sought private professional advice, and this time T.A. was diagnosed with ADHD and a number of disabilities related to learning and memory. Advised by the private specialist that their son would do best in a structured, residential learning environment, the parents enrolled him at a private academy that focuses on educating children with special needs.

T.A.'s parents hired a lawyer and gave the school district written notice of his move to private schooling. The parents and the district were at odds over whether T.A. had a disability that significantly interfered with his educational performance. A hearing officer took evidence in the matter and issued a decision finding that

T.A.'s ADHD adversely affected his educational performance and that the school district failed to meet its obligations under the IDEA. The hearing officer ordered the district to reimburse T.A.'s parents for the cost of the private-school tuition. The district filed suit in federal district, challenging the hearing officer's decision. The **district court** set aside the reimbursement award, ruling that the 1997 amendments categorically barred reimbursement of private-school tuition for students who have not "previously received special education and related services under the authority of a public agency." The Ninth **Circuit Court** of Appeals reversed this decision. It held that the amendments did not impose a categorical bar to reimbursement when a parent unilaterally places in private school a child who has not previously received special-education services through the public school. Instead, such students were eligible for reimbursement, to the same extent as before the 1997 amendments.

The Supreme Court, in a 6-3 decision, upheld the Ninth Circuit. Justice JOHN PAUL STEVENS, writing for the majority, noted that in two prior decisions the Court had upheld private school reimbursement. However, in both cases the students had IEPs and had received public special-education services. In this case, T.A. did not have an IEP nor did he receive any services from the district. The Court found these differences insignificant because its analysis in the earlier cases "depended on the language and purpose of the Act and not the particular facts involved. Moreover, when a child requires special-education services, a school district's failure to propose an IEP of any kind is at least as serious a violation of its responsibilities under IDEA as a failure to provide an adequate IEP." The only question was whether the 1997 amendments had changed the legal landscape.

In 1997, Congress found that substantial gains had been made in the area of special education but that more needed to be done to guarantee children with disabilities adequate access to appropriate services. The 1997 amendments were intended "to place greater emphasis on improving student performance and ensuring that children with disabilities receive a quality public education." The amendments did not change the provision which gives courts broad authority to grant "appropriate" relief, including reimbursement for the cost of private

special education when a school district fails to provide a FAPE. Stevens stated that absent a clear expression elsewhere in the amendments of Congress' intent to **repeal** some portion of that provision or to abrogate the Court's two prior IDEA decisions, it would continue to read the **statute** to authorize the relief T.A. sought.

The district argued that because the statute only discussed reimbursement for children who have previously received special-education services through the public school, the IDEA only authorizes reimbursement in that circumstance. The Court found this argument unpersuasive. Stevens wrote that the amended IDEA explicitly bars reimbursement only when a school district makes a FAPE available by correctly identifying a child as having a disability and proposing an IEP adequate to meet the child's needs. The clause said nothing about the availability of reimbursement when a school district failed to provide a "free appropriate public education" (FAPE).

Justice Stevens also concluded that the school district's reading of the law was at odds with the general remedial purpose underlying IDEA and the 1997 amendments. The express purpose of the act was to "ensure that all children with disabilities have available to them a free appropriate public education that emphasizes special education and related services designed to meet their unique needs." The Court stated that the district's reading of the act would leave parents without an adequate remedy when a school district unreasonably failed to identify a child with disabilities. This "would not comport with Congress' acknowledgment of the paramount importance of properly identifying each child eligible for services." Such a reading "would produce a rule bordering on the irrational." The Court stated that it "would be particularly strange for the act to provide a remedy, as all agree it does, when a school district offers a child inadequate special-education services but to leave parents without relief in the more egregious situation in which the school district unreasonably denies a child access to such services altogether."

Therefore, when a court or hearing officer concludes that a school district failed to provide a FAPE and the private placement was suitable, "it must consider all relevant factors, including the notice provided by the parents and the school district's opportunities for evaluating the child, in determining whether reimbursement for some or all of the cost of the child's private education is warranted."

ELECTION LAW

D.C. Circuit Strikes Down Campaign Finance Law Aimed at Non-Profit Political Committees

The U.S. Court of Appeals for the District of Columbia Circuit in 2009 issued a controversial opinion that struck down regulations issued by the FEDERAL ELECTION COMMISSION aimed at limiting how non-profit entitles could spend and raise money to **advance** their beliefs and positions. The court concluded that these regulations violated the FIRST AMENDMENT rights of EMILY's List, which is a non-profit **entity** that promotes ABORTION rights and supports female pro-choice candidates for office.

Congress passed the Federal Election Campaign Act of 1971 (FECA), Pub. L. No. 92-255, 86 Stat. 3, to limit campaign contributions connected with federal elections. The FECA established limitations on the amounts that entities could contribute and spend on these federal elections. However, entities found ways to circumvent this law, using so-called "soft money" to contribute to campaigns. This soft money included funds that were not subject to limitations on contributions and spending. By comparison, "hard money" includes funds that are subject to the limitations. In response to concerns about the use of soft money, Congress approved the Bipartisan Campaign Reform Act of 2002 (BCRA), Pub. L. No. 107-155, 116 Stat. 81, which (among several provisions) placed restrictions on direct soft-money contributions to candidates. One year after the BCRA's passage, the SUPREME COURT upheld the statute's constitutionality in *McConnell v. FEC*, 540 U.S. 3, 124 S. Ct. 619, 157 L. Ed. 2d 491 (2003).

Many non-profit groups organized under section 527 of the INTERNAL REVENUE CODE (and commonly known as 527s) were exempt from the restrictions in the BCRA. During the 2004 election season, a number of 527 groups were accused of using soft money heavily to influence federal elections. Wealthy individuals were accused of donating large sums to individual non-profit groups, and these groups allegedly spent hundreds of millions of dollars on the 2004 election. Presidential candidates GEORGE W. BUSH and John Kerry both questioned donations made by some of the 527 groups.

The FEC rejected arguments that it should pass regulations banning non-profits from receiving and spending large donations. However, regulations passed by the FEC on November 23, 2004 limited how much money 527 groups could raise and spend. These regulations required non-profits to pay for a large percentage of election-related activities with hard money. In the case of such administrative expenses as rent, utilities, office supplies, and so forth, the non-profit group was required to use at least 50 percent of hard money for funding. In the case of costs for advertisements or other communications used to advocate for a federal candidate, 100 percent of the funds had to come from hard money. The FEC regulations became effective on January 1, 2005.

EMILY's List is a nonprofit political committee that was affected by the new FEC regulation. Shortly after the regulations took effect, EMILY's List asked the U.S. **District Court** for the District of Columbia to temporarily enjoin the FEC from enforcing the new regulation. On February 25, 2005, however, the district court denied request. During the next three years, both parties filed a series of motions, including motions for **summary judgment**. In 2008, Judge Colleen Kollar-Kotelly sided with the FEC, rejecting arguments by EMILY's List that the regulations violated the organization's First Amendment rights. According to the district court's opinion, the regulations were designed to prevent corruption and the appearance of corruption, which were important governmental interests. Because the regulations were closely drawn to match these interests, the court concluded that the regulations did not violate the Constitution. *EMILY's List v. FEC*, 569 F. Supp. 2d 18 (D.D.C. 2008).

EMILY's List then appealed the case to the District of Columbia **Circuit Court** of Appeals. Although each of the judges on the three-judge panel ruled in favor of EMILY's List, two of the judges signed off on a broad holding, while a third judge only concurred with the court's result. The majority opinion written by Judge Brett Kavanaugh and joined by Judge Karen LeCraft Henderson reviewed a series of Supreme Court decisions governing First Amendment limitations on campaign spending. Kavanaugh identified a series of principles established in these Supreme Court cases and summarized the principles as follows: "In reconciling the competing interests, the Supreme Court has generally approved **statutory** limits on *contributions* to

court of appeals reversed the district court's opinion. *EMILY's List v. FEC*, 581 F.3d 1 (D.C. Cir. 2009). Judge Janice Rogers Brown concurred with the court's judgment, agreeing that the FEC had exceeded its statutory authority. However, Brown disagreed strongly with the court's First Amendment analysis, noting that the court was "not content just answering a gratuitous constitutional question. Its holding is broader than even the PLAINTIFF requests."

In October 2009, the FEC was deadlocked in a 3-3 vote about whether to appeal the decision to the court of appeals sitting **en banc**. The FEC's vote meant that the decision stands, thus effectively removing the restrictions on spending by the non-profit groups.

ENTERTAINMENT LAW

NBC Settles Late Night "Tonight Show" Contract

In January 2010, late night television saw its biggest and most galvanizing moment when network television's NBC-TV Entertainment bought out the remainder of host Conan O'Brien's "Tonight Show" contract for $45 million and restored former star host Jay Leno to his old position. This followed a controversial but ostensibly cost-cutting five-month-old experiment that moved Jay Leno up to a "prime-time" 10:00 p.m. slot on the network in the newly-captioned "Jay Leno Show," while O'Brien took over "The Tonight Show" at 11:35 p.m., following local station evening news. Coincidentally, noted a January 22 *New York Times* article, $45 million was "precisely the amount that NBC had promised Mr. O'Brien as a penalty payment if he did not get 'The Tonight Show' when it was first promised to him in 2004."

In 2004, NBC Universal's Chief Executive Officer Jeffrey Zucker made a decision to name O'Brien as Leno's successor to host "The Tonight Show" in five years (June 2009). At that time (2004), Leno had been hosting the show for 17 years and enjoyed top-rank against competitive CBS network host David Letterman ("Late Show with David Letterman). To keep Leno from leaving, NBC offered him an experimental slot at 10:00 p.m. for a newly-formatted pilot, "The Jay Leno Show." Other networks scoffed, as that time slot ("prime-time" television) was generally booked by all networks with scripted,

candidates and political parties as consistent with the First Amendment. The Court has rejected *expenditure* limits on individuals, groups, candidates, and parties, even though expenditures may confer benefits on candidates."

Consistent with these principles, non-profit entities that only make contributions are subject to different standards than those that only make expenditures. Entities that make expenditures are treated like individuals, who have the right to spend an unlimited amount on individual candidates. By comparison, some entities only make contributions to candidates, and these entities are limited in their spending just as political parties are. EMILY's List is hybrid of these two types of entities because EMILY's List makes both contributions and expenditures. The majority of the panel decided that First Amendment rules that apply to political parties do not apply the same way to non-profit entities. The court determined that non-profit groups should be allowed to accept an unlimited amount of funds for their soft-money accounts, and the non-profits should be able to spend an unlimited amount for such expenditures as advertisements, get-out-the-vote efforts, and voter registration drives.

In this case, the court concluded that the regulations unconstitutionally limited EMILY's List from making these expenditures and thus struck down several of the regulations on this ground. The court also determined that the FEC had exceeded its statutory authority in adopting other regulations, and this conclusion negated these additional regulations. Accordingly, the costly dramas (e.g. crime/detective shows). But with much fanfare and promotional advertising, NBC proceeded with its plan; Leno agreed to give it his best effort.

It failed. Just five months into the switch, the network alienated viewers and collected complaints from local stations with shrinking audiences for their evening broadcasts. Following O'Brien's takeover, "The Tonight Show" dropped to second place behind CBS Corporation's "Late Show with David Letterman." According to data from Nielsen, as of late December 2009, O'Brien was averaging 2.84 million viewers per night, compared with Letterman's 3.74 million.

Jeff Gaspin, NBC Entertainment chairman, reportedly told *The New York Times,* of a ratings falloff that was far worse for NBC than expected. In that article, Gaspin said that ratings for NBC's local newscasts—the direct lead-in to O'Brien—were down an average 14 percent among households, and O'Brien was off by 49 percent compared to Leno's audience the year before. Meanwhile, Leno, in his new time slot, had failed to maintain his prior 18-to-49-year-old late night audience—the group prized by advertisers. Leno had previously led Letterman in those audience groups for 14 years, according to Nielsen. The network's troubles came to a head when Philadelphia-based cable-TV giant Comcast Corporation reached a tentative deal to take control, with a 51 percent stake in NBC Universal and parent company General Electric retaining 49 percent.

In early January 2010, the network announced plans to return Leno to the 11:35 p.m. slot (from 10:00 p.m.) and delay "The Tonight Show" by 30 minutes, to 12:05 a.m., to accommodate local news at 11:00. The plan fizzled when O'Brien refused, setting off two weeks of public feuding and laundry-airing, mostly casting Leno as the villain. Oddly enough, the network feud caused audience increases across the network board, as NBC and key players became, themselves, the subject of late-night talk show jokes and news.

On January 21, 2010, NBC announced that O'Brien had signed a $45 million deal to leave the network after refusing the 12:05 a.m. slot. The non-public agreement included a $33 million sum for O'Brien and $12 million for his staff, while clearing the way for Leno to resume his old job. The network further stated that "Late Night With Jimmy Fallon" would continue in its 12:35 a.m. slot.

Although most of the agreement's terms remained confidential, NBC publicly announced that, following a week of negotiations, it was releasing O'Brien from his contract after seven months and that O'Brien would be free to pursue other opportunities after September 1, 2010. The $32.5 million settlement amount essentially constituted a buyout of the remaining two and a half years of O'Brien's guaranteed contract. Leno resumed the helm of "The Tonight Show" on March 1, 2010.

Importantly, the settlement agreement contained a "non-disparagement" clause, legally prohibiting him from saying anything false or disparaging about the network. He was also prohibited, under the terms, from giving interviews or appearing on television for at least 90 days. The clauses were intended to deflect any sabotage or competing interviews of O'Brien airing on the night when Leno resumed the show and in the proximal weeks thereafter.

On May 2, 2010, CBS News aired its new interview with a bearded O'Brien in Seattle, Washington. After leaving the show, O'Brien hibernated briefly at home, then reassembled some of his prior staff, opened a Twitter account, and began planning a nationwide comedy tour. The "Legally Prohibited from Being Funny on Television Tour" was scheduled for 40 performances in 32 cities in the United States and Canada, ending in Radio City Music Hall, New York City, in June 2010.

ENVIRONMENTAL LAW

An amalgam of state and federal statutes, regulations, and common-law principles covering air pollution, water pollution, hazardous waste, the wilderness, and endangered wildlife.

Monsanto v. Geertson Seed Farms

The Plant Protection Act (PPA), 7 U.S.C. §§7701, *et seq.,* provides that the Secretary of the DEPARTMENT OF AGRICULTURE (USDA) may issue regulations "to prevent the introduction of plant pests into the United States or the dissemination of plant pests within the United States,"(§7711(a). The Secretary delegated that authority to the Animal and Plant Health Inspection Service (APHIS). Pursuant to that delegated authority, APHIS issued regulations that governed "the introduction of organisms and products altered or produced through **genetic engineering** that are plant pests or are believed to be plant pests." Under those regulations, certain genetically engineered plants are presumed to be "plant pests" and are therefore "regulated articles" under the Act (until APHIS determines otherwise). Any person may petition APHIS for a determination that a regulated article does not present a plant pest risk and should, therefore, not be subject to the applicable regulations.

When deciding whether to grant non-regulated status to a genetically engineered plant variety, APHIS must comply with the NATIONAL ENVIRONMENTAL POLICY ACT OF 1969 (NEPA), 42 U.S.C. §§ 4321-4347. NEPA, in turn, requires federal agencies, "to the fullest extent possible," to prepare environmental impact statements (EIS) for "every recommendation or report on proposals for legislation and other major Federal actio[n] significantly affecting the quality of the human environment." 42 U.S.C. §4332 (2)(C). (Agencies may substitute an abbreviated "environmental assessment (EA)" in lieu of an EIS if the proposed action will not have a significant impact on the environment.)

As background, the Monsanto Company (Monsanto) owned the INTELLECTUAL PROPERTY rights to the subject alfalfa variety, known as Roundup Ready Alfalfa (RRA). RRA has been genetically engineered to resist the active ingredient (glyphosphate) weed/plant killer in the herbicide Roundup brand. APHIS had originally classified RRA as a regulated article, but in 2004, Monsanto petitioned for non-regulated status of two strains of RRA. APHIS did prepare a draft EA assessing the likely environmental impact, published a notice in the **Federal Register** inviting public comment on the EA, and after considering those comments, issued a Finding of No Significant Impact. It also authorized nearly 300 field trials of RRA conducted over eight years.

Geertson Seed Farms (Geertson) was a conventional alfalfa seed farm. It joined with environmental groups and another seed company, Trask Family Seeds, to file suit against the Secretary of Agriculture and other federal officials in a California federal **district court**. The complaint did not ask for preliminary injunctive relief, resulting in RRA remaining unregulated for another two years, during which time more than 3,000 farmers in 48 states planted an estimated 220,000 acres of RRA.

In *Monsanto Company v. Geertson Seed Farms*, No. 09-475, 561 U.S. ___ (2010), the U.S. SUPREME COURT reviewed a decision by APHIS to deregulate a variety of the RRA genetically engineered alfalfa. The district court had held that APHIS had violated NEPA by not completing an EIS before issuing its deregulation decision (it had decided to unconditionally deregulate the alfalfa variety in question). As a remedy, the court vacated the APHIS decision, ordered APHIS not to act on the deregulation petition until it had completed an EIS, and awarded injunctive relief to stop all *future* planting of the alfalfa variety in question pending the completion of the environmental impact review. The Ninth **Circuit Court** of Appeals affirmed the district court's entry of permanent injunctive relief.

Th U.S. Supreme Court reversed and remanded the decision of the Ninth Circuit. Justice Alito delivered the opinion for the majority. First, both sides had challenged the standing of the others to seek review. The Court summarized Article III (of the Constitution) standing requirements as injury that was (i) concrete, particular, and actual or imminent; (ii) fairly traceable to the challenged action; and (iii) redressable by a favorable ruling. The Court found that Monsanto met all three criteria in that it was injured by its inability to sell or license RRA to prospective customers until APHIS completed its EIS. Geertson Farms, likewise, had established a reasonable probability that their pure, conventional alfalfa crops would be infected (cross-pollination) with the genetically-engineered Roundup Ready gene if RRA were completely deregulated.

Moving on to the merits, the Court held that the district court had abused its discretion in enjoining (imposing an INJUNCTION on) APHIS from effecting a partial deregulation and in prohibiting the planting of RRA pending the agency's completion of its detailed environmental impact review. While the majority found that Geertson and others had standing to sue, the Court held that they did not meet criteria needed for a court to grant a permanent injunction: (1) that they suffered **irreparable injury**; (2) that remedies available under law, such as monetary damages, were inadequate to compensate for injury; (3) that, balancing hardships between parties, a remedy in equity is warranted; and (4) that the PUBLIC INTEREST would not be disserved by a permanent injunction. *eBay Inc. v Merc-Exchange, L.L.C.,* 547 U.S. 388, 126 S. Ct. 1837,

164 L. Ed. 2d 641 (2006). The Court focused on the most important, that the seed farmers could not show IRREPARABLE INJURY if APHIS was allowed to proceed with a partial deregulation.

Finally, the scope of the district court's nationwide injunction was inappropriate, foreclosing even the possibility of a partial and temporary deregulation. Such an injunction was a drastic and **extraordinary remedy** not to be awarded as a matter of course. A less drastic remedy, such as partial or complete vacating (vacatur) of APHIS' deregulation decision, might have been sufficient to remedy their injury.

Justice Breyer, whose brother was the district court judge issuing the injunction, did not participate in the decision. The lone dissenter was Justice Stevens, who opined that the district court did not abuse its discretion, considering the voluminous record it reviewed before making its specific findings.

ERISA

Conkright v. Frommert

The Employee Retirement Income Security Act of 1974 (ERISA) governs most employee pension and retirement benefit plans. In *Conkright v. Frommert,* (formerly captioned as *Alfieri v. Conkright,*) No. 08-810, 559 U.S. ___ (2010), the U.S. Supreme Court held that plan administrators are entitled to a continuing deferential standard of review when interpreting terms of plans, even after having made previous but honest mistakes.

The case involved about 100 employees from the Xerox Corporation, who left the company in the 1980s and received lump-sum distribution at that time of any accrued retirement benefits under the company's Retirement Income Guarantee Plan earned up to that point. The complication came later, when they were rehired by Xerox.

In calculating the rehired employees' entitlement to current benefits, the company's plan administrator needed to account for the past distributions made to them. The plan administrator interpreted the plan as calling for an approach that has come to be known as the "phantom account" method (the methods or calculations of which are not relevant to the Court's decision). The rehired employees filed suit.

The federal district court granted summary judgment for the plan, but this was vacated and remanded by the Second Circuit Court of Appeals. The appellate court found that the plan administrator's interpretation was unreasonable, and further, that the rehired employees had not been provided proper notice that the phantom account method would be used to calculate their pension benefits upon rehire.

On remand, the plan administrator proposed a new interpretation of plan benefits. This time, the proposed plan would account for the time value of the money the rehired employees had previously received (the lump sum distributions), i.e., it would subtract the previously-paid lump sum distribution, plus interest, from the rehired employees' pension benefits. However, the district court declined to apply a deferential standard to this interpretation of the plan, and instead adopted the interpretation proposed by the plaintiff-employees that did not account for the time value of the money. Now, the plan administrators (current and former) appealed.

The Second Circuit affirmed the district court in relevant part, finding that it correctly refused to apply a deferential standard on a remanded matter, and that its decision on the merits was not an abuse of discretion. The U.S. Supreme Court granted review.

Chief Justice Roberts delivered the opinion of the 5-3 majority (with Justice Sotomayor taking no part). The Court reversed the Second Circuit, holding that the district court should have applied a deferential standard of review to the plan administrator's interpretation of the plan, even though it had already been remanded once. The Court noted that it had already addressed the appropriate standard of review for decisions of ERISA plan administrators in a previous case, *Firestone Tire & Rubber v. Bruch,* 489 U.S. 101. In that case, the Court had looked to principles of trust law in holding that when a trust instrument gives a trustee "power to construe disputed or doubtful terms, ... the trustee's interpretation will not be disturbed if reasonable." Under *Firestone* and the present plan, the plan administrator would normally have been entitled to deference when interpreting the plan. However, the Second Circuit had taken upon itself to create its own exception that deference need not apply when a plan administrator's previous interpretation had been found to violate ERISA and the case had then been remanded. To the contrary, said the Court, nothing in the language of the plan, which expressly gave the plan administrator interpretive authority, limited that authority to a one-time first-effort interpretation.

The Court went on to explain that ERISA already represented a "careful balancing" between ensuring fair and prompt enforcement of rights under a plan, and encouragement to create such plans. The plaintiff-employees in this case argued that deference was less important the second time around, after the plan administrator's first interpretation had been found unreasonable. But the Court noted that the other half of the "balancing," i.e., interests in efficiency, predictability, and uniformity, did not just disappear because of a simple honest mistake the first time around. When the district court declined to apply a deferential standard of review on remand, it made the case more complicated than necessary, said the Court.

Finally, plaintiff-employees had argued that plan administrators would adopt unreasonable interpretations in the future, knowing that they would receive deference, and thereby undermining the prompt resolution of benefits disputes. But the Court found the concern as overblown, stating that there would be no reason to require deference in the extreme examples cited by plaintiffs.

Chief Justice Roberts was joined in the majority opinion by Justices Scalia, Kennedy, Thomas, and Alito. Justice Breyer dissented, joined by Justices Stevens and Ginsburg. The dissent basically favored the plaintiffs, opining that the interpretation of the plan shorted them out of considerable benefits, which should prompt more substantive review.

ESTABLISHMENT CLAUSE

Ninth Circuit Rules Upholds Constitutionality of "In God We Trust"

The national motto of the United States is "In God We Trust." Congress established the motto by **statute** and directed the TREASURY DEPARTMENT to place the motto on U.S. coins and currency. Michael Newdow, a California Atheist and the founder and ordained minister of the First Amendmist Church of True Science (FACTS), challenged the constitutionality of the motto and its placement on **legal tender**. He

argued that the motto violated the First Amendment's Establishment Clause and the Religious Freedom Restoration Act of 1993 (RFRA), 42 U.S.C. §§ 2000bb *et seq.* The Ninth **Circuit Court** of Appeals upheld the constitutionality of the motto in *Newdow v. Lefevre.*, 598 F.3d 638 (9th Cir. 2010). In a 2-1 decision, the appeals court relied on a 1970 circuit decision, *Aronow v. United States*, 432 F.2d 242 (9th Cir. 1970), which had previously upheld the constitutionality of the motto.

Newdow filed his lawsuit in California federal **district court**. He asked for an INJUNCTION that would order the removal of the motto from coins and currency and prevent Congress from referencing the motto in any law or act. The U.S. government asked the court to dismiss the lawsuit, arguing that Newdow lacked standing to bring the lawsuit, the binding circuit precedent of *Aronow v. United States*, and the failure to allege facts sufficient to state a claim under the RFRA. The district found that Newdow had standing to but agreed that *Aronow* barred both the Establishment Clause claim and the RFRA claim. Newdow appealed to the Ninth Circuit.

Judge Carlos Bea agreed with the district court that Newdow had standing to seek the removal of the motor from coins and currency. Newdow claimed that he was injured by having to use money that bore the "In God We Trust" motto. This contact was a "concrete, particularized, and PERSONAL INJURY resulting from his frequent, unwelcome contact with the motto." However, he did not have standing to challenge the statute that established the motto itself because the law did not direct the inscription of the motto on any object.

As to the substantive merits of Newdow's two claims, the court found them lacking. For his Establishment Clause claim, Newdow argued that the motto was an endorsement of a monotheistic God by the federal government. In addition, the motto turned him and other Atheists into political outsiders, where belief in God was "good" and disbelief in God was "bad." Judge Bea brought this argument to a close by citing *Aronow*. In that decision the Ninth Circuit ruled that the motto "has nothing to do with establishment of religion. Its use is of a patriotic or ceremonial character and bears no true resemblance to a governmental sponsorship or a religious exercise." The court went on to state that the motto was "excluded from FIRST AMENDMENT significance because the motto has no theological or ritualistic impact." The motto had no more than a "spiritual and psychological value" and "inspirational quality."

Newdow admitted his Establishment Clause claim was virtually identical to the one raise in *Aronow*, but contended that it was not binding precedent. He argued that since the 1970 decision the Supreme Court's Establishment Clause **jurisprudence** had significantly changed. The tests employed by the Court undermined the *Aronow* precedent to the point that it must be set aside. The court disagreed. The Supreme Court's thinking on how to test Establishment Clause issues may have changed but there was not one case where it "called into question the motto's constitutionality." Moreover, in nonbinding statements called **dicta**, the Court had commented several times on the constitutionality of the motto. Newdow argued in the alternative that *Aronow* was not binding because the court had ruled on the merits even though the PLAINTIFF did not have standing to bring the lawsuit. Bea agreed that the SUPREME COURT had barred the practice of "hypothetical jurisdiction" after *Aronow*, but the Court did not overturn the rulings of every case that had been decided using this discredited doctrine. Therefore, *Aronow* remained good law.

The court also found no merit in Newdow's RFRA claim. The RFRA bars the government from placing a substantial burden on a person's exercise of religion unless the government can show the rule is in furtherance of a "compelling governmental interest" and is the "least restrictive means" of furthering that governmental interest. Newdow argued that the use of the motto on coins and currency substantially burdened the free exercise of his religion in two ways. First, Newdow's religion barred him from carrying currency with the national motto. This impeded his ability to purchase goods for his church that required cash payments. Second, because he cannot avoid handling money in his daily life, he was violating a basic tenet of his religion.

The court rejected the RFRA claim because the burdens Newdow cited rested on a single premise: "the motto represents a purely religious dogma and constitutes a government endorsement of religion." This premise was faulty because *Aronow* held that the motto was patriotic rather than religious.

Salazar v. Buono

The erection of religious symbols on public land has led to many lawsuits over the proper interpretation of the First Amendment's Establishment Clause. One such dispute involved the placement of a cross on federal land in the Mojave Nature Reserve in 1934 by members of the VETERANS OF FOREIGN WARS (VFW) to honor American soldiers killed in WORLD WAR I. A 2001 federal lawsuit led a federal court to issue an INJUNCTION barring the presence of the cross on Establishment Clause grounds. While the case was still pending Congress enacted a law that directed the DEPARTMENT OF THE INTERIOR to transfer the cross and the land on which it stands to the VFW in exchange for privately owned land elsewhere in the preserve. The PLAINTIFF challenged the legitimacy of this land transfer in *Salazar v. Buono*, __U.S.__, 130 S. Ct. 1803, 176 L. Ed. 2d 634 (2009). The SUPREME COURT upheld the land transfer and chastised the lower **federal courts** for questioning the motivation of Congress for making the land transfer.

The erection of the cross was on Sunrise Rock in the federal preserve but two private ranches are two miles area from the granite outcropping. The cross had been replaced several times since 1934, most recently by Henry Sandoz in 1998, who owns property in the preserve. The cross stands eight feet tall and is visible from a narrow road. It is not visible from the nearest highway, which is 10 miles away. Easter services have been conducted near the cross since its erection and Sunrise Rock is a popular camping site. At one point a wooden sign was in place that stated the cross stood in memory of the dead of all wars, but in recent times there has been no signage.

Frank Buono, a retired Park Service employee who made regular visits to the preserve, filed a federal lawsuit asking that the cross be removed. Buono claimed to be offended by the presence of a religious symbol on federal land and argued that its presence violated the Establishment Clause. The **district court** agreed and issued an injunction ordering that the cross be removed. While the district court action was being litigated, Congress enacted a law that designated the cross and its adjoining land "as a national memorial commemorating United States participation in World War I and honoring the American veterans of that war." It also directed the Department of the Interior to spend up to $10,000 to acquire a replica of the original cross and its memorial plaque and to install the plaque at a suitable nearby location.

The Ninth **Circuit Court** of Appeals stayed the injunction to the extent that it required the cross to be removed or dismantled but did not forbid alternative methods of complying with the order. The Park Service covered the cross, first with a tarpaulin and later with a plywood box. The appeals upheld the lower court injunction in all other respects. While the appeal was pending, Congress enacted another law on the subject. It directed the Department of the Interior to make a land transfer: government transferred to the VFW its interest in the land that had been designated a national memorial. In return, the government was to receive land elsewhere in the preserve from Henry Sandoz and his wife. Any difference in value between the two parcels would be equalized through a cash payment.

The following the appeal , Buono went back to district court and objected to the land transfer. He sought an injunction to block the transfer. The district examined whether the land transfer was a **bona fide** attempt to comply with the injunction or a sham aimed at keeping the cross in place. It concluded it was an attempt by the government to keep the cross atop Sunrise Rock and so was invalid. The Ninth Circuit **Court of Appeal** upheld this decision.

The Supreme Court overturned the lower court rulings. In a plurality opinion, Justice Anthony Kennedy, writing for Chief Justice John Roberts and Justice Samuel Alito, concluded that the district court could not properly issue an injunction blocking the land transfer because it had ignored all of the circumstances surrounding the issue. The district court had failed to take into account "the context in which the statute was enacted and the reasons for its passage." The erection of the cross by private citizens had been done to honor fallen soldiers; the federal government had not sought to endorse a particular religion. The original injunction banning the cross created a dilemma for the government: "It could not maintain the cross without violating the injunction, but it could not remove the cross without conveying disrespect for those the cross was seen as

honoring." Congress stepped in to resolve this dilemma by enacting the land transfer statute. The lower courts should not have dismissed the law as an evasion, "for it brought about a change of law and a congressional statement of policy applicable to the case." Therefore, the case needed to be remanded to the district court to examine the circumstances again. Justice Kennedy directed the court to "consider less drastic relief than complete invalidation of the statute" if it still found defects in the law but pointedly stated that the court should consider whether there was "continued necessity for injunctive relief." Justices Antonin Scalia and Clarence Thomas concurred in the Court's judgment, but Scalia wrote a separate concurrence that Thomas joined. Scalia argued that Buono had no standing to pursue his injunction.

Justices JOHN PAUL STEVENS and STEPHEN BREYER filed dissenting opinions, with Justices RUTH BADER GINSBURG and SONIA SOTOMAYOR joining Stevens' DISSENT. Stevens argued that the land transfer statute did not cure the Establishment Clause violation. The district court had properly analyzed the statute in light of its original ruling and determined the transfer was a further endorsement of religion in violation of the FIRST AMENDMENT.

ETHICS

The branch of philosophy that defines what is good for the individual and for society and establishes the nature of obligations, or duties, that people owe themselves and one another.

Lawyers Struggle with Ethics of Using Social Media

During the mid- to late-2000s, a new breed of social media sites exploded in popularity. These sites have provided Internet users with new methods to connect to one another and to use software applications that are run on browsers through a network connection rather than on local machines. Lawyers and judges have used these services just as others have, but new questions have arisen about the ethics of communicating through these sites.

Many of the ethical concerns have focused on what is known as cloud computing, which describes a service that stores a user's data externally. For instance, YouTube allows users to upload videos and allows other Internet users to view those videos through an Internet connection. Likewise, Google had a service known as Google Docs that allows users to upload documents and even share these documents with others if so desired. Sites such as Facebook and Twitter allow users to post updates about their lives. Lawyers have begun to use these services not only for personal reasons but also to connect with clients and to market their services. The benefit of using social media for professional communications and marketing purposes is low cost and ease.

However, this use of social media also raises ethical concerns. For instance, a lawyer can use Google Docs to create text documents, spreadsheets, and presentations, and this data is stored on Google's servers. The user can access this information from any computer that has an Internet connection, but Google's terms of service allow the company to disable access to a user's account without giving the user access to the files. Thus, a lawyer who relies on this service loses, to some degree, control over where files are actually located, which could lead to a crisis if the lawyer's account was ever disabled or somehow compromised.

Other commentators have focused their attention on the content of the communications. One of the most popular sites on the Internet is Twitter, which allows uses to make short comments limited to 140 characters. The short comments, known as "tweets," became a phenomenon just as email and blogging exploded in the past. Lawyers may use Twitter to increase their visibility with clients and prospective clients, sharing information about the lawyer's activities and practice area. Few best practices for using social media for this type of communication, though, and a lawyer could encounter problems. Steven Bennett, a partner with the law firm of Jones Day, wrote that lawyers should limit their communications to "anything but general professional news in their Twitter communications, restricting the group of recipients of Twitter communications (or some subset of such communications) and/or providing periodic notice to recipients of the conditions under which the Twitter communications are made."

Social media sites have already caused problems for some lawyers. One Texas judge reportedly caught a lawyer lying about the need for a continuance. The lawyer told the judge that the lawyer's father had died. However, when the judge checked the lawyer's status update on Facebook, the judge discovered the lawyer had actually planned a weekend of drinking and partying. In other instances, lawyers have complained about their opposing counsel or even their own clients. Problems are not limited to the lawyers, either. In one case, the Texas judge discovered an alleged tort victim bragging online about how much money she would make in a lawsuit.

Bennett suggested, "Twitter messages from lawyers, for all their informality, must be treated with the same caution as messages in any other form (including correspondence, memoranda or e-mails). Lawyers must pay particular attention to the risks of revealing privileged or confidential information in Twitter messages, which are often programmed to be sent to a group of friends and acquaintances. Further, despite the informality of the medium, messages that contain what may appear to be legal advice, that operation on the (unstated) premise of an attorney-client relationship, or that may be characterized as a **solicitation** of legal work, may have the unintended consequences of raising PROFESSIONAL RESPONSIBILITY issues or ethics concerns."

Lawyers have also begun to use social media during the course of LITIGATION. In one scenario, a lawyer may depose a witness who has a Facebook account. The lawyer may believe that the witness has information that could be relevant to the lawyer's case. More specifically, the witness' testimony may be adverse to the lawyer's case, and the lawyer may believe that the witness has posted information online that could be used to IMPEACH the witness. On a website such as Facebook, the witness may need to grant access to permit the lawyer to read this information. In some instances, the lawyer may ask a **third party** to try to become an online "friend" with the witnesses, meaning that the witness allows the THIRD PARTY to access the information. According to an **advisory opinion** issued by the Philadelphia Bar Association, the lawyer who asks a third party to access the information in this manner violates rules of professional conduct. The opinion concludes that the only way an attorney can ethically obtain access is to ask the witness directly for access and to disclose the true purpose for such access.

Other bar associations have likewise addressed ethical and legal issues arising from social media. In August, the Florida Board of Bar Examiners announced that it would surf social media sites to try to find adverse information about those applying to become members of the Florida bar. The board said that it would not ask for access up front because such a request would increase the likelihood that applicants would delete information before providing access. The policy limits investigation of social media sites to instances where the applicant has had a history of substance abuse; has had "significant candor concerns," such as lying on a resume; has been accused of engaging in the unlicensed PRACTICE OF LAW; or similar circumstances.

EVIDENCE

Any matter of fact that a party to a lawsuit offers to prove or disprove an issue in the case. A system of rules and standards used to determine which facts may be admitted, and to what extent a judge or jury may consider those facts, as proof of a particular issue in a lawsuit.

Law Enforcement Authorities and Lawyers Use Social Media to Gather Evidence

Social media sites such as Facebook and MySpace have grown to include several million users. Many of these users enjoy connecting with others or reconnecting with old friends, acquaintances, and so forth. However, the sites are progressively being used to gather evidence for use in court and for other similar purposes.

Social media has existed in several forms since the early years of the Internet in the 1990s. Among the many social media sites, MySpace had emerged by 2005 as the largest in the world. Facebook, a competitor of MySpace, became available to those not affiliated with U.S. colleges or universities in 2006, and Facebook developed an enormous following. The website known as Twitter also attracted a huge following during the late 2000s. Each of these social media sites and several others allow users to post updates about their daily lives so that online "friends" know what the users are doing. Several of these sites also allow users to post pictures and videos that the users share with others.

Legal experts generally agree that individuals have no expectation of privacy with regard to information that appears on social media sites,

meaning that law enforcement investigators may use these sites to obtain evidence. During the mid to late 1990s, many incidents involving use of social media in investigations were related to on-campus incidents at COLLEGES AND UNIVERSITIES. In many of these instances, school officials have caught underage students drinking at parties or otherwise committing acts that constituted rules violations.

Social media has especially affected the area of FAMILY LAW. When spouses decide to DIVORCE and arguments over finances and CHILD CUSTODY ensue, lawyers for each spouse will typically look for any advantage they may find. This advantage may come in the form of postings on social media sites. For example, a husband may divulge information about something he bought for his new girlfriend. Likewise, a wife may inform the court that she no longer drinks or smokes, but dated photographs posted to a social media site may show her doing both.

Because this information is so readily available on the Internet, attorneys have begun to offer standard advice to their clients. St. Louis-based attorney Joseph Cordell of Cordell & Cordell told *Time Magazine,* "It's now just routine for us to go over with clients whether they have an active presence on the Web and if they Twitter or have a MySpace page." If so, Cordell advises the clients to scour these pages for anything that an ex-spouse could use against the client. Cordell also said he looks carefully at the pages of the ex-spouse.

Other divorce lawyers take this advice a step further. Ken Alshuler of Portland, Maine told the *Atlanta Journal-Constitution,* "Every client I've seen in the last six months had a Facebook page. And the first piece of advice I give them is to terminate their page immediately." Alshuler is the VICE PRESIDENT of the American Academy of Matrimonial Lawyers, which polled its members and determined that 81 percent said that they had seen an increase in the use of social networking sites. According to the attorneys surveyed, Facebook is by far the most commonly used site to gather online divorce evidence. Altshuler noted, "People don't think about who has access to their Facebook page. A good attorney can have a field day with this information."

In some instances, information posted on social media has been used as evidence in criminal trials. For example, a jury convicted Raul Cortez of committing four murders in McKinney, Texas. Prosecutors introduced evidence that Cortez was a member of a gang based on displays of gang colors and symbols on his MySpace page. Similarly, a burglar in Pennsylvania checked his Facebook page at the site of the crime and left the page open when he left, allowing prosecutors to track him down. In other cases, lawyers have used information on social media sites to discover evidence of insurance **fraud**. For example, a person may claim to be disabled for purposes of receiving an insurance settlement. However, lawyers may find photographs of this individual dancing or engaging in sports, thus proving that the person is making a false claim.

Facebook was at the center of other controversies in 2009 regarding information posted to its site. In March, an emergency medical technician (EMT) named Frank Musarella allegedly took pictures of the body of Caroline Wimmer, who had been beaten and strangled in New York. Musarella, a former detective with the New York Police Department (NYPD), allegedly posted the pictures to his Facebook profile. Authorities arrested Musarella on charges of official misconduct, while Wimmer's parents sued Musarella, the City of New York, the NYPD, and other entities. According to the parents, Facebook and the other defendants violated state and federal privacy laws for posting the pictures. However, legal experts said that Facebook would most likely be immune from liability under the Communications Decency Act of 1996, 47 U.S.C. § 230. In an unusual twist to the story, authorities suspected that Wimmer was strangled by a man upset that Wimmer had spread rumors about him on MySpace.

In at least one case, a social media site helped a user to establish an alibi. In 2009, police arrested a 19-year-old man named Rodney Bradford after suspecting him of committing **robbery**. Bradford told his lawyer that he was on Facebook at the time of the ROBBERY, and the attorney determined that Bradford had written a status update at the time the robbery occurred. The attorney informed the PROSECUTOR assigned to the case, and when the prosecutor confirmed that Bradford had indeed typed the update from his father's house in Harlem, the prosecutor dropped the charges.

EX POST FACTO LAWS

[Latin, "After-the-fact" laws.] *Laws that provide for the infliction of punishment upon a person for some prior act that, at the time it was committed, was not illegal.*

United States v. Carr

In 2006, Congress passed the Sex Offender Registration and Notification Act a part of a comprehensive child-protection **statute**. The act requires sex offenders to register with authorities when these offenders cross state lines. A sex offender who had crossed a state line before the act took effect was subsequently charged with violating the act because he failed to register with local authorities. In 2010, the U.S. SUPREME COURT in a 6-3 decision overturned the offender's conviction, holding that Congress only intended the act to apply prospectively and not retroactively.

In 1994, Congress first required states to maintain a federally compliant system for registration of sex offenders as a condition for states to receive law enforcement funds. Out of concern that state systems were comprehensive, uniform, and effective, Congress enacted the Sex Offender Registration and Notification Act (SORNA) as part of the Adam Walsh Child Protection and Safety Act, Pub. L. No. 109-248, 120 Stat. 590. SORNA makes the act of failing to register as a sex offender the subject of a maximum penalty of ten years imprisonment. The act established a federal criminal offense that applies when the government can prove three elements: (1) that the individual is required under SORNA to register as a sex offender; (2) that the offender "travels in interstate commerce"; and (3) that the offender knowingly fails to register or update a registration. The Attorney General in 2007 determined that SORNA applies to sex offenders who were convicted prior to the statute's enactment.

Thomas Carr was charged with first-degree SEXUAL ABUSE for touching a 14-year-old girl over her clothes. He pleaded guilty to the crime in 2004 and was sentenced to 15 years in prison. All but two of those years were suspended, and he received credit for time already served. Authorities released him on PROBATION in July 2004, and he registered as a sex offender under Alabama law. In either late 2004 or early 2005, Carr moved from Alabama to Indiana, but he did not register under Indiana's sex-offender laws. Three years later, in July 2007, he became involved in a fight in Fort Wayne. Authorities determined that he was a sex offender and discovered that he had not registered as required.

Federal prosecutors on August 22, 2007 filed an INDICTMENT against Carr, charging him with violating SORNA for failing to register. Carr filed a motion to dismiss the indictment, which was filed in the U.S. **District Court** for the Northern District of Indiana. Carr argued that the Ex Post Facto Clause of the U.S. Constitution should prohibit his conviction because he moved from Alabama to Indiana before SORNA's effective date. On November 2, 2007, the district court denied Carr's motion. *United States v. Carr*, No. 1:07-CR-73, 2007 WL 3256600 (N.D. Ind. Nov. 2, 2007). Carr entered a conditional guilty plea but retained the right to appeal. The district court sentenced him to 30 months in prison.

Carr appealed his conviction to the Seventh **Circuit Court** of Appeals. In an opinion by Judge RICHARD POSNER, a panel of the Seventh Circuit rejected Carr's argument that the conviction violated his rights. Posner's opinion acknowledged that one other federal court of appeals—the Tenth Circuit—had previously ruled that SORNA only applies to sex offenders who have traveled in interstate commerce after Congress enacted the statute. In *United States v. Husted*, 545 F.3d 1240 (10th Cir. 2008), the Tenth Circuit focused on Congress' use of the word "travels," which is used in the present tense. According to the Tenth Circuit, Congress clearly intended for the act to apply prospectively based on the words Congress used. Posner disagreed with the Tenth Circuit, however, noting that *Husted*'s result "makes no sense." Posner cited statements from other authorities indicating that use of the present tense does not reveal congressional intent and that present tense may be used to refer to the past, present, and future simultaneously.

In Posner's opinion, applying SORNA's provisions to those who traveled across state lines before the statute took effect was analogous to laws that increase punishment for repeating an offense. The latter category of laws "do not violate the ex post facto clause because even if the law was passed after the DEFENDANT committed his first offense and increases the punishment for a repeat offense, the defendant can avoid the increased punishment by not repeating (and so not being determined by a court to have repeated) the offense." Similarly, Carr's conviction (as well as the conviction of another defendant in the Seventh Circuit case) was based on his failure to register after the Attorney General issued the regulation that applied SORNA to those who crossed state lines before SORNA's effective date. Posner stressed that Carr could have avoided prosecution by registering within a reasonable time after the Attorney General issued the regulation. By concluding that Carr's conviction did not violate the Ex Post Facto Clause, the Seventh Circuit panel upheld his conviction. *United States v. Dixon*, 551 F.3d 578 (7th Cir. 2008).

Carr appealed his conviction to the U.S. Supreme Court, which agreed in March 2009 to review the case. The government continued to argue that the statute applied even if the sex offender's conviction and travel occurred in the past. However, in an opinion by Justice SONIA SOTOMAYOR, the Court disagreed. Sotomayor's opinion, as joined at least in part by six other justices, focused on the use of the word "travels" The Court agreed with the Tenth Circuit's analysis in *Husted* that Congress' use of verb tense was meaningful. Sotomayor noted that had Congress intended for SORNA to apply two of the provisions to preenactment conduct but not the third, Congress "presumably would have varied the verb tenses to convey this meaning." Instead, Congress used the present tense of the verbs in each of the elements, indicating intent for the statute to apply to post-enactment conduct. By reaching this conclusion and reversing Carr's conviction on this ground, the Court did not address Carr's Ex Post Facto Clause argument. *Carr v. United States*, ___ U.S.___, 2010 WL 2160783 (U.S. June 1, 2010).

In his DISSENT, Justice SAMUEL ALITO argued that the decision would hinder law enforcement efforts to find the estimated 100,000 unregistered sex offenders who have evaded authorities. Joining Alito in dissent were Justices CLARENCE THOMAS and RUTH BADER GINSBURG.

Although some organizations expressed disappointment in the opinion, much of the legal commentary focused on how the justices voted. Ginsburg sided with two conservative justices, while Scalia joined Sotomayor's opinion except to the extent that the majority opinion relied on statutory construction.

U.S. v. Marcus

The U.S. SUPREME COURT in May 2010 determined that the conviction of a man for crimes based on activity that occurred in part before the enactment of **statute** prohibiting his activity did not violate the Ex Post Facto Clause of the U.S. Constitution. The DEFENDANT in the case, Glenn Marcus, earned notoriety for profiting on Internet sites focusing on sadism and masochism. In fact, Marcus was dubbed the "S&M Svengali" before his conviction under the Trafficking Victims Protection Act, which became effective in October 2000. At trial, Marcus did not raise the defense that his conviction had violated the Ex Post Facto Clause, but he raised the defense on appeal. The Second **Circuit Court** of Appeals determined that his conviction was unconstitutional because the jury might have considered some of Marcus' activities before the statute took effect. However, the Supreme Court disagreed, ruling that the Second Circuit had applied the incorrect standard.

In 1998, Marcus met a woman named Jodi in an online chat room. Marcus convinced Jodi to meet with him in person, and when they met, Marcus whipped her and carved the word "slave" in her stomach. After meeting for a second time, Marcus convinced Jodi to move from the Midwest to Maryland, where Jodi would live with another woman. Marcus would visit the women frequently, engaging in sexual activity known as BDSM (bondage, dominance/discipline, submission/sadism, and masochism). Marcus also maintained websites that provided videos and stories focusing on various BDSM activities. Throughout 1999, Marcus became increasingly violent during his visits to Jodi and the other woman. When the other woman said she wanted to discontinue the relationship, Marcus threatened that he would show pictures of the woman engaged in sexual acts to the woman's family. Jodi heard the conversation between Marcus and the woman, and Jodi said she feared what Marcus would do if she left.

In 2000, Marcus told Jodi to move to New York, where he required her to create a new website. She worked on the site for several hours each day. Marcus continued to force Jodi to engage in violent sexual activity, and any time that he was unhappy with her work on the website, he would punish her severely. She finally told Marcus she wanted to leave, but he threatened to humiliate her by sending pictures

of her engaged in BDSM activity to her family and the press. In March 2001, he finally said he would allow Jodi to leave, but she had to endure one more punishment. He beat her severely, drugged, her, and had sexual intercourse with her. He photographed the episode and required Jodi to write an entry about the incident on the website. After that time, Jodi did not completely break contact with Marcus, but her interactions with Marcus became less frequent. She broke contact with Marcus in 2003.

Congress addressed concerns about sex trafficking by passing the Trafficking Victims Protection Act (TVPA), Pub. L. No. 106-386, 114 Stat. 1486, which became effective on October 28, 2000. Among its provisions, the TVPA prohibits knowingly using force, threats of force, or coercion to cause a person to engage in a commercial sex act. The term "coercion" under the statute includes "threats of serious harm to or physical restraint against any person" as well as "any scheme, plan, or pattern intended to cause a person to believe that failure to perform an act would result in serious harm to or physical restraint against any person."

Federal prosecutors charged Marcus with violating the TVPA, alleging that Marcus had engaged in acts of sex trafficking, forced labor, and dissemination of obscene materials. The INDICT-MENT alleged that the dates of the offenses (all relating to his activities with Jodi) began in January 1999 and ended in October 2001. On March 5, 2007, a jury found Marcus guilty on the sex trafficking and forced labor charges but not guilty on the other charge. Marcus sought a new trial, arguing that the TVPA should not apply to the facts of his case. The **district court** denied Marcus' motions. *U.S. v. Marcus*, 487 F. Supp. 2d 289 (E.D.N.Y. 2007).

On appeal before the Second Circuit Court of Appeals, Marcus argued for the first time that the Ex Post Facto Clause contained in Article I, Section 9 of the U.S. Constitution prohibited the application of the statute to facts that occurred before the statute's enactment. Since the statute did not become effective until October 2000, the statute could not apply to any activity that occurred before that date. The Second Circuit considered Marcus' activities to be a continuing offense, and in such an instance, the Ex Post Facto Clause is not violated if a statute applies to activity that began before but continued to occur after the statute's enactment. In *United States v. Torres*, 901 F.2d 205 (2d Cir. 1990), the Second

Film director Roman Polanski, in a January 2009 photo.
AP IMAGES

Circuit determined that if it was possible that a jury might have considered pre-enactment conduct when convicting a defendant, then the conviction violates the Ex Post Facto Clause. In Marcus' case, the Second Circuit concluded that it was indeed possible that the jury could have found a violation based solely on activity that occurred before October 2001. Accordingly, the Second Circuit vacated Marcus' conviction. *U.S. v. Marcus*, 538 F.3d 97 (2d Cir. 2008).

The government appealed the case to the U.S. Supreme Court. In an opinion by Justice Steven Breyer, the Court reviewed the Second Circuit's analysis in light of Supreme Court precedent. Under Rule 52(b) of the Federal Rules of **Criminal Procedure**, an **appellate court** can recognize a "plain error that effects substantial rights," even if a party did not bring the claim to the district court's attention. Under Supreme Court precedent, an **appellate** court can correct a plain error under Rule 52(b) only when four criteria are met: (1) there is an "error"; (2) the error is "clear or obvious, rather than subject to reasonable dispute"; (3) the error "affected the appellant's substantial rights, which in the ordinary case means" it "affected the outcome of the district court proceedings"; and (4) "the error seriously affect[s] the fairness, integrity or public reputation of judicial proceedings."

According to Breyer's opinion, the Second Circuit's standard was inconsistent with the third and fourth criteria in the Supreme Court's standard. The Second Circuit's standard would set aside a conviction if there was only a remote possibility that the jury could have considered pre-enactment conduct. However, the Supreme Court's standard requires the error to be prejudicial, meaning there must be a reasonable probability that the error effected the trial's outcome. Because the Second Circuit applied the incorrect standard, the Court reversed the Second Circuit's judgment. *U.S. v. Marcus*, No. 08-1341, 2010 WL 2025203 (U.S. May 24, 2010).

EXTRADITION

The transfer of an accused from one state or country to another state or country that seeks to place the accused on trial.

Extradition of Roman Polanski for 1977 Conviction

In 1977, Roman Polanski, then 43, pleaded guilty in a California court to having sexual intercourse with a 13-year-old girl. At that time, Polanski, an Oscar-winning Hollywood director whose film credits include "The Pianist" "Chinatown," and "Rosemary's Baby," was at the peak of his career. The girl told police that Polanski had raped and sodomized her when they were alone on a 1977 photo shoot. Charged with various offenses, including RAPE, Polanski entered a guilty plea to a single count of **statutory rape** because the girl's parents wanted to spare her the ordeal of testifying at trial. Polanski then spent 42 days of a 90-day stay in a California state prison for psychiatric evaluation. After prison officials released him early, Polanski fled the country in 1978, on the eve of his final sentencing date. He later stated that he believed the judge would have sentenced him to more than the time he already served at the prison.

Indeed, Polanski remained a wanted man under warrant for arrest for 32 years, living in France in relative freedom. On September 26, 2009, he was finally arrested in Zurich, Switzerland and placed in prison there. In December 2009, he was placed on HOUSE ARREST by Swiss authorities (at his western Switzerland ski chalet in Gstaad, with an ankle bracelet and a $4.5 million bond) pending EXTRADITION to the United States to face sentencing for that 1977 conviction. He publicly declared his intentions to resist extradition and retained U.S. defense counsel.

The glitch in his case was two-fold. First, his attorneys alleged prosecutorial and judicial misconduct in the 1977 case. Specifically, they alleged, among other things, that the California judge then handling the case, Judge Lawrence J. Rittenband (who has since passed away) promised that the 90-day psychiatric evaluation at the state prison in Chino, California would be his only sentence in the case, but later reneged. They alleged that Rittenbach was angered by the prison officials' early release of Polanski and planned to order him back to prison at his formal sentencing. They further alleged that Rittenbach was unduly concerned about public response and spoke to the media when he should not have. Finally, they alleged that the extradition request to Swiss authorities concealed certain facts that would show he did not qualify for extradition.

The Los Angeles County District Attorney's Office strongly disputed the claims. But defense counsel responded they had testimonial evidence from the original PROSECUTOR who handled the case, Roger Gunson, describing Judge Rittenbach's misconduct and original intentions to limit Polanski's sentence to the time at Chino. In any event, Judge Peter Espinoza, the supervising judge of the Los Angeles Superior Court's criminal division, rejected defense counsel's motion, ruling that Polanski could not pursue his misconduct claims unless he appeared before the court.

Polanski's attorneys then appealed. In December 2009, the California Second District **Court of Appeal** denied Polanski's petition to have all charges against him dropped, or, in the alternative, that the case be sent back to a lower court for an evidentiary hearing on the prosecutorial misconduct charges. The three-judge panel expressed concern that prosecutors investigate the claims of misconduct and respond to the claims. The panel indicated that evidence and arguments before the court did raise "extremely serious allegations." In the 70-page ruling, the **appellate court** found there was a "substantial probability" that any court reviewing the

allegations would conclude "many, if not all, are true," and if true, they would "demonstrate malfeasance ... and unethical conduct." The justices went so far as to propose that the case be settled without Polanski returning to the United States or serving additional time, by having sentencing conducted with Polanski permissibly *in abstentia*, i.e., represented in court through counsel. The justices suggested that such a sentencing could allow full airing of the misconduct charges.

The matter being remanded back to the Los Angeles Superior Court, Judge Spinoza, in January 2010, denied defense counsel's request that Polanski be sentenced *in abstentia*. He further stated that he agreed with Polanski's lawyers that the prison stay was Polanski's intended sentence, but that "the dignity of the court" required Polanski's surrender.

In February 2010, Swiss authorities indicated that extradition proceedings were on indefinite hold. Justice Ministry deputy director Rudolph Wyss reportedly told the *Los Angeles Times* that California **appellate** courts must first make a final ruling on whether Polanski could be sentenced *in abstentia* before the Swiss government would consider the matter. His comments appeared to focus on a single clause in the 32-page 1995 Switzerland-United States treaty that governs extradition. That clause allows for the return of fugitives convicted of offenses considered crimes in both countries, but "only if the duration of the penalty ... still to be served amounts to at least six months."

In April 2010, the California Second **District Court** of Appeal denied Polanski's appeal to be sentenced *in abstentia*, but did not issue a written opinion. Swiss authorities indicated that they would not move on the extradition proceedings until Polanski had exhausted all further APPELLATE remedies in United States' courts, which could take months or years. In July 2009, Swiss authorities stunned their American counterparts by refusing to extradite Polanski on grounds that the extradition request had missing information. Polanski was then set free, but remains unable to travel to the United States lest he be arrested again.

FAIR TRIAL

Skilling v. United States

In *Skilling v. United States,* No. 08-1394, 561 U.S. ___ (2010), the U.S. Supreme Court reviewed whether (1)Enron executive Jeffrey Skilling, convicted on several fraud-related charges, received a fair trial and (2)whether he had committed "honest-services fraud." After Houston-based Enron Corporation, then the seventh highest-revenue-grossing company in the United States, crashed into bankruptcy in 2001, several of its top executives were criminally prosecuted and convicted of various "white-collar" corporate crimes. Skilling was CEO of Enron from February 2001 until he resigned six months later, in August 2001. Less than 120 days after his departure, Enron spiraled into bankruptcy, with company stock crashing from $90 per share to just pennies. A subsequent government investigation exposed an elaborate conspiracy to inflate short-term stock prices by overstating the company's financial well-being.

In July 2004, a grand jury indicted Skilling, along with Enron founder Ken Lay and former chief accounting officer Richard Causey, of a series of conspiracy and fraud charges, essentially related to securities fraud. The criminal indictment charged, among other things, that the defendants "engaged in a wide-ranging scheme" to deceive investors about Enron's true financial performance by manipulating its publicly-reported financial results and making false and

misleading statements. Count I charged Skilling with conspiracy to commit "honest-services" wire fraud, 18 U.S.C. §§371, 1343, and 1346, by depriving Enron and its shareholders of the intangible right to his honest services. Skilling was additionally charged with more than 25 substantive counts of wire fraud, securities fraud, making false representations to Enron's auditors, and insider trading.

In November 2004, Skilling moved for a change in venue. Submitting news reports about Enron's downfall as well as affidavits from experts who compared community attitudes (toward Enron) in Houston with those of other potential venues, he argued that the media had poisoned potential jurors in Houston. The district court denied the motion, concluding that pretrial publicity did not create a presumption that Skilling would not get a fair trial in Houston. Further, noted the court, media coverage on the whole had been objective and unemotional. The court ruled that effective *voir dire* would address any juror bias.

Indeed, in the months preceding trial, the court favored the more specific and probing questions that Skilling submitted for *voir dire*. With minor changes, the court used his submission instead of the government's to create a 77-question, 14-page form to be completed by 400 potential jurors.

One year later (and three weeks before trial), in December 2005, Skilling again renewed his motion for change of venue. This time, it was based upon the fact that one of his co-defendants, Richard Causey, had pleaded guilty, which, according to Skilling, would further bias the jury pool. Again, the court declined to move the trial to another venue, ruling that the jury questionnaires and *voir dire* provided the needed safeguards to ensure an impartial jury. It also denied Skilling's motion for an attorney-conducted *voir dire*, although it allowed counsel to ask follow-up questions, and gave each defendant two additional peremptory challenges.

Following a four-month trial, the jury found Skilling guilty on 19 of the 25 counts (he was acquitted on the insider trading counts). He appealed on two issues. First, he argued that pretrial publicity and community prejudice precluded a fair trial. Second, he argued that the jury erred in convicting him of the conspiracy to commit honest-services wire fraud.

The Fifth Circuit Court of Appeals held that Skilling had established a sufficient level of pretrial publicity of an inflammatory nature so as to create a rebuttable presumption of juror prejudice. However, upon examination, the court found the *voir dire* to be "proper and thorough" and concluded that the district court had impaneled an impartial jury, therefore rebutting the presumption of jury prejudice. However, it rejected Skilling's second argument that his conduct did not constitute a conspiracy to commit "honest-services" fraud, finding the charge valid. (It did not address the argument that the honest-services statute, if not interpreted to exclude his conduct, was unconstitutionally vague.) Skilling appealed.

The U.S. Supreme Court addressed both issues. Writing for the majority, Justice Ruth Bader Ginsburg held that Skilling had not suffered an unfair trial and the district court did not err in denying him a change of venue. The Court went on to distinguish Skilling's trial from other cases in which a presumption of juror bias had been established, e.g., *Rideau v. Louisiana*, 373 U.S. 723. Most importantly, Skilling's trial took place in Houston, the fourth most-populated city in the nation; any argument that a mere dozen impartial jurors could not be empaneled in Houston was hard to support. Second, none of the news articles contained blatantly prejudicial information, albeit they may have been unkind. Third, unlike *Rideau* and other cases where trial followed swiftly after a widely-reported crime, over

four years elapsed between Enron's bankruptcy and Skilling's trial. The Fifth Circuit had presumed prejudice based on the negative tone and widespread media attention to Enron, but "pretrial publicity—even pervasive, adverse publicity—does not inevitably lead to an unfair trial." (quoting *Nebraska Press Association v. Stuart*, 427 U.S. 539 at 554) Finally, the Court noted that the jury had actually acquitted Skilling of nine counts of insider trading, so it hardly appeared to be prejudiced.

As to the "honest-services" wire fraud charges, the Court outlined the history of the doctrine, distinguishing this type of fraud from traditional fraud in which a defendant is enriched, to the detriment of a victim. The honest-services doctrine targets corruption without the above symmetry; instead, a defendant profits not from a betrayed victim, but from a third party, who had not been deceived, who provides the enrichment to defendant. By 1982, all courts of appeals had embraced the honest-services theory of fraud, sometimes referred to in their cases as the "intangible-rights doctrine." But in 1987, the Supreme Court, in *McNally v. United States*, 483 U.S. 350, restricted the application to cases "limited in scope to the protection of property rights." Congress responded in 1988 by enacting §1346, which provides, in relevant part, "For the purposes of the[e] chapter of the U.S. Code that prohibits, inter alia, mail fraud, §1341, and wire fraud, §1343, the term 'scheme or artifice to defraud' includes a scheme or artifice to deprive another of the intangible right of honest services."

Now, in *Skilling,* the Court held that the statute was not unconstitutionally vague, as Skilling had argued. The Court noted that all the courts of appeals had been divided on how best to interpret the statute, but all had declined to invalidate it as irremediably vague. The Court agreed that §1346 needed to be construed (judicially), not invalidated. Accordingly, the Court held that §1346, proscribing fraudulent deprivations of "the intangible right of honest services," was properly limited to cover only bribery and kickback schemes. In this case, Skilling's alleged misconduct did not involve either of these, and therefore did not fall within the statute's prohibitions. So the Fifth Circuit decision was affirmed in part, reversed in part.

The Court's majority, concurring, and dissention-in-part opinions constituted well over 110 pages. Justice Scalia, joined by Justices Thomas and Kennedy, concurred in part and concurred in the judgment, agreeing with the holding on the fair trial charge and agreeing with the reversal of the Fifth Circuit on the §1346 charge, but for a different reason: he would have found the statute vague. Justice Alito also wrote separately, concurring in part and concurring in the judgment. He opined that a Sixth Amendment impartial jury only requires that "no biased juror is actually seated at trial." Justice Sotomayor, joined by Justices Stevens and Breyer, concurred in part and dissented in part. She agreed with the Court's holding on the honest-services statute, but also opined that Skilling did not receive a fair trial.

FALSE CLAIMS ACT

U.S. ex rel Eisenstein v. City of New York

The federal False Claims Act (FCA) contains "qui tam", or whistleblower, provisions. Qui tam permits citizens with evidence of **fraud** against government contracts and programs to sue, on behalf of the federal government, in order to recover the fraudulently paid funds. In compensation for the risk and effort of filing a case, the whistleblower may be awarded a portion of the funds recovered. The SUPREME COURT has litigated many provisions of the FCA, the most recent in *U.S. ex rel Eisenstein v. City of New York*, __U.S.__, 129 S. Ct. 2230, 173 L. Ed. 2d 1255 (2009). The case involved the status of the United States government and whether it is a "party" to the qui tam LITIGATION if it does not formally intervene in the lawsuit. The Court ruled that even though the government may be aware of the litigation, it is not a party. This meant that the plaintiffs missed an **appellate** filing deadline, as a longer filing period only applied when the U.S. government was a party.

Irwin Eisenstein and four New York City employees filed a FCA qui tam lawsuit against the city, challenging a fee charged by the city to nonresident workers. They argued that the city had deprived the United States of tax revenue that it otherwise would have received if the fee had not been deducted as an expense from the workers' **taxable income**. Therefore, they contended, this violated the FCA, which creates civil liability for "[a]ny person who knowingly presents, or causes to be presented, to an officer or employee of the United States Government ... a false or

fraudulent claim for payment or approval." Under the FCA, the federal government had 60 days to decide whether to intervene in the lawsuit. The government declined to intervened but asked that it receive all pleadings in the case. The **district court** ultimately dismissed the case and the plaintiffs elected to appeal.

However, the Second **Circuit Court** of Appeals noticed that the plaintiffs had filed their appeal 54 days after the entry of the district court's judgment. Under the Federal Rules of APPELLATE Procedure and federal law an appeal generally must filed within 30 days of the **entry of judgment** unless "the United States or an officer or agency thereof is a party." If the United States is a party, the filing period is 60 days. Therefore, if the government was not a party, the appeal would be untimely and would be dismissed. The plaintiffs argued that the appeal was timely filed under the 60-day limit because the United States is a "party" to every FCA suit. New York City contended that the appeal was untimely under the 30-day limit because the United States is not a party to an FCA action absent formal intervention or other meaningful participation. The appellate court ruled in favor of the city and dismissed the appeal as untimely. The Supreme Court agreed to hear Eisenstein's appeals because other circuit courts of appeal had ruled the opposite.

In a unanimous decision, the Court upheld the Second Circuit ruling. Justice CLARENCE THOMAS, writing for the Court, noted that if the United States intervenes, the private citizen has "the right to continue as a party to the action," but the United States acquires the "primary responsibility for prosecuting the action." When the government declines to intervene the private citizen must conduct the action. Despite this clear language, Eisenstein still believed the government was a party to the action. Thomas pointed to the definition of "party" to show that the only way the U.S. could become a party was to file a motion to intervene. To rule otherwise would "render the intervention provisions of the FCA superfluous, as there would be no reason for the United States to intervene in an action in which it is already a party." Congress expressly gave the United States discretion to intervene in FCA actions and the Court concluded that it could not disregard this clear command.

Eisenstein had claimed the U.S. government was a "real party in interest" but Justice

Thomas noted that this was a **term of art** used in federal law "to refer to an actor with a substantive right whose interests may be represented in litigation by another." The fact that Congress chose the term "party" for use in the appellate rules and federal **statute** and not "real party in interest" demonstrated that the 60-day time limit applied only when the United States was an actual "party" in **qui tam actions**. The Court also rejected the claim that the party status of the U.S. government was controlled by the FCA provision that an FCA action be "brought in the name of the Government." The mere fact that the government was named in the case caption was not determinative of party status.

Graham County Soil and Water Conservation District v. U.S. ex rel. Wilson

Though the False Claims Act (FCA) provides citizens with the right to bring qui tam lawsuits against persons who make **fraudulent** payment claims to the U.S. government, the act does place some limitations on this right. One of three explicit exceptions to this right bars **qui tam actions** based upon the public disclosure of allegations or transactions in "a congressional, administrative, or Government Accounting Office [(GAO)] report, hearing, audit, or investigation." 31 U.S.C. § 3730(e)(4)(A). The SUPREME COURT, in *Graham County Soil and Water Conservation District v. U.S. ex rel. Wilson*, __U.S.__, 129 S. Ct. 2824, 174 L. Ed. 2d 551 (2009), was asked to determine whether this exception applied to state and local sources as well as federal sources. The Court concluded that the provision did apply to any government source, thereby narrowing the exception even further than thought.

In 1995 the U.S. DEPARTMENT OF AGRICULTURE (USDA) signed contracts with two counties in North Carolina, authorizing them to perform cleanup and repair work in parts of the counties that had been injured by flooding. USDA paid 75 percent of the cost of the cleanup work. Karen T. Wilson worked for the Graham County Soil and Conservation District, which was partially responsible for the flood repair work. Wilson believed that some officials were committing **fraud** in this effort. She contacted local officials in 1995 and met with USDA agents. Graham County hired a firm to conduct an audit and in 1996 the firm issued a report that identified several potential irregularities in the county's administration of the USDA

contract. Soon after, the North Carolina Department of Environment, Health, and Natural Resources issued a report that identified similar problems. The USDA's Office of Inspector General issued a third report that contained additional evidence of problems.

In 2001 Wilson filed a FCA qui tam action against the Graham County and Cherokee County Soil and Water Conservation Districts as wall as local and federal officials, alleging that the defendants had knowingly submitted false claims for payments. Wilson also alleged that these officials had retaliated against her for her involvement in the FRAUD investigation. The **district court** dismissed her lawsuit, ruling that her claims were based upon allegations publicly disclosed in the county and state reports. Under §3730 these reports constituted administrative reports, audits, or investigations. The Fourth **Circuit Court** of Appeals reversed the decision, holding that the public disclosure exception applied only to federal administrative reports, audits or investigations.

The Supreme Court, in a 7-2 decision, reversed the Fourth Circuit ruling and concluded that state and local administrative reports were included in the §3730 exception. Justice JOHN PAUL STEVENS, writing for the majority, stated that the provision's plain text did not limit it to federal sources. An FCA qui tam action was barred by the **statute** if there was public disclosure of allegations or transactions "in a congressional, administrative, or Government Accounting Office report, hearing, audit, or investigation." The dispute came down to the meaning of the adjective "administrative." The Court of Appeals' ruling was based on its application of a canon of **statutory** interpretation known as *noscitur a sociis*. The literal meaning of the phrase is "it is known by its associates." The appeals court reasoned that the placement of "administrative" in the middle of a list of federal sources strongly suggested that "administrative" should also be limited to federal reports, audits, and investigations. Justice Stevens disagreed, finding the argument unpersuasive. The list of three items, "each quite distinct from the other no matter how construed, is too short to be particularly illuminating."

Stevens relied on the meaning of "administrative "within the larger scheme of the public disclosure bar." Section 3730 also applied to public disclosures arising from criminal, civil, or administrative hearings, and to disclosures by the news media. These additions categories were not limited to federal hearings or national news media. The fact that the administrative exception was sandwiched between the court hearings and news media clauses suggested that state and local administrative sources were just as public as court proceedings and news reports. Stevens believed the exceptions to filing an FCA action were enacted in 1986 to "strike a balance between encouraging private persons to root out fraud and stifling parasitic lawsuits." However, these provisions were inserted into the bill without floor debate as "technical amendments," making the "precise scope" of the provisions "all but opaque."

Justice SONIA SOTOMAYOR, in a dissenting opinion joined by Justice STEPHEN BREYER, argued that the Court had misread the law and had given insufficient weight to "contextual and historical evidence of Congress' purpose in enacting §3730." She supported the Court of Appeals' application of *noscitur a sociis* and rejected the idea that it could not be invoked because the list of items was too short. While agreeing that the legislative record was "incomplete," she concluded that there was enough there "to exercise caution before giving the statutory text its broadest possible meaning—i.e., to encompass not only federal, but also state and local, government sources."

FAMILY LAW

Statutes, court decisions, and provisions of the federal and state constitutions that relate to family relationships, rights, duties, and finances.

Abbott v. Abbott

The Hague Convention on the Civil Aspects of International Child Abduction, along with the implementing statute for signatory United States, requires "Contracting States" (countries/sovereignties) to secure the prompt return of any child to the child's country of habitual residence. The statute addresses children who had been wrongfully abducted to another contracting state in violation of "rights of custody," subject to some exceptions. To that end, the Convention and the International Child Abduction Remedies Act (ICARA), 42 U.S.C. §§ 11601, *et seq.,* prevents a parent from taking a child to another country without the other parent's consent. In *Abbott v.*

Abbott, No. 08-645, 560 U.S. ___ (2010), the U.S. Supreme Court, by a 6-3 decision, held that a non-custodial parent could still have a "right of custody" under the Convention, by reason of that parent's *ne exeat* right. Generally, a *ne exeat* is a court order forbidding a person from leaving a country, state, or jurisdiction of the ordering court. In the present case, the right traced to an order from a court in Chile, another contracting state.

Timothy Abbott, a British citizen, and Jacquelyn Abbott, a U.S. citizen, married in England in 1992 and later had a child in Hawaii, where Timothy worked as an astronomer. In 2002, the family moved to La Serena, Chile, but in 2003, the couple separated. The Chilean courts essentially granted the mother physical CUSTODY of their son, while Mr. Abbott was given "direct and regular visitation." Of particular note in this case, however, was a specific court order prohibiting the child's removal from Chile, by either the father or the mother, without their mutual consent (the subject *ne exeat* order). This order was made pursuant to the Chilean Minors Law, 16,618, art. 49, which stated in relevant part that once a court had determined that one of the parents had VISITATION RIGHTS, that parent's authorization generally "shall also be required" before the child could be taken out of the country.

In 2005, while proceedings in Chilean court were still pending, the mother removed the boy from Chile without permission from either the father or the court. A private investigator hired by the father located the mother and child in Texas. In 2006, the mother filed for DIVORCE in Texas state court. She petitioned the court for modification of the father's visitation in the form of an order limiting him to "supervised visitation" only, and further requesting that she be granted full power to determine the child's place of residence. The father then filed a separate action in Texas state court, asking for visitation rights and an order requiring the mother to SHOW CAUSE why the court should not allow the father to return to Chile with the child. The court denied his relief but granted him "liberal periods of possession" during his stay in Texas.

Mr. Abbott then filed an action in the U.S. **District Court** for the Western District of Texas, seeking his child's return to Chile pursuant to the Convention and enforcement provisions under ICARA. Following a **bench**

trial in 2007, the district court denied relief. It held that the father's *ne exeat)* right was not a "right of custody" right under the Convention, and therefore the requested remedy was not authorized. The Fifth **Circuit Court** of Appeals affirmed, 542 F.3d 1081 (2008). The **appellate court** characterized the father's *ne exeat)* right as one that only conferred "a VETO right over his son's departure from Chile." The three-judge panel further held that only a parent who had custodial rights could invoke the treaty to have a child returned. The U.S. Supreme Court granted **certiorari** to resolve a conflict among other circuit courts of appeals.

Justice Kennedy delivered the opinion of the Court. The Court dissected Convention language, found that the child was under 16 years of age, was an habitual resident of Chile, and that both Chile and the United States were "contracting states." The Court further noted that under ICARA, §11603(b), state or **federal courts** in which a petition alleging international child abduction had been filed were required to "decide the case in accordance with the Convention."

Next, Justice Kennedy looked to the nature of Mr. Abbott's right. He noted that while Chilean law determined the content of his right, the Convention's text and structure determined whether that right was a "right of custody" *ne exeat)* right.

Said the Court,

> The Convention defines 'rights of custody,' and it is that definition that a court must consult. This uniform, text-based approach ensures international consistency in interpreting the Convention … It forecloses courts from relying on definitions of custody confined by local law usage, definitions that may undermine recognition of custodial arrangements in other countries or in different legal traditions, including the civil-law tradition.

Article 5(a) of the Convention defines "rights of custody" to include "the right to determine the child's place of residence." Because Mr. Abbott had direct and regular visitation rights, it followed that he had his own independent *ne exeat)* right, said the high court. Accordingly, held the Supreme Court majority opinion, a parent has a right of custody under the Convention by reason of that parent's *ne exeat)* right.

While noting the contrary conclusions of several courts of appeals (and the Supreme Court of Canada), the Court further noted that a review of INTERNATIONAL LAW showed that courts and other legal authorities in England, Israel, Austria, South Africa, Germany, Australia, and Scotland agree that *ne exeat)* rights are rights of custody within the Convention's meaning. Accordingly, the case was reversed and remanded to the Fifth Circuit.

Joining Justice Kennedy in the majority opinion were Chief Justice Roberts and Justices Scalia, Ginsburg, Alito, and Sotomayor. Justice Stevens filed a dissenting opinion, joined by Justices Thomas and Breyer. He disagreed with the majority's having made what he opined to be a "travel restriction" into a "right of custody" under the Convention. He further opined that the original drafters of the Convention were merely reaching for an international solution to trans-border abductions by non-custodial parents "to establish artificial jurisdictional links … with a view to obtaining custody of a child" (quoting the Convention's Explanatory Report). Stevens' DISSENT noted, "[T]he Court has upended the considered judgment of the Convention's drafters in favor of protecting the rights of noncustodial parents."

Tiger Woods Loses Millions Due to Scandal

Professional golfer Tiger Woods suffered a fall from grace in 2009 and 2010 when he admitted to having numerous extramarital affairs. Rumors swirled that Woods' wife planned to file for DIVORCE, and several companies decided to end their endorsement deals. The scandal could eventually cost Woods hundreds of millions of dollars and could cost the companies that sponsored him even more.

Woods was a child prodigy, having been introduced to golf before the age of two by his father, Earl. As a child, Woods appeared on several television shows and even putted against the late Bob Hope on an episode of the *Mike Douglas Show*. Woods won numerous amateur championships as a teenager, and he eventually enrolled at Stanford University, where he competed on the golf team and also entered several professional golf tournaments, including the Masters in 1995. He left college after two years to become a full-time professional, and in 1997, he won his first major tournament when he won the Masters. During the year he turned professional, he signed multi-million dollar deals with such companies as Nike and Titleist, the latter of which produces golf equipment.

During the next 12 years, Woods fulfilled nearly every expectation the golfing world had set for him. He won 14 major professional golf tournaments, which is only four shy of the record set by legend Jack Nicklaus. Woods became the most marketable athlete in the world and had contracts with numerous companies, including General Motors, General Mills, American Express, and many others. In 2007, Woods signed a deal with Gatorade that reportedly would earn him up to $100 million. In October 2009, *Forbes* magazine reported that Woods had become the first athlete to top the $1 billion mark in prize winnings and endorsements. No other active athlete came close to earning as much as Woods, as his annual income nearly doubled the earnings of golfer Phil Mickelson and basketball star LeBron James. Woods appeared to have a nearly perfect home life as well. In the early 2000s, he met a Swedish model named Elin Nordegren, whom he married in 2004. The couple owned a mansion in Florida, and they had children born in 2007 and 2009.

The image of Woods as a devoted husband and family man took a hit when the tabloid magazine *The National Enquirer* published a story in November 2009 indicating that Woods had engaged in an affair with a nightclub manager named Rachel Uchitel. On November 27, Woods' name appeared in the headlines when he crashed his 2009 SUV into a fire hydrant and tree near his home. He suffered facial injuries and was cited for careless driving. He refused to address the police about the incident, which took place at 2:30 a.m. Elin reportedly helped him out of the car, although some speculated that the two had fought prior to the incident. Woods finally issued a statement on his website, taking blame for the incident but not proving any more details. He said then that he would not participate in any more tournaments in 2009.

Over the next few weeks, numerous women came forward claiming to have had affairs with Woods. One of these women, a cocktail waitress named Jaimee Grubbs, who claimed to have text messages from Woods asking her to remove his name from her phone. Woods issued more statements, first indicating the he regretted certain transgressions and then finally admitting to infidelity. He announced in December that he would take an indefinite leave from the

Tiger Woods speaks at a news conference, May 2010.

AP IMAGES

professional golf tour. Woods checked himself into a facility for treatment for his sexual addictions, and he did not make any public appearances for months after the news first broke. He finally gave a televised speech on February 19, 2010, admitting that he was unfaithful to his wife and apologizing for his behavior. He said then that he expected to return to golf but did not offer a timetable.

Several of the companies that endorsed Woods immediately reconsidered their deals. Accenture and AT&T dropped Woods relatively soon after the news first leaked. Gillette announced that it would phase Woods from the company's ads. In February 2010, less than two weeks after Woods' press conference, Gatorade became the third major sponsor to end relations with Woods. However, Woods retained relationships with other companies, including Nike and Electronic Arts. Although he retained many of his sponsors, the scandal cut into the $110 million he made annually, and some speculated that Woods could lose as much as $180 million if he stayed away from golf for an entire year. A study by two professors at the University of California-Davis indicated that the Woods scandal cost shareholders much more than it did Woods himself. Researchers Victor Stango and Christopher Knittel studied the stock prices of companies associated with Woods before and after the scandal became public knowledge. According to their estimates, the scandal reduced the overall value of these companies by about $12 billion.

Although Woods apologized several times to his wife, Elin, most news accounts reported that she would seek a divorce. The couple had signed a prenuptial agreement under which Elin would reportedly receive $300 million. Several reports indicated that the couple had been in counseling and that it was possible that they would reach a new agreement. However, by April 2010, most news accounts indicated that the marriage was most likely over. Woods participated in the 2010 Masters, placing fourth. However, Elin did not attend the tournament, providing further speculation that the marriage was over.

FEDERAL PREEMPTION

Health Care Services Corporation v. Pollitt

In *Health Care Services Corporation v. Pollitt,* No. 08-3509, the U.S. Supreme Court was asked to address whether the Federal Employees Health Benefits Act (FEHBA), 5 U.S.C. §8901-8914, completely preempted (and therefore made removable to federal court) a state court lawsuit challenging enrollment and health benefits determinations subject to FEHBA. The Supreme Court granted petition for review in October 2009. In February 2010, the Court granted a motion of U.S. Solicitor General Kagan for leave to participate in oral argument as *amicus curiae* (friend of the Court). However, shortly thereafter, the parties settled the case and jointly stipulated to dismiss the writ of certiorari (petition for Supreme Court review). On February 24, 2010, pursuant to Supreme Court Rule 46, the petition was dismissed. The effect of the parties' settlement of the matter and subsequent stipulation to dismiss their petition for Supreme Court review was to keep in place the earlier decision of the Seventh Circuit Court of Appeals, *Pollitt v. Health Care Serv. Corp.,* 558 F.3d 615 (7th Cir. 2009), which was being appealed.

In 2007, Juli Pollitt, a federal employee, filed suit in Illinois state court against Health Care Service Corporation (HCSC) for bad faith conduct in its insurance practices. HCSC managed the health insurance plan Pollitt and others received as part of their federal employee benefits. Pollitt had sued when HCSC stopped paying claims submitted on behalf of Pollitt's son because the Department of Labor (her employer) allegedly advised HCSC that Ms. Pollitt's health coverage was for herself only and not family coverage. HCSC had also sought reimbursement from various health-care providers for services previously rendered to her son. Pollitt, on the other hand, alleged in her complaint that HCSC unilaterally came to this decision on its own, and that its sudden termination of her son's coverage, in combination with demands for reimbursement from medical-care providers, subjected her family to humiliation and financial hardship.

In October 2007, HCSC began paying benefits again for Pollitt's son, but she alleged continued harm in that HCSC had not alerted all the medical providers of the continued coverage, causing them to persist in their collection activities against her.

The district court granted dismissal of the suit, holding that FEHBA "completely preempted" the claim. The Seventh Circuit Court of Appeals vacated that decision and remanded the case. It first noted that preemption was a defense, "and a federal defense does not allow removal." Notwithstanding, the appellate court acknowledged that in cases of "complete preemption," i.e., cases where federal law completely occupies the field at issue, removal is proper. In this case, however, the "complete preemption" doctrine was not warranted because federal law did not completely occupy the field of health insurance coverage for federal workers.

Continuing in its reasoning, the Seventh Circuit noted another possible source of authority for removal, 28 U.S.C. §1442(a)(1), which allows any defendant who acts under the authority of a federal officer, and follows the direction issued by the federal officer, to remove a suit to federal court. But in this case, the parties were in dispute as to whether HCSC had acted under the direction or advice of a federal officer (in this case, the Department of Labor) or had acted "in bad faith" on its own. Therefore, said the Seventh Circuit opinion, the district court erred in relying on HCSC's representation of the facts as a basis for removal.

The remand to district court from the Seventh Circuit was for evidentiary proceedings to determine whether HCSC was merely following a directive from the Department of Labor to terminate Pollitt's son's benefits, in which case it would fall within the purview of the federal officer removal statute, 28 U.S.C. §1442(a)(1); or whether HCSC was acting on its own and was therefore appropriately sued in state court.

The Supreme Court had granted certiorari on the questions, (1)whether the FEHBA completely preempts (and therefore makes removable to federal court) a state court lawsuit challenging enrollment and benefit determinations subject to the exclusive remedies established in FEHBA; and (2)whether the federal officer removal statute, 28 U.S.C. §1442(a)(1), encompasses a lawsuit against a government contractor (HCSC) administering a FEHBA plan, when the contractor is sued for actions taken pursuant to the government contract?

Terms of the settlement between the parties, that resulted in their stipulation to dismiss their petition before the Supreme Court, were not released to the general public.

FEDERAL TORT CLAIMS ACT

Hui v. Castaneda

The Federal Tort Claims Act, (FTCA), 28 U.S.C. §§1346 and 2671-2680, provides that when federal employees are sued for damages from harm caused in the course of their employment, the United States may be substituted as the defendant. Another related provision, 42 U.S.C. §233(a), makes the FTCA an "exclusive remedy" for harm caused by any U.S. Public Health Service (PHS) officer or employee performing medical or related functions "while acting within the scope of his office or employment." Specifically, as relevant here, §233(a) provides

> The [FTCA] remedy against the United States provided by [28 U.S.C. §§1346(b) and 2672] for damage for personal injury, including death, resulting from the performance of medical . . . or related functions . . . by any [PHS] commissioned officer or employee . . . while acting within the scope of his office or employment, shall be exclusive of any other civil action or proceeding by reason of the same subject-matter against the officer or employee."

By way of simple analogy, this might be comparable to a private-sector remedy against a private-sector hospital for suits alleging medical malpractice of its doctors or nurses.

Notwithstanding, in two previous U.S. Supreme Court cases, *Bivens v. Six Unknown Fed. Narcotics Agents,* 403 U.S. 388 (1971) and *Carlson v. Green,* 446 U.S. 14 (1980), the Court recognized implied causes of action outside the scope of FTCA's exclusive remedy provision, for cases involving flagrant violation of an individual's constitutional rights.

Subsequent to the above, Congress passed the Federal Employees Liability Reform and Tort Compensation Act of 1988, 102 Stat. 4563, commonly known as the Westfall Act. It amended the FTCA to make it the "exclusive remedy" for most claims arising out of official conduct of federal employees (expanding the FTCA's reach beyond its §2679(b) "exclusive remedy" for harm resulting from a federal employee's operation of a motor vehicle). A provision within the Westfall Act noted an exception for "a civil action against an employee of the Government . . . brought for a violation of the Constitution of the United States," §2679(b)(2)(A).

In *Hui v. Castaneda,* (re-captioning consolidated cases *Migliaccio v. Castaneda* and *Henneford v. Castaneda*), No. 08-1529, 559 U.S. ___ (2010), the U.S. Supreme Court unanimously reversed both district and appellate court decisions that had permitted a *Bivens* action against PHS medical employees for the death of an under-treated immigrant in federal custody. The Supreme Court, in reversing, held that the immunity provided by §233(a) precluded *Bivens* actions against individual PHS officers or employees for harms arising out of constitutional

Vanessa Castaneda, daughter of Francisco Castaneda, speaks in front of US Supreme Court, March 2010.

AP IMAGES

violations committed within the scope of their office or employment.

Francisco Castaneda had been detained by U.S. Immigration and Customs Enforcement personnel at the San Diego Correctional Facility in March 2006. According to the complaint later filed on his behalf, while in custody, Castaneda brought to the attention of medical personnel working for the Division of Immigration Health Services a painful penile lesion that was growing and emitting a discharge. Between March 2006 and January 2007, Castaneda continued to seek medical treatment, further complaining that the pain was now interfering with urination, defecation, and sleep. He also reported a lump in his groin. A PHS physician's assistant and three outside specialists recommended biopsy to rule out cancer, but Dr. Hui, a civilian PHS employee, denied the requests as "elective," and instead treated him with ibuprofen and antibiotics.

In early 2007, after a fourth specialist recommended biopsy, the procedure was finally authorized. However, before results came back, Castaneda was released from custody on February 5, 2007. One week later, biopsy results confirmed cancer, Castaneda had his penis amputated and began chemotherapy after tests confirmed that cancer had metastasized to his groin. He died in February 2008 after unsuccessful treatment.

Three months prior to his death, Castaneda filed suit in federal district court, raising both medical negligence claims under FTCA and *Bivens* claims for constitutional violations under the Fifth, Eighth, and Fourteenth Amendments, for deliberate indifference to his serious medical needs. (After his death, his sister and daughter continued the action on behalf of his estate.)

Dr. Hui and the other PHS defendants moved to dismiss the claims, asserting absolute immunity under §233(a), even for *Bivens* claims, and asserting that FTCA was the exclusive remedy for harms caused in the course of their medical or related duties. Both the federal district court and the Ninth Circuit Court of Appeals denied the dismissal of the *Bivens* claims, concluding that such claims were not precluded by §233(a), expressly noting that it had been enacted prior to the *Bivens* decision.

Unanimously reversing, the Supreme Court, in an opinion written by newly appointed Justice Sotomayor, poignantly noted that the Court's inquiry began and ended with the text of §233(a), the only immunity invoked by the defendants. The plain language of that text (see above) clearly precluded a *Bivens* action, said the Court. Because the text's phrase "exclusive of any other civil action" is easily broad enough to encompass both known and unknown causes of action, the Court's conclusion was not undermined, said Justice Sotomayor, by the fact that §233(a) preceded *Bivens*..

The fact that the Westfall Act, amending the FTCA several years after the *Bivens* decision, provided an exception from FTCA's exclusive remedy for constitutional violations, does not alter this conclusion, said the Court:

> The Westfall Act's explicit exception for *Bivens* claims is powerful evidence that Congress did not understand the exclusivity provided by [FTCA's] §2679(b)(1) —or the substantially similar §233(a) —to imply such an exception. Given Congress' awareness of pre-existing immunity provisions like §233 when it enacted the Westfall Act, see *United States v. Smith*, 499 U.S. 160,173 (1991), it is telling that Congress declined to enact a similar exception to the immunity provided by §233(a).

Again, beginning and ending its inquiry with the plain language of §233(a), the Court found no *Bivens* exception.

FIFTH AMENDMENT

Supreme Court Rules that Miranda Advisory Question Was Not Misleading

In *Miranda v. Arizona*, 384 U.S. 436, 86 S. Ct. 1602, 16 L. Ed. 2d 694 (1966), the SUPREME COURT extended the right to remain silent to pretrial **custodial interrogation**. The Court held that before a suspect is questioned, the police must apprise the suspect of his or her right to remain silent and that if he or she gives up this right, any statements may be used against the suspect in a subsequent criminal prosecution. Under *Miranda*, suspects also have a FIFTH AMENDMENT right to consult an attorney before they submit to questioning. *Miranda* applies to any situation in which a person is both held in CUSTODY by the police, which means that he or she is not free to leave, and is being interrogated, which means he or she is being asked questions that are designed to elicit an incriminating response. The Supreme Court was called on, in *Florida v. Powell*, __U.S.__, 130 S. Ct. 1195, __L. Ed. 2d__ (2010), to determine whether a *Miranda* advisory was misleading and failed to clearly inform the suspect of his rights. The Florida Supreme Court thought the advisory was misleading but the U.S. Supreme Court ruled that it was sufficient to protect the suspect's Fifth Amendment rights.

In 2004, police in Tampa, Florida, were looking for Kevin Dewayne Powell in connection with a **robbery** investigation. They entered an apartment rented by Powell's girlfriend, spotted Powell, and then search the bedroom. They found a loaded nine-millimeter handgun under the bed. The officers arrested Powell and took him to the Tampa Police headquarters, where they read him the standard Tampa Police Department Consent and Release Form, which embodies the *Miranda* warnings. The form included two statements: "You have the right to talk to a lawyer before answering any of our questions" and "you have the right to use any of these rights at any time you want during this interview." Powell signed the form and then confessed to possessing the handgun, which he was prohibited from possessing because he had previously been convicted of a **felony**. He was charged with a felony for possessing the handgun and he challenged the *Miranda* warnings, claiming that they were deficient because they did not adequately convey his right to the presence of an attorney during questioning. The **district court** denied Powell's motion to suppress his statements and a jury convicted him of the crime.

Powell appealed to the Florida Court of Appeals, again making his *Miranda* warnings argument. The appeals court agreed that the statements were misleading in that it was not clear to Powell that a lawyer could be present throughout the interrogation. Powell believed he was only allowed to have a lawyer present before his questioning. The appeals court certified the question to the Florida Supreme Court as one of great importance. The state supreme court concluded that the two statements were misleading and that Powell's statement could not be used at his trial. The state filed an appeal with the U.S. Supreme Court.

The Court, in a 7-2 decision, reversed the state court decision. Writing for the majority, Justice RUTH BADER GINSBURG noted that that though the elements of *Miranda* warnings are "invariable," the Court had never dictated the words in which the "essential information must be conveyed." In assessing Tampa Bay Police language, the question was whether the warnings "reasonably convey" to a suspect his rights as required by *Miranda*. As to the warnings in this case, the Court concluded that they satisfied this standard. The warnings communicated to Powell that he could consult with a lawyer before answering any particular question and could exercise his RIGHT TO COUNSEL anytime during the interrogation. Combining the two warnings reasonably conveyed to Powell his right to have a lawyer with him at anytime. To reach the opposite conclusion would require the Court to imagine a "counterintuitive and unlikely scenario" that would require Powell to exit and reenter the interrogation room between each question. As to the Florida Supreme Court's conclusion that the first warning suggested to Powell that he could only consult with a lawyer before questioning, Ginsburg declined to find any temporal ambiguity in the language. Moreover, police would not rewrite warnings to introduce such purported ambiguity, for it was in law enforcement's own interest to state *Miranda* warnings clearly, so as to avoid suppression by a trial court.

Justice JOHN PAUL STEVENS, in a dissenting opinion joined by STEPHEN BREYER, argued that the Court did not have jurisdiction to hear the case because the Florida Supreme Court's decision was based on its state constitution rather than the U.S. Constitution's Fifth and Fourteenth Amendments. If a state supreme court decision is based on adequate and independent state-law grounds, the U.S. Supreme Court cannot review it. Stevens' rejected the majority's conclusion that the state decision rested primarily on federal law.

FIRST AMENDMENT

Christian Legal Society v. Martinez

In one of the most significant cases invoking First Amendment arguments, a very divided U.S. Supreme Court held that a state law school could deny official recognition to a religious student organization that required its officers and members to agree to core religious beliefs, in this case, the rejection of "sexually immoral lifestyles," including gay and lesbian lifestyles. *Christian Legal Society v. Martinez*, No. 08-1371, 561 U.S. ___ (2010).

The affected student organization, Christian Legal Society, filed suit, contending that University of California's Hastings College of Law violated its members' right to First Amendment expressive association, free speech, free exercise of religion, and equal protection of the law. Justice Ruth Bader Ginsburg, writing for the majority, rejected the First Amendment and equal protection challenges. Instead, said the Court, the Christian Legal Society was asking for preferential treatment, i.e., exemption from the law school's general policy requirement of non-discrimination for *all* student organizations. The Court limited the question before it as whether a public law school may "condition its official recognition of a student group—and the attendant use of school funds and facilities—on the organization's agreement to open eligibility for membership and leadership to all students?"

The Hastings College of Law, founded in 1878, was the first law school in the University of California's public school system. Through its "Registered Student Organization" (RSO) program, Hastings extended official recognition, with attendant benefits, to student groups. These benefits were not nominal, but included school-approved status, the use of Hastings' name and logo, and use of school facilities and school funds. In exchange, RSOs must comply with certain conditions, including, and relevant here, compliance with the school's Nondiscrimination Policy, which paralleled state law barring discrimination on the basis of, among other things, religion and sexual orientation. As related to the RSO program, Hastings interpreted its policy to mean that RSOs must accept "all comers," that is, it must allow any student to participate, become a member, or seek leadership positions within the RSO, regardless of status or personal beliefs.

Conversely, the Christian Legal Society, the progeny of an existing Christian RSO that, in the 2004-2005 school year, affiliated with a national Christian association that chartered student chapters at law schools around the country, required its members and officers to sign a "Statement of Faith" and conduct their lives in accordance with its principles. Among the tenets was the belief that sexual activity should not occur outside of marriage between a man and a woman. The Christian Legal Society interpreted its bylaws to exclude from affiliation anyone who engaged in "unrepentant homosexual conduct" or who held religious convictions other that those found in the Statement of Faith.

Following this new national affiliation and the concomitant exclusions from membership described above, the Christian Legal Society received notice from Hastings that it would lose its RSO status as an official student group. This meant that it would no longer receive travel costs for the group's leaders to attend national meetings, would lose the use of reserved rooms for meetings, and could not use the school's official Web site to promote itself to students, among other things. The student group filed suit against Hastings in U.S. District Court for the Northern District of California.

The district court upheld the school's nondiscrimination policy for RSOs as an acceptable regulation of Christian Legal Society's conduct, rather than regulation of its speech. The Ninth Circuit Court of Appeals affirmed, holding that the school's nondiscrimination policy was "viewpoint-neutral" and reasonable in light of the school's educational mission. Said the appellate court, "Hastings imposes an open membership rule on all student groups—all groups must accept all comers as voting members even if those individuals disagree with the mission of the group. . .The conditions on recognition are therefore viewpoint-neutral and reasonable."

The Seventh Circuit had held contrary to this, in *Christian Legal Society v. Walker,* 453 F.3d 853 (7th Cir. 2006). Moreover, U.S. Supreme Court precedent has emphasized that the First Amendment generally precluded public universities from denying student organizations access to school-sponsored forums based on their viewpoints. (See, e.g., *Rosenberger v. Rector and Visitors of Univ. of Va.,* 515 U.S. 819, 1995) Accordingly, to resolve conflict, the U.S. Supreme Court granted review.

Indeed, in a majority opinion by Justice Ginsburg, the Supreme Court used the *Rosenberger* case as an example to now rule, as in that case, that its limited public forum decisions provided the appropriate framework for assessing the present free speech and expressive-association claims. Those decisions, including *Rosenberger,* recognized that a governmental entity (in this case, a public college), in regulating property in its charge, may impose restrictions on speech that are reasonable in light of the purposes of the forum and are viewpoint neutral.

The Court held,

In accord with the District Court and the Court of Appeals, we reject [Christian legal Society's] First Amendment challenge. Compliance with Hastings' all-comers policy, we conclude, is a reasonable, viewpoint-neutral condition on access to the student-organization forum … In requiring [Christian Legal Society]—in common with all other student organizations—to choose between welcoming all students [or] forgoing the benefits of official recognition, we hold, Hastings did not transgress constitutional limitations.

The Court made point to note that "[Christian Legal Society], it bears emphasis, seeks not parity with other organizations, but a preferential exemption from Hastings' policy." While the First Amendment protects Christian Legal Society from state prohibition of its expressive activity (however exclusionary it may be), said the Court, "[Christian Legal Society] enjoys no constitutional right to state subvention [support] of its selectivity."

Justice Ginsburg was joined by Justices Stevens, Kennedy, Breyer, and Sotomayor, with Justices Stevens and Kennedy filing concurring opinions. Justice Alito, joined by Chief Justice Roberts along with Justices Scalia and Thomas, dissented. "The proudest boast of our free speech jurisprudence is that we protect the freedom to express 'the thought that we hate,'" quoting from *United States v. Schwimmer*, 279 U.S. 644 (1929). Justice Alito continued, "Today's decision rests on a very different principle: no freedom for expression that offends prevailing standards of political correctness in our country's institutions of higher learning."

Doe v. Reed

The State of Washington has, in its state constitution, a provision to allow citizens to challenge state laws by a referendum. To initiate a referendum, proponents must file a petition with the secretary of state that contains valid signatures of registered Washington voters who would support a ballot initiative, i.e., would support the question of repealing a law being submitted to voters by voting ballot. A valid petition must contain not only signatures, but also signers' addresses and counties in which they are registered to vote. In *Doe v. Reed*, No. 09-559, 561 U.S. ___ (2010), the U.S. Supreme

Washington attorney General Rob McKenna speaks outside the U.S. Supreme Court about whether names on a petition asking for repeal of Wahsington's domestic partnership rights should stay undisclosed, April 2010.

AP IMAGES

Court, in a 8-1 decision, held that the state's Public Records Act did not violate the First Amendment by making public the names of citizens who had signed such petitions.

In May 2009, Washington Governor Christine Gregoire signed into law Senate Bill 5688, which expanded the rights and responsibilities of domestic partners, including same-sex partners. This triggered a protest among citizens not supporting these gay rights, resulting in several efforts to repeal the law. One such group, Protect Marriage Washington, organized as a "state political committee" for the purpose of collecting sufficient petition signatures to place a referendum challenging SB 5688 on the ballot.

Protect Marriage Washington submitted a petition with 137,000 signatures to the secretary of state (a minimum of 120,000 were required to place the referendum on the ballot). In turn, after verifying the signatures as required by law, the secretary of state determined that the petition contained sufficient signatures to qualify the referendum (R-71) for the November 2009 ballot.

Meanwhile, several organizations had contacted the secretary of state with requests to make public the signed R-71 petitions under the Washington Public Records Act, Wash. Rev. Code §42.56.070. That Act, similar in purpose to the federal Freedom of Information Act (FOIA), requires that state and local governments make public records available to citizens.

The petition organizers and certain signers filed a complaint in the U.S. District Court for the Western District of Washington to stop (enjoin) the public release of the petition and signatures. Count I alleged that the Public Records Act was unconstitutional as applied to referendum petitions, and Count II alleged that it was unconstitutional as applied to the Referendum 71 petition in particular, because there was a reasonable probability that release would subject the signers to threats, harassment, and reprisals.

The district court agreed, granting "John Doe #1, *et al.*," plaintiffs, a preliminary injunction preventing release of the signatory information. It based that relief on the likelihood that plaintiffs would succeed on the merits of Count I, and applied a strict scrutiny standard of review to assess the government's interest in releasing the information. It found that the Act was not narrowly tailored to serve a compelling state interest, but instead, burdened core political speech.

But the Ninth Circuit Court of Appeals held that the plaintiffs were unlikely to succeed on their claim that the Public Records Act was unconstitutional as applied to referendum petitions, and therefore reversed. Further, it held that the district court should have applied only an intermediate level of scrutiny, which means that a statute that" incidentally restricts expressive conduct" is nonetheless constitutional under the First Amendment if it "is within the constitutional power of the government to enforce, it furthers an important government interest unrelated to the suppression of free speech, and the incidental restriction on alleged First Amendment freedom is no greater than necessary to justify the interest" [citing *United States v. O'Brien*, 391 U.S. 367 (1968)]. The petitioner-plaintiffs, fighting release of the information, appealed to the U.S. Supreme Court.

Writing for the 8-1 majority , Chief Justice Roberts held that the State of Washington may compel disclosure of the names of citizens who had signed petitions for ballot initiatives. "Disclosure of referendum petitions does not as a general matter violate the First Amendment," he wrote. However, the Court agreed that the compelled disclosure of signatory information on referendum petitions was indeed subject to First Amendment review. Whether a signer is expressing the view that the law subject to the petition should be overturned, or is simply signing on principle, the signature nonetheless expresses the political

view that the question should be considered by the entire electorate. Notwithstanding, the State's interest in preserving the integrity of the electoral process, particularly strong with respect to efforts to root out fraud, is sufficient to defeat an argument that the Public Records Act is unconstitutional with respect to referendum petitions, said the Court.

The plaintiffs nonetheless argued that "the strength of the governmental interest" did not "reflect the seriousness of the actual burden of First Amendment rights." But, said the Court, the plaintiffs' argument rested almost entirely on the supposed harm that would attend any disclosure of information of the R-71 petition. At this stage, the question before the Court was whether disclosure of referendum petitions in general violated the First Amendment. The State had advanced unrebutted arguments that only modest burdens attended the disclosure of a typical petition. Therefore, plaintiffs' broad challenge must be rejected, said the Court.

The lone dissenter, Justice Thomas, opined that, just as confidence in the integrity of our electoral process is essential, "so too is citizen *participation* in those processes." In his view, compelled disclosure of signed referendum and initiative petitions under the state's act "severely burdens those rights and chills citizen participation in the referendum process."

D.C. Circuit Upholds Lobbying Disclosure Statute

Congress passed the Honest Leadership and Open Government Act of 2007 to increase disclosure requirements related LOBBYING organizations. The NATIONAL ASSOCIATION OF MANUFACTURERS (NAM) is an organization that engages in a variety of lobbying efforts on its members behalf, and the new law affected the NAM by requiring the organization to report contributions made by its various members. The NAM brought suit to challenge the law in FIRST AMENDMENT grounds. In 2009, the D.C. **Circuit Court** of Appeals affirmed a decision by a federal **district court** upholding the constitutionality of the **statute**.

Congress has long expressed concerns about groups that put pressure on congressional members through various lobbying efforts. These concerns led to the enactment of the Federal Regulation of Lobbying Act (FRLA) as part of the Legislative Reorganization Act of

1946, ch. 610, 60 Stat. 812. The FRLA required persons who engaged for pay in various lobbying efforts to register with the Clerk of the HOUSE OF REPRESENTATIVES and with the Secretary of the SENATE. The statute also required lobbyists to disclose a variety of information, including names and addresses of the lobbyists and the lobbyists' clients, contributors for the lobbyists and the amounts of the contributions, and similar information. The U.S. SUPREME COURT upheld the constitutionality of the FRLA in *United States v. Harriss*, 347 U.S. 612, 74 S. Ct. 808, 98 L. Ed. 989 (1954), with the Court noting that Congress "merely provided for a modicum of information from those who for hire attempt to influence legislation or who collect or spend funds for that purpose."

The FRLA fell under fire by many critics, including President HARRY S. TRUMAN, because lobbying organizations had already discovered loopholes in the act. However, various reform efforts stalled for several decades. In the early 1990s, Congress heard testimony indicating that corporations and other entities would hide their identities behind coalitions that would lobby Congress but would not divulge the identities of the entities that supported the coalitions. The desire to enhance disclosure requirements led Congress in 1995 to pass the Lobbying Disclosure Act of 1995 (LDA), Pub. L. No. 104-65, 109 Stat. 691. Among the LDA's various provisions were requirements that registrants disclose the names of affiliates, including clients that contribute more than $10,000 towards lobbying activities during a semi-annual period. The statute defines "lobbying activities" as "lobbying contacts and efforts in support of such contacts, including preparation and planning activities, research and other background work that is intended, at the time it is performed, for use in contacts, and coordination with the lobbying activities of others."

In the first year of its passage, the LDA resulted in a significant increase in the number of individuals and organizations registering as lobbyists. Members of Congress, however, continued to express concerns about the LDA's disclosure provisions. During the 2006 congressional elections, a series of lobbying-related scandals led the Senate to consider a bill that would further enhance the disclosure requirements. Both the Senate and the House passed the bill by overwhelming majorities, and then-President GEORGE W. BUSH in 2007 signed into law the Honest Leadership and Open Government Act of 2007 (HLOGA), Pub. L. No. 110-81, 121 Stat. 735.

The HLOGA in part focused on revising provisions in the LDA. The HLOGA changed the reporting requirements for registrants, mandating that any **entity** that contributes more than $5,000 per quarter is subject to the statute. The statute also changed language applying to the level in which an organization must participate in lobbying activities before the organization is subject to the disclosure requirements. Under the HLOGA, an organization that knowingly fails to comply with the disclosure requirements could be subject to a fine of up to $200,000, depending on the severity of the violation. The statute also added the possibility of an offender receiving a criminal penalty, providing that "whoever knowingly and corruptly fails to comply with any provision [of the LDA] shall be imprisoned for not more than 5 years or fined … or both."

NAM was established in 1895 "to promote trade, advocate for economic growth, and represent the interests of its members." The organization is specifically designed to focus its efforts on influencing members of Congress as well as employees and officers of the executive branch of the government. NAM has more than 11,000 corporate members, but NAM has kept its membership list confidential for at least 30 years. NAM also employs about 35 individuals who regularly engage in lobbying activities and whom the organization has identified in filing submitted pursuant to the LDA.

In 2008, NAM challenged the constitutionality of the HLOGA, arguing that the statute's new disclosure requirements violate the First Amendment rights of both the organization and its members. NAM's suit stressed that the organization's efforts often focus on policy positions that may be unpopular with other groups. If NAM had to disclose all of its members, the member companies could be the subject of boycotts, political pressure, shareholder suits, and other actions. NAM expressed concern that the disclosure requirements would lead some companies to cease their support for NAM out of fears that NAM will have to disclose the companies' identities. According to NAM's argument, the HLOGA violated the First

Amendment because it was both overly broad and vague.

NAM made its argument before Judge Colleen Kollar-Kotelly of the U.S. District Court for the District of Columbia. The judge analyzed the case under the **strict scrutiny** standard, which requires the government to prove that a restraint on speech is narrowly tailored to serve a compelling government interest. Kollar-Kotelly concluded that the government could meet both parts of this standard, finding that the government's interest in avoiding appearances of corruption was a compelling government interest. The lower court also concluded that the HLOGA was the least intrusive means of serving this compelling interest. Therefore, the court rejected NAM's challenge. *Nat'l Ass'n of Mfrs. v. Taylor*, 549 F. Supp. 2d 33 (D.D.C. 2008).

NAM repeated its arguments before a three-judge panel of the U.S. Court of Appeals for the District of Columbia. In an opinion written by Merrick B. Garland, the panel agreed with the district court's analysis. The court reviewed the HLOGA under the STRICT SCRUTINY standard, with Garland's opinion citing numerous Supreme Court opinions that set forth the applicable standard. Based on its review of the applicable **case law**, the court rejected NAM's argument and held that the statute did not violate the First Amendment. *Nat'l Ass'n of Mfrs. v. Taylor*, 582 F.3d 1 (D.C. Cir. 2009).

Second Circuit Rules that Valerie Plame Wilson Cannot Reveal Dates of CIA Employment in Her Memoir

The FIRST AMENDMENT gives citizens the right to express their views orally and in writing. Individuals are free to write about their lives without fear that the government will prohibit the disclosure of information. However, when an individual signs an employment agreement that gives the government the right to review any writings in **advance** of publication that deal with government work, the courts generally come down on the side of the government. This is particularly true when a former employee of the CENTRAL INTELLIGENCE AGENCY (CIA) seeks to publish a memoir about her life as a member of the agency. The CIA has been involved in a number of lawsuits where the author objects to the editing of a manuscript by the CIA. The latest such suit involved Valerie Plame Wilson, a former CIA employee, who played a part in the

national debate over whether President GEORGE W. BUSH misled the country about the possibility of Saddam Hussein possessing weapons of mass destruction. When she wrote a memoir about her CIA career, the agency severely edited information that predated 2002. *Fair Game*, as published, contained many blacked out portions of text that the CIA had redacted. She sued to overturn these redactions but the Second **Circuit Court** of Appeals dismissed her claims in *Wilson v. Central Intelligence Agency*, 586 F.3d.2d 171 (2009).

The case grew out of President Bush's 2003 State of the Union address, in which he tried to bolster support for invading Iraq. During his speech, he state that "The British government has learned that Saddam Hussein recently sought significant quantities of uranium from Africa." This claim became the subject of extensive debate after reporters learned that the statement contradicted the findings of former ambassador Joseph Wilson, who had visited Niger in February 2002 at the direction of the government. Journalists pursued this story for months and on July 7, 2003 Wilson published an op-ed piece entitled "What I Didn't Find in Africa." In the piece he said that "some of the intelligence related to Iraq's NUCLEAR WEAPONS program was twisted to exaggerate the Iraqi threat." Soon after publication of this article the White House began an effort to discredit Wilson, telling selected reporters that Wilson's wife, Valerie Plame Wilson, was a CIA operative and that she was involved in sending her husband to Africa. On July 14, syndicated columnist Robert Novak revealed Plame's identity as an intelligence agent, attributing the information to two "senior administration officials." The leak led to an investigation by a special PROSECUTOR, who tried and convicted Lewis "Scooter" Libby, Chief of Staff to VICE PRESIDENT Dick Cheney, on PERJURY charges.

Valerie Plame Wilson realized after the disclosure of her CIA employment that she could no longer work there. She appeared on news and opinion shows and became a prominent **public figure**. The publisher Simon and Shuster offered her a contract to write a memoir about her life as a CIA agent and the effects of the White House scandal some dubbed "Plamegate." Wilson had signed the standard CIA secrecy agreement when she joined the agency. She agreed never to disclose information or materials obtained in the course of her CIA career that were classified. She also agreed to submit for review by the CIA all works,

including works of fiction, that may be based on classified information. The problem for Wilson in writing her memoir was that she would have difficulty writing about her career before the disclosure in 2003 when she was a covert employee. Nevertheless, she wrote her memoir and submitted it to the CIA's Publication Review Board. The board barred her from publishing any passages relating to her pre-2002 agency service. After negotiations between Wilson's lawyers and the CIA broke down, Simon and Schuster published the redacted passages as-is in *Fair Game*, and commissioned a journalist to write an afterword that disclosed what had been put in the public record about Wilson's CIA career. Wilson and her publisher then filed suit against the CIA, asking a New York federal **district court** to overturn the CIA redactions. The district court rejected these claims, relying on the secrecy agreement that Wilson had signed. Wilson then appealed to the Second Circuit.

A three-judge panel of the appeals court unanimously upheld the lower court decision. The appeals court found no merit in Wilson's two main arguments. She first maintained that the CIA had "officially disclosed" her pre-20002 dates of service. She based this on the fact she received, in violation of CIA policy, a letter from the CIA human resources department in 2006 that disclosed her service dates as part of a denial of her application for retirement benefits. The court acknowledged that the CIA may have been negligent in communicating personnel information without proper classification. However, Wilson had shared this letter with a member of Congress who sought to pass a special retirement bill on her behalf. The Congressman had placed the letter in the **Congressional Record**, thereby making the dates of service public.

Wilson also argued that her dates of CIA service were now a matter of such widespread knowledge that it was unreasonable for the CIA to insist on maintaining this information as classified. The court ruled that the evidence of public disclosure did not "deprive information of classified status," and that the CIA had demonstrated a "reasonable basis for maintaining information about Ms. Wilson's pre-2002 Agency service as classified." The CIA had provided classified information to the court, which reviewed it in private. This information convinced the court that the restrictions on publication were legitimate.

U.S. v. Stevens

The SUPREME COURT has permitted few restrictions on the FIRST AMENDMENT right to freedom of expression. These restrictions include OBSCENITY, **defamation**, **fraud**, incitement, and speech integral to criminal conduct. The Court was confronted with the emotional topic of animal cruelty and whether Congress could ban depictions of it. The law, 18 U.S.C. § 48, came in response to the distribution of dog fighting and "crush" videos (the torture and killing of small animals). A distributor of dog fighting videos was charged with violating the **statute** but he challenged the constitutionality of the law. The Supreme Court sided with the video distributor in *U.S. v. Stevens*, __U.S.__, 130 S. Ct. 1577, __ L. Ed. 2d __ (2010), ruling that the law was substantially overbroad and would violate the First Amendment by stifling protected speech.

Congress enacted the law to criminalize the commercial creation, sale, or possession of certain depictions of animal cruelty. It only addressed the portrayals of such cruelty and did not deal with the underlying harmful acts. A person may be sentenced up to five years in prison if he or she knowingly "creates, sells, or possesses a depiction of animal cruelty," if done "for commercial gain" in interstate or foreign commerce. A depiction of "animal cruelty" is defined as one "in which a living animal is intentionally maimed, mutilated, tortured, wounded, or killed," if that conduct violates federal or state law where "the creation, sale, or possession takes place." In an "exceptions clause," the law exempts from prohibition any depiction "that has serious religious, political, scientific, educational, journalistic, historical, or artistic value." The law was designed to shut down the market for "crush videos" that show the intentional torture and killing of cats, dogs, monkeys, mice, and hamsters. These depictions attract persons with a very specific sexual fetish. Though the acts shown in these videos are prohibited by state animal cruelty laws, the videos rarely disclose the identities of the participants, which makes prosecution difficult.

Robert J. Stevens ran a business, "Dogs of Velvet and Steel, and used a website to sell videos of pit bulls fighting each other and attacking other animals. He was charged with violating the animal cruelty law by selling these videos. Stevens asked that the INDICTMENT be dismissed because §48 was on its face invalid under the First Amendment. The court denied the motion and a jury convicted him on all counts. The court sentenced Stevens to 37 months in prison and three years of supervised release. The Third **Circuit Court** of Appeals vacated Stevens's conviction and ruled that §48 was unconstitutional. The appeals court concluded that the law regulated protected speech and that it could not survive the **strict scrutiny** test of constitutional review. Moreover, the court refused to recognize a new category of unprotected speech for depictions of animal cruelty.

The Supreme Court, in an 8-1 decision, agreed that the law was unconstitutional. Chief Justice JOHN ROBERTS, writing for the majority, first noted that the Court had rarely made exceptions to the First Amendment protection of freedom of expression. The government contended that depictions of animal cruelty should be added to this list but Robert rejected its argument that the Court apply a simple balancing test to determine whether the value of the speech outweighed its "societal costs." He called such a "free-floating" test "startling and dangerous." Instead, the Court applied an "overbreadth analysis" to this facial challenge of the law. Under this analysis, a law may be invalidated as overbroad if "a substantial number of its applications are unconstitutional, judged in relation to the statute's plainly legitimate sweep." Therefore, the Court reviewed how broadly §48 was construed.

Roberts found the law created a "criminal prohibition of alarming breadth." The law applied to any depiction including ones where animals are wounded or killed. While maiming, mutilating, and torturing animals conveyed cruelty, wounded or killed did not have any such limitation. Though the law required the depicted conduct to be illegal, there are many state and federal laws that deal with the proper treatment of animals but are not addressed at stopping animal cruelty. For example, the protection of endangered species restricts even the humane killing of animals. In addition, §48 would apply nationally to conduct that is illegal in only one state. Those businesses that sought to comply with the law would face "bewildering maze of regulations from at least 56 separate jurisdictions."

As for the exceptions clause, which the government tried to use to narrow the breadth of the statute, Chief Justice Roberts concluded that it would take an "unrealistically broad reading" of it to make it work. The government stated that any material with "redeeming societal value" or anything more than "scant social value" would be excluded from the reach of §48. However, the text used the term "serious value." Roberts would not stretch the meaning of "serious" to include "scant." The clause also was defective because excepted speech had to fall into one of the listed categories, yet much speech did not. for example, hunting videos. There was no way to explain why hunting videos or depictions of Spanish bullfights would be "inherently valuable" but dogfights were not. The Court rejected the government's claim that it trust federal prosecutors to exercise restraint, noting that when the law was passed the Executive Branch announced that it would interpret §48 to cover only crush videos. The videos that Stevens distributed did not fit this description. Therefore, the law was overbroad and unconstitutional.

Justice SAMUEL ALITO filed a dissenting opinion, calling §48 a "valuable statute" that was enacted to prevent "horrific acts of animal cruelty." He contended that the Court should not have used the overbreadth analysis to invalidate statute. Instead, the Court should have directed the court of appeals to decided whether the videos in question were constitutionally protected.

Fourth Circuit Reverses Verdict Against Westboro Baptist Church

The Fourth **Circuit Court** of Appeals in 2009 reversed a $5 million verdict handed down against the Westboro Baptist Church of Topeka, Kansas. The father of a Marine soldier killed in Iraq had originally prevailed in his suit against the church, which is infamously known for staging protests at the funerals of fallen soldiers on the grounds that God has actually killed the soldiers as punishment for America's tolerance of homosexuality. A panel of the Fourth Circuit concluded that the church's speech was protected by the FIRST AMENDMENT. In March 2010, the U.S. SUPREME COURT agreed to review the case, though the decision will not likely come until 2011.

Westboro Baptist Church was founded in the 1950s by Fred Phelps. The church's congregation consists of about 60 to 70 members, most of whom are related to Phelps. The church created significant controversies in the early 1990s when it began staging protests at such events as funerals of those who have died of AIDS. The group's efforts intensified in the 2000s when church members began to protest at the funerals of soldiers killed in Iraq and related conflicts. Church members display signs such inflammatory messages as, "God Hates the USA" and "America is doomed." Phelps and other church members have said that they stage the protests because it increases the exposure of the message they are trying to send.

Marine Lance Corporal Matthew A. Snyder was killed in action in Iraq on March 3, 2006. His father, Albert, arranged for his funeral on March 10, 2006, held in Westminster, Maryland. On March 8, the Westboro church issued a news release announcing that church members would stage a protest at Snyder's funeral. Phelps, two of his daughters, and four of his grandchildren arrived in Westminster on March 10. The church members did not meet Albert Snyder, nor did Albert actually see the protesters during the funeral itself. The protesters remained several hundred feet away from the church in compliance with a local **ordinance**.

Sometime after the Westboro members returned to Kansas, they posted something of an essay (referred to as an "epic") entitled "The Burden of Marine Lance Cpl. Matthew Snyder." The posting mostly featured references to scripture along with admonitions purportedly directed at Albert Snyder and his former wife. The posting noted that that Albert raised Matthew "for the devil. You taught him that God was a liar." The essay moreover attacked the Snyders for supporting Catholicism. The "epic" concluded that God killed Matthew Snyder so that the Westboro members would have a chance to spread their message at such places as the U.S. Naval Academy, the Maryland Legislature, and the St. John Catholic Church in Westminster.

Albert Snyder said that he became physically ill when he saw coverage of the protests on television. His condition worsened when he saw the posting about Matthew on the Westboro website. Snyder has suffered from depression, and a doctor said the condition worsened because Albert could not go through a normal grieving process. In June 2006, Albert sued Fred Phelps, the Westboro Church, and several of the

Albert Snyder, father of a Marine killed in Iraq, in an interview, April 2010.

AP IMAGES

church's members. Albert alleged five claims based on Maryland state law, including **defamation**, intrusion upon seclusion, publicity given to a private life, intentional infliction of emotional distress, and civil CONSPIRACY.

The defendants argued that its protests involved matters of opinion on public issues. Thus, according to the defendants, the First Amendment should protect their speech. According to their argument, the words used in the protests "are clearly rhetorical, hypothetical, religious and laced with opinion." Moreover, the church argued that "it is impossible to prove or disprove these things, particularly given that doctrinal viewpoints drive the opinions." In October 2007, the U.S. **District Court** for the District of Maryland granted the defendants' motion for **summary judgment** regarding two of the five claims, but the court allowed the other three claims to proceed to trial. A jury awarded the PLAINTIFF a total of $10.9 million in compensatory and **punitive damages**. The district court later reduced the overall amount to $5 million after determining that the punitive damage award was excessive. *Snyder v. Phelps*, 533 F. Supp. 2d 567 (D. Md. 2008).

The defendants appealed the case to the Fourth Circuit. Before a three-judge panel, the defendants repeated their argument that the First Amendment protected their speech. In an opinion written by Judge Robert B. King, the court analyzed the limitations the First Amendment places on tort actions based on state law. In a tort action that involving speech that cannot be interpreted as stating actual facts about the plaintiff, the First Amendment does not permit a private plaintiff to recover. Moreover, the First Amendment prohibits recovery when the speech involves nothing more than "rhetorical hyperbole."

The Fourth Circuit's panel concluded that the First Amendment protected the church's speech on several grounds. First, the court determined that none of the signs displayed at the protest could be interpreted as stating actual and objectively verifiable facts about either Snyder or his son. Moreover, the court determined that the signs only contained "imaginative and hyperbolic rhetoric intended to spark debate about issues with which the Defendants are concerned." Although the court said the "epic" presented a more difficult question, the court concluded that the statements in the online posting were in effect no different than the speech used on the signs. Because the court concluded that the First Amendment protected the protesters' speech, the court reversed the district court and set aside the judgment. *Snyder v. Phelps*, 580 F.3d 206 (4th Cir. 2009).

Albert Snyder vowed to continue the fight and sought a review by the U.S. Supreme Court. The Court agreed to review the case in March 2010, but the Court will not likely hear oral argument until at least the fall of 2010. In late March, the Fourth Circuit disappointed Snyder when the appeals court ordered Snyder to pay the Phelps' court costs, which amounted to more than $16,000. Within weeks, thousands of supporters donated money to help Snyder, and these donations were more than enough to pay for these costs.

FOREIGN SOVEREIGN IMMUNITY ACT

Samantar v. Yousuf

The Foreign Sovereign Immunities Act of 1976 (FSIA), 28 U.S.C. §1604 provides that a "foreign state shall be immune from the jurisdiction" of both federal and STATE COURTS, except as

provided [elsewhere] in the Act." In *Samantar v. Yousuf*, No. 08-1555, 560 U.S. ___ (2010), the U.S. SUPREME COURT separated foreign sovereign states from officials acting on behalf of those foreign states. It ruled that FSIA does not govern whether an individual foreign official has IMMUNITY from suit, as immunity under FSIA attaches only to foreign states and their agencies. The unanimous opinion of the high court affirmed the Fourth **Circuit Court** of Appeals, which held similarly.

In 2004, five Somalians, some of whom were naturalized U.S. citizens, filed a lawsuit in federal **district court** against Mohamed Ali Samantar for offenses he allegedly committed while serving as First VICE PRESIDENT and Minister of Defense of Somalia(1980-1986), and later as its Prime Minister (1987-1990). Samantar was in charge of Somalia's military forces until the military regime collapsed; he then fled Somalia in 1991 and became a resident of Virginia.

In their complaint, plaintiffs alleged that they or their family members were victims of torture and **extrajudicial** killings during the years that Samantar controlled the military. In particular, they alleged that Samantar exercised command and control over members of the Somali military forces who tortured, killed, or arbitrarily detained them or family members. According to their complaint, his personal role ranged from aiding and **abetting** the commission of these abuses, to knowing (or charged with knowing) that these abuses were occurring. The plantiffs sought relief under the Alien Tort **Statute**, 28 U.S.C. §1350, and the Torture Victim Protection Act of 1991, 106 Stat. 73, note following 28 U.S.C. §1350.

For two years, the case languished as the district court stayed the proceedings pending word from the STATE DEPARTMENT as to its interest regarding Samantar's claim of immunity. In 2007, still having heard nothing from the State Department, the district court ruled that it lacked **subject matter jurisdiction** and dismissed the charges against him.

The district court's dismissal was based on the FSIA. The court noted that §1604 of the Act provides that a "foreign state shall be immune from the jurisdiction" of both federal and state courts, except as provided [elsewhere] in the Act," and that the parties had not argued that any exceptions in the Act were applicable. It therefore followed **appellate** decisions holding that immunity extended not only to foreign states, but also to "an individual acting in his official capacity on behalf of a foreign state" (excluding "an official who acts beyond the scope of his authority"). The district court also rejected plaintiffs' arguments that Samantar was necessarily acting beyond the scope of his authority because he allegedly violated INTERNATIONAL LAW (torture and extrajudicial killings).

The Fourth Circuit Court of Appeals reversed the district court, disagreeing that the FSIA governed Samantar's immunity at all. While acknowledging that "the majority view" among circuits was that the FSIA applied to individual officials of a foreign state, it did not share that view. Instead, said the Fourth Circuit, "based on the language and structure of the statute, the FSIA does not apply to individual foreign government agents like [Samantar]." 552 F 3d.371 (2009).

The U.S. Supreme Court unanimously affirmed, Justice Stevens writing for the Court. A great many paragraphs of the opinion were devoted to LEGISLATIVE HISTORY and the transition from **common law** to CODIFICATION, as well as the canon of construction for reading statutes. Ultimately, the Court held,

> There is nothing to suggest we should read 'foreign state' ... to include an official acting on behalf of the foreign state, and much to indicate that this meaning was not what Congress enacted ... The text does not foreclose [Samantar's] reading, but it supports the view of [plaintiffs] and the United States that the [FSIA] does not address an official's claim to immunity.

Indeed, the actual text of the FSIA states, in relevant part, that a foreign state "includes a political subdivision ... or an agency or instrumentality" of that state. Further in the text, it refers to an "agency or instrumentality" as "any entity" having three specific characteristics, none of which lent itself to individuals.

The Court went on to clarify that whether Samantar might be entitled to common-law immunity or whether he had some other valid defense were matters to be addressed on remand to the district court. Here, the Court simply held, plaintiffs had sued Samantar in his personal capacity. They sought damages from his own pockets. Such a case is governed by COMMON LAW and does not fall under the **purview** of the FSIA.

Justice Stevens was joined by Chief Justice Roberts and Justices Kennedy, Ginsburg, Breyer, Alito, and Sotomayor, with Justice Alito filing a separate concurring opinion. Justice Thomas concurred in part and concurred in the judgment. Justice Scalia concurred in the judgment. All three justices who wrote separate concurrences took exception to reliance upon or reference to (in the Court's opinion) legislative history. Justice Alito opined that it was of little or no value; Justice Thomas opined that the court's textual analysis was sufficient alone to resolve the case; Justice Scalia also expressed his non-reliance on legislative history.

FORFEITURE

The involuntary relinquishment of money or property without compensation as a consequence of a breach or nonperformance of some legal obligation or the commission of a crime. The loss of a corporate charter or franchise as a result of illegality, malfeasance, or nonfeasance. The surrender by an owner of her or his entire interest in real property mandated by law as a punishment for illegal conduct or negligence. In old English law, the release of land by a tenant to the tenant's lord due to some breach of conduct, or the loss of goods or chattels (articles of personal property) assessed as a penalty against the perpetrator of some crime or offense and as a recompense to the injured party.

Alvarez v. Smith

The U.S. Constitution directs the **federal courts** to review all "cases and controversies." The SUPREME COURT has interpreted this to mean that for a lawsuit to proceed, parties to the action must show that they have been injured and that a court decision is needed to provide a remedy. If, during a case the parties settle their issues, the court will dismiss the action as moot. It will refuse to make decision unless a party can show that she would likely be subject to future **jeopardy** on the same issue. In cases before it, the Supreme Court usually dismisses cases as moot if the parties have resolved the underlying dispute. Such was the case in *Alvarez v. Smith*, __U.S.__, 130 S. Ct. 576 , __L. Ed. 2d__ (2009), where the Court dismissed the **forfeiture** case after learning at oral argument that the state had returned cars and cash to the parties who had originally challenged the FORFEITURE **statute**. Moreover, the Court vacated the judgment of the court of appeals.

In November 2006, six individuals brought a federal CIVIL RIGHTS action against the city of Chicago, its police chief, and the Cook County state's attorney. Three of the individuals said after their arrests in early 2006, the police had seized their cars without a warrant. The other three plaintiffs alleged that after their arrests in early 2006, the police had seized their cash without a warrant. At the time of the filing of the complaint, the police still had CUSTODY of the property. They claimed that the failure of the state to provide a speedy post-seizure hearing violated the Constitution's Due Process Clause. The six plaintiffs asked the court to certify a **class action**, declare that they had a due process right to a prompt post-seizure probable-cause hearing, declare that the hearing must take place within 10 days of any seizure, and enjoin the defendants' current practice of keeping the property in custody for a longer time without a judicial determination of **probable cause**.

The **district court** rejected the CLASS ACTION request and dismissed the case because the Seventh **Circuit Court** of Appeals' precedent that "the Constitution does not require any procedure prior to the actual forfeiture proceeding." However, on appeal the Seventh Circuit reviewed its precedent and concluded that it could not be applied in this case. The appeals court ruled that the procedures in the Illinois forfeiture statute displayed "insufficient concern for the due process right of the plaintiffs." Given the length of time that could accrue between seizure and a hearing on the propriety of the seizure, "some sort of mechanism to test the validity of the retention of the property is required."

The Supreme Court granted review in February 2009 and after briefs were filed, asked the parties to address the question of mootness at oral argument. At oral argument both sides agreed that there was no longer any dispute about ownership or possession of the property in question. The cars had been returned to the three plaintiffs, while two plaintiffs conceded that the state could keep the cash. The other PLAINTIFF worked out an agreement to keep some of the cash. The lawyer for the state's attorney told the justices that the six cases were over.

In an 8-1 ruling the Court dismissed the case as moot and vacated the Seventh Circuit judgment. Justice STEPHEN BREYER, writing for the majority, noted that under the "cases and controversies" clause, an "'actual controversy must be extant at all stages of review, not merely at the time the complaint is filed." In this case there is no longer any actual controversy between the parties about ownership or possession of the underlying property. Both sides had contended, for different reasons, that there was a continuing controversy. The state's attorney noted that the plaintiffs had filed a motion in district court asking to amend the complaint and include a damages action against the defendants. Breyer rejected this claim because the district court could not consider the motion while the case was before the Court. All the Court had before it were claims for a **declaratory judgment** and an INJUNCTION. The plaintiffs argued that their class action request was still pending but Breyer pointed out that they had not appealed that decision. Therefore, that issue was moot as well.

Justice Breyer agreed that both sides contested the legitimacy of the forfeiture hearing procedure but concluded that the dispute was "no longer embedded in any actual controversy about the plaintiffs' particular legal rights. Rather, it is an abstract dispute about the law, unlikely to affect these plaintiffs any more than it affects other Illinois citizens. And a dispute solely about the meaning of a law, abstracted from any concrete actual or threatened harm, falls outside the scope of the constitutional words "Cases" and "Controversies." The only way the case could continue was if it demonstrated special circumstances. The most common circumstances involved attacks on practices that no longer directly affect the attacking party, but are "capable of repetition" while "evading review." Unlike those cases, the plaintiffs were unlikely to be subjected to forfeiture again. If they were again subjected to forfeiture they could pursue damages actions, which meant there was a means of court review.

The Court vacated the Seventh Circuit decision, even though it did not address the merits of the case. Justice JOHN PAUL STEVENS agreed that the case was moot but dissented on vacating the appeals court decision. He contended the Court should have dismissed the **writ** of **certiorari** as improperly granted and let the Seventh Circuit decision alone.

FOURTH AMENDMENT

Ninth Circuit Rules That Jail's Strip-Search Policy Is Constitutional

The Ninth **Circuit Court** of Appeals in 2010 ruled that a strip-search policy used by the sheriff's office at six county jails in the San Francisco area did not violate the FOURTH AMENDMENT rights of those who were subject to strip searches. The policy in question applies to those who have been arrested and are subject to searches at the time of their booking. A group of arrestees challenged the policy, arguing that standards that apply to convicted prisoners should not apply to those who have been detained but who have not been convicted. The Ninth Circuit disagreed, ruling that the courts should defer to decisions made by prison officials.

The sheriff's office for the County of San Francisco oversees the county's six jails. These prisons hold nearly 50,000 individuals who are booked and processed after their arrests. The jail in question in the Ninth Circuit's case was used as a temporary intake and release facility. The facility was not used to house detainees and did not contain beds. Many of the individuals who passed through this facility were released relatively soon after they are processed. However, those who were not released were transferred to jails that had housing facilities. Those who were transferred became part of the general prison population that consisted of both pretrial detainees as well as convicted offenders.

In April 2000, Sheriff Michael Hennessey instituted a policy under which pretrial detainees were strip searched prior to being released into the general population. The policy required officers to perform the searches in a professional manner, with an officer of the same sex as the detainee performing the search. The person being searched was required "to remove or arrange some or all of his or her clothing so as to permit a visual inspection of the underclothing, breasts, buttocks or genitalia of such person." The policy permitted officers to conduct a visual inspection of an arrestee's body cavity parts, but the policy did not permit a physical search of body cavities.

As a result of the policy, officers discovered a total of 1,574 items of CONTRABAND, including weapons and drugs. At the temporary facility alone between April 2000 and April 2005,

officers discovered drugs and drug paraphernalia on 73 different arrestees. The discovered contraband included handcuff keys, syringes, crack pipes, heroin, crack cocaine, rock cocaine, and marijuana. Weapons included various knives, scissors, a nail, and glass shards. Weapons and contraband were found not only on violent offenders, but also on those accused of such non-violent offenses as public drunkenness, public nuisance, and violations of court orders.

In April 2003, a group of former arrestees brought a **class action** against Hennessey, Hennessey's department, and the City and County of San Francisco. The lead PLAINTIFF was Mary Bull, who was arrested on suspicion of VANDALISM. She was subjected to a strip search, and when she refused to consent, she allegedly was forced to the ground, searched, and left naked in a cold room for 12 hours before being released. She was never charged with a crime. Bull and other members of the class alleged that the defendants had violated their Fourth Amendment rights by conducting unreasonable searches. The CLASS ACTION suit was brought in the U.S. **District Court** for the Northern District of California.

In 2005 and 2006, the district court issued several orders on motions filed by both the plaintiffs and the defendants. On the issue of whether the policy violated the plaintiff's Fourth Amendment rights, the district court concluded that the policy was unconstitutional. *Bull v. City & County of San Francisco*, No. C 03-1840, 2006 WL 449148 (N.D. Cal. Feb. 23, 2006). According to the district court, the blanket policy of conducting strip searches violated principles established in previous Ninth Circuit cases, which had held that strip searches are justified only when prison officials have a reasonable suspicion that a particular arrestee is concealing contraband. Placement in the general jail population was not sufficient justification for the strip search. The district court's decision was later affirmed by a divided panel of the Ninth Circuit. *Bull v. City & County of San Francisco*, 539 F.3d 1193 (9th Cir. 2008).

The Ninth Circuit agreed to review the case *en banc*. In a 6-5 decision, the Ninth Circuit reversed the district court's decision. Writing for the majority, Judge Sandra Ikuta noted that because the policy involved an issue related to institutional security goals within a detention facility, the U.S. Supreme Court's decisions in *Bell v. Wolfish*, 441 U.S. 520, 99 S. Ct. 1861, 60 L. Ed. 2d 447 (1979) and *Turner v. Safley*, 482 U.S. 78, 107 S. Ct. 2254, 96 L. Ed. 2d 64 (1987). In both *Bell* and *Turner*, the Court upheld policies requiring a visual body cavity search of each prisoner who had contact with a visitor. Under both of these decisions, the Court established a principle that the courts should defer to decisions made by corrections officials, noting that the courts are ill-equipped to deal with problems associated with running a corrections facility.

Applying *Bell* and *Turner*, the Court concluded that the San Francisco policy was constitutional. Ikuta's opinion noted that the policy was reasonable "in light of the documented evidence of the ongoing, dangerous, and perplexing contraband-smuggling problem, and given the deference [the court owes] to jail officials' professional judgment." The court acknowledged that official may not have a reasonable suspicion that each individual searched has smuggled a weapon or contraband, but the court held that the policy was still reasonable given the precedent established by the SUPREME COURT. *Bull v. City & County of San Francisco*, 595 F.3d 964 (9th Cir. 2010).

Writing for the DISSENT, Judge Sidney Thomas noted several examples of prison officials abusing their authority by conducting strip searches of such arrestees as a nun arrested for trespassing during an anti-war protest and another person arrested for operating a motor vehicle without a license. The dissent argued that the decision gives jail officials "the unfettered right to conduct mandatory, routine, suspicion-less body cavity search on any citizen who may be arrested for minor offenses, such as violating a leash law or traffic code, and who pose no credible risk for SMUGGLING contraband into the jail." The majority dismissed the dissent's argument, noting that the dissent's "dramatic accounts" of the several individual stories were "misleading and ultimately irrelevant to the case.…"

City of Ontario v. Quon

The FOURTH AMENDMENT to the U.S. Constitution protects "[t]he right of the people to be secure in their persons, houses, papers, and effects, against unreasonable searches and seizures …" In a case garnering widespread attention from employers and employees alike,

as well as the media, a unanimous U.S. SUPREME COURT ruled that the Fourth Amendment did not protect the privacy of text messages that government employees sent to each other by employer-provided electronic paging devices. *City of Ontario, California v. Quon,* No. 08-1332, 560 U.S. ___ (2010). The case has far-reaching significance in an age of electronic communications and open workplaces.

Police Sergeant Jeff Quon was employed by the City of Ontario Police Department. In October 2001, the City acquired 20 alphanumeric pagers capable of sending and receiving text messages. It retained Arch Wireless ("Arch Wireless") Operating Company to provide wireless service for the pagers. Through the contract with Arch Wireless, each pager was allotted a limited number of text characters (25,000) sent or received each month. Usage in excess of that amount would result in additional fees imposed by Arch Wireless. Quon and other members of the police SWAT team were issued pagers to help them mobilize and respond to emergency situations.

Several months prior to the acquisition of the pagers, the City had announced a "Computer Usage, Internet and E-MAIL Policy" that applied to all employees. Among other things, the policy specified that the City "reserves the right to monitor and log all network activity including e-mail and Internet use, with or without notice. Users should have no expectation of privacy or confidentiality when using these resources." (On its face, the policy did not apply to text messaging sent on the pagers, because they were transmitted via independent, external wireless radio frequencies through equipment owned and operated by Arch Wireless.) In March 2000, Jeff Quon signed a statement acknowledging that he had read and understood this policy.

For several months running, Quon and others exceeded their monthly text character allotments and Arch Wireless imposed additional fees, which were passed on to the respective employees. The City's chief of police (Scharf) then attempted to determine whether the existing monthly limit on the number of characters was too low, potentially causing officers to pay fees for work-related messages, or, whether the overages were for personal messages. The City requested message transcripts from Arch Wireless, which provided transcripts of Quon's and another employee's August and September 2002 text messages. The review revealed that many of Quon's messages were not work-related and several were sexually explicit.

Scharf referred the matter to the Internal Affairs department. The investigating officer used Quon's work schedule for those months to redact (black out) from his transcript any messages he sent while off-duty. However, the transcript showed that very few of the messages he sent or received while on duty were related to police business. Quon was disciplined for violating police department rules.

Quon and three other police officers (and others who had exchanged text messages with Quon, including his wife and a department employee with whom Quon was romantically involved) filed suit against the City as well as Arch Wireless. They alleged violation of their Fourth Amendment constitutional rights that protected them against unreasonable searches. They also alleged that Arch Wireless had violated the Stored Communications Act (SCA) by providing transcripts to the City.

Both sides moved for **summary judgment**; the **district court** denied both. Citing *O'Connor v. Ortega*, 480 U.S. 709, 107 S. Ct. 1492, 94 L. Ed. 2d 714 (1987), the court ruled that Quon had a reasonable expectation of privacy in the content of his messages. Whether search of those messages was unreasonable, said the district court, turned on whether Scharf used it for the improper purpose of determining if Quon was using his pager to waste time, or for the legitimate purpose of determining the sufficiency of existing character limits to ensure that officers were not paying for work-related costs. At trial, a jury concluded that Scharf had a legitimate intent, and the court granted the City and Arch Wireless SUMMARY JUDGMENT on the ground that they did not violate the Fourth Amendment.

The U.S. Court of Appeals for the Ninth Circuit reversed. It agreed that Quon had a reasonable expectation of privacy in his text messages. But it concluded that the City's search of them was not reasonable, even though conducted on a legitimate, work-related rationale. The **appellate court** cited what it considered numerous alternative means that were less intrusive and could produce the same needed information. Finally, the **appellate** court concluded that Arch Wireless had violated the SCA by giving the City the transcripts.

Justice Kennedy delivered the opinion for a unanimous Supreme Court. The Court held that Fourth Amendment rights were not violated because the search of Quon's text messages was reasonable. The Amendment protects against arbitrary and invasive governmental acts, without regard to whether the government is investigating a crime or performing some other function.

With respect to the *O'Connor* case, a four-Justice **plurality** had devised a two-step analysis for determining violations. First, because some offices may be so open that no expectation of privacy is reasonable, a court must consider "[t]he operational realities of the workplace" to determine if constitutional rights are implicated. Second, where an employee has a legitimate privacy expectation, an intrusion on that expectation by an employer "for investigatory, work-related purposes, as well as for investigations of work-related misconduct, should be judged by the standard of reasonableness under all the circumstances." (Justice Scalia, in that case, concurred in the judgment but would have dispensed with the "operational realities" inquiry and would have held that government-employer searches to retrieve work-related materials or to investigate employee misconduct, regarded as reasonable and normal in private-sector employment, do not violate the Fourth Amendment.) Accordingly, in the present case, even assuming, *arguendo*, that Quon had a reasonable expectation of privacy in the text messages (not decided herein), the City and Scharf's search was reasonable under either of the *O'Connor* approaches. The Ninth Circuit's "least intrusive" means approach was inconsistent with controlling precedent, said the Court.

Justice Stevens filed a concurring opinion, although expressing reserve for the correctness in approach of the *O'Connor* plurality. Justice Scalia, concurring in part and concurring in the judgment, would eliminate the distinction between messages on public employees' employer-issued pagers and such messages, in general on employer-issued pages. He noted that this case did not require an answer to that threshold question.

FRANCHISE

A special privilege to do certain things that is conferred by government on an individual or a corporation and which does not belong to citizens generally of common right, e.g., a right granted to offer cable television service.

A privilege granted or sold, such as to use a name or to sell products or services. In its simplest terms, a franchise is a license from the owner of a trademark or trade name permitting another to sell a product or service under that name or mark. More broadly stated, a franchise has evolved into an elaborate agreement under which the franchisee undertakes to conduct a business or sell a product or service in accordance with methods and procedures prescribed by the franchisor, and the franchisor undertakes to assist the franchisee through advertising, promotion, and other advisory services.

Mac's Shell Service, Inc. v. Shell Oil Products Co. LLC

Tensions often exist between franchisees and franchisors over the terms of their franchise agreements. Franchisors usually hold the upper hand in such agreements and can make the economic future of franchisees difficult if key terms are changed during the course of the contract. In the retail petroleum industry, Congress addressed widespread concern over increasing numbers of allegedly unfair franchise terminations and nonrenewals by enacting the Petroleum Marketing Practices Act (PMPA) of 1978, 15 U.S.C. §§ 2801 et seq. The PMPA establishes minimum federal standards governing the termination and nonrenewal of petroleum franchises. A franchisor may "terminate" a "franchise" during the term stated in the franchise agreement and may "fail to renew" a "franchise relationship" at the conclusion of that term only if the franchisor provides written notice and takes the action in question for a reason specifically recognized in the **statute**. In 2001, a large group of Massachusetts franchisees of Shell Oil Company filed suit against Shell, arguing that they had been constructively terminated by the company when a volume-based rent subsidy was ended. The SUPREME COURT, in *Mac's Shell Service, Inc.v . Shell Oil Products Co. LLC*, __U.S.__, 130 S. Ct. 1251,176 L. Ed. 2d 36 (2009), ruled that a franchisee cannot recover for constructive termination under the MMPA if the franchisor's allegedly wrongful conduct did not compel the franchisee to abandon its franchise.

Under their franchise agreements with Shell, each franchisee was required to pay Shell monthly rent for use of the service-station premises. For many years, Shell offered the franchisees a rent subsidy that reduced the monthly rent by a set amount for every gallon of motor fuel a franchisee sold above a specified threshold. Shell renewed the subsidy annually through notices that "explicitly provided for cancellation [of the rent subsidy] with thirty days' notice." However, Shell representatives made oral representations to the franchisees that the subsidy or something similar to it would always exist.

The situation changed in 1998, when Shell joined two other petroleum companies to create Motiva Enterprises LLC. This **joint venture** combined the companies' petroleum-marketing operations in the eastern United States. Shell assigned to Motiva its rights and obligations under the franchise agreements. Motiva proceeded to make two major changes. In 2000 it ended the volume-based rent subsidy, which increased the franchisees' rent. Second, as each franchise agreement expired, the company offered the franchisees new agreements that contained a different formula for calculating rent. For some of the franchisees, the annual rent was greater under the new formula.

In July 2001, 63 franchisees filed a suit in federal district against Shell and Motiva, alleging that the discontinuation of the rent subsidy formula was a breach of contract under state law. In addition, the plaintiffs contended the companies had violated the PMPA by constructively terminating their rent subsidies and that Motiva's offer of new franchise agreements that used a different formula for calculating rent amounted to a "constructive nonrenewal" of their franchise relationships. A jury ruled in favor of the plaintiffs but the First **Circuit Court** of Appeals reversed in part and affirmed in part. It upheld the dealers' constructive termination claim, finding that a franchisee did not have to abandon the franchise to qualify for constructive termination under the PMPA. A simple breach of contract by a franchisor or its assignee was sufficient so long as the breach resulted in "such a material change that it effectively ended the lease, even though the [franchisee] continued to operate [its franchise]." The court reversed on the issue of constructive nonrenewal: a franchisee cannot maintain a claim for unlawful nonrenewal under the PMPA "where the franchisee has signed and operates under the renewal agreement complained of."

The Supreme Court, in a unanimous decision, reversed the First Circuit on the constructive termination issue and agreed with its ruling on constructive nonrenewal. Justice SAMUEL ALITO, writing for the Court, stated that text of the PMPA prohibits only that franchisor conduct that has the effect of ending a franchise. As to the word "terminate," Alito looked to the common meaning of the word: "put an end to." Giving the word its ordinary meaning, he concluded that the PMPA is violated only if an agreement for the use of a trademark, purchase of motor fuel, or lease of a premises is "put [to] an end" or "annul[ed] or destroy [ed]." Conduct that does not force an end to the franchise is not prohibited by the PMPA's plain terms. Requiring franchisees to abandon their franchises before claiming constructive termi- nation was also consistent with the general understanding of the doctrine of constructive termination. Alito noted that in EMPLOYMENT LAW, an employee may recover for constructive discharge only If he or she has quit the job. To allow franchisees to use constructive termina- tion without **abandonment** of the franchise would extend the reach of the PMPA beyond its text and structure. The same arguments held true for the constructive nonrenewal theory. Practical arguments also went against both theories. The Court believed the use of these theories would be "indeterminate and unwork- able." It would be difficult to know when a simple breach of contract triggered constructive termination and nonrenewal.

FRAUD

A false representation of a matter of fact—whether by words or by conduct, by false or misleading allegations, or by concealment of what should have been disclosed—that deceives and is intended to deceive another so that the individual will act upon it to her or his legal injury.

Parents of "Balloon Boy" Admit to Hoax

On October 15, 2009, the parents of a six-year- old boy reported that the child had climbed into a helium-filled balloon that had accidentally launched. The balloon soared to an altitude of about 7,000 feet, and authorities raced to try to find a way to bring the balloon down and keep the child safe. When the balloon finally landed, though, the boy was not aboard. After a further search, the boy was discovered hiding in a box

Richard Heene, father of the "balloon boy," January 2010.

AP IMAGES

in his parents' attic in Fort Collins, Colorado. Just days later, investigators said the entire ordeal was nothing but a hoax.

By most accounts, the child's father, Richard Heene, was eager for fame. He and his wife, Mayumi, first met at an acting school in California and had appeared on two episodes of the ABC show "Wife Swap." Richard Heene had pursued several other possible vehicles to star- dom. Prior to appearing on Wife Swap, he had reportedly developed a documentary about chasing tornadoes. He had also attempted to develop a show focusing on Heene's theories about the existence of UFOs and the possibility of life on Mars. He was in discussions at one point with the producers of Wife Swap to produce a show that focused solely on the Heenes. Mayumi Heene is a Japanese citizen, but Richard and the couple's three sons are U.S. citizens.

Richard Heene constructed a dome-shaped balloon that was about 20 feet in diameter. Observers said the balloon looked like a flying saucer commonly seen on old movies. The balloon was apparently tied down with cords and a tether in the family's backyard. The bottom of the balloon had a utility box made out of cardboard and plywood. The family took a video of the balloon's launch. In the video, Richard Heene can be seen inspecting the utility box before releasing the cord that held the balloon down. As the balloon floated into the air, Richard Heene became irate because he thought the balloon was still tethered to the ground. Heene later said that one of his older sons had seen six-year-old Falcon Heene climb into the utility box before the launch. Heene then contacted authorities.

The FEDERAL AVIATION ADMINISTRATION, the U.S. Air Force, and the Colorado NATIONAL GUARD soon became involved in an effort to bring the balloon down. Authorities searched the family's neighborhood in hopes that the boy might not have been in the balloon, but efforts to find the boy failed. The balloon remained in the air for two hours as it drifted south towards the Denver area. Authorities had confirmed with a physics professor that the balloon could have launched and remained airborne with the child inside, and these authorities sought frantically for ways to bring the balloon down. When the balloon finally landed about 12 miles from the Denver International Airport, though, the boy was not inside. Though the utility box had not been breached, authorities feared that the child might have fallen out at some point during the flight.

Search teams began frantic efforts to find the boy. Hours after the ordeal began, though, authorities found Falcon hiding in a box in his attic. He had never been in the balloon and said that he had gone to the attic because his father had yelled at him. The story continued to attract media attention, as Richard and Mayumi Heene appeared at news conferences with Falcon and the other two sons.

On the evening of October 15, the family appeared on the CNN show "Larry King Live," on which reporter Wolf Blitzer was serving as a guest host. During the course of the interview, Blitzer asked Richard whether Falcon had heard his parents calling for him when Falcon was in the attic. Richard turned to Falcon and asked the boy whether he had heard the calls, and the boy responded affirmatively. Richard then asked the boy, "why didn't you come out?" The boy responded, "You guys said that, um, we did this for the show." The parents disregarded the comment, but Blitzer later asked what the child meant by the comment. Richard Heene immediately became defensive, claiming that the boy was talking about the media in general. When Blitzer asked again, Richard said he was "appalled" by the suggestion that the family had made up the episode for publicity.

Investigators said publicly that they did not believe that the incident was a hoax, but within days of the balloon's launching, authorities announced that they planned to press charges against Richard and Mayumi Heene. According to investigators, the parents hatched a plan about Falcon being launched in a balloon to give the parents an opportunity to promote a potential reality television show. Costs for the rescue operation were estimated by some at nearly $2 million, and authorities wanted the family to reimburse the government for these rescue efforts. The sheriff of Larimer County in Colorado, Jim Alderden, announced on October 19 that he wanted to bring **felony** charges. At a news conference, Alderden said, "They put on a very good show for us, and we bought it."

Officers sought a warrant to search the Heene's home. In an AFFIDAVIT filed by the Larimer County Sheriff's Office, sheriff deputies testified that Mayumi Heene confessed to them that the couple made up the incident. The affidavit read, "Mayumi described that she and Richard Heene devised this hoax approximately two weeks earlier … She and Richard had instructed their three children to lie to authorities as well as the media regarding this hoax."

Richard and Mayumi both pleaded guilty to charges related to the incident. Richard agreed to plead guilty to one felony count for attempting to influence a public servant. Mayumi pleaded guilty to a **misdemeanor** charge, which was significant because a felony charge could have resulted in her DEPORTATION. Richard was sentenced to 90 days in jail, which he began serving in January 2010 and completed with in-home detention in April. Mayumi received a 20-day sentence, which she completed on work detail on weekends. The couple was also ordered to pay $36,000 in **restitution** and were prevented from receiving any profits from the hoax.

Former Partner at New Orleans Firm Sentenced to 15 Years for Fraud

James "Jamie" Perdigao for many years was the top billing partner in the elite New Orleans law firm of Adams and Reese. Behind the scenes, though, Perdigao was busy embezzling money. Over the course of many years, Perdigao stole nearly $30 million from his firm and several of the firm's clients. After PLEADING guilty to 30 counts on a variety of charges, a judge in

March 2009 sentenced him to 15 years, eight months in prison.

Perdigao is a native of New Orleans. He graduated with honors from both Tulane University and Tulane Law School. In 1987, he joined the firm of Adams and Reese as a first-year associate. At that time, the firm was known for its work in insurance defense, admiralty, and products liability. However, the firm's focus was about to change. Within seven years of Perdigao's arrival, the firm had expanded to include offices in Washington, D.C., Alabama, and Mississippi. One of the partner's in the firm, Charles "Chuck" Adams, Jr., brought in several major clients, including WorldCom, Inc.

During the early-1990s, the State of Louisiana approved a series of proposals that allowed for the operation of several forms of legal gambling. A major client of Adams and Reese decided to bid on a license that would allow the client to operate a riverboat casino. One of the firm's partners, Robert Vosbein, brought in Perdigao to help with the GAMING issues involving with the bid. At that time, Perdigao was a junior partner who was earning a reputation as a hard-worker and rising star within the firm. Even at that time, Perdigao typically exceeded his annual billing quota.

Perdigao quickly developed a reputation as an expert in gaming law. His list of clients included the likes of Pinnacle, Harrah's Entertainment, Inc., and Bally Gaming International, Inc. Thanks to the work for these clients, Perdigao became the firm's top billing partner for several years in a row. Although members of his firm said he was well-liked, he generally kept to himself and did not reveal information about his social life. In fact, despite earning a substantial salary as a law firm partner, he was known to wear rumpled suits, drive a beat-up car, and live in the same apartment where he had lived since law school.

In reality, Perdigao had begun to embezzle from the firm even as a young associate. Initially, he added time to otherwise legitimate bills. Later, he sent fake invoices to clients and included special return envelopes that he would collect personally from the firm's mail room. He typically deposited these checks into the firm's trust account and then had the firm cut checks to one of several **dummy** companies that Perdigao controlled. These bills were typically small—no more than $15,000—and the firm did not closely audit its trust account. Clients later said they did not notice the extra invoices because they did not seem out of the ordinary, given the amount of legitimate work that Perdigao did for these clients. For instance, Perdigao typically billed Pinnacle for about 1,000 hours of work each year, so the extra bills did not stand out to the company.

In late August 2004, neither Perdigao nor his secretary came to work one day. The accounting department at Boomtown Casino called to question a bill that Perdigao had recently submitted. A temporary employee routed the call to the law firm's accounting department, which could not find the bill or any related documentation. Moreover, time for lawyers other than Perdigao appeared on the bill, but those lawyers would not verify that they had worked on the file. The firm discovered that the invoices sent from Perdigao to several clients looked different from the standard invoices issued by the firm.

Just before Labor Day that year, the firm put Perdigao on mandatory leave and told him not to return to the office pending an investigation. Nevertheless, during the weekend after Perdigao was placed on leave, security cameras caught Perdigao removing about 60 boxes worth of files from the firm. Just a few days later, Perdigao faxed his resignation from the firm and admitted that he had been misappropriating funds. Investigators initially believed that Perdigao took about $1 million, but in meetings between the firm and Perdigao's lawyer, Perdigao agreed to return $9 million. While this negotiation was taking place, though, Perdigao had transferred an additional $19 million to an account in Zurich. Federal authorities arrested Perdigao on October 16, 2004, and agents found about $25,000 in cash and two cashier's checks worth $1.2 million in his car. Prosecutors charged Perdigao with stealing nearly $30 million from the firm and the firm's clients.

For the next four years, Perdigao engaged in an battle with the firm and federal investigators. In 2008, Perdigao filed a 73-page federal RACKETEERING complaint making a number of claims deemed "sensational" by most accounts. Perdigao tried to paint himself as an ethical, hard-working lawyer in a firm that put pressure on him to bend the ethical rules to make more money. Perdigao's case fell apart, however, when authorities discovered that he had hacked into the law firm's computer system. According to authorities, Perdigao had used two of the firm's laptop computers to hack into the computer's network to steal information about his case and to create a false paper trail suggesting that the firm had authorized his **fraudulent** billing practices. After this discovery, U.S. District Judge Eldon Fallon revoked Perdigao's $2 million bond. After having resisted previous plea bargains, Perdigao agreed to plead guilty to 30 counts on a 61-count INDICTMENT.

Several family members and friends asked Fallon for leniency in sentencing Perdigao. According to those who supported Perdigao, he was deeply affected by his parents' DIVORCE while he was a teenager, and he was convinced that he would end up penniless. In a letter to Fallon, Perdigao wrote, "I am not sure what is wrong with my judgment and decision-making process, but it relates somehow to the fact that I don't have much balance in my life. My life was my work. On most nights for many years, I left the office after the night cleaning crew. I never bought a house, never married, never had children." Fallon, however, showed little compassion for Perdigao. At sentencing, Fallon said, "Every Wednesday, I see defendants with no education, no job, no family. You don't fall into that category." In March 2009, Fallon sentenced Perdigao to 15 years, eight months in prison with no possibility of PAROLE.

In an unusual twist the story, Perdigao did not spend the $30 million he had embezzled, and he was able to make full **restitution** to the victims. This puzzled observers, who questioned what motive Perdigao might have had to steal the money if he did not plan to spend it.

Weyhrauch v. United States

In *Weyhrauch v. United States,* No. 08-1196, 561 U.S. ___ (2010),the U.S. Supreme Court vacated the judgment of the Ninth Circuit Court of Appeals and remanded for further consideration in light of another case it had just decided, *Skilling v. United States,* No. 08-1394, 561 U.S. ___ (2010). Both cases involved convictions for the fraudulent deprivation of the "intangible right of honest-services" pursuant to 18 U.S.C. §1346 (see below).

Bruce Weyhrauch was formerly a member of the Alaska House of Representatives. While serving in that capacity (2006), Weyhrauch and other state representatives were working on state tax legislation directly affecting oil production. A subsequent criminal indictment alleged that during this pending legislation, Weyhrauch had been in regular contact with two oil company executives from VECO Corporation, an oil field services company directly impacted by the pending legislation. Although it was not alleged that Weyhrauch took any explicit bribes from VECO, the indictment alleged that Weyhrauch "took actions that were favorable to VECO" in return for an understanding that VECO would employ Weyhrauch after he completed his term in government office.

The government subsequently charged Weyrauch with "honest-services" fraud pursuant to 18 U.S.C. §1346. The criminal complaint alleged that his dealings with VECO deprived the citizens of Alaska of their "intangible right" to his honest service as a government official. The operative language here is derived from the statute, which provides that such intangible rights are violated where a government official or fiduciary performs his or her duties in a manner involving "deceit, self-dealing, bias, or concealment."

Prior to trial, the government sought to introduce evidence that Weyhrauch knowingly concealed a conflict of interest stemming from his dealings with VECO; such conduct, argued the government, supported a violation of §1346. The parties disagreed as to whether Weyhrauch had an affirmative duty to disclose the conflict of interest. Weyhrauch argued that he could not be criminally accountable for conduct that fell within the bounds of ethical rules governing the state body in which he served.

The U.S. District Court for the District of Alaska, acknowledged that the Ninth Circuit Court of Appeals, under which jurisdiction it fell, had no precedent in this matter. The district court further acknowledged a split among other circuit courts of appeals. It decided to adopt the approach taken by the Fifth Circuit, holding that "any duty to disclose sufficient to support the mail and wire fraud charges here must be a duty imposed by state law." Accordingly, concluded the district court, since no law in Alaska required Weyhrauch to disclose his negotiations for future employment with VECO, a company directly affected by pending legislation, the court would deny the government's motion to admit evidence of Weyhrauch's concealing of this conflict of interest to support a §1346 violation. The government then petitioned for an interlocutory appeal on the evidentiary ruling to the Ninth Circuit Court of Appeals. The Ninth Circuit reversed the district court's decision, holding that §1346 "establishes a uniform standard for 'honest services' that governs every public official and that the government does not need to prove an independent violation of state law to sustain an honest services fraud conviction." *United States v. Weyhrauch*, 548 F.3d 1237 (9th Circuit 2009). Weyhrauch then petitioned the Supreme Court for review.

In vacating the judgment of the Ninth Circuit and remanding for further consideration under the newly-decided *Skilling v. United States* case, the Supreme Court directed the Ninth Circuit to consider Weyhrauch's facts in light of its ruling in *Skilling*. In that case,as to the "honest-services" fraud charges, the Court had outlined the history of the doctrine, distinguishing this type of fraud from traditional fraud in which a defendant is enriched, to the detriment of a victim. The honest-services doctrine targets corruption without the above symmetry; instead, a defendant profits not from a betrayed victim, but from a third party, who had not been deceived, who provides the enrichment to defendant. By 1982, all courts of appeals had embraced the honest-services theory of fraud, sometimes referred to in their cases as the "intangible-rights doctrine." But in 1987, the Supreme Court, in *McNally v. United States*, 483 U.S. 350, restricted the application to cases "limited in scope to the protection of property rights." Congress responded in 1988 by enacting §1346, which provides, in relevant part, "For the purposes of the[e] chapter of the U.S. Code that prohibits, inter alia, mail fraud, §1341, and wire fraud, §1343, the term 'scheme or artifice to defraud' includes a scheme or artifice to deprive another of the intangible right of honest services."

Now, in the newly-decided *Skilling* case, the Court held that the statute was not unconstitutionally vague, as Skilling had argued. The Court noted that all the courts of appeals had been divided on how best to interpret the statute, but all had declined to invalidate it as irremediably vague. The Court agreed that §1346 needed to be construed (judicially), not invalidated.

Accordingly, the Court held that §1346, proscribing fraudulent deprivations of "the intangible right of honest services," was properly limited to cover only bribery and kickback schemes. The Ninth Circuit now needed to apply this holding to the facts in *Weyhrauch*..

FREEDOM OF RELIGION

Michigan Supreme Court Allows Trial Judges to Ban Religious Head Scarves in Court

When two constitutional principles are at odds, a court must decide which one should be given deference. Such was the case in Michigan, where a woman who wore a head scarf that covered most of her face had her case dismissed because she would not remove it in court. She contended that wearing her head covering was mandated by her Islamic religious beliefs and thus the ban violated her freedom of religion. Countering this constitutional right was the Sixth Amendment's Confrontation Clause, which requires witnesses to testify in **open court**. That right, plus rules of evidence, militated against allowing someone to cover their face. Witness demeanor and credibility might not be accurately assessed if a person can cover most of her face. The Michigan SUPREME COURT took the issue under consideration as a matter of court administration and in August 2009 issued an amendment to a rule of evidence that gives trial judges the discretion to ban religious head scarves. Dissenting members contended that no one should be prevented from testifying on the basis of clothing worn on the basis of a sincerely held religious belief.

The issue arose in small claims action in Michigan **district court**. The PLAINTIFF, Ginah Muhammad, wore a niqab, a garment that covered her entire face, except for a slit for her eyes. As Muhammad was preparing to testify, the judge asked her to remove her niqab. He stated that "One of the things I need to do as I am listening to testimony is I need to see your face and I need to see what's going on and unless you take [niqab] off, I can't see your face and I can't tell whether you're telling me the truth or not and I can't see certain things about your demeanor and temperament that I need to see in a court of law." Muhammad replied that she was a practicing Muslim and that "this is my way of life and I believe in Koran and God is first in my life. I don't have a problem taking my veil off if it's a female judge." She requested a female judge and said she would not follow the judge's order otherwise. The judge said no female judge was available and suggested that the veil was a "custom thing" rather than a "religious thing." Muhammad strongly objected to that characterization. The judge gave Muhammad a choice between removing the veil and having the case dismissed. She chose not to remove her veil and the case was dismissed the case **without prejudice**. Muhammad then filed a federal CIVIL RIGHTS against the judge in federal district court, alleging a violation of her right of free exercise of religion under the FIRST AMENDMENT and her civil right to access to the courts.

The Michigan Supreme Court proposed an amendment to the Michigan Rules of Evidence and solicited comment from the bench and bar. It also held a public hearing on the matter. On August 25, 2009, the court promulgated the amendment to Rule 611, Mode and Order of Interrogation and Presentation. A new section was added entitled "Appearance of Parties and Witnesses." The section states that "The court shall exercise reasonable control over the appearance of parties and witnesses so as to (1) ensure that the demeanor of such persons may be observed and assessed by the factfinder and (2) ensure the accurate identification of such persons."

The majority of the court believed the amendment was "consistent with the historical importance in our legal system of the trier of fact's assessment of a witness's demeanor and with the constitutional right of a criminal DEFENDANT to confront his accusers face to face." The court noted that a number of U.S. Supreme Court cases had made clear that in criminal cases, defendants had a right to confront witnesses in the courtroom. In one case the trial court permitted two child witnesses against defendant to testify behind a screen that prevented them from seeing the defendant. This violated the Sixth Amendment's Confrontation Clause. In a Texas case, the criminal court of appeals ruled that a witness could not testify while wearing sunglasses, a baseball cap, and a jacked with an upturned collar. The witness was afraid of the defendant and sought to disguise his appearance. The appeals court stated that the observation of the witnesses' demeanor was impaired by his disguise.

The majority also pointed out that some scholars believe that Islamic law accommodates exceptions to the practice of veiling because of "necessity." One of the exceptions is giving testimony. However, two dissenting judges concluded that the rule as promulgated violated a person's freedom of religion. They suggested that one more sentence be added to the new clause: "Provided, however, that no person shall be precluded from testifying on the basis of clothing worn because of a sincerely held religious belief." The two constitutional rights at issue were both fundamental but there were less obtrusive ways to protect people like Muhammad. The case could have been reassigned to a female judge or the male judge could have made a credibility assessment without requiring the removal of the niqab. The dissenters pointed out that court allow the participation of blind jurors and blind judges, so seeing the face of the witness is not mandatory.

GOVERNMENTAL IMMUNITY

Army Corps of Engineers Liable for Hurricane Katrina Levee Failures

In November 2009, U.S. District Court Judge Stanwood Duval, Jr., sitting for the Eastern District of Louisiana, ruled that the U.S. Army Corps Of Engineers, and therefore the U.S. Government, was liable for substantial damages caused when Hurricane Katrina hit the shore of Louisiana and Alabama on August 29, 2005. The finding of liability attached to the Army Corps' "gross" negligence and "myopic" maintenance of the Mississippi River Gulf Outlet (MRGO) shipping channel in the area, leading to failure of the constructed levees intended to hold back floodwaters. The landmark 158-page ruling awarded $719,000 to four plaintiffs from New Orleans' Lower Ninth Ward and neighboring St. Bernard Parish.

Most significantly, being the only such liability suit to actually reach a courtroom, the decision in this case opened the door for thousands more such claims. The district court had refused all lawsuits against the Army Corps for its design of New Orleans' failed levees (part of a storm protection system) because of governmental sovereign immunity. Accordingly, without any court judgments finding liability, the prior Bush administration had refused to negotiate settlements. But Judge Duval allowed this particular case to go forward

because the MRGO was a navigational canal, not part of a storm protection system. The plaintiffs had argued that immunity did not apply to activities regarding the MRGO shipping channel because these "were in direct contravention of professional engineering and safety standards," Judge Duval wrote. ". . . Ignoring safety and poor engineering are not policy [where immunity would attach], and clearly the Corps engaged in such activities."

The six plaintiffs who brought this case all had properties allegedly affected by the MRGO. The judge ruled against one couple, who lived in New Orleans East, but awarded damages ranging from $100,000 to $317,000 to the other plaintiffs, whose properties were in the Lower Ninth Ward and St. Bernard Parish. Under the precedent set by Judge Duval's ruling, thousands more homes and businesses could be entitled to compensation.

The 76-mile long MRGO was built in 1965 as a shortcut from New Orleans to the Gulf of Mexico. During testimony at trial, veteran Louisiana geologist Sherwood Gagliano, a former Corps consultant, testified that the Corps had failed to stop the natural erosion, causing widening of the canal. This, he opined, caused it to eventually bump against (abut) the shore of Lake Borgne on the city's east side. During the hurricane, that failure allowed waves on Lake Borgne to enter the MRGO and travel into the east side of the city. The waves then

battered the storm-protection-designed levees with a level of force against which they were not designed too withstand.

As trial commenced, Judge Duval asked, "You all know what this is about: … What did the Corps know, when did it know it, and when should it have known?" At the end of the trial, his ruling declared, "It is the court's opinion that the negligence of the Corps, in this instance by failing to maintain the MRGO properly, was not policy, but insouciance, myopia, and shortsightedness." (He was referring to the government's defense of sovereign immunity attaching to any federal flood policy decisions.)

In noting that "gross negligence" overrides any claim of immunity, Judge Duvall said the Army Corps was tasked with the protection of life and property. And yet, he continued,

> For over 40 years, the Corps was aware that the Reach II levee protecting Chalmette and the Lower Ninth Ward was going to be compromised by the continued deterioration of the MRGO … The Corps had an opportunity to take a myriad of actions to alleviate this deterioration or rehabilitate this deterioration [such as buttressing the banks with rocks] and failed to do so. Clearly, the expression "talk is cheap" applies here.
>
> … Furthermore, the Corps not only knew, but admitted in 1988, that the MRGO

threatened human life … and yet it did not act in time to prevent the catastrophic disaster that ensued with the onslaught of Hurricane Katrina … The Corps' negligence resulted in the wasting of millions of dollars in flood protection measures and billions of dollars in Congressional outlays to help this region recover from such a catastrophe.

Judge Duvall found that the Army Corps was *not* negligent with respect to its failure to construct a surge protection barrier at the "funnel" where Reach II merged with Reach I and, therefore, was not liable for the flooding of New Orleans East. However, it expressly found that the Corps was not entitled to immunity under §702c of the Flood Control Act of 1928 and was not entitled to the protection of the "due care," "discretionary function," or "misrepresentation" exceptions under the Federal Torts Claim Act.

For its part, in addition to the defense of immunity, the government had maintained that Hurricane Katrina was "an act of God" and argued that its magnitude alone caused the flooding of New Orleans (resulting in hundreds of deaths of residents and an estimated $81 billion in damage across a 90,000-square-mile area in the geographic region). It argued that Katrina was such a massive force that no remedial action on the part of the Corps would have prevented the flooding.

At its Web site (www.mvn.usace.army.mil/oc/katrina_claims), the Army Corps stated that it had received more than 490,000 claim forms seeking recovery from the United States for hurricane storm related damages. It further advised that received forms had been scanned into an electronic database, and acknowledged via correspondence to the claimant(s). However, it further advised, "Until such time as the litigation is completed, including any appellate process, no activity is expected to be taken on any of these claims."

HABEAS CORPUS

[Latin, You have the body.] *A writ (court order) that commands an individual or a government official who has restrained another to produce the prisoner at a designated time and place so that the court can determine the legality of custody and decide whether to order the prisoner's release.*

Beard v. Kindler

The SUPREME COURT has developed a number of doctrines that limit the ability of prisoners to seek federal **habeas corpus** relief. Under the "adequate state ground" doctrine, a federal habeas court will not review a claim rejected by a state court if the decision of the state court rests on a state law ground that is independent of a federal right or law and is adequate to support the judgment. The Court was called on to clarify this doctrine when the lower **federal courts** granted an inmate a habeas petition because the state procedural rule in question was discretionary. In *Beard v. Kindler*, __U.S.__, 130 S. Ct. 612, __L. Ed. 2d__ (2009), the Court rejected such a limitation and concluded that to do otherwise would lead to mandatory rules by states so as to prevent federal review.

In 1982, Joseph Kindler was arrested with Scott Shaw and David Bernstein for **burglary** in Bucks County, Pennsylvania and released on bail. When he found out that Bernstein had agreed to testify against him, Kindler and Shaw savagely beat and drowned him. He was convicted of MURDER and sentenced to death in September 1984. While motions were still pending about the trial and death sentence, Kindler escaped from the maximum-security prison. He fled to Canada, where he was arrested in April 1985 for BURGLARY offenses in Quebec. The Canadian government refused to extradite Kindler because under the treaty with the U.S. it could deny EXTRADITION if the person could face execution. However, the U.S. eventually convinced Canadian authorities to return Kindler. He again frustrated this plan by escaping from his 13th floor cell and rappelling down the building with 13 stories worth of bed sheets tied together. He remained on the loose until September 1988, when he was again arrested by Canadian authorities. He fought extradition in the Canadian courts for three years but was ultimately extradited to Pennsylvania in 1991.

The judge handling Kindler's murder trial had dismissed Kindler's motions in 1984 because of his original escape. In 1991 Kindler sought to reinstate the motions but the court dismissed them and imposed the death sentence. The Pennsylvania Supreme Court upheld the verdict, the death sentence, and the denial of Kindler's post-trial motions. It noted that under the state's fugitive **forfeiture** law, the trial court had the discretion to deny such motions because of Kindler's flouting of authority. Kindler was unsuccessful with a state post-conviction appeal on the same issue and then filed for federal habeas relief. The federal **district court** granted his petition because the state fugitive FORFEITURE rule did not apply and the jury instructions were unconstitutional. The Third **Circuit Court** of Appeals upheld these rulings, stating that fugitive forfeiture rule, because it was discretionary, did not preclude a federal court from ruling on habeas relief.

The Supreme Court, in a unanimous decision (Justice SAMUEL ALITO did not participate in the case), overturned the Third Circuit ruling. Chief Justice JOHN ROBERTS, writing for the Court, stated that for a state rule to be an adequate state ground it had to be "firmly established and regularly followed." This did not mean the rule had to be mandatory, for a discretionary rule could be both "firmly established" and "regularly followed" even if "the appropriate exercise of discretion may permit consideration of a federal claim in some cases but not others." Roberts concluded that to rule otherwise would pose a dilemma for states. They could either "preserve flexibility by granting courts discretion to excuse procedural errors, but only at the cost of undermining the finality of state court judgments. Or States could preserve the finality of their judgments by withholding such discretion, but only at the cost of precluding any flexibility in applying the rules."

The Court noted that states would choose mandatory rules to preserve the "adequate state ground" protection against costly federal habeas review. This would not wise because in some cases discretionary rules are often desirable. Specifically, criminal defendants could lose the opportunity to argue that a "procedural default should be excused through the exercise of judicial discretion." Both federal and STATE COURTS grant the trial judge great discretion. To disregard FEDERALISM and **comity** and remove discretionary rules from the adequate state ground doctrine would be "particularly strange" when similar rules are in effect in the federal courts and in nearly every state. However, the Court made clear that its holding was limited to rejecting the discretionary rules as automatically inadequate under the state ground doctrine. It rejected Pennsylvania's claim as well that all discretionary rules are automatically adequate.

Holland v. Florida

Albert Holland was convicted in 1997 of first-degree MURDER in a Florida state court and was sentenced to death. The Florida SUPREME COURT affirmed the judgment in 2000. Under the Antiterrorism and Effective Death Penalty Act of 1996 (AEDPA), 28 U.S.C. §2244(d), as to post-conviction relief, "[a] 1-year period of limitation shall apply to an application for a **writ** of **habeas corpus** by a person in CUSTODY pursuant to the judgment of a State court." AEDPA further states that "[t]he time during which a properly filed application for State post-conviction ... review" is pending "shall not be counted" against the one-year period. In *Holland v. Florida,* No. 09-5327, 560 U.S. ___ (2010), the U.S. Supreme Court held that "gross negligence" on the part of state-appointed defense counsel provided a basis for tolling that one-year period, in a case where the federal habeas petition was filed late despite repeated instructions from the client (Holland). In other words, the Court ruled that the timeliness provision in the **statute** was subject to equitable tolling in this case. In so holding, the Court reversed the decision of the Eleventh **Circuit Court** of Appeals.

The scheme of interplay between state and federal review is complex. On the date that the U.S. Supreme Court denied direct review of Holland's conviction (534 U.S. 834), October 1, 2001, the AEDPA's one-year period began to run. As the statute further indicates, that time period is tolled during periods of pending state *post-conviction* relief. In November 2001, the state appointed attorney Bradley Collins to represent Holland in all state and federal post-conviction proceedings. But Collins did not file a motion for post-conviction relief until almost ten months later, on September 19, 2002. Even though that filing "stopped the clock" temporarily under AEDPA, it was just 12 days before its one-year limitation period would expire.

Holland's state petition remained pending in STATE COURTS for the next three years. During this time, Holland wrote letters to Collins, asking him to make certain that all his claims would be preserved for any subsequent federal habeas review. Collins wrote back, assuring him that counsel was well aware of state time limitations and federal exhaustion requirements, also telling Holland that if his motion for post-conviction relief was denied, "your state HABEAS CORPUS claims will then be ripe for presentation in a petition for writ of habeas CORPUS in federal court. "

In May 2003, a state court denied relief to Holland; nearly two years later, in February 2005, the Florida Supreme Court heard oral arguments in his case. But by now, his relationship with Collins had deteriorated to the point that he asked the state supreme court to remove Collins from the case. He expressly complained about Collin's failure to communicate with him about the status of his case, and that he had not seen or spoken to Collins since April 2003. He told the court that he had "no idea what is going on with [my] capital case on appeal." The state responded that Holland could not file any *pro se* papers while represented by counsel, including papers seeking new counsel. The Florida Supreme Court agreed and denied Holland's requests. Holland also filed a complaint with the Florida Bar Association, but the complaint was denied.

Collins did argue Holland's appeal before the Florida Supreme Court on February 10, 2005. Holland wrote another letter to Collins, emphasizing the importance of filing a timely habeas corpus in federal court, once the Florida Supreme Court issued its decision. Collins did not reply. Holland wrote two more letters, unanswered. In November 2005, the Florida Supreme Court affirmed the lower court's denial of state habeas relief to Holland. On December 1, 2005, the court issued its mandate, making the decision final. At that point, the AEDPA federal habeas clock resumed ticking, and Holland had but twelve days left. He did not know that his case had been decided.

In January 2006, four weeks after the AEDPA time limit expired, Holland, still unaware that the Florida Supreme Court had ruled in his case, again wrote to Collins, asking for a status of the case. Nine days later, while working in the prison library, he learned that the Florida Supreme Court had decided his case, with a mandate issued, five weeks earlier. He immediately prepared his own *pro se* papers for federal habeas corpus and mailed them to the Federal **District Court** for the Southern District of Florida the next day. In the petition, he advised the court that his appointed counsel had failed to file a timely petition oh his behalf. He also filed a second complaint against Collins with the state bar association.

Collins finally responded in January 2006, advising Holland that the AEDPA time limitation had actually expired before he had even been appointed as counsel to represent Holland. Collins erroneously advised Holland that the clock started ticking on October 5, 2000 when the Florida Supreme Court denied his relief. (Collins was appointed to the case on November 7, 2001.)

In sum, defense counsel was wrong, Holland was right. With legal time expired, Holland's only hope was equitable relief. But the district court refused to toll the AEDPA limitations period for equitable reasons, holding that Holland had not demonstrated due diligence necessary to invoke equitable tolling. The Eleventh Circuit Court of Appeals affirmed. It held that attorney unprofessional conduct, even if it constituted **gross negligence**, did not justify equitable tolling unless there was proof of **bad faith**, dishonesty, **fraud**, mental impairment, etc.

Justice Breyer delivered the 7-2 decision of the U.S. Supreme Court. First, the Court confirmed that the AEDPA **statute of limitations** was indeed subject to equitable tolling. Next, it concluded that the Eleventh Circuit had been "too rigid" in its standard for relief. Instead, the Court noted its own precedent for equitable tolling, *Pace v. DiGuglielmo,* 544 U.S. 408, 418. According to the Supreme Court, a petitioner was entitled to equitable tolling if he could show (1) that he pursued his rights diligently, and (2)some extraordinary circumstances stood in his way. The Court further noted that, while Holland's case may well represent such "extraordinary circumstances," the district court had rejected equitable relief on a lack of diligence. Therefore, a remand to the Eleventh Circuit was necessary to see if such tolling were appropriate or whether an evidentiary hearing and/or other proceedings might indicate that the state should prevail.

Justices Scalia and Thomas dissented. In the view of Justice Scalia, AEDPA's §2244(d) "leaves no room for equitable exceptions, and Holland could not qualify even if it did."

Wood v. Allen

Persons sentenced to death in STATE COURTS may seek a **writ** of **habeas corpus** in federal **district court**, but the federal **statute** granting habeas relief has a number of provisions that make it difficult to obtain. Some of these provisions have appeared at odds with each other, leading to different court decisions. The SUPREME COURT, in *Wood v. Allen*, __U.S.__, 130 S. Ct. 841 , __ L. Ed. 2d__ (2009), declined to reconcile two such provisions by issuing a definitive answer. Instead, the Court used one of the provisions to settle the case before it and left for another day the opportunity to clarify the law.

In 1993, Holly Wood broke into the home of his former girlfriend and shot her in the head and face as she lay in bed. The victim died and Wood was charged with capital MURDER during a first-degree **burglary**. He had three court-appointed lawyers, two of whom had significant trial experience. The third lawyer, Kenneth Trotter, had been admitted to the bar just five months before the trial. After a jury convicted Wood of murder, Trotter was put in charge of the penalty phase. The jury recommended the death penalty on a 10-2 vote and at a separate sentencing hearing the judge imposed the death penalty. Wood's direct appeals to the Alabama **appellate** courts were unsuccessful.

Wood petitioned for state postconviction relief under Alabama Rule of **Criminal Procedure** 32. At his Rule 32 hearing, Wood claimed he was mentally retarded and not eligible for the death penalty, and that Trotter had provided ineffective assistance **of counsel** in violation of the SIXTH AMENDMENT because he had failed to investigate and present evidence of his mental disabilities during the penalty phase of the trial. The state district court concluded that as to Wood's mental retardation claims that he "probably does exhibit significantly subaverage general intellectual functioning," he had failed to show "that he has significant or substantial deficits in his adaptive functioning." The court also denied the ineffective counsel claim because the defense team had made a strategic decision not to pursue evidence of his alleged mental retardation. A doctor had evaluated Wood and his report but the defense had made a strategic decision not to introduce it because it was not in the best interest of Wood's.

Having exhausted his state law remedies, Wood filed a petition for habeas relief in federal district court under 28 U.S.C. §2254(d)(2). This provision states that a federal court may grant a state prisoner habeas relief if his claim was adjudicated on the merits in state court and

"resulted in a decision based on an unreasonable determination of the facts in light of the evidence presented in the State court proceeding." Under §2254(e)(1), "a determination of a factual issue made by a State court [is] presumed to be correct," and the petitioner has "the burden of rebutting the presumption of correctness by clear and convincing evidence." The district court denied all but the ineffective-assistance-of-counsel claim, ruling that the state court's finding that counsel made a strategic decision was an unreasonable determination of the facts. The court further held that Trotter's performance was deficient and had prejudiced Wood. The Eleventh Circuit reversed the district court decision. It ruled that the state court's rejection of Wood's ineffective-assistance claim was neither an unreasonable application of clearly established law nor based on an unreasonable determination of the facts. It also found that the evidence in the Rule 32 hearings supported the state court's strategic-decision finding.

The Supreme Court accepted Wood's petition for **certiorari** as a means to answer whether the state court's strategic-decision determination was reasonable. More importantly, the Court addressed the grounds under which the petition may obtain relief under § 2254(d)(2). One argument is that the petitioner only had to establish that the state-court factual determination on which the decision was based was "unreasonable." The competing argument was that § 2254(e)(1) additionally required a petitioner to rebut a presumption that the determination was correct with clear and convincing evidence. The Court, in a 7-2 decision, declined to answer the latter questions, ruling simply that the state court determination was not unreasonable.

Justice SONIA SOTOMAYOR, writing for the majority, concluded that the state court's factual determination was reasonable even under Wood's reading of §2254(d)(2), so there was no need to explore its relationship with §2254 (e)(1). Having reviewed the evidence, Sotomayor stated that it was not unreasonable to conclude that, after reviewing the doctor's report, Wood's lawyers "made a strategic decision not to inquire further into the information contained in the report about Wood's mental deficiencies and not to present to the jury such information as counsel already possessed about these deficiencies."

Justice JOHN PAUL STEVENS, in a dissenting opinion joined by ANTHONY KENNEDY, argued that there was a "world of difference between a decision not to introduce evidence at the guilt phase of a trial and a failure to investigate mitigating evidence that might be admissible at the penalty phase." He contended that Wood's legal team had declined to investigate "powerful mitigating evidence of Wood's mental deficits for the penalty phrase." This inattention and neglect was enough to demonstrate ineffective assistance OF COUNSEL.

HEALTH CARE

Congress Passes Historic Health Care Reform Law

After months of fierce debating, Congress in March 2010 passed the Patient Protection and Affordable Care Act, which is designed to guarantee medical insurance to a large percentage of Americans who do not have insurance policies. Members of both major parties clashed during the debate, and no Republican member of Congress approved the final bill. Democrats, on the other hand, hailed passage as a major victory, especially for President BARACK OBAMA.

Efforts by the DEMOCRATIC PARTY to ensure universal health care in the United States have been ongoing for several decades. When President BILL CLINTON was elected to office in 1993, one of his most significant goals was to guarantee universal health care coverage by relying on competition between private insurers along with government regulations. However, Clinton was unable to build sufficient support among Democrats to defeat opposition by Republicans. During his eight years in office, Clinton never came close to achieving his goal of health care reform, which was not a priority of his successor, GEORGE W. BUSH.

The health care debate continued in 2008, when Obama and fellow Democratic hopeful HILLARY CLINTON used health care reform as major parts of their platforms. After winning the Democratic primary, Obama promised that health care reform would be one of his top priorities as president. His principal goals included controlling the escalating costs of health care, addressing certain abusive practices of insurance companies, and expanding

insurance coverage to millions without it. Obama vowed at one point to complete health care reform by the end of 2009. However, throughout the spring and summer of 2009, reform plans caused controversy. Obama's initial proposals called for the creation a government-run insurance program to compete with private insurance companies. Many conservatives and industry leaders sharply criticized the so-called "public option," which some decried as a form of SOCIALISM. In an address to Congress in September 2009, though, Obama asked legislators to take quick action on the health care legislation.

By November 2009, House Democrats were on the brink of passing their version of the legislation. In the days before the final vote, the House Democratic leaders had to make several concessions to other Democrats who opposed insurance coverage for abortions. Proponents said that the bill would ensure coverage to 36 million uninsured Americans. To accomplish this goal, the House bill included a public option. On November 7, 2009, the House approved the legislation by a vote of 220-215, with 39 Democrats voting against and only one Republican voting in favor. Democrats cheered the victory, with Representative George Miller (D.-Cal.) proclaiming, "This is our moment to revolutionize health care in this country."

After the House's action, attention turned to the SENATE. Democrats at that time held a 60-seat "super-majority," which would allow the Democrats to overcome a Republican **filibuster** that could have stalled the Senate bill's passage.

House Speaker Nancy Pelosi discusses health care reform, April 2010.

AP IMAGES

In December, the Senate considered its own bill, which was similar to the House counterpart but which contained some key differences. The biggest difference between the two was the absence of a public option in the Senate bill. The Senate and House also differed in terms of funding for the proposals. The Senate met on Christmas Eve for the first time since 1895, and VICE PRESIDENT Joseph R. Biden, Jr. presided over the final roll call. As was the case with the House bill, voting was entirely partisan, as no Republican voted in favor of the bill. However, the Democrats managed to pass the bill by a 60 to 39 margin.

In January 2010, voters in Massachusetts surprisingly elected Republican Scott Brown to replace long-time Senator EDWARD KENNEDY, who died of brain cancer in August 2009. Brown's win meant that the Senate Democrats lost their super-majority, which many believed could hurt chances for the Democrats to complete the process of passing the proposed legislation. Democrats decided not to proceed with a plan that would merge the House and Senate bills into one. Obama in February 2010 organized a bipartisan summit where he unveiled his own health care proposal, which relied heavily on the Senate bill. Commentators suggested that the health care reform effort could be doomed.

Obama continued to push strongly for passage of the bill, and he and other Democratic Congressional leaders held numerous meetings to gain support. By March 2010, Obama promised that he would issue an EXECUTIVE ORDER that would prohibit use of federal funds to support ABORTION services, which helped to gain support from pro-life Democrats in the House. These final actions led the House on March 21, 2010 to approve the Senate bill. Two days later, Obama signed the Patient Protection and Affordable Care Act, Pub. L. No. 111-148. About a week later, both chambers approved the Health Care and Education Reconciliation Act of 2010, Pub. L. No. 111-152, which made a number of fixes to the bills resulting from the compromise that took place during the several months prior to passage of the Patient Protection and Affordable Care Act.

One of the main features of the new legislation is the expansion of coverage to 32 uninsured Americans. Those who are uninsured or self-employed will be able to purchase insurance through state-based insurance exchanges, and the legislation established subsidies for those who make between 133 and 400 percent of the poverty level, which in 2010 was $22,050 for a family of four. Within one year of passage, the federal government would assist states with funding to establish these exchanges, and this funding would be available until 2015. By 2014, separate exchanges would be available for small businesses to purchase coverage. The year 2014 is also significant because by this year, all individuals must purchase health insurance or be subject to a fine. However, illegal immigrants will not be able to pay for health insurance in the new exchanges.

The legislation makes significant reforms to the insurance industry. Within six months of the bill's passage, insurance companies could not deny children coverage due to preexisting conditions. This protection will be extended to all Americans by 2014. Moreover, insurance companies will be required to allow parents to keep their children on the parents' insurance plans until the children turn 26.

The cost of the legislation was a major source of controversy. The legislation will cost an estimated $940 billion over ten years and will be funded through a variety of new taxes, including **excise** taxes on high-end insurance plans. Initial estimates indicate that the legislation will result in a $143 billion reduction in the federal deficit within the first ten years. The second ten years will be more significant, reducing the deficit by an estimated $1.2 trillion.

Lawmakers for both parties—but especially Democrats—faced a backlash for positions taken on the bills. During both 2009 and 2010, several polls showed strong public concern about the health care reforms, and the fact that both chambers passed the legislation on such a strictly partisan basis did not help Democrats to build public support. Opponents, the majority of which are white and conservative, stressed that the legislation was an unprecedented expansion of the federal government. Candidates for Congressional elections in November 2010 used the vote to argue for change in Congress.

Some Republicans who voted against the bill faced pressure from their constituencies, especially in areas where many citizens do not have health care. Others who generally supported the legislation also questioned whether Congress went far enough, especially because the final legislation lacked the public option.

IMMIGRATION

The entrance into a country of foreigners for purposes of permanent residence. The correlative term emigration *denotes the act of such persons in leaving their former country.*

Tenth Circuit Enjoins Enforcement of Oklahoma Immigration Law

Illegal IMMIGRATION into the U.S. has been a concern for decades. Congress, operating under the Constitution's **Supremacy Clause**, has enacted national laws to deal with all aspects of immigration, including the employment of illegal ALIENS. However, the effectiveness of current federal laws on this issue has been questioned, as employers have faced few sanctions for employing people with false identification. Some states have sought to enact tougher laws to address these shortcomings, yet the **federal courts** have concluded that most provisions are preempted by federal law. In *Chamber of Commerce of the United States of America v. Edmondson*, 594 F.3d 742 (2010), the Tenth **Circuit Court** of Appeals upheld most of the provisions of a **preliminary injunction** that bars enforcement of an Oklahoma law dealing with the employment of illegal aliens by state public contractors.

The state legislature enacted the Oklahoma Taxpayer and Citizen Protection Act of 2007, H.B. 1804, which contained provisions that regulated illegal immigration and verification of employment eligibility. The U.S. CHAMBER OF COMMERCE and other state trade associations filed a suit in federal **district court** challenging three sections of the act. Section 7(B) forces businesses to use the federal Basic Pilot Program to verify work authorization status of their employees; if they fail to follow the procedure they will be barred from bidding on state contracts. Section 7(C) makes it a discriminatory practice for an employer to terminate an authorized worker while retaining an employee that the employer knows or reasonably should know is unauthorized to work. Section 9 requires contractors to either verify the work eligibility of their independent subcontractors or withhold certain taxes from those contractors. Otherwise, the contractor is liable to the state for the money not withheld.

The plaintiffs alleged argued that the three provisions were expressly and impliedly preempted by federal law. They asked for a PRELIMINARY INJUNCTION to halt enforcement of these provisions. The district court rejected the claims from the state that the plaintiffs did not have standing to challenge the law and granted the INJUNCTION. The state appealed to the Tenth Circuit and made the same arguments. In a 2-1 decision, the appeals court upheld the injunction as to Section 7 (C) and Section 9, but reversed as to Section 7 (B). The decision was based on an analysis of the interplay between the Oklahoma law and the federal employment verification program.

The appeals court noted that Congress enacted in 1986 the Immigration Reform and Control Act (IRCA), Pub. L. No. 99-603, 100 Stat. 3359, which contained a "comprehensive scheme prohibiting the employment of illegal aliens in the United States." IRCA set out an exhaustively detailed administrative scheme for determining whether an employer has knowingly employed an unauthorized alien. Employers can be subject to civil and criminal penalties for noncompliance. This part of IRCA includes an express **preemption** provision: "The provisions of this section preempt any State or local law imposing civil or criminal sanctions upon those who employ, or recruit or refer for a fee for employment, unauthorized aliens." IRCA also established an extensive employment verification system, known as the I-9 system. Employees must be verified but not independent contractors. Congress also created a "safe harbor" for employers that comply with the I-9 system. Employers who attempt to comply in **good faith** are protected from civil and criminal penalties. In 1996, Congress passed the Illegal Immigration Reform and Immigrant Responsibility Act (IIRIRA), Pub. L. No. 104-208, 110 Stat. 3009-546. This law directed the Attorney General to set up three pilot programs to ensure accurate employment verification. Only the Basic Pilot Program remains in existence. It is an Internet-based system of employment verification in which the employer submits information online to the federal government. The Basic Pilot Program is a voluntary alternative to the I-9 system for most employers. The appeals court noted that the Basic Pilot was far from perfect.

Based on these federal laws and programs, the appeals court examined the three challenged provisions. Under Section 7(C) an employer is subject to court orders, back pay, costs, and ATTORNEY'S FEES if found in noncompliance by firing an authorized employee and retaining an unauthorized program. The court concluded that these were sanctions within the meaning of IRCA's PREEMPTION provision and thus the state law was expressly preempted by federal law.

As to Section 9 and its imposition of requirements when dealing with independent contractors, the court ruled that this was no expressly preempted by federal law. However, under the SUPREMACY CLAUSE a law may be preempted by implication. States are prohibited from enacting laws that make compliance with both federal and state law a physical impossibility or that "stand as an obstacle to the accomplishment and execution of the full purposes and objectives of Congress." The appeals court held that Section 9 interferes with Congress' chosen methods and is therefore preempted.

Section 7(B) requires employers to use one of four methods to verify employment but in reality only the Basic Pilot program would qualify. The majority of the court ruled that this section was not impliedly preempted. Though the Basic Pilot was voluntary on the national level, "it is not reasonable to assume that a mandatory program choice for state public contractors conflicts with Congressional purpose." There was no evidence that federal standards would be compromised by making all state public contractors use the Internet-based program.

Kucana v Holder

The removal or DEPORTATION of an alien from the United States is governed by federal law, much of which has been changed since the 1990s. The Illegal Immigration Reform and Immigrant Responsibility Act (IIRIRA), Pub. L. No. 104-208, 110 Stat. 3009-546 amended the Immigration and Nationality Act (INA), 12 U.S.C. §§ 1101 et seq. codifying certain rules that had been made by the Attorney General that govern the process of reopening removal proceedings. IIRIRA also added a provision stating that no court has jurisdiction to review any action of the Attorney General "the authority for which is specified under this subchapter to be in the discretion of the Attorney General." 8 U.S.C. § 1252(a)(2)(B)(ii). A regulation, amended just months before IIRIRA's enactment, provided that "[t]he decision to grant or deny a motion to reopen ... is within the discretion of the [Board of Immigration Appeals (BIA)]," 8 C.F.R. § 1003.2(a). In *Kucana v. Holder*, __U.S.__, 103 S. Ct. 827, __L. Ed. 2d__ (2010), the SUPREME COURT addressed whether the IIRIRA law change deprived the **federal courts** of jurisdiction to review the administrative denial of a motion to reopen a removal proceeding. A unanimous Court ruled that the changes did not deprive the courts of jurisdiction.

Agron Kucana, a citizen of Albania, entered the United States on a business visa in 1995 and remained after the visa expired. Kucana applied for ASYLUM and the withholding of removal in 1996, claiming he would be persecuted for his political beliefs if he returned to his native country. An immigration judge determined that Kucana was removable and scheduled a hearing to evaluate his eligibility for asylum. When Kucana failed to appear for the hearing, the judge immediately ordered his removal in absentia. Kucana filed a motion to reopen, explaining that he had missed his hearing because he had overslept. The judge denied the motion, and the BIA affirmed in 2002. Kucana did not seek **judicial review**, nor did he leave the United States.

Kucana filed a second motion to reopen his removal proceedings in 2006, arguing that conditions in Albania had worsened but the BIA again denied the motion. The court concluded that the political climate had gotten much better since 1997. Kucana then petitioned the Seventh **Circuit Court** of Appeals, alleging that the BIA had abused its discretion. The appeals court denied the petition, concluding that it lacked jurisdiction. Under the IIRIRA provision, JUDICIAL REVIEW was barred not only for administrative decisions made discretionary by **statute**, but also "when the agency's discretion is specified by a regulation rather than a statute." Because other circuit courts had ruled differently, the Supreme Court agreed to hear Kucana's appeal.

The Court, in a unanimous decision, held that the Seventh Circuit interpretation was incorrect. Justice RUTH BADER GINSBURG, writing for the Court, noted that the motion to reopen is an "important safeguard" intended "to ensure a proper and lawful disposition" of immigration proceedings. In addition, federal courts had reviewed administrative decisions denying motions to reopen removal proceedings since at least 1916. Ginsburg concluded that the attorney general did not have the discretion to decide whether a motion to reopen should be granted. A close textual reading of the statute led the Court to conclude that the statute had not removed federal court jurisdiction. The fact that Congress, when it enacted the IIRIRA, did not address the issue of federal court review, led to the conclusion that Congress intended to leave the pre-IIRIRA law in effect. Ginsburg stated that the BIA has broad discretion, conferred by the Attorney General, "to grant

or deny a motion to reopen," but courts retain jurisdiction to review, with due respect, the Board's decision. In her view this decision by Congress to keep judicial oversight was unsurprising, as this procedural safeguard was to insure a proper and lawful **disposition** of immigration proceedings.

To reach its overall conclusion, the Court applied a basic principle of **statutory** construction–the presumption favoring judicial review of administrative action. Ginsburg stated that when a statute is "reasonably susceptible to divergent interpretation," the Court will adopt a reading "that executive determinations generally are subject to judicial review." The Court noted that it had "consistently applied this interpretive guide to legislation regarding immigration, and particularly to questions concerning the preservation of federal-court jurisdiction." There was no clear and convincing evidence that Congress intended to restrict jurisdiction on motions to reopen. A contrary interpretation would "free the Executive to shelter its own decisions from abuse-of-discretion **appellate court** review simply by issuing a regulation declaring those decisions "discretionary." Such an extraordinary delegation of authority cannot be extracted from the statute Congress enacted."

Nijhawan v. Holder

Noncitizens convicted of crimes in the U.S. are likely to deported. In many cases the criminal sentence is less punitive than the threat of DEPORTATION. Under 8 U.S.C. § 1252(a)(2)(B)(ii) any "alien who is convicted of an aggravated **felony** at any time after admission is deportable." A related **statute** defines "aggravated felony" in terms of a set of listed offenses that includes "an offense that … involves **fraud** or deceit in which the loss to the victim or victims exceeds \$10,000." §1101(a)(43)(M)(i). The SUPREME COURT, in *Nijhawan v. Holder*, __U.S.__, 129 S. Ct. 2294, 174 L. Ed. 2d 22 (2009) had to decide whether an alien who was convicted of a felony where no finding of loss was required could be deported based on the Board of IMMIGRATION Appeals (BIA) judge's inquiry into the financial loss associated with the crime. The Court held that the statute's \$10,000 threshold referred to the particular circumstances in which an offender committed a FRAUD or deceit crime on a particular occasion rather than to an element of the fraud or deceit crime.

Manoj Nijhawan migrated to the United States in 1985. In 2002 he was indicted for conspiring to commit **mail fraud**, wire fraud, bank fraud, and **money laundering**. A jury convicted him on all counts but none of criminal statutes in question required a finding of any particular amount of victim loss. Although the jury made no finding about the amount of the loss, at sentencing Nijhawan stipulated that the loss exceeded $100 million. The court then imposed a sentence of 41 months in prison and required **restitution** of $683 million.

In 2005 the federal government began a removal action, arguing that because Nijhawan had been convicted of an "aggravated felony," under 8 U. S. C. §1227(a)(2)(A)(iii), he must be deported. The immigration judge found that Nijhawan's conviction was for crimes of fraud and deceit and that the sentencing stipulation and restitution order showed that the victims' loss exceeded $10,000. Therefore, Nijhawan's conviction fell within the immigration statute's "aggravated felony" definition. The Board of Immigration Appeals upheld this reading of the statute, as did the Third **Circuit Court** of Appeals.

The Third Circuit pointed out in its decision that the statutes of conviction were silent as to amounts. Despite this silence, the appeals court concluded that the determination of loss amounts for "aggravated felony" purposes "requires an inquiry into the underlying facts of the case." However, other circuit courts of appeal had come to different conclusions as to whether the $10,000 threshold in refers to an element of a fraud statute or to the factual circumstances surrounding commission of the crime on a specific occasion. Three circuits held that the fact-based/circumstance specific approach was appropriate, while three other circuits approved of the definitional/categorical approach. The Supreme Court agreed to hear the case to resolve this conflict.

In a unanimous decision, the Court came down on the fact-based/circumstance specific approach. Justice STEPHEN BREYER, writing for the court, noted that Nijhawan had argued for the categorical approach, believing the statute's language referred to a generic kind of crime, not a crime as committed on a particular occasion.

This interpretation would avoid the practical difficulty of determining the nature of prior conduct from what may be a brief paper record, which might only be a **statutory** section number and a guilty plea; or, if there was a more extensive record, searching through that record for evidence of underlying conduct. Finally, Nijhawan contended that the categorical approach, since it covers only criminal statutes with a relevant monetary threshold, not only provides assurance of a finding on the point, but also gives the DEFENDANT had an opportunity to present evidence about the amount of loss.

Justice Breyer found no merit in these arguments. He concluded that the "fraud and deceit" provision lent itself to a "circumstance-specific" interpretation. The provision "lists certain other "offenses" using language that almost certainly does not refer to generic crimes but refers to specific circumstances." The statute also had other provisions that contained qualifying language that called for circumstance-specific application. Most important was the clause dealing with "an offense that … involves fraud or deceit in which the loss to the victim or victims exceeds $10,000." The Court concluded that the language of the provision was consistent with a circumstance-specific approach because the words "in which" (which modify "offense") can refer to the conduct involved "in" the commission of the offense of conviction, rather than to the elements of the offense.

IMMUNITY

Exemption from performing duties that the law generally requires other citizens to perform, or from a penalty or burden that the law generally places on other citizens.

Ninth Circuit Upholds Decision Limiting the Use of Tasers

The use of tasers by law enforcement officers has become more and more popular. However, some persons who have been shot with a tasers have filed CIVIL RIGHTS lawsuits, alleging that police have used excessive force when using the device. The Ninth **Circuit Court** of Appeals entered this new area of the law in *Bryan v. McPherson*, 590 F.3d 767 (2009). The appeals court ruled that a police officer did not have

IMMUNITY from a civil suit because his use of the taser against the victim was unconstitutional.

Carl Bryan, a 21-year old Californian, was driving with his brother to his parents' house in San Diego County when he was stopped by a California Highway Patrolman. The officer issued a ticket speeding ticket. Bryan, who was dressed only in a t-shirt and boxer shorts, became emotionally distressed, crying, moping, and eventually removing his t-shirt. He resumed his trip and, as he entered Coronado, Bryan was stopped at an intersection by Coronado police officer Brian McPherson. McPherson was stationed at the intersection to enforce seat-belt regulations. He stepped in front of Bryan's car and signaled him to stop. Bryan realized that he did not have his seat-belt bucked and by the time McPherson reached his car Bryan's anger at himself was growing. He complied with the officer's instructions to turn off his radio and pull over. Once parked, he hit his steering wheel and yelled expletives at himself for receiving a second citation that day. He then stepped out of his car.

As he stood outside his car, clad only in boxer shorts and tennis shoes, Bryan grew more agitated, yelling gibberish and hitting his thighs. McPherson was standing 20 to 25 feet away from Bryan. McPherson later stated that he had told Bryan to remain in his car but Bryan claimed not to have heard this command. However, the main factual dispute was whether Bryan made any movement toward McPherson. The officer said Bryan took one step toward him but Bryan denied he had. The physical evidence indicated that Bryan was facing away from McPherson. At this point, without warning, McPherson shot Bryan with his taser gun. The probes embedded in the side of his upper left arm. The electrical current immobilized him and he fell to the ground face first, fracturing four teeth and suffering facial contusions. Bryan was charged with resisting arrest and opposing an officer in the performance of his duties. Following a trial that ended with a HUNG JURY, the PROSECUTOR dismissed the charges.

Bryan filed a federal civil rights suit under 42 U.S.C. § 1983, against McPherson, the Coronado Police Department, and the city itself. Bryan alleged that McPherson had used excessive force when he shot his taser gun. McPherson asked the federal **district court** to dismiss him from the lawsuit by claiming

qualified immunity. For an officer to obtain qualified immunity, the officer must show that his conduct did not violate a constitutional right. If a violation did occur, the officer could still be immune if the constitutional right was not "clearly established in light of the specific context of the case." The district court concluded that McPherson was not entitled to immunity because a reasonable jury could conclude that Bryan presented no immediate danger to the officer and that no use of force was necessary. The court did dismiss the city and the department from the lawsuit. McPherson appealed to the Ninth Circuit, claiming the judge erred in denying him immunity.

The three-judge panel unanimously upheld the district court ruling. Judge Kim Wardlow, writing for the court, grounded her analysis on whether the officer's actions were objectively reasonable in light of the facts and circumstances confronting him. The amount of force used by McPherson when employing the taser was significant—the stainless steel barbs that penetrated Bryan's skin led to the delivery of a 1200 volt charge of electricity into his muscles. The electrical impulse instantly shuts down a victim's central nervous system, paralyzing the muscles throughout the body. This rendered Bryan limp and helpless. Bryan also suffered excruciating pain as he fell to the ground. The injuries from his fall compounded the severity of the taser shot. Though tasers have been classified by the courts a non-lethal force, Wardlow stated that this term was not synonymous with non-excessive force. All force "must be justified by the need for the specific level of force employed."

In this case the use of the taser was not justified because Bryan did not pose an immediate threat to the safety of McPherson. Bryan's behavior was erratic and volatile but from his lack of clothes he clearly was unarmed. He did not threaten the officer verbally or physically and he was at least 20 feet from McPherson. The entry wound in Bryan's arm indicated he had turned away from the officer when McPherson shot the taser. If he had been moving toward the officer the wound should have been in his chest. In addition, the minor nature of the traffic stop, which is punishable by a fine, could not serve as a justification for the use of physical force.

The appeals court concluded that McPherson had violated Bryan's clearly established rights to be free from unreasonable searches and seizures. As to whether this right was clearly established in the context of the case, the court acknowledged that there was no "direct legal precedent dealing with this precise factual scenario." However, where an officer's conduct "so clearly offends an individual's constitutional rights, we do not need to find closely analogous **case law** to show that a right is clearly established." No reasonable officer, faced with the same situation as McPherson, would have concluded that using the taser without warning was justified. The court returned the case to the district court, where Bryan could bring his allegations before a jury.

IMPEACHMENT

To accuse; to charge a liability upon; to sue. To dispute, disparage, deny, or contradict; as in to impeach a judgment or decree, or impeach a witness; or as used in the rule that a jury cannot impeach its verdict. *To proceed against a public officer for crime or misfeasance, before a proper court, by the presentation of a written accusation called articles of impeachment.*

House Impeaches Judge Samuel B. Kent

The HOUSE OF REPRESENTATIVES in June 2009 voted to IMPEACH disgraced judge Samuel B. Kent, who had been convicted on six counts of charges of SEXUAL ABUSE and OBSTRUCTION OF JUSTICE. It marked the first time since 1989 that the House had impeached a member of the judiciary. Kent is also the only federal judge ever indicted for alleged sexual crimes. Kent resigned shortly after the House passed its resolution, and the SENATE did not hold a trial.

Kent was a graduate of the University of Texas School of Law. He engaged in private practice in Galveston, Texas before President GEORGE H.W. BUSH appointed Kent to serve as judge for the Galveston Division of the U.S. **District Court** for the Southern District of Texas. Kent was the only judge at the Galveston courthouse, meaning that he had substantial authority over courthouse employees. In 2001, the chief judge of the Southern District of Texas reassigned 85 cases from Kent's **docket**. Though the court did not provide a reason for the action, each of the cases was being handled by

the same attorney, Richard Melancon, who was a close friend of Kent.

Kent ran into more trouble in 2007. Cathy McBroom, deputy clerk in the Galveston Division, filed a judicial misconduct complaint against Kent with the U.S. Court of Appeals for the Fifth Circuit. According to McBroom's complaint, Kent had sexually assaulted her on several occasions. The Fifth Circuit responded by appointing a special investigative committee to review the complaint. During the investigation, allegations also arose that Kent had abused a secretary named Donna Wilkerson. When the committee interviewed Kent about the accusations, he said that his only non-consensual contact with anyone was a single kiss with Wilkerson. According to Kent, once Wilkerson told him that his advances were unwelcome, he ceased any further contact.

After a few months of investigation, the Judicial Council for the Fifth Circuit suspended Kent for four months, during which time he continued to receive pay. When he returned to the bench in January 2008, he was assigned to the Houston Division of the Southern District of Texas. At that time, the Fifth Circuit did not divulge any facts related to the case. By December 2007, though, the Fifth Circuit acknowledged that Kent was the subject of a criminal investigation by the JUSTICE DEPARTMENT.

On August 28, 2008, a federal **grand jury** in the Southern District of Texas indicted Kent on three counts, including abusive sexual contact and attempted aggravated sexual abuse. According to the INDICTMENT, Kent had intentionally touched several private areas of McBroom and also attempted to force her to engage in a sexual act. On January 6, 2009, the GRAND JURY issued a superseding indictment that repeated the three counts related to his acts towards McBroom and added two more counts for alleged acts involving Wilkerson. The grand jury also added a sixth count for obstruction of justice based on Kent's lying to investigators in 2007 about the allegations. Further allegations suggested that Kent told Wilkerson that he had lied to investigators and attempted to persuade her to do the same.

As part of a plea agreement, Kent pleaded guilty to the obstruction of justice charge. Prosecutors agreed to drop the remaining five counts. However, prosecutors required Kent to sign a factual statement in which he acknowledged that he had engaged in non-consensual sexual contact with both McBroom and Wilkerson. Kent stated under oath that the facts set forth in the statement were indeed accurate.

At sentencing in May 2010, both McBroom and Wilkerson testified. According to McBroom, Kent first attacked her when he returned to work in an intoxicated state. McBroom said that Kent did not care that security officers might hear what was happening because Kent wielded so much authority that others were afraid of him. McBroom stated that Kent engaged in "evil and deliberate manipulation" and that she was "utterly disgusted" by his actions. As a result of his abuse, McBroom's marriage failed. Wilkerson told a similar story, indicating that his abuse of her began five days after she started working for the court.

Kent apologized in court to his family and his staff, but he failed to apologize to the two women. Kent said that he had been sober for 26 months and that he thought he could emerge from the situation a better person. Though prosecutors recommended a 36-month sentence, Judge C. Roger Vinson sentenced Kent to 33 months in prison, along with fines and **restitution** paid to McBroom and Wilkerson. At sentencing, Vinson told Kent, "Your wrongful conduct is a huge black X on your own record. It's a smear on the legal profession, and, of course, it's a stain on the justice system itself. And, importantly, it is a matter of grave concern within the **Federal courts**." Kent began to serve his sentence in Massachusetts in June 2009.

Members of Congress demanded Kent's resignation from the bench, because until he resigned or was impeached, he could continue to draw his annual salary of $174,000. Kent attempted to claim that he suffered from a mental disability and refused to step down. On May 12, just one day after his sentencing, the House passed a resolution to establish a committee to determine whether Kent should be impeached. The Fifth Circuit later recommended that Kent should not be given disability status and should be impeached. Kent submitted his resignation on June 2, 2009, but the resignation would not be effective until June 1, 2010. The House proceeded to conduct hearings on the matter. The House Judiciary Committee on June 10 decided to send four **articles of impeachment** to the full House.

Under Article I of the U.S. Constitution, the House has the sole power to impeach civil

U.S District Judge Samuel Kent leaves federal court in Houston, May 2009.
AP IMAGES

officers of the United States, including judges. Grounds for IMPEACHMENT include TREASON, BRIBERY, or "other high Crimes and Misdemeanors." Until Kent's case, the last federal judge to be impeached was Walter L. Nixon, Jr., who had committed PERJURY before a grand jury and was removed as a judge with the U.S. District Court of the Southern District of Mississippi in 1989.

The full House on June 19 impeached Kent by a vote of 389-0. The Senate immediately took action to prepare for a trial, but after Kent met with Senate officials at the prison where he is being housed, Kent submitted a second resignation, effective June 30. President BARACK OBAMA accepted the resignation, and the Senate later ended the impeachment trial.

Kent became the 14th judge in U.S. history to be impeached.

INTELLECTUAL PROPERTY

Former College Players Sue Video Game Maker

Technology used in video games has evolved to the point that video game producers can create virtual likenesses of real people that appear to be nearly identical to real-life counterparts. In the case of sports titles, consumers have shown a strong preference for games that offer an authentic simulation of real leagues and real teams. Although several college sports have

Quarterback Sam Keller at the NFL Combine, February 2008.

AP IMAGES

been replicated in video game form, producers are limited in their ability to virtually recreate actual players because of prohibitions against commercial use of the college player's name, picture, or likeness. The video game producers have found ways around these rules by not using a player's name but instead only featuring the player's number. Several former athletes think that their likenesses have been appropriated, though, and have sued the biggest producer of college sports games.

The National Collegiate Athletic Association (NCAA) serves as the governing body for all of college sports. Many colleges and the NCAA use the Collegiate Licensing Company (CLC) to handle their commercial trademark, licensing, and marketing. Many NCAA rules focus on retaining amateur status for college athletes, and so these rules focus heavily on prohibiting activities that would allow college athletes to profit from their athletic endeavors. The NCAA's **bylaws** prohibit commercial licensing of an athlete's name, picture, or likeness, and so neither the NCAA nor the CLC may license the use of a player who still has amateur status under the NCAA rules.

The NCAA is a significant business, earning revenues of $614 million in 2007-08. The vast majority of these revenues come from the sale

of television and marketing rights, including licensing rights for such items as apparel and video games. The athletes themselves, however, earn nothing from these agreements. In fact, players are required to sign an AFFIDAVIT stating that they understand the rules for maintaining amateur status, including the prohibition against selling their names, pictures, and like-nesses.

Electronic Arts is the largest producer of sports-related video games. Through its brand name EA Sports, the company produces such college sports titles as NCAA Football and NCAA Basketball. Neither of these sports titles includes the names of the players but instead features nameless players with only their jersey numbers. The game's depictions of the players is detailed enough that it includes identifiable skin tones, hair color, and hair style. The game likewise displays player profiles that show a player's height, weight, hometown, and so forth. The profiles are similar in most respects to the videos games focused on professional sports, except that for the most part, the professional sports titles feature the actual names of the players.

Sam Keller was a quarterback who played for Arizona State University and the University of Nebraska during the mid-2000s. In May 2009, he filed a class-action lawsuit against Electronic Arts, the NCAA, and the CLC, arguing that these defendants misappropriated Keller's and other athletes' likenesses and vio-lated the plaintiff's right of publicity through the production of the NCAA Football title. Keller filed the suit in the U.S. **District Court** for the Northern District of California and requested damages in excess of $5 million.

Keller's complaint alleges that EA Sports uses the actual players in the game but simply removes the name. In Keller's case, he wore number 9 at Arizona State University in 2004 and 2005. In EA Sports' NCAA Football games that corresponded to those seasons, the game features an Arizona State quarterback who wears number 9 and has the "same height, weight, skin tone, hair style, handedness, home state, play style (pocket passer), visor prefer-ence, and facial features" as Keller, according to the complaint. Keller transferred to Nebraska, and during a season in which he sat out, he wore #5. In the EA Sports game the following year, the game features a Nebraska quarterback wearing number 5 who is identical in nearly every respect to Keller.

Keller's complaint also refers to several examples of how the games actually feature real players. For instance, a running back named Eugene Jarvis wore number 6 when he played for Kent State in 2008. Jarvis' size was rather unusual for a college football running back, as he stood at only 5'5" and weighed only 170 pounds. In the 2009 version of NCAA Football, the game features a running back at Kent State wearing number 6, standing at 5'5", and weighing only 170 pounds.

In addition to these similarities, the game also allows users to edit the virtual players to include real names. In fact, several websites provide files that allow gamers to upload entire rosters with actual player names into the game. According to Keller's complaint, both the NCAA and EA Sports blatantly circumvent the prohibitions against using athlete's names and likenesses because without the realism, the game would not be as profitable. Keller's attorney told *USA Today*, "I think it's pretty clear they're taking the players' likenesses and using them in the game. It's also pretty clear that the NCAA prohibits that. There's not supposed to be misappropriation, or an APPROPRIATION, of players' names or players' likenesses for profit. And so we think we have a pretty strong case that they've misappropriated, in violation of state law, these players' likenesses."

Several other former college athletes filed their own suits in the months that followed Keller's action. In June 2009, former Rutgers quarterback Ryan Hart and former California quarterback Troy Taylor filed their own suits, which are similar to Keller's suit. A more obscure player named Byron Bishop, who played guard for North Carolina in the late 2000s, also filed a suit in September 2009, making many of the same allegations.

Electronic Arts has faced similar complaints in the past few years. In November 2008, a jury awarded a group of retired professional football players a total of $28.1 million (later reduced to $26.25 million) after a union representing the players allowed their names and likenesses to appear in a video game known as Madden NFL. In 2009, former player Jim Brown tried to sue Electronic Arts on similar grounds, but a Los Angeles judge threw his case out, concluding

that use of the athletes' likenesses in the game was a form of expression protected by the FIRST AMENDMENT.

INTERNET

A worldwide telecommunications network of business, government, and personal computers.

Microsoft Sues Family Members in an Internet Fraud Case

In a case that is the first of its kind, Microsoft in 2009 sued two brothers and their mother, claiming that these family members engaged in an online ad **fraud** scheme. Microsoft has claimed damages of $750,000 in the case. Online advertisers applauded the move, noting that this type of case is important in curbing the practice known as click FRAUD.

Most of the major online search engines, including Google, Yahoo, and Microsoft, use the same basic online advertising models. In one of the most common advertising models, known as "keyword bidding", advertisers agree to pay a certain amount of money each time an Internet user clicks on an advertisement that appears on a search engine's site. The amount that the advertiser agrees to pay depends on the advertiser's "bid", which relates to where the ad appears on the site when a user enters certain words or phrases. For instance, a company may want to advertise its services for discount car rentals. The company could enter a bid for the amount it would be willing for a search engine user to click on its ad. If the company bids more than any other company, the company's ad will appear at the top of the list of sponsored sites, which appears on the same page as the search engine results. The advertiser might bid, for instance, $40 for the keyword phrase "cheap car rental." If the advertiser outbids others, the advertiser's ad will appear above other sponsored sites, and when a user clicks on the link in the sponsored site area, the advertiser will be charged up to the amount of the bid (the actual amount charged varies depending on what the other bids were). The advertiser will generally establish an advertising budget with the search engine through which the advertiser establishes the maximum amount it is willing to spend on ads during a given period of time.

This pay-per-click system is subject to abuse. One fairly common type of fraud is known as "competitor click fraud." This occurs when a perpetrator uses a variety of methods to click on a competitor's sponsored links, meaning that the competitor is charged frequently. The effort is designed to exhaust the competitor's advertising budget, thus meaning that the competitor's ads will no longer appear at the top of the list of sponsored sites. The perpetrator's links may then rise up the list of these sponsored sites, even though the perpetrator paid less per click than the competitor. In the example above, a perpetrator that only bid $25 on a keyword phrase might engage in competitor click fraud to exhaust the budget of the competitor that bid $40 per click. When the budget runs out, the perpetrator's link may appear closer to the top of the list, which means that the site will have increased traffic without having to spend as much as the competitor spent on its bid.

Microsoft operates a search engine that uses a pay-per-click form of advertising. In 2008, advertisers in the auto insurance industry complained to Microsoft that the number of clicks on their ads had risen dramatically. The advertiser noted that the clicks occurred with keyword phrases commonly used by auto insurance advertisers, such as "auto insurance," "car insurance," "cheap car insurance," and "auto insurance quote." Microsoft noted that a spike in the use of exactly the same keywords was very unusual and typically resulted from a **fraudulent** pay-per-click scheme. Investigators at Microsoft noticed similar patterns related to searches for the online game known as World of Warcraft.

It took Microsoft investigators some time to track down the perpetrators of the fraud. The investigators determined that the perpetrators were using a variety of networks to disguise the perpetrator's identity and to make it appear as if the traffic was being generated by humans rather than through an automated process. After months of attempting to determine the source of the fraud, the investigators determined that the perpetrators for the auto insurance fraud were the same as those running the World of Warcraft fraud. Further investigation revealed that a man from Vancouver, B.C. named Eric Lam was in a unique position to be involved in both the auto insurance market and the World of Warcraft market. Using seven different Microsoft ad accounts, Lam allegedly took a fee for directing traffic to auto insurance sites. Others implicated the scheme included

Lam's brother, Gordon Lam, and their mother, Melanie Suen.

According to Microsoft, Lam and the other perpetrators made about $250,000 in profits from their efforts. The scheme was more costly to Microsoft itself, which had to credit back $1.5 million to advertisers who had been affected. Microsoft also claimed that the company suffered damage to its business, reputation, and goodwill. The company filed suit against Eric Lam, Gordon Lam, and Melanie Suen in the U.S. **District Court** for the Western District of Washington on June 15, 2009. Microsoft sought $750,000 in damages, along with an INJUNCTION prohibiting the defendants from engaging in the fraudulent conduct. According to Microsoft attorney, "part of our responsibility as an industry leader is to bring enforcement in this area. What we've seen in this particular area of online advertising is there is a significant amount of fraud."

Advertisers applauded the suit, noting that Microsoft was addressing a problem that had plagued the industry for years. According to industry sources, about one out of every seven clicks is fraudulent.

"Spam King" Pleads Guilty to Spamming and Fraud Scheme

In the 1990s and 2000s, Alan Ralsky developed a reputation as one of the most notorious sources of the commercial mass of email known as spam. Federal investigators finally caught up to Ralsky, indicting him along with ten others in an international **fraud** scheme involving spam mail. In 2009, Ralsky pleaded guilty to several charges and received a sentence of more than four years in prison.

The tremendous rise in the popularity of the Internet and use of email led marketers to develop a number of methods for sending unsolicited bulk advertising, popularly referred to as spam. By the 2000s, roughly half of email messages sent in the United States was in the form of spam. States attempted to combat the problem by enacting anti-spam legislation, but these statutes generally failed to reduce the amount of spam. Many spam messages are sent from servers overseas or through several different PROXY servers, making it difficult to enforce these statutes and stop the so-called spammers. In 2003, Congress responded to the problem by enacting a law known as Controlling the ASSAULT of Non-Solicited PORNOGRAPHY and Marketing (CAN-SPAM) Act of 2003, Pub. L. No. 108-187, 117 Stat. 2719. The law established criminal and civil penalties for violators, but most have viewed the law as ineffective in slowing down the distribution of spam messages.

During the 1990s, Alan Ralsky was charged with and served time for a number of crimes, including selling unregistered SECURITIES and committing **felony** bank FRAUD. By the 2000s, his schemes had evolved into the distribution of spam. In December 2002, Ralsky did what few other spammers would ever consider doing by granting an interview with the *Detroit News* and openly discussing his company's distribution of spam. After the article was published and later posted on a website known as Slashdot.org. Users of the website reportedly turned the tables on Ralsky by signing him up for hundreds of ads, catalogs, and brochures (the print equivalent of online spam), which apparently irritated Ralsky and led him to threaten to sue those who signed him up for the material.

Ralsky's trouble with the junk mail did not cause him to end is online spamming activities. In 2005, the FEDERAL BUREAU OF INVESTIGATION opened a probe into Ralsky's business operation. The investigation also involved the U.S. Postal Inspection Service and the INTERNAL REVENUE SERVICE. During the investigation, agents discovered an extensive and elaborate spamming operation. Agents alleged that Ralsky ran a so-called "pump and dump" scheme. In this scheme, Ralsky and other defendants sent spam email touting **penny stocks** from China. The spam was designed to fraudulently increase the price of the stock, and when the stock price had risen, the defendants sold the stock at the inflated prices. Ralsky used a number of methods to evade spam-fighting tools and to trick email recipients to open these messages. Moreover, Ralsky and others used a tool known as a "botnet," to send the spam. To set up this botnet, the defendants caused a network of computers to be infected with malicious software (known as malware), which caused the computer to send the spam messages. As computers were added to this network, the number of spam messages increased. Investigators estimated that the defendants made a profit of $3 million in the operation.

In January 2008, the JUSTICE DEPARTMENT announced that Ralsky had been indicted along

Alan M. Ralsky, in a July 2002 photo.
AP IMAGES

with ten others. Also charged with Ralsky was Scott K. Bradley, who is Ralsky's son-in-law and was the chief financial officer of Ralsky's company. One other DEFENDANT was also from Michigan, in addition to five defendants from California and another from Arizona. Others charged included one defendant from Russia and another from Vancouver, Canada. The 41-count INDICTMENT included several violations, including CONSPIRACY, fraud in violation of the CAN-SPAM Act, computer fraud, **mail fraud**, wire fraud, and **money laundering**. At the time the indictment was announced, U.S. Attorney Stephen J. Murphy stated, "Today's charges seek to knock out one of the largest illegal spamming and fraud operations in the country, an international scheme to make money by manipulating stock prices through illegal spam E-MAIL promotions." Assistant Attorney General Alice S. Fisher added, "The flood of illegal spam continues to wreak havoc on the online marketplace and has become a global criminal enterprise. It clogs consumers' email boxes with scams and unwanted messages and imposes significant costs on our society."

In June 2009, the FBI announced that Ralsky and five others had pleaded guilty to the charges related to their roles in the scheme. Ralsky entered into a plea agreement under which he faced up to 87 months in prison and a fine of $1 million. Bradley also faced a significant sentence of up to 78 months in prison and a $1 million fine. On November 23, 2009, U.S. District Judge Marianne O. Battani sentenced Ralsky to 51 months in prison and fined Ralsky $250,000. As part of the plea agreement, Ralsky also agreed to help prosecutors with cases against others involved in Ralsky's scheme.

According to Richard Cox of the website Spamhaus.org, spam advertising bogus stock took a hit after Ralsky's indictment. However, Cox did not think that Ralsky's conviction would curb practices that Ralsky used. Cox said, "If you look at the fact he was paying money to people to develop botnets - and the cost to millions of innocent people around the world who had to pay lots of money every time they had to repair their computer to fix the damage caused by his spam Trojans – even the maximum time he could get under this agreement is not nearly enough."

JUVENILE LAW

An area of the law that deals with the actions and well-being of persons who are not yet adults.

Graham v. Florida

The SUPREME COURT plays an important role in society by deciding whether certain categories of crimes or offenders can be subjected to types of criminal punishment. The Constitution's EIGHTH AMENDMENT bars "cruel and unusual punishments" but only the Court gets to decide these questions. In 2002 it held that mentally retarded persons may not be executed and in 2005 it ruled that persons who committed criminal offenses before age 18 may not be sentenced to death. In 2008 the Court ruled that a person convicted of raping a child may not be subjected to CAPITAL PUNISHMENT. In 2010 the Court again decided an important Eighth Amendment case when it ruled in *Graham v. Florida*, __U.S.__, 130 S. Ct. 2011, 176 L. Ed. 2d 825 (2010), that juvenile offenders cannot be sentenced to life in prison without parole for non-homicide crimes. The Court looked to the sentencing laws and practices of the states and of foreign nations.

At age 16, Terrance Jamar Graham attempted to rob a restaurant with three other teen-accomplices in Jacksonville, Florida. One of the accomplices hit the restaurant manager several times in the head with a metal bar but the manager's cries for help led the youths to run away with no money. Graham was arrested and the PROSECUTOR elected under Florida law to charge Graham as an adult rather than a juvenile. The **felony** charges lodged against Graham included armed **burglary** with ASSAULT, a first-degree felony carrying a maximum of life imprisonment without the possibility of parole, and attempted armed **robbery**, carrying a maximum of 15 years' imprisonment. The trial court accepted a plea bargain in which the court withheld **adjudication** of guilt on both charges and sentenced Graham to three years PROBATION. Graham was also required to serve the first year of his probation in the county jail. Less than six months after leaving jail and 34 days short of his 18th birthday, he was arrested for participating in a home invasion ROBBERY. Graham denied that he had been involved but the arrest triggered a probation violation hearing.

The judge who presided at Graham's probation violation hearing was not the same judge who had accepted the guilty plea and plea agreement. At the hearing Graham maintained his innocence on the home invasion robbery but admitted probation violations by fleeing the police in a car the night of the invasion. The prosecution put before the court evidence relating to the home invasion. The trial court found that Graham had violated his probation by participating in the home invasion, possessing a firearm, and associating with persons involved in criminal activity. The minimum sentence Graham could have received was five years in prison. The maximum was life imprisonment. The Florida Department of Corrections recommended that Graham receive only 4 years in prison, while the prosecution recommended 30 years on the armed BURGLARY charge and 15 years on the attempted armed robbery count. The judge chose to sentence Graham to life imprisonment with no possibility of parole. The Florida Court of Appeals upheld the sentence, concluding that Graham was incapable of rehabilitation and the Florida Supreme Court denied review.

The Supreme Court, in a 6-3 decision, overturned the state decision and ruled categorically that juvenile offenders may not be sentenced to life imprisonment without the possibility of parole for non-homicide offenses. Justice ANTHONY KENNEDY, writing for the majority, noted the Court's earlier rulings that banned capital punishment for juvenile offenders and persons with mental retardation. In cases involving categorical rules, the Court considers "objective **indicia** of society's standards, as expressed in legislative enactments and state practice" to determine whether there is a national consensus against the sentencing practice at issue. It then looks to the "standards elaborated by controlling precedents and by the Court's own understanding and interpretation of the Eighth Amendment's text, history, meaning, and purpose." It then exercises its independent judgment as to whether the punishment violates the Eighth Amendment.

Employing this analysis, Kennedy pointed out that 37 states and the District of Columbia permitted sentences of life without parole for a juvenile non-homicide offender in some circumstances, while sevens states permitted such sentences but only for HOMICIDE offenses. Only six states barred life without parole for any juvenile offenders. Despite these statistics, Kennedy concluded that in actual practice very few juvenile offenders were serving life without parole sentences for non-homicide crimes. Only 129 juvenile offenders were currently serving such sentences and 77 of those offenders were in Florida. Of the remaining 52 offenders, they were imprisoned in just 10 states and the federal system. This sentence was rarely imposed and its rarity matched the death sentences that had been pronounced for juveniles and mentally-retarded persons.

The Court also concluded that no theory of **penology** justified life without parole sentences

for juvenile non-homicide offenders. The Court had concluded in the juvenile death sentence case that persons under 18 have limited culpability due to their youth and immaturity. Justice Kennedy stated that nothing had changed in five years to change this conclusion. Applying different penological theories, including retribution and deterrence, the Court found them all deficient in justifying life without parole for juveniles. In addition, it noted that the United States was the only country in the world this type of sentence. Therefore, it imposed a categorial rule banning the sentencing practice.

Justice CLARENCE THOMAS, in a dissenting opinion joined by Justices ANTONIN SCALIA and SAMUEL ALITO, argued that the Court had imposed its own values on a sentencing practice adopted by most of the 50 states. He stated that "I am unwilling to assume that we, as members of this Court, are any more capable of making such moral judgments than our fellow citizens. Nothing in our training as judges qualifies us for that task, and nothing in Article III gives us that authority."

JUVENILE SENTENCING

Sullivan v. Florida

In May 2010, after having heard oral arguments several months earlier, the U.S. SUPREME COURT dismissed (as "improvidently granted") its earlier grant of **certiorari** in the case of *Sullivan v. Florida,* No. 08-7621, 560 U.S. ___ (2010). It offered no further opinion in the matter. However, the case was the second to be brought before the court in conjunction with the sentencing of juveniles/minors (to life in prison, without PAROLE) for non-homicide crimes. Both cases challenged the sentencing under the **Cruel and Unusual Punishment** Clause of the EIGHTH AMENDMENT to the U.S. Constitution.

In May 2010, the Supreme Court rendered its decision in the companion case, *Graham v. Florida,* No. 08-7412, 560 U.S. ___ (2010). It held that the CRUEL AND UNUSUAL PUNISHMENT prohibition of the Eighth Amendment did not permit a juvenile offender to be sentenced to life in prison without parole for a non-homicidal crime. (Graham, a repeat offender, committed his first serious crime at age 16; while on PROBATION for that crime, he was involved in another armed **robbery** in which he held a gun to a victim's head, then led police on a lengthy car chase through residential streets. He was 18 when sentenced to life without parole.) Since Sullivan was also a (much younger) juvenile when he committed a violent crime, his challenged sentence fell within the **purview** of the *Graham v. Florida*, decision; hence, the dismissal.

Joe Harris Sullivan was only 13 years old when he was convicted of sexual **battery** in a Florida court and sentenced to life without parole. Although merely pubescent, he committed a very adult crime. He and two other juveniles had broken into the empty home of an elderly woman and stolen jewelry and coins. Later that same day, Sullivan and one of the other accomplices returned to the same house, ostensibly to steal more, but this time the woman was home. Sullivan forcibly removed the woman to a bedroom, where he beat and raped her.

Sullivan was tried as an adult and convicted of two counts of sexual BATTERY, two counts of **burglary** of a dwelling, and grand theft. Since (despite his young age) Sullivan had an extensive criminal record, the trial court concluded that an adult sentence was appropriate, and sentenced him to life without parole. His conviction was upheld by the Florida District **Court of Appeal** in 1991, and the Supreme Court of Florida denied review.

Sixteen years later, in 2007, the U.S. Supreme Court rendered its decision in *Roper v. Simmon*, prohibiting states from imposing death penalties on juvenile offenders. Sullivan seized this opportunity to file a motion for post-conviction relief, arguing that *Roper* rendered his life sentence unconstitutional under the Eighth (and extended to states by the Fourteenth) Amendment. The trial court denied the claim, noting that *Roper* did not ban sentences of life without parole, and that the state supreme court had already decided not to extend *Roper* to such a sentence. The Florida **District Court** of Appeal affirmed the sentence without opinion/comment, and the Supreme Court of Florida, under Florida law, declined review.

Sullivan then petitioned the U.S. Supreme Court, which granted CERTIORARI (review) in 2009. His appeal attracted national legal attention, and various *amicus curiae* (friends of the court) filed supporting briefs. Collectively, his appeal and the *amicus* briefs essentially acknowledged that *Roper* did, in fact, only address the constitutionality of death sentences for minors. Notwithstanding, they argued, the Supreme

Court had longstanding constitutional **jurisprudence** requiring that a youth's developmental status be considered in construing Eighth Amendment rights. Further, they argued, life without parole was contrary to the concept of a rehabilitative juvenile justice system. Juveniles have distinct psychological and social needs and traits, they argued, and have less capacity for reasoned or logical judgment, are more vulnerable to peer pressure and negative external influences, and do not have fully-formed personal identities. These factors make juveniles, as a class, less CULPABLE for crime and more amenable to rehabilitation. Therefore, the argument continued, life without parole for them served no legitimate **penology** purpose of deterrence, rehabilitation, punishment, or retribution.

But Florida Attorney General Bill McCollum urged the Court not to hear the case. He argued that in the past, the Court had "recognized that a state is permitted to make 'a societal decision that when a person who has previously committed a **felony** commits yet another felony, he should be subjected to the admittedly serious penalty of INCARCERATION for life, subject only to the state's judgment as to whether to grant him parole.'"

Other *amicus* briefs supported the state and states' rights in general, arguing that the Court should avoid a categorical ban on sentencing juveniles to life without parole. The arguments pointed out that the Court had never categorically exempted a class of offenders from a particular punishment other than death. Further, in support of states' rights, others argued that states which have consciously and deliberatively adopted such measures (as life without parole) did so as part of a considered legislative response to the growing problem of juvenile crime. Amici also argued that in appropriate cases, life without parole is proportionate to the crime(s) committed, and that Sullivan's crimes were particularly heinous and violent. Finally, they argued that life without parole served to protect innocent children, the most frequent victims of juvenile crime, and also gave other crime victims some closure in knowing that the juveniles would not be released back into a world already burdened with recidivist crimes.

But, in *Graham*, the Supreme Court decided in favor of considering the special needs of juveniles, thus rendering the issues raised in *Sullivan* redundant and moot.

KAGAN, ELENA

Elena Kagan, who had become the U.S. solicitor general in March of 2009, was nominated to replace Justice JOHN PAUL STEVENS on the U.S. Supreme Court in May of 2010. Kagan, whom President Barack Obama first nominated and the Senate confirmed to represent the United States before the Supreme Court, had drawn widespread praise as the innovative dean of Harvard Law School for five years. She also served a variety of advisory roles advising the administration of President Bill Clinton during the 1990s.

Kagan, born and raised in New York, graduated from Hunter College High School in 1977 and earned her bachelor's degree four years later from Princeton University. Kagan received her master's degree in philosophy from Oxford University's Worcester College in 1983 and her law degree from Harvard University three years later. Kagan was a supervising editor for the *Harvard Law Review*. In the late 1980s, Kagan worked as an associate for Washington, D.C., law firm Williams & Connolly. She was also a law clerk for Judge Abner J. Mikva of the U.S. Court of Appeals for the District of Columbia Circuit and for Supreme Court Justice Thurgood Marshall. Kagan was an adviser to Massachusetts Governor Michael S. Dukakis during his 1988 presidential campaign.

Kagan began her academic career at the University of Chicago School of Law as an assistant professor in 1991. She became a

tenured law professor in 1995. Also in 1995, Kagan began a four-year stretch in the White House. Her titles included associate counsel to the president, deputy assistant to the president for domestic policy, and deputy director of the Domestic Policy Council. Her coverage areas included education, crime, and public health. Kagan joined Harvard as a law professor in 1999. Four years later, she became law school dean in a surprise move by then-university president Larry Summers, succeeding Robert C. Clark. Drake Bennett of the Boston Globe called Kagan "a relative outsider in a school that values its traditions."

Kagan inherited a Harvard Law School that despite its storied reputation had experienced its share of strife. It included ideological divisions, oversized classes, and a perception that its approach to teaching law was too rigid. "Its students felt estranged; its faculty was fractious, aging, and unable to agree whom to hire or how to modernize," Bennett wrote. Over five years, however, Kagan "galvanized the place with her ambition and adroit management style, knitting together the faculty, charming the students, and attracting top-flight talent to the school." Early on, Kagan made small but significant quality-of-life changes at the school that included free coffee in classroom buildings and free tampons in the women's bathrooms. She added a beach volleyball court outside the student center and converted it to a skating rink during the winter. "As it turned out, you can buy more student

U.S. Supreme Court nominee Elena Kagan with President Barack Obama and Vice President Joe Biden, May 2010.

AP IMAGES

1986	Received law degree from Harvard
2003	Became dean of Harvard Law School
2009	Named U.S. Solicitor General
2010	Nominated to replace John Paul Stevens on U.S. Supreme Court

happiness per dollar by giving people free coffee than anything else I've discovered," Kagan told Bennett.

Academically, Kagan overhauled the curriculum, expanded the faculty, and coordinated the design of a complex that was under construction in 2009. She also made more accessible the legal "clinics" where students could get courtroom experience, and encouraged careers in public service. Kagan oversaw the hiring of high profile public law scholars, sometimes in the face of opposing law school factions. They included Jack Goldsmith, a former White House lawyer in the administration of President George W. Bush, and administrative law expert John Manning. "Both hires have helped assuage complains that Harvard marginalized conservative views,"

Bennett wrote. Kagan ran Harvard Law with experimentation a constant theme. "Before, every possible change had to be weighed against hundreds of years of illustrious history. Now changes are weighed by asking whether it might make something better," Elizabeth Warren told Bennett. Warren, a bankruptcy law professor who chaired Harvard Law's admissions committee, later in 2009 became chair of the congressional oversight panel that monitored the U.S. banking bailout.

Shortly before his inauguration in January of 2009, Obama, himself a 1991 Harvard Law graduate, named Kagan solicitor general. The Senate confirmed her by a 61-31 vote on March 19. Her former Harvard boss, Summers, is also in the Obama administration as director of the National Economic Council. Upon the announcement of Justice Stevens' retirement, Obama selected Kagan to replace him, despite her never having served as a judge and as a practicing lawyer for only two years, points quickly raised by those opposed to her nomination. As of July 2010, Kagan had been approved by the House Judiciary Committee by a vote of 13-6, with all 12 committee Democrats and 1 Republican voting in favor, and the remainder of Republicans voting against her.

LABOR LAW

Granite Rock v. International Brotherhood of Teamsters

The U.S. Supreme Court case of *Granite Rock Co. v. International Brotherhood of Teamsters*, No. 08-1214, 561 U.S. ___ (2010) resolved whether a labor dispute between parties could be brought into federal district court or needed to be arbitrated, where the parties disagreed as to whether a new collective bargaining agreement had been ratified.

Granite Rock Company, a California concrete and building materials company in business since 1900, employed about 800 persons under different labor contracts with several unions. Granite Rock and Local 287 of the International Brotherhood of Teamsters ("Teamsters") were parties to a 1999 labor agreement that expired in April 2004. The parties had reached an impasse while attempting to negotiate a new agreement. On June 9, 2004, Local 287 members initiated a strike.

The strike continued until July 2, 2004, at which time the parties finally agreed to the terms of a new collective bargaining agreement. The new agreement contained a no-strike clause but did not directly address union members' liability for any strike-related damages incurred by Granite in the interim period before the new agreement was negotiated but after the old agreement had expired.

At the end of the negotiating session, Local 287's union representative approached Granite Rock about executing a separate "back-to-work" agreement that would, among other things, hold union members harmless for damages incurred during that interim period. The representative neither made such a separate agreement a condition of Local 287's ratification of the new collective bargaining agreement, nor a condition for Local 287's decision to stop picketing. Accordingly, Local 287 had neither a back-to-work agreement nor a hold-harmless agreement in place when it voted to ratify the new collective bargaining agreement on July 2, 2004.

Meanwhile, the Teamsters advised Local 287 to continue with the strike until Granite Rock agreed to a hold-harmless agreement. Granite Rock refused and informed Local 287 members that continued strike activity was in violation of the no-strike clause contained in the new agreement. Local 287 and the Teamsters responded by announcing a company-wide strike that involved numerous facilities and workers, including members of other Teamsters' locals.

Granite Rock then sued both the Teamsters and Local 287. It invoked federal jurisdiction in the district court under §301 of the Labor Management Relations Act of 1947 (LMRA), under which it sought strike-related damages for the unions' alleged breach of contract. It also asked for an injunction against the continuing strike because the hold-harmless dispute (about which the parties never agreed upon) was an arbitrable grievance under the newly-negotiated agreement.

Local 287 conceded §301(a) jurisdiction but countered that the new collective bargaining agreement was never properly ratified by a vote of Local 287's members. Therefore, it argued, the new agreement's no-strike clause did not provide a basis for a §301 claim. Granite Rock amended its complaint to add charges against the Teamsters for tortious interference with the new agreement, and the unions moved to dismiss.

The district court dismissed the tortious interference claims on the ground that §301 supports a federal cause of action only for breach of contract claims. It, however, denied defendants' motion to order arbitration on the issue of when the new agreement was ratified (Granite Rock contended July 2, 2004; Local 287 alleged August 22). The district court concluded that a jury needed to decide this. Subsequently, a jury concluded that the new agreement was ratified on July 2, 2004, and the court then ordered arbitration to proceed on Granite Rock's breach of contract claims. The Ninth Circuit Court of Appeals affirmed the dismissal of the tortious interference claims, but reversed the order to arbitrate, holding that the entire ratification-date dispute should have been arbitrated under the new agreement's arbitration clause. The reason the appellate court held that the arbitration clause covered the ratification-date dispute was because the clause covered strike-related claims, and national policy favored arbitration for ambiguous arbitration clauses

The U.S. Supreme Court reversed in part, affirmed in part, and remanded. First, it held that the parties dispute over the effective ratification date was a matter for federal court and not an arbitrator. Whether parties have agreed to arbitrate is an issue for judicial determination. Writing for the 7-2 majority, Justice Thomas noted that the presumption that a dispute is arbitrable should only be applied where it reflects, and derives its legitimacy from, a judicial conclusion that the parties agreed to arbitrate in the first place. This resolution included whether the parties' ever formed an express agreement, whether the agreement was legally enforceable, and that is was best

construed to encompass the dispute. Further, the question of when the agreement was formed is one for judicial determination because ist constituted a "judicial conclusion" needed to employ the framework for even determining arbitrability.

The Court affirmed the Ninth Circuit's refusal to recognize a cause of action under §301 of the LMRA, because granite Rock had not yet exhausted other available means of redress, such as state-law tort claims, unfair labor practice claims, and federal common-law breach of contract claims. Therefore, a cognizable LMRA cause of action was premature.

Justice Thomas was joined by Chief Justice Roberts and Justices Scalia, Kennedy, Ginsburg, Breyer, and Alito, and Justices Stevens and Sotomayor joined in concluding that the LMRA did not recognize a new common-law cause of action. However, Justice Sotomayor, joined by Justice Stevens, opined that the parties' new agreement did cover the dispute in question. Therefore, judicial determination should have been limited to determining whether (1) the parties had an agreement to arbitrate, and (2) whether the agreement covered the dispute.

New Process Steel v. National Labor Relations Board

The Taft-Hartley Act, enacted in 1947, among other things, increased the size of the National Labor Relations Board (Board) from three members to five. 29 U.S.C. §153(a). Concurrently, it amended §3(b) of the National Labor Relations Act to increase the quorum requirement for Board decisions from two members to three, and to allow the Board to delegate its authority to groups of at least three members [29 U.S.C.§153(b)]. The question before the U.S. Supreme Court in *New Process Steel v. National Labor Relations Board*, No. 08-1457, 560 U.S. ___ (2010), was whether, following an authorized delegation of the Board's powers to a three-member group, two members of that group could continue to exercise that delegated authority once the group's (and the Board's) membership falls to two. A narrowly-divided Court ruled that it could not.

Since January 2008, feuding between Congress and the White House had resulted in unfilled vacancies on the Board. In December 2007, the Board had four members and one vacancy. However, it anticipated two more vacancies at the end of year. Acting on that, on December 20, 2007, the Board made two delegations of authority, effective at midnight on December 28, 2007. First it delegated to the general counsel a continuing authority to initiate and conduct litigation, which normally required case-by-case approval of the Board. Second, and relevant here, the Board delegated to "Members Liebman, Schaumber and Kirsanow, as a three-member group," all of the Board's powers, in anticipation of the adjournment of the 1st Session of the 110th Congress." On December 31, 2007, Member Kirsanow's recess appointment expired. Starting January 1, 2008, Members Liebman and Schaumber became the only members of the Board.

The two remaining Board members continued to render more than 400 labor decisions. At least 60 challenges to two-member rulings had been filed in federal appellate courts. One of those challenges was from New Process Steel, which operated four steel-processing plants in the United States and one in Mexico.

The union representing employees at New Process Steel's Butler, Indiana plant failed to reach an agreement over a new contract (collective bargaining agreement). The union filed unfair labor practice claims with the National Labor Relations Board, claiming that New Process Steel failed to honor its collective bargaining agreement to deal with the union representative as the exclusive representative of the employees in the plant. The two-member panel of the Board agreed with the union. National Steel appealed and raised the argument that the Board's decision was invalid because 29 U.S.C. §153(b) of the national Labor Relations Act (see above) required that three of the five members of the Board shall "at all times" constitute a quorum.

The Seventh Circuit Court of Appeals, in agreement with the First and Second Circuit Courts of Appeals, upheld the validity of two-member rulings. It reasoned that the Board had power to delegate its authority to a delegee group of three members; therefore, two sitting members of that delegee three-member group constituted a quorum. On the other hand, the Circuit Court of Appeals for the D.C. Circuit had held, in *Laurel Baye Healthcare v. NLRB*, that 29 U.S.C. §153(b) of the National Labor Relations Act required a three-member quorum at all times. To resolve the split among circuits,

the U.S. Supreme Court granted certiorari (review).

Justice Stevens delivered the opinion of the Court, reversing and remanding to the Seventh Circuit. The 5-4 majority held that, under the NLRB, when the Board delegates its authority, the delegee group must maintain a membership of three in order to exercise that delegated authority. That delegated authority significantly includes the major power to render decisions in labor disputes under the NLRB.

Relying on the plain language of the statute, the Board may only delegate its powers to a "group of three or more members." That clause is best read, said the Court, to mean that the delegee group of three is to *maintain* a membership of three in order for the delegation to remain valid. In fact, wrote Justice Stevens, that was the only way to harmonize and give meaningful effect to §3(b)'s provisions, including, (1) the above-quoted delegation clause, (2) the Board quorum requirement, mandating that "three members of the Board shall, at all times, constitute a quorum of the Board," (3) the delegated group provision, stating that "two members shall constitute a quorum" of any delegee group, and (4) the vacancy clause.

The Court dismissed as "unconvincing" the government's other arguments, including that the group quorum requirement and vacancy clause, read together, permitted two members of a three-member group to constitute a quorum even when there was no third member; that the vacancy clause established that a vacancy within the *group* [" ...of three"] has no effect; or that reading the statute to authorize the Board to act with only two members advanced Congress' objective of Board efficiency.

Justice Stevens was joined in the majority opinion by Chief Justice Roberts and Justices Scalia, Thomas, and Alito. Justice Kennedy, joined in dissent by Justices Sotomayor, Ginsburg, and Breyer, opined that "nothing in the statute suggests that a delegation to a three-member group expires when one member's seat becomes vacant."

LAWYERS

A person, who through a regular program of study, is learned in legal matters and has been licensed to practice his or her profession. Any qualified person who prosecutes or defends causes in courts of record or other judicial tribunals of the United States, or of any of the states, or who renders legal advice or assistance in relation to any cause or matter.

Lawyers and Law Firms Struggle Through Difficult Financial Times

Law firms in 2009 and 2010 continued to struggle through challenging financial times. Clients became skeptical of the high fees that firms charged, and both large and small firms had to find ways to cut costs. During 2009 alone, firms across the country laid off more than 5,200 lawyers.

For many years, the high-end salaries of new lawyers at large law firms dominated the headlines. By 2007, more than 50 of the largest law firms paid new associates salaries of $160,000, leading many prospective law students and lawyers to expect a six-figure salary when they entered practice. However, even in 2007, the reality was that the majority of new lawyers made significantly less than $100,000. Between 1988 and 2007, the legal sector grew at a rate of only 1.2%, which was half the growth rate of the economy as a whole. Whereas some new graduates earned more than $100,000 a year, others struggled to find jobs making as much as $50,000 per year.

Unfortunately for both lawyers and law students, the recession that began in late 2007 and worsened in 2008 caused major problems that many large firms. Clients faced with their own financial problems looked to cut legal costs, and these businesses started to remove their business from larger firms and started using smaller firms that did not charge as much. Large firms not only instituted hiring freezes, but they cut salaries and laid off a number of lawyers. Some firms were forced to fold. Many of the lawyers who were laid off believed that their employment would always be stable. The result of the economic downturn was that many of these lawyers had to rethink their career options. Experts stressed that those with law degrees would likely have employment security but may lack job security in individual positions. Some large firm lawyers, including partners, chose to leave those firms to start or join smaller boutique firms that offered greater stability. Some experienced lawyers left law practice altogether.

Statistics compiled in late 2009 by the *National Law Journal* painted a bleak picture. In the nation's largest 250 law firms, the total number of lawyers shrank by 5,259 lawyers. The decline marked the first time since 1993 that the total number of lawyers decreased. Moreover, the 4.0% decline was the largest since the magazine started collecting data in 1978. Fifteen of the top 75 law firms on the list laid off 100 or more attorneys, and some large firms laid off 200 or more. The law firm of Fried, Frank, Harris, Shriver, and Jacobson, which has offices in several large cities, reduced its total number of attorneys by 26.4%, from 636 in 2008 to 468 in 2009. The firm of Latham & Watkins laid off the largest number of attorneys by releasing a total of 444 lawyers.

With experienced lawyers having difficulty with their careers, new lawyers faced even greater challenges. Many large firms did not hire law students to work as summer associates, and a number of those firms that did hire summer associates did not offer permanent positions to these law students. In other instances, firms offered the summer associates jobs but deferred the hiring for a year after the student graduated from law school. The practice of firms deferring hires affected other options for these students. More students decided to compete for job serving as judicial clerks, thus increasing competition for these clerkships.

Other law students faced even greater challenges. Some students had such difficulty finding jobs as attorneys that they accepted positions as paralegals. In New York, some law school graduates even had trouble finding work in law firms as paralegals or legal assistants. One law firm reported that when the firm posted an advertisement for an administrative assistant position, the firm received dozens of resumes from law graduates. The firm decided to hire a college graduate, though, out of concern that the law graduate would leave as soon as a lawyer position became available. Some new law graduates decided to start their own solo practices, but this can be a difficult decision to make, especially when a student has accumulated a large amount of student loan debt.

Although some signs suggested that legal market was improving in late 2009 and the early part of 2010, other statistics continued to be discouraging. According to the National

Association of Law Placement (NALP), recruiting efforts at law school campuses "nose-dived" in the fall, which is when most firms engage in recruiting efforts. The NALP estimated that between 3,200 and 3,700 graduating law students nationally faced deferrals, meaning that the students would go without work for at least a year after graduation (though firms often offer a stipend to those who receive deferrals). The NALP also expects the legal market to struggle until at least 2012.

As for those deciding to enter the legal profession, a number of commentators have suggested that prospective law students should look carefully at how much they spend on a LEGAL EDUCATION. Students expecting to make $160,000 when they enter the profession may be inclined to take out large student loans, but few make anywhere close to $160,000. According to U.S. News and World Report, most first-year associates at small firms earn between $49,750 and $73,000 per year, while new attorneys at midsize firms make between $71,500 and $100,750. Earning more than these amounts simply is not a realistic expectation for many new lawyers.

The declines in salaries and opportunities for lawyers corresponds with other stories of growing dissatisfaction among lawyers with the PRACTICE OF LAW. According to a survey conducted by AMERICAN BAR ASSOCIATION, only four out of ten lawyers would recommend a legal career to others.

LEGAL EDUCATION

Law School Rankings May Hurt Efforts Towards Diversity

Each spring, the magazine U.S. News and World Report publishes an issue ranking graduate programs across the United States. Prospective students and prospective employers rely on these rankings when they, respectively, decide which law schools to attend or which students to interview for jobs. The rankings have been heavily criticized because of the criteria used. In 2009, a study revealed that because the rankings rely so heavily on statistics that tend to favor certain types of applicants, these rankings have had an adverse effect on law school's efforts towards diversity.

U.S. News and World Report first published rankings of COLLEGES AND UNIVERSITIES in 1983.

In 1987, the magazine issued its first ranking of law schools. The next set of rankings was published in 1990, and they have been published annually since then. In 1987, Harvard ranked number one, but in each year since 1990, Yale Law School has taken the top spot. Although the specific order typically changes from one year to the next, Harvard, Yale, and 12 other students have made up what is known as the Top 14 (or T14). In addition to Harvard and Yale, the other schools in this list include: University of California, Berkeley School of Law; University of Chicago Law School; Columbia University Law School; Cornell University Law School; Duke University School of Law; Georgetown University Law Center; University of Michigan Law School; New York University School of Law; Northwestern University School of Law; University of Pennsylvania Law School; Stanford Law School; and University of Virginia School of Law.

U.S. News measures a number of objective criteria. The magazine includes such numbers as the median LAW SCHOOL ADMISSION TEST (LSAT) score of each school's students, along with median undergraduate grade point average, acceptance rate, student/faculty ratio, employment statistics, bar passage rate, and expenditures. The magazine also polls faculty and administrators from each law school and lawyers at several large law firms to gauge each school's overall reputation. These subjective reputation scores count for 40 percent of the overall score used to rank each school. The magazine uses the overall scores to give each law school a number. For schools in the top 100, the magazine lists schools in order of their ranking. The magazine places other schools below the top 100 into either the third tier or fourth tier, but the magazine does not rank the schools in order.

The rankings have had an undeniable effect on how many law schools operate. These rankings not only affect decisions made by prospective law students about where to attend law school, but the rankings also affect decisions on which faculty law school's should hire. In some instances, law schools have fired administrators when the schools have slipped in the rankings. Schools focus heavily on increasing their statistics to give them a better chance to improve in the rankings. In fact, some schools have been accused of improperly manipulating their statistics. For example, some schools have been accused of hiring their own students temporarily after these students graduate for the sole purpose of boosting the schools' employment statistics.

The rankings do not measure a number of attributes that may be important to some applicants. For example, applicants should take into account the cost of a program, quality of instruction, geographical location, areas of specialization, clinical opportunities, library services, and facilities when deciding which law schools to attend. *U.S. News* rankings either do not take these factors into account, or these factors only have a minimal effect on the actual rankings. The AMERICAN BAR ASSOCIATION (ABA), Association of American Law Schools (AALS), and Law School Admission Council (LSAC) have either refused to participate in the rankings or have openly criticized the rankings or ranking methodology. The LSAC stresses that *U.S. News and World Report* arbitrarily weighs the various factors. Carl C. Monk, former executive director of the AALS, called the rankings "a misleading and deceptive, profit-generating commercial enterprise that compromises U.S. News and World Report's journalistic integrity."

In 2009, two sociologists named Wendy Espeland and Michael Sauder studied the effect of the rankings. Espeland and Sauder reiterated concerns of others, noting: "Rankings not only influence individual decisions about where to apply and attend law school, but also organizational decisions such as whom to admit or hire, how to evaluate the work of subordinates, peers, and superiors, and how to think about status and specialization in the field of LEGAL EDUCATION. Rankings subtly, powerfully, and enduringly shape perceptions of ability and achievement."

Espeland and Sauder published their findings in the Fall 2009 edition of the *Southern California Review of Law and Social Justice*. The authors focused much of their attention on use of LSAT scores and grade point averages in admissions decisions. Previous studies have shown that members of certain racial groups and those with certain economic backgrounds tend to perform worse on standardized tests compared with other students. Moreover, other studies have shown that LSAT scores

are unreliable indicators of achievement in law school or after law school. Nevertheless, schools focus heavily on boosting the median LSAT scores and grade point averages of their entering students because of the effect of these statistics on the rankings. Moreover, though schools often set aside scholarship money for members of underrepresented and disadvantaged groups, the money is more typically used to bring in students with higher LSAT scores, according to the Espeland and Sauder study.

Bob Morse, the director of data research for *U.S. News and World Report*, disagreed with the report's conclusions. Morse noted that because the rankings measure median scores rather than average scores, schools are not punished for admitting students with very low scores. For instance, if a school admits 100 students in a class, and the median LSAT score of this class were 160, admitting a student with an LSAT score of 150 (or lower) would have no effect on the rankings. According to Morse, "The median gives schools considerable flexibility to accept students with very low LSAT and undergraduate grades without lowering the school's actual LSAT and and grade-point average—and in turn, without negatively affecting their *U.S. News* rankings.

The *U.S. News* does include a separate diversity index, but this index is not measured as part of the overall *U.S. News* rankings. Morse said factoring diversity into the rankings would be difficult but that the magazine would be open to suggestions from legal educators about how diversity could be incorporated.

LEGAL RESEARCH

Ensuring Authenticity of Online Legal Resources Causes Issues for Government Providers

Legal information has been available on a many government websites since the 1990s. The U.S. GOVERNMENT PRINTING OFFICE (GPO) produced a site known as GPO Access, which has provided online access to a wide **array** of legislative, executive, and administrative documents. State governments followed suit. When states suffered budgetary problems due to the recession of the late 2000s, though, some state governments stopped printing official versions of laws and relied exclusively on the online versions. This practice has caused problems because the online versions may not have been verified to be authentic. States as a general matter have been slow to authenticate their online information, but GPO has created a new website featuring authenticated information.

Many legal resources have traditionally appeared in official and unofficial forms. An official version of a law means that it was produced through the authority of the government. In the case of the federal government, official sources are authorized by **statute** and are produced by GPO. For instance, for statutes currently in force, Congress requires publication of the United States Code (also referred to as the Code of Laws of the United States), which is produced by GPO. Under 1 U.S.C. § 204, "The matter set forth in the edition of the Code of Laws of the United States current at any time shall, together with the then current supplement, if any, establish **prima facie** the laws of the United States, general and permanent in their nature...." Many states produce similar official sources, with a state's SECRETARY OF STATE often overseeing the publication of these sources.

On some sites, such as GPO Access, users can retrieve different version of the legal materials. For instance, if a user on GPO Access wants to retrieve the text of an administrative regulation, the user can do so by accessing the CODE OF FEDERAL REGULATIONS in either a text form or a portable document file (PDF) form. The PDF form is essentially a digital photocopy of the print version of a source, appearing exactly as the print source does. Assuming that the PDF version is in fact identical to the authentic official print source, the PDF version is typically more reliable for legal researchers than other forms of the law. Several state government sites also provide PDF versions of their laws.

It is difficult, however, to verify whether an online version indeed accurately reflects the actual text of the law. A user who retrieves the text of a law in PDF form from a government website may assume that the law must be accurate. However, it is possible that the version retrieved could be different than what the actual law is. The issue is whether the law retrieved is actually the authoritative text of that law, and unless the source has been authenticated, the users cannot completely rely on the text. A

committee of the American Association of Law Libraries (AALL) defines an authentic legal resource as, "An authentic text is one whose content has been verified by a government **entity** to be complete and unaltered when compared to the version approved or published by the content originator. Typically, an authentic text will bear a certificate or mark that conveys information as to its certification, the process associated with ensuring that the text is complete and unaltered when compared with that of the content originator. An authentic text is able to be authenticated, which means that the particular text in question can be validated, ensuring that it is what it claims to be."

In 2007, the AALL issued a report that summarized the online publication of laws from all 50 states and the District of Columbia. According to the report, a significant percentage of states provided official version of sources online, but none of these sources were authenticated according to AALL's definition. Based on this conclusion, the AALL concluded that "[S]tate online primary legal resources are therefore not sufficiently trustworthy." AALL continued to track the status of the government websites between 2007 and 2010. An AALL report issued in February 2010 showed that a handful of states had made changes to the publication of their materials. According to this report, "[A] few states have made changes to online legal publications, including adding official and authentic notations to the information, making the information more accessible, and even eliminating print publications in favor of online only. One of the most significant changes noted in the 2009-10 update is the addition of disclaimers to many state Web sites regarding authentication and official format of the information online."

Concerns over the authenticity of online legal information has not been limited to law librarians or other academics. One judge referred to the AALL report as a "timely wake-up call for work that needs to be done to ensure the integrity and trustworthiness of electronically transmitted and maintained legal documents and information." This judge expressed concerns about preserving the integrity of all types of legal materials, including the current and archived versions of various laws. Denley Chew, counsel for the Federal Reserve Bank of

New York, echoed concerns about authenticity, telling an audience at an AMERICAN BAR ASSOCI- ATION conference that he did not think the problem would be resolved until someone lost a $10 million case based on an inaccurate version of the law.

GPO may have resolved any concerns over the authenticity of federal information with the creation of the Federal Digital System, also known as FDsys. Throughout 2009 and 2010, GPO has moved collections of materials from the 15-year-old GPO Access to the new FDsys site, available at http://www.gpo.gov/fdsys. Moreover, GPO is digitally signing each of these collections, meaning that these collections will be properly authenticated.

Google and Other Companies Offer New Free Sources for Legal Information

Recent years have seen a significant growth in the amount of free legal information available on different Internet websites. One of the newest sites to provide access to such information is Google Scholar, as the company announced in 2009 that it had developed a database that allowed users to search for cases from the state and federal levels. With the development of these databases on Google Scholar, along with other open source sites, Internet users can find a substantial amount of information that previously was difficult to find except on subscription databases or in print resources.

Judicial opinions issued by state and **federal courts** are published in various repor- ters. Some states publish what are considered official reporters, meaning that the state has identified a specific source that provides the authoritative text of the published opinions. During the late nineteenth century, an innova- tor named John B. West formed the West Publishing Company, which began to publish cases through a system of reporters that covered various regions. Over time, West's National Reporter System covered virtually every **appellate** jurisdiction in the United States. Although the reporters in the National Reporter System are not considered official, these reporters for many years were the only standard source for judicial opinions in states that did not publish official reporters.

By the 1970s, the Internet was in its infancy, but more information was appearing in elec- tronic form. In 1973, a company named Mead

Data Central developed a system known as LEXIS, which provided access to New York and Ohio judicial opinions. By 1980, the database had expanded to include all state and federal cases. West developed its own system, Westlaw, which was launched in 1975. Westlaw and LEXIS have added many databases over the years and remain the top two systems used by lawyers and law schools in the United States. However, use these systems involves substantial costs. Large law firms typically pay more than a million dollars annually to access the databases. Smaller firms pay less (and have more restricted access), but costs to smaller firms still runs in the thousands per year. Ordinary citizens are typically either unable or unwilling to pay the costs to use these databases. Some other companies have produced alternative subscrip- tion databases, which are usually less expensive but which are also less comprehensive.

Since the 1990s, a number of Internet sources have provided free access to legal materials. However, many of these sites were not comprehensive, and most did not cover opinions other than those from the highest courts in the various jurisdictions. Several courts—both state and federal—provide access to opinions on their websites, but these opinions are often difficult to search. Moreover, these cases were limited to a single court rather than to an entire jurisdiction. For instance, a researcher in Texas can search for several Texas SUPREME COURT decisions on that court's website. How- ever, if the researcher wants to find cases from a lower **appellate court** in Texas, he or she must visit the websites of each of the lower courts. Given that several of these lower courts do not provide access to their opinions, this means of searching cases is often ineffective.

In 2004, Google released Google Scholar to provide access to the full text of articles published in top American and European journals. Some of the articles appear in traditional web format (i.e., text format using hypertext markup language, or HTML), while others appear in portable document file (PDF) format. Google also attempts to rank the relevance of various document by taking into account the search terms used, the journal in which an article was published, and how often and how recently an article was published. In addition to journals, Google Scholar also contains abstracts of various books.

In November 2009, Google announced that it had expanded Google Scholar to include the text of legal opinions and law journals. Google's announcement stated, "As many of us recall from our civics lessons in school, the United States is a common law country. That means when judges issue opinions in legal cases, they often establish precedents that will guide the rulings of other judges in similar cases and jurisdictions. Over time, these legal opinions build, refine and clarify the laws that govern our land. For average citizens, however, it can be difficult to find or even read these landmark opinions. We think that's a problem: Laws that you don't know about, you can't follow—or make effective arguments to change."

Google Scholar allows users to search cases by both case name and by subject matter. When a user enters a search, such as "separate but equal," the user sees a list of relevant cases. The top two cases for this search are *Brown v. Board of Education*, 347 U.S. 483, 74 S. Ct. 686, 98 L. Ed. 873 (1954) and *Plessy v. Ferguson*, 163 U.S. 537, 16 S. Ct. 1138, 41 L. Ed. 256 (1896). The list of cases displayed after a search also includes a "How Cited" link, which shows a list of cases that have cited the case that appears in the result list. This feature allows users to see how other courts have applied principles in the case.

Although legal opinions are often difficult for non-lawyers to understand completely, the developers of Google Scholar think that the opinions are nevertheless accessible in terms of language. "As we worked to build this feature, we were struck by how readable and accessible these opinions are," the announcement said. "Court opinions don't just describe a decision but also present the reasons that support the decision. In doing so, they explain the intricacies of law in the context of real-life situations. And they often do it in language that is surprisingly straightforward, even for those of us outside the legal profession. In many cases, judges have gone quite a bit out of their way to make complex legal issues easy to follow."

Google Scholar is not alone among relatively new sites that provide access to judicial opinions and other materials. One site, OpenJurist, provides access to nearly 650,000 opinions from the U.S. Supreme Court and the lower federal courts. Another site, Justia, similarly provides full-text access to federal cases dating back to 1950.

LIBEL

Two torts that involve the communication of false information about a person, a group, or an entity such as a corporation. Libel is any defamation that can be seen, such as a writing, printing, effigy, movie, or statue. Slander is any defamation that is spoken and heard.

Tenth Circuit Upholds Dismissal of Libel Suit Against Author John Grisham

The Tenth **Circuit Court** of Appeals in February 2010 affirmed a district court's dismissal of a libel suit brought against author John Grisham. The plaintiffs in the case included a state district attorney, a former police officer, and a former state criminologist, each of whom were involved in two wrongful conviction cases. These cases were the subject of several books, and the plaintiffs claimed that statements made in these books were false and defamatory, among other allegations. The Tenth Circuit concluded that statements in these books were privileged and were not **libelous** as a result.

In 1982, a woman named Debra Sue Carter was raped and murdered in her apartment in Ada, Oklahoma. Four years after the attack, police officer Gary Rogers and others arrested Ronald Williamson and Dennis Fritz for Carter's MURDER. Oklahoma District Attorney William Peterson tried the case, which was based on a collection of hair and semen samples, Williamson's statement to police that he had committed a murder, and testimony given by jailhouse informants. Criminologist Melvin Hett testified at trial that the hair belonged to Williamson and Fritz, who were convicted of murder by a jury in 1988. Williamson was sentenced to death, while Fritz received a life sentence.

In 1995, four days before Williamson's scheduled execution, Judge Frank H. Seay of the U.S. **District Court** for the Eastern District of Oklahoma issued an order granting a petition for **writ** of **habeas corpus** in Williamson's case. *Williamson v. Reynolds*, 904 F. Supp. 1529 (E.D. Okla. 1995). Two years later, the Tenth Circuit affirmed the district court's opinion. *Williamson v. Ward*, 110 F.3d 1508 (10th Cir. 1997). The district court ordered DNA testing of the hair and semen samples, and the results showed that the men had been wrongly convicted. Another man, Glen Dale Gore, was later found guilty of the crimes. Williamson suffered from mental illness and alcoholism, and he died in 2004. Before Williamson's death, both he and Fritz recovered large settlement amounts from both the City of Ada and the State of Oklahoma.

Two different books focused on the wrongful convictions of Williamson and Fritz. In 2006, popular author John Grisham published *The Innocent Man*, which focuses on Williamson's life story. The book largely blames Peterson, Rogers, and Hett for the conviction, noting that the criminal justice system in Oklahoma condones "bad police work, junk science, faulty EYEWITNESS identifications, bad defense lawyers, lazy prosecutors, [and] arrogant prosecutors." A second book was written by Fritz and is entitled *Journey Toward Justice*. Fritz's book provides a recount of his experience from the time he was arrested to the time of his **exoneration** and release. The story was also featured in a chapter of attorney Barry Scheck's book entitled *Actual Innocence* as well as a book that focused on a similar crime in Ada during the 1980s.

Following the publication of these books in 2006, Peterson, Hett, and Rogers sued several of the authors and publishers on four claims, including **defamation**, false light publicity, civil CONSPIRACY, and intentional infliction of emotional distress. The claims focused on a total of 71 statements contained in three books. The plaintiffs contended that the defendants had engaged in a "massive joint defamatory attack" against the plaintiffs, motivated by the defendants' anti-death penalty views. The plaintiffs brought the case in the U.S. District Court for the Eastern District of Oklahoma.

The defendants filed motions to dismiss pursuant to Rule 12(b)(6) of the Federal Rules of **Civil Procedure**. Much of the district court's focus was on the defamation claims. Oklahoma law applies broad protection for speech against claims for libel brought by public officials. Under Oklahoma law, unless a DEFENDANT has made a false ALLEGATION regarding criminal behavior, a person who criticizes a public

official on a matter of public concern is absolutely protected from a libel claim. In reviewing statements in the books in question, the district court determined that none of the statements provided the basis to sustain a libel claim. The court wrote, "While the plaintiffs in this case may feel the sting of criticism, because of the enormous constitutional obstacle concerning political speech, they do not plausibly assert any statement which entitles them to relief." The court likewise concluded that the plaintiffs had not alleged facts that supported the other claims, so the court dismissed the entire action. *Peterson v. Grisham*, No. CIV-07-317-RAW, 2008 WL 4363653 (E.D. Okla. Sept. 17, 2008).

The plaintiffs appealed the case to the Tenth Circuit Court of Appeals. The Tenth Circuit reiterated that the plaintiffs had a difficult standard to satisfy because the plaintiffs were public officials. The court noted that several of the statements did not concern any of the plaintiffs and could not serve as the basis for a libel claim under any standard. Other statements simply did not accuse the plaintiffs of committing a crime. The court noted, "Plaintiffs expect us to scale a mountain of inferences in order to reach the conclusion that defendants' statements impute criminal acts to plaintiffs and render the **statutory** privilege...inapplicable. We decline to engage in such inferential analysis, or to take a myriad of other analytical leaps plaintiffs ask us to make. Any connection between defendants' statement and an accusation of criminal activity is far too tenuous for us to declare them unprivileged...."

The court also determined that the same privilege that applies to libel cases also applies to the torts of intentional infliction of emotional distress and false light invasion of privacy. Accordingly, the court dismissed those claims, as well as the claim for civil conspiracy. *Peterson v. Grisham*, 594 F.3d 723 (10th Cir. 2010).

MINOW, MARTHA

On June 11, 2009, Harvard University President Drew Faust announced that law professor Martha Minow had been appointed as Dean of Harvard Law School. Minow has been a member of the Harvard Law faculty since 1981 and is a former professor of BARACK OBAMA. Minow was considered as a potential candidate to replace Justice JOHN PAUL STEVENS, but the nomination went to the woman whom Minow replaced as dean at Harvard, Elena Kagan.

Minow received her undergraduate degree from the University of Michigan in 1975. She received a master's degree in education from Harvard University in 1976 and then enrolled at Yale Law School, from which she graduated in 1979. She served as a clerk with Judge David Bazelon of the U.S. Court of Appeals for the D.C. Circuit before serving as a clerk for Justice THURGOOD MARSHALL of the U.S. SUPREME COURT. After serving her two clerkships, she joined the Harvard Law faculty in 1981 as an assistant professor. The school promoted her to full professor in 1986. She has been named both the William Henry Bloomberg Professor of Law (2003) and the Jeremiah Smith, Jr. Professor of Law (2005). She also holds an appointment as a lecturer at the Harvard Graduate School of Education.

She published extensively as a faculty member, focusing her research efforts on such topics international HUMAN RIGHTS, equality, religion, managing mass LITIGATION, FAMILY LAW, EDUCATION LAW, and the privatization of military, schooling, and other governmental activities. She has written or served as a major editor on 16 books. She has also written dozens of scholarly articles that have appeared in a wide variety of leading journals, including *Harvard Law Review*, *University of Pennsylvania Law Review*, *California Law Review*, and *Columbia Law Review*. She has likewise given many presentations and written a number of editorials, with most appearing in the *Boston Globe*. The courses she has taught have likewise been diverse, including **civil procedure**, **constitutional law**, nonprofit organizations, family law, law and education, **jurisprudence**, and the legal profession.

At the time of her appointment, Faust said of Minow: "Martha Minow has been an intellectual leader, a devoted teacher and mentor, a collaborative colleague, and an exemplary institutional citizen across her nearly three decades of service on the Harvard Law School faculty. She's a scholar of remarkable intelligence, imagination, and scope, with a passion for LEGAL EDUCATION and a deep sense of how the law can serve essential public purposes. She has played an important and influential role in the institutional life of the Law School and the University over the years, and I am delighted that she has agreed to serve as dean during a critical time in the long and storied history of the School."

From 2003 to 2006, Minow served as the co-chair of Harvard Law School's curriculum-reform committee. This committee's efforts led to significant changes not only in Harvard's first-year curriculum but also the curriculum at other law schools. She has also served as a senior fellow with the Harvard Society of Fellows; as a member of the Harvard University Press Board of Syndics; as acting director of Harvard's Safra Foundation Center for Ethics; and as co-chair of the Harvard Project on Justice, WELFARE, and Economics. In 2005, the Law School honored Minow with the Sacks-Freund Award for Teaching Excellence. She has also received an honorary doctorate of law from the University of Toronto and an Honorary Doctorate of Education from Wheelock College.

Minow said of her appointment: "In this time of both challenge and promise for this country and for the world, Harvard Law School faculty, students, staff, and graduates are already playing pivotal roles in the search for financial stability, national security, peaceful international relations, and legal order. I am eager to help the remarkable community of people at the Harvard Law School, in concert with colleagues across Harvard and beyond, continue to pursue the promise of the **rule of law**, the ideal of justice, the practical solution of problems, and ever deeper understandings of legal institutions and commitments."

Minow replaced Kagan, who had served as dean from 2003 until 2009. Kagan left the position when Obama appointed her to serve as **Solicitor General** in 2009. One year later, Justice John Paul Stevens announced that he would retire, and Obama considered a number of potential replacements, including Minow. During his 2008 presidential campaign, Obama had identified Minow as one of his law professors who had changed his life. Minow as also credited as "one of the very first people to identify" Obama as a future leader, according to a source close to Obama. The president had already appointed Mionw to serve on the LEGAL SERVICES CORPORATION, which is a government-sponsored organization that provides legal assistance to low-income Americans. However, in May 2009, Obama chose Kagan as his nominee.

Minow took over as dean of Harvard Law at a time when the school was suffering from difficult financial times. Just before she took over as dean, the law school announced that it

1979	Received law degree from Yale
1985	Became full professor at Harvard
2005	Received Sacks-Freund Award for teaching excellence
2009	Became dean of Harvard Law School

would receive a significant reduction in returns on its **endowment**, leading to cuts in every department. Nevertheless, she was able to introduce new programs that would address student concerns aid to students who were having difficulty finding jobs or who wished to enter the public service. "My goals are to help the Harvard Law School continue to be the leader in legal education in the world, which includes continuing to enhance the student experience, continuing to enhance the faculty, [and] managing during a turbulent economic time," she told the *Harvard Law Record* in November 2009.

MIRANDA RIGHTS

Maryland v. Schatzer

The SUPREME COURT has continued to deal with the parameters of **custodial interrogation** that it first set out in *Miranda v. Arizona*, 384 U.S. 436, 86 S. Ct. 1602, 16 L. Ed. 2d 694 (1966). The right to remain silent and the right to have a lawyer present during a police interrogation remain firmly set in **constitutional law** but questions as to when such protections are triggered and how long they remain in effect have continued to bedevil the Court. In *Maryland v. Schatzer*, __U.S.__, 130 S. Ct. 1213, __L. Ed. 2d__ (2010), the Court was called on to determine whether an inmate who invoked his *Miranda* rights could have voluntary statements suppressed that he made three years later while in prison. The Court ruled that the statements could be admitted into evidenced and announced a new rule: when a person has been released from CUSTODY after invoking his FIFTH AMENDMENT rights, these protections expire after 14 days.

In 2003, Michael Schatzer, Sr., was serving time in a Maryland prison for a child SEXUAL

ABUSE crime. A social worker alerted police to a report that Schatzer had sexually abused his three-year-old son. A detective went to the prison and read Schatzer his *Miranda* warnings. The inmate initially waived his rights but changed his mind and ended the interview. In 2006 the same social worker referred more specific allegations about Schatzer abusing his son to police. The son, now eight, provided details to the social worker and a different police detective about the abuse. The social worker and detective went to the prison and met with Schatzer in a private room. This time he waived his *Miranda* rights and discussed the allegations. He admitted to one ALLEGATION, denied a more serious one, and agreed to submit to a POLYGRAPH examination. Five days later the exam was administered, but not before Schatzer again waived his rights. Informed that he had failed the test, Shatzer confessed to a sexual ASSAULT on his son but then requested a lawyer.

Schatzer was charged with several counts of sexual abuse and assault. He challenged the admissibility of his confession, claiming that the police had violated the rule established in *Edwards v. Arizona* , 451 U.S. 477, 101 S. Ct. 1880. 68 L. Ed. 2d 378. (1981). In that case the Supreme Court stated that: "[W]hen an accused has invoked his right to have counsel present during CUSTODIAL INTERROGATION, a valid waiver of that right cannot be established by showing only that he responded to further police-initiated custodial interrogation even if he has been advised of his rights.... [He] is not subject to further interrogation by the authorities until counsel has been made available to him, unless the accused himself initiates further communication, exchanges, or conversations with the police." Schatzer contended that even though almost three years elapsed between interrogations, police could not use his statements unless a lawyer was present. The trial court rejected Schatzer's argument and in a **bench trial** (no jury) convicted him of the sexual abuse of his son. The Maryland Court of Appeals overturned the conviction, agreeing that "the passage of time alone is insufficient to [end] the protections under *Edwards.*" Schatzer's release back into the general prison population between interrogations did not constitute a break in custody.

The U.S. Supreme Court, in a unanimous decision, overturned the state court decision. Justice ANTONIN SCALIA, writing for the Court,

reviewed the history and scope of *Miranda* and noted the importance of *Edwards* . However, he concluded that at some point *Miranda* custody must end. Otherwise, "every *Edwards* prohibition of custodial interrogation of a particular suspect would be eternal." Extending the "protective umbrella" of *Edwards* was out of the question when a break in custody was of sufficient duration. It seemed clear that more than two years between interrogations was a sufficient duration but the Court resolved to end any doubt or future LITIGATION as to the amount of time that would pass constitutional muster. Scalia stated that case-by-case **adjudication** was impractical. Moreover, "law enforcement officers need to know, with certainty and beforehand, when renewed interrogation is lawful." Though he acknowledged that it was unusual to set precise time limits on police action, it had been done before. Therefore, *Edwards* protection must end 14 days after the person is released from custody. The Court believed this was "ample time for the suspect to get reacclimated to his normal life, consult with friends and counsel, and shake off any residual coercive effects of prior custody." As for Schatzer, his release back into the general prison population in 2003 triggered the time limit. Therefore, his 2006 statement was properly admitted into evidence.

Berghuis v. Thompkins

Perhaps one of the most often quoted or cited cases ever decided by the U.S. SUPREME COURT is that of *Miranda v. Arizona,* 384 U.S. 436. (1966). Over the ensuing years, virtually every adult American and most youths have gained some concept of what constitutes their "Miranda Rights," including their right to remain silent and to obtain legal counsel when being questioned by police. In *Berghuis v. Thompkins,* No. 08-1470, 560 U.S. ___ (2010), the U.S. Supreme Court took a major step in refining those rights.

In February 2001, police officers in Southfield, Michigan questioned Van Chester Thompkins about a shooting that had occurred almost a year prior. During that 2000 shooting, one man died from multiple gunshot wounds, but another survived and later testified. Thompkins, a suspect, had fled to Ohio. He was later apprehended and arrested in Ohio. While awaiting transfer to Michigan, two Michigan police officers traveled to Ohio to interrogate him. At the beginning of the roughly three-hour session, one of the officers presented Thompkins with a form derived from the *Miranda* rule, entitled, "Notification of Constitutional Rights and Statement." One of the officers, Detective Helgert, asked Thompkins to read out loud the fifth warning listed on the form, to which Thompson complied. The fifth warning stated, "You have the right to decide at any time before or during questioning to use your right to remain silent and your right to talk with a lawyer while you are being questioned." (Helgert later said his request to Thompkins was to ensure that Thompkins could read and understand English.) Helgert then read the other four warnings out loud to Thompkins and asked him to sign the form to demonstrate that he understood those rights. Thomkins declined to sign the form. (The record contained conflicting evidence as to whether Thompkins then verbally confirmed that he understood the rights listed on the form.)

In any event, the officers then began an interrogation. At no point during the interrogation did Thompkins state that he did not wanted to talk to police, that he wanted to remain silent, or that he wanted an attorney. However, he remained "[l]argely" silent during the next three hours. Periodically, he did verbally respond to a few questions with a verbal "yeah" or "no" or "I don't know." On occasion, he nodded his head in response.

Near the end of the interrogation, Helgert asked Thompkins, "Do you believe in God?" Thompkins' eyes welled with tears as he responded, "Yes." Helgert then asked, "Do you pray to God?" Thompkins again verbally responded, "Yes." Helgert asked, "Do you pray to God to forgive you for shooting that boy down?" Thompkins again said, "Yes. "

Later, at Thompkins' criminal trial, defense counsel moved to suppress Thompkins' incriminating statements, arguing that he had invoked his FIFTH AMENDMENT right to remain silent, that he had not waived that right, and that his inculpatory statements were involuntary. The trial court denied the motion to suppress.

Thompkins' defense was that another DEFENDANT, who drove the van in which Thompkins and another ACCOMPLICE were riding at the time of the shooting, was the shooter. The driver, Eric Purifoy, had been convicted of firearm offenses but acquitted of MURDER and ASSAULT. He testified at Thompkins' trial that he did not see who fired the shots. Defense counsel did not ask for a jury instruction that it could consider evidence of the outcome of Purifoy's trial only to assess his credibility and not to establish Thompkins' guilt. The jury ultimately found Thompkins guilty. He was sentenced to life in prison without PAROLE.

The trial court denied Thompkins' request for a new trial based on ineffective counsel (for failing to request a limiting jury instruction about the outcome of Purifoy's trial), deeming it as nonprejudicial. The Michigan Court of Appeals rejected both his ineffective counsel claim and his *Miranda* claim.

Thompkins next tried for habeas relief through federal **district court**, but that request was denied, the court concluding that Thompkins had not invoked his right to remain silent (at the interrogation) and was not coerced into making statements. Further, the district court found that under the Antiterrorism and Effective Death Penalty Act of 1996 (AEDPA) 28 U.S.C. §2254(d)(1), which limits habeas relief, the state **appellate court** had not been unreasonable in finding that he had waived his right to remain silent.

But the Sixth **Circuit Court** of Appeals reversed, holding that the state court applied the law in an objectively unreasonable manner. It granted Thompkins' petitions on both the *Miranda* and ineffective counsel claims.

A divided U.S. Supreme Court endorsed the state court's opinion, thereby effectively finding it "reasonable" under AEDPA's more deferential standard of review. Writing for the majority, Justice Kennedy held that Thompkins' silence during his interrogation did not invoke his right to remain silent. The Court cited a previous case, *Davis v. United States,* 512 U.S. 452, which held that a suspect's *Miranda* RIGHT TO COUNSEL must be invoked "unambiguously." In that case, the Court ruled that if an accused made "ambiguous or equivocal" statements or no statement at all, the police could continue the interrogation and were not required to clarify the accused's intent. Now, in *Thompkins,* there was no principled reason to adopt a different standard for determining when an accused had invoked his *Miranda* right to remain silent and the *Miranda* right to counsel (at issue in the *Davis* case. Both rights protect against compulsory SELF-INCRIMINATION by requiring an interrogation to cease when either right is invoked. Both require unambiguous assertion by the accused. If Thompkins had told the police that he wanted to remain silent or that he did not want to talk, he would have invoked his right to end the questioning. He did neither. In sum, said the Court, after giving a *Miranda* warning, police may interrogate a suspect who has neither invoked nor waived his *Miranda* rights.

The Court also agreed with the state court as to the ineffective counsel claim, reiterating that a defendant must show both deficient performance as well as prejudice. Here, Thompkins did not show prejudice, even under *de novo* review of the record [AEDPA, 28 U.S.C. §2254(a)].

Justice Sotomayor filed a strong DISSENT, joined by Justices Stevens, Ginsburg, and Breyer. "Today's decision turns *Miranda* upside down," she wrote. "Criminal suspects must now unambiguously invoke their right to remain silent—which, counterintuitively, requires them to speak. At the same time, suspects will be legally presumed to have waived their rights even in they have given no clear expression of their intent to do so."

MURDER

The unlawful killing of another human being without justification or excuse.

Former Police Officer Indicted for His Wife's Murder

Drew Peterson, a former police sergeant in Bolingbrook, Illinois, was indicted in May 2009 for the death of his third wife. By that time, he had already been a suspect in the disappearance of his fourth wife, who was first reported missing in October 2007. The media has followed Peterson's case closely due not only to the nature of the alleged crimes, but also to Peterson's willingness to answer questions publicly.

Peterson was originally from the Chicago area before being trained as a police officer in Virginia. In 1977, he began his career with the police department in Bolingbrook, Illinois, a suburb of Chicago. Early in his career, he won his department's "Police Officer of the Year" award, but by 1985, he faced allegations that he had failed to report a bribe, had been

Drew Peterson leaves court, July 30, 2008.
AP IMAGES

disobedient, and had committed other acts of misconduct. The Bolingbrook Police Department initially fired Peterson, but official charges were later dismissed after a judge determined that the department lacked evidence to convict Peterson. In 1986, the department reinstated Peterson.

Peterson was married to his first wife, Carol Brown, from 1974 to 1980. He later married Victoria Connolly, but the two were divorced in 1992. Years after she and Peterson divorced, Connelly alleged that Peterson had abused both her and her daughter. At the end of his marriage to Connelly, Peterson was allegedly involved with Kathleen Savio, and two months after his DIVORCE was finalized, he married Savio. His marriage to Savio lasted until their divorce was finalized in October 2003. Just as he did when he divorced his second wife, Peterson did not remain single for long, as he married Stacy Ann Cales two weeks after his divorce to Savio was finalized.

Between 2002 and 2004, police were reportedly called 18 different times for domestic disturbance incidents between Peterson and Savio. In early 2004, Peterson and Savio were still working to complete the final stages of the divorce settlement. However, on March 1, 2004, neighbors found Savio's body in a bathtub of her home. Her head had a half-inch gash in the back of it. Peterson was a suspect in the death, and a coroner's jury was convened to review the evidence. One member of the jury was a police officer who knew Peterson and who reportedly told other jurors that Peterson was not the type

TESTIMONY FROM THE GRAVE: THE DREW PETERSON LAW AND HEARSAY EXCEPTIONS IN HOMICIDE CASES

In July 2010, Illinois prosecutors found themselves backed up against a wall despite the passage of legislation they thought would help them: the state's new law allowing hearsay evidence if prosecutors can prove that the defendant killed the victim to prevent him or her from testifying. Dubbed by the media as the "Drew Peterson Law" or "Drew's Law," it was codified in 2009 as 725 ILCS5/115-10.6, after the Illinois legislature passed the law in November 2008. The law's infamous namesake, Drew Peterson, a retired Chicago police sergeant who has been married four times, was charged with the murder of his third wife, Kathleen Savio. He also remained a key suspect in the disappearance of his fourth wife, Stacy Peterson, who, as of July 2010, was still missing. Peterson denied all charges.

Third wife Savio's 2004 death was originally ruled an accidental drowning after her body was found in an empty bathtub. After fourth wife Stacy Peterson's disappearance in late 2007, Savio's body was exhumed and her death reinvestigated. Two more autopsies were performed, one by the state and one by a private examiner hired by her family. Both examinations resulted in Savio's death being changed from accidental to criminal; the state subsequently ruled it a homicide and charged Drew Peterson.

Prior to Stacy's disappearance, she allegedly had voiced serious doubts about Savio's demise, hinting that her husband Drew might have played a role. She specifically commented on his 29 years'

experience as a policeman and statements he had made boasting that he knew how to conceal or cover up wrongdoing. She further intimated to several persons, including family members and a pastor, that she feared the same fate as Savio. Savio's family claimed that she, too, had told them that she feared her husband would kill her.

There is no physical evidence linking Peterson to either Savio's death or Stacy Peterson's disappearance. Therefore, prosecutors were relying on Illinois' new law to introduce "testimony from the grave" against Peterson in the Savio murder trial, and connect his fourth wife's disappearance through the same evidentiary tactic.

During pretrial hearings in Peterson's pending murder trial for the death of his third wife (Savio)), prosecutors produced nearly 70 witnesses, mostly family members, friends, and clergy, to testify that both women were afraid of Peterson and hinted at their beliefs that he might kill them. In a landmark evidentiary ruling on hearsay earlier in 2010, Judge Stephen White agreed with prosecutors and found that a preponderance of evidence suggested that Peterson killed Savio and caused Stacy's disappearance. (The evidentiary hearing only required a "preponderance" finding; whereas at trial, Peterson would still need to be found guilty "beyond a reasonable doubt.") This left open the door for the hearsay evidence of the above witnesses.

But in May 2010, Judge White barred the testimony of a majority of the hearsay witnesses, finding that they "did not provide sufficient safeguards of reliability." Under Drew's Law, prosecutors must prove the reliability of the hearsay evidence they intend to introduce.

Five weeks later, in an unrelated case, the Illinois Supreme Court upheld the conviction of Eric Hanson, sentenced to death for the 2005 murder of four relatives. The state high court unanimously held that common law did not require judges to weigh a hearsay statement's reliability.

However, in July 2010, Judge White refused to reconsider his decision in light of the Hanson case. Although prosecutors had requested that he consider admitting the hearsay statements under both common law and Drew's Law, he concluded, in his opinion, that he was bound by guidelines established under Drew's Law. As to Hanson, Judge White noted that he had been convicted prior to the passage of Drew's Law and therefore faced a different standard. "[W]hen you codify common law ... that codification (in this case, Drew's Law) takes precedence over the common law," White said.

Later in July 2010, prosecutors delayed Peterson's trial to allow for appeal of the judge's ruling on the hearsay evidence.

Overcoming Hurdles to Admitting Inculpatory Hearsay Evidence
Hearsay evidence, i.e., "second-hand"

who would hurt his wife. Based on the coroner's jury conclusion, the death was ruled an accidental drowning.

On the morning of October 29, 2007, Stacy Peterson went missing. Drew Peterson claimed that Stacy had called him on the previous evening to tell him she was leaving him for another man. Drew also alleged that she had left her car at a local airport. During the next several

months, both the Illinois State Police and the FEDERAL BUREAU OF INVESTIGATION became involved in the search for Stacy Peterson, but authorities could not find sufficient evidence to charge Drew with a crime related to Stacy's disappearance. He resigned from the Bolingbrook Police Department shortly after Stacy went missing, and he began to receive a monthly **pension** of $6,068.

statements that one person allegedly made to another, are generally inadmissible at trial as unreliable: courts want the person who made the statements to testify, not the person who simply heard the statement (of another). In 2004, the U.S. Supreme Court ruled, in *Crawford v. Washington,* that hearsay evidence violated a defendant's Sixth Amendment right to confront witnesses against him or her. In another (domestic violence) case, the Court held that if a defendant likely committed a crime making it impossible for a victim to testify, statements given to law enforcement officers were admissible.

Both armed with, and hindered by, the results in these cases, courts have increasingly established exceptions to the hearsay rules of evidence and other hearsay laws. As the list of "hearsay exceptions" continues to grow over the years, the Drew Peterson Law adds a new dimension to their potential application, especially in cases where hearsay could be used to show a witness or victim's state of mind.

The Doctrine of Forfeiture by Wrongdoing Federal law had already been updated in the late 1990s when the so-called "forfeiture by wrongdoing" doctrine was codified in federal courts as a hearsay exception. Federal Rule of Evidence 804(b)(6) now makes admissible "[a] statement offered against a party that has engaged or acquiesced in wrongdoing that was intended to, and did, procure the unavailability of the declarant as a witness." Because many state rules of evidence parallel federal rules, states began to adopt and codify similar hearsay exceptions.

There is generally accepted, as well, a common-law theory of "forfeiture by wrongdoing." In other words, the theory finds that otherwise-excludable hearsay evidence may be admissible because defendants had forfeited both their rights to confrontation under the Sixth Amendment, and hearsay rights, by their own wrongdoing in preventing such testimony.

But once a state codifies the doctrine, the common-law theory of forfeiture by wrongdoing may not be available for prosecutors. In *Chavez v. State,* No. 1D08-1532 (Fla. App. 2009) the First District Court of Appeal of Florida held that application of common-law forfeiture by wrongdoing hearsay exceptions were actually precluded under Florida's Evidence Code, Section 90.804(1) (that a declarant is not "unavailable" for purposes of the unavailable witness hearsay exceptions, if the unavailability was due to the wrongdoing of a party preventing the witness from attending or testifying). Other states have adopted evidence codes expressly incorporating the doctrine, e.g., California, Delaware, Hawaii, Kentucky, Maryland, Michigan, North Dakota, Ohio, Oregon, Pennsylvania, Tennessee, and Vermont.

New Prosecutorial Hurdles Despite the enactment of many state evidence codes supporting forfeiture by wrongdoing theories, evidentiary burdens remain. Key among them are the dichotomies that exist in burdens of proof. To meet Sixth Amendment scrutiny, most jurisdictions agree that the doctrine requires the state to prove the specific intent of the wrongdoer in preventing the witness from testifying. Proving specific intent, as an element of the wrongdoing, generally requires proof

beyond a reasonable doubt. Yet many state codes fail to specify that in their language. Moreover, under the common-law forfeiture by wrongdoing doctrine, it was generally accepted that only a preponderance of evidence was necessary to proffer evidence at the evidentiary hearing stage. Additionally, there are varying levels of burden of proof for the reliability of proffered hearsay evidence.

In some states, those gaps have been narrowed or closed by case precedent. For example, in *Roberts v. State,* 894 N. E.2d 1018 (Ind. App.2008), the Indiana appellate court held that "a party, who has rendered a witness unavailable for cross-examination through a criminal act, including homicide, may not object to the introduction of hearsay statements by the witness as being inadmissible." In *State v. Mason,* 162 P.3d 396 (Wash. 2007), the appellate court held that equity compelled the adoption of the doctrine of forfeiture by wrongdoing where the defendant was unable to confront a witness who was unavailable due to defendant's own action. Similar holdings can be found in Wisconsin's *State v. Jensen,* 727 N.W.2d 518 (2007) and Michigan's *People v. Bauder,* 712 N. W.2d 506 (Mich. Ct. App. 2006).

In any event, until the U.S. Supreme Court is presented with a controversy ripe for this issue, states may continue to struggle in reconciling common law with exclusive statutory language or judicial precedent. The bottom line is that, whether guilty or innocent of murder, Drew Peterson has become the poster boy for raising awareness of the potential pitfalls behind hearsay exclusions, exceptions, and common-law underpinnings of the forfeiture by wrongdoing doctrine.

The investigation into Stacy's disappearance led authorities to exhume Savio's body on November 16, 2007, to undergo forensic testing. According to several reports, the examiner concluded that Savio died of drowning after a struggle. The Illinois State Attorney General said publicly that the incident was a MURDER made to look like an accident. The investigation continued for more than a year. Representatives

of Savio's estate in April 2009 filed a $300,000 **wrongful death** suit against Peterson for Savio's death. About a month later, prosecutors charged Peterson with first-degree murder. Peterson pleaded not guilty to the charges, and bail was set for $20 million.

Because both of Peterson's wives had died, anything that they said to others would constitute **hearsay** and would be inadmissible evidence at trial. Because of this, the Illinois Legislature passed a law allowing a judge to admit HEARSAY evidence in first-degree murder cases when a PROSECUTOR could prove that a DEFENDANT killed a victim to prevent the victim from testifying. Based on this law, a judge in Joliet, Illinois held a hearing in January 2010 to determine if any statements made by Savio to others could be admitted. One of Savio's co-worker's testified that Peterson had once thrown Savio to the floor, grabbed her throat, and told her that he could kill her. Other witnesses also testified that Savio had told them that Peterson had threatened her life. According to these witnesses, they were hesitant to call the police because Peterson himself was a police officer. One of Stacy Peterson's neighbors later testified that Stacy said that Drew would kill her.

Even after his arrest, Peterson remained willing to discuss the case publicly, appearing on a local radio show and writing messages on the website Twitter. Even during his first court appearance, Peterson made smart-aleck comments, telling reporters that the jumpsuit issued by the prison was a "spiffy outfit." Peterson responded publicly that he was not going to back off making comments. He told Matt Lauer of NBC, "Would it be better if I hid my head down and tried to hide my face and hunched and had tears in my eyes? I mean, no, that's just not me."

Peterson remained in the news during the spring of 2010. In April, two members of his defense team resigned, citing "irreconcilable differences" with their co-counsel. Peterson then hired lawyer Joseph Lopez, who has represented members of the mafia in the past and is known by the nickname "The Shark." In an effort to pay his legal bills, Peterson also put his Harley Davidson motorcycle for sale on Ebay.

NECESSARY AND PROPER CLAUSE

United States v. Comstock

Article I, §8, cl.18 of the U.S. Constitution (the "Necessary and Proper Clause) expressly provides the federal government, i.e., Congress in this case, to enact laws that are "necessary and proper for carrying into execution" other powers vested by the Constitution. In *United States v. Comstock,* No. 08-1224, 560 U.S. ___ (2010), the question before the U.S. SUPREME COURT was whether Congress had exceeded such powers by enacting the Adam Walsh Protection and Safety Act of 2006, 18 U.S.C. §4248, which permits indefinite civil commitment of mentally ill "sexually dangerous" sex offenders following their prison terms. Enumerating five different considerations, the Court concluded, by a 7-2 margin, that Congress did have such power. In so holding, the Court reversed the decision of the U.S. Court of Appeals for the Fourth Circuit, which had upheld the federal district court's dismissal of federal commitment petitions against five prisoners.

Under the challenged law, §4248 (the only section at issue herein) authorized the federal government to effect a civil commitment of a criminally-incarcerated prisoner, beyond the completion of his or her prison sentence, if that person was "sexually dangerous." To accomplish this, the Attorney General must certify that such a person in federal CUSTODY is "sexually dangerous" and then file such certification with the **district court** having jurisdiction over the federal facility holding the prisoner. Thereafter, the district court must determine, by clear and convincing evidence, whether that person is "sexually dangerous." Any subsequent post-prison civil confinement under the law will continue until either (1) the person's mental condition improves to the point that he or she is deemed no longer dangerous, or, (2) a state assumes responsibility for the person's custody, care, and treatment, in which case, the person is transferred to the custody of that state. The law also provides for six-month psychiatric and judicial reviews at the request of the confined person.

Graydon Earl Comstock, Jr. was the first of five persons to challenge the constitutionality of 18 U.S.C. §4248. He and four other men (Shane Catron, Thomas Matherly, Marvin Virgil, and Markis Revland) remained confined in a medium-security federal corrections facility in North Carolina more than two years past the end of their prison terms. In Comstock's case, the Attorney General had certified that he was "sexually dangerous" six days prior to the end of his 37-month prison sentence for receiving CHILD PORNOGRAPHY.

In late 2006, the government instituted commitment proceedings against the five men in the Federal District Court for the Eastern District of North Carolina. Each of the five moved to dismiss the proceeding on constitutional grounds. They argued a plethora of constitutional violations of, among others, the Fifth, Sixth, and Eighth Amendments, as well as substantive and **equal protection**. Ultimately, the district court accepted two of their arguments, one that the government should be held to a proof **beyond a reasonable doubt**, and one alleging that Congress exceeded its Article I legislative powers; accordingly, it dismissed the government's petitions on these grounds. The Fourth **Circuit Court** of Appeals affirmed on the legislative powers ground, but declined to address the standard-of-proof question or any of the other constitutional arguments. 551 F.3d 274.

The U.S. Supreme Court granted **certiorari** (review) on the question of Congress' authority under Article I, §8, cl.18 of the Constitution (the "Necessary and Proper Clause). The First and Eighth Circuit Courts of Appeals having decided in the government's favor in similar cases, a split of authority among circuits further compelled review.

Justice Breyer delivered the opinion of the Court. In reversing the Fourth Circuit and holding that indeed, Congress had the authority to enact the federal civil-commitment program outlined in the Adam Walsh Protection and Safety Act, the Court expounded on five separate considerations which compelled that conclusion.

First, the Court noted that going back nearly 200 years, the Court has always acknowledged that the federal government was one of enumerated powers, but "must also be entrusted with ample means for their execution." [*McCulloch v. Maryland*, 4 Wheat. 316 (1819). Then the Court cited numerous cases showing that federal legislative authority is always accompanied by broad power to enact laws that are "convenient, or useful" or specifically "conducive" to the specifically-enumerated power's "beneficial exercise. Further, in determining whether the NECESSARY AND PROPER CLAUSE authorizes a particular federal **statute**, there must be "means-ends rationality" between the statute and the source of federal power. But, said the Court, the Constitution leaves the choice of means to the judgment of Congress. If it can be seen that the means adopted are really calculated to attain the end, then other specifics [e.g., the degree of necessity, the closeness in relationship between means and end, etc.] "are matters for congressional determination alone." (citing *Burroughs v. United States,* 290 U.S. 534).

Second, the Court noted that Congress has long been involved in the delivery of mental health care to federal prisoners. In fact, the only real difference between §4248 and the more general §4246 (which, since 1949, authorized post-sentence detention of federal prisoners who suffered mental illness and were thereby dangerous) is that §4248 focuses specifically on "sexually dangerous" prisoners.

Third, the Court found sound reasons for enactment of §4248. As custodian of its prisoners, the federal government has the constitutional power to act as necessary to protect citizens in nearby and other communities from the dangers such prisoners may pose. Fourth, the Court rejected a TENTH AMENDMENT violation argument, simply noting that the Tenth Amendment does not "reserve to the States" those powers that are delegated to the United States by the Constitution, including those delegated under the Necessary and Proper Clause. Finally, the Court found that §4248 was sufficiently narrow in scope, and therefore represents a reasonably adapted and narrowly tailored means of pursuing the government's legitimate interest, as federal custodian, in the responsible administration of its prison system.

Justice Breyer was joined in the majority opinion by Chief Justice Roberts and Justices Stevens, Ginsburg, and Sotomayor. Justices Kennedy and Alito filed separate opinions concurring in the judgment. Justice Thomas, joined by Justice Alito, dissented. The DISSENT more narrowly read the Necessary and Proper Clause as authorizing only those enactments that "carr[y] into Execution" one or more of the federal powers enumerated in the Constitution. According to the dissent, the Adam Walsh Protection and Safety Act did not carry into execution any enumerated power.

ORIGINAL JURISDICTION

The authority of a tribunal to entertain a lawsuit, try it, and set forth a judgment on the law and facts.

South Carolina v. North Carolina

States that are separated from each other by rivers sometimes become engaged in legal disputes as to who controls these waters. The U.S. Constitution grants the SUPREME COURT general or **original jurisdiction** over federal lawsuits between the states. The Court serves as a trial court and must be the finder of fact. However, the Court always appoints a SPECIAL MASTER, who acts as the finder of fact and files a report with the Court as to these findings and to conclusions of law. Once the report is filed the Supreme Court reviews the report and the "exceptions" the states make to the report. In *South Carolina v. North Carolina*, __ U.S.__, 130 S. Ct. 854, __L. Ed. 2d__ (2010), South Carolina sought an equitable **apportionment** with North Carolina of the Catawba River's waters. However, three nonstate entities—the Catawba River Water Supply Project (CRWSP), Duke Energy Carolinas, LLC, and the city of Charlotte, N. C.—sought to intervene in the lawsuit. The Special Master granted all three motions to intervene and South Carolina filed exceptions with the Supreme Court as to the motions. The Court reviewed the exceptions, upholding two of the motions and reversing the other one.

In 2007, South Carolina filed with the Supreme Court its complaint against North Carolina concerning the Catawba River. It claimed that North Carolina had authorized upstream transfers of water from the Catawba River basin that exceed North Carolina's equitable share of the river. South Carolina stated that this had been done pursuant to a North Carolina **statute** that requires any person seeking to transfer more than 2 million gallons of water per day (mgd) from the Catawba River basin to obtain a permit from the North Carolina Environmental Management Commission. The commission had issued permits to Charlotte for the transfer of up to 33 mgd, and one to the North Carolina cities of Concord and Kannapolis for the transfer of 10mgd. In addition, the complaint alleged, that the statute "grandfathers" a 5 mgd transfer by the CRWSP, and "implicitly authorize[s]" an unknown number of transfers of less than 2 mgd. South Carolina claimed that the effect of these upstream transfers was to deprive it of its equitable share of the Catwaba River's water, especially during times of drought or low river flow.

The Court appointed a Special Master to hear the case. CRWSP, Duke Energy, and Charlotte filed motions to intervene in the matter. In granting the motions, the Special Master filed a report that explained her reasons. She noted that the Court had long exercised jurisdiction over nonstate parties in original actions between two or more states. Using prior Court standards on intervention, she also looked at cases where the Court allowed nonstate entities to be named as defendants by the complaining state. From these sources she distilled a broad rule: "nonstate entities may become parties to such original disputes in appropriate and compelling circumstances, such as where the nonstate **entity** is the instrumentality authorized to carry out the wrongful conduct or injury for which the complaining state seeks relief, where the nonstate entity has an independent property interest that is directly implicated by the original dispute or is a substantial factor in the dispute, where the nonstate entity otherwise has a direct stake' in the outcome of the action within the meaning of the Court's cases discussed above, or where, together with one or more of the above circumstances, the presence of the nonstate entity would **advance** the full exposition' of the issues."

In a 5-4 decision, the Court upheld **intervenor** status for CRWSP and Duke Energy, but removed Charlotte from the lawsuit. Justice SAMUEL ALITO, writing for the majority, declined to adopt the Special Master's "appropriate and compelling circumstances" intervention rule. Instead, Alito employed a standard used by the Court for almost 60 years. Under this standard "An intervenor whose state is already a party should have the burden of showing some compelling interest in his own right, apart from his interest in a class with all other citizens and creatures of the state, which interest is not properly represented by the state." Alito admitted that the standard for intervention was high but this was entirely appropriate. The Court has

limited resources to play the role of fact-finder in these disputes.Moreover, in matters involving sovereign states, the Court must be wary of allowing nonstate entities to become involved as parties.

Employing this standard, the Court concluded that CWSP should be allowed to intervene because it is a bistate entity that supplies water from the river to North Carolina's Union County and South Carolina's Lancaster County. It had demonstrated a compelling interest in protecting the viability of its operations, which were premised on a fine balance between the joint venture's two participating counties. Duke Energy also had a compelling interest to intervene. Among other interests, it operated 11 dams and reservoirs in both states that generate electricity for the region and control the river's flow. The city of Charlotte failed the test because its interest was not "sufficiently unique." The state of North Carolina would be able to represent the city's interests.

Chief Justice JOHN ROBERTS filed an opinion, which was joined by Justices Thomas, Ginsburg, and Sotomayor that concurred in the use of the compelling interest standard and the denial of Charlotte's intervention but dissented as to the intervention of the other two entities. Roberts concluded that the majority had misapplied its standard, thereby producing a result that was "literally unprecedented." The Court had "never before granted intervention in such a case to an entity other than a State, the United States, or an Indian tribe. Never. That is because the apportionment of an interstate waterway is a sovereign dispute, and the key to intervention in such an action is just thatsovereignty."

PATENTS

Rights, granted to inventors by the federal government, pursuant to its power under Article I, Section 8, Clause 8, of the U.S. Constitution, that permit them to exclude others from making, using, or selling an invention for a definite, or restricted, period of time.

Bilski v. Kappos

The law of PATENTS is complex, requiring the courts to apply and interpret the federal patent laws using a variety of methods. One goal of **judicial review** in this area of the law is to promote certainty as to what methods will be applied to determine whether a patent should be issued. The SUPREME COURT, in *Bilski v. Kappos*, __ U.S. __, __ S. Ct. __, __ L. Ed. 2d __, 2010 WL 2555192 (2010).

Bernard Bilski and Rand Warsaw filed an application with the U.S. Patent Office, seeking to patent an invention they claimed that explained how commodities buyers and sellers in the energy market can protect, or hedge, against the risk of price changes. Their application included a mathematical formula that underpinned their concept. The patent examiner rejected the application, concluding that the invention was not implemented on a specific apparatus or machine. Instead, the claimed invention only manipulated an abstract idea and solved a purely mathematical problem. The Board of Patent Appeals and Interferences

upheld the examiner's ruling and inventors then filed a lawsuit in the Federal **Circuit Court** of Appeals in Washington, D.C. This court reviews all patent lawsuits.

The Federal Circuit affirmed the decision but the appeals court was divided over what test to apply when examining a process. The court first rejected its prior test for determining whether a claimed invention was a patentable "process" under Patent Act. This test determined whether the invention produced a "useful, concrete, and tangible result." The majority of the court endorsed a "machine or transformation" test as the sole test for determining patent eligibility for a process. Under this test, a process is patent eligible if: (1) it is tied to a particular machine or apparatus, or (2) it transforms a particular article into a different state or thing. The inventors had not tied their process to a machine, thereby making their claim ineligible for a patent.

The Supreme Court unanimously agreed with the Federal Circuit's decision that the process could not be patented but it was divided on what test should be applied. The majority rejected the use of the machine or transformation test as the sole test for analyzing a process patent application. Justice ANTHONY KENNEDY, writing for the majority, noted that §101 provides four independent categories of inventions or discoveries that are patent eligible: processes, machines, manufactures, and compositions of matter. These broad categories have

WeatherWise CEO Rand Warsaw talks in a conference room about his company's Supreme Court patent case.

AP IMAGES

been limited by the Supreme Court with three exceptions: laws of nature, physical phenomena, and abstract ideas. In the majority's view, the machine or transformation test was not the sole means of evaluating a patent application. Justice Kennedy stated that the Court was "unaware of any ordinary, contemporary, common meaning of 'process' that would require it to be tied to a machine or the transformation of an article." In addition, he denied that the Court had endorsed the machine-or-transformation test as the exclusive test.

The Court then examined whether §101 categorically excluded a business method as a "process" under the act. Justice Kennedy found that the act "may include at least some methods of doing business." In addition, the categorical exclusion was further undermined by the fact that federal law "explicitly contemplates the existence of at least some business method patents." However, Kennedy did concede that the law did not suggest "broad patentability of such claimed inventions." Turning to the Bilski-Warsaw application, the Court concluded that their method could not be patented because it was an abstract idea. Under prior Court precedent the mathematical formula in the application clearly was an abstract idea, just like the algorithms at issue in two prior Court cases. Having decided the case on prior precedent, the majority declined to define further what constituted a patentable "process. "

Justice JOHN PAUL STEVENS, in a concurring opinion joined by Justices RUTH BADER GINS-BURG, STEPHEN BREYER, and SONIA SOTOMAYOR, stated that business methods should never be

patentable, no matter what the test. He pointed out that until the 1990s, business methods were not patentable and concluded that "although a process is not patent-ineligible simply because it is useful for conducting business, a claim that merely describes a method of **doing business** does not qualify as a "process" under §101."

PATRIOT ACT

Holder v. Humanitarian Law Project

The U.S. Supreme Court's first review of the somewhat controversial USA PATRIOT Act, specifically involving 18 U.S.C. §2339, resulted in a Court affirmation of the Act's criminal prohibition against providing "material support" to terrorists. *Holder, Attorney General, v. Humanitarian Law Project,* No. 08-1498, 561 U.S. ___ (2010). That provision had been challenged on constitutional grounds as violating the First Amendment's right to free speech and association, and the Fifth Amendment's Due Process Clause against vagueness in statutory terms. Both arguments, continuing over a 12-year litigation period, failed, according to the Court's application of them to the facts in this case.

In 18 U.S.C. §2339B(a)(1), Congress expressly prohibited the providing of "material support or resources" to certain foreign organizations that engage in terrorist activity. The prohibition is premised upon a finding that the specified organizations "are so tainted by their criminal conduct that any contribution to such an organization facilitates that conduct." [Antiterrorism and Effective Death Penalty Act of 1996 (AEDPA), §301(a)(7), 110 Stat. 1247] The authority to designate an entity as a "foreign terrorist organization rests with the Secretary of State, subject to judicial review.

In relevant part, §2339A(b)(1) reads,

The term 'material support or resources' means any property, tangible or intangible, or service, including currency or monetary instruments or financial securities, financial services, lodging, training, expert advice or assistance, safehouses, false documentation or identification, communications equipment, facilities, weapons, lethal substances, explosives, personnel . . ., and transportation (excepting medicine or religious materials.

Section §2339B and the definition of "material support or resources" have been amended and clarify that a violation of this provision requires a knowledge of a foreign group's designation as a terrorist organization or knowledge of its commission of terrorist acts. The terms "training," "expert advice or assistance," and "personnel" are also expressly defined.

The Secretary of State had designated the Partiya Karkeran Kurdistan (PKK) and the Liberation Tigers of Tamil Eelam (LTTE) as "foreign terrorist organizations." Both aim to establish independent states for, respectively, the Kurds in Turkey and the Tamils in Sri Lanka. Of import, both groups engage in political and humanitarian activities. But each has also committed numerous terrorist attacks, some of which have harmed American citizens. Key to this case was that plaintiffs in this case (two U.S. citizens and six domestic organizations, including the Humanitarian Law Project) argued that their "material support" to these terrorist organizations was to support the terrorists' lawful, non-violent political and humanitarian activities, not their violent terrorist acts.

Specifically, plaintiffs claimed they wanted to train PKK members to use international law to resolve disputes; teach PKK members how to petition the United Nations for relief, and engage in political advocacy in support of these groups of Kurds and Tamils.

U.S. District Court Judge Audrey Collins agreed with plaintiffs and partially enjoined the enforcement of the "material support" provision against them, holding that the portions addressing training, expert advice or assistance, personnel, and service were too vague. In December 2007, the Ninth Circuit Court of Appeals affirmed. It reasoned that such a ban on "material support or resources" could effectively and unconstitutionally be used to prosecute those who train members of such groups about peaceful resolution of their disputes, or lobbying the United Nations for disaster relief, for example. After this decision, both sides cross-petitioned for certiorari (Supreme Court review).

Chief Justice Roberts delivered the opinion of the Court. First, and most importantly, it held that the material support statute, §2339B, was constitutional as applied to the particular forms of support that plaintiffs had sought to provide to the terrorist organizations. "Providing material support to a designated foreign terrorist organization—even seemingly benign support—bolsters the terrorist activities of that organization," Justice Roberts wrote. The Court went on to add, "We do not, however, address the resolution of more difficult cases that may arise under the statute in the future."

More specifically, as to the First Amendment free speech and association challenge, plaintiffs had argued that the statute should be read to require proof that they intended to further the terrorist organizations' illegal activities. But the Court found this inconsistent with the actual language of §2339B, which only prohibited "knowingly" providing material support. Congress chose "knowledge" about an organization's connections to terrorist activities, not a specific intent to further those terrorist activities, as the necessary mental state for a violation. Also, other sections immediately surrounding §2339B do refer to "intent" to further terrorist activities, so this was not vagueness or oversight in the language.

As to the Fifth Amendment argument of "vagueness," said the Court, the statutory terms at issue here, e.g., "training," "expert advice or assistance," "personnel," and "service," were quite different from the sorts of terms that the Court has previously struck down, such as "indecent" or "annoying," because these terms required "wholly subjective arguments without statutory definitions, narrowing context, or settled legal meanings." (quoting from *United States v. Williams,* 553 U.S. 285 at 304) Said the Court, although the terms at issue here may not be clear in every application, they were very clear in their application to plaintiffs' proposed conduct.

In summary, the problem with plaintiffs' arguments as to what they had intended to "materially support" was this: whether terrorist organizations could meaningfully segregate support of their legitimate activities from support of their terrorist activities. But, noted the Court, Congress had already removed that argument when it enacted §2339B, for it found that the specified organizations "are so tainted by their criminal conduct that any contribution to such an organization facilitates that conduct."

Justice Breyer dissented, joined by Justices Ginsburg and Sotomayor. He opined that this line of cases required the Court to consider how to apply the First Amendment where national security was at stake. "In my view," he wrote, "the government has not met its burden of showing that an interpretation of the statute that would prohibit this speech-and-association-related activity serves the Government's compelling interest in combating terrorism."

❖ PELOSI, NANCY

The first woman to serve in a top leadership role in a major U.S. political party, California Congresswoman Nancy Pelosi became the Democratic Party's minority leader of the House of Representatives in 2002 and speaker of the House in 2007.

Born in 1940 as Nancy D'Alesandro in Baltimore, Pelosi inherited her family's political tradition. Her father, Thomas D'Alesandro, Jr., served as the mayor of Baltimore from 1947 through 1959. Later, her brother, Thomas D'Alesandro III, also became Baltimore's mayor, from 1967 to 1971.

The young woman met her future husband while attending Trinity College in Washington, D.C. After they married, they moved to San Francisco and started a family. Her husband also had a family with political leanings, with a brother winning a seat on the city's board of supervisors. The Pelosis had five children, and after her youngest entered school Pelosi became involved in local Democratic Party politics.

Starting with house parties and door-to-door campaigning, Pelosi eventually became Northern California party chairwoman. She became a close ally of Democratic politician, Congressman Phillip Burton, who represented San Francisco. In 1983, Burton died, and his wife, Sala, won a special election to finish his term in office. But when she was diagnosed with cancer, Sala Burton asked Pelosi to run for her seat. Pelosi won a special election in 1987 and was re-elected every two years after that from California's Eighth District.

Pelosi represents one of the country's most left-leaning Congressional districts, encompassing most of San Francisco. Reflecting the concerns of her constituency, which strongly favors gay rights, Pelosi sponsored a bill creating a special housing opportunities program for people infected with Acquired Immune Deficiency Syndrome, or AIDS. In related work, she

Nancy Pelosi.
AP IMAGES

championed programs to expand access to Medicaid for people with the HIV virus, to increase funding for HIV- and AIDS-related healthcare, and to spur development of an HIV vaccine.

She also filed bills that helped nonprofit organizations create affordable housing and insured access to healthcare coverage for people with disabilities. She promoted the creation of a national network to track the chronic disease effects of environmental pollutants. Advocating increased investment in health research, she led the fight for double funding for the National Institutes of Health and beat back efforts to reduce funding for family planning programs abroad.

Pelosi served on the House's Appropriations and Intelligence committees. Pelosi met with leaders of intelligence services in the United States and in allied countries and advocated stronger efforts to stop nuclear proliferation. After the September 11, 2001, terrorist attacks, Pelosi wrote a bill creating the independent 9/11 commission, and despite her liberal stance on domestic matters, Pelosi supported the U.S. Patriot Act.

Pelosi has also served on House ethics and banking committees, and has campaigned and raised funds for other Democratic candidates across the country. In 2001, she was elected House minority whip, the second-highest party post.

When Richard Gephardt resigned as the party's minority leader in 2002 to run for president in 2004, Pelosi was selected to replace him. Despite her liberalism, Pelosi appealed to all wings of the party, working closely with moderate party whip Steny Hoyer. She also routinely helped junior party members gain media exposure and integrate them into the legislative process.

After the Democrats lost the 2004 presidential election, the job of leading the opposition to the Bush Administration fell to Pelosi and Senate minority leader Harry Reid. Pelosi played a key role in organizing the Democrats' successful opposition to Bush's 2005 proposal to partially privatize the Social Security system. During 2006, she proved very successful at raising money for Democratic candidates for Congress. Democrats won a majority of the House in the 2006 elections, after 12 years in the minority, so Pelosi moved from minority leader to speaker of the House.

As speaker, Pelosi led Democrats to pass a flurry of legislation in their first 100 days in power, including ethics reform that placed new restrictions on lobbyists, an increase in the minimum wage, and enactment of all the anti-terrorism reforms recommended by the Sept. 11 commission. She angered some of the most combative members of her party by refusing to consider impeachment of Bush.

Pelosi and Reid led the Democratic effort in the spring of 2007 to pass a bill that set a deadline of October 1, 2007, for the United States to begin withdraw troops from Iraq, but Bush vetoed the bill. Faced with an impasse, Pelosi and Reed abandoned their attempts to pressure Bush to accept a deadline. Many Democrats joined with Republicans to continue funding the war without restrictions. Pelosi, however, announced that she would not vote for the war funding bill.

Political observers questioned how much Pelosi had accomplished in her first year as speaker. They questioned her partisan legislative battling, since many key Democratic initiatives had been vetoed by Bush or stopped by Republican filibusters in the Senate. However, in early 2008, Pelosi quickly agreed with Bush on a plan to stimulate the economy with tax rebates, upsetting some Democrats who favored a different economic strategy. Some observers felt the decision would be a turning point in her speakership, toward bipartisan compromise.

In November of 2008, Democrat Barack Obama was elected President of the United States. Pelosi agreed with Obama's decision to investigate the causes of the financial crisis that occurred in the fall of 2008; supported his "cash for clunkers" program that was intended to take gas guzzling cars off the road and provide incentives for people to buy more efficient cars; and supported the confirmation of Judge Sonia Sotomayor as a member of the Supreme Court. On November 4, 2009, Pelosi was re-elected to her Congressional seat in the 8th District of California, defeating Republican Dana Walsh. In March 2010, Pelosi steered passage of landmark healthcare overhaul legislation by a 219-212 vote in the House.

1940	Born, Baltimore, Maryland
1987	First elected to Congress as a representative of California's 8th District
2002	Elected House Democratic leader
2007	Elected first female speaker of the House
2010	Helped drive passage of landmark healthcare reform legislation

POLITICAL PARTIES

The Rise of the Tea Party Movement

In early April 2010, a CBS/*New York Times* survey revealed that 18 percent of Americans considered themselves members or supporters of what had come to be identified as a united "Tea Party Movement." If truth be told, this rise among the American populace of persons who identified with the movement was, in reality, a vast, multifaceted, and fragmentized collection of disgruntled persons who did not always agree on why they were united. They knew they were unhappy with the way things were in America, but they didn't always agree on what things were wrong, or how to fix them. Like a snowball going downhill, what began as a loose gathering of persons unhappy with the federal government, picked up other stragglers unhappy with this and that, coalesced with still other disgruntled groups, broadened their complaint base to pluck up even more protesters, then sped downhill, surprising even themselves at how much political debris and fallout they left in their wake. The above description is neither rhetoric nor opinion: it comes from the mouths of many Tea Party members.

Most Tea Party members do not even know how or when the movement started. As of 2010, the group represented mostly conservative voters, former or current members of the Republican Party or independents, who were unhappy with the Obama administration. But others say the movement started in 2008, with liberals protesting then-president George W. Bush's policies on immigration and taxation.

In any event, by mid-2010, the perception of those aligned with the movement appeared to consist of persons identifying with right-sided, conservative political views that focused on a

united distrust of the federal government and "Washington" in general. They saw Washington as a threat, "a place where crisis is manipulated—even manufactured—by both parties to grab power," noted David Barstow in his February 16, 2010 article covering the movement for *The New York Times*. According to Barstow, the Movement "has become a platform for conservative populist discontent, a force in Republican politics for revival, as it was in the Massachusetts Senate election [where a Republican took over the Democratic seat held for decades by the late Senator Edward M. "Ted" Kennedy], or for division."

"People who are closely identified with the tea party movement feel very much this sense of betrayal," said J. Walker Smith, executive vice-president of market research firm Futures Company. In a July 2010 *Washington Post* article, Smith said that tea party members dislike and distrust Wall Street, the automobile industry, President Obama, even [surprisingly] the Republican Party. There is a sense of betrayal by institutions and people who had invested their trust in them, said Smith.

The Republican Party did not readily adopt the movement, considered too right-wing and exclusionary for some Party members. But

following the disastrous 2008 elections, internal splintering between moderates and the far right seemed to fade against the new hope for a united front, with former vice-presidential candidate Sarah Palin as the flagship helmsperson. Notwithstanding, not every person who identified with the movement was ready to embrace her, or some of the tenets she touted at public speaking events and fundraisers. As the movement continued to strike up acquaintances and alliances with the likes of Friends for Liberty, the John Birch Society, Glenn Beck's 9/12 Project, and the Oath Keepers (a new player in a resurgent militia movement), as many prospective members became alienated as were inspired.

In March 2010, *Forbes* magazine columnist Bruce Bartlett published his assessment in "The Misinformed Tea Party Movement," concluding that, for an [alleged} anti-tax group, "they don't know much about taxes." Randomly canvassing persons in a crowd of 300 to 500 alleged Tea Party demonstrators on Capitol Hill on March 16, his friend and several interns garnered some surprising results. When asked how much the federal government got in taxes, as a percentage of the gross domestic product (GDP), the average response was "42 percent," and the median response was "40 percent." In truth, according to Congressional Budget Office (CBO) data, the highest figure for all federal taxes since 1970 occurred in 2000, when it rose to 20.6 percent of GDP, dropping to the high teens since then, e.g., 17.5 percent in 2008. The highest figure ever recorded in all of American history was 20.9 percent at the peak of World War II in 1944. When asked what the typical family making $50,000 per year paid in federal income taxes, the average response was $12,710; the median response, $10,000. But according to IRS tax tables, a single person with taxable income of $50,000 in 2009 would owe $8,694, while a married couple filing jointly would owe just $6,669. Home ownership and having children reduced the tax even further.

Still, in theory at least, the Tea Party Movement represents a significant undercurrent within American politics. Although it easily defies definition, largely because there is no single Tea Party, but rather a loose conglomeration of hundreds of autonomous Tea Party groups who don't always share principles and tenets in common, the movement has attracted international attention. Said Barstow," . . . Tea Party events have become a magnet for other groups and causes—including gun rights activists, anti-tax crusaders, libertarians, militia organizers, the 'birthers' who doubt President Obama's citizenship, Lyndon LaRouche supporters and proponents of the sovereign states movement."

PONZI SCHEME

A fraudulent investment plan in which the investments of later investors are used to pay earlier investors, giving the appearance that the investments of the initial participants dramatically increase in value in a short amount of time.

Bernard Madoff Sentenced to 150 Years in Prison

Bernard Madoff spent nearly three decades, and perhaps more, bilking clients in a giant **Ponzi scheme** that cost these clients an estimated $65 billion. In 2009, Madoff received the maximum sentence allowed, as federal judge imposed a 150-year sentence after Madoff pleaded guilty to charges related to his operation. In 2009 and 2010, investors continued to try to recover at least part of the money they had given to Madoff, and inspectors continued to evaluate why the U.S. SECURITIES AND EXCHANGE COMMISSION (SEC) had failed to uncover the scheme long before 2008.

Investigators believe that Madoff's PONZI SCHEME dated back to the 1980s. In a Ponzi scheme such as Madoff's, investors are promised a high rate of return on what they believe are legitimate investments. However, those running the Ponzi scheme actually use money brought in from new clients to pay the other investors. The entire scheme is thus dependent on bringing in new clients because the money invested is not really backed by SECURITIES. In Madoff's case, he attracted clients from throughout several parts of the world, and his list of celebrity investors included director Steven Spielberg, Hall of Fame pitcher Sandy Koufax, and actors John Malkovich, Kyra Sedgwick, and Kevin Bacon. Madoff's investors continually made money, though his company's average rate of return of 10% was low compared with most Ponzi schemes. Even as the markets started taking a downturn in 2007 and 2008, Madoff's investors still believed they were making money.

Those investigating the SEC's response to suspicions about Madoff's enterprise concluded that the SEC had plenty of opportunities to expose the scheme. In 2005, a regional office with the SEC in New York examined Madoff's practices. The SEC reportedly relied on inexperienced staffers to conduct the investigation, including using a recent law school graduate to serve as a lead staff attorney. These investigators should have discovered evidence of the scheme during their review of the files, but the investigators largely discounted such evidence. Madoff also reportedly both impressed and intimidated the investigators by referring to names of high-ranking officials in the SEC.

Even when the SEC received complaints in 2006, the investigators failed to discover the scheme. The investigators did not understand the markets well enough to see through Madoff's explanations for his "incredibly consistent returns" over a number of years. In May 2006, though, Madoff reportedly thought he had been caught. He was questioned by federal agents and gave these agents his account number with the Depository Trust Co., an independent clearing agency. Had the agents checked the account thoroughly, they would have discovered that Madoff was not trading in the volume of securities that he led his investors to believe. According to a report filed by the SEC's inspector general office in 2009, Madoff thought "thought it was the endgame, over." However, the inexperienced staff members did not review the case thoroughly and missed the chance to expose the scheme.

In September 2009, Inspector General H. David Kotz issued a report indicating that Madoff had given implausible explanations for his investment success. SEC Chairwoman Mary Schapiro issued a statement in which she stated, "It is a failure that we continue to regret, and one that has led us to reform in many ways how we regulate markets and protect investors. We have been reviewing our practices and procedures, addressing shortcomings, and implementing the lessons learned."

Madoff's enterprise did not fall apart until November 2008, when investors started to panic and attempted to redeem the money they had invested with Madoff. Madoff in December 2008 after Madoff had admitted to his sons that his business was a giant Ponzi scheme, and his sons informed authorities. In March 2009, Madoff pleaded guilty to 11 charges, including: investment advisor **fraud**, **mail fraud**, wire FRAUD, international **money laundering**, domestic MONEY LAUNDERING, false statements, PERJURY, false filing, and theft from an employee benefit plan.

Although Madoff acknowledged had he had made a "terrible mistakes," and that he had "left a legacy of shame." However, victims told the court that he had shown little remorse for the damage he had caused. A victim named Carla Hilschhorn of New Jersey told the court that her life had become a "living hell," with her mother depending on SOCIAL SECURITY and her daughter having to work two jobs to pay for college tuition. Other victims told stories of how they lost their life savings and had to rely on WELFARE to survive. Madoff said that he had deceived his family, including his wife, brothers, and children. However, he would not identify accomplices, which made it difficult for prosecutors to build cases against others. Moreover, the **receiver** of Madoff's firm told the court that Madoff was not helping to identify assets.

On June 29, 2009, U.S. District Judge Denny Chin sentenced Madoff to 150 years in prison, which was the maximum allowed by law. Crowds gathered near the courthouse in Manhattan cheered when news of the sentence was announced. Chin noted that Madoff's crimes were "extraordinarily evil" and that the sentence was appropriately symbolic. Chin added, "This was not merely a bloodless financial crime that occurred on paper, but one that took a staggering toll. The breach of trust here was massive." Madoff requested that he serve his sentence at a prison in the northeast, but he was later sentenced to the Butner Federal Correctional Institution in North Carolina. In December 2009, Madoff was allegedly assaulted by another prisoner and was treated for facial injuries. Prison officials, however, denied the report, and his attorney declined to answer questions.

In 2010, authorities continued to try to recover money to return to Madoff's investors. Much of the focus has been on assets held by Madoff's brothers and sons, each of whom are reportedly the subject of a tax fraud investigation by federal prosecutors. Authorities have also sought to recover assets from one of Madoff's top aides, Frank DiPascali, who by April 2010 had already forfeited more than a $1 million.

❖ POST, ROBERT C.

Yale Law School in 2009 named the sixteenth dean in its history when the school announced the appointment of law professor Robert C. Post to the position. Post had been a faculty member of the law school since 2003 and replaced Harold Hongju Koh, who became legal advisor to the U.S. STATE DEPARTMENT in 2009.

Post earned an A.B., *summa cum laude* from Harvard College in 1969, studying the history of American civilization. He later attended Yale Law School from which he earned the Michael Egger Prize and served as note editor of the *Yale Law Journal*. He earned his law degree in 1977. He held two prestigious judicial clerkships after graduation, including one with Chief Judge David L. Bazelon of the U.S. Court of Appeals for the District of Columbia and another with Justice William Brennan of the U.S. SUPREME COURT. (Coincidentally, Martha Minow, who was appointed dean of Harvard Law School at nearly the same time as Post, also had a clerkship with Bazelon—although several years later—before clerking at the Supreme Court.) Post completed his education in 1980 by receiving his Ph.D. from Harvard in 1980.

From 1980 to 1982, he served in the LITIGATION department of the law firm of Williams & Connelly in Washington, D.C. He moved into academia in 1983, joining the faculty of the University of California at Berkeley (Boalt Hall) as an acting professor of law. In 1987, he became a full professor of law, and in 1994, he was appointed the Alexander F. and May T. Morrison Professor of Law. In 2003, Post returned to Yale as the David Boies Professor of Law.

While in California, Post also served as general counsel to the American Association of University Professors from 1992 to 1994, and he remains a consultant for the association. He served on the California's Independent Panel on Redistricting, established by former California Governor Pete Wilson in 1991. He is a fellow with the American Academy of Arts and Sciences, and he also serves as Librarian for the organization. He is a member of the American Law Institute, a **trustee** of the National Humanities Center. He has been awarded fellowships with the John Simon Guggenheim Memorial Foundation and the American Council of Learned Societies. In 1998, he received the Hughes-Gossett Award for the best article appearing in the *Journal of Supreme Court History*.

Post has written extensively in his ares of focus, which include **constitutional law**, FIRST AMENDMENT, LEGAL HISTORY, and **equal protection**. He has written or served as editor on nine books, including *For the Common Good: Principles of American Academic Freedom*, written with University of Illinois law professor Matthew M. Finkin and published by Yale University Press in 2009. He also wrote *Prejudicial Appearances: The Logic of American Antidiscrimination Law* (written with K. Anthony Appiah, Judith Butler, Thomas C. Grey, and Reva Siegel and published by Duke University Press in 2001), and *Constitutional Domains: Democracy, Community, Management* (published by Harvard University Press in 1995). Several of his dozens of articles have appeared in top law journals. His best-known articles include "Roe Rage: Democratic Constitutionalism and Backlash" (with Reva Siegel,

Harvard Civil-Rights Civil-Liberties Law Review, 2007); "Federalism, **Positive Law**, and the Emergence of the American Administrative State: Prohibition in the Taft Court Era" (*William & Mary Law Review*, 2006); "Foreword: Fashioning the Legal Constitution: Culture, Courts, and Law" (*Harvard Law Review*, 2003); and "Subsidized Speech" (*Yale Law Journal*, 1996). Post has also published in nonlegal journals, including the *New England Journal of Medicine*.

In 2004, Yale appointed Koh to serve as dean. Koh had served on the Yale faculty since 1985, and from 1998 to 2001, he also served as U.S. Assistant SECRETARY OF STATE for Democracy, HUMAN RIGHTS and Labor during the administration of President BILL CLINTON. With the return of a Democrat to the presidency in 2008, Koh was tapped to serve again in a position within the cabinet. President BARACK OBAMA appointed Koh as legal advisor to the U.S. State Department, as confirmed by the SENATE on June 25, 2009. As Koh awaited news of his confirmation during the spring of 2009, Kate Stith, the Lafayette S. Foster Professor of Law at Yale served as the acting dean. The school convened a nine-member search committee, which was chaired by law professor Paul Kahn.

By the middle of June 2009, Post had emerged as the leading candidate for the deanship. The school announced his appointment on June 22, and he assumed his duties on July 1. Yale President Richard C. Levin said of the appointment, "Professor Post, who returned to Yale in 2003 as the David Boies Professor of Law, is a distinguished scholar of CONSTITUTIONAL LAW, in particular the First Amendment, EQUAL PROTECTION, and legal history. As a leading scholar and a respected citizen of the legal profession, he is ideally positioned to move the Yale Law School forward. He is greatly admired by his colleagues for his wisdom and judgment, and his commitment to sustaining the excellence of the Law School is unwavering." Both Koh and Stith also commended Post, with Stith noting that Post "is dedicated to world-class scholarship, to excellence in public and private service, and to sustaining our special community."

Post accepted the challenge associated with his new position, commenting, "I am humbled and honored to be asked to serve as dean of Yale Law School, a community that I loved as a student and that I have loved even more as a

1977	Received law degree from Yale
1980	Received PhD. from Harvard
2003	Joined Yale law faculty
2009	Became dean of Yale Law School

faculty member. I am eager to work with our faculty, staff, students, and alumni to deepen Yale Law School's commitment to scholarly excellence, outstanding education, and the achievement of professional and public ideals."

PRACTICE OF LAW

Law Firms May Need to Consider Their Business Models in the Wake of the Recession

The recession of the late 2000s had a significant effect on the economics of running a law firm. Although concerns over the rates that law firms charges have existed for several years, economic setbacks severely cut into the profitability of these firms. Some firms have responded by considering new alternatives, but experts have suggested that firms may need to completely overhaul their business models to survive in the future.

Large law firms have traditionally operated under the same basic business model. A small group of partners typically make most of the management decisions and earn the most money based on the firm's profits. In 2006, the average profit per partner at the largest law firms topped more than $1 million. Other partners have much less authority than the managing partners and also earn much less than these partners. These firms typically recruit new lawyers by hiring top law students to work as summer associates, and firms make their initial hiring decisions based on the performance of these summer associates. New lawyers usually remain associates for five to seven years, after which the firms decide whether the promote the associate to a partner position or to release the associate to find work elsewhere.

Salaries of associates at the largest firms skyrocketed between the late 1990s and the late 2000s, jumping from a median of $80,000 in 1997 to $160,000 (plus bonuses) in 2007. Firms usually employ a lock-step system of pay, meaning that firms pay associates based on years of service rather than on performance. Although only a percentage of these associates will be promoted to partner, the lock-step system of payment ensures that these associates would remain employed for several years, often at salaries greater than $200,000 per year. Despite these relatively high salaries, associates in general have reportedly been dissatisfied with their careers, often because of the system that ensures that only some of the associates will become partners. At some firms, the percentage of those making partners is quite small.

To be able to pay rising salaries to new associates, and to ensure that the firm's partners continued to earn greater profits, firms continually raised their rates throughout the 2000s. When the firms' clients had to address the recession that began in late 2007, however, the clients looked carefully at their legal costs. In-house legal departments at corporations determined that they could save on legal costs by relying less on the large firms with high billing rates and relying more on smaller firms. The larger firms saw their profits shrink, which led the firms to take cost-saving measures, such as freezing the hiring of new associates or laying off associates and partners. In 2009, the total number of lawyers at the top 250 law firms in the United States shrank by more than 5,000.

Law firms considered a number of strategies to address the economic downturn. Many of these strategies focused on recruiting, hiring, and promotion practices related to associates. Associate salaries fell at many firms in 2009 and 2010, and a few firms announced that they would abandon lock-step method of paying associates. Meanwhile, firms have also experimented by moving away from hourly billing rates (which are often $400 or more for partners at large firms) to a flat fee based on the types of services provided in a given case. Other strategies have focused on reducing costs by looking carefully at the use of new technologies. Still other firms have changed their hiring tracks, employing some new lawyers on a "partnership track" while hiring others at a lower salary to perform more routine matters, such as reviewing documents during the course of LITIGATION.

Although these plans and others may help law firms survive in the short term, commentators suggest that none of the proposals will be sustainable in the long-term. In an article written for the *National Law Journal*, legal consultant Joel Henning called reform ideas "insepid and inadequate." He noted, "There is a lot of talk about moving away from billable hours, but alternative fee arrangements are neither new nor making much headway. Greater use of contract lawyers, offshoring, fewer equity partners, a cutback in associate salaries and more differentiation in associate pay and promotions—are all being discussed and even modestly implemented. But all of this has been around for at least a decade, and none of it has so far done much to make clients happier either about their legal bills or the quality of the services they pay for."

Henning endorsed an approached suggested by Larry Ribstein, a University of Illinois law professor. According to Ribstein, firms lack a "coherent business model," and he questioned what value the larger and most costly law firms add when compared with the services and cost of smaller firms. Ribstein also questioned the basic law firm business structure, which relies on financing provided by the firm's partners and banks, but not from other outside sources. According to Ribstein, this is a "preindustrial model of financing the firm." In a paper entitled "Regulating the Evolving Law Firm," Ribstein make several recommendations for major reforms, including allowing firms to seek outside financing for litigation. According to Ribstein, outside financiers "would have strong incentives to make value-maximizing litigation decisions." Ribstein also made more radical suggestions, including a proposal to allow law-related firms to sell shares to the public. Under current rules, such an option would not be possible because non-lawyers cannot own business interests in firms. However, a large firm in Australia made a successful **public offering**, and Ribstein believes that American law firms would benefit from such an option.

PREVAILING PARTY

The litigant who successfully brings or defends an action and, as a result, receives a favorable judgment or verdict.

Hardt v. Reliance Standard Life Insurance Company

In the U.S. legal system, each litigant generally pays his own attorney's fees, whether he wins or loses his case. This principle has come to be known as the American Rule. However, attorneys' fees may be awarded under specific statutes authorizing them (state or federal), or binding contracts that express this intent. When statutes or contract provisions do provide for the awarding of attorneys' fees and costs, they generally award them to "a prevailing party" in the LITIGATION. In an earlier U.S. SUPREME COURT case, *Buckhannon Board & Care Home, Inc. v. West Virginia Dept. of Health and Human Resources,* 532 U.S. 598, the Court explained that a fee claimant was a "prevailing party" only if he had obtained "an enforceable judgmen[t] on the merits" or "a court-ordered consent decree[e]."

One of the federal statutes generally authorizing the award of "a reasonable attorney's fee and costs ... to either party" is the EMPLOYEE RETIREMENT INCOME SECURITY ACT of 1974 (ERISA) 29 U.S.C. §1001, *et seq.* In *Hardt v. Reliance Standard Insurance Company,* No. 09-448, 560 U.S. ___ (2010), the U.S. Supreme Court held that a party need not be a "prevailing party" under §1132(g)(1) of ERISA to request fees, and a court, in its discretion, may award such fees and costs as long as the requesting party achieved "some degree of success on the merits."

Bridget Hardt had been working as an executive assistant to the president of textile manufacturer Dan River, Inc. when, in 2000, she began experiencing neck and shoulder pain. She eventually was diagnosed with carpal tunnel syndrome and underwent unsuccessful surgeries on both her wrists. When pain persisted, she stopped working in early 2003. Later that year, Hardt applied for long-term disability benefits from her employer's insurance program plan, which was subject to ERISA. Although her company administered the plan, Reliance Standard Life Insurance Company ("Reliance") provided underwriting for any benefits awarded, and rendered the decisions as to whether claimants qualified for benefits under the plan.

Reliance provisionally approved Hardt's claim, pending further evaluation of her performance in functional capacities testing; it wanted to assess the impact of her carpal tunnel syndrome and neck pain on her ability to work. After observing her physical limitations in conjunction with her medical history, an evaluator concluded that Hardt was able to perform some amount of sedentary work. Based on this finding, Reliance determined that Hardt was not totally disabled within the meaning of benefits eligibility under the employee plan, and denied her claim.

Hardt filed an administrative appeal, and Reliance, in reconsidering her claim, found her totally disabled from her regular occupation, and awarded her temporary disability benefits for 24 months.

Meanwhile, while this appeal was still pending, Hardt began to experience new symptoms, ultimately diagnosed as small fiber neuropathy, and her functional capabilities decreased. She applied for SOCIAL SECURITY disability benefits, supported by doctors' statements that she was unable to return to full gainful employment because of pain and functional limitations. After exhausting her administrative remedies, Hardt file suit against Reliance in federal **district court**, alleging that Reliance had violated ERISA by denying her benefits claim.

Although the district court denied Hardt's motion for **summary judgment**, it did state on record that it found "compelling evidence" supporting her claim that she was totally disabled, and that it was inclined to rule in her favor but wanted to give Reliance fair chance to address the issue. Therefore, it remanded to Reliance, giving it 30 days to consider all the evidence and act on Hardt's application for benefits accordingly, or else the court would enter judgment in Hardt's favor. Reliance complied, ultimately awarding Hardt benefits.

Hardt then filed a motion under 29 U.S.C. §1132(g)(1), one of the fee-shifting statutes that applies in most ERISA cases. The actual language of the **statute** provides that a court "... in its discretion may allow a reasonable attorney's fee and costs ... to either party." The district court awarded Hardt fees, concluding that Hardt had attained the requisite status of "prevailing party." Reliance appealed.

The Fourth **Circuit Court** of Appeals reversed and vacated the award. It held that Hardt had failed to establish that she qualified as a "prevailing party" under the rule articulated in *Buckhannon, see above.* In Hardt's case, said the **appellate court**, the district court's remand order did not require Reliance to award benefits to Hardt, so this was not an "enforceable judgment on the merits."

The U.S. Supreme Court did not agree, with all nine justices concurring. Writing for the Court,

Justice Thomas pointed out that nothing in the language of §1132(g)(1) required a fee claimant to be a "prevailing party" to be eligible for award of attorney's fees. In fact, the words "prevailing party" do not even appear in the provision. To the contrary, the express language of the statute grants district courts discretion to award fees "to either party." Justice Thomas further pointed out that the very next section in the statute, of §1132(g)(2) (governing the availability of attorneys' fees in ERISA actions to recover delinquent employer contributions to a multi-employer plan), expressly allows such awards only to plaintiffs who obtain "a judgment in favor of the plan." By contrast, no such limiting language appears in the subject §1132(g)(1).

Instead, said the Court, a court may award fees and costs under §1132(g)(1) as long as the fee claimant has achieved "some degree of success on the merits." (quoting *Ruckelshaus v. Sierra Club,* 463 U.S. 680). Here, as in that case (involving another statute), because Congress failed to use precise language, a fee claimant need only show "some degree of success on the merits" in order to petition a court for such an award. Although Hardt did not win SUMMARY JUDGMENT, the district court did note on record that it was inclined to find in her favor, based on the evidence. Hardt also obtained the relief she sought, disability benefits, after the district court remand to Reliance, which reconsidered and reversed its earlier denial of benefits. Accordingly, Hardt qualified for attorney's fees under the statute.

Justice Thomas was joined by Chief Justice Roberts and Justices Scalia, Kennedy, Ginsburg, Breyer, Alito, and Sotomayor. Justice Stevens filed a separate opinion, concurring in part and concurring in the judgment. He would have preferred that the Court's decision stand alone, without reliance on *Ruckelshaus,* opining that the text, structure, and history of each statute should be examined individually rather than concluding that Congress intended the same approach under one as under another.

PRIVACY

Ninth Circuit Allows Paris Hilton's Privacy Suit to Proceed

In 2007, celebrity Paris Hilton sued greeting-card maker Hallmark, alleging that Hallmark had misappropriated Hilton's image, had

infringed her registered trademark by using the phrase "that's hot", and falsely designated the origin of Hilton's trademark. A federal **district court** dismissed the trademark INFRINGEMENT claim but denied Hallmark's motions to dismiss the remaining claims. In 2009, the Ninth **Circuit Court** of Appeals likewise rejected Hallmark's arguments, thus allowing Hilton's claim to proceed to trial.

Hilton is the great-granddaughter of Conrad Hilton, the founder of Hilton Hotels. Paris Hilton became a celebrity in her own right during the 2000s through a number of different exploits, including modeling and acting. In 2003, Hilton and another socialite named Nicole Richie were first featured in a reality-based television program called *The Simple Life*. Both Hilton and Richie both lived lives of privilege, and the show played on their backgrounds by requiring them to live as average people. For instance, the two had to work various jobs to pay for food and so forth. In one show, Hilton and Richie worked at fast-food restaurant. The women were also known for saying the phrase "that's hot" anytime they found something interesting or amusing. Hilton

registered this phrase with the U.S. PATENT AND TRADEMARK OFFICE.

Hilton was frequently the subject of parody during the 2000s. For example, in the movie "Epic Movie," a character that looked like Hilton utters the phrase "I'm so hot" after leaving a store, only to be crushed by one of the film's protagonists. In another example, an editorial cartoon mocked Hilton's INCARCERA-TION for violating terms of PROBATION by showing her pointing to a prison uniform and asking, "That's hot, but do you, like, have it in pink?"

Hallmark was first established in Missouri in 1910. The company is one of the best-known producers of greeting cards for holidays and other occasions. Hallmark cards focus not only on holiday themes but also on subjects of current issues with social and political relevance. The wide range of subjects covered by Hallmark cards include, for example, WORLD WAR II, Prohibition, Vietnam, and the atomic bomb. Many of the cards feature parody and satire. One such card included a cartoon depicting the body of a waitress in an apron serving a plate of food to a patron.

A photograph of Hilton's head was super-imposed over the top of the waitress's body. The card shows the character saying, "Don't touch that, it's hot." The customer responds, "What's hot?" The character replies, "That's hot." Inside the card, a message reads, "Have a smokin' hot birthday."

In her suit against Hallmark, Hilton alleged two claims based on federal trademark law, including trademark infringement and false designation of origin under 15 U.S.C. § 1125(a). A third claim was based on the theory of misappropriation of publicity under California **common law**. Hallmark filed motions to dismiss or strike each claim. On December 17, 2007, Judge Percy Anderson of the U.S. District Court for the Central District of California dismissed the trademark infringement claim but denied Hallmark's motions related to the other two claims. With regard to these remaining claims, Anderson concluded that the court needed more facts before he could rule on the issues related to the claims.

Hallmark appealed the district court's ruling regarding the false designation of origin and misappropriation claims (Hilton did not dispute the dismissal of the trademark infringement claim). In its brief, Hallmark opened its argument by noting: "In this action, Hilton is not going after a company that slapped her name on a product label or used a song of hers in an advertisement. Rather, Hilton seeks to impose liability on a personal expression company engaging in speech—through the historically rich communication medium of a greeting card—that comments on a self-described cultural "icon" and admitted subject of PUBLIC INTEREST. The Card caricatures Hilton by grafting an oversized photograph of her head onto a cartoon body, injecting her into an absurd situation, and creating a fictional dialogue to accompany the visual image for the purpose of commenting on her.

Hallmark based part of its argument on the application of a California law known as an "anti-SLAPP" law, which prohibits a "strategic lawsuit against public participation." The purpose for such a law is to bar plaintiffs from bringing meritless lawsuits designed to deter a DEFENDANT from exercising his or her FIRST AMENDMENT right on a matter of public interest. California's anti-SLAPP law provides: "[a] **cause of action** against a person arising from

any act of that person in furtherance of the person's right of petition or free speech under the United States or California Constitution in connection with a public issue shall be subject to a special motion to strike, unless the court determines that the PLAINTIFF has established that there is a probability that the plaintiff will prevail on the claim."

Hallmark argued that it was exercising its First Amendment right by producing the card and that Hilton's suit was designed to chill the company's exercise of this right. For Hallmark's argument to prevail, the company had to prove that its acts were in furtherance of the company's constitutional right of petition or free speech in connection with a public issue. If the company could meet this threshold, then the court had to determine whether the plaintiff had demonstrated a probability of prevailing on the claim. The Ninth Circuit reviewed California **case law** and concluded that Hallmark had indeed acted in furtherance of its free speech rights by creating the card. However, the court concluded that Hilton had shown a probability that she would succeed on her privacy claim, which was sufficient to defeat Hallmark's motion. After rejecting Hallmark's other arguments, the court remanded the case to the district court for further proceedings. The court issued its original decision on August 31, 2009 and then filed an amended opinion on March 23, 2010. *Hilton v. Hallmark Cards*, No. 08-55443, 2010 WL 1039872 (9th Cir. March 23, 2010).

PROBATE

The court process by which a will is proved valid or invalid. The legal process wherein the estate of a decedent is administered.

Brooke Astor's Son Convicted in Estate-Handling Fraud

Beloved New York socialite, multimillionaire, and philanthropist Brooke Astor died in 2007 at the age of 105. In a sensationalized trial that brought in many celebrities and famous persons to testify, Astor's only child, Anthony D. Marshall, was convicted in October 2009 of first-degree **grand larceny** for defrauding his elderly mother out of millions of dollars during her last years. Also convicted was Marshall's lawyer, Francis X. Morrissey, accused, among other things, of forging Ms. Astor's signature to a 2004 **codicil** to her will. At the time of Astor's death, her estate was valued at $180 million. She also controlled the **disposition** of a trust set up by her third husband, Vincent Astor, worth several million more. While still living, she had already given away nearly $200 million of his estate to charities.

The highly-publicized drama surrounding the case had actually started a few years earlier, while Astor was still alive, when grandson Phillip Marshall filed for guardianship of his grandmother in **probate** court. (*In Re Brooke Russell Astor,* Surrogate's Court, Westchester County, New York) In that 2006 probate proceeding, Phillip accused his father of gross neglect and mistreatment of her, as well as mismanagement of her financial affairs. A court-appointed evaluator ultimately concluded that Astor had not been mistreated. Nonetheless, the matter was settled with an agreement in which Mr. and Mrs. Marshall relinquished control of Astor's financial affairs both before and after her death. (As her only child, Marshall had managed her financial affairs during her lifetime under a POWER OF ATTORNEY. He also was named executor of her will, along with co-executors Mrs. Marshall and attorney Morrissey.) The probate settlement further established that henceforward, Astor's close personal friend, Mrs. Annette de la Renta (wife of famed fashion designer Oscar de la Renta) would serve as **guardian** of Astor's personal affairs, while JPMorgan Chase would handle her finances. Finally, the settlement suspended (until after her death) any claims that Marshall has mismanaged his mother's financial affairs.

Following Astor's death, the old claims resurfaced during a will contest in the Westchester Surrogate's Court. Attorneys for several ultimate charitable beneficiaries of Astor's estate (including the Metropolitan Museum of Art, the New York Public Library, and the Astor, Lenox, and Tilden Foundations) contested the validity of two codicils to Astor's will that essentially divested their bequests, and, during discovery, requested the release of several documents from Marshall and Morrissey. Soon, the New York Attorney General began investigating the allegations, and the indictments followed. Most charges accused Marshall and Morrissey of exercising UNDUE INFLUENCE and coercion upon Astor, who suffered from Alzheimer's Disease, to change her will to shift millions of dollars to her son instead of

Anthony Marshall arrives at court for his sentencing, December 2009.

AP IMAGES

intended charitable beneficiaries. Several counts also accused Marshall of stealing several million dollars from Astor during her lifetime.

In probate court, Marshall appealed the denial of his petition for a **protective order** to stay discovery of the requested documents, pending resolution of any related criminal proceedings against him. As justification for protection, Marshall had asserted that compelling release of the documents would violate his FIFTH AMENDMENT **privilege against self-incrimination**. But a New York **appellate court** disagreed, stating, in relevant part, " . . . Because it is undisputed that the **appellant** was not compelled to create the documents at issue here, his Fifth Amendment PRIVILEGE AGAINST SELF-INCRIMINATION would not be violated by the fact alone that the [documents] on their face might incriminate him." (Decision and Order D23190, May 19, 2009, *In the Matter of Brooke Russell Astor,* 2008-00767, 2008-09412, SUPREME COURT of the State of New York **Appellate** Division: Second Judicial Department.)

Meanwhile, criminal trial proceeded, focusing on charges that Mr. Marshall, 85, and Morrissey, 66, conspired to have Ms. Astor, while in a fragile mental state, sign two codicils to her 2002 will. Both codicils would have greatly enhanced her **bequest** to Marshall as well as increased the fees he would collect as executor of her will. Both codicils were executed in 2004, when Astor was 102 years old. Morrissey was additionally accused of forging Astor's signature on the second CODICIL.

In Astor's case, the first challenged codicil bequeathed her residuary estate to Marshall outright. Prior to that codicil, her residuary estate had been put in a trust for the benefit of various charities. The second codicil would have required Astor's REAL ESTATE holdings to be sold upon her death, thereby enhancing Marshall's fees as well as those of his wife and Morrissey, co-executors.

In addition to the will-related charges, Marshall was accused of stealing artwork from Astor and using estate funds to pay the captain of his yacht as well as an employee of his theatre production company. He was further accused of abusing his power of attorney (later surrendered as part of the probate settlement) for giving himself a retroactive lump-sum raise of $1 million for managing his mother's finances, representing an increase of more than 200 percent from what she had originally designated for him.

The trial lasted five months and produced approximately 18,000 pages of transcript in addition to thousands of pages of exhibits. But nothing captured the media's attention more than the list of well-recognized public figures who appeared as witnesses for the prosecution. These included Mrs. De la Renta, former SECRETARY OF STATE HENRY KISSINGER, Barbara Walters, and David Rockefeller. Dozens of witnesses were called to testify about personal experiences indicating that Astor lacked capacity to sign the codicils, in addition to personal knowledge of alleged incidents of mistreatment by Marshall or his plans to inflate his inheritance from Astor's estate. (It was Mrs. De la Renta and Mr. Rockefeller who had originally helped grandson Phillip prepare the guardianship petition that first alleged Marshall's mistreatment of Astor.) Several witnesses further opined that Marshall was motivated by pressure from his wife, Charlene, although she was not indicted.

Ultimately, after 12 days of deliberation, a jury of eight women and four men convicted Marshall on 14 of the 16 counts of **fraud**, CONSPIRACY, theft, and **abuse of power**. The most serious conviction was for grand **larceny**,

which carried a mandatory minimum of one year imprisonment. He was acquitted on a second GRAND LARCENY charge for selling a painting from Astor's art collection for $10 million and keeping $2 million commission on the sale. Prosecutors had contended that he had received Astor's permission to sell it only by convincing her that she needed the money. In December 2009, Marshall was sentenced to one to three years in prison for each of the 14 convictions (to be served consecutively).

Morrissey was convicted on several charges of FRAUD and conspiracy in addition to one count of forging Astor's signature to one of the codicils. In addition to a sentence of one to three years' imprisonment for six convictions (to be served consecutively), Morrissey's license to practice law was revoked by the State of New York Bar Association. (Morrissey previously had his license suspended for two years in 1995 and was the subject of other civil LITIGATION alleging that he used undue influence in courting wealthy elderly persons, ultimately coaxing them into bequeathing him valuable property from their estates. Morrissey did estate planning for Astor as well.)

In December 2009, defense attorneys filed a motion asking the trial judge to have the convictions reversed and spare their client prison time. The appeal cited the judge's refusal to talk with a juror who had sent out a note saying she felt threatened by another juror. The trial court denied the motion but granted Marshall's application to remain free on bond pending an appeal. In February 2010, Marshall's attorneys filed an appeal to have the convictions reversed and a new trial scheduled. As of June 2010, the criminal appeal as well as probate case were still pending.

PRODUCT LIABILITY

The responsibility of a manufacturer or vendor of goods to compensate for injury caused by a defective good that it has provided for sale.

Toyota Forced to Recall Millions of Cars

By 2009, Toyota Motor Company had grown into the world's largest and most profitable automobile maker. However, the company's reputation—and bottom line—suffered damage due to a series of recalls prompted by concerns about defects that cause Toyota cars to accelerate unintentionally. By the end of January 2010, Toyota had recalled about 5.2 million cars in the United States and nine million throughout the world.

Although most of Toyota's recent problems began in August 2009, the National Highway Traffic Safety Administration (NHTSA) throughout the 2000s had investigated several concerns about acceleration problems with Toyota cars. In 2003 and 2004, NHTSA received complaints about claims of unintended acceleration on certain Lexus brands. During the entire year in 2004, Toyota cars accounted for 20 percent of the total number of complaints filed for unintended acceleration. The NHTSA conducted several investigations, but most of these investigations resulted in findings that the cars had no defects.

By 2007, some Toyota-brand cars continued to have unintended acceleration problems. In March 2007, the NHTSA investigated a claim that the pedals on the 2007 Lexus ES350 had become entrapped by the car's floor mat. The agency's investigation became more intense when a 2007 Camry was involved in a fatal accident caused by the floor mat entrapping the gas pedal. After the NHTSA informed Toyota of the **entrapment** problem, Toyota announced a recall of 55,000 floor mats from 2007 and 2008 Camry and certain Lexus models. Because of concerns over safety, the magazine *Consumer Reports* downgraded its vehicle quality ratings for three models manufactured by Toyota. Nevertheless, by the end of 2007, Toyota had surpassed Ford Motor Company as the second largest manufacturer in the U.S. market, and Toyota had nearly unseated General Motors as the leading automaker in the world.

On August 28, 2009, an off-duty California High Patrol officer named Mark Saylor was traveling with this family in Santee, California, near San Diego. He was driving a 2009 Lexus ES350, which suddenly accelerated out of Saylor's control. The car struck another vehicle, fell down an embankment, and caught fire. One of the passengers, Saylor's brother-in-law, was able to call 911 as the car sped along the highway at more than 100 miles per hour. The passenger said that the car would not slow down. When the car burst into flames, each member of the family was killed. A local Lexus dealer had given the car to Saylor on loan while Saylor's vehicle was being serviced. Representatives of Toyota as well as local authorities suspected that the car may have had the wrong floor mats installed.

In October 2009, Toyota CEO Akio Toyoda publicly apologized to the Saylor family for the accident.

Nearly two months after the accident, the NHTSA and local authorities revealed the results of an investigation showing that a set of rubber floor mats intended for the Lexus RX 400 had been placed over the top of the stock floor mats used for the Lexus ES350. When the rubber mats became jammed against the gas pedal, the car accelerated uncontrollably. The tests also showed that the brakes in the car Saylor was driving were nearly destroyed and that the gas pedal had become "bonded" to the floor mat. Toyota issued a press release indicating that the company would recall certain vehicles because of the floor-mat issue, but the company stated that the cars did not have defects. The NHTSA publicly criticized Toyota for the statement, stressing that the floor-mat recall would not correct the vehicle's underlying defect.

On November 25, 2009, Toyota recalled 3.8 million vehicles because of the problems with the floor mats. On the same day, the company announced that it would redesign the floor mats and would install a brake-override system on new vehicles so that when an operator hits the brake, the system cuts off the car's throttle. Earlier in the month, the company admitted that it had set aside $5.6 billion to address the problems with the unintended acceleration.

Four days after the company's announcement, though, the *Los Angeles Times* reported that several Toyota drivers complained about acceleration issues that had nothing to do with

Toyota executive vice president Takeshi Uchiyamada speaking on Capitol Hill, March 2010.

AP IMAGES

floor mats. In one story, a driver named Eric Weiss said that he had problems with acceleration on his 2008 Toyota Tacoma. Based on advice given by his Toyota dealer, Weiss removed the floor mats from his truck, but Weiss said he was involved in an accident when his truck suddenly accelerated and struck the rear end of a BMW. "The brakes squealed and the engine roared," he said. "I don't want to drive the truck anymore, but I don't want anyone else to, either."

Concerns about the acceleration issued continued in 2010. On January 21, 2010, the company announced a recall of 2.3 additional vehicles because of problems of gas pedals. The company claimed that the recall was unrelated to the floor-mat recall, but the company acknowledged that 1.7 vehicles would be affected by both recalls. Toyota expanded its recall to cover cars sold in Europe and China. On January 26, the company announced that it would cease sales of the car brands affected by the January 21 recall. One day later, U.S. Transportation Secretary Ray LaHood told the press that the government had asked Toyota to stop selling the recalled vehicles until the company could fix the problems. Toyota stood to lose $1.5 million in profit for each week that the sales freeze continued.

Toyota's woes continued during the spring of 2010. In March, the owner of a Toyota Prius called 911 when the accelerator in his Toyota Prius became stuck. The car accelerated to more than 90 miles per hour even when the driver continually applied the brake. The driver was able to stop the car only after a patrol officer said to apply both the brake and the emergency brake. In April, *Consumer Reports* determined that the 2010 Lexus GX460 SUV was a safety risk because of an increased risk that the vehicle would roll over. Toyota responded immediately to the report by recalling the 9,400 units already sold and temporarily suspending sales of the vehicle. The company made changes to the vehicle's electronic stability-control software and resumed sales two weeks after announcing the recall.

Officials with the NHTSA said in April that Toyota knew about the gas pedal problems as early as September 2009 but failed to report the problem to the agency. Because of this failure, these officials said they would seek to fine Toyota a total of $16.4 million. Toyota's U.S. sales

declined amid stories of the recalls, but the company responded by investing $1 billion in sales incentives. The recalls also did not prevent Toyota from turning a profits during the **fiscal** year that ended in March 2010. In May, the company announced that it had made a profit of $209 billion between March 2009 and March 2010.

PROPERTY LAW

Stop the Beach Renourishment, Inc. v. Florida Department of Environmental Protection

Owners of beachfront property in Florida have long had rights associated with their property and its relationship to the water. Pursuant to a state **statute**, a state agency in Florida decided to restore some Florida beaches, and this restoration would have an effect on the property owner's enjoyment of their land. The SUPREME COURT in June 2010 decided that the Florida agency's decision, along with the judgments of the Florida courts, did not constitute a taking of the property in violation of the owners' constitutional rights. *Stop the Beach Renourishment, Inc. v. Florida Department of Environmental Protection*, No. 08-1151 (June 17, 2010).

Under Florida **common law**, the boundary between privately owned land and land reserved for the public was the mean-high water line (MHWL). The land seaward of this line was held in trust for the public for the purpose of bathing, fishing, and navigation. Conversely, private beachfront property owners own what is known as littoral property, and these owners had certain rights at COMMON LAW. For instance, these owners have the right to access to the water, to use water for certain purposes, and to have an unobstructed view of the water. Florida courts have recognized that property rights of littoral owner cannot be taken without **just compensation**.

Florida law also established principles that applied when changes to the land occurred. In some circumstances, a property owner could take title to new dry land added as a result of changes to the beach. When new dry land appears gradually and imperceptibly, this is known as **accretion**. Conversely, a change that occurs suddenly is known as an **avulsion**. When an accretion occurs, resulting in an increase in new dry land, the MHWL changes. Under the common law, the property owner would automatically take ownership in the new land added by the accretion. However, when an avulsion took place, the MHWL remained as it was before the event took place, so the property owner would not take title to the new land.

The State of Florida in 1961 addressed problems associated with beach erosion with the enactment of the Beach and Shore Preservation Act, Fla. Stat. §§ 161.011-.45 (2005). This statute authorized the state's Environmental Protection Department to engage in processes for restoring and renourishing the beach. The department has the authority to determine which beaches have become critically eroded and to pay for up to 75 percent of the costs to restore and renourish a beach. Under the statute, the department establishes an erosion control line (ECL), which establishes the boundary between publicly owned land and privately owned land. Once the department establishes the ECL, the common law rules for accretion no longer apply.

In 1995, Hurricane Opal caused massive damage to the beaches in the City of Destin and Walton County. The result of the hurricane was that the beaches severely eroded. Destin and Walton County decided to restore the beach by depositing sand and then maintaining the deposited sand through renourishment. The City of Destin and Walton County sought permits that would allow the restoration of 6.9 miles of beach. A survey established the MHWL at the coastline that was going to be restored, and the department used this line as the ECL. The effect of this was that the ECL would establish the boundary between public and private land even after the state deposited many tons of sand along the beachfront, resulting in up to 75 feet of new dry land. Moreover, any new land added as a result of gradual change would also belong to the public because the ECL would not change under the statute.

Stop the Beach Renourishment (STBR) is a non-profit association consisting of six owners of beachfront property affected by the proposal. STBR challenged the action in an administrative hearing, but an administrative law judge ruled in favor of the department. STBR then appealed the case to a Florida appeals court, which determined that the department's decision would be an unconstitutional taking and remanded the case to the department. The Florida Supreme Court agreed to review the case. According to the Florida Supreme Court, the doctrine of avulsion rather than the doctrine of accretion allowed the state to reclaim the restored beach on the public's behalf. The Florida Supreme Court concluded that the department's action did not infringe on a vested PROPERTY RIGHT, and so the action did not amount to an unconstitutional taking. *Walton County v. Stop the Beach Renourishment, Inc.*, 998 So. 2d 1102 (Fla. 2008).

Although the case mostly involved questions of state law, the U.S. Supreme Court agreed to review the case because of questions of whether the Florida Supreme Court's decision constituted a taking. The question of whether there is such a concept as a judicial taking was a rather novel question, so the case drew some interest. All of the justices agreed that the Florida Supreme Court's decision did not constitute a taking, but no majority opinion emerged. Justice ANTONIN SCALIA and three other justices concluded that if a person has an established property right that is no longer recognized because of a judicial decision, then the court has unconstitutionally taken the property in violation of the FIFTH AMENDMENT of the U.S. Constitution. It did not matter to the **plurality** that the action involved the judicial branch of government rather than the legislative or executive branches. In the present case, however, the plurality also concluded that the property owners had no right to the filled-in land because the state had the right to repair its own beaches and claim the new dry land that resulted from restoration.

Justices ANTHONY KENNEDY and STEPHEN BREYER filed concurring opinions, with both questioning the concept of a judicial taking.

PROSECUTORIAL MISCONDUCT

Pottawattamie County v. McGhee

In *Pottawattamie County v. McGhee Health Care Services Corporation v. Pollitt*, No. 08-1065, the U.S. Supreme Court was asked to address whether a prosecutor violated a criminal defendant's "substantive due process" rights by procuring false testimony during a criminal investigation and introducing that same testimony against the defendant at trial. The U.S. Supreme Court granted certiorari (review) based on a split among lower circuit courts on the topic. However, following oral arguments before the Court in late 2009, a reported $12 million settlement resulted in a petition for dismissal of Supreme Court review. The petition was dismissed, pursuant to Supreme Court Rule 46, in early 2010. The Eighth Circuit Court of Appeals had affirmed the district court's denial of immunity for the prosecutors, finding that the alleged facts were "sufficient to state a substantive due process claim," and that the constitutional right against such prosecutorial conduct was "clearly established."

In 1978, Pottawattamie County, Iowa prosecutors Joseph Hrvol and David Richter successfully obtained murder convictions and life sentences against defendants Curtis McGhee and Terry Harrington for the murder of a retired police officer who was working as an auto dealership security guard. Police had initially focused on another person of interest, Charles Gates, a man identified by two witnesses as being near the scene "with a shotgun and a dog," but attention shifted to McGhee and Harrington after yet another person of interest, 16-year-old Kevin Hughes, was questioned. Hughes, who already had a lengthy criminal history, was facing charges for auto theft and possible involvement in the policeman's murder. Detectives offered not to charge Highes with the murder as well as other pending criminal charges, if he cooperated in the investigation. They also intimated that he could be eligible for a $5000 reward for information regarding the policeman's murder.

Hughes' unreliability as a credible witness began to unravel shortly thereafter, when two other men he expressly implicated were proved innocent through police investigation. Hughes further had initially stated to police that he did not think McGhee or Harrington were involved in the murder. Nonetheless, he subsequently implicated them in a series of stories that proved inaccurate. Using Hughes as their main witness, along with his friends and associates and jailhouse informants, the prosecutors brought murder charges against McGhee and Harrington. Both were convicted and sentenced to life imprisonment.

In post-conviction relief, the Iowa Supreme Court in 2003 overturned the convictions due to prosecutorial failure to provide defense counsel with exculpatory information, to wit, evidence of alternative suspects, which the court held was a due process violation. Prosecutors decided not to retry Harrington; McGhee, whose conviction was based on the same facts in evidence, entered a plea to second-degree murder in exchange for a sentence of time served. Both men at that time had served 25 years each. They filed suit in the U. S. District Court for the Southern District of Iowa against Pottawattamie County and the two county prosecutors, Hrvol and Richter. They alleged that defendants had coerced false witness testimony from Kevin Hughes (see above) during the criminal investigation, subjected them to false charges and false arrest, introduced false testimony at trial, and withheld exculpatory evidence. Their suit was filed under 42 U.S.C. §1983, which creates a cause of action against state and local government officials for constitutional violations.

The district court dismissed the claims based on the withholding of exculpatory evidence, but would not grant immunity to the extent that claims arose from allegations of coercing false testimony and introducing perjured testimony at trial, which the court found to constitute due process violations. In 2008, the Eighth Circuit Court of Appeals affirmed, going a little further in its analysis. It distinguished immunity attaching to the prosecutors during trial from the absence of immunity for pre-trial acts, which it characterized as "investigatory." The court then found that the prosecutors' alleged coercion of testimony from Hughes and other informants was investigatory and did not fall within "a distinctly prosecutorial function." Thus, the prosecutors enjoyed no immunity from these claims of violating due process rights. *McGhee v. Pottawattamie County*, 547 F.3d 922 (8th Cir. 2008).

Attorneys for Pottawattamie County and the prosecutors petitioned for Supreme Court review, pointing to a split among circuit courts of appeals regarding the scope and extent of absolute immunity. The question before the Court was captioned as whether a prosecutor may be subjected to a civil trial and potential damages for a wrongful conviction and incarceration where the prosecutor allegedly violated a criminal defendant's "substantive due process" rights by procuring false testimony during the criminal investigation, and then introduced that same testimony against the criminal defendant at trial.

The subsequent $12 million settlement from Potawattamie County to McGhee and Harrington rendered the issue moot.

PUBLIC UTILITIES

Businesses that provide the public with necessities, such as water, electricity, natural gas, and telephone and telegraph communication.

NRG Power Marketing, LLC v. Maine Public Utilities Commission

The Federal Power Act (FPA), 16 U.S.C. §§ 824 **et seq.** gives the Federal Energy Regulatory Commission (FERC) the authority to regulate the sale of electricity in interstate commerce. Under the FPA, regulated utilities must file rate schedules, or tariffs, with FERC. FERC is also involved with setting the terms and prices for services to electricity purchasers. Utilities may additionally set rates with individual electricity purchasers through bilateral agreements. Both the rate schedules and the contracts must be filed with FERC. The SUPREME COURT, in two 1956 decisions, set out the standard that the FERC must use in reviewing contracts. This standard was reaffirmed in a 2008 decision: freely negotiated contracts for the sale of electricity under the FPA were presumed to be reasonable and just, in the absence of a showing that the rates impaired the PUBLIC INTEREST. However, the **Circuit Court** of Appeals for the District of Columbia ruled after this decision that the standard for challenging a contract only applied to for disputes involving contracting parties. The Supreme Court, in *NRG Power Marketing, LLC v. Maine Public Utilities Commission,* __ U.S. __, 130 S. Ct. 693, __L. Ed. 2d__ (2010), overruled this limitation, holding that the standard applied to all challenges of energy contracts.

The case arose out a long-standing problem with the reliability of the power grid in New England. In 2006, the FERC approved a comprehensive settlement agreement that established rate-setting mechanisms for sales of energy capacity . The agreement also stated that the *Mobile-Sierra* public interest standard would govern rate challenges. This standard was named for two 1956 Supreme Court cases dealing with utility rate regulation where rates are set by contract rather than rate schedules: *United Gas Pipe Line Co. v. Mobile Gas Serv. Corp. (Mobile),* 350 U.S. 332, 76 S. Ct. 373, 100 L. Ed. 373 (1956); *Fed. Power Comm'n v. Sierra Pac. Power Co. (Sierra),* 350 U.S. 348, 76 S. Ct. 368, 100 L. Ed. 388 (1956). Under this standard, the FERC must presume that an electricity rate established through a freely-negotiated, **bilateral contract**

meets the "just and reasonable" requirement set forth in the FPA. This presumption may be overcome only if FERC determines that the contract causes serious harm to the public interest. In *Morgan Stanley Capital Group Inc. v. Pub. Util. Dist. No. 1,* 554 U.S. __, 128 S. Ct. 2733, 171 L. Ed. 2d 607 (2008), the Supreme Court reaffirmed the standard.

In the New England energy case, 107 participants approved the settlement and 8 opposed. The FERC approved the settlement agreement, "finding that as a package, it presents a just and reasonable outcome for this proceeding consistent with the public interest." The *Mobile-Sierra* provision, FERC explicitly determined, "appropriately balances the need for rate stability and the interests of the diverse entities would be subject to an auction system. Six of the parties objecting to the settlement filed an appeal in the D.C. Circuit Court of Appeals. The court refused to overturn the settlement but it ruled that the *Mobile-Sierra* standard applied only to contracting parties. Both sides appealed to the Supreme Court.

In an 8-1 decision, the Court upheld the agreement and ruled that the *Mobile-Sierra* standard applied to contracting and noncontracting parties alike. Justice RUTH BADER GINSBURG, writing for the Court, concluded that the reasoning in *Morgan Stanley* "strongly suggested" that the D.C. Circuit had misperceived the aim and diminished the force of the *Mobile-Sierra* standard. The public interest standard was not a standard independent of, and sometimes at odds with, the "just and reasonable" standard; instead, the public interest standard defined "what it means for a rate to satisfy the just-and-reasonable standard in the contract context." The FERC must presume just and reasonable a contract rate resulting from fair, arms-length negotiations; it made no sense that noncontracting parties could escape that presumption. In addition, the *Mobile-Sierra* standard was designed to protect third parties: it directs the FERC to reject a contract rate that "seriously harms the consuming public." Limiting the standard to contracting parties would diminish the "animating purpose of *Mobile-Sierra,* which was to promote the stability of supply arrangements. Without stability, the health of the power industry would be put in doubt. Justice Ginsburg concluded that a standard limited to contracting parties and "inoperative as to everyone elseconsumers, advocacy groups, state utility commissions, elected officials acting *parens patriae* could scarcely provide the stability *Mobile-Sierra* aimed to secure.

In a dissenting opinion, Justice JOHN PAUL STEVENS stated that this is "the third chapter in a story about how a reasonable principle, extended beyond its foundation, becomes bad law." Stevens agreed that *Mobile-Sierra* was decided correctly but he noted that he had dissented in *Morgan Stanley*. In that second chapter he concluded that the Court had imposed another burden on those who challenged utility rates. In this third chapter, the "Court applies a ruleone designed initially to protect the enforceability of freely negotiated contracts against parties who seek a release from their obligationsto impose a special burden on third parties exercising their **statutory** right to object to unjust and unreasonable rates. This application of the rule represents a quantum leap from the modest origin set forth in the first chapter of this tale."

RACIAL DISCRIMINATION

Louisiana Judge Denies Marriage License to Interracial Couple

A **justice of the peace** in Louisiana came under pressure from state lawmakers and national advocacy groups when he denied a marriage license to an interracial couple. The judge, who is white, tried to explain that he was concerned about children of interracial marriages. However, Louisiana lawmakers acted quickly to renounce the act, and the judge finally resigned. The couple also filed a lawsuit against the judge in federal court in Louisiana.

Laws banning interracial marriages have an infamous but long history in the United States. Many statutes banning interracial marriage and interracial sex used the term "miscegenation" to describe these acts as crimes. In many states, **miscegenation** was a **felony** punishable by a prison term. In 1959, a couple in Virginia pleaded guilty to having been married illegally and then returning to Virginia, which banned interracial marriages. The couple received a **suspended sentence** on a one-year prison term under the condition that the couple left the state.

The AMERICAN CIVIL LIBERTIES UNION filed suit on the couple's behalf, arguing that the **statute** violated the couple's FOURTEENTH AMENDMENT rights. In an opinion by Chief Justice EARL WARREN, the Court reversed the convictions. Warren wrote: "Marriage is one of

the 'basic CIVIL RIGHTS of man,' fundamental to our very existence and survival.... To deny this fundamental freedom on so unsupportable a basis as the racial classifications embodied in these statutes, classifications so directly subversive of the principle of equality at the heart of the Fourteenth Amendment, is surely to deprive all the State's citizens of liberty without **due process of law**. The Fourteenth Amendment requires that the freedom of choice to marry not be restricted by invidious racial DISCRIMINATION. Under our Constitution, the freedom to marry, or not marry, a person of another race resides with the individual and cannot be infringed by the State." *Loving v. Virginia*, 388 U.S. 1, 87 S. Ct. 1817, 18 L. Ed. 2d 1010 (1967).

In Louisiana, a JUSTICE OF THE PEACE is elected to a six-year term by the people. A justice of the peace can conduct marriage ceremonies and has jurisdiction over civil matters that do not exceed $5,000. A person holding such a position must have a high school diploma or GED, and the person must be able to read and write the English language. The person does not have to be a lawyer to serve as justice of the peace.

Since 1975, Keith Bardwell served as the justice of the peace in Hammond, Louisiana. In October 2009, a woman named Beth Humphrey approached Bardwell's wife about Bardwell holding a marriage ceremony for Humphrey and her boyfriend. Towards the end of the conversation, Bardwell's wife asked Humphrey if the relationship was interracial. When Humphrey replied that it was, Bardwell's wife said that Bardwell would refuse to sign a marriage license to an interracial couple. A shocked Humphrey had to ask a justice of the peace from nearby Tickfaw to hold the ceremony, and Humphrey and her boyfriend, Terence McKay were eventually married.

Bardwell openly admitted in interviews that he refused to sign marriage certificates for interracial couples. He claimed that he is not a racist but said that he concern is about the children of such marriages. According to Bardwell, neither white nor black communities readily accept the children of an interracial marriage. "I don't do interracial marriages because I don't want to put children in a situation they didn't bring on themselves," he told the *Hammond Star*. "In my heart, I feel the children will later suffer." Bardwell later defended his actions on the CBS television program "The Early Show" on October 19.

Humphrey and McKay found abundant support from such groups as the American Civil Liberties Union (ACLU) and the National Association for the **Advancement** of Colored People (NAACP). The ACLU immediately sent a letter to the state's judiciary committee asking for an investigation. Louisiana Governor Bobby Jindal and Senator Mary Landrieu (D.-La.) quickly called for Bardwell to resign. Several who commented on the case noted that President BARACK OBAMA is the offspring of an interracial marriage.

The pressure for Bardwell to resign intensified throughout the month of October. The story made national headlines, with nearly anyone who commented noting that Bardwell's position was absurd. On November 3, Bardwell finally resigned, saying at the time of his resignation that he did not plan to run for reelection when his term was supposed to expire in 2014. The state's SUPREME COURT appointed an interim justice to serve in Bardwell's place. At the time of Bardwell's resignation, Landrieu noted, "Bardwell has finally consented to the will of the vast majority of Louisiana citizens and nearly every governmental office in Louisiana. Bardwell's refusal to issue marriage licenses to interracial couples was out of step with our Louisiana values and reflected terribly on our state. We are better off without him in public service."

On October 20, 2009, Humphrey and McKay filed a civil suit against Keith Bardwell and his wife, Beth. The plaintiffs alleged violations of several provisions of the U.S. and Louisiana constitutions. In addition to their allegations against Keith Bardwell, Humphrey and McKay alleged that Beth Bardwell "acted to aid and **abet** and conspire with DEFENDANT, Keith Bardwell, a public official, to deprive plaintiffs of their right to marry." The plaintiffs have sought monetary damages for their **mental anguish** and emotional distress caused by Bardwell's refusal to sign the marriage license. The Bardwells filed an answer on February 5, 2010. In their answer, the Bardwells denied several of the plaintiff's allegations and stressed that the couple's damages and expenses were "self-inflicted."

RACKETEERING

Billionaire Sex Offender Sues Disgraced Attorney Charged with Running a Ponzi Scheme

A bizarre case in Florida has pitted a billionaire who was previously convicted of a sex offense against disbarred lawyer accused of running a billion-dollar **Ponzi scheme**. The billionaire, Jeffrey Epstein, accused Scott Rothstein of lying to potential clients about personal-injury lawsuits Rothstein was bringing against Epstein so that the clients would invest money to earn interest in these suits. Epstein brought an action for civil RACKETEERING, seeking more than $15,000 in damages along with injunctive relief. Attorneys for several young women who were allegedly victimized by Epstein have said that the suit is designed to scare them rather than Rothstein.

Epstein founded his own financial management firm, J. Epstein and Co., in 1982. He had several high-profile clients, friends, and associates. For example, he flew former president BILL CLINTON and actors Kevin Spacey and Chris Tucker to Africa in 2002 to promote an anti-AIDS rally. He pledged millions of dollars to a number of charities and was a member of several boards. He was known for traveling in the company of young women who purportedly served as his personal assistants.

In 2005, allegations arose that Epstein had molested a 14-year-old girl. Police began investigation that involved searching Epstein's

Palm Beach mansion. This investigation led to further allegations that Epstein had paid a number of underage girls to engage in sexual activity with him. Investigators found photos of young nude girls, including girls who had been interviewed by the investigators. Police in 2006 filed a **probable cause** AFFIDAVIT indicating that Epstein should be charged with four counts of having sex with minors and one count of CHILD MOLESTATION.

Epstein hired high profile lawyers, including Gerald B. Lefcourt, ALAN DERSHOWITZ, and KENNETH STARR. Prosecutors presented evidence to a **grand jury**, which in 2006 returned only one charge of **felony solicitation** of PROSTITUTION. Epstein initially pleaded not guilty to the charge. Police in Palm Beach immediately argued that the prosecutors had given Epstein preferential treatment due to his wealth. Epstein and his lawyers engaged in plea negotiations, and in June 2008, he pleaded guilty to a single charge of soliciting a prostitute. He was sentenced to 18 months in prison, of which he served 13 months. He is required to register as a sex offender.

Rothstein built his law practice from the ground up, and he eventually became managing partner of the Rothstein Rosenfeldt Adler law firm, which employed 70 attorneys and a large staff. He lived a lavish lifestyle, owning several expensive homes in the Fort Lauderdale, Florida area. Around 2005, though, Rothstein allegedly began running a PONZI SCHEME in which he would attract investors with promises of high returns and then use the new investment money to pay other investors. According to the allegations, investors would pay a certain amount of money up front to an individual who was likely to receive money from a court settlement. The investor would then receive a high rate of return (typically 20 to 30 percent) only a few months later.

The FEDERAL BUREAU OF INVESTIGATION caught on to Rothstein's scam, and in December 2009, Rothstein turned himself in to authorities. The Florida SUPREME COURT permanently disbarred him on November 25. After turning himself in, Rothstein cooperated with authorities, and he change his plea to guilty on five counts related to the Ponzi scheme in January 2010. The Ponzi scheme allegedly cost investors as much as $1.6 billion. Rothstein's sentencing was scheduled for May 2010.

Epstein entered the picture in December 2009 when he filed a suit against Rothstein and an attorney employed by Rothstein in **circuit court** in Palm Beach. Also named in the action was a woman represented by Rothstein and Edwards in a **civil action** against Epstein. According to Epstein's allegations, Rothstein claimed to investors to represent several client who were involved in SEXUAL HARASSMENT suits against Epstein. Rothstein allegedly told the investors that Epstein had agreed to pay $200 million to settle the various suits. In reality, Rothstein's firm only represented three women bringing suits against Epstein. The story was designed, according to Epstein, to lure investors to pay money up front for the chance to recover a larger amount once Epstein settled the cases.

Lawyers for Epstein's victims said that Epstein's only motivation for filing the suit was to scare the victims themselves. According to these lawyers, Epstein wants to make his victims look bad by associating them with Rothstein. Epstein argued it his suit that the girl, identified only as "L.M.," changed her story between the time she was first interviewed and the time she was deposed as part of her civil suit.

Epstein's legal problems continued in late 2009 and 2010. In December 2009, he settled a case against another accuser for an undisclosed amount, and at that time he faced more than a dozen cases from other women he allegedly abused. Epstein ran into more problems in March 2010 when investigators discovered a journal apparently containing the names of hundreds of teenage girls who were Epstein's victims. The journal had been in the possession of Alfredo Rodriguez, Epstein's former property manager. Rodriguez later attempted to sell the journal for $50,000, but the person to whom he tried to sell the journal alerted authorities.

In April 2010, reports surfaced that Epstein had made damaging statements in a 22-minute interview with reporter George Rush of the *New York Daily News*. According to reports, Epstein discusses SEXUAL ABUSE of underage girls, noting that he had come "close to crossing a line" when it came to having sex with the girls. Attorneys for a girl who has filed suit against Epstein submitted a court filing asking for access to the tape. The newspaper fought the request, arguing that the tape was confidential.

RAILROADS

Union Pacific Railroad v. Brotherhood of Locomotive Engineers and Trainmen General Committee of Adjustment, Central Region

The U.S. railroad industry is heavily regulated by the federal government. Under the Railway Labor Act (RLA) railroad employees and employers must use federally-created procedures to resolve labor disputes, including ARBITRATION. To administer arbitration, Congress established the National Railroad Adjustment Board (NRAB), a 34-person private board representing the companies and employees in equal numbers. A three-person arbitration panel consists of a company board member, an employee board member, and a third "neutral" arbitrator. NRAB created regulations to govern the arbitration process and required that both sides exhaust the grievance procedures in their **collective bargaining agreement**. The question arose whether NRAB could dismiss an employee claim for lack of jurisdiction if there was no proof in the record that the sides had conducted a settlement conference. The NRBA believed it must dismiss the claims but the SUPREME COURT rejected this approach in *Union Pacific Railroad v. Brotherhood Of Locomotive Engineers and Trainmen General Committee Of Adjustment, Central Region* , __U.S.__, 130 S. Ct. 584 , __L. Ed. 2d__ (2009). The Court concluded that the failure to show that the sides had conference was not a jurisdictional issue and had no bearing on the resolution of the grievance.

Union Pacific Railroad charged five of its employees with disciplinary violations. Their union, the Brotherhood of Locomotive Engineers and Trainmen started grievance proceedings pursuant to the COLLECTIVE BARGAINING AGREEMENT. After grievance proceedings had been exhausted, the union claimed that all five claims had been conferenced with the railroad. The railroad later claimed that only two had been conferenced. The union rejected the railroad's offer and sought arbitration from the NRAB. The union submitted its paperwork to the board and each submission included the required documents. Neither the union nor the railroad mentioned in their filings that conferencing was a disputed matter for the board to resolve. Under board regulations both sides were instructed to "set forth all relevant,

argumentative facts." Prior to the hearing on the employees' claims, an arbitrator associated with the railroad industry raised an objection on his own initiative that there was no proof of conferencing. Union Pacific agreed, though it had not raised an objection previously, and the neutral arbitrator adjourned the hearing and asked the union to submit of evidence of conferencing. The union provided phone logs and handwritten notes but argued that the objection was untimely and that Union Pacific had forfeited its claim on this issue. The arbitration panel dismissed the employees' claims because it had concluded that no new evidence could be submitted once an arbitration claim was filed.

The union took the matter to federal district, which upheld the board's order. The Seventh **Circuit Court** of Appeals reversed this decision, concluding that a written record of conferencing was not a prerequisite for arbitrating a claim before the NRAB. However, in justifying this ruling the appeals court ignored the union's statute-based argument that the panel mistakenly ruled that it lacked jurisdiction over the case. Instead, the court reversed on the grounds that NRAB's proceeding was incompatible with due process. The Supreme Court agreed to hear the railroad's appeal to determine whether the appeals court's constitutional argument was correct. Other circuit courts of appeal had preferred to use **statutory** grounds to resolve similar issues.

The Court, in a unanimous decision, rejected the Seventh Circuit's constitutional analysis. Justice RUTH BADER GINSBURG, writing for the Court, stated that nothing in the federal law "elevates to jurisdictional status the obligation to conference minor disputes or to prove conferencing." The union was entitled to a vacation of the board's order under the law and therefore there was no due process constitutional issue "alive in this case." However, the Court concluded that it was important to educate the lower courts and administrative boards over what should be properly typed "jurisdictional." Ginsburg noted that there was a substantial difference between jurisdiction and claim-processing rules. Congress had authorized the NRAB to prescribe rules for presenting and processing claims, but "Congress alone controls the Board's jurisdiction." In this case the board's false premise that it lacked jurisdiction to hear the claims had taken the board beyond its congressional mandate. Unless Congress specifically states in a law that the courts or administrative bodies do not have jurisdiction to hear a case, the rules that a board prescribes are no more than claim-processing regulations that do not deprive a body from hearing the case.

Justice Ginsburg pointed out that conferencing is often conducted informally and is no way "jurisdictional." Therefore, the failure to submit proof of conferencing cannot itself be considered jurisdictional. The RLA and NRAB regulations could not "plausibly be read to require, as a prerequisite to the NRAB's exercise of jurisdiction, submission of proof of conferencing. Instructions on party submissions are claim-processing, not jurisdictional, rules." The board was entitled to reject the introduction of new information about the employee's grievance at the arbitration stage, but "conferencing is not a fact bearing on the merits of a grievance. Moreover, the RLA respects the parties' right to order for themselves the conference procedures they will follow."

RELIGION

Dad Has Court Trouble for Taking Child to Catholic Church

A Chicago man in 2009 and 2010 found himself at the center of a controversy for taking his daughter to church. Joseph Reyes, a Catholic, had been married to a Jewish woman. When the two separated, Reyes decided to take his three-year-old daughter to a Catholic church and even had her Baptized. A court enjoined Reyes from taking his daughter to the church, but he proceeded to do so anyway. Because of his action, Reyes faced possible criminal CONTEMPT charges. However, the court in April 2010 decided that the father could take his child to the church.

Reyes, a military veteran who fought in Afghanistan and who is now studying law, was a Catholic before he married Rebecca Reyes in 2004. To please his wife's family, Joseph Reyes agreed to convert to Judaism, though he later said he never stopped practicing Catholicism. The couple had a daughter, and when the couple separated in 2008, Rebecca gained sole CUSTODY of the girl. For one seven-month period, Joseph did not see his daughter. When

he finally gained VISITATION RIGHTS, Joseph decided to take his daughter to a Catholic church and to have her baptized. Joseph decided to send a picture of the baptism to Rebecca, who was incensed because she wanted her daughter to be raised Jewish. Rebecca asked a judge to issue a TEMPORARY RESTRAINING ORDER that would prohibit Joseph from taking the daughter to anything other than a Jewish church. According to Rebecca Reyes, exposing the child to another religion would cause irreparable harm. Joseph Reyes' attorney said he "almost fell out of [his] chair" after reading the petition for the RESTRAINING ORDER. "I thought maybe we were in Afghanistan and this was the Taliban. This is America. We have a FIRST AMENDMENT right of freedom of religion."

Rebecca Reyes, who has custody of the couple's child, Ela, was upset not only with where the child attended church but also with Joseph's decision not to consult Rebecca. Rebecca's attorney told ABC News, "[I]t wasn't just a religious thing per se; it was the idea that he would suddenly, out of nowhere without any discussion and have the girl baptized. [Rebecca] looked at it as basically an ASSAULT on her little girl." The attorney noted that Joseph had ever been an especially devout Christian. When Joseph decided to take his daughter to church in violation of the order, he called the media to record the event. Video clips of Joseph's church attendance with his daughter later appeared on the Internet site YouTube. In one of the videos, Joseph says, "I am taking her to hear the teachings of perhaps the most prominent Jewish rabbi in the history of this great planet of ours." Rebecca responded that she thought he was "just trying to exert some power."

For his act of defying the court order, Joseph in February 2010 was arraigned on a charge of criminal contempt, which could have resulted in jail time. Experts commented that the order was rather unusual. According to law professor Eugene Volokh of the UCLA School of Law, a parent with visitation rights "usually has the right to expose the child to his religious beliefs, teach the child his religion, to take the child to religious services, unless there seems to be likely psychological or physical harm stemming from that exposure." University of Chicago law professor Emily Buss added, "Even if [one] parent has more authority in the form of more custody, the other parent can [usually] ... still expose the child to his or her religion even if it was not the religious practices within the family when it was intact."

The case earned national attention, as the story was the focus of stories in several newspapers and other media outlets. Joseph appeared on such televisions shows as "Good Morning America," and attorneys for both sides defended their clients' respective positions in quotes to the press. Rebecca also appeared in the media, granting an interview with such media sources as ABC News.

In March 2010, Joseph filed a motion in Cook County **Circuit Court**, asking the judge to dismiss the contempt charges against Joseph. The motion asserts that the order prohibiting Joseph from exposing the girl to a religion other than the Jewish faith is too vague. In the motion, Joseph's attorneys asked a series of rhetorical questions about what it means to expose a child to another religion. For instance, the motion questions whether the order would prohibit such acts as taking the child to buy Christmas presents, taking the child on an Easter Egg hunt, or taking the child into a church building where no ceremony is being held. The motion also asserts that the court could not sufficiently define what the Jewish religion is, noting that Illinois courts apply what is known as the ecclesiastical ABSTENTION DOCTRINE, under which a court will not make a decision on the matter of religion.

About a month later, Cook County Judge Renee Goldfarb ruled that Joseph could take his daughter to "church services if he so chooses" and also that he would have visitation on the Christian holidays of Christmas and Easter. According to the order, the judge found no evidence that taking the girl to a Catholic church would cause her harm. Instead, the judge determined that it was in the child's best interest to allow Joseph to take her to his own church. On the other hand, Goldfarb was critical of how Joseph handled the situation, writing, "Joseph chose to make three-year-old Ela the center of his own media event, as seen on every local news channel, print media and national news channels during his visitation. Joseph chose to dispense three-year-old Ela's picture to the media."

Although the issue of whether Joseph could take the girl to church was settled, as of May 2010, he still faced the criminal contempt charges.

RICO

The Racketeer Influenced and Corrupt Organizations Act, a set of federal laws (18 U.S.C.A. § 1961 et seq. [1970]) specifically designed to punish criminal activity by business enterprises.

Hemi Group, LLC, v. City of New York

The Racketeer Influenced and Corrupt Organizations Act (RICO), 18 U.S.C. §§ 1961-1968, is a powerful tool for government in its fight against illegal activities. However, the SUPREME COURT has been reluctant to expand the reading of RICO. In *Hemi Group, LLC, v. City of New York,*, __U.S.__, 130 S. Ct. 983, __L. Ed. 2d__ (2010), the Court rejected the application of RICO because the alleged illegal activity could not be show to be the **proximate cause** of the alleged injury to the city of New York.

Hemi Group, a New Mexico company that sells cigarettes online, did not file reports as required by the federal Jenkins Act about the purchasers of cigarettes. This requirement was imposed because purchasers do not pay state and local sales taxes for the cigarettes. The city of New York imposes a $1.50 tax on each pack of cigarettes possessed within the city for sale or use. When purchasers buy cigarettes from in-state vendors, the seller is responsible for charging, collecting, and remitting the tax. Online vendors like Hemi are not required to collect the tax. Instead, the city is responsible for recovering, directly from the customers, taxes on cigarettes sold outside New York. To aid in collection of the taxes, which can be a difficult task, the state of New York agreed to share Jenkins Act information with the city. The act requires out-of-state cigarette sellers to register and to file a report with state tobacco tax administrators listing the name, address, and quantity of cigarettes purchased by state residents. Hemi failed to file reports with the state of New York, leading the city to file a civil RICO action in federal **district court**, alleging that Hemi's conduct had deprived the city of tens, if not hundreds, of millions of dollars per year in tax revenue.

Hemi moved the court to dismiss the lawsuit and the court agreed. It concluded that Hemi owner and officer Kai Gachupin did not have an individual duty to file Jenkins Act reports, and thus could not have committed the alleged predicate acts (mail and wire **fraud**) required by RICO. That meant that the City could not establish that Hemi and Gachupin formed an "enterprise" as required to establish RICO liability. The Second **Circuit Court** of Appeals reversed this decision. It ruled that city had established that Gachupin and Hemi operated as an "enterprise" and that the enterprise committed the predicate RICO acts of mail and wire FRAUD, based on the failure to file the Jenkins Act material with the state. The appeals court also found that the city's asserted injury, lost tax revenue, was "business or property" under RICO, and that it had been caused by the mail and wire fraud. Hemi appealed to the Supreme Court.

The Court, in a 5-3 decision, with Justice SONIA SOTOMAYOR not participating, overruled the Second Circuit. Chief Justice JOHN ROBERTS, writing for the majority, addressed whether the city's asserted injury came about "by reason of" the allegedly **fraudulent** conduct, as required by RICO. Roberts concluded that the city could not satisfy the RICO causation requirement that any injury the city suffered must be "by reason of" the alleged frauds. The PROXIMATE CAUSE for the city's alleged injury requires "some direct relation between the injury asserted and the injurious conduct alleged." In this case the city's causal theory was "far more attenuated" than those rejected in prior Court RICO decisions.

Roberts found that the city's theory of liability rested "not just on separate *actions*, but separate actions carried out by separate *parties.*" The city's theory would rest on the Court's extension of RICO liability to situations where the defendant's fraud on "the **third party** (the state) has made it easier for a *fourth* party (the taxpayer) to cause harm to the PLAINTIFF (the city). "The fourth-party taxpayers only caused harm to the city if they decided not to pay taxes they were legally obligated to pay. Therefore, Hemi's obligation was to file Jenkins Act reports with the state, not the city, and the city's harm was directly caused by the customers, not Hemi. Roberts concluded that the Court "has never before stretched the causal chain of a RICO violation so far, and declines to do so today."

Justice STEPHEN BREYER, in a dissenting opinion joined by Justices JOHN PAUL STEVENS and ANTHONY KENNEDY, argued that the failure of Hemi to provide the state with the names and addresses of its New York City cigarette customers proximately caused the city to lose tobacco tax revenue. The fact that Hemi misrepresented the situation to the state, not the city, did not significantly separate the MISREPRESENTATION from the harm. The state signed a contact agreed to share the tobacco customer information with the city. The state was a conduit, "indeed roughly analogous to a postal employee. This Court has recognized specifically that "under the **common law** a fraud may be established when the DEFENDANT has made use of a THIRD PARTY to reach the target of the fraud."

SARBANES-OXLEY ACT

Free Enterprise Fund v. Public Company Accounting Oversight Board

In the wake of several major accounting and securities fraud scandals, Congress passed the anti-fraud Sarbanes-Oxley Act of 2002, P.L. 107-204, 116 Stat. 745 (codified in various chapters and sections of the U.S. Code). Among other things, the Act created a Public Company Accounting Oversight Board (PCAOB), to be paid for by fees collected on publicly traded companies, according to their size. The Board replaced the accounting industry's own internal regulators, and now had independent subpoena power to facilitate its own regulation, oversight, and discipline of accountants and accounting firms. An important provision in the Act created greater financial disclosure mandates and increased the criminal penalties for securities fraud. The Sarbanes-Oxley Act also provided for the Securities and Exchange Commission (SEC) to appoint the chairman and four directors of the PCAOB.

Notwithstanding, the Act itself came under criticism and constitutional scrutiny when pro-business, anti-tax/fee plaintiffs (the Free Enterprise Fund) brought suit alleging that the creation of the PCAOB violated the Appointments Clause of the U.S. Constitution (Article II, §2, cl. 2) as well as the constitutionally-mandated separation of powers. The constitutional challenges were grounded in the fact that the PCAOB was a government-created entity with expansive powers to govern an entire industry. Its Board members, in turn, were appointed by SEC, itself a government-created entity. Both Board members and SEC officials could only be removed from office "for cause," which became the subject matter under appeal herein.

A federal district court upheld the constitutionality of the Act and the PCAOB, and its decision was affirmed by the U.S. District Court of Appeals for the D.C. Circuit in 2008. *Free Enterprise Fund v. Public Company Accounting Oversight Board*, 537 F.3d 667 (D. C. Cir. 2008). However, the U.S. Supreme Court modified that result. In *Free Enterprise Fund v. Public Company Accounting Oversight Board*, No. 08-861, 561 U.S. ___ (2010) it affirmed in part and reversed in part, holding that the Act's dual "for-cause" limitations on removal of PCAOB members contravened the Constitution's separate of powers. However, the Court also held that the unconstitutional provisions were severable from the remainder of the Act, and therefore, the remainder of the Act was "fully operative as a law."

It all started when the PCAOB inspected one of the member accounting firms of the Free Enterprise Fund and released a report critical of its auditing procedures. The PCAOB then began its own investigation, as empowered. The Free Enterprise fund then sued the PCAOB, asking for a declaratory judgment preventing the

PCAOB from exercising those powers. The complaint alleged that the Sarbanes-Oxley Acct was unconstitutional as violating the separation of powers, because it conferred executive power on PCAOB members without subjecting them to Presidential control. Further, they argued, PCAOB members were insulated from presidential control by two layers of protection: board members could only be removed by the SEC for good cause, but SEC members could only be removed by the President for good cause. The complaint alleged that this also violated the Constitution's Appointments Clause, which requires that officers be appointed by the President with the Senate's advice and consent, or, in the case of "inferior officers," by "the President alone, … the Courts of Law, or … the Heads of Departments."

After affirming that the district court had jurisdiction to render its decision, the U.S. Supreme Court addressed the substance of the arguments raised. Writing for the 5-4 majority, Chief Justice Roberts declared that, indeed, the Act's double-layered "for-cause" limitations on the removal of PCAOB members did violate the Constitution's separation of powers. Article II, §1, cl. 1 provides that "[t]he executive Power shall be vested in a President of the United States of America." Since 1789, this has been understood to mean that the president was empowered to hold executive officers accountable and to remove them if necessary. Likewise, the Court has held that principal executive officers may be restrained in their ability to remove their own inferior officers. But the question before the Court in this case was whether those separate layers of protection could be combined.

The Sarbanes-Oxley Act not only protects PCAOB members from removal except for good cause, but removes from the President any decision on whether good cause exists, wrote Justice Roberts. That decision is vested with the SEC. In turn, SEC commissioners are not subject to the President's direct control and can only be removed by the President for cause. But if the SEC cannot remove a PCAOB member at will, the President cannot hold the SEC fully accountable for the PCAOB's conduct, so the power is impotent. Without the ability to oversee the PCAOB or to attribute its failures to those whom the President can directly oversee, the President is no longer the judge of the PCAOB's conduct. He can neither ensure that the laws are faithfully executed nor hold responsibility for any PCAOB member's breach of faith. Such diffusion of power carries with it a diffusion of accountability, without an effective chain of command, said the Court." We hold that such multilevel protection from removal is contrary to Article II's vesting of the executive power in the President."

Notwithstanding this holding, the Court continued, the unconstitutional provisions regarding removal ("tenure provisions") are severable from the rest of the Act. Having concluded that the removal restrictions ("for cause" only) for PCAOB members are invalid, the Court held that the PCAOB may continue to function as before, but henceforth, PCAOB members may be removed at will by the SEC.

Finally, the PCAOB's appointment is consistent with the Appointments Clause because the SEC is a "Department" under that Clause, and the several commissioners are the SEC's "Head." PCAOB members are "inferior officers" directly controlled by SEC. This meets the requirement of the Appointments Clause that officers be appointed by the President with the Senate's advice and consent, or, in the case of "inferior officers (in this case, the PCAOB)," by "the President alone,. . .the Courts of Law, or … the Heads of Departments (in this case, the SEC)."

Chief Justice Roberts was joined in the majority by Justices Scalia, Kennedy, Thomas, and Alito. Justice Breyer dissented, in which he was joined by Justice Stevens, Ginsburg, and Sotomayor. While Justice Breyer agreed that PCAOB members were "inferior officers," he disagreed that the Act unconstitutionally interfered with the President's executive powers.

❖ SCHILL, MICHAEL H.

On January 1, 2010, Michael H. Schill officially became the 14th dean at the University of Chicago Law School. Schill had previously served as dean and professor of law at UCLA School of Law, where he was "wildly successful," especially when it came to fundraising. Schill has also had faculty posts at New York University and the University of Pennsylvania.

He grew up in upstate New York, where Schill's father was an assistant manager at a clothing factory. Schill lived much of his life in the northeast, and despite the fact that nobody in his family had attended college, his father told him repeatedly that he would attend Harvard. Instead, Schill attended Princeton University, which gave him a substantial scholarship. He received an A.B. from Princeton in 1980. He then enrolled at Yale Law School, from which he earned a **juris doctor** degree in 1984. He worked as a law clerk with Judge Marvin Katz of the U.S. **District Court** for the Eastern District of Pennsylvania. He then took a position as an attorney in New York with the law firm of Fried, Frank, Harris, Schriver, and Jacobson.

In 1987, Schill interviewed for positions with several law schools, including UCLA, but he remained in the northeast by accepting a position with the law faculty at the University of Pennsylvania Law School. He earned tenure at Pennsylvania by 1992 and became a full professor. In 1995, Schill left Pennsylvania and returned to New York when he accepted a position as Professor of Law and Urban Planning at the New York University School of Law. He also served as the director of the Furman Center on REAL ESTATE and Urban Policy, which is part of both NYU's law school and the Wagner School of Public Service. In 2003, he was also named the Wilf Family Professor in PROPERTY LAW at NYU.

As a faculty member, Schill became an expert in property law, real estate and housing policy, deregulation, finance, and DISCRIMINA-TION. He published extensively, writing four books (as of 2010) along with more than 40 articles in a variety of academic journals. Many of his articles address urban housing conditions and revitalizing urban areas. He has served as a member of dozens of community boards and councils, along with many university commit-tees as the various institutions with which he has been affiliated.

In 2004, Schill had the opportunity to become the dean at the UCLA School of Law. In a 2006 interview, he said that colleagues told him not to accept the job. Each of the previous deans at UCLA had come from its own faculty, and in 2004, 11 of the current faculty were being recruited by other law schools. Moreover, state support for UCLA's law school had dropped significantly between 2000 and 2004. During a ten-year period between 1996 and 2006, tuition increased from $7,800 to $25,000. Moreover, UCLA had an **endowment** of only $44 million, which was tiny compared with competitors such as the University of Virginia (with an endowment of $250 million) and the University of Michigan (with an endowment of $252 million).

Despite the challenges, Schill accepted the UCLA position, taking over as dean in 2004. Only four of the 11 faculty who were being courted elsewhere ended up leaving UCLA, and the school was able to recruit several other top scholars under Schill's leadership. In his first two years, he met with about 3,000 graduates in an effort to increase overall donations. He spent much of his time in face-to-face fundraising, and the effort paid off. Between 2005 and 2006, the law school's total gifts increased from $6.1 million to $9.2 million. In 2008, the UCLA law school launched a campaign in which it sought to raise $100 million for its endowment. In 2009, the law school received a $1.5 million gift to establish the Michael H. Schill Endowed Chair in Law, which would be awarded to a "legal scholar of the highest academic and professional caliber."

Just months later, though, Schill had announced to the UCLA law school community that he had accepted the position of dean of the University of Chicago Law School. While some within the UCLA community were surprised by Schill's departure, the University of Chicago Law School community was ecstatic. Professor Eric Posner, who served as chair of the search committee, commented, "We hit the jackpot with Mike Schill. Throughout his scholarly and administrative career, he has always displayed a profound commitment to the intellectual values at the core of the law school's mission, At the same time, he's one of the most talented academic administrators in the country, who has received extraordinary accolades for his leadership, integrity and devotion to the best in legal education."

Schill replaced Saul Levmore on January 1, 2010. Just two weeks after officially taking over the position, Schill commented that he would lead the University of Chicago Law School on a major campaign that would like raise between $150 and $200 million. When asked why the school needs to much money, Schill replied, "We are way under-endowed compared to our peer schools—Harvard, Yale, Columbia, Stan-ford, NYU. The law school has generated the most important idea to affect law in the past

1984	Received law degree from Yale
1995	Joined New York University School of Law faculty
2004	Became dean of UCLA Law School
2010	Became dean of University of Chicago Law School

50 years: law and economics. I want to improve some of the connectivity of faculty and students between the law school and other departments in social sciences and the business school. It has been reduced in past 10 to 15 years. I also want to identify areas that we'll grow in faculty—law and economics, INTERNATIONAL LAW, **constitutional law**. I want to find the resources to make it possible."

SEARCH AND SEIZURE

In international law, the right of ships of war, as regulated by treaties, to examine a merchant vessel during war in order to determine whether the ship or its cargo is liable to seizure.

A hunt by law enforcement officials for property or communications believed to be evidence of crime, and the act of taking possession of this property.

Safford Unified School District #1 v. Redding

The SUPREME COURT has been sympathetic toward public school officials who have enforced strict anti-drug policies. The Court has permitted officials to search student lockers without a warrant and have upheld mandatory drug tests for student athletes. However, the Court drew a line at strip searching students. In *Safford Unified School District #1 v. Redding,* __U.S.__, 129 S. Ct. 2633, 174 L. Ed. 2d 354 (2009), the Court held that strip searches were not permitted when there was no showing that the degree of intrusion was justified by the perceived threat.

The search in question involved a 13-year-old girl, who was subjected to a search of her bra and underpants by school officials acting on reasonable suspicion that she had brought forbidden prescription and over-the-counter drugs to school. School officials questioned the student about four white prescription-strength ibuprofen 400-mg pills, and one over-the-counter blue naproxen 200-mg pill, all used for pain and inflammation but which were banned under school rules without **advance** permission. The student denied any knowledge about the pills but permitted school officials to search her backpack. Finding nothing in the backpack, the assistant principal instructed his female assistant to take the girl to the school nurse and tell the nurse to look for pills in the student's clothes. At the nurse's office the two women told the student to remove her jacket, shoes, and shoes. Again finding nothing, they told her to remove her stretch pants and T-shirt, which did not have pockets. They then told her to pull her bra out and to the side and shake it, and to pull out the elastic on her underpants. These actions exposed her breasts and pelvic area to some degree. The officials did not find any CONTRABAND.

The student's mother filed a § 1983 damages lawsuit against the principal, administrative assistant, the nurse, and the school district, alleging that the officials had conducted a strip search in violation of the FOURTH AMENDMENT **Search and Seizure** Clause. The **district court** dismissed the case, concluding that there had been no constitutional violation. However, the Ninth **Circuit Court** of Appeals ruled that the strip search was unjustified under the Fourth Amendment test for searches of children by school officials set out in the Supreme Court's decision in *New Jersey v. T.L.O.*,,469 U.S. 325, 105 S. Ct. 733, 83 L. Ed. 2d 720 (1985). Having established a violation, the appeals court examined whether any of the three individual defendants were entitled to qualified IMMUNITY. However, the principal was denied immunity because he was an independent decisionmaker.

The Supreme Court, in a unanimous decision, acknowledged that school officials had a right to inspect for drugs in the backpack but beyond that, searches cannot be "excessively intrusive." Justice DAVID SOUTER, writing for the Court, stated that The student's "subjective expectation of privacy against such a search is inherent in her account of it as embarrassing, frightening, and humiliating. The reasonableness of her expectation is indicated by the consistent experiences of other young people similarly searched, whose adolescent vulnerability intensifies the patent intrusiveness of the exposure." Souter noted studies by school psychologists showing strip searches of teens can result in serious emotional injury.

However, the indignity of the search alone was not reason enough make it a Fourth Amendment violation. It must be demonstrated that the search was unreasonable in relation to the "scope to the circumstances which justified the interference in the first place." In this case, Justice Souter found that "content of the suspicion failed to match the degree of intrusion." The drugs in question were already known and the school officials knew of the "limited threat" the drugs posed. In addition, the principal could not have suspected the student was hiding drugs in her underwear: "nondangerous school contraband does not raise the specter of stashes in intimate places, and there is no evidence in the record of any general practice among Safford Middle School students of hiding that sort of thing in underwear." The combination of these deficiencies defeated a finding that the search was reasonable.

As to the question of immunity, a school official searching a student is "entitled to qualified immunity where clearly established law does not show that the search violated the Fourth Amendment." To be established clearly, however, there is no need that "the very action in question [have] previously been held unlawful." On the issue of student strip searches, Souter acknowledged that the circuit courts of appeal had been divided. The Court concluded that "these differences of opinion from our own are substantial enough to require immunity for the school officials in this case." The Court cautioned that it did not "suggest that entitlement to qualified immunity is the guaranteed product of disuniform views of the law in the other federal, or state, courts, and the fact that a single judge, or even a group of judges, disagrees about the contours of a right does not automatically render the law unclear if we have been clear." On the issue of student strip searches the lower court decisions had been numerous, and well-reasoned both in the majority and dissenting opinions. The law was sufficiently in doubt to prevent it from being "clearly established." Therefore, all three school officials were immune from the civil lawsuit. Though the individuals were dismissed, the lawsuit continued against the school

district, which does not have the protection of immunity.

SECOND AMENDMENT

McDonald v. City of Chicago, Illinois

In a landmark decision, the U.S. SUPREME COURT in 2010 ruled that the SECOND AMENDMENT applied to the states through the Due Process Clause of the FOURTEENTH AMENDMENT. The Court decided the case two years after ruling that the Second Amendment guaranteed the right to bear arms as an individual right. By applying this principle to the states, the Court struck down a Chicago **ordinance** that banned possession of guns in the home.

The Second Amendment states: "A well regulated MILITIA, being necessary to the security of a free State, the right of the people to keep and bear Arms, shall not be infringed." For many years after its **ratification**, text of this amendment was seldom construed by the courts, and no clear doctrine about how the amendment should apply emerged from **case law**. The Supreme Court finally tackled the text of the amendment in *District of Columbia v. Heller*, 554 U.S. ___, 128 S. Ct. 2783, 171 L. Ed. 2d 637 (2008). In that case, the Court reviewed the constitutionality of a District of Columbia ordinance that effectively banned handguns. In an opinion by Justice ANTONIN SCALIA, the Court determined that the Second Amendment established individual rights to bear arms. As such, the Court ruled that the D.C. ordinance violated the Second Amendment.

Because the District of Columbia is a federal jurisdiction, the Court did not have to consider whether the Second Amendment applies to the states. Many cities have enacted restrictions on the possession of handguns, similar to the D.C. ordinance considered in *Heller*. The City of Chicago enacted such an ordinance, which provided that "[n]o person shall … possess … any firearm unless such person is the holder of a valid registration certificate for such firearm." The ordinance in turn prohibited registration of most of these handguns, which had the effect of banning handgun possession for those who resided in the city. The City of Oak Park had a similar ordinance that made it "unlawful for any person to possess … any firearm." The ordinance defined firearm to include "pistols, revolvers, guns and small arms … commonly known as handguns." Evidence showed that the City of Chicago enacted its handgun restriction in 1982 in an effort to protect its citizens from harm caused by firearms. However, statistics presented to the Court showed that the MURDER rate in Chicago had increased since the city enacted its ban.

Three Chicago residents who wanted to keep handguns in their homes for protection challenged the firearm laws on Second Amendment grounds. These residents, along with the Illinois State Rifle Association and the Second Amendment Foundation, Inc., filed suit in the U.S. **District Court** for the Northern District of Illinois. The plaintiffs wanted the district court to declare that the handgun ban violated both the Second and Fourteenth Amendments to the Constitution. In a separate action, the NATIONAL RIFLE ASSOCIATION (NRA) and two residents of Oak Park filed suit to challenge the Oak Park regulation. The NRA also filed a third action against the City of Chicago.

The same district judge, Milton I. Shadur, heard each of the three cases. Shadur noted that the Seventh **Circuit Court** of Appeals had ruled in 1982 that handgun bans were constitutional, and he noted that the Supreme Court in *Heller* had passed on the question of whether the Second Amendment applied to the states through the Due Process Clause of the Fourteenth Amendment. The plaintiffs appealed the decision to the Seventh Circuit, which affirmed the district court's ruling. The Seventh Circuit noted that the "Supreme Court has rebuffed requests to apply the second amendment to the states." Because the Seventh Circuit was unwilling to predict how the Second Amendment would apply under the Supreme Court's modern selective **incorporation doctrine** under the Fourteenth Amendment, the **appellate court** affirmed the district court's conclusion. *567 F.3d 856 (7th Cir. 2009).*

The Supreme Court agreed to review the case, and it turned out to be one of the most closely watched disputes in the Court's 2009 term. An amicus curiae brief filed by four members of Congress was signed by 58 senators and 251 representatives, which marked the highest number of members of Congress to sign such a brief. Advocacy groups, including the NRA on one side and the Brady Campaign to Prevent Gun Violence on the other, watched the decision closely and commented on it frequently.

The Court issued its decision on June 28, 2010 in a 214-page opinion, thanks to lengthy opinions written by Justice CLARENCE THOMAS and JOHN PAUL STEVENS. Justice SAMUEL ALITO wrote the majority opinion. The petitioners had asked the Court to recognize that the **Privileges and Immunities** Clause of the Fourteenth Amendment, which would have the same effect as the Court's recognition that the Fourteenth Amendment incorporates the BILL OF RIGHTS through the Due Process Clause. However, the Court has long held that the PRIVILEGES AND IMMUNITIES Clause protects a very limited range of rights, and Alito rejected the argument. Alito importantly determined that the Due Process Clause indeed incorporated the rights recognized in *Heller*, so the decision was applicable to the states. Based on this decision, the Court reversed the Seventh Circuit's judgment and remanded the case for further proceedings.

Thomas issued a long concurrence in which he argued that the Privileges and Immunities Clause of the Fourteenth Amendment should apply to the states. Thomas concluded his opinion by stating that the "the right to keep and bear arms is guaranteed by the Fourteenth Amendment as a privilege of American citizenship." Dissents written by Stevens and STEPHEN BREYER argued that the Court's decision in *Heller* was incorrect and that the right to bear arms is not a FUNDAMENTAL RIGHT that should apply to the states.

The decision will likely lead to more LITIGATION as parties challenge local firearm restrictions.

SECURITIES

Evidence of a corporation's debts or property.

Jones v. Harris Associates L.P.

Investment advisers who manage mutual funds are typically paid handsomely for their work. Not surprisingly, shareholders at times object to the level of compensation paid to advisers. The Investment Act of 1940 , 54 Stat. 789, imposed regulations on investment companies, including mutual funds. Under §36(b) of the act an adviser has a **fiduciary** duty with "respect to the receipt of compensation for services." This means that advisers hold the shareholder's money in trust and have a legal duty to the shareholders not to abuse their position and pay themselves exorbitant amounts. The courts have wrestled with the appropriate standard to use when assessing whether an adviser has charged a disproportionately large fee, yet the SUPREME COURT only addressed the issue in case *Jones v. Harris Associates L.P.*, __ U.S. __, 130 S. Ct. 1418, __ L. Ed. 2d __ (2010). The Court adopted a standard first announced by the Second **Circuit Court** of Appeals in 1982, resolving a split among the circuit courts of appeals.

A group of shareholders in three different mutual funds sued Harris Associates, an investment adviser, which managed the three funds. The shareholders alleged that Harris Associates had violated §36(b) by charging fees that were "disproportionate to the services rendered" and "not within the range of what would have been negotiated at arm's length in light of all the surrounding circumstances." The federal **district court** dismissed the complaint. Applying the standard adopted by the Second Circuit in *Gartenberg v. Merill Lynch Asset Management, Inc.*, 694 F.2d 923 (1982), the court ruled that the plaintiffs had failed to raise a triable issue of fact as to whether the fees were so disproportionately large that they could not have been the result of arm-length bargaining. The court compared the fees charged to the plaintiffs with those that Harris Associates charged its other clients. It also compared the fees to those charged by similar mutual funds. The Seventh Circuit Court of Appeals upheld the dismissal on other grounds and explicitly disapproved of using the *Gartenberg* approach. The appeals court used trust law to reach its conclusion, finding that an investment adviser must make full disclosure and "play no tricks" but it is not subject to a cap on compensation.

The Supreme Court, in a unanimous decision, rejected the Seventh Circuit reasoning and endorsed the *Gartenberg* standard. Justice SAMUEL ALITO, writing for the court, reviewed the history and application of the Investment Act of 1940 provision on compensation. He noted that an investment adviser creates the **mutual fund**, selects the fund's directors, manages the fund's investments, and provides other services. Because the adviser and the fund are intertwined, the fund "'cannot as a practical matter sever its relationship with the adviser. Therefore, the forces of arm's-length bargaining do not work in the MUTUAL FUND industry in the same manner as they do in other sectors of the American economy.' "Therefore, the Investment Act of 1940 was passed to correct abuses

by investment advisers. Though the Court had not addressed the standard for reviewing compensation, Alito pointed to the fact that most appeals courts and the SECURITIES AND EXCHANGE COMMISSION (SEC) had recognized the *Gartenberg* standard.

Gartenberg had defined "fiduciary duty" with respect to compensation, something Congress had failed to address. The Second Circuit stated that to violate §36(b) the investment adviser "must charge a fee that is so disproportionately large that it bears no reasonable relationship to the services rendered and could not have been the product of arm's-length bargaining." To make this determination, a court must examine the adviser's cost in providing the service, the "the extent to which the adviser-manager realizes economies of scale as the fund grows larger, and the volume of orders which must be processed by the manager." *Gartenberg* explicitly excluded from consideration the price charged by other similar funds because competition among advisers for the business of managing a fund may be "virtually non-existent." Justice Alito concluded that the framework in *Gartenberg* was correct in its basic formulation and should be used by all **federal courts**.

Merck & Co., Inc. v. Reynolds

Plaintiffs seeking recovering for injuries must file their lawsuits within a specified amount of time. Statutes of limitations protect defendants from cases that may have gone stale over time and where witnesses are unavailable and memories are hazy. State and federal laws set time periods for different types of civil actions. Though the **statute of limitations** for a particular area of law may appear to be clear, the courts are regularly asked to clarify whether a PLAINTIFF has waited too long. Such was the case in *Merck & Co., Inc. v. Reynolds*, __U.S.__, 130 S. Ct. 1784, 176 L. Ed. 2d 582 (2010)., where the SUPREME COURT examined the time period set for filing a private SECURITIES **fraud** action under §10(b) of the Securities Exchange Act of 1934. The DEFENDANT pharmaceutical company challenged the lawsuit, arguing that it was not timely under federal law. The Court ruled that the lawsuit was timely, as the plaintiffs did not have sufficient knowledge of the facts to file their complaint under the shorter of two limitations provisions.

A group of investors sued Merck, an international pharmaceutical company, for securities

FRAUD involving the company's alleged **fraudulent** MISREPRESENTATION of the risks of heart attacks accompanying the use of Merck's pain-killing drug, Vioxx. Once these risks were disclosed to the public, the value of Merck stock went down. Under 28 U.S.C. §1658(b), a private right of action" that "involves a claim of fraud, deceit, manipulation, or contrivance in contravention of a regulatory requirement concerning the securities laws … may be brought not later than the earlier of" 2 years after the discovery of the facts constituting the violation, or 5 years after such violation. The complaint was filed in November 2003, and Merck did not dispute that it was filed within five years of the alleged violation. However, Merck claimed that the "2 years after the discovery of facts constituting the violation" should be applied. Therefore, the key issue was whether the plaintiffs had or could have discovered the facts constituting the violation prior to November 2001.

The federal **district court** agreed with Merck and dismissed the complaint as untimely because the plaintiffs should have been alerted to the possibility of Merck's misrepresentations prior to November 2001. In addition, the court found that the plaintiffs had failed to undertake a reasonably diligent investigation at that time. The court pointed out three major circumstances that justified its conclusion. First, in March 2000 a study was published that compared Vioxx with the painkiller naproxen. The study showed adverse cardiovascular results for Vioxx, which Merck suggested might be due to the absence of a benefit conferred by naproxen rather than a harm caused by Vioxx. Second, the FOOD AND DRUG ADMINISTRATION (FDA) issued a warning letter that was released to the public on September 21, 2001. The letter stated that Merck's Vioxx marketing with regard to the cardiovascular results was "false, lacking in fair balance, or otherwise misleading." Third, pleadings were filed in products-liability actions in September and October 2001 that alleged that Merck had concealed information about Vioxx and intentionally downplayed its risks. These three events put the plaintiffs on notice under the **statute** of limitations. However, the Third **Circuit Court** of Appeals reversed the decision. The appeals court ruled that the pre-November 2001 events did not suggest that Merck acted with **scienter**, an element of a §10(b) violation. (SCIENTER refers to a person knowingly committing the act in

question. In this case, events did not show that Merck had knowingly concealed troubling news about Vioxx.) Therefore, these events did not commence the running of the limitations period.

The Supreme Court unanimously voted to affirm the Third Circuit ruling. Justice STEPHEN BREYER, writing for the Court, acknowledged the shadings of the word "discovery," but stated that "Limitations period does not begin to run until the plaintiff thereafter discovers or a reasonably diligent plaintiff would have discovered "the facts constituting the violation," including scienter—irrespective of whether the actual plaintiff undertook a reasonably diligent investigation." In this case scienter was a fact crucial to the plaintiffs prevailing on the merits of their claims. In a §10(b) action, scienter refers to "a mental state embracing intent to deceive, manipulate, or defraud," and is a necessary element in proving a violation. Proving scienter is difficult: "where §10(b) is at issue, the relation of factual falsity and state of mind is more context specific."

Applying this yardstick to the case, the Court found that prior to November 2001 the plaintiffs did not discover, nor could Merck show that a reasonably diligent plaintiff could have discovered the facts constituting the violation. The three circumstances used by the district court were also not dispositive. None of them showed whether Merck possessed fraudulent intent. Without such a demonstration of scienter, the limitations period could not be triggered.

SENTENCING

The postconviction stage of the criminal justice process, in which the defendant is brought before the court for the imposition of a penalty.

Barber v. Thomas

Federal sentencing provisions, specifically, §212(a)(2) of the Sentencing Reform Act, enacting 18 U.S.C. §3624(b), allow that a "prisoner … serving a term of imprisonment of more than one year … may receive credit toward the service of [that] sentence … of up to 54 days at the end of each year," subject to the Bureau of Prison's (BOP) "determination … that, during that year," the prisoner had behaved in an exemplary fashion. Credit "for the last year or portion of a year of the term of imprisonment [is] prorated ... " In *Barber v. Thomas,* No. 09-5201, 560 U.S. ___ (2010), the U.S. SUPREME COURT addressed the methodology for implementing and applying those provisions. It concluded that the BOP's method for calculating good time credit reflected the most natural reading of the **statute**, and was therefore lawful.

Michael Barber was sentenced to 320 months in federal prison for drug trafficking and weapons possession. Tahir Jihad-Black was sentenced to 262 months in prison for being a convicted felon in possession of a firearm. Both were eligible to have their sentences reduced based on good behavior.

The BOP had been applying this statute by using a methodology that awarded 54 days of credit at the end of each year the prisoner served, and setting those days aside. When the difference between time remaining in the sentence and credit days earned was less than one year, the BOP awarded a prorated amount of credit for that final year (proportional to the awards in other years).

The BOP calculated Barber's scheduled release date as March 29, 2016, based on the maximum award of 1,254 days of accumulated good time credit for time served. But if good time credit were to be based on the sentence imposed, and not the time actually served, Barber could accrue a credit of 1,440 days. Likewise, the BOP calculated a release date for Black of May 21, 2016, based on a maximum award of 1,027 good time credit days. But if good time credit were to be based on the sentence imposed rather than time served, the maximum available good time credit would be 1,179 days.

Both men and several others challenged the BOP's interpretation of that statute. The specific **statutory** language at issue was the phrase, [that inmates could receive up to 54 days off their sentences for] "each year of the prisoner's term of imprisonment." The prisoners urged an interpretation that this phrase referred to the total sentence imposed by the court. The BOP operated on the interpretation that it referred to the prisoner's actual time served. Otherwise, argued BOP, prisoners would receive good behavior credit for years they did not end up serving. The federal **district court** ruled that

BOP's interpretation was lawful and denied the petitions.

The Ninth **Circuit Court** of Appeals affirmed and denied habeas relief. It also consolidated cases in order to petition the U.S. Supreme Court for review, as differing opinions had come forth from other circuits.

The Supreme Court, in a 6-3 opinion, held that the Sentencing Reform Act did not require the BOP to calculate credit for good time served based on the length of the sentence imposed (rather than on the time actually served). Justice Breyer, writing for the majority, concluded, "The statute's language and its purpose, taken together, convince us that the BOP's calculation method is lawful." This conclusion followed pages of the opinion dedicated to analysis of the provision. The Court reasoned that, as §3624(b) directed the BOP to award the credit "at the end of each year" of imprisonment {i.e., not a single cumulative number based on the length of the sentence imposed,) the prisoners' approach could not be reconciled with the statute. As BOP had argued (and the Court agreed), such an interpretation (the awarding of credit for sentence imposed) proffered by the prisoners would mean a prisoner could receive credit for a year/years that he actually did not spend in prison. That interpretation also was at odds with the specific statutory language that provided for calculation of credit "at the end of each year." Accordingly, because the BOP's method of calculation applied the statute as its language was most naturally read, which also appeared consistent with the statute's basic purpose, this interpretation was preferable to the dissenting opinion's alternative interpretation.

That dissenting interpretation was written by Justice Kennedy, joined by Justices Stevens and Ginsburg. They concluded that any ambiguities in the law should favor the inmates. Citing that the majority's interpretation would disadvantage nearly 200,000 federal prisoners "who have behaved the best" and cost taxpayers "untold millions of dollars," the DISSENT opined that "Absent a clear congressional directive, the statute ought not to be read as the Court reads it."

United States v. Dillon

The U.S. SUPREME COURT in 2005 determined that parts of the federal sentencing scheme were unconstitutional because judges were permitted to impose sentences based on facts that were not proven **beyond a reasonable doubt** before a jury. The Court did not strike down the Federal Sentencing Guidelines in their entirety, and lower **federal courts** have struggled with questions about how the guidelines and sentencing statutes continue to apply. In *Dillon v. United States*, No. 09-6338, 2010 WL 2400109 (June 17, 2010), the Court determined that federal district courts do not have authority to modify a sentence below the range established by the Federal Sentencing Guidelines.

The Supreme Court's case focused on Percy Dillon, who was convicted in 1993 on charges related to possession of 500 grams of powder cocaine and 50 grams of crack cocaine. He was also convicted of intent to distribute, CONSPIRACY to distribute, and use of a firearm during a drug-related offense. At the time of his offense, the Federal Sentencing Commission had adopted a rule establishing that courts should treat possession of one gram of crack cocaine as equivalent to possession of 100 grams of powder cocaine. The U.S. **District Court** for the Western District of Pennsylvania determined that Dillon that the range of Dillon's sentencing under the Federal Sentencing Guidelines fell between 322 and 387 months. Dillon received the lowest sentence of 322 months (just over 26 years), though the district court at the time stressed that the sentence was too harsh. The Third **Circuit Court** of Appeals later affirmed Dillon's sentence.

In 2007, the Federal Sentencing Commission revised its rule regarding the ratio of crack to powder cocaine, reducing this ratio from 100-to-1 to 20-to-1. The Commission also made the amendment to the guidelines retroactive. Under 18 U.S.C. § 3582(c)(2), a district court may reduce a final sentence when the sentence is based on a provision that has been amended subsequently. Such reductions must be consistent with policy statements issued by the Commission at the time of the amendment. Following the Commission's decision to amend the ratio, Dillon filed a motion *pro se* to reduce his sentence pursuant to 18 U.S.C. § 3582(c)(2). The district court recalculated and reduced Dillon's sentence to 270 months. However, the district court concluded that it could not reduce the sentence any further.

Prior to the Supreme Court's decision in *United States v. Booker*, 543 U.S. 220, 125 S. Ct.

738, 160 L. Ed. 2d 621 (2005), federal district courts were bound by the provisions of the Federal Sentencing Guidelines. These Guidelines have been produced by the Federal Sentencing Commission pursuant to federal **statute**. District court judges were able to make independent factual determinations that could affect individual sentences, even though prosecutors had not proven these facts BEYOND A REASONABLE DOUBT. In *Booker*, the Court ruled that the mandatory sentencing regime was unconstitutional because it violated the SIXTH AMENDMENT to the U.S. Constitution. The Court in *Booker* specifically invalidated two sections of the federal sentencing statute, including one that required a court to impose a sentence pursuant to the Guidelines.

Under 18 U.S.C. § 3582(c)(2), if the Sentencing Commission lowers a sentencing range for a certain crime, then a district court reduce a person's term of imprisonment according to the reduced sentencing range. However, this statute does not allow district courts to reduce a sentence below the guideline range. Most lower federal courts have concluded that the ruling only applies to initial sentencing and did not apply to reduction of sentences. The most significant exception was the Ninth Circuit, which ruled in *United States v. Hicks*, 472 F.3d 1167 (9th Cir. 2007) that *Booker* had rendered the Federal Sentencing Guidelines as advisory in all contexts.

Dillon requested a reduction of his sentence, and the district court reduced his sentence to 270 months. The district court concluded that it lacked jurisdiction to reduce the sentence below the range established in the Federal Sentencing Guidelines. Dillon then appealed the decision to the Third Circuit yet again. A three-judge panel agreed with the majority of federal circuits that *Booker* did not apply to reductions of sentences, noting that the Supreme Court made no reference to 18 U.S.C. § 3582(c)(2) when it struck down other provisions of the federal sentencing **statutory** scheme.

The Supreme Court granted **certiorari** to review the decision. In an 7-1 decision, with Justice SAMUEL ALITO choosing not to participate, the Court affirmed the Third Circuit's decision. Writing for the majority, Justice SONIA SOTOMAYOR reviewed *Booker*'s affect on the entire federal sentencing scheme and noted that *Booker* focused on two principal statutory provisions. Unlike those provisions (dealing with the imposition of a sentence and the standard of **appellate** review for that sentence), 18 U.S.C. § 3582(c)(2) does not allow a judge to conduct a plenary resentencing proceeding. In other words, the judge's decision is limited to a review of the revised sentencing guideline and the policy implicated by the revision of the guideline. Sotomayor wrote, "Given the limited scope and purpose of § 3582(c)(2), we conclude that proceedings under that section do not implicate the interests identified in Booker. Notably, the sentence-modification proceedings authorized by § 3582(c)(2) are not constitutionally compelled. We are aware of no constitutional requirement of retroactivity that entitles defendants sentenced to a term of imprisonment to the benefit of subsequent Guidelines amendments. Rather, § 3582(c)(2) represents a congressional act of lenity intended to give prisoners the benefit of later enacted adjustments to the judgments reflected in the Guidelines."

Justice JOHN PAUL STEVENS wrote the lone DISSENT, arguing that the reasoning underlying *Booker* should also apply to reduction of sentences under 18 U.S.C. § 3582. The majority's opinion, according to Stevens, was "manifestly unjust" because it failed to take into account the policy implications addressed in *Booker*.

United States v. Dolan

Congress enacted the Mandatory Victims **Restitution** Act to require federal district courts to compensate VICTIMS OF CRIME. The **statute** requires a **district court** to determine a victim's losses no more than 90 days after sentencing. In June 2010, the U.S. SUPREME COURT issued a ruling in a case where a district court had estimated the victim's losses at a hearing that took place more than 90 days after sentencing. In a 5-4 decision, the Court ruled that the district court's failure to order restitution within 90 days did not deprive the district court of the authority to order restitution at the later hearing. *Dolan v. United States*, No. 09-367, 2010 WL 2346548 (June 14, 2010).

The petitioner in the case was Brian Dolan, who was convicted of a crime involving the beating of a hitchhiker at the Mescalera Indian Reservation in New Mexico. Dolan and the hitchhiker engaged in an argument that turned into a physical altercation. Dolan severely injured the hitchhiker in the fight, causing a broken nose, broken wrist, fractured leg, a spinal injury, broken ribs, and a hematoma in the victim's head. Dolan left the hitchhiker at the side of the road and drove off. Dolan told his sister of the incident, and the sister informed the Bureau of Indian Affairs police. The police rescued the injured hitchhiker and later arrested Dolan.

Under the Mandatory Victims Restitution Act, 18 U.S.C. § 3664(d)(5), a district court is required to issue an order setting forth the amount of restitution a convicted criminal must pay to a victim. The statute provides: "If the victim's losses are not ascertainable by the date that is 10 days prior to sentencing, the attorney for the Government or the PROBATION officer shall so inform the court, and the court shall set a date for the final determination of the victim's losses, not to exceed 90 days after sentencing. If the victim subsequently discovers further losses, the victim shall have 60 days after discovery of those losses in which to petition the court for an amended restitution order. Such order may be granted only upon a showing of **good cause** for the failure to include such losses in the initial claim for restitutionary relief."

Dolan pleaded guilty to the charges according to a plea agreement, which also stated that the district court "may order" restitution. On July 30, 2007, the U.S. District Court for the District of New Mexico sentenced Dolan to 21 months in prison and three years of supervised release. At that time, the district court acknowledged that it was required to order restitution but that it did not have enough facts to make the determination. More specifically, the court left the "matter open, pending receipt of additional information." The court on August 8, 2007 entered its final judgment but stated that the court had not received information that would allow it to order restitution at that time.

On October 5, 2007, less than a month before the expiration of the 90-day period, a probation office reported that had enough information to calculate the appropriate restitution amount, which was set at $105,559.78. The district court received documentation supporting this amount, and the probation office even noted to the district court that the 90-day period for imposing the restitution order expired after October 28, 2007. However, the district court failed to act by this date. Instead, the court held the hearing regarding the restitution order on February 4, 2008, well after the 90 days had expired. Dolan's attorney argued that the court no longer had authority to order restitution because the time period had passed. The court, however, rejected this argument, noting that while the court erred in not complying with the statute, the statute did not deprive the court of jurisdiction for failing to order restitution in a timely manner.

Dolan appealed the restitution order to the Tenth **Circuit Court** of Appeals. A three-judge panel of the Tenth Circuit agreed with the district court, noting, "Rather than creating a jurisdictional bar to untimely restitution orders, the MVRA's deadline seeks to prod the government into ensuring victims swift compensation. Sometimes, of course, the government is not so easily prodded." *United States v. Dolan*, 571 F.3d 1022 (10th Cir. 2009). The Tenth Circuit's decision conflicted with decisions in the Seventh and Eleventh Circuits, which had held that failure to order restitution in a timely manner deprived the district court of jurisdiction to issue the order.

The Supreme Court agreed to review the case to resolve the split between the circuits. The case featured an unusual split among the justices. Conservatives SAMUEL ALITO and CLARENCE THOMAS along with liberals RUTH BADER GINSBURG and Sonya Sotomayor joined the majority opinion written by Justice STEPHEN BREYER. The majority acknowledged that the statute uses the word "shall" in mandating that the court issue restitution within 90 days of sentencing. However, the majority found several instances where the Court has not read statutes to bar judges from taking an action after the expiration of a **statutory** deadline. Moreover, the majority determined that the purpose behind the statute did not support the argument that failure by the court to act within the prescribed time deprived the court of jurisdiction. Moreover, the Court noted, "to read the statute as depriving the sentencing court of the power to order restitution would harm those-the victims of crime-who likely bear no responsibility for the deadline's being missed and whom the statute also seeks to benefit." The majority rejected Dolan's argument that its ruling would cause prejudice to the DEFENDANT. Accordingly, the Court affirmed the restitution order.

Chief Justice JOHN ROBERTS, joined by three other justices, dissented. According to Roberts, the majority's opinion effectively rewrote the statute because failing to meet the 90-day deadline had "no consequence whatsoever." Roberts attacked the reasoning offered by the majority, arguing that the "Court runs through a series of irrelevancies that cannot trump the clear statutory text."

Johnson v. United States

The Armed Career Criminal Act of 1984 (ACCA), 18 U.S.C. § 924(e)(1), imposes a minimum 15-year prison term if the offender's prior criminal record includes at least three convictions for "violent felonies" or "serious drug offenses." ACCA continues to generate numerous appeals concerning the scope of its application because the law is dependent on state **criminal law** definitions, which differ from state to state. The latest case to reach the U.S. SUPREME COURT, *Johnson v. United States*, __U.S.__, 130 S. Ct. 1265, 176 L. Ed. 2d 1 (2010), involved whether the ACCA term "violent felony" could include a simple **battery** conviction that involved no more than touching another person. The Court held that absent physical force, simple BATTERY did not qualify as a violent **felony** under ACCA.

Curtis Johnson pleaded guilty to the federal crime of knowingly possessing ammunition after having been convicted of a felony. The government sought to enhance his sentence by invoking the provisions of ACCA. Under the law a person who violates the federal ammunition possession law and who has three previous convictions for a "violent felony" must be imprisoned for 15 years. The term violent felony is defined as any crime punishable by imprisonment for a term exceeding one year" that: "(i) has as an element the use, attempted use, or threatened use of physical force against the person of another; or "(ii) is **burglary**, ARSON, or EXTORTION, involves use of explosives, or otherwise involves conduct that presents a serious potential risk of physical injury to another." The government alleged that Johnson had five prior felony convictions and that three of them, including a 2003 Florida battery, made him eligible for ACCA sentencing. Johnson disputed only the battery conviction, arguing that simple battery under Florida law is usually a first-degree **misdemeanor**. Because he had prior felony convictions the battery charge was raised to a third-degree felony. Under the battery law the state can prove the charge in one of three ways: the DEFENDANT intentionally caused bodily harm, that he intentionally struck the victim, or that he merely "actually and intentionally touched" the victim. The federal **district court** found nothing in the record to reflect which of the three acts was in issue, so it defaulted to the least serious act of intentionally touching the victim. The court concluded that the felony was "violent" for ACCA purposes and sentenced Johnson to a 15-year prison term. The Eleventh **Circuit Court** of Appeals upheld the decision and the Supreme Court agreed to hear Johnson's appeal.

The Supreme Court, in a 7-2 decision, overruled the Eleventh Circuit. Justice ANTONIN SCALIA, writing for the majority, noted that Florida has a law similar to ACCA and that the Florida Supreme Court had ruled that the element of "actually and intentionally touching" under Florida's battery law is satisfied by any intentional physical contact, "no matter how slight." Even a tap on the shoulder without consent establishes a violation. Scalia stated that the Court was bound by this interpretation of law in deciding whether a felony conviction for battery under Florida law met ACCA's definition of a "violent felony."

ACCA does not define "physical force," so the Court had to determine its ordinary meaning. In the end Scalia found that in the context of ACCA's definition of "violent felony, "physical force" meant violent force "capable of causing physical pain or injury to another person." This definition was reinforced by the fact that simple battery generally is punishable as a misdemeanor. The Court concluded that it was unlikely Congress would "select as a **term of art** defining 'violent felony' a phrase that the **common law** gave peculiar meaning only in its definition of a misdemeanor.

The government argued that to require violent force rather than force would undermine the purpose of ACCA when applied to other misdemeanor crimes such as DOMESTIC VIOLENCE. The Court disagreed, believing this exaggerated the practical effect of its decision. A federal district court can consult the trial record to determine "which **statutory** phrase was the basis for the conviction." Though in many cases state and local records from battery convictions may be incomplete but such absence of records will often frustrate other examinations of prior convictions. Justice

Scalia concluded that it "is implausible that avoiding that common-enough consequence with respect to the single crime of battery, under the single **statute** that is the Armed Career Criminal Act, caused Congress to import a TERM OF ART that is a comical misfit with the defined term 'violent felony.'"

Justice SAMUEL ALITO, in a dissenting opinion joined by Justice CLARENCE THOMAS, argued that the traditionally-defined crime of battery "fell squarely within the plain meaning of ACCA." The Court should not have imposed its own definition of "physical force" on the statute.

United States v. O'Brien and Burgess

Martin O'Brien and Arthur Burgess each pleaded guilty in federal **district court** to charges arising from a failed attempt to rob an armored car in Boston. They each had carried a firearm during the attempted **robbery**. The firearms included a pistol, a semi-automatic ASSAULT rifle, and a second pistol that had been modified to operate as a fully automatic gun (specifically, an AK-47, a Sig-Sauer, and a Cobray pistol). Count Three of their indictment(s) charged them with using a firearm in furtherance of a crime of violence, which carried a mandatory minimum prison sentence of five years. 18 U.S.C. §924(c). A fourth count had been added, charging that the Cobray pistol (also listed in Count Three) was a machine gun. The significance is that under 18 U.S.C. §924(c)(1)(B)(ii), if the weapon is a machine-gun, the **statutory** minimum sentence is 30 years. In *United States v. O'Brien and Burgess,* No. 08-1569, 560 U.S. ___ (2010), the SUPREME COURT was asked to decide whether the fact that a firearm was a machine-gun was an element of a crime, to be proved to the trier of fact **beyond a reasonable doubt**, or a sentencing factor to be proved to the judge at sentencing.

At O'Brien's and Burgess' PRETRIAL CONFERENCE, the district court ruled that machine-gun possession was an element of a crime and needed to be proved by the government BEYOND A REASONABLE DOUBT. Conversely, the government argued that it represented merely a sentencing enhancement factor. Ultimately, the government conceded that it could not prove, beyond a REASONABLE DOUBT, that O'Brien and Burgess had knowledge that the Cobray had been modified to operate automatically (as a machine gun). The government then moved to dismiss Count Four, and the defendants pleaded guilty to the remaining charges.

However, at sentencing, the government again insisted that the court mete the 30 year mandatory sentence, on the ground that the court could find the necessary facts as to possession of a machine gun by a **preponderance of evidence**, and without a specific finding that the defendants knew that the gun was automatic. In support, the government argued that if O'Brien and Burgess were convicted of carrying a firearm under Count Three (which they pleaded guilty to), the court could determine at sentencing that the Cobray was a machine gun, thus activating the 30-year minimum sentence. The government reasoned that since defendants had already pleaded guilty to possessing the Cobray, and this was a sentencing hearing, not a trial, a PREPONDERANCE OF EVIDENCE burden was all that was needed. The district court rejected this argument, sentencing O'Brien to a 102-month prison sentence and Burgess to a 84-month prison sentence. The government appealed.

The U.S. Court of Appeals for the First Circuit affirmed. It looked to *Castillo v. United States*, 530 U.S. 120 (2000) for guidance, which held that the machine gun provision in an earlier version of 18 U.S.C. §924(c) constituted an element of a crime and not a sentencing factor. Even though the **statute** was subsequently revised, it found that "Absent a clearer or more dramatic change in language or LEGISLATIVE HISTORY expressing a SPECIFIC INTENT to assign judge or jury functions, we think that *Castillo* is close to binding," and any reconsideration of the issue should be left to [the appellate] Court." There was a split of opinion among circuit courts of appeals, most taking an opposite view from that of the First Circuit. The U.S. Supreme Court accepted **certiorari** (review).

A unanimous Supreme Court agreed. Justice Kennedy delivered the opinion for the Court, affirming the lower court order. "The immense danger posed by machine guns, the moral depravity in choosing the weapon, and the substantial increase in the minimum sentence provided by the statute support the conclusion that this prohibition is an element of the crime, not a sentencing factor," said the Court. As such, it must be proved to the trier of fact (jury or, in a **bench trial**, judge) beyond a reasonable doubt.

Importantly, the Court acknowledged that the current structure of the amended §924(c) favored the treatment of a machine gun provision as a sentencing factor, more than was true in *Castillo*. This was partly due to the textual positioning of the provision between the sentencing factors provided in (A)(ii) and (iii) and those in (C)(i) and (ii). But that structural point was overcome by the substantial weight of other factors in *Castillo*, in addition to the principle that Congress would not enact so significant a change without a clear indication of its intent and purpose to do so.

Justice Stevens filed a separate concurring opinion. Justice Thomas filed a separate opinion concurring in the judgment. Justice Stevens opined that the simplest and most correct way to resolve this matter is to recognize that mandating the imposition of a sentence more severe than a judge would otherwise have discretion to impose should be treated as an element of the offense. Justice Thomas, referring to *Harris v. United States*, 536 U.S. 545 (2002), said, "If a sentencing fact either 'raises the floor or raises the ceiling' of the range of punishments to which a DEFENDANT is exposed, it is, 'by definition [an] elemen[t].'"

Millennium Bomber Must Be Resentenced

The sentencing of people convicted of crimes is a process that culminates in a decision by a trial judge. For most of U.S. history, judges had broad discretion to increase or reduce a sentence. This was changed when the federal government and individual states passed laws that required an independent agency to formulate sentencing guidelines. The guidelines combine the criminal history of the person with the severity of the crimes for which the person has been convicted. Federal judges objected to the fact that they had little discretion to alter a sentence. The SUPREME COURT ultimately ruled that the guidelines were unconstitutional. A judge was, however, still required to look at the guidelines and the sentence was to reviewed by an **appellate court** using a reasonableness standard. The Ninth Circuit, in *United States v. Ressam*, 593 F.3d 1095 (2010), was called on to review the reasonableness of the sentence imposed on Ahmed Ressam, the so-called "Millennium Bomber." Prosecutors objected to Ressam's 22-year sentence, claiming it was too short. The trial judge had reduced Ressam's sentence because he had cooperated with the government following his conviction and had supplied information about terrorists and terrorist organizations. The Ninth Circuit reversed the sentencing, and in an unusual move, directed that Ressam be resentenced by another federal **district court** judge.

Ressam is an Algerian national who trained as a terrorist in Afghanistan in the late 1990s. He became part of a five-person cell charged with carrying out an operation against a target in the United States—an airport or a consulate—before the end of 1999. Ressam entered Canada in February 1999 carrying $12,0000 in cash, a chemical used in the manufacture of explosives, and a notebook with instructions on how to put together explosives. After the other members of the cell failed to join him, Ressam decided to carry out the operation with a conspirator already living in Canada. He chose Los Angeles International Airport (LAX) as the target. He and his ACCOMPLICE drove to Victoria, British Columbia, with a trunkful of bomb components. However, a U.S. Customs Inspector discovered what was in the trunk and arrested Ressam.

Before being tried on nine TERRORISM counts, which could result in a **statutory** maximum sentence of 130 years in prison, the government offered Ressam a sentence of 25 years imprisonment in exchange for a guilty plea. Ressam turned down the offer and the site of his trial was moved to Los Angeles to avoid possible prejudice by public sentiment in the Seattle area. In 2001 he was convicted on all counts by a jury. The then-mandatory sentencing guidelines for these convictions was 65 years to life. Prior to sentencing, Ressam approached the prosecutors and offered to cooperate with the government in the investigation of terrorist activities. In return he sought a sentence of between 10 to 15 years. The government negotiated with Ressam and both agreed that neither side would request a sentence of less than 27 years imprisonment.

Ressam signed an agreement pledging total cooperation. He met with government agents 22 times in 2001 and testified as a prosecution witness against his co-conspirator. He also provided information that led to the INDICTMENT of two others for terrorist acts. However, by the end of 2001 Ressam started to become uncooperative. When the time came for sentencing, the judge sentenced Ressam to 22 years in prison. Ressam appealed his conviction and the government cross-appealed, challenging the sentence. The U.S. Supreme Court ultimately upheld his conviction and the Ninth Circuit vacated his sentence. The district court again sentenced Ressam to 22 years imprisonment. The government appealed to the Ninth Circuit.

In a 2-1 decision, a three-judge panel tossed out the sentence. The appeals court noted that the government had argued that the sentence was substantively unreasonable in light of facts of the case. However, the court concluded that the district court judge had committed procedural error in imposing a sentence "that is significantly below the Sentencing Guidelines range." The district court had failed to "remain cognizant" of the sentencing guidelines throughout the sentencing process. It had failed to adequately explain its reasons for imposing a sentence "two-thirds less than the low end of the advisory Guidelines range." Ressam was a long-time, trained terrorist who had plotted to commit an act of mass destruction on January 1, 2000. Moreover, the district court had overstated the value of Ressam's cooperation. These and other mistakes and omission required the court to set aside the sentence. On remand the court directed that another judge handle the sentencing because the sentencing judge had twice ruled incorrectly. Moreover, the judge believed his first sentence was "correct," despite the appeals court ruling. After spending over 10 years on this case, the judge's views were "too entrenched to allow for the appearance of fairness on remand."

SIXTH AMENDMENT

Berghuis, Warden v. Smith

One of the many rights secured by the SIXTH AMENDMENT to the U.S. Constitution is that criminal defendants are to be tried by an impartial jury drawn from sources reflecting a fair cross section of the community. In *Berghuis v. Smith*, No. 08-1402, 559 U.S. ___ (2010), the U.S. SUPREME COURT unanimously upheld a Michigan Supreme Court decision that rejected an African-American defendant's claim that African-Americans were systematically excluded from jury pools in his county. In upholding the Michigan decision, the high court ended a seesaw of decisions alternately affirming then reversing the claim. The Sixth **Circuit Court** of Appeals had reversed the Michigan Supreme

Court, but now found itself subjected to reversal and remand.

In 1993, DEFENDANT Diapolis Smith was convicted of MURDER by an all-white jury in the Kent County Circuit Court, Michigan. The murder occurred at a bar in the city of Grand Rapids, also located in Kent County. At that time, approximately 85 percent of the population of Grand Rapids, the largest city in Kent County, was African-American.

At *voir dire* for Smith's trial, between 60 and 100 potential jurors comprised the venire panel, but only two or three of them were African-American. At that time, African-Americans constituted about 7.2 percent of the county's population. Smith unsuccessfully objected to the jury pool (a "fair-cross-section claim"), was ultimately convicted, and appealed.

The Michigan Court of Appeals remanded to the trial court to conduct an evidentiary hearing on the fair-cross-section claim. The hearing produced facts showing that all **felony** charges in Kent County were tried in the single Circuit Court, whereas misdemeanors were prosecuted in 12 geographically-distributed district courts throughout the county. To fill the jury pool, the county sent questionnaires to prospective jurors. At the evidentiary hearing, the **court administrator** testified that about five percent of questionnaires were returned as undeliverable, and another 15 to 20 percent were not answered. However, evidence also showed that the jury system in place at the time assigned prospective jurors first to the local district courts, and only after those needs were filled, to the county-wide circuit court, which heard all felony cases. In his appeal, Smith referred to this as a "siphoning" procedure.

Shortly after Smith's *voir dire*, the county changed its procedure and adopted a circuit-court-first assignment order for jurors. It did so specifically with the belief that the district courts did in fact take most of the minority jurors, leaving very few for circuit court. Within the first year following the change, the means used by the county to measure under-representation showed palpable improvement.

Notwithstanding, the trial court, after the evidentiary hearing, concluded that Smith had not shown that either the juror assignment order or any other part of the jury selection process had systematically excluded African-Americans. It again denied his claim.

The "systematic exclusion" language comes from an earlier Supreme Court case, *Duren v. Missouri*, 439 U.S. 357 (1979). In that case, the Court had set out three prongs to establish a **prima facie** violation of the Sixth Amendment's right to a fair cross-section claim: (1) that the group allegedly excluded be a "distinctive" group in the community; (2) that the representation of this group in jury pools is not fair and reasonable in light of the number of such persons in the community; and (3) that the alleged under-representation is due to a systematic exclusion of the group in the jury selection process.

Again the case went back to the Michigan Court of Appeals, which reversed the trial court and ordered a new trial, using the newer circuit-court-first order of assignment. Next, the Michigan Supreme Court reversed the **appellate court**, instead agreeing with the trial court that Smith had not made out a PRIMA FACIE Sixth Amendment violation. The state high court noted that the U.S. Supreme Court had specified no preferred method for measuring whether representation of a distinctive group in a jury pool was fair and reasonable. Looking on a case-by-case basis of lower federal court decisions, the Michigan Supreme Court concluded that Smith had failed to establish a legally significant disparity, and even giving him the benefit of the doubt, he nonetheless failed to show, by any measurement, systematic exclusion.

From there, Smith headed to federal court under a petition of **habeas corpus**. Under the Antiterrorism and Effective Death Penalty Act (AEDPA) of 1996, **federal courts** are prohibited from granting habeas relief unless the state court's **adjudication** "resulted in a decision that was contrary to, or involved an unreasonable application of, clearly established Federal law, as determined by the Supreme Court of the United States," 28 U.S.C. §2254(d)(1), or resulted in a decision that was based on an unreasonable determination of the facts in light of the evidence presented in the state court proceeding, 28 U.S.C. §2254(d)(2). Finding no fault in the Michigan's court's ADJUDICATION, the federal **district court** dismissed Smith's petition.

The matter was then appealed to the Sixth Circuit Court of Appeals, which reversed, holding that the prior district-court-first assignment order in Kent County significantly reduced the number of African-Americans available for circuit court jury duty. Further, it found no important **state interest** supporting the district-court-first system. Therefore, Smith was entitled to relief.

Finally, the U.S. Supreme Court put the matter to rest, ruling that the Sixth Circuit had erred in ruling that the Michigan Supreme Court's decision "involve[d] an unreasonable application o[f] clearly established Federal Law." Justice Ginsburg delivered the opinion for a unanimous Court (Justice Thomas wrote a separate concurring opinion.) The Court noted that its earlier *Duren* decision hardly established, much less "clearly" so, that Smith met the criteria outlined in that case. Further, neither *Duren* nor any other Supreme Court case specified the test or method to be used by courts in determining under-representation (as the Michigan Supreme Court also had noted). The Michigan Supreme Court was therefore far from "unreasonable" (as required by AEDPA). Further, the Supreme Court had never 'clearly established" that a jury selection process as the kind identified by Smith could give rise to a fair-cross-section claim.

Having reversed the Sixth Circuit, the Supreme Court remanded the case for review consistent with its holding.

Briscoe v. Virginia

In *Briscoe v. Virginia*, No. 07-11191, 559 U.S. ___ (2009), a case concerning the Confrontation Clause of the SIXTH AMENDMENT to the U.S. Constitution, the U.S. SUPREME COURT, in a **per curiam** opinion, vacated the judgment of the Supreme Court of Virginia and remanded the case for consideration under *Melendez-Diaz v. Massachusetts*, 557 U.S. ___, 129 S. Ct. 2527, 174 L. Ed. 2d 314 (2009). The Supreme Court gave no further opinion in the matter.

The Sixth Amendment guarantees that the accused (in relevant part) shall have the right " . . . to be confronted with the witnesses against him." This has been interpreted by courts over the years as not only guaranteeing a right to know the identity of those offering inculpating evidence, but also, the right to confront (i.e., cross-examine) them.

The Virginia Supreme Court had consolidated three similar but unrelated cases, including Briscoe's, that of Sheldon Cypress, and Michael Magruder. *Magruder v. Commonwealth*, 657 S.E.2d 113 (Va. 2008). (Magruder was not part of the appeal to the Supreme Court). All three involved offenses involving drug possession and/or trafficking. More importantly, what the cases had in common was that a state forensic scientist had prepared a written certificate of analysis confirming the seized substances as illegal drugs. Prosecutors then entered into evidence these "certificates of analysis."

Both Cypress and Briscoe had objected to these certificates at trial, arguing that they were "testimonial" and were inadmissible unless the preparer (forensic scientist) testified at trial. Both cited an earlier U.S. Supreme Court case, *Crawford v. Washington*, 541 U.S. 36, 124 S. Ct. 1354, 158 L. Ed. 2d 177 (2004), for the general rule that so-called "testimonial" evidence could not be introduced at trial unless a DEFENDANT had a chance to cross-examine the witness providing the evidence.

But Virginia Code Section 19.2-187.1, (challenged in the present consolidated cases) permits defendants to call the forensic scientists as witnesses at trial. Specifically, Virginia Code Section 19.2-187.01 allows prosecutors to submit such certificates of analysis without the need for live testimony. Additionally, Section 19.2-187.1 provides an opportunity for any defendant against whom such certificate of analysis has been admitted into evidence to call the person who performed the analysis and question him as though he were called as an adverse witness. Neither Cypress nor Briscoe had called the respective forensic scientists who prepared the certificates of analysis, and both were convicted.

In February 2009, the Virginia Supreme Court denied the appeals, holding that the above Virginia **statute** adequately protected the appellants' Sixth Amendment's Confrontation Clause because they could either object under the statute or call the forensic analyst as a witness for the defense. Further, as the statute adequately put them on notice of the charges against them, they could also choose to waive their right to confront the witness.

It was true that the cited Virginia statute afforded defendants the opportunity to call forensic analysts (who prepare such certificates of analysis regarding the nature of seized substances) as witnesses. Briscoe had argued that the statute was unconstitutional because it shifted the burden from the prosecution, who must present its witnesses in its CASE IN CHIEF, to the defendant, who is compelled to call the forensic analyst as a witness adverse to the prosecution.

But prosecutors for the Commonwealth argued on appeal that Briscoe had waived his Sixth Amendment right when he failed to utilize the protective provisions of Virginia's statute. Following the Supreme Court's decision in *Melendez-Diaz.* the Virginia General Assembly amended Virginia Code 19.2-187, herein relied upon.

However, the Virginia Supreme Court did not consider Briscoe's case under *Melendez-Diaz.* In that case, also decided in 2009, the U.S. Supreme Court expressly held that such certificates of analysis fell within "the core class of testimonial statements" precisely covered by the Confrontation Clause. Therefore, a defendant must have an opportunity to cross-examine the forensic scientists who prepared them. Melendez-Diaz had been arrested while engaged in a cocaine sale in a parking lot. At his criminal trial, the bags of cocaine were introduced by prosecution along with drug analysis certificates/reports prepared by a lab technician who had analyzed them and identified them as cocaine. Relying on *Crawford v. Washington,* (as Briscoe had in the present case), Melendez-Diaz appealed but the Massachusetts Supreme Court denied his appeal.

On remand from the U.S. Supreme Court,, the Virginia Supreme Court needed to determine whether Virginia Code 19.2-187 complies with the Court's interpretation of the Confrontation Clause's requirements, as articulated in *Melendez-Diaz.*

SOTOMAYOR, SONIA

Sotomayor Takes Seat as the First Hispanic Supreme Court Justice

With Justice DAVID SOUTER retirement from the SUPREME COURT in 2009, President BARACK OBAMA took the opportunity not only to appoint another female to the Court, but also to appoint the first Hispanic-American to the Court. SONIA SOTOMAYOR survived the confirmation process during July 2009, and Chief Justice JOHN ROBERTS administered her oath on August 8, 2009. Sotomayor became the Court's 111th justice in history.

Sotomayor was raised in the Bronx borough of New York City in 1954. She became one of the first Hispanic-Americans to attend

Princeton Univeristy, from which she graduated *summa cum laude* in 1976. She then attended Yale Law School, where she was an editor of the >*Yale Law Journal* and served as managing editor of the *Yale Studies in World Public Order*. She became a member of the New York bar in 1980.

Sotomayor worked as an assistant district attorney from 1979 until 1984, when she joined the relatively small LITIGATION firm of Pavia & Harcourt in Manhattan. In 1990, a managing partner at the firm recommended that she apply for a position on the federal judiciary. One year later, President GEORGE H.W. BUSH nominated Sotomayor for a spot on the U.S. **District Court** for the District of New York, and the U.S. SENATE confirmed her nomination on August 11, 1992. Her most famous decision involved the Major League Baseball strike of 1994 and 1995. In *Silverman v. Major League Baseball Player Relations Committee, Inc.*, 880 F. Supp. 246 (S.D.N.Y. 1995), she ruled that the league could not unilaterally implement a new collective-bargaining agreement and use replacement players. Her ruling effectively ended the strike just before the start of the 1995 season.

After serving on the bench for seven years, President BILL CLINTON nominated her for a position on the Second **Circuit Court** of Appeals. The Senate approved her nomination by a vote of 67-29 in 1998. As an **appellate** judge, she heard appeals in more than 3,000 cases and wrote nearly 380 opinions. She earned a reputation as a centrist who wrote lengthier opinions than her counterparts. She was also known for being more blunt towards the attorneys who argued cases before the Second Circuit.

Souter announced in April 2009 that he would retire from the Court. On May 25, 2009, Obama informed Sotomayor that she would be his candidate. During her confirmation process in the summer of 2009, several Republican members of the SENATE JUDICIARY COMMITTEE attempted to derail her candidacy by attacking her credibility. She received harsh criticism for commenting in a speech in 2001 at the University of California at Berkeley that "I would hope that a wise Latina woman with the richness of her experiences would more often than not reach a better conclusion than a white male who hasn't lived that life." Despite some controversy about what she meant by this quote, polls showed that the majority of

Americans thought she was qualified to serve on the Court, and the Senate Judiciary Committee eventually confirmed her nomination by a vote of 13-6. Patrick Leahy (D.-Ver.), the chair of the Senate Judiciary Committee, commented, "It is distinctively American to continually refine our union, moving us closer to our ideals. Our union is not yet perfected, but with this confirmation, we will be making progress."

Several leading Republicans continued to oppose her confirmation, as did some advocacy groups. Among her most vocal opponents included the NATIONAL RIFLE ASSOCIATION and those who oppose ABORTION rights. Democrats on the Senate, however, where unanimous in their approval of Sotomayor, and a small number of Republicans decided to vote against party lines and in favor of her confirmation. Several of these Republicans were concerned about the backlash from Hispanic voters for those senators who voted against Sotomayor. Moreover, others noted that a Republican president, Bush, had been the first to nominate Sotomayor to the federal bench. The Senate on August 6 confirmed her nomination by a vote of 68-31, representing a higher percentage of votes than was the case with SAMUEL ALITO, who was confirmed by a vote of 58-42 in 2005. Obama applauded the vote, commenting, "With this historic vote, the Senate has affirmed that Judge Sotomayor has the intellect, the temperament, the history, the integrity and the independence of mind to ably serve on our nation's highest court."

Sotomayor remained relatively quiet during the period following her confirmation. She watched the Senate's vote on television, according to a White House spokesperson, and she was sworn in by Chief Justice John Roberts at a private ceremony on August 8. One of her first public appearances after being sworn in was to throw out the first pitch at a New York Yankee game in September. She became the third female to serve on the Court, joining Ruth Bader Ginsberg as one of two active females on the Court. She is also a Roman Catholic, and her appointment increased the number of Catholics to six.

The Supreme Court's first hearing with Sotomayor as a justice was the case of *Maryland v. Shatzer* (08-680), which involved a question of how long a suspect's request for a lawyer should be considered valid. Sotomayor, like

Supreme Court Justice Sonia Sotomayor outside the court, September 2009.

AP IMAGES

other justices, appeared to be skeptical of arguments that once a suspect has requested counsel that the police should not be able to approach the suspect until an attorney has been provided. She wrote the Court's first opinion of the 2009 term in the case of *Mohawk Industries v. Carpenter*, ___ U.S. ___, 130 S.Ct. 599, ___ L. Ed. 2d ___ (2009), which was decided on December 8.

SOVEREIGN IMMUNITY

The legal protection that prevents a sovereign state or person from being sued without consent.

Republic of Iraq v. Beaty

U.S. citizens in most cases cannot sue a foreign government in U.S. courts, as they possess **sovereign immunity**. The Foreign Sovereign Immunities Act of 1976 (FSIA), 28 U.S.C. § 1604, prohibits suits against other countries in American courts, with certain exceptions. One exception, removed a foreign state of IMMUNITY in any suit arising from acts of TERRORISM that occurred when the state was designated as a sponsor of terrorism. In 1990, Iraq was designated as a sponsor of terrorism but Congress removed Iraq from this status in 2003, following the invasion by the U.S. and its allies and the removal of Saddam Hussein as dictator. It did so because the government wanted Iraqi-government assets to be used in the reconstruction of the country. However, several lawsuits that had been filed prior to the

2003 invasion were not dismissed by the **federal courts**. Congress responded with another law but again a federal appeals court concluded that suits filed while Iraq was still a sponsor of terrorism could continue. The U.S. SUPREME COURT, in *Republic of Iraq v. Beaty*, __U.S.__,129 S. Ct. 2183, 173 L. Ed. 2d 1193 (2009).

Bob Simon, a correspondent for CBS News and other Americans alleged that they had been captured and horribly mistreated by Iraqi officials during the 1991 Gulf War. They filed suit in early 2003 in federal **district court**, seeking damages for their injuries. A second group of plaintiffs, Kenneth Beaty and others, filed suit around the same time, alleging similar abuses after the conclusion of the Gulf War. Soon after the regime of Saddam Hussein was toppled in 2003, Congress enacted an emergency military APPROPRIATION which included included a PROVISO clause authorizing the President to "make inapplicable with respect to Iraq [§]620A of the Foreign Assistance Act of 1961 or any other provision of law that applies to countries that have supported terrorism." President GEORGE W. BUSH exercised this authority but in 2004 the D.C. **Circuit Court** of Appeals ruled that the proviso did not permit the President to waive the terrorism immunity exception for claims arising from actions Iraq took while designated as a sponsor of terrorism.

Congress responded in 2008 by repealing the entire terrorism exception to FISA and replacing it with a new exception that was very similar to the original one. The law declared that nothing in the 2003 proviso sought to remove the jurisdiction of any court but authorized the President to waive any provisions of this new exception with respect to Iraq under certain conditions. President Bush signed the law and that same day waived all of its provisions as to Iraq. Iraq and the U.S. government sought to have the federal district court dismiss the Simon and Beaty lawsuits in light of this waiver but the court declined. The D.C. Circuit again refused to dismiss the lawsuits.

The Supreme Court, in a unanimous decision, overturned the appeals court ruling. Justice ANTONIN SCALIA, writing for the Court, held that the district court lost jurisdiction over both lawsuits in May 2003, when the President waived the terrorism exception for Iraq. Scalia noted that "to a layperson the notion of the President's suspending the operation of a valid law might seem strange. But the practice is well established, at least in the sphere of foreign affairs." The granting of this authority made sense because prior to the enactment of FISA the Executive Branch had to make the granting or denial of foreign immunity on a case-by-base basis. Having freed the government from diplomatic pressures created by this case-by-case approach, Congress deemed it "prudent to afford the President some flexibility in unique circumstances such as these." The court of appeals had resisted this construction by looking beyond the proviso in question and finding support in other sections of the 2008 act.

Scalia rejected this "highly sophisticated effort" by the appeals court, finding it "neither necessary or successful." He found that the principal clause granted the President the power to waive the provision. The President consequently concluded that exposing Iraq to billions of dollars in damages would jeopardize the law's goal of reconstructing the country. The courts should be wary, therefore, "of overriding apparent **statutory** text supported by executive interpretation in favor of speculation about a law's true purpose."

Having established that the actions had been properly taken, Scalia addressed whether the plaintiffs could still pursue their claims. The plaintiffs had argued that the courts should disfavor retroactive application of such a change in law. The Court found nothing in the wording of the 2008 law that suggested Congress meant to allow the lawsuits to proceed. As a policy matter, it made no sense to drain the Iraqi treasury at a time when every dollar could aid reconstruction and convert it "into a compensation scheme for a few of Saddam's victims." Therefore, the district court lost jurisdiction over the cases in May 2003 when the President signed the waiver and "immunity kicked back in."

SPEEDY TRIAL

Bloate v. United States

The SIXTH AMENDMENT to the U.S. Constitution guarantees the right to a "speedy and public trial" in all criminal prosecutions. In furtherance thereof, Congress enacted the SPEEDY TRIAL Act of 1974, which requires federal criminal trials to commence within 70 days of a defendant's INDICTMENT or initial appearance, 18 USC §§3161(c)1. If that deadline is not met, a DEFENDANT is entitled to dismissal of the charge against him.

Under the Act, certain delays resulting from " … proceedings concerning the defendant" are automatically excluded from the 70-day period, Subsection §3161(h)(1), (to prevent defendants from running out the clock). Eight subparagraphs in subsection (h)(1) enumerate specific purposes/circumstances qualifying for automatic excludability from the 70-day limit. Under a different subsection, (h)(7), a **district court** may exclude delays resulting from a continuance it grants, provided it makes certain findings on record as required by Subsection §3161(h)(7).

In *Bloate v. United States,* No. 08-728, 559 U.S. ___ (2010), the U.S. SUPREME COURT held that time spent to prepare pretrial motions on behalf of a defendant was not automatically excluded from the 70-day period. In so holding, the high court reversed the opinion of the Eighth **Circuit Court** of Appeals (and effectively, seven other circuit courts of appeals that had similarly held such time as automatically excludable). Only the Fourth and Sixth Circuits had previously held that time spent in preparation of pretrial motions was outside the scope of §3161(h)(1). The conflict among circuits prompted the Supreme Court to grant review.

In *Bloate,* police officers had been surveilling an apartment building for drug activity when they observed Bloate and a female enter a vehicle in front of the apartments and drive away. After observing several traffic violations, officers stopped Bloate. As they approached the vehicle, they observed two small bags of (what appeared to be) cocaine on Bloate's lap. The officers read *Miranda* warnings to Bloate, after which he made inculpatory statements but denied any association with the apartment building. His girlfriend admitted she lived there and consented to a search. During the search, officers found several items belonging to Bloate, including cocaine, three firearms, ammunition, and a bulletproof vest. He was arrested the next day. A federal **grand jury** later indicted him on **felony** firearms violations and possession with intent to distribute more than five grams of cocaine. The August 24 (2006) indictment started the 70-day clock under the Speedy Trial Act.

On September 7, defense counsel filed a motion to extend the court-ordered September 13 deadline for filing pretrial motions. The **Magistrate** Judge granted the motion, extending the deadline to September 25. But on September 25, defense filed a "Waiver of Pretrial Motions." On October 4, the magistrate held a hearing to consider this "waiver," ultimately determining that the waiver was voluntary and intelligent. On November 8, defense moved to continue the trial date, which the court granted, rescheduling for December 18. However, prior to trial, the parties prepared a plea agreement, and the court scheduled a hearing on the matter for December 20. At the hearing, defendant backed out of the plea and requested a new attorney. This, too, was granted, new counsel was appointed, and trial again rescheduled for February 26, 2007.

One week before trial (and 179 days after the indictment), on February 19, 2007, defense counsel moved to have the indictment dismissed, claiming the 70-day time limit had elapsed. The district (trial) court excluded the time from September 7 to October 4 (see preceding paragraph) as "within the extension of time granted to file pretrial motions," i.e., pretrial motion preparation time. It also excluded other periods of time, e.g., for continuances, and stated on the record the applicable subsections under §3161(h) as well as the court's determination that the continuances were necessary and "obviously outweighed the best interest of the public and the defendant to a Speedy Trial." After calculating the remaining unexcludable time, the court denied the motion. Following one more continuance (necessitated by a **docket** change in an unrelated case), a jury convicted Bloate on both charges after a two-day trial. He was sentenced to concurrent 30-year terms of imprisonment.

On appeal, the Eighth Circuit upheld the district court's denial of Bloate's motion to dismiss for a Speedy Trial Act violation. In affirming the district court's various exclusions (from the 70-day period), the **appellate court** agreed with the exclusion of the time from September 7 (when defense counsel filed a motion to extend the September 13 deadline for pretrial motions) through October 4 (when the district court held a hearing to determine that defendant's waiver was voluntary and intelligent). Although the district court did not articulate which section of the Speedy Trial

Act supported the exclusion, the Eighth Circuit expressly noted that "pretrial motion preparation time" was automatically excluded under §3161(h)(1), under the umbrella of certain delays resulting from ". . .proceedings concerning the defendant," provided that "the [district] court specifically grants time for that purpose." 534 F.3d at 897. Seven other Courts of Appeals had similarly interpreted Subsection(h)(1).

Accordingly, and to resolve conflict among circuits, the Supreme Court granted review on the narrow question involving the automatic exclusion of time spent on preparing pretrial motions.

Justice Thomas delivered the opinion of the Court. In reversing and remanding to the Eighth Circuit, the Court held that time granted to *prepare* pretrial motions was not automatically excludable under Subsection (h)(1).

The delay at issue in the present case, noted the Court, was governed by Subsection (h)(1)(D), enumerating a category as automatically excludable a "delay resulting from any pretrial motion, from the filing of the motion through the conclusion of the hearing on, or other prompt **disposition** of, such motion." Since Congress had expressly articulated the boundaries of the above automatic exclusion, anything falling outside of those parameters, e. g., preparation time for pretrial motions, was not excludable unless determined so under a different subsection. In other words, other pretrial motion-related delays were excludable only if they resulted in a continuance under Subsection (h)(7). Since the Eighth Circuit did not address (nor the government assert in its brief) whether any other provision of the Act [e.g., subsection (h)(7)] could support exclusion, the Supreme Court did not consider or rule on this.

Subsection (h)(7) specifically provides that delay "resulting from a continuance granted by any judge" is excludable only if the judge finds that "the ends of justice served by taking such action outweigh the best interest of the public and the defendant in a speedy trial" and records those findings.

The government had argued that if a district court failed to make the necessary (h)(7) findings or express them on record, such failure could lead to a windfall gain for a defendant who induces delay beyond the 70-day limit. But the Court noted that the district court could

always dismiss **without prejudice**, thereby affording the Government an opportunity to refile charges or reindict the defendant.

Justice Thomas was joined by Chief Justice Roberts and Justices Stevens, Scalia, Kennedy, Ginsburg, and Sotomayor. Justice Ginsburg filed a concurring opinion in which she expressly noted that nothing in the majority opinion barred the Eighth Circuit, on remand, from sustaining the indictment and conviction because, even if the time excluded for preparation of pretrial motions (28 days) was excluded, the number of days for purposes of the Act would be 65, still under the 70-day threshold.

Justice Alito, joined by Justice Breyer, dissented. He sided with the eight circuit courts of appeal, who interpreted the provision as allowing exclusion for any "period of delay resulting from other proceedings concerning the defendant, including but not limited to. . ." the eight specific types of delays enumerated in subparagraphs (A)-(h).

STANDARD OF REVIEW

Renico v. Letts

In enacting the Antiterrorism and Effective Death Penalty Act of 1996 (AEDPA), 28 U.S.C. §2254 *et seq.*, Congress clearly intended "to prevent defendants (and **federal courts**) from using **habeas corpus** review as a vehicle to second guess the reasonable decisions of state courts," noted Chief Justice Roberts, Jr. in writing the majority 6-3 opinion for the case of *Renico v. Letts,* No. 09-338, 559 U.S. ___ (2010). Notwithstanding, the U.S. SUPREME COURT reviews several HABEAS CORPUS cases each term. While this is yet another of those cases, involving multiple **appellate** decisions alternately affirming or reversing the previous level, it is instructive for Justice Roberts' careful delineation of the appropriate standard of review to be used.

In 1996, DEFENDANT Reginald Lett was in a Detroit liquor store when an argument broke out between his friend, Charles Jones, and a taxicab driver who Jones claimed wrongfully ejected him from the cab. Lett left the liquor store, retrieved a handgun from another friend in the parking lot, returned to the liquor store and shot the taxicab driver in the head and chest. He was charged with first-degree MURDER and possession of a firearm during the commission of a **felony**.

During two days of deliberation at his 1997 murder trial, the jury sent seven notes to the judge, including one that said the jury could not agree on a verdict. The judge called the jury back into the courtroom, along with the PROSECUTOR and defense counsel, then on record, questioned the jury foreperson, who advised again that the jury was unable to reach a unanimous verdict. The judge declared a MISTRIAL, dismissed the jury, and scheduled a new trial. At Lett's second trial, a new jury deliberated for just a little more than three hours, but unanimously convicted him of second-degree murder.

The crux of Lett's original appeal to the Michigan Court of Appeals was that the trial judge had declared a mistrial in the first trial without necessity for doing so, and therefore, the **Double Jeopardy** clause of the FIFTH AMENDMENT prevented the state from trying him a second time. The Court of Appeals agreed.

Next, the Michigan Supreme Court reversed. Using U.S. Supreme Court precedent, it went all the way back to *United States v. Perez,* 9 Wheat. 579, for the holding that a defendant may be retried following a deadlocked jury, providing the trial court exercised "sound discretion" in concluding a deadlock existed and thus found a "manifest necessity" for a mistrial. Further, said the Michigan Supreme Court, under *Arizona v. Washington,* 434 U.S. 497, an **appellate court** must generally defer to a trial court's determination that a deadlock existed. Finding that the trial court had not abused discretion in declaring a mistrial, the Michigan Supreme Court made note of several facts, including the sufficient two-day jury deliberations, the numerous jury notes to the judge, including one indicating a heated disagreement among jurors, and foreperson's statement that the jury could not reach a verdict.

Letts next filed a petition for federal habeas review. However, now he claimed that the Michigan Supreme Court's rejection of his double **jeopardy** claim was "an unreasonable application of ... clearly established Federal law, as determined by the Supreme Court of the United States" (quoting language from the AEDPA) and therefore, he was not barred by AEDPA from getting federal habeas relief. The federal **district court** agreed, and so did the Sixth **Circuit Court** of Appeals.

The U.S. Supreme Court reversed the Sixth Circuit Court of Appeals, effectively reinstating the decision of the Michigan Supreme Court. Significantly, Chief Justice Roberts said this,

> It is important at the outset to define the question before us. That question is not whether the trial judge should have declared a mistrial. It is not even whether it was an **abuse of discretion** for her to have done so—the applicable standard on direct review. The question under AEDPA is instead whether the determination of the Michigan Supreme Court that there was no ABUSE OF DISCRETION was 'an unreasonable application of—clearly established Federal law.' §2254(d)(1).

The Court went on to note that it had previously explained, in *William v. Taylor,* 529 U.S. 362 (2000), that an unreasonable application of federal law is different from an incorrect application of federal law. This meant that a federal habeas court could not grant relief simply because it concluded, in its own judgment, that the relevant state court decision applied clearly established federal law erroneously or incorrectly. Rather, it must have applied it in an "objectively unreasonable" manner. This distinction created a substantially higher threshold for obtaining relief, than under a *de novo* review. AEDPA thus imposed a "highly deferential standard for evaluating state-court rulings." *Lindh v. Murphy,* 521 U.S. 320 (1997), and "demands that state-court decisions be given the benefit of the doubt." *Woodford v. Visciotti,* 537 U.S. 19 (2002).

Justice Roberts then went on to explain, "[W]e do not deny that the trial judge could have been more thorough before declaring a mistrial." True, the judge could have addressed more questions to the foreperson, or granted additional time for deliberations, or consulted with the parties' counsel before making her decision. However, as Justice Roberts noted, none of this was *required,* under either the AEDPA or Supreme Court precedent for DOUBLE JEOPARDY. In sum, "Whether or not the Michigan Supreme Court's opinion reinstating Lett's conviction in this case was *correct,* it was clearly *not unreasonable.*" Accordingly, the judgment of the Sixth Circuit was reversed and the case remanded.

Chief Justice Roberts was joined in the majority opinion by Justices Scalia, Kennedy, Thomas, Ginsburg, and Alito. Justice Stevens dissented, in which he was joined by Justice Sotomayor, and in which Justice Breyer joined in part. The DISSENT cited numerous historical instances where **common law** courts went to great lengths to force juries to reach a verdict, as a mistrial should be reserved only for the most "extraordinary and striking circumstances."

STATUTE OF LIMITATIONS

A type of federal or state law that restricts the time within which legal proceedings may be brought.

Krupski v. Costa Crociere

Statutes of limitations generally dictate the amount of time within which a person may BRING SUIT against another person or **entity**. It follows that a timely lawsuit must also name the proper party as DEFENDANT. What happens when a complaint is timely filed with the court under the applicable **statute** of limitation, but the lawsuit names the wrong party-defendant? Rule 15(c) of the Federal Rules of **Civil Procedure** governs when an amended PLEADING "relates back" to the date of a timely filed original pleading, and therefore itself is still timely, even though it was filed outside an applicable **statute of limitations**. In *Krupski v. Costa Crociere*, No. 09-337, 560 U.S. ___ (2010), the U.S. SUPREME COURT held that Rule 15 could save an otherwise untimely amended pleading naming a different defendant, because the newly-named defendant "knew or should have known that the action would have been brought against it, but for a mistake concerning the proper party's identity." (Rule 15(c). This was so even though the PLAINTIFF knew or should have known of her mistake in naming the wrong party-defendant. Importantly, the Supreme Court ruled that relating back under Rule 15(c)(1)(C) depended upon what the party to be added knew or should have known, and not the amending party's knowledge or timeliness in seeking to amend the pleading.

In early 2007, Wanda Krupski booked a trip with Costa Cruise Lines. On February 21, 2007, she tripped over a cable on the cruise ship and fractured her femur. Upon her return home, she retained legal counsel and sought compensation for her injuries. Her passenger ticket, issued by Costa Cruise Lines, expressly stated that it was the sole contract between each passenger and the carrier. However, the ticket expressly identified "Costa Crociere S.p.A." as

the carrier. The ticket extended all defenses, limitations, extensions " ... that may be invoked by the CARRIER ... "to agents, subsidiaries, successors, etc., as well as "Costa Cruise Lines N.V., identified as the "sales and marketing agent for the CARRIER and the issuer of this Passage Ticket Contract." The ticket "contract" further required injured parties to submit written notice of any claim to the carrier or its agent; to file lawsuits within one year of injury; to file claims with a specific federal **district court** in Florida, designated as the exclusive forum for lawsuits such as Krupski's: and to serve the carrier within 120 days after filing.

In July 2007, Krupski's lawyer notified Costa Cruise Lines of Krupski's claim. A claims administrator for Costa Cruise Lines responded by requesting additional information "[i]n order to facilitate our future attempts to achieve a pre-litigation settlement." The parties did not settle, however, and three weeks before the expiration of the one-year limitations period, on February 1, 2008, Krupski filed an action against Costa Cruise Lines in the Florida district court designated in the ticket. Costa Cruise Lines was served three days later.

In its answer to the complaint, filed February 25, 2008 (after the limitations period had expired) Costa Cruise Lines asserted that it was not the proper defendant and named Costa Crociere as its principal and the actual carrier. In March 2008, Costa Cruise listed Costa Crociere as an interested party in its corporate disclosure statement. Finally, in May 2008, Costa Cruise Lines filed for **summary judgment**, again stating that Costa Crociere was the proper defendant.

On June 13, 2008, Krupski responded to the motion for SUMMARY JUDGMENT by requesting limited discovery to determine if Costa Cruise should be dismissed. She simultaneously moved to amend her complaint to add Costa Crociere as a defendant. Summary judgment was denied, and Krupski was permitted to amend her complaint, adding Costa Crociere. After Costa Crociere was served, the district issued an order dismissing Costa Cruise Lines pursuant to stipulation of the parties.

Shortly thereafter, Costa Crociere, represented by the same legal counsel who had represented Costa Cruise Lines, filed for dismissal, claiming that the one-year limitation had expired, and that the amended complaint did not "relate back" under Rule 15(c), making the action untimely. U.S.C. §1692, *et seq.*

Rule 15(c)(1)(C)(i) lays out three requirements to be met before an amended complaint naming a new defendant can relate back to the original pleading. First, the claim against the new defendant must arise "out of the conduct, transaction, or occurrence set out—or attempted to be set out—in the original pleading." Second, within the period allowed for serving the summons and complaint (generally 120 days from the filing of the complaint), the newly-named defendant must have "received such notice of the action that it will not be prejudiced in defending on the merits." And last, the plaintiff must show, within that period (in this case, 120 days) that the newly-named defendant "knew or should have known that the action would have been brought against it, but for a mistake concerning the proper party's identity."

The district court found that Krupski had met the first two criteria, but also found that Krupski had not made a mistake in identifying the proper party. Rather, it held that because Costa Cruise Lines had informed Krupski that Costa Crociere was the proper defendant, starting with its answer to the complaint and two times after, and Krupski nevertheless delayed for months her motion to amend her complaint, she knew of the proper defendant and made no mistake. The Eleventh **Circuit Court** of Appeals affirmed. While noting that Costa Cruise Line's information to Krupski came after the expiration of the STATUTE OF LIMITATIONS, it still noted that all the relevant information about proper party defendants was spelled out right there in Krupski's ticket. Krupski had given that ticket to her legal counsel well before the time period expired. Therefore, Krupski knew or should have known of Costa Crociere's identity as the proper defendant. Even if, for the sake of argument, she first learned from Costa Cruise Line's answer to the complaint, she waited another 133 days to seek leave to amend.

The U.S. Supreme Court, however, pointed out that Rule 15's language refers to the newly-named party, not the amending party. Relation back, under the Rule, depends on what the party to be added knew or should have known, not on the amending party's knowledge or timeliness in seeking to amend a pleading *see*

above. On the face of Krupski's complaint, she (mistakenly) identified Costa Cruise Lines as the entity that "owned, operated, managed, supervised, and controlled" the ship on which she was injured. Therefore, Costa Crociere, through its agent Costa Cruise Lines, should have known that it avoided suit within the limitation period only because of Krupski's misunderstanding about which "Costa" was in charge of the ship. Finally, once Krupski met the Rule's three criteria, the Rule mandates a relation back; it does not leave that to a court's equitable discretion. Therefore, the Eleventh Circuit also erred in holding that Krupski's undue delay in seeking leave to amend her pleading justified denial of the request. The Supreme Court reversed the Eleventh Circuit and remanded the case to the district court.

Justice Sotomayor delivered the opinion for the unanimous Court. However, Justice Scalia wrote a separate opinion, concurring in part and concurring in the judgment. He did not support the majority's use of the Notes of the Advisory Committee to the Federal Rules of CIVIL PROCEDURE to reach its decision.

SUBJECT MATTER JURISDICTION

Morrison v. National Australia Bank

In *Morrison v. National Australia Bank Ltd.,* No. 08-1191, 561 U.S. ___ (2010), the U.S. SUPREME COURT unanimously held that U.S. laws against SECURITIES **fraud** do not apply to trans-national securities dealings. Therefore, foreign plaintiffs could not pursue FRAUD charges in federal **district court** for securities purchased on foreign exchanges. Accordingly, the district court had no **subject matter jurisdiction** over the matter and was correct in dismissing the suit.

National Australia Bank, Ltd. (National), a foreign bank whose "ordinary shares" (the equivalent of **common stock** in this country) were not traded on any stock exchange in the United States, purchased a Florida-based company, HomeSide Lending Inc. in 1998. Home-Side Lending was in the business of servicing mortgages, e.g., collecting monthly payments. In 2001, National was forced to significantly write down the value of HomeSide Lending's assets, causing a sharp decline in the value of National shares.

A group of Australians who had purchased National shares before the write-downs filed suit in federal district court in New York against National, HomeSide, and company officers. The suit alleged securities fraud under §10(b) of the Securities and Exchange Act of 1934 (providing for a private **right of action**) and SEC Rule 10b-5. Specifically, the complaint alleged that HomeSide and its officers had manipulated financial models to make the company's mortgage-servicing assets appear more valuable, and that National and its chief executive officer (CEO) knew of this deception. After the plaintiffs purchased shares, National reduced the value of HomeSide's assets by $2.2 billion, citing "mistakes" on the part of HomeSide. This caused the share value to plummet, in turn, causing financial loss to the plaintiffs. The plaintiffs argued that U.S. courts should hear the case because HomeSide Lending was a Florida company, and the alleged fraud was committed in the United States.

The district court granted a motion to dismiss, based on Federal Rule of **Civil Procedure** 12(b)(1) for lack of SUBJECT MATTER JURISDICTION, in that the alleged domestic acts were, at most, a link in a securities fraud that concluded abroad.

The Second **Circuit Court** of Appeals affirmed the dismissal. Specifically, it ruled that U.S. courts had jurisdiction only if a defendant's alleged wrongdoing in the United States was "more than merely preparatory" to the fraud. In this case, the **appellate court** concluded, any losses suffered by investors were the result of decisions made in Australia than by what happened in Florida.

There had been a split among circuit courts of appeals on what is refered to as "foreign-cubed" lawsuits, and the Supreme Court granted **certiorari** (review). Although the Court unanimously affirmed the decision and the district court's dismissal, it found error in the lower courts' rulings.

Justice Scalia delivered the opinion for the unanimous Court. He narrowed the question before the Court as "whether §10(b) of the Securities Exchange Act of 1934 provides a **cause of action** to foreign plaintiffs suing foreign and American defendants for misconduct in connection with securities traded on foreign exchanges." In short, the answer was no.

The Court held that the Second Circuit erred in considering §10(b)'s extra-territorial reach in order to raise a question of subject matter jurisdiction, as whatever conduct §10(b) reached was a merits question, while subject matter jurisdiction referred to a tribunal's power to hear a case. Nonetheless, the end result was the same, because §10(b) did not provide a CAUSE OF ACTION to foreign plaintiffs suing foreign and American defendants for misconduct in connection with securities traded on foreign exchanges. Accordingly, it was not necessary to remand in view of that error because the same analysis justified dismissal under Rule 12(b)(6), FAILURE TO STATE A CLAIM.

It was a "longstanding principle of American law" that legislation of Congress, unless a contrary intent appeared, was meant to apply within the territorial jurisdiction of the United States, said the Court. The Second Circuit had disregarded this presumption against **extraterritoriality** and decided it had the right to discern what Congress intended to be §10(b)'s reach or application. Similar decisions, said the Court, have occurred over many decades in many courts, resulting in a plethora of "tests" to determine congressional intent. Rather, said the Court, it would apply the presumption against EXTRATERRITORIALITY in all cases, thereby preserving a stable background against which Congress could legislate with predictable effect.

Because SEC Rule 10b-5 was promulgated under §10(b), it followed that the Rule did not extend beyond the reach of the section as well. Thus, if §10(b) was not extraterritorial, neither was Rule 10b-5, and the Rule's reach did not extend beyond conduct encompassed by §10(b)'s prohibitions.

Regarding the allegations of wrongful conduct in the United States (HomeSide and its executives allegedly engaged in deceptive conduct and misleading statements in Florida) the Court noted that the focus of the Securities and Exchange Act was not on the place where deception occurred or originated,, but rather, on purchases and sales of securities in the United States. Section 10(b) applies only to transactions in securities listed on domestic exchanges, and domestic transactions in other securities. The proposed test employed by the government and the Second Circuit, that a jurisdictional violation occurred where the fraud involved significant and material conduct in the United States, was without textual support, said the Court.

Justices Stevens and Ginsburg concurred in the judgment, but noted reluctance in the

Court's formulating a new "transactional test" that limited §10(b)'s reach only to transactions of securities listed on domestic exchanges or domestic transactions in other securities. "[F]ederal courts have been construing §10(b) in a different manner for a long time," said the concurring opinion, "... as to warrant the **abandonment** of their doctrine." Justice Sotomayor took no part in either consideration or decision in the case.

SUPREMACY CLAUSE

The clause of Article VI of the U.S. Constitution that declares that all laws and treaties made by the federal government shall be the "supreme law of the land."

Haywood v. Drown

State and federal governments have sought to reduce the number of civil lawsuits filed by prisoners. Congress passed the Prison LITIGATION Reform Act of 1995 (PLRA), 28 U.S.C.A. § 1932, which placed a number of restrictions on prisoners who used the federal CIVIL RIGHTS **statute**, 42 U.S.C.A. § 1983, to pursue actions challenging prison conditions. Under the PLRA, prisoners must exhaust all administrative remedies before they are allowed to file a § 1983 lawsuit or any other **civil action** based on a federal law in federal court. Once filed, a federal **magistrate** will determine whether the prisoner has met the PLRA conditions. If not, the court will dismiss the lawsuit. The State of New York took a different approach, enacting a provision in its Correction Law that prohibits state trial courts from hearing any § 1983 lawsuit for damages against correction officers. A prisoner challenged the law, contending that it violated the Constitution's **Supremacy Clause**. The SUPREME COURT agreed with the prisoner, ruling in *Haywood v. Drown*, __U.S. __, 129 S. Ct. 2108, 173 L. Ed. 2d 920 (2009), that the state could not selectively remove certain § 1983 actions from its courts of **general jurisdiction**.

Keith Haywood, an inmate at New York's Attica Correctional Facility, started two 1983 actions against several correction employees, alleging that they had deprived him of his civil rights at three disciplinary hearings and one altercation. He filed the suits in State Supreme Court, the state's trial court of GENERAL JURISDICTION. The court dismissed the actions, citing the provision of the Correction Law for its lack

of jurisdiction to hear the case. The intermediate court of appeals upheld this ruling, as did the state's highest court, the New York Court of Appeals. The court of appeals believed that there was no SUPREMACY CLAUSE violation because the law treated state and federal damages actions against correction officers equally; neither action could be brought in state court.

The Supreme Court, in a 5-4 decision, overruled the New York court. Justice JOHN PAUL STEVENS, writing for the majority, acknowledged that the purpose of the state law provision was to stop prisoner lawsuits that were largely frivolous and vexatious. New York did provide an alternate procedure for the prisoner, allowing the inmate to file the claim for damages in the state's **court of claims**. Stevens pointed out, however, that in this court the inmate is not provided the same relief and same options as in a state trial court. An inmate must file a claim within 90 days of the alleged injury; he is not entitled to a jury trial, **punitive damages**, or attorney's fees. In addition, the inmate cannot seek an INJUNCTION.

Justice Stevens stated that the Court had long held that federal law "is as much the law of the several States as are the laws passed by their own legislature." Although § 1983 was enacted during RECONSTRUCTION to help newly freed slaves protect their rights in federal court, the Court has ruled that such actions can be heard in state court as well. The only way New York could justify its law was by demonstrating it was a "neutral rule of judicial administration." Otherwise, the states lack the authority "to nullify a federal right or **cause of action** they believe is inconsistent with their local policies."

The Court concluded that the state's policy of prohibiting prisoner lawsuits for damages was not a neutral rule of **judicial administration**. The law was contrary to the intent of Congress that all persons who violate federal rights while acting under color of state law should be held liable for damages. Justice Stevens admitted that prior Court decisions had not been clear as to what was an acceptable neutral rule. He stated that "equality of treatment" does not equal neutrality. Just because there was the absence of DISCRIMINATION in the law did not mean the law was neutral: "A jurisdictional rule cannot be used as a device to undermine federal law, no matter how evenhanded it may appear." Ensuring the equality of treatment is just the beginning and not the end of the Supremacy Clause. Therefore, the state could not bar inmates from filing § 1983 lawsuits in state court.

Justice CLARENCE THOMAS, in a dissenting opinion joined by Chief Justice JOHN ROBERTS and Justices ANTONIN SCALIA and SAMUEL ALITO, contended that the state had the absolute right to refuse to hear a § 1983 action or any other federal action that it selected. Justice Thomas reviewed the history of the Constitutional Convention and the drafting of the Supremacy Clause, concluding that "the States have the unfettered authority to determine whether their local courts may entertain a federal cause of action." Once the state chooses to do so, "it is the end of the matter as far as the Constitution is concerned."

TERRORISM

The unlawful use of force or violence against persons or property in order to coerce or intimate a government or the civilian population in furtherance of political or social objectives.

Ninth Circuit Takes a Broad View of Government's Power to Detain Guantanamo Bay Detainees

The Ninth **Circuit Court** of Appeals in January 2010 adopted a broad view of the government's power to detain terrorist suspects at Guantanamo Bay in Cuba. The decision was the first test of the Supreme Court's decision in *Boumediene v. Bush*, ___ U.S. ___, 128 S. Ct. 2229, 171 L. Ed. 2d 41 (2008), in which the Court held the Guantanamo detainees were entitled to **habeas corpus** rights. The result of the Ninth Circuit's decision was that the United States could continue to hold a detainee who had not actually fired a shot in combat.

The case involved Ghaleb Nassar Al-Bihani, who is a native of Saudi Arabia and a citizen of Yemen. A local sheikh issued a religious decree (known as a fatwa) to support Afghanistan's Taliban government in its war against rival Northern Alliance. Al-Bihani first visited a family friend in Pakistan, and the friend escorted Bihani to Afghanistan. Al-Bihani received training from the terrorist organization Al Qaeda before joining one of the Taliban's military units near Khwaje Ghar. Following the SEPTEMBER 11TH ATTACKS in 2001, the United

States and allied forces bombed the area where Al-Bihani was stationed. Although he was issued a weapon and had received combat training, he served as a cook and never fired the weapon in combat. Al-Bihani ended up near the Pakistan border before surrendering to a commander of the Northern Alliance, which later gave Al-Bihani to U.S. forces. The United States transferred Bihani to Guantanamo Bay in 2002, and he has remained there since then.

In 2004, the SUPREME COURT held in *Rasul v. Bush*, 542 U.S. 466, 124 S. Ct. 2686, 159 L. Ed. 2d 548 (2004) that 28 U.S.C. § 2241 extended habeas jurisdiction of U.S. courts to ALIENS held at Guantanamo Bay. Following the decision, Bihani filed a petition seeking HABEAS CORPUS relief with the U.S. **District Court** for the District of Columbia. However, Congress passed the Military Commissions Act of 2006 (MCA), Pub. L. No. 109-366, 120 Stat. 2600, which withdrew jurisdiction of U.S. courts to hear habeas petitions of Guantanamo Bay detainees. The district court stayed Bihani's petition.

Two years after Congress enacted the MCA, the Court rendered a decision in *Boumediene v. Bush,,*553 U.S. 723, 128 S. Ct. 2229, 171 L. Ed. 2d 41 (2008). The Court in *Boumediene* reviewed the MCA to determine its constitutionality, particularly as the **statute** applied to habeas cases that were pending at the time of the statute's enactment. In a splintered 5-4 opinion written by Justice ANTHONY KENNEDY, the Court held that the MCA was unconstitutional as it applied to the pending cases. The Court concluded that Guantanamo Bay detainees could proceed with their habeas challenges under procedures that the district court should craft to account for special circumstances related to the detention of terrorist suspects.

The district court responded to the *Boumediene* decision by adopting procedures to apply to Al-Bihani's case. In a case management order, the court established that the government had the burden to prove by a preponderance of the evidence that Al-Bihani's detention was legal. Moreover, the order required the government to explain the legal basis for Al-Bihani's detention. to share the documents pertaining to factual allegations, and to turn over exculpatory evidence found as the government prepared its case. *Al Bihani v. Bush*, 588 F. Supp. 2d 19 (D.D.C. 2008).

After holding hearings on the matter, the district court considered the sufficiency of the evidence that the government had presented in the case. The government argued that it had to prove Al-Bihani was an "enemy combatant" to justify his detention. The district court had previously adopted the following as a definition of an ENEMY COMBATANT: "An 'enemy combatant' is an individual who was part of or supporting Taliban or al Qaeda forces, or associated forces that are engaged in hostilities against the United States or its coalition partners. This includes any person who has committed a belligerent act or has directly supported hostilities in aid of enemy armed forces." In support of its argument that Al-Bihani met this definition, the government asserted that he: (1) had stayed a guesthouse affiliated with Al Qaeda in Afghanistan; (2) had received combat training at an Al Qaeda camp; and (3) had supported the Taliban in its fight against the Northern Alliance and later against the United States. Al-Bihani disputed the allegations, arguing that though he was in Afghanistan, he merely served as a cook and kitchen aid. The court, however, determined that the government had presented sufficient evidence to prove that Al-Bihani had been part of or supportive of Al Qaeda forces. *Al Bihani v. Obama*, 594 F. Supp. 35 (D.D.C. 2009).

Al-Bahini appealed the case to the U.S. Court of Appeals for the District of Columbia. On appeal, he argued that under INTERNATIONAL LAW, the United States would be authorized to detain him only if he had either belonged to an

official state MILITIA or had committed a direct hostile act, such as firing a weapon. Since he did not belong to a militia and had not fired a weapon, he argued, he was merely a civilian who could not be detained. Al-Bahini also argued that the military unit to which he belonged was not subject to attack by U.S. forces and, moreover, that the conflict in which he was detained ended when the Taliban lost control of Afghanistan.

Al-Bahini's arguments were premised on the application of international law that he asserted should limit the application of U.S. law. However, a panel of the D.C. Circuit Court rejected this premise, asserting that Congress never intended international law to limit the president's war-time powers. The panel instead applied federal statutes in concluding that the U.S. has authority to retain him as an enemy combatant. The court also rejected his argument that the habeas proceedings adopted by the district court were insufficient. *Al-Bihani v. Obama*, 590 F.3d 866 (D.C. Cir. 2010).

Unless the opinion is reversed on appeal to the full D.C. Circuit Court or to the U.S. Supreme Court, the decision will control future detention cases brought before the D.C. District Court.

THEFT

A criminal act in which property belonging to another is taken without that person's consent.

Shoplifters Who Confessed on Dr. Phil Show Convicted

A California couple who appeared on the syndicated television show *Dr. Phil* and admitted to being professional shoplifters were convicted in 2009 and sentenced to terms in federal prison. The case raised questions about why the couple appeared on the show in the first place, whether the show's portrayal of the couple's shoplifting habits were accurate, what the show's host and producers should have done in response to the confessions.

The host of *Dr. Phil* is Phil McGraw, who had a career as a clinical psychologist before becoming a celebrity. He appeared on segments of the *Oprah Winfrey Show* and became popular enough to begin his own show. The show's topic are diverse, as McGraw covers subjects such as marriage, children, and weight loss. The show has been in syndication since 2002 and is broadcast in several countries. Most of the episodes are serious in tone, and many of the guests appear on the show in an effort to seek help for their various problems. The show has an audience of about five million viewers.

In November 2008, a couple calling themselves Allen and Laura appeared on the show. According to Laura, the couple brought in about $10,000 per month by shoplifting and that during a seven-year period, they amassed nearly $1 million. Though many of the goods they stole were small items, such as diapers and shoes, they also stole much larger items, such as computers and desks. On the show, Allen showed the camera a new lawn mower, which he claimed that he simply loaded into the back of his truck. They said they had worked in several states, including Nevada, Arizona, North Dakota, and South Dakota.

Allen described several methods by which he and his wife stole goods. "I have some pants that have pockets down at the bottom, and I would keep the actual store bags that they use," he said on the show. "We would get somewhere where I know the camera is not looking, quickly put stuff in bags and just go out so it looks like we paid for it. The other time is what we call 'buy one, get one' where my wife and I would go into a retail store. She would go in first and buy the item. She would have her receipt, she would hand me the receipt, and I would go get the same exact item, and I would walk out with it. If I would get stopped at the door, I would have my receipt right there. What are you going to do about it?"

The couple videotaped themselves as they went on a shoplifting spree. Laura remained in the car with the couple's three children while Allen went into stores to steal merchandise. The couple said they were stealing small items, such as Lego toys. Laura estimated that they had hit about 27 stores over the course of a weekend and would make about $4,000 to $5,000. During the shoplifting spree, the couple would fill up their trunk with merchandise and then mail the merchandise to their home. Once they returned home, they sold the merchandise online by using such services as Ebay and PayPal.

Laura told McGraw that she had not feared getting caught. However, the couple acknowledged that by transporting stolen goods across state lines, they had committed federal crimes.

When McGraw asked why the couple agreed to appear on the show, Allen responded, "Putting it out in the open and knowing that everybody has seen us now, it will help us to not want to go to the stores, because we're going to feel like they're going to recognize us now. I think it's something to help us to stop, because my cover's blown." McGraw also asked what they expected would happen to their children if they were caught, to which Laura replied, "We're going to lose them."

McGraw also interviewed security expert who is hired by stores to research methods for theft protection. The experts said the two were definitely professional shoplifters and that they could expect to face an INDICTMENT of "several thousand" counts. McGraw also noted that the Allen and Laura did not appear to be kleptomaniacs but rather appeared to be professional thieves. The fact that the couple shoplifted items in large quantities, stole items of value, and planned to get away with their crimes were signs of professional shoplifters, according to McGraw.

The couple's actual names were Matthew Allen Eaton and Laura Eaton. In March 2009, federal agents raided the couple's home in San Marcos, California. One week before the raid, an Internet auction site featured toys made by the Lego Group toy company, and the address connected to the sale was the Eaton's address. The agents did not immediately make an arrest, saying that the raid was just part of an ongoing investigation. Authorities found more than 500 boxes of toys in the house. In September 2009, a federal **grand jury** indicted the couple on charges of transporting stolen items across state lines. Agents working on the case were as dumbfounded as McGraw as to why the Eatons confessed on television. One agent said, "In 20 years of **fraud** cases, I've never seen anything like this: a taped confession before a national audience."

Records revealed that Matthew Eaton had held several jobs, including positions as a security guard, supervisor at a gas station, and owner of an auto-detailing business. Laura Eaton was a home-care helper for the disabled. The couple was indigent at the time of their arrest and were represented by public defenders. The couple's children were sent to live with relatives. The couple alleged that the producers of *Dr. Phil* had promised to help the Eatons by providing psychological care and a legal defense fund. However, the show's producers denied making such promises.

In March 2010, U.S. District Judge Irma Gonzalez sentenced Matthew Eaton to 27 months in prison and sentenced Laura to one year and one day in prison. Gonzalez showed little pity for the Eatons, calling Matthew Eaton "despicable." The judge also said she did not believe Laura's statement that the couple did not use their children as part of the scheme.

VOTING RIGHTS ACT

*An enactment by Congress in 1965 (42 U.S.C.A. §
1973 et seq.) that prohibits the states and their
political subdivisions from imposing voting qua-
lifications or prerequisites to voting, or standards,
practices, or procedures that deny or curtail the
right of a U.S. citizen to vote because of race, color,
or membership in a language minority group.*

Ninth Circuit Overturns Washington State Felony Disenfranchisement Law

In a 2-1 decision, a panel of the Ninth **Circuit
Court** of Appeals ruled that the State of
Washington's constitutional provision regarding
felony disenfranchisement violates Section 2 of
the Voting Rights Act (VRA), 42 U.S.C. §§ 1973–
1973aa-6. All states have laws that bar or
temporarily restrict persons convicted of felonies
from voting. The appeals court in *Farrakhan v.
Gregoire*, 590 F.3d 989 (9th Cir.2010) became the
first court to rule that because of racial DISCRIMI-
NATION in the state's criminal justice system, a
felony disenfranchisement law results in the
denial of the right to vote on account of race.

The Ninth Circuit overturned a 2006 federal
district court ruling. The district court had held
that the state's felony disenfranchisement provision did not violate the Voting Rights Act. The
court had "no doubt that members of racial
minorities have experienced discrimination in
Washington's criminal justice system. It addition, it found telling the fact that the state did

not introduce any evidence to rebut the discrimination claims. Nevertheless, the court found
that "Washington's history, or lack thereof, of
racial bias in its electoral process and in its
decision to enact the felon disenfranchisement
provisions, counterbalance the contemporary
discriminatory effects that result from the
day-to-day functioning of Washington's criminal
justice system." In addition, the court concluded
that under Section 2 of the Voting Rights Act, the
"totality of the circumstances" did not support a
finding that the state's felon disenfranchisement
law results in racial discrimination.

The Ninth Circuit ruled that the Voting
Rights Act could be applied to felony disenfranchisement laws. The burden was on the plaintiffs
to prove racial discrimination. In this case the
plaintiffs had demonstrated that racial minorities
were overrepresented in the felon population
based upon factors that cannot be explained by
non-racial reasons. The plaintiffs had relied on
two academic studies, one statewide and one
from Seattle, to show that racial and ethnic
minority populations were disproportionally
stopped, search, arrested, convicted, and incarcerated in the state. One scholar stated that these
disparities were not "fully warranted by race or
ethnic differences in illegal behavior.

The state did not try to refute these facts,
concentrating instead on attacking the credibility of the plaintiffs' experts as to the ultimate
effect of Washington's felon disenfranchisement

law. It raised three claims, first attacking the extrapolation of the Seattle study findings to the entire state. The appeals court rejected this argument, noting that a large proportion of the state's minority population resides in Seattle and surrounding King County. It also found no merit in the state's claim that the district court's finding of discrimination was based solely on statistical disparity. The appeals court pointed out the EXPERT TESTIMONY that linked statistical disparity and disproportionality in the criminal justice system with discrimination. Finally, the court held that the plaintiffs did not need to show that bias in the criminal justice system was connected to the "ability of protected minorities to participate effectively in the political process." Under the law, disenfranchisement was automatic.

Based on the findings of fact, the court concluded that "Section 2 of the VRA demands that such racial discrimination not spread to the ballot box." The state claimed that even if there was racial bias in the criminal justice system because voters fully control whether they forfeit their right to vote under the felon disenfranchisement law. As long as voters "refrain from committing a felony," they will retain their right to vote. The appeals court dismissed this claim, stating that Section 2 gives those already disenfranchised the right to seek legal **redress**. Given the "uncontroverted showing" by plaintiffs of discrimination, the state law had to be struck down.

The dissenting member of the panel pointed out that Washington had enacted an amendment in 2009 that provides that the State will provisionally restore voting rights to felons convicted in Washington STATE COURTS so long as the individual is no longer under the authority of the Department of Corrections, and to those convicted of federal felonies or felonies in other states as long as the person is no longer incarcerated. The judge noted that as a result, "we are left to consider the Voting Rights Act challenge of only those felons still serving their prison terms. Both the parties and the courts have seemingly considered felons generally, as a single group; the bifurcation of classes of felons came about as a consequence of this new legislation. Thus, within this LITIGATION, no court has addressed whether these two sets of individuals present meaningful analytical differences."

Northwest Austin Municipal Utility District Number One v. Holder

State and local governments covered by Section 5 of the Voting Rights Act have expressed concerns in recent years that federal oversight of elections was either no longer needed or unconstitutional. The constitutionality of Section 5 was argued before the SUPREME COURT in *Northwest Austin Municipal Utility District Number One v. Holder*, __U.S.__, 129 S. Ct. 2504, 174 L. Ed. 2d 140 (2009). In a unanimous decision, the Court declined to address the constitutional question, resting its decision on an interpretation of the Voting Rights Act provision. Based on **statutory** interpretation, the Court held that all political subdivisions may seek removal of Section 5 coverage, even those that did not register voters.

Northwest Austin Municipal Utility District Number One was created in 1987 to provide city services to residents of a portion of Travis County, Texas. It is governed by a board of five members, elected to staggered terms of four years. The district does not register voters but it is responsible for its own elections. For administrative reasons alone, those elections are run by Travis County. Because the district is located in Texas, it is subject to the obligations of Section 5, although there was no evidence that it had ever discriminated on the basis of race.

The district filed suit in the **District Court** for the District of Columbia, seeking relief under the statute's so-called "bailout provisions." These provisions permit the federal court to remove an election unit from the oversight of Section 5. The district also argued that if it lost on this argument, it would argue Section 5 was unconstitutional. The three-judge panel rejected both claims, finding that under Section 5, only a "State or political subdivision" is permitted to seek removal from the Voting Rights Act provision. The court concluded that the district was not a political subdivision because that term includes only "counties, parishes, and voter-registering subunits." As to the constitutionality of Section 5, the court concluded that the 25-year extension of Section 5 was constitutional both because "Congress ... rationally concluded that extending [Section]5 was necessary to protect minorities from continued racial DISCRIMINATION in voting" and because "the 2006 Amendment qualifies as a congruent and proportional response to the continuing problem of racial discrimination in voting."

After the the Supreme Court agreed to hear the district's appeal, A large number of briefs were filed by state and local governments that addressed the constitutional question. Writing for the Court, Chief Justice JOHN ROBERTS stated that the "constitutional question has attracted ardent briefs from dozens of interested parties, but the importance of the question does not justify our rushing to decide it. Quite the contrary: Our usual practice is to avoid the unnecessary resolution of constitutional questions."

Roberts lauded the "historic accomplishments" of the Voting Rights Act but noted that Section 5 "which authorizes federal intrusion into sensitive areas of state and local policy-making, imposes substantial 'federalism costs.' "Section 5 went beyond the prohibition of the FIFTEENTH AMENDMENT by "suspending all changes to state election law—however innocuous—until they have been precleared by federal authorities in Washington, D. C." The preclearance requirement applies broadly and in particular to every political subdivision in a covered State, no matter how small. Though the **statute** had played a large part in eliminating racial discrimination in voting, "past successes alone" were not adequate justification for retaining preclearance requirements.

Robert reviewed the contemporary relevance of some of the data that was used to support enactment of the law in 1965 and expressed concern that the law did not take into account current political conditions. He noted that in 2009 the "racial gap in voter registration and turnout" was lower in the states originally covered by Section 5 than it was nationwide. The utility district contended that these deficiencies showed that Congress had gone beyond the authority of the Fifteenth Amendment in imposing Section 5 procedures on all political subdivisions. The Court rejected this constitutional challenge because of the "well-established principle governing the prudent exercise of this

Court's jurisdiction that normally the Court will not decide a constitutional question if there is some other ground upon which to dispose of the case." Because the district could obtain the relief it sought through its statutory argument, the Court declined to rule on the constitutional issue. However, Justice CLARENCE THOMAS, in a concurring opinion, contended the Court should have decided the case on constitutional grounds.

Turning to the language of Section 5, the Roberts pointed out that the district was a political subdivision of the State of Texas in the "ordinary sense of the term." However, the act stated that "where registration for voting is not conducted under the supervision of a county or parish, the term shall include any other subdivision of a State which conducts registration for voting." The district panel had ruled that because the utility district did not register voters, it could not seek a bailout from the act through Section 5. Roberts rejected this interpretation. It would, in the Court's view, only make sense if the provision was read in isolation from the rest of the law and the Court's prior decisions. Based on specific precedent, the structure of the Voting Rights Act, and underlying constitutional concerns," the Court concluded that it was compelled to reading the bailout provision broadly.

Roberts looked to prior Court decisions that permitted political subdivisions like school boards to obtain Section 5 removal. In addition, an amendment to the act in 1982 overhauled the removal provisions. Congress decided that a jurisdiction covered because it was within a covered state need not remain covered for as long as the state did. If the subdivision met the bailout requirements, it could bail out, even if the state could not. Because piecemeal bailout was now permitted, it made no sense to conclude that Section 5 treated every governmental unit as the state itself. Therefore, the Court held that the Voting Rights Act permits all political subdivisions, including the utility district, to seek relief from its preclearance requirements.

WHISTLEBLOWER

The disclosure by a person, usually an employee, in a government agency or private enterprise; to the public or to those in authority, of mismanagement, corruption, illegality, or some other wrong-doing.

Texas Nurse Found Not Guilty for Reporting Doctor

A nurse employed by a hospital in a small Texas town faced the possibility of spending 10 years in prison for reporting to state regulators that a doctor had practiced bad medicine. The nurse stood trial in February 2010, but a jury took less than hour to decide that the nurse was not guilty. The case made news nationally, with national organizations condemning the decision to go forward with the prosecution. The nurse and one of her colleagues responded by filing a civil lawsuit in federal court against several of the parties responsible for bringing the **criminal action**.

Anne Mitchell was a nurse at the Winkler Memorial Hospital in Kermit, Texas for about 25 years. Kermit is a town of about 5,200 near the New Mexico border, and the county in which the town is located has a difficult time attracting doctors and nurses. In fact, Winkler County employs a total of only three doctors and about a dozen nurses. In 2008, the Winkler Memorial Hospital hired Dr. Rolando G. Arafiles Jr., who had attended medical school in the Philippines and received medical training

in Baltimore and Buffalo. Arafiles is reportedly a proponent of alternative forms of medicine, such as the use of herbal supplements. The hospital hired Arafiles even though the Texas Medical Board in April 2007 had fined Arafiles for actions related to his job to oversee medical care at a weight-loss clinic. According to the order, Arafiles and supervised a physician assistant and oversaw the protocol for using phentermine and amphetamine, which are used respectively as an appetite suppressant and as a treatment for obesity.

Mitchell and a fellow nurse, Vickilyn Galle, said that they began to see a pattern of improper procedures. The nurses said they saw Arafiles perform a skin graft in the emergency room, even though Arafiles did not have surgical privileges. Arafiles also sutured a rubber tip to a patient's crushed fingers in an action that the Texas DEPARTMENT OF STATE Health Services later said was inappropriate. The nurses likewise reported that Arafiles would send email messages to patients about an herbal supplement that he sold on the side. The nurses reported their concerns to hospital administrators, but the nurses said the administrators did not take adequate action.

Under Texas law, a nurse may report complaints about physicians to the Texas Medical Board. Section 301.4025 of the Texas Occupations Code provides, "In a written, signed report to the appropriate licensing board or accrediting body, a nurse may report a

Anne Mitchell appears in the Andrews, Texas courthouse, February 11, 2010.

AP IMAGES

licensed health care practitioner, agency, or facility that the nurse has reasonable cause to believe has exposed a patient to substantial risk of harm as a result of failing to provide patient care that conforms to: (1) minimum standards of acceptable and prevailing professional practice, for a report made regarding a practitioner; or (2) **statutory**, regulatory, or accreditation standards, for a report made regarding an agency or facility." Consistent with this **statute**, Mitchell and Galle decided to send a letter to Texas Medical Board. In this letter, the nurses noted six cases of concern, identified only by the file numbers and not by the patient names. The nurses drafted the letter on a hospital computer but submitted the letter anonymously.

The Texas Medical Board informed Arafiles of the anonymous complaint against him. He turned to a friend, Winkler County Sheriff Robert Roberts, who credits Arafiles from saving his life after suffering a heart attack. Roberts obtained a SEARCH WARRANT to search the nurses' work computers, and he found the letter sent to the medical board. From that point, county PROSE-CUTOR Scott M. Tidwell decided to press charges against Mitchell and Galle, claiming that the nurses had committed the crime of "misuse of official information." The charges were based on section 39.06 of the Texas Penal Code, which

establishes: "A public servant commits an offense if with intent to obtain a benefit or with intent to harm or DEFRAUD another, he discloses or uses information for a nongovernmental purpose that: (1) he has access to by means of his office or employment; and (2) has not been made public."

Both Mitchell and Galle had been fired from their jobs in June 2009, and neither were able to find other positions. Nursing organizations came to their defense, though, raising about $40,000 for the nurses' legal fees. The executive director of the Texas Medical Board, Mari E. Robinson, also criticized the prosecution, saying it would have "a significant chilling effect" on reporting of MALPRACTICE claims. The prosecutor dropped the case against Galle but decided to proceed against Mitchell, who faced 10 years in prison and a $10,000 fine if convicted.

The case caused a fierce debate in Kermit, and because of various conflicts of interest in the dispute, the case was moved several miles away to a court in Andrew, Texas. The prosecution tried to claim that Mitchell had sent the letter in **bad faith** and that she had sent the report intending to harm Arafiles' reputation. Witnesses for the prosecution testified that Mitchell had called Arafiles a "witch doctor." The defense countered with evidence of various concerns about Arafiles, including testimony from other nurses who said that Mitchell's complaints were legitimate. In the end, the jury sided with Mitchell, with individual jurors even questioning why she was prosecuted in the first place. According to the jury foreman, Harley D. Tyler, "We just didn't see the wrongdoing of sending the file numbers in, since she's a nurse."

Attorneys for Mitchell and Galle noted that the result of the criminal prosecution had not made the nurses whole and that they would press on with the civil trial. The nurses have sued the county, the hospital, the sheriff, the doctor, and the prosecutor.

WHITE COLLAR CRIME

Former Attorney Receives 99-Year Sentence for Investment Scam

Edward Digges Jr. was once the top billing partner at a large law firm in Maryland during the 1980s. However, he had a dramatic fall from grace as he ended up serving time in a federal prison for a series of scams he perpetrated while at the firm. Years later, Digges once again devised a scam involving investments in credit-card terminals. In 2010, a jury in Collin County, Texas convicted Digges on charges of SECURITIES fraud and sentenced him to 99 years in prison.

Digges' story has its origins in the early 1980s. He was a graduate of Princeton University and the University of Maryland School of Law. By the time he was in his mid-30s, he had represented major companies such as Mazda Motor Corp. and Bell Helicopter Textron, Inc., and he had written a form book on Maryland **civil procedure**. He was a managing partner with the Maryland law firm of Piper & Marbury, which had been hired by Texas-based Dresser Industries to defend the company in a number of lawsuits related to asbestos. In 1984, Digges left Piper & Marbury, forming a new firm known as Digges, Wharton & Levin, and the new firm handled Dresser's representation. As of 1988, Dresser was involved in more than 1,000 asbestos cases and was represented by Digges, Wharton & Levin in each of them.

Executives with Dresser became concerned about the size of the law firm's bills. When the company performed an audit of the firm in May 1988, auditors discovered a number of discrepancies that led executives to believe that the company had been significantly overcharged. The company's attempts to negotiate with the law firm failed, and Dresser quickly discharged the law firm. In February 1989, Dresser sued the law firm and the individual partners for LEGAL MALPRACTICE. Evidence from this case revealed that the firm had engaged in what a court later dubbed "value billing," through which partners charged the client what the partners thought the services were worth. However, since Dresser had agreed on an hourly billing structure, the firm had to adjust the hours upward so that the hours matched the amount billed. One associate with the firm billed more than 24 hours in a single day on several occasions in 1988. The law firm also inflated a number of other charges. For instance, the firm had once spent $400 on LEXIS online research charges. However, the firm billed—and Dresser had paid— more than $66,000 for the same charges.

On August 30, 1989, a federal **district court** in Maryland ruled in favor of Dresser on claims of FRAUD, deceit, and breach of contract. *Dresser Industries, Inc. v. Digges*, Civ. No. JH-89-485, 1989 WL 139234 (D. Md. Aug. 30, 1989). The court awarded Dresser a total of more than $3.6 million and held each partner jointly and severally liable. In November 1989, Digges was indicted for **mail fraud** based on his activities with the firm. He was disbarred by the Maryland State Bar Association in January 1990, five days before he pled guilty to the MAIL FRAUD charge. A court sentenced him to 30 months in prison, and the court ordered him to pay $1 million in **restitution** to Dresser.

Digges' former partners and colleagues were puzzled what would lead to such a dramatic fall from grace. He was reportedly thought of as a solid family man and talented litigator. His father was a partner with a law firm in LaPlata, Maryland. Moreover, nobody found evidence that his judgment had been impaired by drugs, alcohol, or mental illness. However, some speculated that he was driven strictly by greed. One partner testified during the trial that Digges had withdrawn more than a million dollars from client accounts to renovate his farm on Maryland's Atlantic shore.

More than 16 years after his disbarment, Digges was accused of masterminding another scam. In 2003, Digges established what was called the Millennium Terminal Investment Program. In this program, he attempted to find individuals who would invest their money in credit card terminals, which are typically used by merchants in retail businesses to swipe credit and debit cards. Digges promised the investors they would receive at least a 12 percent return on their investment, and after five years, he promised he would return the original investment of $5,000. Digges falsely stated that other individuals managed the program, hiding the fact that Digges had been disbarred for **fraudulent** activity in the past.

In 2003 and 2004, state securities commissioners in Pennsylvania and Maryland issued orders instructing Digges's business to stop selling the credit-card terminal investments. Officials in Ohio in 2004 also concluded that the scheme violated Ohio securities law. However, Digges continued to sell the investments by using different companies. In 2006, the SECURITIES AND EXCHANGE COMMISSION finally became involved, filing a civil complaint against Digges. The complaint alleged that Digges had sold the investment to more than 275 individuals and had raised more than $15 million. Reports later indicated that the scam had financed Digges' personal expenses, including a boat and a Jaguar. The program never earned a profit, and any amounts that investors received had come from the money taken in from new investors, making the scam a so-called **Ponzi scheme**.

The Texas State Securities Board began to review Digges' company in 2005. The investigation revealed that about 130 of Digges' investors came from Texas, and several of these investors put substantial amounts of money into Digges' company. One investor named Jesse C. Dotson invested $495,000 in the scam, and several others likewise put in more than $100,000 each. The investigation led to Digges' prosecution in Collin County, Texas. Digges served as his own counsel at trial but was unsuccessful at defending himself. A jury found him guilty on a series of charges related to the scheme and sentenced him to 99 years in prison.

Individual investors were unable to collect more than a small percentage of the money they put in. Texas Securities Commissioner Denise Voigt Crawford noted that the sentence would ensure that Digges would never DEFRAUD citizens again. However, she stressed that the case "highlights the importance of checking the background of any financial professional you choose to do business with, and the importance of obtaining full disclosure before investing."

Commerical Law

CREDIT CARDHOLDERS' BILL OF RIGHTS ACT OF 2008 (EXCERPTS)

To amend the Truth in Lending Act to establish fair and transparent practices relating to the extension of credit under an open end consumer credit plan, and for other purposes.

Be it enacted by the Senate and House of Representatives of the United States of America in Congress assembled,

SEC. 2. CREDIT CARDS ON TERMS CONSUMERS CAN REPAY.

(a) Universal Default Eliminated- Chapter 2 of the Truth in Lending Act (15 U.S.C. 1631 et seq.) is amended by inserting after section 127A the following new section:

(a) Universal Default Eliminated for Credit Already Outstanding- No creditor may use any adverse information concerning any consumer, including any information in any consumer report (as defined in section 603) or any change in the credit score of the consumer, as the basis for increasing any annual percentage rate of interest applicable to the outstanding balance on a credit card account of the consumer under an open end consumer credit plan at the time of any such increase, other than actions or omissions of the consumer that are directly related to such account.

(b) Any-Time Any-Reason Changes in Terms Eliminated-

(1) IN GENERAL- No creditor may change any term of the contract or agreement applicable with respect to any credit card account of the consumer under an open end consumer credit plan until renewal of the contract or agreement except for the specific material reasons, and subject to specific limitations, that are contained in the contract or agreement with respect to such term at the time the account is opened.

(2) EXCEPTION FOR INCREASES IN CREDIT LIMIT- Paragraph (1) shall not apply with respect to any increase in the amount of credit authorized to be extended under an account described in such paragraph.

(1) ADVANCE NOTICE OF CREDIT CARD ACCOUNT RATE INCREASES REQUIRED- In the case of any credit card account under an open end consumer credit plan, no increase in any annual percentage rate of interest, for any reason other than an increase due to the expiration of any introductory percentage rate of interest, or due solely to a change in another rate of interest to which such rate is indexed, may take effect before the end of the 45-day period beginning on the date notice of such increase is sent to the cardholder.

(2) RIGHT TO CANCEL WITHOUT INCREASE IN APR ON OUTSTANDING BALANCE- Any consumer who receives a notice from a creditor pursuant to paragraph (1) with respect to a credit card account under an open end consumer credit plan shall have the right–

(A) to cancel the credit card, by mail, telephone, or electronic communication and without penalty or the imposition of any fee with respect to such cancellation, at any time during the period beginning on the date the consumer receives the notice pursuant to paragraph (1) and ending on the date the consumer receives the third periodic statement with respect to such account after the effective date of the increase; and

(B) to pay any outstanding balance on the credit card account that accrued before the effective date of the increase at the annual percentage rate and repayment period in effect before the notice was received.

(3) NOTICE REQUIREMENTS-

(A) INITIAL NOTICE REQUIREMENT- The notice required under paragraph (1) with respect to an increase in any annual percentage rate of interest shall–

(i) be made in a clear and conspicuous manner; and

(ii) contain a brief statement of the right of the consumer to cancel the account and pay the balance at the annual percentage rate in effect before the increase in accordance with paragraph (2) and the mailing address, telephone-number, and Internet address and Worldwide Web site at which the consumer may make any such cancellation.

(B) SUBSEQUENT NOTICES REQUIRED IN PERIODIC STATEMENTS- Each periodic statement provided to the consumer with respect to the credit card account after a notice is provided under paragraph (1) until the third periodic statement with respect to such account after the effective date of the increase shall also contain the information required in such notice.

(C) PRO FORMA NOTICES DO NOT MEET NOTICE REQUIREMENT- A notice that terms may change, or will change, for any or no reason does not constitute a notice for purposes of this subsection.

(4) PAYMENT OF POST-INCREASE EX-TENSIONS OF CREDIT- If any consumer obtains an extension of credit on a credit card account on or after the effective date of the increase in the annual percentage rate for which a notice was provided in accordance with paragraph (1) and subsequently cancels the account under paragraph (2), the outstanding balance of such credit that was extended on or after the effective date of the increase shall be subject to repayment at the increased rate in effect at the time of the extension of credit.

Murder

"DREW'S LAW" (EXCERPT)

Provides that a statement is not rendered inadmissible by the hearsay rule if it is offered against a party that has killed the declarant in violation of the first degree murder statute intending to procure the unavailability of the declarant as a witness in a criminal or civil proceeding. Provides that while intent to procure the unavailability of the witness is a necessary element for the introduction of the statements, it need not be the sole motivation behind the murder which procured the unavailability of the declarant as a witness. Provides that the murder of the declarant may, but need not, be the subject of the trial at which the statement is being offered. Provides that if the murder of the declarant is not the subject of the trial at which the statement is being offered, the murder need not have ever been prosecuted. Provides that the admissibility of the statements shall be determined by the court at a pretrial hearing. Establishes criteria which such statement may be admitted into evidence.

Executive Orders: 2009

The order number is given first, followed by subject and Federal Register page number and date of publication.

Executive Order 13489: Presidential Records; 74 FR 4669, January 26, 2009

Executive Order 13490: Ethics Commitments by Executive Branch Personnel; 74 FR 4673, January 26, 2009

Executive Order 13491: Ensuring Lawful Interrogation; 74 FR 4673, January 26, 2009

Executive Order 13492: Review and Disposition of Individuals Detained at the Guantanamo Bay Naval Base and Close of Detention Facilities; 74 FR 4897, January 27, 2009

Executive Order 13493: Review of Detention Policy Options; 74 FR 4901, January 27, 2009

Executive Order 13494: Economy in Government Contracts; 74 FR 6101, February 4, 2009

Executive Order 13495: Nondisplacement of Qualified Workers Under Service Contracts; 74 FR 6103, February 4, 2009

Executive Order 13496: Notification of Employee Rights Under Federal Labor Laws; 74 FR 6107, February 4, 2009

Executive Order 13497: Revocation of Certain Executive Orders Concerning Regulatory Planning and Review; 74 FR 6113, February 4, 2009

Executive Order 13498: Amendments to Executive Order 13199 and Establishment of the President's Advisory Council for Faith-Based and Neighborhood Partnerships; 74 FR 6533, February 9, 2009

Executive Order 13499: Further Amendments to Executive Order 12835, Establishment of the National Economic Council; 74 FR 6979, February 11, 2009

Executive Order 13500: Further Amendments to Executive Order 12859, Establishment of the Domestic Policy Council; 74 FR 6981, February 11, 2009

Executive Order 13501: Establishing the President's Economic Recovery Advisory Board; 74 FR 6893, February 11, 2009

Executive Order 13502: Use of Project Labor Agreements for Federal Construction Projects; 74 FR 6985, February 11, 2009

Executive Order 13503: Establishment of the White House Office of Urban Affairs; 74 FR 8139, February 24, 2009

Executive Order 13504: Amending Executive Order 13390; 74 FR 8431, February 24, 2009

Executive Order 13505: Removing Barriers to Responsible Scientific Research Involving Human Stem Cells; 74 FR 10667, March 11, 2009

Executive Order 13506: Establishing a White House Council on Women and Girls; 74 FR 11271, March 16, 2009

Executive Order 13507: Establishment of the White House Office of Health Reform; 74 FR 17071, April 13, 2009

Executive Order 13508: Chesapeake Bay Protection and Restoration; 74 FR 23099, May 15, 2009

Executive Order 13509: Establishing a White House Council on Automotive Communities and Workers; 74 FR 30903, June 26, 2009

Executive Order 13510: Waiver Under the Trade Act of 1974 With Respect to the Republic of Belarus; 74 FR 32047, July 6, 2009

Executive Order 13511: Continuance of Certain Federal Advisory Committees; 74 FR 50909, October 1, 2009

Executive Order 13512: Amending Executive Order 13390; 74 FR 50911, October 2, 2009

Executive Order 13513: Federal Leadership on Reducing Text Messaging While Driving; 74 FR 51225, October 6, 2009

Executive Order 13514: Federal Leadership in Environmental, Energy, and Economic Performance; 74 FR 52117, October 8, 2009

Executive Order 13515: Increasing Participation of Asian Americans and Pacific Islanders in Federal Programs; 74 FR 53635, October 19, 2009

Executive Order 13516: Amending Executive Order 13462; 74 FR 56521, November 2, 2009, then corrected in 74 FR 56521, November 2, 2009

Executive Order 13517: Amendments to Executive Orders 13183 and 13494; 74 FR 57239, November 5, 2009

Executive Order 13518: Employment of Veterans in the Federal Government; 74 FR 58533, November 13, 2009

Executive Order 13519: Establishment of the Financial Fraud Enforcement Task Force; 74 FR 60123, November 19, 2009

Executive Order 13520: Reducing Improper Payments; 74 FR 62201, November 25, 2009

Executive Order 13521: Establishing the Presidential Commission for the Study of Bioethical Issues; 74 FR 62671, November 30, 2009

Executive Order 13522: Creating Labor-Management Forums to Improve Delivery of Government Services; 74 FR 66203, December 14, 2009

Executive Order 13523: Half-Day Closing of Executive Departments and Agencies on Thursday, December 24, 2009; 74 FR 66563, December 16, 2009

Executive Order 13524: Amending Executive Order 12425 Designating Interpol as a Public International Organization Entitled To Enjoy Certain Privileges, Exemptions, and Immunities; 74 FR 67803, December 21, 2009

Executive Order 13525: Adjustments of Certain Rates of Pay; 74 FR 69231, December 30, 2009

Executive Order 13526: Classified National Security Information; 75 FR 707, January 5, 2010, then corrected in 75 FR 1013, January 8, 2010

Executive Order 13527: Establishing Federal Capability for the Timely Provision of Medical

Countermeasures Following a Biological Attack; 75 FR 737, January 6, 2010

Executive Orders: 2010

Executive Order 13528: Establishment of the Council of Governors; 75 FR 2053, January 14, 2010

Executive Order 13529: Ordering the Selected Reserve and Certain Individual Ready Reserve Members of the Armed Forces to Active Duty; 75 FR 3331, January 21, 2010

Executive Order 13530: President's Advisory Council on Financial Capability; 75 FR 5481, February 3, 2010

Executive Order 13531: National Commission on Fiscal Responsibility and Reform; 75 FR 7927, February 23, 2010

Executive Order 13532: Promoting Excellence, Innovation,and Sustainability at Historically Black Colleges and Universities; 75 FR 9749, March 3, 2010

Executive Order 13533: Providing an Order of Succession Within the Department of Defense; 75 FR 10163, March 5, 2010

Executive Order 13534: National Export Initiative; 75 FR 12433, March 16, 2010

Executive Order 13535: Ensuring Enforcement and Implementation of Abortion Restrictions in the Patient Protection and Affordable Care Act; 75 FR 15599, March 29, 2010

Executive Order 13536: Blocking Property of Certain Persons Contributing to the Conflict in Somalia; 75 FR 19869, April 15, 2010

Executive Order 13537: Interagency Group on Insular Affairs; 75 FR 20237, April 19, 2010

Executive Order 13538: Establishing the President's Management Advisory Board; 75 FR 20895, April 22, 2010

Executive Order 13539: President's Council of Advisors on Science and Technology; 75 FR 21973, April 27, 2010

Executive Order 13540: Interagency Task Force on Veterans Small Business Development; 75 FR 22497, April 29, 2010

Executive Order 13541: Temporary Organization To Facilitate a Strategic Partnership With the Republic of Iraq; 75 FR 26879, May 12, 2010

Executive Order 13542: Providing an Order of Succession Within the Department of Agriculture; 75 FR 27921, May 18, 2010

Executive Order 13543: National Commission on the BP Deepwater Horizon Oil Spill and Offshore Drilling; 75 FR 29397, May 26, 2010

Executive Order 13544: Establishing the National Prevention, Health Promotion, and Public Health Council; 75 FR 33983, June 16, 2010

Executive Order 13545: President's Council on Fitness, Sports, and Nutrition; 75 FR 37283, June 28, 2010

Executive Order 13546: Optimizing the Security of Biological Select Agents and Toxins in the United States; 75 FR 39439, July 8, 2010

Executive Order 13547: Stewardship of the Ocean, Our Coasts, and the Great Lakes; 75 FR 43023, July 22, 2010

Executive Order 13548: Increasing Federal Employment of Individuals With Disabilities; 75 FR 45039, July 30, 2010

BIBLIOGRAPHY

AFFIRMATIVE ACTION

Ricci v. DeStefano

Covington, Robert and Decker, Kurt. *Employment Law in a Nutshell.* Saint Paul, MN: West Group. 2002. Second Edition.

Lewis, Jr., Harold and Norman, Elizabeth. *Civil Rights Law and Practice.* Saint Paul, MN: West Gropu. 2004.

Vieira, Norman. *Constitutional Civil Rights in a Nutshell.* Saint Paul, MN.: West Group. 1998.

ANTITRUST LAW

American Needle, Inc. v. National Football League

Mauro, Tony. "High Court Broadsides NFL in Antitrust Case." *National Law Journal.* May 25, 2010.

"Throwing the Rule Book at the N.F.L." *New York Times.* May 26, 2010.

ARBITRATION

Jackson v. Rent-a-Center West

Gans, David H. "Why the Supreme Court's Decision in Rent-a-Center v. Jackson Matters". Constitutional Accountability Center. June 22, 2010.

Horton, David. "The Mandatory Core of Section 4 of the Federal Arbitration Act." *In Brief: The Online Magazine of the Virginia Law Review.* April 2, 2010.

Stolt-Nielsen v. AnimalFeeds International

"Stolt-Nielsen S.A. v. AnimalFeeds International," Cornell University School of Law Available at http://www.law.cornell.edu/supct/cert/08-1198.html

Stolt-Nielsen S.A. v. AnimalFeeds International, No. 08-1198, Available at www.supremecourt.gov/opinions/09.pdf/08-1198.pdf

The Oyez Project. "Stolt-Nielsen S.A. v. AnimalFeeds International," U.S. Supreme Court Media Report, 1 June 2010. Available at http://www.oyez.org/cases/2000-2009/2009/2009_08_1198

ATTORNEY-CLIENT PRIVILEGE

Mohawk Industries, Inc. v. Carpenter

Chemerinsky, Erwin. 2007. *Federal Jurisdiction.* 5th ed. Boston: Aspen.

Little, Laura. 2007. *Federal Courts Examples & Explanations.* Boston: Aspen.

Wright, Charles Alan. 2002. *Law of Federal Courts.* 6th ed. St. Paul, Minn.: West Group.

ATTORNEY

Second Circuit Affirms Conviction of Civil Rights Attorney

Carmella, Jay. "Second Circuit Affirms Civil Rights Lawyer Lynee Stewart Conviction." *Jurist,* 17 November 2009.

Jones, Ashby. "Lynne Stewart's Conviction Upheld; StewartOrdered to Jail." *Wall Street Journal,* 17 November 2009.

United States v. Stewart, No. 06-5015 (2009), available at http://www.ca2.uscourts.gov/decisions/isysquery/6f9dbbc4.5cf8

ATTORNEY'S FEES

Astrue v. Ratliff

Astrue v. Ratliff, Cornell University School of Law Available at http://www.law.cornell.edu/supct/cert/08-1322.htm

229

Astrue v. Ratliff, Available at www.supremecourt.gov/ opinions/08-1322.htm

Astrue v. Ratliff, No. 08-1322, Available at www. supremecourt.gov/opinions/09pdf/08-1322.pdf

"Court Grants Fee-Shifting Case." *On the Docket,* U.S. Supreme Court Media Report, 30 September 2009. Available at http://otd.oyez.org/cases/2009/ astrue-v-ratliff

"Justices Back Clients Over Attorneys in Fee-Shifting Case." *On the Docket,* U.S. Supreme Court Media Report, 14 June 2010. Available at http://otd .oyez.org/cases/2009/astrue-v-ratliff

PERDUE V. KENNY A.

Biggs, Keith. 2009. *Lawyers Costs and Fees: Fees and Fixed Costs in Civil Actions.* 15th Ed. London: Tottel Publising.

MacKinnon, F.B. 2008. *Contingent Fees for Legal Services: Professional Economics and Responsibilities.* Edison, N.J.: Aldine Transaction.

Parker, Kristine. 2007. *Inside Lawyers' Ethics.* New York: Cambridge Univ. Press.

BANKRUPTCY

HAMILTON V. LANNING

Hamilton v. Lanning, Cornell University School of Law Available at http://www.law.cornell.edu/ supct/cert/08-998.htm

Hamilton v. Lanning, Available at www .supremecourt.gov/opinions/08-998.htm

Hamilton v. Lanning, Available at www .supremecourt.gov/opinions/09pdf/08-998.pdf

The Oyez Project. "Hamilton v. Lanning." U.S. Supreme Court Media Report, accessed on 3 June 2010. Available at http://www.oyez.org/cases/ 2000-2009/2009/2009_08_998

"Supreme Court Decides 'Hamilton v. Lanning.'" Martindale Legal News, June 2010. Available at http://www.martincale.com/legal-news

MILAVETZ, GALLOP & MILAVETZ, P.A. V. U.S.

Blum, Brian. 2006. *Bankruptcy and Debtor/Creditor.* 4th Ed. Boston: Aspen Publishers.

Elias, Stephen. 2007. *How to File for Chapter 7 Bankruptcy.* 14th Ed. San Francisco: Nolo Press.

Epstein, Richard. 2005. *Bankruptcy and Related Law in a Nutshell.* 7th Ed. St. Paul: West.

UNITED STUDENT AID FUNDS, INC. V. ESPINOSA

Blum, Brian. 2006. *Bankruptcy and Debtor/Creditor.* 4th Ed. Boston: Aspen Publishers.

Elias, Stephen. 2007. *How to File for Chapter 7 Bankruptcy.* 14th Ed. San Francisco: Nolo Press.

Epstein, Richard. 2005. *Bankruptcy and Related Law in a Nutshell.* 7th Ed. St. Paul: West.

SCHWAB V. REILLY

Blum, Brian. 2006. *Bankruptcy and Debtor/Creditor.* 4th Ed. Boston: Aspen Publishers.

Elias, Stephen. 2007. *How to File for Chapter 7 Bankruptcy.* 14th Ed. San Francisco: Nolo Press.

Epstein, Richard. 2005. *Bankruptcy and Related Law in a Nutshell.* 7th Ed. St. Paul: West.

BANKS AND BANKING

CUOMO, ATTORNEY GENERAL OF NEW YORK V. CLEARING HOUSE ASSOCIATION LLC

Epstein, Richard. 2007. *Federal Preemption.* AEI Press.

O'Reilly, James. 2006. *Federal Preemption of State and Local Law.* American Bar Association.

Zimmerman, Joseph. 2006. *Congressional Preemption.* State University of New York Press.

BLACKMAIL

DAVID LETTERMAN PART OF AN EXTORTION PLOT

Daly, Michael. "Robert 'Joe' Halderman's Dream of $2M Payday Became His Own Nightmare." *New York Daily News.* October 4, 2009.

Italiano, Laura. "Letterman Blackmail 'Revenge'" *New York Post.* October 7, 2009.

CABLE TELEVISION

D.C. CIRCUIT OVERTURNS FCC CABLE OWNERSHIP RULE

National Cable and Telecommunications Association. Available online at <www.ncta.com> (accessed April 25, 2010).

Robichaux, Mark. 2002. *Cable Cowboy: John Malone and the Rise of the Modern Cable Business.* New York: John Wiley.

Parsons, Patrick. 2008. *Blue Skies: A History of Cable Television.* Philadelphia: Temple Univ. Press.

CAMPAIGN FINANCE

CITIZENS UNITED V. FEDERAL ELECTION COMMISSION

Barron, Jerome, Dienes, Thomas. 2004. *First Amendment Law in a Nutshell, 3rd ed.* West Group.

Currinder, Marian. 2008. *Money In the House: Campaign Funds and Congressional Party Politics.* Boulder: Westview Press.

Farber, Daniel. 2002. *The First Amendment: Concepts and Insights.* Foundation Press.

LaRaja, Raymond J. 2008. *Small Change: Money, Political Parties, and Campaign Finance Reform.* Lansing: University of Michigan Press.

Pinaire, Brian. 2008. *The Constitution of Electoral Speech.* Palo Alto: Stanford Law Books.

CAPITAL PUNISHMENT

SMITH V. SPISAK

Cammack, Mark. 2006 *Advanced Criminal Procedure in a Nutshell.* 2d ed. St. Paul, Minn.: Thomson West.

CLASS ACTION

SHADY GROVE ORTHOPEDIC ASSOCIATES, P.A. V. ALLSTATE INSURANCE CO.

Chemerinsky, Erwin. 2007. *Federal Jurisdiction.* 5th ed. Boston: Aspen.

Little, Laura. 2007*Federal Courts Examples & Explanations..* Boston: Aspen.

Wright, Charles Alan. 2002. *Law of Federal Courts.* 6th ed. St. Paul, Minn.: West Group.

COMITY

LEVIN V. COMMERCE ENERGY

"Court Rules in Ohio Tax Dispute." *On the Docket,* U.S. Supreme Court Media Report, 1 June 2010. Available at http://otd.oyez.org/cases/2009/levin-v-commerce-energy

"Court Takes Ohio Tax Case." *On the Docket,* U.S. Supreme Court Media Report, 2 November 2009 2010. Available at http://otd.oyez.org/cases/2009/levin-v-commerce-energy

Levin v. Commerce Energy, Cornell University School of Law Available at http://www.law.cornell.edu/supct/cert/09-223.htm

Levin v. Commerce Energy, Inc., No. 09-223, Available at www.supremecourt.gov/opinions/09-223.htm

Levin v. Commerce Energy Inc., No. 09-223, Available at www.supremecourt.gov/opinions/09pdf/09-223.pdf

COMMERCIAL LAW

CONGRESS PASSES THE CREDIT CARD ACCOUNTABILITY RESPONSIBILITY AND DISCLOSURE ACT OF 2009

Press Release. "Fact Sheet: Reforms to Protect American Credit Card Holders." May 22, 2009. http://www.whitehouse.gov/the_press_office/Fact-Sheet-Reforms-to-Protect-American-Credit-Card-Holders/

Sidel, Robin. "Credit-Card Fees: The New Traps." *Wall Street Journal.* February 20, 2010.

CONFLICT OF LAWS

KAWASAKI KISEN KAISHA V. REGAL-BELOIT

"Court Rules in Cargo Liability Case." *On the Docket,* U.S. Supreme Court Media Report, 21 June 2010. Available at http://otd.oyez.org/cases/2009/kawasaki-kisen-kaisha-v-regal-beloit-union-pacific-railroad...

"Justices Will Hear Cargo Case." *On the Docket,* U.S. Supreme Court Media Report, 20 October 2009. Available at http://otd.oyez.org/cases/2009/kawasaki-kisen-kaisha-v-regal-beloit-union-pacific-railroad...

Kawasaki Kisen Kaisha v. Regal-Beloit, Cornell University School of Law Available at http://www.law.cornell.edu/supct/cert/08-1553ZS.html

Kawasaki Kisen Kaisha v. Regal-Beloit, No. 08-1553, Available at www.supremecourt.gov/opinions/08-1553.htm

Kawasaki Kisen Kaisha v. Regal-Beloit, No. 08-1553, Available at www.supremecourt.gov/opinions/09pdf/08-1553.pdf

CONSTITUTIONAL LAW

KIYEMBA V. OBAMA

Barnes, Robert. "Supreme Court Dismisses Case Involving Resettlement of Guantanamo Detainees" *The Washington Post.* March 2, 2010.

Bravin, Jess. "Supreme Court Dismisses Uighurs' Appeals." *Wall Street Journal.* March 2, 2010.

CONTEMPT

HORNE V. FLORES

Abernathy, Scott. 2007. *No Child Left Behind and the Public Schools.* Ann Arbor, Mich.: University of Michigan Press.

Yudof, Mark G., David L. Kirp, and Betsy Levin. 2001. *Educational Policy and the Law.* 4d ed. San Francisco: Wadsworth.

COPYRIGHT

MUSIC PUBLISHERS' ASSOCIATION FILES COPYRIGHT INFRINGEMENT SUITS AGAINST ONLINE PUBLISHERS OF SONG LYRICS

Christman, Ed. "Publishers File Suit Against Lyric Sites." Billboard.biz. August 24, 2009.

Miller, Jay. "Music Publishers Group Files Copyright Suit." *Wall Street Journal.* August 24, 2009.

REED ELSEVIER, INC. V. MUCHNICK

Klien, Sheldon. 2009. "Introduction to Trademarks: Patents, Copyrights, Trademarks and Literary Property Course Handbook Series." *Practicing Law Institute* Pat 123.

Miller, Arthur, and Davis, Michael. 2007. *Intellectual Property-Patents, Trademarks And Copyright in a Nutshell.* St. Paul, Minn.: Thomson West.

CORRUPTION

CONVICTION OF FORMER CONGRESSMAN WILLIAM JEFFERSON

"Former Congressman William J. Jefferson Sentenced to 13 Years in Prison for Bribery and Other Charges." U.S. Department of Justice Press release, 13 November 2009. Available at http://washingtondc.fbi.gov/dojpressrel/pressrel09/wfo111309b.htm

Markon, Jerry and Brigid Schulte. "Jury Convicts Former Congressman Jefferson of Bribery." *Washington Post,* 5 August 2009.

Stout, David. "Ex-Rep. Jefferson Convicted in Bribery Scheme." *New York Times,* 6 August 2009.

FORMER NEW YORK POLICE COMMISSIONER SENTENCED TO PRISON

Dolnick, Sam. "Kerik Is Sentenced in Corruption Case." *New York Times,* 18 February 2010.

Gearty, Robert and Greg B. Smith. "Bernard Kerik Pleads Guilty to Lying About Payoff..." *New York Daily News,* 5 November 2009.

Linzer, Dafna. "Kerik, Indicted on Corruption Charges, Pleads Not Guilty." *Washington Post,* 10 November 2007.

CRIMINAL LAW

NBA STAR GILBERT ARENAS PLEADS GUILTY TO GUN CHARGE

"Arenas Suspended Indefinitely." ESPN.com. January 7, 2010.

Beck, Howard. "Wizards' Arenas Is Charged with Felony." *New York Times.* January 15, 2010.

CRIMINAL PROCEDURE

BLACK V. UNITED STATES

Bravin, Jess. "Justices Question Antifraud Law." *Wall Street Journal.* December 9, 2009.

Liptak, Adam. "A Question of When Dishonesty Becomes Criminal." *New York Times.* October 12. 2009.

DEATH AND DYING

NUMEROUS LEGAL ISSUES SURROUND MICHAEL JACKSON'S DEATH

Pawlowski, A. "Battles Over Jackson's Kids, Assets May Loom." CNN.com. June 26, 2009.

Yoshino, Kimi and Andrew Blankstein. "'Lethal Levels' of Anesthetic Propofol Killed Michael Jackson." *Los Angeles Times.* August 24, 2009.

DEBTOR AND CREDITOR

JERMAN V. CARLISLE

"Court Rules Against Debt Collector in 'Bona Fide Error' Case." *On the Docket,* U.S. Supreme Court Media Report, 21 April 2010. Available at http://otd.oyez.org/cases/2009/jerman-v-carlisle

"Court Takes Debt Collection Case." *On the Docket,* U.S. Supreme Court Media Report, 29 June 2009. Available at http://otd.oyez.org/cases/2009/jerman-v-carlisle

Jerman v. Carlisle, Cornell University School of Law Available at http://www.law.cornell.edu/supct/cert/08-1200.htm

Jerman v. Carlisle, No. 08-1200, Available at www.supremecourt.gov/opinions/08-1200.htm

DEPORTATION

CARACHURI-ROSENDO V. HOLDER

Carachuri-Rosendo v. Holder, Cornell University School of Law Available at http://www.law.cornell.edu/supct/cert/09-60.htm

Carachuri-Rosendo v. Holder, No. 08-1200, Available at www.supremecourt.gov/opinions/09-60.htm

Carachuri-Rosendo v. Holder, No. 07-8521, Available at www.supremecourt.gov/opinions/09pdf/09-60.pdf

The Oyez Project. "Carachuri-Rosendo v. Holder." U.S. Supreme Court Media Report. Available at http://www.oyez.org/cases/2000-2009/2009/2009_09_60

DISPARATE IMPACT

LEWIS V. CITY OF CHICAGO

"Court Backs African-Americans in Firefighter Discrimination Case." *On the Docket,* U.S. Supreme Court Media Report, 24 May 2010. Available at http://otd.oyez.org/cases/2009/lewis-v-city-of-chicago

Lewis v. City of Chicago, Cornell University School of Law Available at http://www.law.cornell.edu/supct/cert/08-974.htm

Lewis v. City of Chicago, Available at www.supremecourt.gov/opinions/08-974.htm

Lewis v. City of Chicago, Available at www.supremecourt.gov/opinions/09pdf/08-974.pdf

The Oyez Project. "Lewis v. City of Chicago." U.S. Supreme Court Media Report, accessed on 3 June 2010. Available at http://www.oyez.org/cases/2000-2009/2009/2009_08_974

DIVERSITY JURISDICTION

HERTZ CORP. V. FRIEND

Chemerinsky, Erwin. 2007. *Federal Jurisdiction.* 5th ed. Boston: Aspen.

Little, Laura. 2007. *Federal Courts Examples & Explanations.* Boston: Aspen.

Wright, Charles Alan. 2002. *Law of Federal Courts.* 6th ed. St. Paul, Minn.: West Group.

DOUBLE JEOPARDY

BOBBY V. BIES

Cammack, Mark. 2006 *Advanced Criminal Procedure in a Nutshell.* 2d ed. St. Paul, Minn.: Thomson West.

Garcia, Alfredo. 2002. *The Fifth Amendment: A Comprehensive Approach.* Westport, Conn.: Greenwood Press.

Stuart, Gary L. 2008 *Miranda: The Story of America's Right to Remain Silent.* Tucson, Ariz.: Univ. of Arizona Press.

DRUGS AND NARCOTICS

CALIFORNIA SUPREME COURT STRIKES DOWN LEGISLATIVE AMENDMENT TO MEDICAL MARIJUANA LAW

Jonas, Stephen. Ed. 2007. *An Introduction to the U.S. Health Care System.* 6th ed. New York: Springer.

Pozgar, George. 2006. *Legal Aspects of Health Care Administration.* 10th ed. New York: Jones and Bartlett.

EDUCATION LAW

FOREST GROVE SCHOOL DISTRICT V. T.A.

Goren, William. *Understanding the Americans with Disabilities Act, 2nd Edition.* 2007, American Bar Association.

Mezey, Susan. *Disabling Interpretations: The Americans With Disabilities Act In Federal Court.* 2005, University of Pittsburgh Press.

Tucker, Bonnie, and Milani, Adam. *Federal Disability Law in a Nutshell, 3rd Edition.* 200, West Publishing.

ELECTION LAW

D.C. CIRCUIT STRIKES DOWN CAMPAIGN FINANCE LAW AIMED AT NON-PROFIT POLITICAL COMMITTEES

Jerome, Sara. "Election Spending: Reformers on Flood Watch." *National Journal.* Nov. 6, 2009.

Wilson, Reid. "FEC Won't Appeals EMILY's List Ruling." TheHill.com. Oct. 22, 2009.

ENTERTAINMENT LAW

NBC SETTLES LATE NIGHT "TONIGHT SHOW" CONTRACT

Carter, Bill. "Fingers Still Pointing, NBC and O'Brien Reach a Deal." *The New York Times,* 22 January 2010.

Kroft, Steve. "Conan Breaks Silence on 'Tonight Show,' NBC Exit-60 Minutes." CBS News, 2 May 2010, Avaiable at http://www.cbsnews.com/stories/2010/05/02/60minutes/main6454416.shtml

Remondi, Chiara and Andy Fixmer. "O'Brien Signs Accord to Leave 'Tonight; Leno Returns.'" Bloomberg *Businessweek,* 21 January 2010.

Sergeant, Jill. "NBC Ends Late Night Wars; Conan is Out, Leno is Back." Reuters Press Release, 21 january 2010.

ENVIRONMENTAL LAW

MONSANTO V. GEERTSON SEED FARMS

"Court Grants GM Alfalfa Case." *On the Docket,* U.S. Supreme Court Media Report, 15 January 2009. Available at http://otd.oyez.org/cases/2009/monsanto-v-geertson-seed-farms

"Justices Lift Ban on Sale of Biotech Crop." *On the Docket,* U.S. Supreme Court Media Report, 21 June 2010. Available at http://otd.oyez.org/cases/2009/monsanto-v-geertson-seed-farms

Monsanto v. Geertson Seed Farms, Cornell University School of Law Available at http://www.law.cornell.edu/supct/cert/09-475-ZS.html

Monsanto v. Geertson Seed Farms, No. 09-475, Available at www.supremecourt.gov/opinions/09-475.htm

Monsanto v. Geertson Seed Farms, Available at www.supremecourt.gov/opinions/09pdf/09-475.pdf

ERISA

CONKRIGHT V. FROMMERT

Conkright v. Frommert, Cornell University School of Law Available at http://www.law.cornell.edu/supct/cert/08-810.htm

Conkright v. Frommert, No. 08-810, Available at www.supremecourt.gov/opinions/08-810.htm

Conkright v. Frommmert, Available at www.supremecourt.gov/opinions/09pdf/08-810.pdf

"Court Sides With Pension Plan Administrator in ERISA Case." *On the Docket,* U.S. Supreme Court Media Report, 21 April 2010. Available at http://otd.oyez.org/articles.../court-sides-pension-plan-administrator-erisa-case-april-21-2010

ESTABLISHMENT CLAUSE

NINTH CIRCUIT RULES UPHOLDS CONSTITUTIONALITY OF "IN GOD WE TRUST"

Barron, Jerome, Dienes, Thomas. *First Amendment Law in a Nutshell, 3rd ed.* West Group, 2004.

Farber, Daniel. *The First Amendment: Concepts and Insights.* Foundation Press, 2002.

SALAZAR V. BUONO

Barron, Jerome, Dienes, Thomas. 2004. *First Amendment Law in a Nutshell, 3rd ed.* West Group.

Farber, Daniel. 2002. *The First Amendment: Concepts and Insights.* Foundation Press.

ETHICS

LAWYERS STRUGGLE WITH ETHICS OF USING SOCIAL MEDIA

Bennett, Steven C. "Look Who's Talking." *NYSBA Journal.* May 2009.

Pudlow, Jan. "On Facebook? FBBE May Be Planning a Visit." *Florida Bar News.* September 1, 2009.

LAW ENFORCEMENT AUTHORITIES AND LAWYERS USE SOCIAL MEDIA TO GATHER EVIDENCE

Hartstein, Larry. "Facebook a Treasure Trove for Divorce Lawyers." *Atlanta Journal-Constitution.* February 11, 2010.

Luscombe, Belinda. "Facebook and Divorce: Airing the Dirty Laundry." *Time.* June 22, 2009.

EX POST FACTO LAWS

UNITED STATES V. CARR

"Court: No Backdating Sex Offender Registry." UPI.com. June 1, 2010.

Richey, Warren. "Registry Law Doesn't Apply to All Sex Offenders, Supreme Court Rules." *Christian Science Monitor.* June 1, 2010.

U.S. V. MARCUS

Hamblett, Mark. "Supreme Court Upsets 2nd Circuit 'Plain Error" Ruling.' Law.com. May 25, 2010.

Mears, Bill. "High Court Restores Conviction of 'S&M' Svengali." CNN.com. May 24, 2010.

EXTRADITION

EXTRADITION OF ROMAN POLANSKI FOR 1977 CONVICTION

Cieply, Michael. "Polanski breaks Long Silence on His Extradition." *New York Times*, 3 May 2010

Jones, Ashby. "California Court Boosts Effort to Extradite Roman Polanski." *Wall Street Journal*, 23 April 2010.

Ryan, Harriet. "Swiss Official Says Roman Polanski Extradition Proceedings on Indefinite Hold." *Los Angeles Times*, 13 February 2010.

"U.S. Court Urges Misconduct Probe into Polanski Case." Reuters press release, 21 December 2009.

accessed on 3 June 2010. Available at http://www.reuters.com/articles/idUSTRE5BK34F20091222

FAIR TRIAL

SKILLING V. UNITED STATES

Skilling v. United States, Cornell University School of Law Available at http://www.law.cornell.edu/supct/cert/08-1394.htm

Skilling v. United States, No. 08-1394, Available at www.supremecourt.gov/opinions/08-1394.htm

Skilling v. United States, No. 07-8521, Available at www.supremecourt.gov/opinions/09pdf/08-1394.pdf

The Oyez Project. "Skilling v. United States." U.S. Supreme Court Media Report, accessed on 28 June 2010. Available at http://www.oyez.org/cases/2000-2009/2009/2009_08_1394

FALSE CLAIMS ACT

U.S. EX REL EISENSTEIN V. CITY OF NEW YORK

Cooper, Cynthia. 2009. *Extraordinary Circumstances: The Journey of a Corporate Whistleblower.* New York: Wiley.

Johnson, Roberta Ann. 2004. *The Struggle Against Corruption: A Comparative Study.* New York: Palgrave Macmillan.

West, Robin. 2009. *Advising the Qui Tam Whistleblower: From Identifying a Case to Filing Under the False Claims Act.* 2d ed. Chicago: American Bar Association.

GRAHAM COUNTY SOIL AND WATER CONSERVATION DISTRICT V. U.S. EX REL. WILSON

Cooper, Cynthia. 2009 *Extraordinary Circumstances: The Journey of a Corporate Whistleblower.* New York: Wiley.

Johnson, Roberta Ann. 2004. *The Struggle Against Corruption: A Comparative Study.* New York: Palgrave Macmillan.

West, Robin. 2009. *Advising the Qui Tam Whistleblower: From Identifying a Case to Filing Under the False Claims Act.* 2d ed. Chicago: American Bar Association.

FAMILY LAW

ABBOTT V. ABBOTT

Abbott v. Abbott, Cornell University School of Law Available at http://www.law.cornell.edu/supct/cert/08-645.html

Abbott v. Abbott, No. 07-8521, Available at www.supremecourt.gov/opinions/09pdf/08-645.pdf

"Justices Rule in International Child Custody Case."
On the Docket, U.S. Supreme Court Media Report,
17 May 2010. Available at http://www.oyez.org/
cases/2000-2009/2009/2009_08_645

TIGER WOODS LOSES MILLIONS DUE TO SCANDAL

McKay, Hollie. "Elin Nordegren and Tiger Woods
Talking Divorce 'Daily,' Source Says," FOXNews.
com. April 20, 2010.

"Tiger Woods Apologizes as Gossip Magazine
Reports Affair." CNN.com. December 2, 2009.

FEDERAL PREEMPTION

HEALTH CARE SERVICES CORPORATION V. POLLITT

Health Care Service Corporation v. Pollitt, Cornell
University School of Law Available at http://www.
law.cornell.edu/supct/cert/08-3509.htm

The Oyez Project. "Health Care Service Corp. v.
Pollitt, U.S. Supreme Court Case Summary & Oral
Arguments." U.S. Supreme Court Media Report,
accessed on 3 June 2010. Available at http://www.
oyez.org/cases/2000-2009/2009/2009_09_38

Pollitt v. Health Care Service Corp., 558 F.3d 615 (7th
Cir. 2009) Available at www.findlaw.com

FEDERAL TORT CLAIMS ACT

HUI V. CASTANEDA

Hui v. Castaneda, Cornell University School of Law
Available at http://www.law.cornell.edu/supct/
cert/08-1529.htm

Hui v. Castaneda, No. 08-1529, Available at www.
supremecourt.gov/opinions/08-1529.htm

Hui v. Castaneda, No. 08-1529, Available at www.
supremecourt.gov/opinions/09pdf/08-1529.pdf

"Justices Will Hear Federal Tort Claims Act Case."
On the Docket, U.S. Supreme Court Media Report,
30 September 2009. Available at http://otd.oyez.
org/cases/2009/migliaccion-v-castaneda-hennefor-
v-castaneda

The Oyez Project. "Hui v. Castaneda." U.S. Supreme
Court Media Report, accessed on 30 May 2010.
Available at http://www.oyez.org/cases/2000-
2009/2009/2009_08_1529

FIFTH AMENDMENT

SUPREME COURT RULES THAT MIRANDA ADVISORY QUESTION WAS NOT MISLEADING

Cammack, Mark. 2006 *Advanced Criminal Procedure
in a Nutshell.* 2d ed. St. Paul, Minn.: Thomson
West.

Garcia, Alfredo. 2002. *The Fifth Amendment:
A Comprehensive Approach.* Westport, Conn.:
Greenwood Press.

Stuart, Gary L. 2008 *Miranda: The Story of America's
Right to Remain Silent.* Tucson, Ariz.: Univ. of
Arizona Press.

FIRST AMENDMENT

CHRISTIAN LEGAL SOCIETY V. MARTINEZ

Christian Legal Society v. Martinez, Cornell University
School of Law Available at http://www.law.cornell.
edu/supct/cert/08-1371.htm

Christian Legal Society v. Martinez, No. 08-1371,
Available at www.supremecourt.gov/opinions/
08-1371.htm

Christian Legal Society v. Martinez, No. 08-1371,
Available at www.supremecourt.gov/opinions/
09pdf/08-1371.pdf

"Court Rules Against Student Religious Group." *On
the Docket,* U.S. Supreme Court Media Report, 28
June 2010. Available at http://otd.oyez.org/cases/
2009/christian-legal-society-v-martinez

"Court Will Hear Student Religioius Group Case."
On the Docket, U.S. Supreme Court Media
Report, 7 December 2009. Available at http://otd.
oyez.org/cases/2009/christian-legal-society-v-
martinez

DOE V. REED

"Court Backs State on Compelled Disclosure of
Petition Signatures." *On the Docket,* U.S. Supreme
Court Media Report, 24 June 2010. Available at
http://otd.oyez.org/cases/2009/john-doe-1-v-reed

"Court Will Hear Case on the Compelled Disclosure
of Petitoin Signatures." *On the Docket,* U.S.
Supreme Court Media Report, 15 January 2010.
Available at http://otd.oyez.org/cases/2009/john-
doe-1-v-reed

Doe v. Reed, Cornell University School of Law
Available at http://www.law.cornell.edu/supct/
cert/09-559.htm

Doe v. Reed, No. 09-559, Available at www
.supremecourt.gov/opinions/09-559.htm

Doe v. Reed, No. 09-559, Available at www
.supremecourt.gov/opinions/09pdf/09-559.pdf

D.C. CIRCUIT UPHOLDS LOBBYING DISCLOSURE STATUTE

Weaver, Russell L. and Donald E. Lively. 2009.
Understanding the First Amendment. 3d ed. New
Providence, N.J.: LexisNexis.

Vile, John R., David Hudson Jr. and David Schultz,
eds. 2009. *Encyclopedia of the First Amendment.*
Washington, D.C.: CQ Press.

SECOND CIRCUIT RULES THAT VALERIA PLAME WILSON CANNOT REVEAL DATES OF CIA EMPLOYMENT IN HER MEMOIR

Barron, Jerome, Dienes, Thomas. *First Amendment
Law in a Nutshell, 3rd ed.* West Group, 2004.

Farber, Daniel. *The First Amendment: Concepts and Insights.* Foundation Press, 2002.

U.S. v. Stevens

Barron, Jerome, Dienes, Thomas. 2004. *First Amendment Law in a Nutshell* 3rd Ed. St. Paul, Minn.: West Group.

Farber, Daniel. 2002. *The First Amendment: Concepts and Insights.* Rochester, New York: Foundation Press.

Fourth Circuit Reversed Verdict Against Westboro Baptist Church

Fuller, Nicole. "Church Wins Round in Court." *The Baltimore Sun.* September 25, 2009.

Sommers, Adam. "Support Grows for Dad of Slain Marine Told to Pay Westboro Baptist Church, Which Cheered Son's Death. *New York Daily News.* March 31, 2010.

FOREIGN SOVEREIGN IMMUNITY ACT

Samantar v. Yousuf

"Justices Reject Immunity for Former Somali PM." *On the Docket,* U.S. Supreme Court Media Report, 1 June 2010. Available at http://otd.oyez.org/cases/2009/samantar-v-yousuf

Samantar v. Yousuf, Cornell University School of Law Available at http://www.law.cornell.edu/supct/cert/08-1555.htm

Samantar v. Yousuf, No. 08-1555, Available at www.supremecourt.gov/opinions/08-1555.htm

Samantar v. Yousuf, No. 08-1555, Available at www.supremecourt.gov/opinions/09pdf/08-1555.pdf

FORFEITURE

Alvarez v. Smith

Edgeworth, Dee. 2009. *Asset Forfeiture,* 2nd Ed., Chicago: American Bar Association.

FOURTH AMENDMENT

Ninth Circuit Rules That Jail's Strip-Search Policy Is Constitutional

Egelko, Bob. "S.F.'s Jail Strip-Search Policy Ruled OK." *San Francisco Chronicle.* February 10, 2010.

Levine, Dan. "9th Circuit Sides with San Francisco Sheriff Over Strip Searches". Law.com. February 11, 2010.

City of Ontario v. Quon

"Court Takes On Privacy of Text Messages." *On the Docket,* U.S. Supreme Court Media Report, 14 December 2009. Available at http://otd.oyez.org/cases/2009/ontario-v-quon

City of Ontario v. Quon, Cornell University School of Law. Available at http://www.law.cornell.edu/supct/cert/08-1332.htm

City of Ontario, California v. Quon, No. 08-1332, Available at www.supremecourt.gov/opinions/08-1332.htm

City of Ontario, California v. Quon, Available at www.supremecourt.gov/opinions/09pdf/08-1332.pdf

"Justices OK Search of Government Text Messages." *On the Docket,* U.S. Supreme Court Media Report, 17 June 2010. Available at http://otd.oyez.org/cases/2009/ontario-v-quon

FRANCHISE

Mac's Shell Service, Inc. v. Shell Oil Products Co. LLC

Barkoff, Rupert. 2009. *Fundamentals of Franchisng,* 3rd. Ed. Chicago: American Bar Association.

Skrocki, Anthony. 2006. *Contracts in a Nutshell.* 6th Ed. St. Paul, Minn: Thomson West.

FRAUD

Parents of "Balloon Boy" Admit to Hoax

Duke, Alan. "Balloon Hoax Dad Must Pay Restitution." CNN.com. April 21, 2010.

Stelter, Brian. "Calling Story of Boy and Balloon a Hoax, Sheriff Seeks Felony Charges." *New York Times.* October 19, 2009.

Former Partner at New Orleans Firm Sentenced to 15 Years for Fraud

Johnson, Allen Jr. "The Confession Doesn't Always End the Mystery." *New Orleans Magazine.* June 2009.

McCollam, Douglas. "The Boy Wonder." *American Lawyer.* June 1, 2009.

Weyhrauch v. United States

Weyhrauch v. United States, Cornell University School of Law Available at http://www.law.cornell.edu/supct/cert/08-1196.htm

Weyhrauch v. United States, No. 08-1196, Available at www.supremecourt.gov/opinions/08-1196.htm

Weyhrauch v. United States, No. 08-1196, Available at www.supremecourt.gov/opinions/09pdf/08-1196.pdf

FREEDOM OF RELIGION

Michigan Supreme Court Allows Trial Judges to ban Religious Head Scarves in Court

Graham, Michael. 2003. *Federal Rules of Evidence in a Nutshell.* 6th ed. St. Paul, MN: West Group.

LaFave, Wayne R., Jerold H. Israel, and Nancy J. King, eds. 2003. *Criminal Procedure.* 4th ed. St. Paul, Minn.: West Group.

Rothstein, Paul. 2003. *Evidence in a Nutshell.* 5th ed. St. Paul, MN: West Group.

Sawczyn, Gerald W., and Sarah K. Eddy. 2002. "Sixth Amendment at Trial." *Georgetown Law Journal* 90 (May).

Tomkovicz, James J. 2002. *The Right to the Assistance of Counsel: A Reference Guide to the United States Constitution.* Westport, Conn.: Greenwood.

GOVERNMENTAL IMMUNITY

ARMY CORPS OF ENGINEERS LIABLE FOR HURRICANE KATRINA LEVEE FAILURES

Fausset, Richard. "Judge Says U.S. Liable in Katrina," *Los Angeles Times,* 19 November 2009.

Hayes, Ashley. "Court" Army Corps of Engineers Liable for Katrina Flooding," *CNN News,* 18 November 2009. Available at http://www.cnn.com/2009/US/11/18/louisiana.katrina.lawsuit

Johnson, Patrik. "Army Corps Liable for Katrina Damage, US Court Finds." *Christian Science Monitor,* 19 November 2009.

"Katrina Canal Breaches Consolidated Litigation." *In re; Robinson,* U.S. District Court-Eastern District of Louisiana. Accessed 13 June 2010. Available at http://www.laed.uscourts.gov/Canal/Cases/Canal Cases.htm

"Katrina Claims Information." U.S. Army Corps of Engineers. Accessed 13 June 2010. Available at site (www.mvn.usace.army.mil/oc/katrina_claim

HABEAS CORPUS

BEARD V. KINDLER

Federman, Cary. 2006. *The Body And the State: Habeas Corpus And American Jurisprudence.* New York, NY: State University of New York Press.

Frank, Jerome. 1973. *Courts on Trial.* Princeton, NJ: Princeton University Press.

Freedman, Eric. *Habeas Corpus: Rethinking the Great Writ of Liberty. 2003.* New York: New York Univ. Press.

HOLLAND V. FLORIDA

"Court OKs Equitable Tolling in Death Penalty Cases." *On the Docket,* U.S. Supreme Court Media Report, 14 June 2010. Available at http://otd.oyez.org/cases/2009/holland-v-florida

Holland v. Florida, Cornell University School of Law Available at http://www.law.cornell.edu/supct/cert/09-5327.htm

Holland v. Florida, No. 09-5327, Available at www.supremecourt.gov/opinions/09-5327.htm

Holland v. Florida, Available at www.supremecourt.gov/opinions/09pdf/09-5327.pdf

"Justices Will Rule on 'Gross Negligence' in Habeas Case." *On the Docket,* U.S. Supreme Court Media Report, 13 October 2009. Available at http://otd.oyez.org/cases/2009/holland-v-florida

WOOD V. ALLEN

Palmer, John. 2006. *Constitutional Rights of Prisoners.* 8th ed. New York: Anderson Pub. Co.

Tomkovicz, James J. 2002. *The Right to the Assistance of Counsel: A Reference Guide to the United States Constitution.* Westport, Conn.: Greenwood.

HEALTH CARE

CONGRESS PASSES HISTORIC HEALTH CARE REFORM LAW

Herszenhorn, David M. "A Grand Achievement, or a Lost Opportunity?" *New York Times,* March 24, 2010.

Nagourney, Adam. "Lawmakers Face Fallout at Home from Health Vote," *New York Times,* March 28, 2010.

Somashekhar, Sandhya and Perry Bacon, Jr. "Those Angry About Health-Care Generally Concerned About the Country's Direction" *Washington Post* April 2, 2010.

IMMIGRATION

TENTH CIRCUIT ENJOINS ENFORCEMENT OF OKLAHOMA IMMIGRATION LAW

Phelan, Margaret and Gillespie, James. *Immigration Law Handbook.* Oxford University Press, 2007.

Scaros, Constantinos. *Learning About Immigration Law.* Thomson Delmaer Learning, 2006.

Weissbrodt, David and Danielson, Laura. *Immigration Law and Procedure in a Nutshell, 5th Edition.* West Group, 2005.

KUCANA V HOLDER

Phelan, Margaret and Gillespie, James. *Immigration Law Handbook.* Oxford University Press, 2007.

Scaros, Constantinos. *Learning About Immigration Law.* Thomson Delmaer Learning, 2006.

Weissbrodt, David and Danielson, Laura. *Immigration Law and Procedure in a Nutshell, 5th Edition.* West Group, 2005.

IMMIGRATION

NIJHAWAN V. HOLDER

Phelan, Margaret and Gillespie, James. *Immigration Law Handbook.* Oxford University Press, 2007.

Scaros, Constantinos. *Learning About Immigration Law.* Thomson Delmaer Learning, 2006.

Weissbrodt, David and Danielson, Laura. *Immigration Law and Procedure in a Nutshell, 5th Edition.* West Group, 2005.

IMMUNITY

NINTH CIRCUIT UPHOLDS DECISION LIMITING THE USE OF TASERS

Cammack, Mark and Garland, Norman. *Advanced Criminal Procedure in a Nutshell.* West Publishing Co. 2001.

Dash, Samuel. *The Intruders: Unreasonable Searches and Seizures from King John to John Ashcroft.* Rutgers University Press. 2004.

Long, Carolyn. *Mapp V. Ohio: Guarding Against Unreasonable Searches And Seizures.* University Press of Kansas. 2006.

IMPEACHMENT

HOUSE IMPEACHES JUDGE SAMUEL B. KENT

Flood, Mary. "Kent Sentenced to 33 Months Behind Bars," *Houston Chronicle.* May 12, 2009.

MacLean, Pamela A. "Federal Judge Pleads Guilty to Obstruction, Steps Down" Law.com. February 23, 2009.

INTELLECTUAL PROPERTY

FORMER COLLEGE PLAYERS SUE VIDEO GAME MAKER

Associated Press. "Keller Sues EA Sports Over Images" ESPN.com. May 8, 2009.

Wieberg, Steve. "Ex-QB Sues NCAA, EA Sports Over Use of Athletes' Likenesses." *USA Today*, May 7, 2009.

INTERNET

MICROSOFT SUES FAMILY MEMBERS IN AN INTERNET FRAUD CASE

Chan, Sharon Pian. "Microsoft Sues Two Brothers, Mother for Online Ad Fraud." *Seattle Times.* June 16, 2009.

Clifford, Stephanie. "Microsoft Sues Three in Click-Fraud Scheme." *New York Times* June 16, 2009.

INTERNET

"SPAM KING" PLEADS GUILTY TO SPAMMING AND FRAUD SCHEME

Krebs, Brian. "Accused Spam King Alan Ralsky Pleads Guilty." *Washington Post: Security Fix*, June 23, 2009.

Press Release. "Detroit Spammer and Four Co-Conspirators Plead Guilty to Multi-Million Dollar E-mail Stock Fraud Scheme." Federal Bureau of Investigation (June 22, 2009).

JUVENILE LAW

GRAHAM V. FLORIDA

Gardner, Martin R. 2009. *Understanding Juvenile Law.* Newark, N.J.: LexisNexis.

JUVENILE SENTENCING

SULLIVAN V. FLORIDA

Juvenile Law Center. "U.S. Supreme Court Declares Juvenile Life Without Parole for Non-homicide Cases Unconstitutional." 17 May 2010 http://www.jlc.org/litigation/63/

"Life Without Parole: Sullivan v. Florida." *On the Docket*, U.S. Supreme Court Media Report, May 2009. Available at http://otd.oyez.org/cases/life-without-parole/sullivan-v-florida

Sullivan v. Florida, Cornell University School of Law Available at http://www.law.cornell.edu/supct/cert/08-7621.htm

Sullivan v. Florida, No. 08-7621, Available at www.supremecourt.gov/opinions/08-1200.htm

The Oyez Project. "Sullivan v. Florida." U.S. Supreme Court Media Report, accessed on 3 June 2010. Available at http://www.oyez.org/cases/2000-2009/2009/2009_08_7621

LABOR LAW

GRANITE ROCK V. INTERNATIONAL BROTHERHOOD OF TEAMSTERS

Granite Rock v. International Brotherhood of Teamsters, Cornell University School of Law. Available at http://www.law.cornell.edu/supct/cert/08-1214.htm

Granite Rock v. International Brotherhood of Teamsters, No. 08-1214, Available at www.supremecourt.gov/opinions/08-1214.htm

Granite Rock v. International Brotherhood of Teamsters, No. 08-1214, Available at www.supremecourt.gov/opinions/09pdf/08-1214.pdf

The Oyez Project. "Granite Rock v. International Brotherhood of Teamsters." U.S. Supreme Court Media Report, accessed on 30 June 2010. Available at http://www.oyez.org/cases/2000-2009/2009/2009_08_1214

NEW PROCESS STEEL V. NATIONAL LABOR RELATIONS BOARD

"Divided Court Finds Two-person Labor Board Can't Make Decisions." *On the Docket*, U.S. Supreme Court Media Report, 17 June 2010. Available at http://otd.oyez.org/cases/2009/new-process-steel-v-national-labor-relations-board

"Justices to Decide Legality of Two-person Labor Board." *On the Docket*, U.S. Supreme Court Media Report, 2 November 2009. Available at http://otd.oyez.org/cases/2009/new-process-steel-v-national-labor-relations-board

New Process Steel v. National Labor Relations Board, Cornell University School of Law Available at http://www.law.cornell.edu/supct/cert/08-1457.htm

New Process Steel v. National Labor Relations Board, No. 08-1457. Available at www.supremecourt.gov/opinions/08-1457.htm

New Process Steel v. National Labor Relations Board, No. 08-1457, Available at www.supremecourt. gov/opinions/09pdf/08-1457.pdf

LAWYERS

LAWYERS AND LAW FIRMS STRUGGLE THROUGH DIFFICULT FINANCIAL TIMES

Efrati, Amir. "A Stingier Job Market Awaits New Attorneys." *Wall Street Journal.*. September 24, 2007.

Jones, Leigh. "So Long, Farewell." *National Law Journal.* November 9, 2009.

LEGAL EDUCATION

LAW SCHOOL RANKINGS MAY HURT EFFORTS TOWARDS DIVERSITY

Espeland, Wendy and Michael Sauder. "Rankings and Diversity." *Review of Law and Social Justice.* 18. Fall 2009.

Sloan, Karen. "Law School Rankings Complicate Diversity Efforts, Research Suggests." *Law.com* March 1, 2010.

LEGAL RESEARCH

ENSURING AUTHENTICITY OF ONLINE LEGAL RESOURCES CAUSES ISSUES FOR GOVERNMENT PROVIDERS

American Association of Law Libraries. *2009-2010 Updates to the State-by-State Report on Authentication of Online Legal Resources.* February 2010.

Stevens, Ruth S. and Jane Edwards. "State Primary Law Materials in a Digital Era." *Michigan Bar Journal.* July 2009.

GOOGLE AND OTHER COMPANIES OFFER NEW FREE SOURCES FOR LEGAL INFORMATION

"Finding the Laws That Govern Us," The Official Google Blog. November 17, 2009. Available online at http://googleblog.blogspot.com/2009/11/ finding-laws-that-govern-us.html

Krazit, Tom. "Legal Opinions Now Available in Google Scholar." CNet.com. November 17, 2009. Available online at http://news.cnet.com/8301-30684_3-10399895-265.html

LIBEL

TENTH CIRCUIT UPHOLDS DISMISSAL OF LIBEL SUIT AGAINST AUTHOR JOHN GRISHAM

Grisham, John. *The Innocent Man.* New York: Doubleday, 2006.

Hylton, Susan. "Suit Brought by Oklahoma Lawman Against Author John Grisham Dismissed." *Tulsa World.* Feb. 1, 2010.

Kranish, Michael. "Harvard Law Dean Considered for Supreme Court." *Boston Globe.* April 14, 2010.

"Martha Minow Appointed Dean of Harvard Law School." *Harvard Magazine.* June 11, 2009.

MIRANDA RIGHTS

MARYLAND V. SCHATZER

Cammack, Mark. 2006 *Advanced Criminal Procedure in a Nutshell.* 2d ed. St. Paul, Minn.: Thomson West.

Garcia, Alfredo. 2002. *The Fifth Amendment: A Comprehensive Approach.* Westport, Conn.: Greenwood Press.

Stuart, Gary L. 2008 *Miranda: The Story of America's Right to Remain Silent.* Tucson, Ariz.: Univ. of Arizona Press.

BERGHUIS V. THOMPKINS

Berghuis v. Thompkins, Cornell University School of Law Available at http://www.law.cornell.edu/ supct/cert/08-1470

Berghuis v. Thompkins, No. 08-1470, Available at www.supremecourt.gov/opinions/08-1470.htm

Berghuis v. Thompkins, No. 07-8521, Available at www.supremecourt.gov/opinions/09pdf/ 08-1470.pdf

The Oyez Project. "Berghuis v. Thompkins." U.S. Supreme Court Media Report, accessed on 3 June 2010. Available at http://www.oyez.org/cases/ 2000-2009/2009/2009_08_1470

MURDER

FORMER POLICE OFFICER INDICTED FOR HIS WIFE'S MURDER

Associated Press. "Drew Peterson Pleads Not Guilty to Murdering 3rd Wife." *Chicago Tribune.* May 18, 2009.

Babwin, Don. "Witness Testifies Drew Peterson Threw Wife to Floor & Threatened to Kill Her." *Chicago Tribune.* January 19, 2010.

TESTIMONY FROM THE GRAVE: THE DREW PETERSON LAW AND HEARSAY EXCEPTIONS IN HOMICIDE CASES

Chavez v. State, No. 1D08-1532 (Fla. App. 2009) Available at http://www.findlaw.com

Chen, Stephanie. "Peterson's Defense Team Challenges 'Drew's Law.'" CNN News, 19 January 2010. Available at www.cnn.com/2010/CRIME/ 01/19/Illinois.drew.peterson.hearsay/index.html

"Peterson, Courts Await Ruling on 'Drew's Law.'" NPR local news, KPCC. Available at http://www .npr.org/

St. Clair, Stacy and Steve Schmadake. "Table Turns for Peterson Case Prosecutor." *The Chicago Tribune,* 11 July 2010.

Wall, Craig. "Drew Peterson Trial Delayed; Peterson Could Be Released Thursday." FOX Chicago News and the Associated Press, 7 July 2010. Available at http://www.myfoxchicago.com/dpp/news/metro/drew_peterson/drew-peterson-trial-delayed-20100707 7

NECESSARY AND PROPER CLAUSE

UNITED STATES V. COMSTOCK

The Oyez Project. "United States v. Comstock, U.S. Supreme Court Case Summary & Oral Argument." U.S. Supreme Court Media Report, accessed on 3 June 2010. Available at http://www.oyez.org/cases/2000-2009/2009/2009_08_1224

United States v. Comstock, Cornell University School of Law Available at http://www.law.cornell.edu/supct/cert/08-1224.htm

United States v. Comstock, Available at www.supremecourt.gov/opinions/09pdf/08-1224.pdf

ORIGINAL JURISDICTION

SOUTH CAROLINA V. NORTH CAROLINA

Arnold, Craig, and Jewell, Leigh. Ed. *Beyond Litigation: Case Studies in Water Rights Disputes.* Environmental Law Institute, 2002.

Sherk, George. *Dividing the Waters: The Resolution of Interstate Water Conflicts in the United States.* Springer, 2000.

Wright, Kennth. Ed. "Water Rights." *American Water Works Association, 1998.*

PATENTS

BILSKI V. KAPPOS

Klien, Sheldon. 2009. "Introduction to Trademarks: Patents, Copyrights, Trademarks and Literary Property Course Handbook Series." *Practicing Law Institute* Pat 123.

Miller, Arthur, and Davis, Michael. 2007. *Intellectual Property-Patents, Trademarks And Copyright in a Nutshell.* St. Paul, Minn.: Thomson West.

PATRIOT ACT

HOLDER V. HUMANITARIAN LAW PROJECT

"Court Backs Ban on 'Material Support' to Foreign Terrorist Groups." *On the Docket,* U.S. Supreme Court Media Report, 21 June 2010. Available at http://otd.oyez.org/cases/2009/holder-v-humanitarian-law-project

Holder v. Humanitarian Law Project, Cornell University School of Law. Available at http://www.law.cornell.edu/supct/cert/08-1498.htm

Holder v. Humanitarian Law Project, No. 08-1498, Available at www.supremecourt.gov/opinions/08-1498.htm

Holder v. Humanitarian Law Project, No. 08-1498, Available at www.supremecourt.gov/opinions/09pdf/08-1498.pdf

"Justices to Take a Look at PATRIOT Act." *On the Docket,* U.S. Supreme Court Media Report, 30 September 2009. Available at http://otd.oyez.org/cases/2009/holder-v-humanitarian-law-project

POLITICAL PARTIES

THE RISE OF THE TEA PARTY MOVEMENT

Barstow, David. "Tea Party Lights Fuse for Rebellion on the Right." *The New York Times,* 16 February 2010.

Bartlett, Bruce."The Misinformed Tea Party Movement." *Forbes,* 18 March 2010.

Gardner, Amy. "Tea Party Movement's Energy, Anger make it Target for Admakers." *Washington Post,* 6 July 2010.

Martin, Michael. "What the Tea Party Movement is Really About." *NPR News,* 19 April 2010. Available at http://www.npr.org/templates/story/story.php?storyId=126109933

McGrath, Ben. "The Rise of Tea Party Activism." *The New Yorker,* 1 February 2010.

PONZI SCHEME

BERNARD MADOFF SENTENCED TO 150 YEARS IN PRISON

Glovin, David. "Bernard Madoff Gets 150 Years in Jail for Epic Fraud." Bloomberg.com. June 29, 2010.

Press Release. "Robert C. Post '77 Named Dean of Yale Law School. Available online at http://opa.yale.edu/news/article.aspx?id=6763

Scheer, David. "SEC Never Did 'Competent' Madoff Probe, Report Finds." Bloomberg.com. September 2, 2010.

PRACTICE OF LAW

LAW FIRMS MAY NEED TO CONSIDER THEIR BUSINESS MODELS IN THE WAKE OF THE RECESSION

Henning, Joel. "A Broken Business Model." *National Law Journal.* August 17, 2009.

Ribstein, Larry E. "Regulating the Evolving Law Firm." Available online at http://www.law.georgetown.edu/legalprofession/documents/ribsteinevolvinglawfirm.pdf

Slater, Dan. "At Law Firms, Reconsidering the Model for Associates' Pay." *New York Times.* April 1, 2010.

PREVAILING PARTY

HARDT V. RELIANCE STANDARD LIFE INSURANCE COMPANY

Hardt v. Reliance Standard Life Insurance Co., Cornell University School of Law Available at http://www.law.cornell.edu/supct/cert/09-448-1200.htm

Hardt v. Reliance Standard Life Insurance Co., No. 9-448, Available at www.supremecourt.gov/opinions/09pdf/09-448.pdf

The Oyez Project. "Hardt v. Reliance Standard Life Ins." U.S. Supreme Court Media Report, accessed on 3 June 2010. Available at http://www.oyez.org/cases/2000-2009/2009/2009_09_448

PRIVACY

NINTH CIRCUIT ALLOWS PARIS HILTON'S PRIVACY SUIT TO PROCEED

Jones, Ashby. "'That's Hot': Paris Hilton Wins 'Hallmark' Decision at Ninth Circuit." *Wall Street Journal Blog.* August 31, 2009. Available online at http://blogs.wsj.com/law/2009/08/31/thats-hot-paris-hilton-wins-hallmark-decision-at-ninth-circuit/tab/article/

Stempel, Jonathan. "Court: Paris Hilton Can Pursue Hallmark Lawsuit." Reuters.com, August 31, 2009.

PROBATE

BROOKE ASTOR'S SON CONVICTED IN ESTATE-HANDLING FRAUD

"Anthony Marshall Convicted of Larceny in Astor Case." *New York Times,* 9 October 2009.

Barron, James. "Brooke Astor's Son Is Sentenced to Prison." *New York Times,* 22 December 2009.

Eligon, John. "Astor's Son to Stay Free During Appeal." *New York Times,* 12 January 2010.

Eligon, John. "Brooke Astor's Son Guilty in Scheme to Defraud Her." *New York Times,* 9 October 2009.

In the Matter of Brooke Russell Astor, > 2008-00767, 2008-09412, Supreme Court of the State of New York Appellate Division: Second Judicial Department Available at http://www.courts.state.ny.us/courts/ad2/calendar/webcal/decisions/2009/D23190.pdf

PRODUCT LIABILITY

TOYOTA FORCED TO RECALL MILLIONS OF CARS

Bensinger, Ken and Ralph Vartabedian. "Data Point to Toyota's Throttles, not Floor Mats." *Los Angeles Times.* November 29, 2009.

Vartabedian, Ralph. "Toyota to Fix 'Very Dangerous' Gas Pedal Defects" *Los Angeles Times* November 26, 2009.

PROPERTY LAW

STOP THE BEACH RENOURISHMENT, INC. V. FLORIDA DEPARTMENT OF ENVIRONMENTAL PROTECTION

Bravin, Jess. "Court Rules State Owns Restored Beach." *Wall Street Journal.* June 18, 2010.

Savage, David G. "Supreme Court Rejects Florida Beach Owners' Claim." *Los Angeles Times.* June 17, 2010.

PROSECUTORIAL MISCONDUCT

POTTAWATTAMIE COUNTY V. MCGHEE

Pottawattamie County v. McGhee, Cornell University School of Law. Available at http://www.law.cornell.edu/supct/cert/08-1065.htm

The Oyez Project. "Justices Accept Case on When Prosecutors Can Be Sued." *On the Docket,* U.S. Supreme Court Media Report, accessed on 3 June 2010. Available at http://www.oyez.org/cases/2009/pottawattamie-coounty-v-mcghee

Pottawattamie County v. McGhee Pollitt v. Health Care Service Corp., 547 F.3d 922 (8th Cir. 2008) Available at www.findlaw.com

PUBLIC UTILITIES

NRG POWER MARKETING, LLC V. MAINE PUBLIC UTILITIES COMMISSION

Federal Energy Regulatory Commission. Available online at www.ferc.gov (accessed May 7, 2010).

Hunt, Sally. 2002. *Making Competition Work in Electricity.* New York: John Wiley.

RACIAL DISCRIMINATION

LOUISIANA JUDGE DENIES MARRIAGE LICENSE TO INTERRACIAL COUPLE

Ellzey, Don. "JP Refuses to Marry Couple." *Hammond Star.* October 15, 2009.

Louis, Errol. "Racial Progress, Before Our Eyes: A National Conversation on Race is Happening, Without Obama." *New York Daily News.* October 18, 2009.

RACKETEERING

BILLIONAIRE SEX OFFENDER SUES DISGRACED ATTORNEY CHARGED WITH RUNNING A PONZI SCHEME

Dargan, Michele. "Jeffrey Epstein's Taped Interview with 'NY Daily News' Contains 'Damning Admissions," Lawyer Says," *Palm Beach Daily News,* April 28, 2010.

Musgrave, Jane. "Victims' Lawyers Say Sex Offender's Lawsuit Aimed at Scaring Female Victims." *Palm Beach Post.* December 8, 2009.

RAILROADS

UNION PACIFIC RAILROAD V. BROTHERHOOD OF LOCOMOTIVE ENGINEERS AND TRAINMEN GENERAL COMMITTEE OF ADJUSTMENT, CENTRAL REGION

Chemerinsky, Erwin. 2007. *Federal Jurisdiction.* 5th ed. Boston: Aspen.

Little, Laura. 2007. *Federal Courts Examples & Explanations.* Boston: Aspen.

Wright, Charles Alan. 2002. *Law of Federal Courts.* 6th ed. St. Paul, Minn.: West Group.

RELIGION

DAD HAS COURT TROUBLE FOR TAKING CHILD TO CATHOLIC CHURCH

Cuomo, Chris, Lauren Pearle, Felicia Patinkin, and Susan Clarke, "Dad Pleads Not Guilty on Violating Court Order for Taking Daughter to Church." ABCNews.com. February 16, 2010.

Weiss, Debra Cassens. "Law Student Charged with Contempt for Exposing Daughter to Christianity." *ABA Journal.* February 17, 2010.

RICO

HEMI GROUP, LLC, V. CITY OF NEW YORK

Bastista, Paul. 2005. *Civil RICO Practice Manual.* 2nd Ed. Boston: Aspen Publishers.

Dietz, Laura Hunter. 2002. "Checklist of Acts Which Constitute Racketeering Activity; Federal Law Violations" *American Jurisprudence.* 2d ed. Extortion Sec. 120.

SARBANES-OXLEY ACT

FREE ENTERPRISE FUND V. PUBLIC COMPANY ACCOUNTING OVERSIGHT BOARD

Free Enterprise Fund v. Public Company Accounting Oversight Board, No. 08-861, Available at www .supremecourt.gov/opinions/08-861.htm

Free Enterprise Fund v. Public Company Accounting Oversight Board, No. 08-861, Available at www .supremecourt.gov/opinions/09pdf/08-861.pdf

Free Enterprise Fund v. Public Company Accounting Oversight Board, Cornell University School of Law Available at http://www.law.cornell.edu/supct/ cert/08-861.html

Free Enterprise Fund v. Public Company Accounting Oversight Board, U.S. Supreme Court Media, Available at http://www.oyez.org/cases/2000- 2009/2009/2009_08_861

Jones, Leigh. "Chicago Law School's New Dean Has Big Plans." *National Law Journal.* January 13, 2010.

Press Release. "Schill Appointment Next Dean of University of Chicago Law School." Available online at http://news.uchicago.edu/news.php? asset_id=1705

SEARCH AND SEIZURE

SAFFORD UNIFIED SCHOOL DISTRICT #1 V. REDDING

Cammack, Mark and Garland, Norman. *Advanced Criminal Procedure in a Nutshell.* West Publishing Co. 2001.

Dash, Samuel. *The Intruders: Unreasonable Searches and Seizures from King John to John Ashcroft.* Rutgers University Press. 2004.

Long, Carolyn. *Mapp V. Ohio: Guarding Against Unreasonable Searches And Seizures.* University Press of Kansas. 2006.

SECOND AMENDMENT

McDONALD V. CITY OF CHICAGO, ILLINOIS

Barnett, Randy. "The Supreme Court's Gun Showdown." *Wall Street Journal.* June 29, 2010.

Liptak, Adam. "Justices Extend Firearm Rights in 5-to-4 Ruling." *New York Times.* June 28, 2010.

SECURITIES

JONES V. HARRIS ASSOCIATES L.P.

Hazen, Thomas. 2006. *Securities Regulation in a Nutshell,* 9th Ed., West Group.

Palmiter, Allen. 2005. *Security Regulation, 3rd Ed.* Aspen Publishers.

Soderquist, Larry, and Gabaldon, Theresa. 2006. *Securities Law: Concepts and Insights,* 3rd Ed. Foundation Press.

MERCK & CO., INC. V. REYNOLDS

Hazen, Thomas. 2006. *Securities Regulation in a Nutshell,* 9th Ed., West Group.

Palmiter, Allen. 2005. *Security Regulation, 3rd Ed.* Aspen Publishers.

Soderquist, Larry, and Gabaldon, Theresa. 2006. *Securities Law: Concepts and Insights,* 3rd Ed. Foundation Press.

SENTENCING

BARBER V. THOMAS

Barber v. Thomas, Cornell University School of Law Available at http://www.law.cornell.edu/supct/ cert/09-5201.htm

Barber v. Thomas, Available at www.supremecourt. gov/opinions/09-5201

Barber v. Thomas, Available at www.supremecourt. gov/opinions/09pdf/09-5201.pdf

"Court Clarifies Calculations for 'Good-time Credits.'" *On the Docket,* U.S. Supreme Court Media Report, 7 June 2010. Available at http://otd. oyez.org/cases/2009/barber-v-thomas

"Justices Take Sentencing Reform Act Case." *On the Docket,* U.S. Supreme Court Media Report, 30 November 2009. Available at http://otd.oyez.org/ cases/2009/barber-v-thomas

UNITED STATES V. DILLON

Ward, Paula Reed. "Cocaine Sentencing Inequity Goes to Top Court." *Pittsburgh Post-Gazette.* March 28, 2010.

Ward, Paula Reed. "Model Prisoner Loses Bid for Reduced Term." *Pittsburgh Post-Gazette.* June 22, 2010

UNITED STATES V. DOLAN

Branham, Lynn S. *The Law and Policy of Sentencing and Corrections in a Nutshell,* 8th ed. St. Paul, Minn.: West, 2010.

Youderian, Annie. "Supreme Court Tackles Restitution Deadline." Courthouse News Service. April 20, 2010.

JOHNSON V. UNITED STATES

Branham, Lynm. 2005. *The Law of Sentencing and Corrections in a Nutshell.* St. Paul, Minn: West Group.

Tonry, Michael. 2004. *Sentencing Matters.* New York: Oxford University Press.

UNITED STATES V. O'BRIEN AND BURGESS

"Justices Hold Machine Gun Mandatory Minimum Cannot Apply Without Jury." *On the Docket,* U.S. Supreme Court Media Report, 24 May 2010. Available at http://otd.oyez.org/cases/2009/us-v-obrien-and-burgess

"Justices Take Sentence Enhancement Case." *On the Docket,* U.S. Supreme Court Media Report, 30 September 2009. Available at http://otd.oyez .org/cases/2009/us-v-obrien-and-burgess

United States v. O'Brien and Burgess, Cornell University School of Law Available at http://www. law.cornell.edu/supct/cert/08-1569.htm

United States v. O'Brien and Burgess, Available at www.supremecourt.gov/opinions/08-1569.htm

United States v. O'Brien and Burgess, Available at www.supremecourt.gov/opinions/09pdf/ 08-1569.pdf

MILLENNIUM BOMBER MUST BE RESENTENCED

Branham, Lynm. *The Law of Sentencing and Corrections in a Nutshell.* West Group, 2005.

Stith, Kate. *Fear of Judging: Sentencing Guidelines in the Federal Courts.* University of Chicago Press, 1998.

Tonry, Michael. *Sentencing Matters.* Oxford University Press, 2004.

SIXTH AMENDMENT

BERGHUIS, WARDEN V. SMITH

Berghuis v. Smith, Cornell University School of Law Available at http://www.law.cornell.edu/supct/ cert/08-1402.html

Berghuis v. Smith, No. 08-1402, Available at www. supremecourt.gov/opinions/08-1402.htm

The Oyez Project. "Berghuis v. Smith." U.S. Supreme Court Media Report, accessed on 3 June 2010.

Available at http://www.oyez.org/cases/ 2000-2009/2009/2009_08_1402

BRISCOE V. VIRGINIA

Briscoe v. Virginia, Cornell University School of Law Available at http://www.topics.law.cornell.edu/ supct/cert/07-11191

Briscoe v. Virginia, No. 07-11191, Available at www .supremecourtus.gov/docket/07-11191.html

"Court Releases Per Curiam Opinion in Crime Lab Case." *On the Docket,* U.S. Supreme Court News Media, 25 January 2010. Available at http://otd. oyez/2000-2009/2009/2009_07_11191.htm

SOTOMAYOR, SONIA

Liptak, Adam. "The Newest Justice Takes Her Seat." *New York Times.* September 9, 2009.

Savage, Charlie. "Sotomayor Confirmed by Senate, 68-31." *New York Times.* August 7, 2009.

SOVEREIGN IMMUNITY

REPUBLIC OF IRAQ V. BEATY

Cooper-Hill, James. 2006. *The Law of Sovereign Immunity and Terrorism,* New York: Oxford Univ. Press.

Grant, John, and Barker, J. Craig. 2009 *Parry and Grant Encyclopaedic Dictionary of International Law,* 3rd Ed., New York: Oxford Univ. Press.

SPEEDY TRIAL

BLOATE V. UNITED STATES

Bloate v. United States, Cornell University School of Law Available at http://www.law.cornell.edu/ supct/cert/08-728.html

Bloate v. United States, No. 08-728, Available at www .supremecourtus.gov/docket/08-728.htm

"Bloate v. United States." U.S. Supreme Court Media Report, accessed on 3 June 2010. Available at http://www.oyez.org/cases/2000-2009/2009/ 2009_08_728

STANDARD OF REVIEW

RENICO V. LETTS

The Oyez Project. "Renico v. Lett." U.S. Supreme Court Media Report, accessed on 3 June 2010. Available at http://www.oyez.org/cases/ 2000-2009/2009/2009_09_338

Renico v. Lett, Cornell University School of Law Available at http://www.law.cornell.edu/supct/ cert/09-338.htm

Renico v. Lett, No. 08-1200, Available at www .supremecourt.gov/opinions/09pdf/09-338.pdf

STATUTE OF LIMITATIONS

KRUPSKI V. COSTA CROCIERE

Krupski v. Costa Crociere, S.P.A., Cornell University School of Law Available at http://www.law.cornell.edu/supct/cert/09-337.htm

Krupski v. Costa Crociere, S.P.A., Available at www.supremecourt.gov/opinions/09-337.htm

Krupski v. Costa Crociere, S.P.A., Available at www.supremecourt.gov/opinions/09pdf/09-337.pdf

The Oyez Project. "Krupski v. Costa Crociere, S.P.A." U.S. Supreme Court Media Report, accessed on 14 June 2010. Available at http://www.oyez.org/cases/2000-2009/2009/2009_09337

SUBJECT MATTER JURISDICTION

MORRISON V. NATIONAL AUSTRALIA BANK

"Justices Rule Australian Bank Can't Be Sued in U.S." *On the Docket,* U.S. Supreme Court Media Report, 24 June 2010. Available at http://otd.oyez.org/cases/2009/morrison-v-national-australia-bank

"Justices Will Hear 'Foreign-cubed' Case." *On the Docket,* U.S. Supreme Court Media Report, 30 November 2009. Available at http://otd.oyez.org/cases/2009/morrison-v-national-australia-bank

Morrison v. National Australia Bank, Cornell University School of Law Available at http://www.law.cornell.edu/supct/cert/08-1191.htm

Morrison v. National Australia Bank, Ltd., No. 08-1191, Available at www.supremecourt.gov/opinions/08-1191.htm

Morrison v. National Australia Bank, Ltd., No. 08-1191. Available at www.supremecourt.gov/opinions/09pdf/08-1191.pdf

SUPREMACY CLAUSE

HAYWOOD V. DROWN

Lewis, Jr., Harold and Norman, Elizabeth. *Civil Rights Law and Practice.* Saint Paul, MN: West Group. 2004.

Palmer, John. *Constitutional Rights of Prisoners. 8th Edition.* Anderson Pub. Co. 2006.

Vieira, Norman. *Constitutional Civil Rights in a Nutshell.* Saint Paul, MN.: West Group. 1998.

TERRORISM

NINTH CIRCUIT TAKES A BROAD VIEW OF GOVERNMENT'S POWER TO DETAIN GUANTANAMO BAY DETAINEES

Grigg, Dicky. "Guantanamo: It is Not About Them—It is About Us." *The Advocate.* Spring 2010.

Means, Brian R. *Federal Habeas Manual.* Eagan, Minn.: Thomson/West. 2009.

THEFT

SHOPLIFTERS WHO CONFESSED ON DR. PHIL SHOW CONVICTED

Perry, Tony. "Grand Jury Indicts Couple Who Bragged About Shoplifting." *Los Angeles Times.* September 20, 2009.

"Shoplifting Confessions." Dr. Phil.com. Available online at http://drphil.com/shows/show/1171

VOTING RIGHTS ACT

NINTH CIRCUIT OVERTURNS WASHINGTON STATE FELONY DISENFRANCHISEMENT LAW

Currie, David. *Federal Jurisdiction in a Nutshell.* West Group, 1999.

Lewis,Jr., Harold and Norman, Elizabeth. *Civil Rights Law and Practice.* West Group, 2004.

Vieira, Norman. *Constitutional Civil Rights in a Nutshell.* West Group, 1998.

NORTHWEST AUSTIN MUNICIPAL UTILITY DISTRICT NUMBER ONE V. HOLDER

Currie, David. *Federal Jurisdiction in a Nutshell.* West Group, 1999.

Lewis,Jr., Harold and Norman, Elizabeth. *Civil Rights Law and Practice.* West Group, 2004.

Vieira, Norman. *Constitutional Civil Rights in a Nutshell.* West Group, 1998.

WHISTLEBLOWER

TEXAS NURSE FOUND NOT GUILTY FOR REPORTING DOCTOR

James, Susan Donaldson, Steve Osunami, and Michael Murray. "Nurse Whistle-Blower Not Guilty for Reporting Doctor."

Sack, Kevin. "Nurse to Stand Trial for Reporting Doctor." *New York Times.* February 7, 2010.

WHITE COLLAR CRIME

FORMER ATTORNEY RECEIVES 99-YEAR SENTENCE FOR INVESTMENT SCAM

Barbee, Darren. "Man Sentenced to 99 Years for Defrauding Nearly 130 in Ponzi Scheme." *Fort Worth Star-Telegram.* February 20, 2010.

Watt, Chad Eric. "Pervasiveness, Prosecution of White-Collar Crime Rising." *Dallas Business Journal.* February 19, 2010.

Abandonment: The surrender, relinquishment, disclaimer, or cession of property or of rights. Voluntary relinquishment of all right, title, claim, and possession, with the intent of not reclaiming it.

The giving up of a thing absolutely, without reference to any particular person or purpose, as vacating property with the intention of not returning, so that it may be appropriated by the next comer or finder. The voluntary relinquishment of possession of thing by owner with intention of terminating ownership, but without vesting it in any other person. The relinquishing of all title, possession, or claim, or a virtual, intentional throwing away of property.

Term includes both the intention to abandon and the external act by which the intention is carried into effect. In determining whether one has abandoned property or rights, the intention is the first and paramount object of inquiry, for there can be no abandonment without the intention to abandon.

Abandonment differs from surrender in that surrender requires an agreement, and also from forfeiture, in that forfeiture may be against the intention of the party alleged to have forfeited.

Abet: To encourage or incite another to commit a crime. This word is usually applied to aiding in the commission of a crime. To abet another to commit a murder is to command, procure, counsel, encourage, induce, or assist. To facilitate the commission of a crime, promote its accomplishment, or help in advancing or bringing it about.

In relation to charge of aiding and abetting, term includes knowledge of the perpetrator's wrongful purpose, and encouragement, promotion or counsel of another in the commission of the criminal offense.

A French word, *abeter*–to bait or excite an animal.

Abuse Of Discretion: A failure to take into proper consideration the facts and law relating to a particular matter; an arbitrary or unreasonable departure from precedents and settled judicial custom.

Abuse Of Power: Improper use of authority by someone who has that authority because he or she holds a public office.

Accretion: The act of adding portions of soil to the soil already in possession of the owner by gradual deposition through the operation of natural causes.

The growth of the value of a particular item given to a person as a specific bequest under the provisions of a will between the time the will was written and the time of death of the testator–the person who wrote the will.

Actual Notice: Conveying facts to a person with the intention to apprise that person of a proceeding in which his or her interests are involved, or informing a person of some fact that he or she has a right to know and which the informer has a legal duty to communicate.

Adjudication: The legal process of resolving a dispute. The formal giving or pronouncing of a judgment or decree in a court proceeding; also the judgment or decision given. The entry of a decree by a court in respect to the parties in a case. It implies a hearing by a court, after notice, of legal evidence on the factual issue(s) involved. The equivalent of a determination. It indicates that the claims of all the parties thereto have been considered and set at rest.

Administrative Agency: An official governmental body empowered with the authority to direct and supervise the implementation of particular legislative acts. In addition to *agency*, such governmental bodies may be called commissions, corporations (e.g., FDIC), boards, departments, or divisions.

Advancement: A gift of money or property made by a person while alive to his or her child or other legally recognized heir, the value of which the person intends to be deducted from the child's or heir's eventual share in the estate after the giver's death.

Advance: To pay money or give something of value before the date designated to do so; to provide capital to help a planned enterprise, expecting a return from it; to give someone an item before payment has been made for it.

Adversary Proceeding: Any action, hearing, investigation, inquest, or inquiry brought by one party against another in which the party seeking relief has given legal notice to and provided the other party with an opportunity to contest the claims that have been made against him or her.

Advisory Opinion: An opinion by a court as to the legality of proposed legislation or conduct, given in response to a request by the government, legislature, or some other interested party.

Affirmative Action: Employment programs required by federal statutes and regulations designed to remedy discriminatory practices in hiring minority group members; i.e., positive steps designed to eliminate existing and continuing discrimination, to remedy lingering effects of past discrimination, and to create systems and procedures to prevent future discrimination; commonly based on population percentages of minority groups in a particular area. Factors considered are race, color, sex, creed, and age.

Affirmative Defense: A new fact or set of facts that operates to defeat a claim even if the facts supporting that claim are true.

Antitrust Law: Legislation enacted by the federal and various state governments to regulate trade and commerce by preventing unlawful restraints, price-fixing, and monopolies, to promote competition, and to encourage the production of quality goods and services at the lowest prices, with the primary goal of safeguarding public welfare by ensuring that consumer demands will be met by the manufacture and sale of goods at reasonable prices.

Appellant: A person who dissatisfied with the judgment rendered in a lawsuit decided in a lower court or the findings from a proceeding before an administrative agency, asks a superior court to review the decision.

Appellate Court: A court having jurisdiction to review decisions of a trial-level or other lower court.

Appellate: Relating to appeals; reviews by superior courts of decisions of inferior courts or administrative agencies and other proceedings.

Apportionment: The process by which legislative seats are distributed among units entitled to representation. Determination of the number of representatives that a state, county, or other subdivision may send to a legislative body. The U.S. Constitution provides for a census every ten years, on the basis of which Congress apportions representatives according to population; but each state must have at least one representative. *Districting* is the establishment of the precise geographical boundaries of each such unit or constituency. Apportionment by state statute that denies the rule of one-person, one-vote is violative of equal protection of laws.

Also, the allocation of a charge or cost such as real estate taxes between two parties, often in the same ratio as the respective times that the parties are in possession or ownership of property during the fiscal period for which the charge is made or assessed.

Array: The entire group of jurors selected for a trial from which a smaller group is subsequently chosen to form a petit jury or a grand jury; the list of potential jurors.

Articles Of Impeachment: Formal written allegations of the causes that warrant the criminal trial of a public official before a quasi-political court.

Assign: To transfer to another, as to assign one's right to receive rental income from property of another. To designate for a particular function, as to assign an attorney to defend an indigent in a criminal prosecution. To specify or point out, as to assign errors in a lower court proceeding on a writ of error that is submitted to request a court to reverse the judgment of the lower court.

Attorney-Client Privilege: In law of evidence, client's privilege to refuse to disclose and to prevent any other person from disclosing confidential communications between the client and his or her attorney. Such privilege protects communications between attorney and client made for the purpose of furnishing or obtaining professional legal advice or assistance. That privilege that permits an attorney to refuse to testify as to communications from the client though it belongs to the client, not the attorney, and hence the client may waive it. In federal courts, state law is applied with respect to such privilege.

Avulsion: The immediate and noticeable addition to land caused by its removal from the property of another, by a sudden change in a water bed or in the course of a stream.

Bad Faith: The fraudulent deception of another person; the intentional or malicious refusal to perform some duty or contractual obligation.

Battery: At common law, an intentional unpermitted act causing harmful or offensive contact with the person of another.

Bench Trial: A trial conducted before a judge presiding without a jury.

Beneficial Interest: Profits or advantages from property derived from the terms of a trust agreement.

Bequest: A gift of personal property, such as money, stock, bonds, or jewelry, owned by a decedent at the time of death which is directed by the provisions of the decedent's will; a legacy.

Beyond A Reasonable Doubt: The standard that must be met by the prosecution's evidence in a criminal prosecution: that no other logical explanation can be derived from the facts except that the defendant committed the crime, thereby over-coming the presumption that a person is innocent until proven guilty.

Bilateral Contract: An agreement formed by an exchange of promises in which the promise of one party is consideration supporting the promise of the other party.

Bill Of Lading: A document signed by a carrier (a transporter of goods) or the carrier's representative and issued to a consignor (the shipper of goods) that evidences the receipt of goods for shipment to a specified designation and person.

Bona Fide: [*Latin, In good faith.*] Honest; genuine; actual; authentic; acting without the intention of defrauding.

Burglary: The criminal offense of breaking and entering a building illegally for the purpose of committing a crime therein.

Bylaws: The rules and regulations enacted by an association or a corporation to provide a framework for its operation and management.

Carriers: Individuals or businesses that are employed to deliver people or property to an agreed destination.

Case Law: Legal principles enunciated and embodied in judicial decisions that are derived from the application of particular areas of law to the facts of individual cases.

Cause Of Action: The fact or combination of facts that gives a person the right to seek judicial redress or relief against another. Also, the legal theory forming the basis of a lawsuit.

Certiorari: [*Latin, To be informed of.*] At common law, an original writ or order issued by the Chancery of King's Bench, commanding officers of inferior courts to submit the record of a cause pending before them to give the party more certain and speedy justice.

A writ that a superior appellate court issues on its discretion to an inferior court, ordering it to produce a certified record of a particular case it has tried, in order to determine whether any irregularities or errors occurred that justify review of the case.

A device by which the Supreme Court of the United States exercises its discretion in selecting the cases it will review

Circuit Court: A specific tribunal that possesses the legal authority to hear cases within its own geographical territory.

Civil Action: A lawsuit brought to enforce, redress, or protect rights of private litigants (the plaintiffs and the defendants); not a criminal proceeding.

Civil Procedure: The methods, procedures, and practices used in civil cases.

Class Action: A lawsuit that allows a large number of people with a common interest in a matter to sue or be sued as a group.

Closing Argument: The final factual and legal argument made by each attorney on all sides of a case in a trial prior to a verdict or judgment.

Codicil: A document that is executed by a person who had previously made his or her will, to modify, delete, qualify, or revoke provisions contained in it.

Collateral: Related; indirect; not bearing immediately upon an issue. The property pledged or given as a security interest, or a guarantee for payment of a debt, that will be taken or kept by the creditor in case of a default on the original debt.

Collective Bargaining Agreement: The contractual agreement between an employer and a labor union that governs wages, hours, and working conditions for employees and which can be enforced against both the employer and the union for failure to comply with its terms.

Comity: Courtesy; respect; a disposition to perform some official act out of goodwill and tradition rather than obligation or law. The acceptance or adoption of decisions or laws by a court of another jurisdiction, either foreign or domestic, based on public policy rather than legal mandate.

Commerce Clause: The provision of the U.S. Constitution that gives Congress exclusive power over trade activities between the states and with foreign countries and Indian tribes.

Common Law: The ancient law of England based upon societal customs and recognized and enforced by the judgments and decrees of the courts. The general body of statutes and case law that governed England and the American colonies prior to the American Revolution.

The principles and rules of action, embodied in case law rather than legislative enactments, applicable to the government and protection of persons and property that derive their authority from the community customs and traditions that evolved over the centuries as interpreted by judicial tribunals.

A designation used to denote the opposite of statutory, equitable, or civil; for example, a common-law action.

Common Stock: Evidence of participation in the ownership of a corporation that takes the form of printed certificates.

Comptroller: An officer who conducts the fiscal affairs of a state or municipal corporation.

Congressional Record: A daily publication of the federal government that details the legislative proceedings of Congress.

Constitutional Law: The written text of the state and federal constitutions. The body of judicial precedent that has gradually developed through a process in which courts interpret, apply, and explain the meaning of particular constitutional provisions and principles during a legal proceeding. Executive, legislative, and judicial actions that conform with the norms prescribed by a constitutional provision.

Court Administrator: An officer of the judicial system who performs administrative and clerical duties essential to the proper operation of the business of a court, such as tracking trial dates, keeping records, entering judgments, and issuing process.

Court Of Appeal: An intermediate federal judicial tribunal of review that is found in thirteen judicial districts, called circuits, in the United States.

A state judicial tribunal that reviews a decision rendered by an inferior tribunal to determine whether it made errors that warrant the reversal of its judgment.

Court Of Claims: A state judicial tribunal established as the forum in which to bring certain types of lawsuits against the state or its political subdivisions, such as a county. The former designation given to a federal tribunal created in 1855 by Congress with original jurisdiction–initial authority– to decide an action brought against the United States that is based upon the Constitution, federal law, any regulation of the executive department, or any express or implied contracts with the federal government.

Criminal Action: The procedure by which a person accused of committing a crime is charged, brought to trial, and judged.

Criminal Law: A body of rules and statutes that defines conduct prohibited by the government because it threatens and harms public safety and welfare and that establishes punishment to be imposed for the commission of such acts.

Criminal Procedure: The framework of laws and rules that govern the administration of justice in cases involving an individual who has been accused of a crime, beginning with the initial investigation of the crime and concluding either with the unconditional release of the accused by virture of acquittal (a judgment of not guilty) or by the imposition of a term of punishment pursuant to a conviction for the crime.

Cruel And Unusual Punishment: Another name for cruelty, or for the intentional, hostile infliction of physical or mental suffering upon another individual, which is a ground for divorce in many states.

Custodial Interrogation: Questioning initiated by law enforcement officers after a person is taken into custody or otherwise deprived of his or her freedom in any significant way, thus requiring that the person be advised of his or her constitutional rights.

Declaratory Judgment: Statutory remedy for the determination of a justiciable controversy where the plaintiff is in doubt as to his or her legal rights. A binding adjudication of the rights and status of litigants even though no consequential relief is awarded.

Defamation: Any intentional false communication, either written or spoken, that harms a person's reputation; decreases the respect, regard, or confidence in which a person is held; or induces disparaging, hostile, or disagreeable opinions or feelings against a person.

Dicta: Opinions of a judge that do not embody the resolution or determination of the specific case before the court. Expressions in a court's opinion that go beyond the facts before the court and therefore are individual views of the author of the opinion and not binding in subsequent cases as legal precedent. The plural of *dictum.*

Disposition: Act of disposing; transferring to the care or possession of another. The parting with, alienation of, or giving up of property. The final settlement of a matter and, with reference to decisions announced by a court, a judge's ruling is commonly referred to as disposition, regardless of level of resolution. In criminal procedure, the sentencing or other final settlement of a criminal case. With respect to a mental state, denotes an attitude, prevailing tendency, or inclination.

District Court: A designation of an inferior state court that exercises general jurisdiction that it has been granted by the constitution or statute which created it. A U.S. judicial tribunal with original jurisdiction to try cases or controversies that fall within its limited jurisdiction.

Docket: A written list of judicial proceedings set down for trial in a court.

To enter the dates of judicial proceedings scheduled for trial in a book kept by a court.

Doing Business: A qualification imposed in state long-arm statutes governing the service of process, the method by which a lawsuit is commenced, which requires nonresident corporations to engage in commercial transactions within state borders in order to be subject to the personal jurisdiction of state courts.

Double Jeopardy: A second prosecution for the same offense after acquittal or conviction or multiple punishments for same offense. The evil sought to be avoided by prohibiting double jeopardy is double trial and double conviction, not necessarily double punishment.

Due Process Of Law: A fundamental, constitutional guarantee that all legal proceedings will be fair and that one will be given notice of the proceedings and an opportunity to be heard before the government acts to take away one's life, liberty, or property. Also, a constitutional guarantee that a law shall not be unreasonable, arbitrary, or capricious.

Dummy: Sham; make-believe; pretended; imitation. Person who serves in place of another, or who serves until the proper person is named or available to take his place (e.g., dummy corporate directors; dummy owners of real estate).

Duress: Unlawful pressure exerted upon a person to coerce that person to perform an act that he or she ordinarily would not perform.

En Banc: [*Latin, French. In the bench.*] Full bench. Refers to a session where the entire membership of the court will participate in the decision rather than the regular quorum. In other countries, it is common for a court to have more members than are usually necessary to hear an appeal. In the United States, the Circuit Courts of Appeal usually sit in panels of judges but for important cases may expand the bench to a larger number, when the judges are said to be sitting *en banc.* Similarly, only one of the judges of the U.S. Tax Court will typically hear and decide on a tax controversy. However, when the issues involved are unusually novel or of wide impact, the case will be heard and decided by the full court sitting *en banc.*

Endowment: A transfer, generally as a gift, of money or property to an institution for a particular purpose. The bestowal of money as a permanent fund, the income of which is to be used for the benefit of a charity, college, or other institution.

Entity: A real being; existence. An organization or being that possesses separate existence for tax purposes. Examples would be corporations, partnerships, estates, and trusts. The accounting entity for which accounting statements are prepared may not be the same as the entity defined by law.

Entity includes corporation and foreign corporation; not-for-profit corporation; profit and not-for-profit unincorporated association; business trust, estate, partnership, trust, and two or more persons having a joint or common economic interest; and state, U.S., and foreign governments.

An existence apart, such as a corporation in relation to its stockholders.

Entity includes person, estate, trust, governmental unit.

Entrapment: The act of government agents or officials that induces a person to commit a crime he or she is not previously disposed to commit.

Entry Of Judgment: Formally recording the result of a lawsuit that is based upon the determination by the court of the facts and applicable law, and that makes the result effective for purposes of bringing an action to enforce it or to commence an appeal.

Equal Protection: The constitutional guarantee that no person or class of persons shall be denied the same protection of the laws that is enjoyed by other persons or other classes in like circumstances in their lives, liberty, property, and pursuit of happiness.

Estoppel: A legal principle that precludes a party from denying or alleging a certain fact owing to that party's previous conduct, allegation, or denial.

Et Seq.: An abbreviation for the Latin *et sequentes* or *et sequentia*, meaning "and the following."

Excise: A tax imposed on the performance of an act, the engaging in an occupation, or the enjoyment of a privilege. A tax on the manufacture, sale, or use of goods or on the carrying on of an occupation or activity, or a tax on the transfer of property. In current usage the term has been extended to include various license fees and practically every internal revenue tax except the income tax (e.g., federal alcohol and tobacco excise taxes).

Exoneration: The removal of a burden, charge, responsibility, duty, or blame imposed by law. The right of a party who is secondarily liable for a debt, such as a surety, to be reimbursed by the party with primary liability for payment of an obligation that should have been paid by the first party.

Extrajudicial: That which is done, given, or effected outside the course of regular judicial proceedings. Not founded upon, or unconnected with, the action of a court of law, as in extrajudicial evidence or an extrajudicial oath.

That which, though done in the course of regular judicial proceedings, is unnecessary to such proceedings, or interpolated, or beyond their scope, as in a extrajudicial opinion.

Extraordinary Remedy: The designation given to such writs as habeas corpus, mandamus, and quo warranto, determined in special proceedings and granted only where absolutely necessary to protect the legal rights of a party in a particular case, as opposed to the customary relief obtained by the maintenance of an action.

Extraterritoriality: The operation of laws upon persons existing beyond the limits of the enacting state or nation but still amenable to its laws. Jurisdiction exercised by a nation in other countries by treaty, or by its own ministers or consuls in foreign lands.

False Pretenses: False representations of past or present material facts, known by the wrongdoer to be false, made with the intent to defraud a victim into passing title in property to the wrongdoer.

Federal Courts: The U.S. judicial tribunals created by Article III of the Constitution, or by Congress, to hear and determine justiciable controversies.

Federal Register: A daily publication that makes available to the public the rules, regulations, and other legal notices issued by federal administrative agencies.

Felony: A serious crime, characterized under federal law and many state statutes as any offense punishable by death or imprisonment in excess of one year.

Fiduciary: An individual in whom another has placed the utmost trust and confidence to manage and protect property or money. The relationship wherein one person has an obligation to act for another's benefit.

Filibuster: A tactic used by a LEGISLATIVE representative to hinder and delay consideration of an action to be taken on a proposed bill through prolonged, irrelevant, and procrastinating speeches on the floor of the House, Senate, or other legislative body.

First Instance: The initial trial court where an action is brought.

Fiscal: Relating to finance or financial matters, such as money, taxes, or public or private revenues.

Foreclosure: A procedure by which the holder of a mortgage–an interest in land providing security for the performance of a duty or the payment of a debt–sells the property upon the failure of the debtor to pay the mortgage debt and, thereby, terminates his or her rights in the property.

Forfeiture: The involuntary relinquishment of money or property without compensation as a consequence of a breach or nonperformance of some legal obligation or the commission of a crime. The loss of a corporate charter or franchise as a result of illegality, malfeasance, or nonfeasance. The surrender by an owner of her or his entire interest in real property mandated by law as a punishment for illegal conduct or negligence. In old English law, the release of land by a tenant to the tenant's lord due to some breach of conduct, or the loss of goods or chattels (articles of personal property) assessed as a penalty against the perpetrator of some crime or offense and as a recompense to the injured party.

Forthwith: Immediately; promptly; without delay; directly; within a reasonable time under the circumstances of the case.

Fraud: A false representation of a matter of fact–whether by words or by conduct, by false or misleading allegations, or by concealment of what should have been disclosed–that deceives and is intended to deceive another so that the individual will act upon it to her or his legal injury.

Fraudulent: The description of a willful act commenced with the specific intent to deceive or cheat, in order to cause some financial detriment to another and to engender personal financial gain.

General Jurisdiction: The legal authority of a court to entertain whatever type of case comes up within the geographical area over which its power extends.

General Verdict: A decision by a jury that determines which side in a particular controversy wins, and in some cases, the amount of money in damages to be awarded.

Genetic Engineering: The human manipulation of the genetic material of a cell.

Good Cause: Legally adequate or substantial grounds or reason to take a certain action.

Good Faith: Honesty; a sincere intention to deal fairly with others.

Grand Jury: A panel of citizens that is convened by a court to decide whether it is appropriate for the government to indict (proceed with a prosecution against) someone suspected of a crime.

Grand Larceny: A category of larceny–the offense of illegally taking the property of another–in which the value of the property taken is greater than that set for petit larceny.

Gross Negligence: An indifference to, and a blatant violation of, a legal duty with respect to the rights of others.

Guardian: A person lawfully invested with the power, and charged with the obligation, of taking care of and managing the property and rights of a person who, because of age, understanding, or self-control, is considered incapable of administering his or her own affairs.

Habeas Corpus: [*Latin, You have the body.*] A writ (court order) that commands an individual or a government official who has restrained another to produce the prisoner at a designated time and place so that the court can determine the legality of custody and decide whether to order the prisoner's release.

Hearsay: A statement made out of court that is offered in court as evidence to prove the truth of the matter asserted.

Incorporation Doctrine: A constitutional doctrine whereby selected provisions of the Bill of Rights are made applicable to the states through the Due Process Clause of the Fourteenth Amendment.

Indicia: Signs; indications. Circumstances that point to the existence of a given fact as probable, but not certain. For example, *indicia of partnership* are any circumstances which would induce the belief that a given person was in reality, though not technically, a member of a given firm.

Interlocutory: Provisional; interim; temporary; not final; that which intervenes between the beginning and the end of a lawsuit or proceeding to either decide a particular point or matter that is not the final issue of the entire controversy or prevent irreparable harm during the pendency of the lawsuit.

Intervenor: An individual who is not already a party to an existing lawsuit but who makes himself or herself a party either by joining with the plaintiff or uniting with the defendant in resistance of the plaintiff's claims.

Involuntary Manslaughter: The act of unlawfully killing another human being unintentionally.

Irreparable Injury: Any harm or loss that is not easily repaired, restored, or compensated by monetary damages. A serious wrong, generally of a repeated and continuing nature, that has an equitable remedy of injunctive relief.

Irrevocable: Unable to cancel or recall; that which is unalterable or irreversible.

Issue Preclusion: A concept that refers to the fact that a particular question of fact or law, one that has already been fully litigated by the parties in an action for which there has been a judgment on the merits, cannot be re-litigated in any future action involving the same parties or their privies (persons who would be bound by the judgment rendered for the party).

Jeopardy: Danger; hazard; peril. In a criminal action, the danger of conviction and punishment confronting the defendant.

Joint Venture: An association of two or more individuals or companies engaged in a solitary business enterprise for profit without actual partnership or incorporation; also called a joint adventure.

Judicial Administration: The practices, procedures, and offices that deal with the management of the administrative systems of the courts.

Juris Doctor: The degree awarded to an individual upon the successful completion of law school.

Jurisprudence: From the Latin term *juris prudentia*, which means "the study, knowledge, or science of law"; in the United States, more broadly associated with the philosophy of law.

Just Compensation: Equitable remuneration to the owner of private property that is expropriated for public use through condemnation, the implementation of the governmental power of eminent domain.

Justice Of The Peace: A judicial officer with limited power whose duties may include hearing cases that involve civil controversies, conserving the peace, performing judicial acts, hearing minor criminal complaints, and committing offenders.

Larceny: The unauthorized taking and removal of the personal property of another by a person who intends to permanently deprive the owner of it; a crime against the right of possession.

Legal Tender: All U.S. coins and currencies–regardless of when coined or issued–including (in terms of the Federal Reserve System) Federal Reserve notes and circulating notes of Federal Reserve banks and national banking associations that are used for all debts, public and private, public charges, taxes, duties, and dues.

Libelous: In the nature of a written defamation, a communication that tends to injure reputation.

Liquidate: To pay and settle the amount of a debt; to convert assets to cash; to aggregate the assets of an insolvent enterprise and calculate its liabilities in order to settle with the debtors and the creditors and apportion the remaining assets, if any, among the stockholders or owners of the corporation.

Magistrate: Any individual who has the power of a public civil officer or inferior judicial officer, such as a justice of the peace.

Mail Fraud: A crime in which the perpetrator develops a scheme using the mails to defraud another of money or property. This crime specifically requires the intent to defraud, and is a federal offense governed by section 1341 of title 18 of the U.S. Code. The mail fraud statute was first enacted in 1872 to prohibit illicit mailings with the Postal Service (formerly the Post Office) for the purpose of executing a fraudulent scheme.

Mandamus: [*Latin, We comand.*] A writ or order that is issued from a court of superior jurisdiction that commands an inferior tribunal, corporation, municipal corporation, or individual to perform, or refrain from performing, a particular act, the performance or omission of which is required by law as an obligation.

Market Value: The highest price a willing buyer would pay and a willing seller would accept, both being fully informed, and the property being exposed for sale for a reasonable period of time. The market value may be different from the price a property can actually be sold for at a given time (market price). The market value of an article or piece of property is the price that it might be expected to bring if offered for sale in a fair market; not the price that might be obtained on a sale at public auction or a sale forced by the necessities of the owner, but such a price as would be fixed by negotiation and mutual agreement, after ample time to find a purchaser, as between a vendor who is willing (but not compelled) to sell and a purchaser who desires to buy but is not compelled to take the particular article or piece of property.

Mediation: A settlement of a dispute or controversy by setting up an independent person between two contending parties in order to aid them in the settlement of their disagreement.

Mental Anguish: When connected with a physical injury, includes both the resultant mental sensation of pain and also the accompanying feelings of distress, fright, and anxiety. As an element of damages implies a relatively high degree of mental pain and distress; it is more than mere disappointment, anger, worry, resentment, or embarrassment, although it may include all of these, and it includes mental sensation of pain resulting from such painful emotions as grief, severe disappointment, indignation, wounded pride, shame, despair, and/or public humiliation. In other connections, and as a ground for divorce or for compensable damages or an element of damages, it includes the mental suffering resulting from the excitation of the more poignant and painful emotions, such as grief, severe disappointment, indignation, wounded pride, shame, public humiliation, despair, etc.

Merit System: System used by federal and state governments for hiring and promoting governmental employees to civil service positions on the basis of competence.

Miscegenation: Mixture of races. A term formerly applied to marriage between persons of different races. Statutes prohibiting marriage between persons of different races have been held to be invalid as contrary to the equal protection Clause of the Constitution.

Misdemeanor: Offenses lower than felonies and generally those punishable by fine, penalty, forfeiture, or imprisonment other than in a penitentiary. Under federal law, and most state laws, any offense other than a felony is classified as a misdemeanor. Certain states also have various classes of misdemeanors (e.g., Class A, B, etc.).

Mitigating Circumstances: Circumstances that may be considered by a court in determining culpability of a defendant or the extent of damages to be awarded to a plaintiff. Mitigating circumstances do not justify or excuse an offense but may reduce the severity of a charge. Similarly, a recognition of mitigating circumstances to reduce a damage award does not imply that the damages were not suffered but that they have been partially ameliorated.

Money Laundering: The process of taking the proceeds of criminal activity and making them appear legal.

Monopoly: An economic advantage held by one or more persons or companies deriving from the exclusive power to carry on a particular business or trade or to manufacture and sell a particular item, thereby suppressing competition and allowing such persons or companies to raise the price of a product or service substantially above the price that would be established by a free market.

Mutual Fund: A fund, in the form of an investment company, in which shareholders combine their money to invest in a variety of stocks, bonds, and money-market investments such as U.S. Treasury bills and bank certificates of deposit.

Of Counsel: A term commonly applied in the practice of law to an attorney who has been employed to aid in the preparation and management of a particular case but who is not the principal attorney in the action.

Of Record: Entered on the appropriate official documents maintained by a governmental body and that are usually available for inspection by the public.

Open Court: Common law requires a trial in open court; "open court" means a court to which the public has a right to be admitted. This term may mean either a court that has been formally convened and declared open for the transaction of its proper judicial business or a court that is freely open to spectators.

Ordinance: A law, statute, or regulation enacted by a municipal corporation.

Original Jurisdiction: The authority of a tribunal to entertain a lawsuit, try it, and set forth a judgment on the law and facts.

Penny Stocks: Inexpensive issues of stock, typically selling at less than $1 a share, in companies that often are newly formed or involved in highly speculative ventures.

Penology: The science of prison administration and rehabilitation of criminals.

Pension: A benefit, usually money, paid regularly to retired employees or their survivors by private business and federal, state, and local governments. Employers are not required to establish pension benefits but do so to attract qualified employees.

Per Curiam: [*Latin, By the court.*] A phrase used to distinguish an opinion of the whole court from an opinion written by any one judge.

Plurality: The opinion of an appellate court in which more justices join than in any concurring opinion.

The excess of votes cast for one candidate over those votes cast for any other candidate.

Ponzi Scheme: A fraudulent investment plan in which the investments of later investors are used to pay earlier investors, giving the appearance that the investments of the initial participants dramatically increase in value in a short amount of time.

Positive Law: Those laws that have been duly enacted by a properly instituted and popularly recognized branch of government.

Preemption: A doctrine based on the Supremacy Clause of the U.S. Constitution that holds that certain matters are of such a national, as opposed to local, character that federal laws preempt or take precedence over state laws. As such, a state may not pass a law inconsistent with the federal law.

A doctrine of state law that holds that a state law displaces a local law or regulation that is in the same field and is in conflict or inconsistent with the state law.

Preliminary Injunction: A temporary order made by a court at the request of one party that prevents the other party from pursuing a particular course of conduct until the conclusion of a trial on the merits.

Preponderance Of Evidence: A standard of proof that must be met by a plaintiff if he or she is to win a civil action.

Price-Fixing: The organized setting of what the public will be charged for certain products or services agreed to by competitors in the marketplace in violation of the Sherman Anti-Trust Act (15 U.S.C.A. § 1 et seq.).

Prima Facie: [*Latin, On the first appearance.*] A fact presumed to be true unless it is disproved.

Privilege Against Self-Incrimination: The right, under the Fifth Amendment to the U.S. Constitution, not to be a witness against oneself in a criminal proceeding.

Privileges And Immunities: Concepts contained in the U.S. Constitution that place the citizens of each state on an equal basis with citizens of other states in respect to advantages resulting from citizenship in those states and citizenship in the United States.

Probable Cause: Apparent facts discovered through logical inquiry that would lead a reasonably intelligent and prudent person to believe that an accused person has committed a crime, thereby warranting his or her prosecution, or that a cause of action has accrued, justifying a civil lawsuit.

Probate: The court process by which a will is proved valid or invalid. The legal process wherein the estate of a decedent is administered.

Protective Order: A court order, direction, decree, or command to protect a person from further harassment, service of process, or discovery.

Proximate Cause: An act from which an injury results as a natural, direct, uninterrupted consequence and without which the injury would not have occurred.

Public Figure: A description applied in libel and slander actions, as well as in those alleging invasion of privacy, to anyone who has gained prominence in the community as a result of his or her name or exploits, whether willingly or unwillingly.

Public Offering: An issue of securities offered for sale to the public.

Punitive Damages: Monetary compensation awarded to an injured party that goes beyond that which is necessary to compensate the individual for losses and that is intended to punish the wrongdoer.

Purview: The part of a statute or a law that delineates its purpose and scope.

Qui Tam Actions: Civil actions maintained by private persons on behalf of both themselves and the government to recover damages or to enforce penalties available under a statute prohibiting specified conduct. The term *quitam* is short for the latin *qui tam pro domino rege quam pro se ipso in hac parte sequitur,* which means "who brings the action for the king as well as for himself."

Ratification: The confirmation or adoption of an act that has already been performed.

Receiver: An archaic term, used in common law and civil law countries, to designate an individual who holds and conceals stolen goods for thieves. Currently an independent individual appointed by a court to handle money or property during a lawsuit.

Redress: Compensation for injuries sustained; recovery or restitution for harm or injury; damages or equitable relief. Access to the courts to gain reparation for a wrong.

Repeal: The annulment or abrogation of a previously existing statute by the enactment of a later law that revokes the former law.

Restitution: In the context of criminal law, state programs under which an offender is required, as a condition of his or her sentence, to repay money or donate services to the victim or society; with respect to maritime law, the restoration of articles lost by jettison, done when the remainder of the cargo has been saved, at the general charge of the owners of the cargo; in the law of torts, or civil wrongs, a measure of damages; in regard to contract law, the restoration of a party injured by a breach of contract to the position that party occupied before she or he entered the contract.

Right Of Action: The privilege of instituting a lawsuit arising from a particular transaction or state of facts, such as a suit that is based on a contract or a tort, a civil wrong.

Robbery: The taking of money or goods in the possession of another, from his or her person or immediate presence, by force or intimidation.

Rule Of Law: Rule according to law; rule under law; or rule according to a higher law.

Scienter: [*Latin, Knowingly.*] Guilty knowledge that is sufficient to charge a person with the consequences of his or her acts.

Search And Seizure: In international law, the right of ships of war, as regulated by treaties, to examine a merchant vessel during war in order to determine whether the ship or its cargo is liable to seizure.

A hunt by law enforcement officials for property or communications believed to be evidence of crime, and the act of taking possession of this property.

Solicitation: Urgent request, plea, or entreaty; enticing, asking. The criminal offense of urging someone to commit an unlawful act.

Solicitor General: An officer of the U.S. Department of Justice who represents the U.S. government in cases before the U.S. Supreme Court.

Sovereign Immunity: The legal protection that prevents a sovereign state or person from being sued without consent.

State Action: A requirement for claims that arise under the Due Process Clause of the Fourteenth Amendment and civil rights legislation, for which a private citizen seeks relief in the form of damages or redress based on an improper intrusion by the government into his or her private life.

State Interest: A broad term for any matter of public concern that is addressed by a government in law or policy.

Statute: An act of a legislature that declares, proscribes, or commands something; a specific law, expressed in writing.

Statute Of Limitations: A type of federal or state law that restricts the time within which legal proceedings may be brought.

Statutory Rape: Sexual intercourse by an adult with a person below a statutorily designated age.

Statutory: Created, defined, or relating to a statute; required by statute; conforming to a statute.

Strict Scrutiny: A standard of judicial review for a challenged policy in which the court presumes the policy to be invalid unless the government can demonstrate a compelling interest to justify the policy.

Subject Matter Jurisdiction: The power of a court to hear and determine cases of the general class to which the proceedings in question belong.

Substantive Law: The part of the law that creates, defines, and regulates rights, including, for example, the law of contracts, torts, wills, and real property; the essential substance of rights under law.

Summary Judgment: A procedural device used during civil litigation to promptly and expeditiously dispose of a case without a trial. It is used when there is no dispute as to the material facts of the case and a party is entitled to judgment as a matter of law.

Supremacy Clause: The clause of Article VI of the U.S. Constitution that declares that all laws and treaties made by the federal government shall be the "supreme law of the land."

Suspended Sentence: A sentence given after the formal conviction of a crime that the convicted person is not required to serve.

Taxable Income: Under the federal tax law, gross income reduced by adjustments and allowable deductions. It is the income against which tax rates are applied to compute an individual or entity's tax liability. The essence of taxable income is the accrual of some gain, profit, or benefit to a taxpayer.

Term Of Art: A word or phrase that has special meaning in a particular context.

Third Party: A generic legal term for any individual who does not have a direct connection with a legal transaction but who might be affected by it.

Trustee: An individual or corporation named by an individual, who sets aside property to be used for the benefit of another person, to manage the property as provided by the terms of the document that created the arrangement.

U.S. Code: A multivolume publication of the text of statutes enacted by Congress.

Unconscionable: Unusually harsh and shocking to the conscience; that which is so grossly unfair that a court will proscribe it.

Venue: A place, such as the territory from which residents are selected to serve as jurors.

A proper place, such as the correct court to hear a case because it has authority over events that have occurred within a certain geographical area.

Without Prejudice: Without any loss or waiver of rights or priveleges.

Writ: An order issued by a court requiring that something be done or giving authority to do a specified act.

Wrongful Death: The taking of the life of an individual resulting from the willful or negligent act of another person or persons.

A.	Atlantic Reporter	ACS	Agricultural Cooperative Service
A. 2d	Atlantic Reporter, Second Series	ACT	American College Test
AA	Alcoholics Anonymous	Act'g Legal Adv.	Acting Legal Advisor
AAA	American Arbitration Association; Agricultural Adjustment Act of 1933	ACUS	Administrative Conference of the United States
		ACYF	Administration on Children, Youth, and Families
AALS	Association of American Law Schools	A.D. 2d	Appellate Division, Second Series, N.Y.
AAPRP	All African People's Revolutionary Party	ADA	Americans with Disabilities Act of 1990
AARP	American Association of Retired Persons	ADAMHA	Alcohol, Drug Abuse, and Mental Health Administration
AAS	American Anti-Slavery Society	ADC	Aid to Dependent Children
ABA	American Bar Association; Architectural Barriers Act of 1968; American Bankers Association	ADD	Administration on Developmental Disabilities
		ADEA	Age Discrimination in Employment Act of 1967
ABC	American Broadcasting Companies, Inc. (formerly American Broadcasting Corporation)	ADL	Anti-Defamation League
		ADR	Alternative dispute resolution
		AEC	Atomic Energy Commission
ABM	Antiballistic missile	AECB	Arms Export Control Board
ABM Treaty	Anti-Ballistic Missile Treaty of 1972	AEDPA	Antiterrorism and Effective Death Penalty Act
ABVP	Anti-Biased Violence Project	A.E.R.	All England Law Reports
A/C	Account	AFA	American Family Association; Alabama Freethought Association
A.C.	Appeal cases		
ACAA	Air Carrier Access Act		
ACCA	Armed Career Criminal Act of 1984	AFB	American Farm Bureau
		AFBF	American Farm Bureau Federation
ACF	Administration for Children and Families	AFDC	Aid to Families with Dependent Children
ACLU	American Civil Liberties Union	aff'd per cur.	Affirmed by the court
ACRS	Accelerated Cost Recovery System	AFIS	Automated fingerprint identification system

AFL	American Federation of Labor	Ann. Dig.	Annual Digest of Public International Law Cases
AFL-CIO	American Federation of Labor and Congress of Industrial Organizations	ANRA	American Newspaper Publishers Association
AFRes	Air Force Reserve	ANSCA	Alaska Native Claims Act
AFSC	American Friends Service Committee	ANZUS	Australia-New Zealand-United States Security Treaty Organization
AFSCME	American Federation of State, County, and Municipal Employees	AOA	Administration on Aging
		AOE	Arizonans for Official English
AGRICOLA	Agricultural Online Access		
AIA	Association of Insurance Attorneys	AOL	America Online
		AP	Associated Press
AIB	American Institute for Banking	APA	Administrative Procedure Act of 1946
AID	Artificial insemination using a third-party donor's sperm; Agency for International Development	APHIS	Animal and Plant Health Inspection Service
		App. Div.	Appellate Division Reports, N.Y. Supreme Court
AIDS	Acquired immune deficiency syndrome	Arb. Trib., U.S.-British	Arbitration Tribunal, Claim Convention of 1853, United States and Great Britain Convention of 1853
AIH	Artificial insemination using the husband's sperm		
AIM	American Indian Movement		
AIPAC	American Israel Public Affairs Committee	Ardcor	American Roller Die Corporation
AIUSA	Amnesty International, U.S.A. Affiliate	ARPA	Advanced Research Projects Agency
AJS	American Judicature Society	ARPANET	Advanced Research Projects Agency Network
ALA	American Library Association		
Alcoa	Aluminum Company of America	ARS	Advanced Record System
		Art.	Article
ALEC	American Legislative Exchange Council	ARU	American Railway Union
		ASCME	American Federation of State, County, and Municipal Employees
ALF	Animal Liberation Front		
ALI	American Law Institute		
ALJ	Administrative law judge	ASCS	Agriculture Stabilization and Conservation Service
All E.R.	All England Law Reports		
ALO	Agency Liaison	ASM	Available Seatmile
A.L.R.	American Law Reports	ASPCA	American Society for the Prevention of Cruelty to Animals
ALY	*American Law Yearbook*		
AMA	American Medical Association		
		Asst. Att. Gen.	Assistant Attorney General
AMAA	Agricultural Marketing Agreement Act	AT&T	American Telephone and Telegraph
Am. Dec.	American Decisions	ATFD	Alcohol, Tobacco and Firearms Division
amdt.	Amendment		
Amer. St. Papers, For. Rels.	American State Papers, Legislative and Executive Documents of the Congress of the U.S., Class I, Foreign Relations, 1832–1859	ATLA	Association of Trial Lawyers of America
		ATO	Alpha Tau Omega
		ATTD	Alcohol and Tobacco Tax Division
		ATU	Alcohol Tax Unit
AMS	Agricultural Marketing Service	AUAM	American Union against Militarism
AMVETS	American Veterans (of World War II)	AUM	Animal Unit Month
		AZT	Azidothymidine
ANA	Administration for Native Americans	BAC	Blood alcohol concentration

BALSA	Black-American Law Student Association	CAFE	Corporate average fuel economy
BATF	Bureau of Alcohol, Tobacco and Firearms	Cal. 2d	California Reports, Second Series
BBS	Bulletin Board System	Cal. 3d	California Reports, Third Series
BCCI	Bank of Credit and Commerce International	CALR	Computer-assisted legal research
BEA	Bureau of Economic Analysis		
Bell's Cr. C.	Bell's English Crown Cases	Cal. Rptr.	California Reporter
Bevans	United States Treaties, etc. *Treaties and Other International Agreements of the United States of America, 1776–1949* (compiled under the direction of Charles I. Bevans, 1968–76)	CAP	Common Agricultural Policy
		CARA	Classification and Ratings Administration
		CATV	Community antenna television
		CBO	Congressional Budget Office
		CBS	Columbia Broadcasting System
BFOQ	Bona fide occupational qualification	CBOEC	Chicago Board of Election Commissioners
BI	Bureau of Investigation		
BIA	Bureau of Indian Affairs; Board of Immigration Appeals	CCC	Commodity Credit Corporation
		CCDBG	Child Care and Development Block Grant of 1990
BID	Business improvement district	C.C.D. Pa.	Circuit Court Decisions, Pennsylvania
BJS	Bureau of Justice Statistics	C.C.D. Va.	Circuit Court Decisions, Virginia
Black.	Black's United States Supreme Court Reports	CCEA	Cabinet Council on Economic Affairs
Blatchf.	Blatchford's United States Circuit Court Reports		
BLM	Bureau of Land Management	CCP	Chinese Communist Party
BLS	Bureau of Labor Statistics	CCR	Center for Constitutional Rights
BMD	Ballistic missile defense		
BNA	Bureau of National Affairs	C.C.R.I.	Circuit Court, Rhode Island
BOCA	Building Officials and Code Administrators International	CD	Certificate of deposit; compact disc
		CDA	Communications Decency Act
BOP	Bureau of Prisons		
BPP	Black Panther Party for Self-defense	CDBG	Community Development Block Grant Program
Brit. and For.	British and Foreign State Papers	CDC	Centers for Disease Control and Prevention; Community Development Corporation
BSA	Boy Scouts of America		
BTP	Beta Theta Pi		
Burr.	James Burrows, *Report of Cases Argued and Determined in the Court of King's Bench during the Time of Lord Mansfield* (1766–1780)	CDF	Children's Defense Fund
		CDL	Citizens for Decency through Law
		CD-ROM	Compact disc read-only memory
		CDS	Community Dispute Services
BVA	Board of Veterans Appeals	CDW	Collision damage waiver
c.	Chapter	CENTO	Central Treaty Organization
C³I	Command, Control, Communications, and Intelligence	CEO	Chief executive officer
		CEQ	Council on Environmental Quality
C.A.	Court of Appeals	CERCLA	Comprehensive Environmental Response, Compensation, and Liability Act of 1980
CAA	Clean Air Act		
CAB	Civil Aeronautics Board; Corporation for American Banking		
		cert.	*Certiorari*

CETA	Comprehensive Employment and Training Act	CLEO	Council on Legal Education Opportunity; Chief Law Enforcement Officer
C & F	Cost and freight		
CFC	Chlorofluorocarbon	CLP	Communist Labor Party of America
CFE Treaty	Conventional Forces in Europe Treaty of 1990	CLS	Christian Legal Society; critical legal studies (movement); Critical Legal Studies (membership organization)
C.F. & I.	Cost, freight, and insurance		
C.F.R	Code of Federal Regulations		
CFNP	Community Food and Nutrition Program		
CFTA	Canadian Free Trade Agreement	C.M.A.	Court of Military Appeals
CFTC	Commodity Futures Trading Commission	CMEA	Council for Mutual Economic Assistance
Ch.	Chancery Division, English Law Reports	CMHS	Center for Mental Health Services
CHAMPVA	Civilian Health and Medical Program at the Veterans Administration	C.M.R.	Court of Military Review
		CNN	Cable News Network
		CNO	Chief of Naval Operations
CHEP	Cuban/Haitian Entrant Program	CNOL	Consolidated net operating loss
CHINS	Children in need of supervision	CNR	Chicago and Northwestern Railway
CHIPS	Child in need of protective services	CO	Conscientious Objector
		C.O.D.	Cash on delivery
Ch.N.Y.	Chancery Reports, New York	COGP	Commission on Government Procurement
Chr. Rob.	Christopher Robinson, *Reports of Cases Argued and Determined in the High Court of Admiralty* (1801–1808)	COINTELPRO	Counterintelligence Program
		Coke Rep.	Coke's English King's Bench Reports
		COLA	Cost-of-living adjustment
		COMCEN	Federal Communications Center
CIA	Central Intelligence Agency		
CID	Commercial Item Descriptions	Comp.	Compilation
		Conn.	Connecticut Reports
C.I.F.	Cost, insurance, and freight	CONTU	National Commission on New Technological Uses of Copyrighted Works
CINCNORAD	Commander in Chief, North American Air Defense Command		
		Conv.	Convention
C.I.O.	Congress of Industrial Organizations	COPA	Child Online Protection Act (1998)
CIPE	Center for International Private Enterprise	COPS	Community Oriented Policing Services
C.J.	Chief justice	Corbin	Arthur L. Corbin, *Corbin on Contracts: A Comprehensive Treatise on the Rules of Contract Law* (1950)
CJIS	Criminal Justice Information Services		
C.J.S.	Corpus Juris Secundum		
Claims Arb. under Spec. Conv., Nielsen's Rept.	Frederick Kenelm Nielsen, *American and British Claims Arbitration under the Special Agreement Concluded between the United States and Great Britain, August 18, 1910* (1926)	CORE	Congress on Racial Equality
		Cox's Crim. Cases	Cox's Criminal Cases (England)
		COYOTE	Call Off Your Old Tired Ethics
		CPA	Certified public accountant
		CPB	Corporation for Public Broadcasting, the
CLASP	Center for Law and Social Policy	CPI	Consumer Price Index
		CPPA	Child Pornography Prevention Act
CLE	Center for Law and Education; Continuing Legal Education	CPSC	Consumer Product Safety Commission

Cranch	Cranch's United States Supreme Court Reports	D.C.	United States District Court; District of Columbia
CRF	Constitutional Rights Foundation	D.C. Del.	United States District Court, Delaware
CRR	Center for Constitutional Rights	D.C. Mass.	United States District Court, Massachusetts
CRS	Congressional Research Service; Community Relations Service	D.C. Md.	United States District Court, Maryland
CRT	Critical race theory	D.C.N.D.Cal.	United States District Court, Northern District, California
CSA	Community Services Administration		
CSAP	Center for Substance Abuse Prevention	D.C.N.Y.	United States District Court, New York
CSAT	Center for Substance Abuse Treatment	D.C.Pa.	United States District Court, Pennsylvania
CSC	Civil Service Commission	DCS	Deputy Chiefs of Staff
CSCE	Conference on Security and Cooperation in Europe	DCZ	District of the Canal Zone
		DDT	Dichlorodiphenyl-tricloroethane
CSG	Council of State Governments	DEA	Drug Enforcement Administration
CSO	Community Service Organization		
CSP	Center for the Study of the Presidency	Decl. Lond.	Declaration of London, February 26, 1909
C-SPAN	Cable-Satellite Public Affairs Network	Dev. & B.	Devereux & Battle's North Carolina Reports
CSRS	Cooperative State Research Service	DFL	Minnesota Democratic-Farmer-Labor
CSWPL	Center on Social Welfare Policy and Law	DFTA	Department for the Aging
CTA	Cum testamento annexo (with the will attached)	Dig. U.S. Practice in Intl. Law	Digest of U.S. Practice in International Law
Ct. Ap. D.C.	Court of Appeals, District of Columbia	Dist. Ct.	D.C. United States District Court, District of Columbia
Ct. App. No. Ireland	Court of Appeals, Northern Ireland	D.L.R.	Dominion Law Reports (Canada)
Ct. Cl.	Court of Claims, United States	DMCA	Digital Millennium Copyright Act
Ct. Crim. Apps.	Court of Criminal Appeals (England)	DNA	Deoxyribonucleic acid
		Dnase	Deoxyribonuclease
Ct. of Sess., Scot.	Court of Sessions, Scotland	DNC	Democratic National Committee
CTI	Consolidated taxable income	DOC	Department of Commerce
CU	Credit union	DOD	Department of Defense
CUNY	City University of New York	DODEA	Department of Defense Education Activity
Cush.	Cushing's Massachusetts Reports	Dodson	Dodson's Reports, English Admiralty Courts
CWA	Civil Works Administration; Clean Water Act	DOE	Department of Energy
DACORB	Department of the Army Conscientious Objector Review Board	DOER	Department of Employee Relations
		DOJ	Department of Justice
		DOL	Department of Labor
Dall.	Dallas's Pennsylvania and United States Reports	DOMA	Defense of Marriage Act of 1996
DAR	Daughters of the American Revolution	DOS	Disk operating system
DARPA	Defense Advanced Research Projects Agency	DOT	Department of Transportation
DAVA	Defense Audiovisual Agency	DPT	Diphtheria, pertussis, and tetanus

DRI	Defense Research Institute	ESRD	End-Stage Renal Disease Program
DSAA	Defense Security Assistance Agency	ETA	Employment and Training Administration
DUI	Driving under the influence; driving under intoxication	ETS	Environmental tobacco smoke
DVD	Digital versatile disc	et seq.	*Et sequentes* or *et sequentia* ("and the following")
DWI	Driving while intoxicated		
EAHCA	Education for All Handicapped Children Act of 1975	EU	European Union
		Euratom	European Atomic Energy Community
EBT	Examination before trial		
E.coli	Escherichia coli	Eur. Ct. H.R.	European Court of Human Rights
ECPA	Electronic Communications Privacy Act of 1986	Ex.	English Exchequer Reports, Welsby, Hurlstone & Gordon
ECSC	Treaty of the European Coal and Steel Community		
EDA	Economic Development Administration	Exch.	Exchequer Reports (Welsby, Hurlstone & Gordon)
EDF	Environmental Defense Fund	Ex Com	Executive Committee of the National Security Council
E.D.N.Y.	Eastern District, New York		
EDP	Electronic data processing	Eximbank	Export-Import Bank of the United States
E.D. Pa.	Eastern-District, Pennsylvania		
EDSC	Eastern District, South Carolina	F.	Federal Reporter
		F. 2d	Federal Reporter, Second Series
EDT	Eastern daylight time		
E.D. Va.	Eastern District, Virginia	FAA	Federal Aviation Administration; Federal Arbitration Act
EEC	European Economic Community; European Economic Community Treaty		
		FAAA	Federal Alcohol Administration Act
EEOC	Equal Employment Opportunity Commission	FACE	Freedom of Access to Clinic Entrances Act of 1994
EFF	Electronic Frontier Foundation	FACT	Feminist Anti-Censorship Task Force
EFT	Electronic funds transfer	FAIRA	Federal Agriculture Improvement and Reform Act of 1996
Eliz.	Queen Elizabeth (Great Britain)		
Em. App.	Temporary Emergency Court of Appeals	FAMLA	Family and Medical Leave Act of 1993
ENE	Early neutral evaluation	Fannie Mae	Federal National Mortgage Association
Eng. Rep.	English Reports		
EOP	Executive Office of the President	FAO	Food and Agriculture Organization of the United Nations
EPA	Environmental Protection Agency; Equal Pay Act of 1963		
		FAR	Federal Acquisition Regulations
ERA	Equal Rights Amendment	FAS	Foreign Agricultural Service
ERDC	Energy Research and Development Commission	FBA	Federal Bar Association
		FBI	Federal Bureau of Investigation
ERISA	Employee Retirement Income Security Act of 1974		
		FCA	Farm Credit Administration
ERS	Economic Research Service	F. Cas.	Federal Cases
ERTA	Economic Recovery Tax Act of 1981	FCC	Federal Communications Commission
ESA	Endangered Species Act of 1973	FCIA	Foreign Credit Insurance Association
ESF	Emergency support function; Economic Support Fund	FCIC	Federal Crop Insurance Corporation

FCLAA	Federal Cigarette Labeling and Advertising Act	FmHA	Farmers Home Administration
FCRA	Fair Credit Reporting Act	FMLA	Family and Medical Leave Act of 1993
FCU	Federal credit unions		
FCUA	Federal Credit Union Act	FNMA	Federal National Mortgage Association, "Fannie Mae"
FCZ	Fishery Conservation Zone		
FDA	Food and Drug Administration	F.O.B.	Free on board
		FOIA	Freedom of Information Act
FDIC	Federal Deposit Insurance Corporation	FOMC	Federal Open Market Committee
FDPC	Federal Data Processing Center	FPA	Federal Power Act of 1935
		FPC	Federal Power Commission
FEC	Federal Election Commission	FPMR	Federal Property Management Regulations
FECA	Federal Election Campaign Act of 1971	FPRS	Federal Property Resources Service
Fed. Cas.	Federal Cases		
FEHA	Fair Employment and Housing Act	FR	Federal Register
		FRA	Federal Railroad Administration
FEHBA	Federal Employees Health Benefit Act	FRB	Federal Reserve Board
FEMA	Federal Emergency Management Agency	FRC	Federal Radio Commission
		F.R.D.	Federal Rules Decisions
FERC	Federal Energy Regulatory Commission	FSA	Family Support Act
		FSB	Federal'naya Sluzhba Bezopasnosti (the Federal Security Service of Russia)
FFB	Federal Financing Bank		
FFDC	Federal Food, Drug, and Cosmetics Act	FSLIC	Federal Savings and Loan Insurance Corporation
FGIS	Federal Grain Inspection Service	FSQS	Food Safety and Quality Service
FHA	Federal Housing Administration	FSS	Federal Supply Service
FHAA	Fair Housing Amendments Act of 1998	F. Supp.	Federal Supplement
		FTA	U.S.-Canada Free Trade Agreement of 1988
FHWA	Federal Highway Administration	FTC	Federal Trade Commission
FIA	Federal Insurance Administration	FTCA	Federal Tort Claims Act
		FTS	Federal Telecommunications System
FIC	Federal Information Centers; Federation of Insurance Counsel	FTS2000	Federal Telecommunications System 2000
FICA	Federal Insurance Contributions Act	FUCA	Federal Unemployment Compensation Act of 1988
FIFRA	Federal Insecticide, Fungicide, and Rodenticide Act	FUTA	Federal Unemployment Tax Act
FIP	Forestry Incentives Program	FWPCA	Federal Water Pollution Control Act of 1948
FIRREA	Financial Institutions Reform, Recovery, and Enforcement Act of 1989	FWS	Fish and Wildlife Service
		GAL	Guardian ad litem
FISA	Foreign Intelligence Surveillance Act of 1978	GAO	General Accounting Office; Governmental Affairs Office
FISC	Foreign Intelligence Surveillance Court of Review	GAOR	General Assembly Official Records, United Nations
FJC	Federal Judicial Center	GAAP	Generally accepted accounting principles
FLSA	Fair Labor Standards Act		
FMC	Federal Maritime Commission	GA Res.	General Assembly Resolution (United Nations)
FMCS	Federal Mediation and Conciliation Service	GATT	General Agreement on Tariffs and Trade

GCA	Gun Control Act	HIRE	Help through Industry Retraining and Employment
Gen. Cls. Comm.	General Claims Commission, United States and Panama; General Claims United States and Mexico	HIV	Human immunodeficiency virus
Geo. II	King George II (Great Britain)	H.L.	House of Lords Cases (England)
Geo. III	King George III (Great Britain)	H. Lords	House of Lords (England)
GHB	Gamma-hydroxybutrate	HMO	Health Maintenance Organization
GI	Government Issue	HNIS	Human Nutrition Information Service
GID	General Intelligence Division	Hong Kong L.R.	Hong Kong Law Reports
GM	General Motors	How.	Howard's United States Supreme Court Reports
GNMA	Government National Mortgage Association, "Ginnie Mae"	How. St. Trials	Howell's English State Trials
GNP	Gross national product	HUAC	House Un-American Activities Committee
GOP	Grand Old Party (Republican Party)	HUD	Department of Housing and Urban Development
GOPAC	Grand Old Party Action Committee	Hudson, Internatl. Legis.	Manley Ottmer Hudson, ed., *International Legislation: A Collection of the Texts of Multipartite International Instruments of General Interest Beginning with the Covenant of the League of Nations* (1931)
GPA	Office of Governmental and Public Affairs		
GPO	Government Printing Office		
GRAS	Generally recognized as safe		
Gr. Br., Crim. Ct. App.	Great Britain, Court of Criminal Appeals		
GRNL	Gay Rights-National Lobby	Hudson, World Court Reps.	Manley Ottmer Hudson, ea., *World Court Reports* (1934–)
GSA	General Services Administration	Hun	Hun's New York Supreme Court Reports
Hackworth	Green Haywood Hackworth, *Digest of International Law* (1940–1944)	Hunt's Rept.	Bert L. Hunt, *Report of the American and Panamanian General Claims Arbitration* (1934)
Hay and Marriott	Great Britain. High Court of Admiralty, *Decisions in the High Court of Admiralty during the Time of Sir George Hay and of Sir James Marriott, Late Judges of That Court* (1801)	IAEA	International Atomic Energy Agency
		IALL	International Association of Law Libraries
		IBA	International Bar Association
HBO	Home Box Office	IBM	International Business Machines
HCFA	Health Care Financing Administration	ICA	Interstate Commerce Act
H.Ct.	High Court	ICBM	Intercontinental ballistic missile
HDS	Office of Human Development Services	ICC	Interstate Commerce Commission; International Criminal Court
Hen. & M.	Hening & Munford's Virginia Reports		
HEW	Department of Health, Education, and Welfare	ICJ	International Court of Justice
		ICM	Institute for Court Management
HFCA	Health Care Financing Administration	IDEA	Individuals with Disabilities Education Act of 1975
HGI	Handgun Control, Incorporated	IDOP	International Dolphin Conservation Program
HHS	Department of Health and Human Services	IEP	Individualized educational program
Hill	Hill's New York Reports		

IFC	International Finance Corporation	ITT	International Telephone and Telegraph Corporation
IGRA	Indian Gaming Regulatory Act of 1988	ITU	International Telecommunication Union
IJA	Institute of Judicial Administration	IUD	Intrauterine device
IJC	International Joint Commission	IWC	International Whaling Commission
ILC	International Law Commission	IWW	Industrial Workers of the World
ILD	International Labor Defense	JAGC	Judge Advocate General's Corps
Ill. Dec.	Illinois Decisions	JCS	Joint Chiefs of Staff
ILO	International Labor Organization	JDL	Jewish Defense League
IMF	International Monetary Fund	JNOV	Judgment *non obstante veredicto* ("judgment nothing to recommend it" or "judgment notwithstanding the verdict")
INA	Immigration and Nationality Act		
IND	Investigational new drug	JOBS	Jobs Opportunity and Basic Skills
INF Treaty	Intermediate-Range Nuclear Forces Treaty of 1987	John. Ch.	Johnson's New York Chancery Reports
INS	Immigration and Naturalization Service	Johns.	Johnson's Reports (New York)
INTELSAT	International Telecommunications Satellite Organization	JP	Justice of the peace
		K.B.	King's Bench Reports (England)
Interpol	International Criminal Police Organization	KFC	Kentucky Fried Chicken
Int'l. Law Reps.	International Law Reports	KGB	Komitet Gosudarstvennoi Bezopasnosti (the State Security Committee for countries in the former Soviet Union)
Intl. Legal Mats.	International Legal Materials		
IOC	International Olympic Committee		
IPDC	International Program for the Development of Communication	KKK	Ku Klux Klan
		KMT	Kuomintang (Chinese, "national people's party")
IPO	Intellectual Property Owners		
IPP	Independent power producer	LAD	Law Against Discrimination
IQ	Intelligence quotient	LAPD	Los Angeles Police Department
I.R.	Irish Reports		
IRA	Individual retirement account; Irish Republican Army	LC	Library of Congress
		LCHA	Longshoremen's and Harbor Workers Compensation Act of 1927
IRC	Internal Revenue Code		
IRCA	Immigration Reform and Control Act of 1986	LD50	Lethal dose 50
		LDEF	Legal Defense and Education Fund (NOW)
IRS	Internal Revenue Service		
ISO	Independent service organization	LDF	Legal Defense Fund, Legal Defense and Educational Fund of the NAACP
ISP	Internet service provider		
ISSN	International Standard Serial Numbers		
		LEAA	Law Enforcement Assistance Administration
ITA	International Trade Administration	L.Ed.	Lawyers' Edition Supreme Court Reports
ITI	Information Technology Integration	LI	Letter of interpretation
ITO	International Trade Organization	LLC	Limited Liability Company
		LLP	Limited Liability Partnership
ITS	Information Technology Service	LMSA	Labor-Management Services Administration

LNTS	League of Nations Treaty Series	MHSS	Military Health Services System
Lofft's Rep.	Lofft's English King's Bench Reports	Miller	David Hunter Miller, ea., *Treaties and Other International Acts of the United States of America (1931–1948)*
L.R.	Law Reports (English)		
LSAC	Law School Admission Council		
LSAS	Law School Admission Service	Minn.	Minnesota Reports
		MINS	Minors in need of supervision
LSAT	Law School Aptitude Test	MIRV	Multiple independently targetable reentry vehicle
LSC	Legal Services Corporation; Legal Services for Children	MIRVed ICBM	Multiple independently targetable reentry vehicled intercontinental ballistic missile
LSD	Lysergic acid diethylamide		
LSDAS	Law School Data Assembly Service		
LTBT	Limited Test Ban Treaty	Misc.	Miscellaneous Reports, New York
LTC	Long Term Care		
MAD	Mutual assured destruction	Mixed Claims Comm., Report of Decs	Mixed Claims Commission, United States and Germany, Report of Decisions
MADD	Mothers against Drunk Driving		
MALDEF	Mexican American Legal Defense and Educational Fund	M.J.	Military Justice Reporter
		MLAP	Migrant Legal Action Program
Malloy	William M. Malloy, ed., *Treaties, Conventions International Acts, Protocols, and Agreements between the United States of America and Other Powers (1910–1938)*	MLB	Major League Baseball
		MLDP	Mississippi Loyalist Democratic Party
		MMI	Moslem Mosque, Incorporated
		MMPA	Marine Mammal Protection Act of 1972
Martens	Georg Friedrich von Martens, ea., *Noveau recueil général de traités et autres actes relatifs aux rapports de droit international* (Series I, 20 vols. [1843–1875]; Series II, 35 vols. [1876–1908]; Series III [1909–])	Mo.	Missouri Reports
		MOD	Masters of Deception
		Mod.	Modern Reports, English King's Bench, etc.
		Moore, Dig. Intl. Law	John Bassett Moore, *A Digest of International Law*, 8 vols. (1906)
Mass.	Massachusetts Reports	Moore, Intl. Arbs.	John Bassett Moore, *History and Digest of the International Arbitrations to Which United States Has Been a Party*, 6 vols. (1898)
MCC	Metropolitan Correctional Center		
MCCA	Medicare Catastrophic Coverage Act of 1988		
MCH	Maternal and Child Health Bureau	Morison	William Maxwell Morison, *The Scots Revised Report: Morison's Dictionary of Decisions* (1908–09)
MCRA	Medical Care Recovery Act of 1962		
MDA	Medical Devices Amendments of 1976	M.P.	Member of Parliament
		MP3	MPEG Audio Layer 3
Md. App.	Maryland, Appeal Cases	MPAA	Motion Picture Association of America
M.D. Ga.	Middle District, Georgia		
Mercy	Movement Ensuring the Right to Choose for Yourself	MPAS	Michigan Protection and Advocacy Service
		MPEG	Motion Picture Experts Group
Metc.	Metcalf's Massachusetts Reports	mpg	Miles per gallon
MFDP	Mississippi Freedom Democratic party	MPPDA	Motion Picture Producers and Distributors of America
MGT	Management		

MPRSA	Marine Protection, Research, and Sanctuaries Act of 1972	NCAA	National Collegiate Athletic Association
M.R.	Master of the Rolls	NCAC	National Coalition against Censorship
MS-DOS	Microsoft Disk Operating System	NCCB	National Consumer Cooperative Bank
MSHA	Mine Safety and Health Administration	NCE	Northwest Community Exchange
MSPB	Merit Systems Protection Board	NCF	National Chamber Foundation
MSSA	Military Selective Service Act	NCIP	National Crime Insurance Program
N/A	Not Available		
NAACP	National Association for the Advancement of Colored People	NCJA	National Criminal Justice Association
NAAQS	National Ambient Air Quality Standards	NCLB	National Civil Liberties Bureau
NAB	National Association of Broadcasters	NCP	National contingency plan
		NCSC	National Center for State Courts
NABSW	National Association of Black Social Workers	NCUA	National Credit Union Administration
NACDL	National Association of Criminal Defense Lawyers	NDA	New drug application
		N.D. Ill.	Northern District, Illinois
NAFTA	North American Free Trade Agreement of 1993	NDU	National Defense University
NAGHSR	National Association of Governors' Highway Safety Representatives	N.D. Wash.	Northern District, Washington
		N.E.	North Eastern Reporter
NALA	National Association of Legal Assistants	N.E. 2d	North Eastern Reporter, Second Series
NAM	National Association of Manufacturers	NEA	National Endowment for the Arts; National Education Association
NAR	National Association of Realtors	NEH	National Endowment for the Humanities
NARAL	National Abortion and Reproductive Rights Action League	NEPA	National Environmental Protection Act; National Endowment Policy Act
NARF	Native American Rights Fund	NET Act	No Electronic Theft Act
NARS	National Archives and Record Service	NFIB	National Federation of Independent Businesses
NASA	National Aeronautics and Space Administration	NFIP	National Flood Insurance Program
NASD	National Association of Securities Dealers	NFL	National Football League
		NFPA	National Federation of Paralegal Associations
NATO	North Atlantic Treaty Organization	NGLTF	National Gay and Lesbian Task Force
NAVINFO	Navy Information Offices		
NAWSA	National American Woman's Suffrage Association	NHL	National Hockey League
		NHRA	Nursing Home Reform Act of 1987
NBA	National Bar Association; National Basketball Association	NHTSA	National Highway Traffic Safety Administration
NBC	National Broadcasting Company	Nielsen's Rept.	Frederick Kenelm Nielsen, *American and British Claims Arbitration under the Special Agreement Concluded between the United States and Great Britain, August 18, 1910* (1926)
NBLSA	National Black Law Student Association		
NBS	National Bureau of Standards		
NCA	Noise Control Act; National Command Authorities		

NIEO	New International Economic Order	NSC	National Security Council
NIGC	National Indian Gaming Commission	NSCLC	National Senior Citizens Law Center
NIH	National Institutes of Health	NSF	National Science Foundation
NIJ	National Institute of Justice	NSFNET	National Science Foundation Network
NIRA	National Industrial Recovery Act of 1933; National Industrial Recovery Administration	NSI	Network Solutions, Inc.
		NTIA	National Telecommunications and Information Administration
NIST	National Institute of Standards and Technology	NTID	National Technical Institute for the Deaf
NITA	National Telecommunications and Information Administration	NTIS	National Technical Information Service
		NTS	Naval Telecommunications System
N.J.	New Jersey Reports		
N.J. Super.	New Jersey Superior Court Reports	NTSB	National Transportation Safety Board
NLEA	Nutrition Labeling and Education Act of 1990	NVRA	National Voter Registration Act
NLRA	National Labor Relations Act	N.W.	North Western Reporter
NLRB	National Labor Relations Board	N.W. 2d	North Western Reporter, Second Series
NMFS	National Marine Fisheries Service	NWSA	National Woman Suffrage Association
No.	Number	N.Y.	New York Court of Appeals Reports
NOAA	National Oceanic and Atmospheric Administration	N.Y. 2d	New York Court of Appeals Reports, Second Series
NOC	National Olympic Committee	N.Y.S.	New York Supplement Reporter
NOI	Nation of Islam		
NOL	Net operating loss	N.Y.S. 2d	New York Supplement Reporter, Second Series
NORML	National Organization for the Reform of Marijuana Laws	NYSE	New York Stock Exchange
		NYSLA	New York State Liquor Authority
NOW	National Organization for Women	N.Y. Sup.	New York Supreme Court Reports
NOW LDEF	National Organization for Women Legal Defense and Education Fund	NYU	New York University
		OAAU	Organization of Afro American Unity
NOW/PAC	National Organization for Women Political Action Committee	OAP	Office of Administrative Procedure
NPDES	National Pollutant Discharge Elimination System	OAS	Organization of American States
NPL	National priorities list	OASDI	Old-age, Survivors, and Disability Insurance Benefits
NPR	National Public Radio		
NPT	Nuclear Non-Proliferation Treaty of 1970	OASHDS	Office of the Assistant Secretary for Human Development Services
NRA	National Rifle Association; National Recovery Act		
NRC	Nuclear Regulatory Commission	OCC	Office of Comptroller of the Currency
NRLC	National Right to Life Committee	OCED	Office of Comprehensive Employment Development
NRTA	National Retired Teachers Association	OCHAMPUS	Office of Civilian Health and Medical Program of the Uniformed Services
NSA	National Security Agency		

OCSE	Office of Child Support Enforcement	OWRT	Office of Water Research and Technology
OEA	Organización de los Estados Americanos	P.	Pacific Reporter
OEM	Original Equipment Manufacturer	P. 2d	Pacific Reporter, Second Series
OFCCP	Office of Federal Contract Compliance Programs	PAC	Political action committee
OFPP	Office of Federal Procurement Policy	Pa. Oyer and Terminer	Pennsylvania Oyer and Terminer Reports
OIC	Office of the Independent Counsel	PATCO	Professional Air Traffic Controllers Organization
OICD	Office of International Cooperation and Development	PBGC	Pension Benefit Guaranty Corporation
OIG	Office of the Inspector General	PBS	Public Broadcasting Service; Public Buildings Service
OJARS	Office of Justice Assistance, Research, and Statistics	P.C.	Privy Council (English Law Reports)
OMB	Office of Management and Budget	PC	Personal computer; politically correct
OMPC	Office of Management, Planning, and Communications	PCBs	Polychlorinated biphenyls
ONP	Office of National Programs	PCIJ	Permanent Court of International Justice
OPD	Office of Policy Development		Series A-Judgments and Orders (1922–30)
OPEC	Organization of Petroleum Exporting Countries		Series B-Advisory Opinions (1922–30)
OPIC	Overseas Private Investment Corporation		Series A/B-Judgments, Orders, and Advisory Opinions (1931–40)
Ops. Atts. Gen.	Opinions of the Attorneys-General of the United States		Series C-Pleadings, Oral Statements, and Documents relating to Judgments and Advisory Opinions (1923–42)
Ops. Comms.	Opinions of the Commissioners		Series D-Acts and Documents concerning the Organization of the World Court (1922–47)
OPSP	Office of Product Standards Policy		Series E-Annual Reports (1925–45)
O.R.	Ontario Reports		
OR	Official Records	PCP	Phencyclidine
OSHA	Occupational Safety and Health Act	P.D.	Probate Division, English Law Reports (1876–1890)
OSHRC	Occupational Safety and Health Review Commission	PDA	Pregnancy Discrimination Act of 1978
OSM	Office of Surface Mining	PD & R	Policy Development and Research
OSS	Office of Strategic Services	Pepco	Potomac Electric Power Company
OST	Office of the Secretary		
OT	Office of Transportation	Perm. Ct. of Arb.	Permanent Court of Arbitration
OTA	Office of Technology Assessment	PES	Post-Enumeration Survey
OTC	Over-the-counter	Pet.	Peters' United States Supreme Court Reports
OTS	Office of Thrift Supervisors		
OUI	Operating under the influence	PETA	People for the Ethical Treatment of Animals
OVCI	Offshore Voluntary Compliance Initiative	PGA	Professional Golfers Association
OWBPA	Older Workers Benefit Protection Act	PGM	Program
		PHA	Public Housing Agency

Phila. Ct. of Oyer and Terminer	Philadelphia Court of Oyer and Terminer	RC	Regional Commissioner
PhRMA	Pharmaceutical Research and Manufacturers of America	RCRA	Resource Conservation and Recovery Act
PHS	Public Health Service	RCWP	Rural Clean Water Program
PIC	Private Industry Council	RDA	Rural Development Administration
PICJ	Permanent International Court of Justice	REA	Rural Electrification Administration
Pick.	Pickering's Massachusetts Reports	Rec. des Decs. des Trib. Arb. Mixtes	G. Gidel, ed., *Recueil des décisions des tribunaux ar-bitraux mixtes, institués par les traités de paix* (1922–30)
PIK	Payment in Kind		
PINS	Persons in need of supervision		
PIRG	Public Interest Research Group	Redmond	Vol. 3 of Charles I. Bevans, *Treaties and Other Interna-tional Agreements of the United States of America, 1776–1949* (compiled by C. F. Redmond) (1969)
P.L.	Public Laws		
PLAN	Pro-Life Action Network		
PLC	Plaintiffs' Legal Committee		
PLE	Product liability expenses	RESPA	Real Estate Settlement Procedure Act of 1974
PLI	Practicing Law Institute		
PLL	Product liability loss	RFC	Reconstruction Finance Corporation
PLLP	Professional Limited Liability Partnership		
		RFRA	Religious Freedom Restoration Act of 1993
PLO	Palestine Liberation Organization		
		RIAA	Recording Industry Association of America
PLRA	Prison Litigation Reform Act of 1995		
		RICO	Racketeer Influenced and Corrupt Organizations
PNET	Peaceful Nuclear Explosions Treaty		
		RLUIPA	Religious Land Use and Institutionalized Persons Act
PONY	Prostitutes of New York		
POW-MIA	Prisoner of war-missing in action		
		RNC	Republican National Committee
Pratt	Frederic Thomas Pratt, *Law of Contraband of War, with a Selection of Cases from Papers of the Right Hon-ourable Sir George Lee* (1856)	Roscoe	Edward Stanley Roscoe, ed., *Reports of Prize Cases De-termined in the High Court Admiralty before the Lords Commissioners of Appeals in Prize Causes and before the judicial Committee of the Privy Council from 1745 to 1859* (1905)
PRIDE	Prostitution to Independence, Dignity, and Equality		
Proc.	Proceedings		
PRP	Potentially responsible party		
PSRO	Professional Standards Review Organization	ROTC	Reserve Officers' Training Corps
PTO	Patents and Trademark Office	RPP	Representative Payee Program
PURPA	Public Utilities Regulatory Policies Act		
		R.S.	Revised Statutes
PUSH	People United to Serve Humanity	RTC	Resolution Trust Corp.
		RUDs	Reservations, understandings, and declarations
PUSH-Excel	PUSH for Excellence		
PWA	Public Works Administration	Ryan White CARE Act	Ryan White Comprehensive AIDS Research Emergency Act of 1990
PWSA	Ports and Waterways Safety Act of 1972		
Q.B.	Queen's Bench (England)	SAC	Strategic Air Command
QTIP	Qualified Terminable Interest Property	SACB	Subversive Activities Control Board
Ralston's Rept.	Jackson Harvey Ralston, ed., *Venezuelan Arbitrations of 1903* (1904)	SADD	Students against Drunk Driving
		SAF	Student Activities Fund

SAIF	Savings Association Insurance Fund	SGLI	Servicemen's Group Life Insurance
SALT	Strategic Arms Limitation Talks	SIP	State implementation plan
SALT I	Strategic Arms Limitation Talks of 1969–72	SLA	Symbionese Liberation Army
		SLAPPs	Strategic Lawsuits Against Public Participation
SAMHSA	Substance Abuse and Mental Health Services Administration	SLBM	Submarine-launched ballistic missile
Sandf.	Sandford's New York Superior Court Reports	SNCC	Student Nonviolent Coordinating Committee
S and L	Savings and loan	So.	Southern Reporter
SARA	Superfund Amendment and Reauthorization Act	So. 2d	Southern Reporter, Second Series
SAT	Scholastic Aptitude Test	SPA	Software Publisher's Association
Sawy.	Sawyer's United States Circuit Court Reports	Spec. Sess.	Special Session
		SPLC	Southern Poverty Law Center
SBA	Small Business Administration	SRA	Sentencing Reform Act of 1984
SBI	Small Business Institute	SS	*Schutzstaffel* (German, "Protection Echelon")
SCCC	South Central Correctional Center		
SCLC	Southern Christian Leadership Conference	SSA	Social Security Administration
Scott's Repts.	James Brown Scott, ed., *The Hague Court Reports,* 2 vols. (1916–32)	SSI	Supplemental Security Income
		START I	Strategic Arms Reduction Treaty of 1991
SCS	Soil Conservation Service; Social Conservative Service	START II	Strategic Arms Reduction Treaty of 1993
SCSEP	Senior Community Service Employment Program	Stat.	United States Statutes at Large
S.Ct.	Supreme Court Reporter	STS	Space Transportation Systems
S.D. Cal.	Southern District, California	St. Tr.	State Trials, English
S.D. Fla.	Southern District, Florida	STURAA	Surface Transportation and Uniform Relocation Assistance Act of 1987
S.D. Ga.	Southern District, Georgia		
SDI	Strategic Defense Initiative	Sup. Ct. of Justice, Mexico	Supreme Court of Justice, Mexico
S.D. Me.	Southern District, Maine		
S.D.N.Y.	Southern District, New York	Supp.	Supplement
SDS	Students for a Democratic Society	S.W.	South Western Reporter
		S.W. 2d	South Western Reporter, Second Series
S.E.	South Eastern Reporter		
S.E. 2d	South Eastern Reporter, Second Series	SWAPO	South-West Africa People's Organization
SEA	Science and Education Administration	SWAT	Special Weapons and Tactics
		SWP	Socialist Workers Party
SEATO	Southeast Asia Treaty Organization	TDP	Trade and Development Program
SEC	Securities and Exchange Commission	Tex. Sup.	Texas Supreme Court Reports
		THAAD	Theater High-Altitude Area Defense System
Sec.	Section		
SEEK	Search for Elevation, Education and Knowledge	THC	Tetrahydrocannabinol
		TI	Tobacco Institute
SEOO	State Economic Opportunity Office	TIA	Trust Indenture Act of 1939
		TIAS	Treaties and Other International Acts Series (United States)
SEP	Simplified employee pension plan		
Ser.	Series	TNT	Trinitrotoluene
Sess.	Session	TOP	Targeted Outreach Program

TPUS	Transportation and Public Utilities Service	UNESCO	United Nations Educational, Scientific, and Cultural Organization
TQM	Total Quality Management		
Tripartite Claims Comm., Decs. and Ops.	Tripartite Claims Commission (United States, Austria, and Hungary), Decisions and Opinions	UNICEF	United Nations Children's Fund (formerly United Nations International Children's Emergency Fund)
TRI-TAC	Joint Tactical Communications	UNIDO	United Nations Industrial and Development Organization
TRO	Temporary restraining order	Unif. L. Ann.	Uniform Laws Annotated
TS	Treaty Series, United States	UN Repts. Intl. Arb. Awards	United Nations Reports of International Arbitral Awards
TSCA	Toxic Substance Control Act		
TSDs	Transporters, storers, and disposers	UNTS	United Nations Treaty Series
TSU	Texas Southern University	UPI	United Press International
TTBT	Threshold Test Ban Treaty	URESA	Uniform Reciprocal Enforcement of Support Act
TV	Television		
TVA	Tennessee Valley Authority		
TWA	Trans World Airlines	U.S.	United States Reports
UAW	United Auto Workers; United Automobile, Aerospace, and Agricultural Implements Workers of America	U.S.A.	United States of America
		USAF	United States Air Force
		USA PATRIOT Act	Uniting and Strengthening America by Providing Appropriate Tools Required to Intercept and Obstruct Terrorism Act
U.C.C.	Uniform Commercial Code; Universal Copyright Convention		
		USF	U.S. Forestry Service
U.C.C.C.	Uniform Consumer Credit Code	U.S. App. D.C.	United States Court of Appeals for the District of Columbia
UCCJA	Uniform Child Custody Jurisdiction Act	U.S.C.	United States Code; University of Southern California
UCMJ	Uniform Code of Military Justice		
UCPP	Urban Crime Prevention Program	U.S.C.A.	United States Code Annotated
UCS	United Counseling Service	U.S.C.C.A.N.	United States Code Congressional and Administrative News
UDC	United Daughters of the Confederacy		
UFW	United Farm Workers	USCMA	United States Court of Military Appeals
UHF	Ultrahigh frequency		
UIFSA	Uniform Interstate Family Support Act	USDA	U.S. Department of Agriculture
UIS	Unemployment Insurance Service	USES	United States Employment Service
UMDA	Uniform Marriage and Divorce Act	USFA	United States Fire Administration
UMTA	Urban Mass Transportation Administration	USGA	United States Golf Association
U.N.	United Nations	USICA	International Communication Agency, United States
UNCITRAL	United Nations Commission on International Trade Law		
UNCTAD	United Nations Conference on Trade and Development	USMS	U.S. Marshals Service
		USOC	U.S. Olympic Committee
UN Doc.	United Nations Documents	USSC	U.S. Sentencing Commission
UNDP	United Nations Development Program	USSG	United States Sentencing Guidelines
UNEF	United Nations Emergency Force	U.S.S.R.	Union of Soviet Socialist Republics

UST	United States Treaties	Wend.	Wendell's New York Reports
USTS	United States Travel Service	WFSE	Washington Federation of
v.	*Versus*		State Employees
VA	Veterans Administration	Wheat.	Wheaton's United States
VAR	Veterans Affairs and		Supreme Court Reports
	Rehabilitation Commission	Wheel. Cr. Cases	Wheeler's New York Criminal
VAWA	Violence against Women Act		Cases
VFW	Veterans of Foreign Wars	WHISPER	Women Hurt in Systems of
VGLI	Veterans Group Life		Prostitution Engaged in
	Insurance		Revolt
Vict.	Queen Victoria (Great	Whiteman	Marjorie Millace Whiteman,
	Britain)		*Digest of International Law,*
VIN	Vehicle identification number		15 vols. (1963–73)
VISTA	Volunteers in Service to	WHO	World Health Organization
	America	WIC	Women, Infants, and
VJRA	Veterans Judicial Review Act		Children program
	of 1988	Will. and Mar.	King William and Queen
V.L.A.	Volunteer Lawyers for the		Mary (Great Britain)
	Arts	WIN	WESTLAW Is Natural; Whip
VMI	Virginia Military Institute		Inflation Now; Work
VMLI	Veterans Mortgage Life		Incentive Program
	Insurance	WIPO	World Intellectual Property
VOCAL	Victims of Child Abuse Laws		Organization
VRA	Voting Rights Act	WIU	Workers' Industrial Union
WAC	Women's Army Corps	W.L.R.	Weekly Law Reports, England
Wall.	Wallace's United States	WPA	Works Progress
	Supreme Court Reports		Administration
Wash. 2d	Washington Reports, Second	WPPDA	Welfare and Pension Plans
	Series		Disclosure Act
WAVES	Women Accepted for	WTO	World Trade Organization
	Volunteer Service	WWI	World War I
WCTU	Women's Christian	WWII	World War II
	Temperance Union	Yates Sel. Cas.	Yates's New York
W.D. Wash.	Western District, Washington		Select Cases
W.D. Wis.	Western District, Wisconsin	YMCA	Young Men's Christian
WEAL	*West's Encyclopedia of Amer-*		Association
	ican Law; Women's Equity	YWCA	Young Women's Christian
	Action League		Association